The Complete Adventures in the Connaught Rangers

The Complete Adventures in the Connaught Rangers
The 88th Regiment during the Napoleonic Wars by a serving officer

William Grattan

Two Original Unabridged Volumes in One Edition

*The Complete Adventures in the Connaught Rangers
The 88th Regiment during the Napoleonic
Wars by a serving officer*
by William Grattan

First published under the title
Adventures of the Connaught Rangers in two volumes

Leonaur is an imprint
of Oakpast Ltd

Copyright in this form © 2009 Oakpast Ltd

ISBN: 978-1-84677-726-4 (hardcover)
ISBN: 978-1-84677-725-7 (softcover)

http://www.leonaur.com

Publisher's Notes

In the interests of authenticity, the spellings, grammar and place names used have been retained from the original editions.

The opinions of the authors represent a view of events in which he was a participant related from his own perspective, as such the text is relevant as an historical document.

The views expressed in this book are not necessarily those of the publisher.

Contents

Preface	7
Answer to Some Attacks in Robinson's *Life of Picton*	9
The Author Leaves the Depot at Chelmsford	14
General Picton Takes the Command of the 3rd Division	22
Inefficiency of the Spanish	31
Movements of the French	37
Lord Wellington Obliged to Give Battle	42
Battle of Busaco	48
Retreat of Massena's Army From Portugal	68
Battle of Fuentes d'Onore	79
General Brennier's Escape From Almeida	91
Olivenza Surrenders	102
Second Siege of Badajoz	114
Affair of El Bodon	130
Retreat of the French Army	144
Third Division at the Siege of Ciudad Rodrigo	154
Progress of the Siege	166
Storm of Ciudad Rodrigo	174
Army Rest in Cantonments	192
Preparations Against Badajoz	209
Badajoz Taken	225

Calamities of War	282
Movements of Marshal Marmont	299
Complete Defeat of the French Army	316
Disgraceful Conduct of the Portuguese Dragoons	336
The British Army Approach Madrid	353
Lord Wellington in the Plaza de los Toros	368
The Retreat From Burgos	379
Jokes of the Connaught Rangers	399
Wolves	415
Adventures on the Road	429
The Connaught Rangers Embark for Canada	445
Our Ship is Separated From the Fleet	466
Our Ship Visited by a Privateer	477
Arrival at the Mouth of the St. Lawrence	487
A Love Adventure	496
Ragged Heroes	505
The Connaught Rangers Set Sail for Europe.	519
Conclusion	524
Appendix	546

Preface

I believe It was Rousseau who said that Prefaces were seldom, if ever, read. I myself do not see any great use in one, but as it is the fashion to say something—by way, I suppose, of telling the reader why the Author published at all—I shall merely state that as I sat one evening in company with a friend who had served in India, but who had never been in the Peninsula during our struggle there, he requested me to give him some description of our proceedings in general, but particularly an account of my own regiment, of which he had heard so much. I told him a good many anecdotes, to all of which he paid great attention. "Can you write them," said he, as well as you tell them?" I replied that I could not say, as I had never thought of doing so.

"Well then," was his answer, "if you write them only half as well as you tell them, rely on it they will be read."

I have made the attempt, and the reception which the pages I now present to the public may meet with, will prove whether I was right or wrong in following my friend's advice.

W. G.

Answer to Some Attacks in Robinson's *Life of Picton*

This writer of the late Sir Thomas Picton's life has shown how very little he understood the subject he wrote upon, and his information, which appears to be principally derived from informants whose names he declines to publish, is so awfully faulty, that he is led into all sorts of errors; and his book, in consequence, assumes more the appearance of a romance than of a history; but he is so witty at the expense of "The Connaught Rangers," that it becomes my duty, as an officer of that corps, and the author of the present work, to notice one or two of his observations.

In attempting to place General Picton in "the next niche to his mighty leader," he makes him appear as one more fitted for a lunatic asylum than the commander of the "fighting division," and in his attempts to brand "The Connaught Rangers" with infamy, he labours hard to gain a verdict from his readers in favour of his being himself placed beside the General in his retirement. An extract or two from the work will give a sample of the entire.

It is well known in the army, that, for four years and upwards, Picton commanded the third division in the Peninsula, and it is as well known that, during this long period, not one officer of the 88th Regiment ever received promotion through his recommendation. Mr. Robinson, it would seem, thinks some sort of excuse should be made for this conduct on the part of General Picton, and he endeavours to prove that "The Connaught Rangers" were so wretched a body of nearly naked, half-armed adventurers, as to be utterly unworthy of any mark of favour from their General; yet, strange to say, his reproaches, if true—which they are not— would cast a much greater share of blame on his "hero" than on

"The Connaught Rangers;" because, if what Mr. Robinson says be correct, General Picton should have reported that regiment as a dangerous one to employ against the enemy, and had he applied to the different French regiments the 88th were opposed to, there is not a shadow of doubt on my mind but that they would have said the same, and pronounced "The Connaught Rangers" to be a "dangerous regiment in battle."

In vol. 2., page 127, Mr. Robinson informs us that "one regiment in particular, the 88th, or Connaught Rangers, as brave and steady a fighting set of fellows as ever handled a musket, were perhaps as determined a ban
d of marauders as ever sacked a city or robbed a poultry-yard," &c. &c.

Now there is nothing extraordinary in this. The 88th Regiment, one of the strongest in the army, we are told were "as determined" as their comrades. What of all this? "The Connaught Rangers "would not give a pin's point to be told this, no more than they would to be told they were as loyal to their colours as any other regiment,—for when other corps lost from one hundred to four hundred men by desertion, "The Connaught Rangers "did not lose one man! Thus it would be no compliment to tell the 88th that it was as loyal as any other corps, any more than it is a disgrace to them to tell them they were as great marauders as their neighbours. Had Mr. Robinson told his readers that the 88th were the most determined robbers, there would be something exciting in it, but, as it is, he has told us nothing that the army did not know already!

During the war, a British infantry soldier required three years to accomplish his complete discipline, by which time he had cost his country about £88; what an odd number, by the way, as we are speaking of the 88th! Thus, for every soldier who deserts to the enemy, the nation loses the sum I mention. Now, a loss of one hundred men, at £88 per man, would amount to £8,800, and if we state the number of desertions which took place in some regiments at three hundred—I have heard it was nearer to four hundred,—we shall find that the loss to the country amounted to the enormous sum, for one regiment alone, of £26,400! This £26,400 sterling would pay for a larger quantity of poultry than was picked up in the Peninsula by the entire of "the fighting division," so that, supposing the British nation had to pay—which it had not—for that portion which fell to the lot of "The Connaught Rangers," I think Mr. Robinson—as an impartial historian—might, as a set-off against the cocks and hens, instead of a set-to amongst them, have told of the wonderful attachment and loyalty of "The Connaught Rangers," and omitted the "poultry-yard." It would have been more dignified in him, as the historian of a "Roman hero!" and he might have left the cocks and hens to fight their own battle, and not commenced his "main" against "the fighting division," by "feathering the pit" with "The Connaught Rangers," and trying to out-crow them! [1]

In speaking of the elevation to the peerage of some general officers, amongst whom the name of Picton did not appear, his biographer remarks:

> Can it then be a matter of surprise that Sir Thomas Picton, who was greedy of honour, and who was fond of the remark, and often made it, that he never envied anybody excepting when he did something great, should now experience a feeling of silent reproach and degradation, when he saw his services passed over, and a decided preference shown to those officers with whom he thought he had at least equal claim?

Nothing can be more natural than those feelings of Sir Thomas Picton; he must have felt keenly the neglect he met with; but, I wonder if it ever occurred to him or his biographer, that a body of

---

1. Brigade Order.—St. John's, May 19, 1815.
"No men having deserted from the 88th Regiment, they will not be required to attend at Chambly, for the purpose of witnessing the execution of the sentence of a General Court Martial on several deserters."
Brigade Order.—St. John's, May 26, 1815.
"Major-General Sir Thomas Brisbane was much pleased this day with the general appearance and movements of the 88th Regiment. He cannot refrain from expressing how much and how sincerely he regrets losing a regiment with which he has so long served, and which has conducted itself so creditably since its arrival in this country; but he confidently looks forward to have it again in his brigade. The circumstance of the regiment never having lost a man by desertion, is highly honourable to it, and can never be forgotten by the Major-General."
(Signed,)   J. Campbell, Brigade Major."

some forty gallant officers, and a battalion of from eight hundred to one thousand devoted soldiers, had any feeling for the neglect and injustice they had all experienced from him during the many years he commanded them?

Not one of the gallant men that composed this body, was ever so much as noticed by Picton for good conduct; and it is well known in the army that many deserved it; but, according to his biographer, "Picton had a strong sense of justice!"

In vol. 2., we find the following:—

> The officers of the division exhibited, however, a more substantial but not more convincing proof of the esteem in which they held him; and it will hardly be believed by those who have heard that Sir Thomas Picton never reported the services of any officer under his command, or attempted to procure for them any reward, that those very officers whom he is thus accused of baring neglected, before the division was broken up, subscribed amongst themselves a sum amounting to nearly £1600, for the purpose of presenting 'Old Picton' with a service of plate, &c., &c.

Whoever said that Sir Thomas Picton "never reported the services of any officer under his command," must be a block-head. Had Picton not recommended "any," then all would have been equally aggrieved, and it is not likely we should have heard anything of the vote of plate; but not one officer of the 88th having been noticed, much less recommended by Picton, not one officer of that corps subscribed one sixpence towards the purchase of plate for "Old Picton."

One more extract from Mr. Robinson's work, and I have done with him and it:—

> Vol. 2., —"But this was not all," added our informant, "for frequently, just before going into battle, it would be found, upon inspection, that one-half of the 88th Regiment were without ammunition, having acquired a pernicious habit of exchanging the cartridges for *aqua ardente*, and substituting in their places pieces of wood, cut and coloured to resemble them."

According to Mr. Robinson, the 88th fought with coloured

wood in lieu of powder and ball, yet they invariably defeated their veteran opponents! [2] Taking it for granted that such was the case, (what a compliment, by the way, Mr. Robinson has unintentionally paid them!) I boldly assert that every officer in that regiment should have been promoted, ay, and promoted so rapidly that their transfer to other corps would have followed as a matter of course, for it would have been contrary to all military practice to have had one regiment with a super-abundance of field-officers and captains, (for, if Mr. Robinson's account be true, the officers should have filled those ranks!) and their initiating the soldiers of the corps they would be transferred to, into the arcana of beating the best troops in the known world with bits of wood, would have considerably eased their new comrades of the burden which, in the shape of lead, they had been wont to carry; would have been a great saving to the British nation, would have stamped themselves as men of unheard-of talent, and would have placed their commander. Sir Thomas Picton—where?

Not in the "next niche to his mighty leader." No, not in the "next niche," but far, far above not only him, but above all the heroes of modem as well as of ancient times! This would have been a new species of tactics developed to the world. It would have called forth the admiration of surrounding nations. It would have cast into the shade all the performances that had preceded it, and our children's children, in place of lisping out—as I hope they will do—the name of "Nelson" and "the wooden walls" of old England, would warble from their infant throats the name of "Picton," and the "wooden balls" of old England!

---

2. See Appendix.

CHAPTER 1

The Author Leaves the Depot at Chelmsford

On the 10th day of October 1809 I left the depot at Chelmsford, and proceeded to Portsmouth for the purpose of joining the first battalion of my regiment (the 88th) in Portugal.

The newspapers announced that a fleet of transport vessels would sail in a few days from Portsmouth for Lisbon, and although I belonged to the second battalion, at that period stationed at Gibraltar, I waived all ceremony, and without asking or obtaining leave from the general in command at Chelmsford (General Colburn), I took the first coach for London, where I arrived that evening, and the next day reached Portsmouth.

I waited upon Colonel Barlow, who commanded at Hilsea, and from him received an order to be admitted on board a transport ship named the *Samaritan*. No questions were asked as to my qualification for this request, as it was much easier in those days to get out to Portugal than return from it. I then requested of the Colonel that he would give me an order for "embarkation money," which I told him I understood was allowed to officers on going to Portugal. He laughed at the demand, and treated me with so little courtesy that I was glad to be rid of him.

I have said the name of the ship in which I was to make my first voyage was the *Samaritan*. So it was. But it most certainly could not be fairly called the *Good Samaritan*, for a more crazy old demirep of a ship never floated on the water. She was one of those vessels sent out, with many others at this period, to be ready to convey our army to England in the event of any disaster occurring to it.

On board of her were ten or a dozen officers, who, like myself, had seen little of the world. We had no soldiers on board, and an inadequate ship's crew; but those deficiencies were amply made up for by the abundance of rats which infested the vessel, and which not only devoured a great portion of our small supply of provisions, but nearly ourselves into the bargain. One officer, ill from seasickness, was well-nigh losing half of his nose, and another had the best part of his great toe eaten away. Providence, however, at length decreed that we should soon be rid of these torments, and on the 29th day of October the Rock of Lisbon presented itself to our view.

It is difficult to convey to the eye, much less to the imagination of those who have not seen it, a more imposing or beautiful sight than Lisbon presents when seen from the deck of a vessel entering the Tagus; its northern bank, upon which the city stands, sweeping with a gentle curve along the extent of the city, shows to great advantage the vast pile of buildings, including palaces, convents, and private dwellings, standing like a huge amphitheatre before the view of the spectator; the splendid gardens and orange groves, the former abounding with every species of botanical plant, while the latter, furnishing the eye with a moving mass of gold, presents a *coup d'œil* which may be felt or conceived, but which cannot be described.

Our vessel had scarcely reached the river when a pilot boat came alongside of us, and for the first time I had an opportunity of looking at the natives of Portugal. I confess I was inexpressibly disgusted; the squalid appearance of those half-amphibious animals, their complexion, their famished looks, and their voracious entreaties for salt pork, gave me but a so-so opinion of the patriots I had heard of and read of with so much delight and enthusiasm. Their bare throats, not even with muscle to recommend them, their dark eyes portraying more of the assassin than the patriot, and their teeth, white no doubt in comparison with their dark hides, was sufficient to stamp them in my eyes as the most ill-looking set of cut-throats I had ever beheld. Their costume, too, is anything but striking, except strikingly ugly. Short *demi* petticoat trousers of white linen, a red sash, and their arms and legs naked, give them the appearance of a race of bad bred North American Indians. On landing at Lisbon, your foot once upon *terra firma*—

> The cloud-cap'd towers,
> The gorgeous palaces—

and the fine gardens all vanish, not into thin air, but into the most infernal pestiferous atmosphere that ever unfortunate traveller was compelled to inhale. Here is a hideous change from what the first view led you to expect. It is, indeed, "love at first sight."

You are scarcely established in the first street, when you behold a group of wretches occupied in picking vermin from each other; while, sitting beside them, cross-legged, holding a distaff and spindle in her left hand, and fanning her *fogareioro* with her right, is a woman who sells chestnuts to any one whose stomach is strong enough to commence the process of mastication in so filthy a neighbourhood.

The appearance of everything in Lisbon is so novel to an Englishman, that he is at a loss what most to fix his attention upon. But the number of beggars and the packs of half-famished dogs which infest the streets are in themselves sufficient to afford food for the mind, if not for either the beggars or the dogs. The latter crowd the streets after nightfall and voraciously devour the filth which is indiscriminately thrown from the different windows, and it is a dangerous service to encounter a pack of those famished creatures.

> In every country there are customs known,
> Which they preserve exclusively their own;
> The Portuguese, by some odd whim infected,
> Have Cloacina's temple quite rejected.

The French general, Junot, whatever his other faults might be, did a good thing in ridding Lisbon of this nuisance. On the fourth day after his arrival he ordered all dogs found in the streets after nightfall to be shot; and the proprietor of every door before which was found any dirt, after a certain hour in the morning, he caused to pay a fine according to the quantity found in front of his premises. But Junot had been too long driven from Lisbon to have his orders respected at the period I write of, and we were in consequence subjected to the annoyance of being poisoned by the accumulated filth, or to the danger of being devoured by the herds of dogs who seemed to consider these windfalls as their particular perquisite.

The beggars, offensive as they were, were less so than the dogs, because in Portugal, as in most countries professing the Roman Catholic religion, the giving of alms is considered an imperative duty; and according to their means, all persons supply the wants of the poor. From the gates of the convents, and from the kitchens of the higher classes, food is daily distributed to a vast number of mendicants, and those persons actually conceive they have a right to such donations; long habit has in fact sanctioned this right, and secure of the means to support their existence, they flock daily to their respective stations, awaiting the summons which calls them to the portal to receive the pittance intended for them. Thus it is that strangers suffer less inconvenience from this description of persons than they otherwise would, for the laziness of these wretches is so great, that although they will not hesitate to beg alms from a passing stranger, they will barely move from their recumbent posture to receive it, much less offer thanks for it.

Satisfied with my first evening's excursion, I returned to the hotel where we had bespoken our dinner and beds. The former was excellent; good fish, for which Lisbon is proverbial, *ragoûts*, and game, all well served up, gave us a *gout* for our wine. We discussed the merits of divers bottles, and it was late ere we retired to our chamber, I was going to say place of rest but never was word more misplaced, had I made use of it. Since the hour of my recollection, up to the moment that I write these lines, I never passed such a night. From the time I lay down, in hopes of rest, until the dawning of morning, I never, for five minutes at a time, closed my eyes. Bugs and fleas attacked me with a relentless fury, and when I arose in the fair daylight, to consult my looking-glass, I had scarcely a feature recognisable. I was not, however, singular, for all my companions had shared the same fate. But it was absolutely necessary, before we attempted to perambulate the streets, that something should be done to render our appearance less horrible.

We accordingly summoned the landlord with the view of ascertaining the name of some medical person who could administer to our wants; but he laughed at the idea of calling in surgical aid for so trifling a matter, which he said, and I believe him, was an everyday occurrence at his hotel. He recommended to us a man, as he was pleased to say, "well skilled in such cases," and one who had made a comfortable competency by his close residence to the hotel we occupied. The person who could have doubted the latter part of our host's harangue must have indeed been casuistical, because the number of patients which, to our own ears, not our sight, for sight we had none, fell to him in one night, was a sufficient guarantee that his yearly practice must be something out of the common.

The person thus described, and almost as soon introduced, was no other than the far-famed Joze Almeida Alcantaro de Castreballos, half-brother to the celebrated Louiranna well known in Lisbon. A man, who as he himself jocosely said, had taken many a British officer by the nose. He was, in fact, neither more nor less than a common barber, who gained a livelihood by shaving, bleeding, and physicing his customers.

The Portuguese barbers are like those of other countries, great retailers of scandal, and amply stocked with a fund of amusing conversation. They know everything, or seem to know everything, which, to nine-tenths of those they meet, is the same thing! This fellow told us all the news of the day, and added to it a thousand inventions, which his own fertile imagination supplied. He described the retreat of Wellington from Talavera as one caused by the want of the Portuguese army to co-operate with him: and if his account was to be given credit to, the whole world put together did not contain such an army as that of Portugal. He said that General Peacock, who commanded in Lisbon, invented stories every day, and that no intelligence from the army ought to be considered sterling, except what emanated from his (the barber's) shop. But then, said he, shrugging up his shoulders, and in broken English. "It is not one very uncommon ting, to see one Peacock spreading a tail!" He laughed at his pun, and so did we; but I have since heard that the merit of it did. not belong to him.

"But, gentlemen," resumed the barber, "I come here as a professional man, not as a wit, though for that matter I am as much one as the other—but to the point, gentlemen! you seem to have suffered, and I am the man, able, ready, and willing to serve you. Look here," said he, holding up a white jar, having a superscription on the outside to the following effect: "*bixas boas*" (good leeches): "I am none of your quacks, that come unprepared! I do not want to write a prescription that will cost my customers a mint of money! Well did I know what you stood in need of when you sent for your humble servant. Within the last ten days, that is to say, since the arrival of the fleet of transports from Portsmouth, I have given employment to one thousand leeches in this very house. This hotel has made my fortune, and now, with the blessing of God and the Virgin Mary, I'll add to the number, already made use of, one hundred more, on the faces of those to whom I have the honour of addressing myself."

There was so much truth and sound sense in what the barber said, that we all submitted to the operation of leeching, which was of material service to us. Old Wright of the 28th, already, from a wound, blind of one eye, now began to peep a little with the other, and it was amusing enough to those who could see it, to witness the coquetting between him and the barber. Indeed it would be difficult to say which of them was most pleased—he who received his sight, or he who was the means of restoring it. Quantities of cloths, steeped in warm water, were applied to our faces, and the crimson hue with which every basin was tinctured showed but too plainly that the "*bixas boas*" of the barber Joze, were of the right sort.

We kept our rooms the entire day, ate a moderate and light dinner, and at an early hour retired to our chambers, not without some misgivings of another night-attack. But the barber assured us there was no danger; and whether it was that the vermin, which nearly devoured us on the preceding night, had gorged themselves, or that the applications which Joze Almeida had administered to our wounded faces was of that nature to give them a nausea towards us, I know not, but, be this as it may, we enjoyed, unmolested, a comfortable night's repose, and in the morning our features had resumed their original shape and appearance.

We were seated at breakfast when the barber again made his appearance. He congratulated us upon our recovery, received his fee, which was extremely moderate, and took his leave. I have not since seen him, or is it likely I ever shall. In 1809 he was approximating to his sixtieth year; now thirty-seven years added to sixty would make him rather an elderly person. However, should he be still alive, and able to fulfil the functions of his calling as well as he did when I met with him, I recommend him to all those who may visit Lisbon and require his aid; on the other hand, should he be no longer in the land of the living, I have paid his memory a just tribute—but not more than he deserved.

At twelve o'clock I took a *calash* and reported myself to Major Murphy of the 88th, who commanded at Belem. By him I was received with great kindness, and asked to dine with him at six o'clock. I returned to our hotel, where I found my companions awaiting my arrival. Although not perfectly restored to their good looks, they agreed to accompany me in a stroll through the town, which was a different quarter from that we had before explored. It was more obscure, and overstocked with beggars of every grade.

At six o'clock I arrived at Major Murphy's quarters at Belem, where were several officers of the depot, amongst them the Honourable Captain Powis, of the 83rd; he was considered to be one of the pleasantest men in the army, and young as I then was in the world, it may be supposed I was quite charmed with him; he gave us several imitations; he was, in truth, a most agreeable person.

Just as we were about to enter the dining-room a note was handed to Murphy from the celebrated priest Fernando: he was an intimate friend of Murphy, and called the 88th his own regiment, because when that corps landed in Lisbon it was quartered in the convent of which Fernando was the head. Nothing could exceed his kindness and hospitality, and, being the principal of the Inquisition, he was a man of great authority. His note was in these words:—

Priest Fernando will cum dis day in boat to dine with Mr. Major Murphy.

He was as good as his word, for the note had been scarcely read aloud by Murphy when Fernando made his appearance. He was a remarkably handsome man, about forty years of age; full of gaiety and spirits, a great talker, a prodigious feeder, and a tremendous drinker. So soon as I was introduced to him he took out a book from his pocket which he opened and handed to me, requesting that I would write down my name in it. This book contained the name of every officer in the first battalion, and according as any died, or were either killed or wounded in action, it was regularly noted after his name. His conduct was of the most disinterested kind, and one of his first questions invariably was—"Did we want money?" It was late before we broke up, and next day an order was issued, directing us to be in readiness to march to join the army on the day but one following.

It did not require many hours' preparation to complete our arrangements, as there were several experienced officers to accompany the detachment, and they not only brought their own animals and provisions, but aided us by their advice in the purchase of ours. At the appointed hour all was in readiness, and the detachment, consisting of fifteen officers and two hundred and twenty men, composed of different regiments, marched from Belem, and embarked on the quay in boats which were prepared to carry us to Aldea Gallega. A short sail soon brought us across the Tagus, and towards evening we disembarked and took up our quarters at Aldea for the night.

Our route, which was made by easy marches, was uninterrupted by any circumstance worthy of notice. We passed through the different towns of the Alemtejo, in each of which we were hospitably received by the inhabitants; not so on our arrival at Badajoz, the headquarters of Lord Wellington. Nothing could exceed the dogged rudeness of the Spaniards; and it was with difficulty we could obtain anything even for money. Civility was not to be purchased on any terms, and one of the detachment was killed in a fracas with some drunken muleteers. Next morning we left this inhospitable town, and each party took their respective routes, with the view of rejoining their regiments. Mine, the 88th, was stationed at Monforte, distant one march from Badajoz, and here, for the first time, I saw the "Connaught Rangers."

CHAPTER 2

General Picton Takes the Command of the 3rd Division

The 88th at this period, although one of the strongest and most effective regiments in the army, did not count more than five hundred bayonets. The fatigues of the late campaign, and the unhealthiness and debility of many of the soldiers in consequence, caused a material diminution in our ranks; added to this, the country in the neighbourhood of the Guadiana was swampy and damp, and what between ague, dysentery, and fever, the hospitals were in a few weeks overstocked. Not less than ten thousand were on the sick list, or about one-third of the entire force, as borne on the muster-rolls; and there was a great paucity of medical officers; many of those had been left at Talavera with the wounded, that were of necessity obliged to be abandoned, and others, either catching the contagion that raged throughout the country, or infected by their close attendance in the hospitals, were lost to us.

The consequence was that the men and officers died daily by tens and fifteens, and this mortality was not confined to the old soldiers alone, for the young militia men, who now joined the army from England, suffered equally with those who were half starved on the retreat from Talavera, and during the occupation of the bridge of Heribisbo. For several days the rations of those soldiers consisted of half a pound of wheat, in the grain, a few ounces of flour twice in the week, and a quarter of a pound of goat's flesh; and regiments which a few weeks before were capable of exertions that were never equalled during the remainder of the Peninsular contest, were now unable to go through an ordinary march.

It was not to be wondered at that men who had so suffered should be now attacked with disease when all excitement was over, and a reaction of the system was the natural consequence; but the young men who joined from England at this period could not be so classed, and as it was manifest that the air of the country was unwholesome, Lord Wellington decided upon marching his army to the north-eastern frontier; yet before quitting the Alemtejo it was necessary that the safety of Seville should be guaranteed by a sufficient Spanish force.

The complete overthrow of the Spanish army, commanded by General Areizaga, on the plain of Ocaña, was one of the most remarkable and fatal that occurred during the terrible contest in the Peninsula, and went well nigh to put an end to the war. In this battle the Spaniards lost nearly all their artillery, and twenty thousand men were made prisoners. Lord Wellington did all that was possible to prevent this catastrophe; but his advice was unheeded, and the fatal results of this battle, which he forewarned the Supreme Junta were sure to take place, were fulfilled to the letter, and from this period no offensive movement was made by the Spaniards.

Early in December the army left the Alemtejo, and by the first week in January the 3rd Division was distributed in the different villages in the neighbourhood of Trancoso. The villages of Alverca and Frayadas, distant about two miles from each other, were allotted for the 88th Regiment. Midway between the two was a plain of considerable extent, and upon this plain the regiment exercised every day for several hours.

At the end of six weeks Colonel Wallace had his battalion in the most perfect state of discipline that it is possible to conceive; the men left in hospital were speedily joining the ranks, and the stragglers which were from necessity left behind in the north of Portugal were now coming in fast to their different regiments. It may be remembered that the troops commanded by Lord Beresford in the spring of 1809 suffered great fatigues in their advance through the province of Tras os Montes; the 88th Regiment formed a portion of this army.

The march upon Amarante, the passage of the Douro, and the occupation of Oporto, are justly ranked high among the many brilliant achievements of the Duke of Wellington; nevertheless the very nature of the service in which this portion of the army was engaged unquestionably tended to put to severe trial the discipline of every corps employed in it.

The rapidity and length of the marches—the very unfavourable state of the weather—the obstacles presented by the nature of the country in the Tras os Montes, where the men were frequently obliged to use torchlight to avoid the risk of being dashed to pieces in the craggy paths they were forced to traverse—the hospitality of the peasantry, who, totally ignorant of the imperious demands of military duty, were loud in commiserating and anxious to alleviate the hard fate of their deliverers thus compelled to march through their country at unseasonable hours, and in such inclement weather, all offered temptations to straggling, which it is not at all wonderful that the men in many instances yielded to.

The best regulated army during a campaign, even if carried on under the most favourable circumstances, always becomes more or less relaxed in its discipline; and when it is considered that the wreck of the 88th Regiment, after its capture at Buenos Ayres, was made up by drafts from the second battalion, that a few short months only were allowed it to recruit and reorganise before it was again employed in Portugal, it may be matter of regret, but certainly not of surprise, that it did not form an exception to the general rule. In fact many men were left behind, and some period of repose was necessary to remedy these irregularities, but that repose could not be obtained, for, towards the end of June, the whole disposable British force was marched into Spain, and on the 27th and 28th of July was fought the battle of Talavera de la Reyna.

Meanwhile many stragglers were left behind. Some preferred remaining with the Portuguese, and never joined the army again. Nevertheless, many of the good soldiers who had been worn down by fatigue and were obliged to make a short stay, soon rallied, followed the track of their different regiments, and joined them by sixes and sevens. Others of a different stamp preferred remaining where they were, and continued under the hospitable roofs that had given them shelter, and made themselves useful to the inhabitants by assisting them to till their fields and gardens. Others, fatigued with the sameness of the scene, went through the country under pretence of seeking their different regiments, and in many instances committed acts that were disgraceful; and, strange to say, not the slightest effort was made to look after those stragglers and collect them.

Several of these men were shot by the peasants, while others were made prisoners and were marched by the militia of the country to the nearest British depot. There they were either flogged, hanged, or shot, according to the nature of their different offences. Others were sent under escorts to whatever corps they belonged. All this relaxation of discipline commenced, as we have shown, in the early part of 1809, while the regiments of which those marauders formed a portion, between that period and the end of the year, had marched over hundreds of miles, fought a battle in the heart of Spain, occupied a line of posts on the Guadiana, and finally, after the lapse of ten months, took up new ground on the north-eastern frontier of Portugal.

It was at this time, and when the 3rd Division were stationed as has been described, that General Picton joined the army. It would be impossible to deny that a very strong dislike towards the general was prevalent. His conduct at the island of Trinidad, while Governor of that colony, and the torture inflicted, by his order, on Louise Calderon, a torture which, by the way, had been given up in our army as being worse than flogging, had impressed all ranks with an unfavourable opinion of the man. Besides this, the strong appeal made by Mr. Garrow, the Attorney-General, to the jury by whom he was tried and found guilty, was known to all, and a very general, and I do believe a very unjust clamour was raised against him. From what I have just written it will be seen in what sort of estimation General Picton was held, and as we of his division had never seen him, his first appearance before his troops was looked for with no little anxiety.

Our wishes were soon gratified, for, in a few days after his arrival at Francosa, a division order was issued stating that on a certain day, which was named, the division should be under arms and ready to receive the general.

Punctual to the appointed time, General Picton reached the ground, accompanied by his staff; every eye was turned towards him, and, as first impressions are generally very strong and very lasting, his demeanour and appearance were closely observed. He looked to be a man between fifty and sixty, and I never saw a more perfect specimen of a splendid-looking soldier. In vain did those who had set him down in their own minds as a cruel tyrant, seek to find out such a delineation in his countenance. No such marks were distinguishable; on the contrary, there was a manly open frankness in his appearance that gave a flat contradiction to the slander, and in truth Picton was not a tyrant, nor did he ever act as such during the many years that he commanded the 3rd Division.

But if his countenance did not depict him as cruel, there was a caustic severity about it, and a certain curl of the lip that marked him as one who rather despised than courted applause. "The stern countenance, robust frame, caustic speech, and austere demeanour," told in legible characters that he was one not likely to say a thing and not do as he said. In a word, his appearance denoted him as a man of strong mind and strong frame.

The division went through several evolutions, and performed them in a very superior manner indeed; the line marching and the echelon movements, for which the 88th, under Wallace, was so celebrated, seemed to surprise the general; he however said little. Once he turned to Wallace and said, in rather a disagreeable tone, "Very well, sir." The parade was about to be dismissed, and the General about to return to his quarters, when two marauders of the 88th were brought up in charge of a detachment of Portuguese militia. They had stolen a goat on their march up to join their regiment. The complaint was at once made to Picton, who ordered the men to be tried by a drum-head court-martial on the spot. This was accordingly done; the men were found guilty, and flogged on the moment in presence of the general.

This act was considered by all as not good taste in General Picton on his first appearance amongst his troops; the offence committed by the soldiers could have been as well punished in front of their own regiment as in the presence of the entire division; and, besides this, there was no necessity for the General's remaining to witness the punishment. This act on his part caused those who had formed a favourable opinion from his appearance to waver, and the word "tyrant" was more than muttered by many of the division.

So soon as the two soldiers were removed after having received the number of lashes it was thought necessary to inflict, the general addressed the brigade in language not of that bearing which an officer of his rank should use, for turning to the 88th he said, "You are not known in the army by the name of 'Connaught Rangers,' but by the name of 'Connaught footpads!'" He also made some remarks on their country and their religion.

Language like this was enough to exasperate the lowest soldier, equally with the colonel, who had done so much for the regiment during his command; and Colonel Wallace, directly the parade was over, waited on General Mackinnon, who commanded the brigade, and requested that he would go to General Picton, and intimate to him that he conceived the abusive language which he had made use of towards the 88th was not just to the corps, or to himself as commanding officer of it.

Mackinnon was a strict disciplinarian, but a man of an extremely mild temper, and he felt greatly annoyed at what had taken place. He readily complied with Colonel Wallace's request, and received for answer from Picton, that he would remove those impressions when he again had an opportunity of assembling the division.

A long period elapsed before the division was again brought together, and when it was Picton neglected, or perhaps forgot, to fulfil the promise he had made. Immediately after the parade Wallace reminded General Mackinnon of what had before passed on the subject, and Mackinnon, for the second time, waited on Picton. The latter requested that Wallace should call upon him, which was immediately complied with, and then took place a memorable interview which led to the apology made by Picton to Wallace, but which has been scoffed at by the biographer of Picton in his letter addressed to the editor of the *United Service Journal*, for May 1836.[1]

When Wallace reached Picton's quarters he found the general alone; a long conversation took place, which Colonel Wallace never repeated to me, nor was it necessary that he should, because my rank did not entitle me to such disclosure, but I have reason to think that it was very animated, and what I am now about to write I have from under Colonel (now General) Wallace's own hand. It is as follows:—

After a conversation which it is here unnecessary to reca-

---
1. Appendix No. 1

pitulate, General Picton paused for a little and said, 'Well, will you dine with me on —?'

I replied, 'Most certainly, General, I shall be happy to do so.' When I went to dinner on the day appointed, I found almost all the superior officers of Picton's division, and the troops quartered in the vicinity of Pinhal, assembled. General Picton then addressed himself to Colonel Mackinnon, commanding the brigade, and said, 'I understand that Colonel Wallace has taken offence at some observations made by me relative to the corps he commands, when addressing the division. I am happy to find that I have been misinformed as to their conduct for some time past; and I feel it but justice to him and them, to say that I am satisfied every attention has been paid to the conduct and appearance of the corps. I certainly did hear, on my way up to the army, of irregularities that had been committed, but I am happy to say that I have had every occasion to be satisfied with the general conduct of the corps since my joining the division.'

I made no reply, but bowed to the General. Dinner was announced, and General Picton came up to me and asked me to sit beside him at dinner. There ought always to be a deference given to a general of division by an officer inferior in rank, and under these circumstances I considered General Picton's conduct to have been arranged in a very gentlemanlike and handsome manner. From that period General Picton and myself were always on the best terms, and though from prejudice he often signified that he suspected the Connaught Boys were as ready for mischief as any of their neighbours, he always spoke of them to me as good soldiers while I was with his division.

Thus ended the matter, and I never knew or heard that Picton ever again made use of a harsh expression towards the regiment; indeed his biographer says that he often gave them "unqualified praise." Perhaps he did, but for nearly four years that Picton commanded the 3rd Division, not one officer of the 88th was ever promoted through his recommendation, though it is well known in the army that many deserved it.

Shortly after this period a laughable circumstance took place between Picton and a soldier of the 88th, which put the general in great good humour, and he often repeated the story as a good joke. He was riding out one day, accompanied by his *aide-de-camp*, near the river Coa, when he saw, on the opposite bank of the river, a man of the Connaught Rangers with a huge goat on his back.

We had received but scanty rations for some days previously, and such a windfall as the old goat was not to be neglected. I am not prepared to state whether it was the cries of the animal, or the stench of his hide—for the wind was from that point—attracted Picton to the spot; howbeit, there he was.

It would be difficult to say, with truth, whether the general was most angry or hungry, but he seemed, in either case, resolved not only to capture the goat, but also the "boy." That he would have done the one or the other, perhaps both, there can be little doubt, had it not been that a stream, whose banks had been the theatre of other scenes of contest, separated the parties. This stream was the Coa, and although its different fordable points were well known to Picton, his *vis-à-vis* neighbour was by no means ignorant of some of the passes; and as the general had not time to consult his chart, and find out the nearest "ford," nor inclination to plunge into the river, he made a furious, but quite an ineffectual, attack of words against the "Connaught boy."

"Pray, sir," said, or rather roared Picton, addressing the soldier, "what have you got there?"

Sol. "A thieving puckawn, sir."

Pic. "A what?"

Sol. "A goat, sir. In Ireland we call a buck-goat a puckawn. I found the poor baste sthraying, and he looks as if he was as hungry as myself."

Pic. "What are you going to do with him, sir?"

Sol. "Do with him, is it? To bring him with me, to be sure! Do you think I'd lave him here to starve?"

Pic. "Ah! you villain, you are at your old tricks, are you? I know you, though you don't think it!"

Sol. "And I know you, sir, and the 'boys of Connaught' know you too, and I'd be sorry to do anything that would be displaising to your honour; and, sure, iv you'd only let me, I'd send your sarvent a leg iv him to dhress for your dinner, for by my sowl your honour looks could and angry—hungry I mane."

He then held up the old goat by the beard, and shook it at Captain Tyler, the general's *aide-de-camp*, and taking it for granted that he had made a peace-offering to the general, or, probably, not caring one straw whether he had or not, went away with his burden, and was soon lost sight of amongst a grove of chestnut-trees.

"Well," said Picton, turning to Tyler, who was nearly convulsed with laughter, "that fellow has some merit. What tact and what humour! He would make a good out-post soldier, for he knows, not only how to forage, but to take up a position that is unassailable."

"Why yes, sir," said Tyler, "when he held up the goat's head, he seemed to beard us to our faces; and his promise of sending you a leg was a capital ruse!"

"It was, faith," replied Picton, "and if the fellow is found out, he will, I suppose, endeavour to make me the 'scape-goat'"

Picton used to often tell this story as one of the best things of the sort he had ever met with.

It is a remarkable circumstance that a few days before the battle of Waterloo, Picton met Wallace in London, when he spoke highly of the regiment, and said if it returned from America in time to join the army under the Duke of Wellington (being then on their passage home), and if he joined the army, the 88th would be one of the first regiments he would ask for his division.

These matters have been mentioned thus fully by me in order to disprove the assertions made by the biographer of Sir Thomas Picton. The next chapter will touch on the events that took place previously, and subsequently to the invasion of Portugal by the army commanded by the Prince of Esling.

CHAPTER 3

Inefficiency of the Spanish

The unfortunate termination of the campaign of 1809 in Germany and Spain is fresh in the recollection of most people; the memorable battles of Esling, Asperne, and Wagram, decided the fate of Austria; and the hard-earned victory of Talavera was not productive of any results which could induce even the most sanguine to hope for a favourable issue to the Peninsular contest. The want of energy and union amongst the Spaniards themselves, and Lord Wellington having, from experience, little or no reliance on any efforts the generals and troops of that nation would make in co-operative movement with him, declined to have more to do with them.

He thus looked calmly on at the ill-judged movements and operations of the different Spanish generals. He had calculated in his own mind what the end would be; he did not conceal his opinion from the Spanish generals and the Spanish government, and the result proved he was correct in the opinion he had formed. Everything he foresaw turned out to be but too true, and three or four battles which the Spanish generals not only risked, but courted, terminated in the total overthrow of each of them.

Those events took place towards the end of the year 1809, and it may be presumed from the circumstance of our army being prepared to move upon Portugal, that Lord Wellington was belied by the Spanish government when it was announced by them that the British troops would act in concert with the Spanish armies in this ill-arranged campaign.

The fact is, that his lordship positively refused to co-operate with them in this rash campaign; yet, if he was to judge, as it was expected he would, by their muster-rolls, he ought to have joined heart and hand in the struggle they had resolved to rush into; and if all was to be credited, the Spaniards could bring into battle over one hundred thousand combatants. But of what description of troops were they? They were men half clothed, half armed, and nearly famished. They were about to enter the lists with the best soldiers Europe could boast of, and they were commanded by men as arrogant as they were ignorant. So far from joining in this mad enterprise, Lord Wellington was occupied in arranging measures that brought the Peninsular contest to a triumphant result.

When his lordship moved his army from the Guadiana its numbers counted about thirty thousand, but those under arms scarcely reckoned twenty thousand; the remainder were in hospital, and many of those in the ranks were but ill able to carry their knapsacks and firelocks, having not yet recovered from the effects of past illness.

In the month of January, 1810, Lord Wellington established his headquarters at Viseu, in Upper Beira, and the different brigades of cavalry and infantry were quartered in the neighbouring villages. General Hill was left with five thousand British, and about as many Portuguese, at Abrantes; and with his army posted as has been described, the British general awaited the development of the French marshal's plan of invasion. In February the Duke of Elchingen made a demonstration against Cuidad Rodrigo, and at the same time the Duke of Treviso threatened Badajos; General Hill advanced from Abrantes to Portalegre; and Lord Wellington reinforced the ground between Guarda and Pinhal.

General Robert Crawford, with the light division, passed to the other bank of the Coa, and those different movements plainly denoted that the invasion of Portugal was not only expected, but likely soon to take place. A panic seized the Portuguese regency, and this body were loud in their clamours for additional British troops; but they were rebuked and silenced by Lord Wellington, who more than hinted to them that the promises made by them were not kept; with respect to the native troops, he said that nothing was executed with vigour; and as regarded the British force, there were scarcely half enough carriages to supply their wants. Lord Wellington recommended those measures to be looked to before any additional troops were asked for.

From the different dispositions made by the French marshal, it was supposed he would invade Portugal by the northern line,— that is to say, by old Castile rather than by Andalusia; but this was an error. Though not present with the army, Napoleon directed its movements, and as usual his plans were gigantic; and it was not one portion of the Peninsula, but the entire, that was destined to feel the force of his vast power. A multitude of veterans, fresh, and flushed with their victories in Germany, were thronging into Spain, reinforcing the different corps, and following the track of those that had preceded them; and so overwhelming were their numbers, that it became a matter of doubt with many, whether Portugal would, or could, be defended at all.

The magnitude of the reinforcements that had arrived, and were arriving, from France, nut it out of the question that the Spanish armies could act on the offensive. Their defeat and dispersion, one after another, the preceding autumn, had placed them *hors de combat*, or nearly so; and Lord Wellington's whole attention was occupied with the defence of Portugal.

The amount of the French force at this period in the Peninsula counted over three hundred and sixty thousand troops of all arms; but the army commanded by Massena, and called "the army of Portugal," did not amount to ninety thousand. The amount of the British and Portuguese forces has been already stated to be about fifty-five thousand men; and it will be recollected that of the Portuguese army scarcely one man in one hundred had ever discharged a musket against an enemy. Lisbon, Abrantes, and Belem Castle, on the Tagus; Figueras and Raiva de Pena Cova, on the Mondego; and Oporto and Lomego, on the Douro,—were the principal depots formed by Lord Wellington; and his magazines of consumption were established at Viseu, Celerias, Condeixa, Lurie, Thomar, and Almeida.

The only means of conveyance for the transport of stares and provisions, were several hundred cars, belonging to the peasants, and about twelve thousand hired mules, which were formed into regular brigades. I have given this brief sketch of the amount of the enemy's force, as likewise the force and means which were at Lord Wellington's disposal to resist the torrent that was about to be launched against him; and before entering into the events that subsequently followed, I mean to give a description of the celebrated lines of Torres Vedras, scarcely known, at the period I write of, to the British army; totally unheard of by the French army; and, even now, but imperfectly understood by a great portion of the British people. Nevertheless, those lines were the principal cause of the triumphant issue of the never-to-be-forgotten Peninsular contest. They saved Portugal; they saved Spain; they enabled the European powers to rally, and finally to crush the greatest military power, and the greatest military chief that Europe, or perhaps the world, ever saw; and they saved England from invasion—perhaps conquest

The invincible men who defended those lines, aided no doubt by Portuguese and Spanish soldiers, afterwards fought for a period of four years, during which time they never suffered one defeat; and from the first commencement of this gigantic war to its final and victorious termination, the Peninsular army fought and won nineteen pitched battles, and innumerable combats; they made or sustained ten sieges, took four great fortresses, twice expelled the French from Portugal; preserved Alicant, Carthagena, Cadiz, and Lisbon: they killed, wounded, and took about two hundred thousand enemies, and the bones of forty thousand British soldiers lie scattered on the plains and mountains of the Peninsula!

Yet those heroes, who, for a series of nearly six years, fought and conquered the best soldiers in the known world, soldiers that were commanded by Massena, Soult, Marmont, Victor, Ney, Jourdan, and a host of others, whose names, coupled with their deeds, made them the terror of Europe; these men, I say, who performed those wonderful deeds, and who received the thanks of parliament on fifteen different occasions, have been denied a medal for their services; and, strange to say, the Duke of Wellington, who commanded them, has never advocated their claims, but, on the contrary, has done much to prevent their being granted. The gallant Duke of Richmond, however, has presented a petition to Her Majesty, signed by hundreds of Peninsular officers, and it is hoped and believed that the queen will grant the prayer of their petition, the more so as medals have been given to the army that fought in India and in China. The services of those armies no doubt have been great, and are well worthy of a medal, but the battles fought by them, and the description of troops they combated against, has been compared by a writer, in the comparison of those conquered by the Peninsular army, as "ossa to a wart."

The lines of Torres Vedras consisted of three distinct ranges of defence. The first, extending from Alhandra on the Tagus to the mouth of the Zizandra on the sea-coast, was, following the inflections of the hills, twenty-nine miles long. The second, traced at a distance, varying from six to ten miles in rear of the first, stretched from Quintella on the Tagus to the mouth of the St Lorenza, being twenty-four miles in length. The third, intended to cover a forced embarkation, extended from Passo d'Arcos on the Tagus to the tower of Junquera on the coast: here an outer line, constructed on an opening of three thousand yards, enclosed an entrenched camp designed to cover the embarkation with fewer troops, should the operation be delayed by bad weather; and within this second camp. Fort St. Julian's (whose high ramparts and deep ditches defied an escalade) was armed and strengthened to enable a rear guard to protect both itself and the army.

The nearest point of the second line was twenty- four miles from these works at Passo d'Arcos, and some parts of the first line were two long marches distant; but the principal routes led through Lisbon, where measures were taken to retard the enemy and give time for the embarkation.

Of these stupendous lines, the second, whether regarded for its strength or importance, was undoubtedly the principal, and the others only appendages, the one as a final place of refuge, the other as an advanced work to stem the first violence of the enemy, and enable the army to take up its ground on the second line without hurry or pressure. Massena having, however, wasted the summer season on the frontiers, the first line acquired such strength, both from labour and from the fall of rain, that Lord Wellington resolved to abide his opponent's charge there.

The ground presented, being, as it were, divided into five parts or positions, shall be described in succession from right to left. 1st. From Alhandra to the head of the valley of Calandrix. This distance, of about five miles, was a continuous and lofty ridge, defended by thirteen redoubts, and for two miles rendered inaccessible by a scarp sixteen to twenty feet high, executed along the brow.

2nd. From the head of the vale of Calandrix to the Pé de Monte. This position, also five miles in length, consisted of two salient mountains, forming the valley of Aruda, that town being exactly in the mouth of the pass.

Only three feeble redoubts, totally incapable of stopping an enemy for an instant, were constructed here. 3rd. The Monte Agraca. This lofty mountain overtopped the adjacent country in such a manner, that from its summit the whole of the first line could be distinctly observed. The right was separated from the Aruda position by a deep ravine which led to nothing, the left overlooked the village and valley of Zibreira, and the centre overhung the town of Sobral. The summit of this mountain was crowned by an immense redoubt, mounting twenty-five guns, and having three smaller works, containing nineteen guns.

4th. From the valley of Zibreira to Torres Vedras. This position was seven miles long. The ground being rough and well defined, and the valley in front watered by the Zizandre, now become a considerable river, it presented a fine field of battle for a small army.

The account here given of these celebrated lines; is taken from the third volume of Colonel Napier's *History of the Peninsular War,* and by him from Colonel Jones's *Sieges in the Peninsula.* It is but right that I should state this fact, as otherwise the reader might give me credit for a degree of knowledge that I have no claim to, or wish to affect.

CHAPTER 4

Movements of the French

Andalusia was invaded, and this seemed the signal for a simultaneous movement of the host of French troops which occupied Spain. Cadiz and Seville were menaced by Victor, while Mortier appeared before Badajoz. Ney summoned Rodrigo, and Bonnet entered the Asturias. At the same time Loison occupied Leon. Thus it might be said that almost the entire of Spain from the base of the Pyrenees to the walls of Cadiz was covered with a mighty moving mass of French soldiers.

These astounding preparations paralysed the Spaniards; and in the British army it was generally believed that the entire force would embark on its reaching Lisbon. The same was asserted in England; the Portuguese dreaded it; the French army universally believed it, and the British ministers seem to have entertained the same opinion; for at this time an officer of engineers arrived at Lisbon, whose instructions, received personally from Lord Liverpool, though unknown to Lord Wellington, commenced thus: "as it is probable that the army will embark in September."[1] At this period (June 1810) the Prince of Esling was still at Madrid, but the first siege of Ciudad Rodrigo was entrusted to Marshal Ney. The garrison amounted to about six thousand men, and was commanded by the Spanish general, Herrasti, an old and gallant man who had served his country with honour for more than half a century. The town was amply supplied with artillery, provisions, and stores of all kinds; and the vigorous resistance which was expected, was made by Herrasti and his brave garrison.

General Robert Crawford, with his superb division, occupied

1. Napier.

the line of the Coa, while General Cole, with the fourth division, and Picton with the third, were posted at Guarda and Pinhal; and these troops were directed to be in readiness to render any support that could with safety be given to the Spanish governor.

The sixth Corps, counting about thirty thousand, were occupied in the siege; and on the 25th of June the French batteries opened against the fortress.

The fire of this day alone caused the garrison a loss of nearly seven hundred men; but though no way daunted, Herrasti sent a note by a peasant imploring assistance, and the Marquis of Romana arrived at the head quarters of Lord Wellington and in the strongest terms urged his lordship to acquiesce, but the thing was impossible.

Lord Wellington positively refused to send even one division. The moment was a trying one, but the refusal was unavoidable, and though Lord Wellington was blamed not only by the Spaniards and Portuguese, but by his own army, and taunted by the French marshal in his proclamations, nothing could move him from his original plan, and by this steel-hardiness and moral courage, the Peninsula was saved.

On the 27th Massena joined the army before Ciudad Rodrigo and summoned the governor to surrender. The summons was refused, and the fire against the place continued until the 1st of July. On that day fresh batteries were constructed, and heir fire was so powerful that nearly all the guns of the fortress were silenced. Nevertheless the governor and his brave garrison did all that men could do to remedy the damage and reorganize the disabled guns, but in vain; the different outworks were carried, and the convent of Santa Cruz, in the suburbs, was taken, and again retaken by the garrison, but it finally remained with the French.

The town took fire in several places, and a mine which had been constructed by the French, exploded, and throwing down several yards of the wall, filled the ditch with the ruins, and showed to the assaulting army a wide and practicable breach.

> At this moment, three French soldiers of heroic courage suddenly running out of the ranks, mounted the breach, looked into the town, and having thus, in broad daylight, proved the state of affairs, discharged their muskets, and with matchless

fortune retired unhurt to their comrades.²

The column of assault was now formed; the three men who had so gallantly proved the breach, were present, and their example, as likewise the presence of Marshal Ney, tended greatly to excite them; and, with loud shouts, they desired to be let forward; but at this moment the signal of surrender waved from the walls, and the old governor was seen standing, with his head uncovered, on the ruins of a place he had so gallantly defended.

Thus fell the fortress of Ciudad Rodrigo, after sustaining a siege of upwards of a month. Its gallant defence reflected great credit on both the governor and garrison, and the delay it caused the French army was of the greatest importance to Lord Wellington's plan of resistance, because the heavy rains which were almost sure to fall in the autumn would greatly aid in the defence of the country.

After his capture of Rodrigo, Massena lost no time in laying siege to Almeida, and it was hoped that this town, which was, though by no means a model of perfection, a more regularly constructed fortress than Ciudad Rodrigo, would hold out at least as long, in which case the season would be very &r advanced before Massena could reach the lines of Torres Vedras, and the rivers of the country, many of them capricious in their rising and falling, would be so swollen, that it would add tenfold to the difficulties of an invading army.

The force which Massena assembled before Almeida was so small in comparison with that collected for the siege of Ciudad Rodrigo, that it has been said Lord Wellington meditated a sudden attack on his lines with the view of raising the siege, carrying off the French battering train, and bringing away the garrison; but the terrible disaster which now took place rendered the attempt impossible.

On the 26th of August the fire of three score heavy cannon opened against the fortress; these guns were mounted in several batteries, and in a short time a great portion of the town was in flames, and it was found impossible, in the confusion that prevailed, to put a stop to the calamity. Nevertheless, the guns of the garrison replied with vigour, and but little damage was done to the walls; towards evening the filing on both sides abated considerably, and

---

2. Napier

the houses that had taken fire were entirely consumed.

A comparative quiet now prevailed, but towards midnight a terrible explosion was heard, the castle was rent into a thousand pieces, and the entire town disappeared as if swallowed by an earthquake. This tremendous crash was heard at a distance of many leagues, and as a matter of course, the governor. Colonel Cox, was obliged to surrender the place.

There can be no doubt that a treasonable plot had been set on foot by some of the Portuguese officers, and suspicion was fixed on two, one named Bernardo Costa, the other, José Bareiros; the latter deserted to the French, but Costa was tried by a court-martial and shot in accordance with his sentence.

While these events were taking place, a variety of movements with our advance and that of the enemy occurred. Upon one occasion a portion of the 14th Dragoons came in contact with a body of the enemy's infantry, and their commanding officer. Colonel Talbott, fell in the midst of a square against which he made a gallant, but fruitless charge. But this was of little import in comparison with what took place with the light division, under Crawford, on the banks of the Coa. His force consisted of four thousand infantry, a thousand cavalry, and a brigade of guns.

The force opposed to him was about six times his own number, but yet he, with a hardihood bordering on rashness, held his post, and fought a very dangerous battle—contrary to orders, I believe—and lost upwards of three hundred men, with nearly thirty officers, and had it not been for the superior description of the troops he commanded, the division would have been destroyed to a man. The French, it is true, lost three times the number Crawford did; but what of that? Massena could have better spared one thousand men than Wellington one hundred!

It has been said that Crawford fully expected Picton would have joined him with the third division, stationed at Pinhal. The division of Picton were within hearing of the fire, but not a man was ordered to move to the support of Crawford. The wounded men and officers of the light division came into Pinhal in the best manner they could; some on foot, others on cars, and the third division were much excited at not. being allowed to join their old companions.

Colonel Wallace held the 88th in readiness, as I believe did every other officer commanding a battalion, and the division could have assembled and marched in ten minutes had any order been given to that effect. However, the light division, after performing more than could have been expected, even from it, and doing so alone, without the aid which it looked for, and which might have been afforded it, held their ground, and sustained no disaster, but on the contrary inflicted a severe loss on the enemy, and covered itself with glory.

CHAPTER 5

Lord Wellington Obliged to Give Battle

The two frontier towns, Ciudad Rodrigo and Almeida, being in the possession of Marshal Massena; Crawford driven across the Coa, and no troops sent by the British general to dispute his right to the ground he had gained, satisfied him that his advance would be, for a time at least, unmolested.

He was thus left at liberty to make choice of his line of operations, and the line of the Mondego was the one he pitched upon. He suddenly assembled his army; thirteen days bread was issued to each soldier, and this, in itself, is sufficient to prove what a superior army the French must have been. To attempt the same with British troops would be quite hopeless.

The Prince of Esling did not fail to issue proclamations to the inhabitants of Portugal of the most friendly nature. He represented Lord Wellington as a man devoid of feeling and courage, as one who only sought to enslave Portugal, and one, although backed as he was by the brave men of that nation, dreaded an encounter with the French troops—so few in number! These appeals were in many instances attended to, and the French portion, or at least those in the interest of the Lisbon cabinet, did not fail to take advantage of it, and an old priest of the name of Souza was the leading man in everything that marred the combinations of the British general

When Lord Wellington determined to defend Portugal against this invasion, he asked but little from the government of that kingdom. He only required that they would supply their own troops; that they would follow his advice in rendering the country as inhospitable as it could be to an invading army; that all persons, not disposed to remain in their abodes, should destroy everything which would conduce to the support and maintenance of the invaders; and that in every place the different mills should be rendered useless. He pointed out to the government, clearly and distinctly, his objects in so advising them; but he was unheeded, and so far from being convinced that he had taken a right view of the matter, those men—traitors they may be called, and traitors they were—had the presumption to tell him, not only that he should fight a battle, but where and when he ought to fight it.

Lord Wellington was not slow in putting down this cabal, but he had more to dread from its reaction than from the force that outwardly assailed him. With the latter he could cope, and had made his arrangements so to do, but the undercurrent at Lisbon shackled his plans.

Besides all this, many military men censured him for allowing Ciudad Rodrigo and Almeida to be lost without striking a blow in their defence, and many officers wrote to their friends in England the opinions they held on these points. Those letters were published in the newspapers, and caused a great deal of inquietude in the mind of the public; but his lordship read them all—unmoved, and his only observation was—that he hoped it would not occur again.

Now, had Lord Wellington given battle at either of the places named, his army would have been lost. The Prince of Esling never brought into play more than thirty thousand men at those sieges. He thus had nearly fifty thousand veteran troops in hand, with a cavalry little short of twelve thousand. To oppose this formidable army of veterans, the English general could, at most, bring thirty thousand men. General Hill was away, observing Reynier's corps, and even taking into calculation the fifteen thousand men he commanded, and supposing him to be on the spot, what could induce Lord Wellington to fight a pitched battle in a flat country, with an army, one half of which were Portuguese, and who had never seen a shot fired, against the best troops that Europe ever saw, with a cavalry double the number of those he could bring into the field?

Besides this, unless there was a certainty of a very great success, the thing could not be risked. A great plan of defensive operations, after months of the most mature deliberation, had been fixed upon, and it would be an act of insanity in the man who would give up what he considered as certain, for a chance where there were ten to one against him.

The plans of the French generals were well laid; they were ably seconded by their faction in the cabinet of Lisbon; and had the British commander been caught in the snare and advanced to the Agueda; much less the Tonnes, it would not have, given Lord Liverpool much uneasiness as to the number of transport ships necessary to convey the army home.

The third division, under Picton, were stationary at Pinhal. Crawford, after his gallant fight, was, with his division, in the different villages in our front, and a quiet calm succeeded the first outburst. There was an inactivity in the movements of the enemy, notwithstanding that the soldiers had been supplied with bread for many days; and a curious incident took place at the time that is worthy of mention. It shows the good terms upon which the British and French officers stood in regard to each other.

Colonel Napier of the 50th regiment, who had been badly wounded at Comma, and who had been treated with much attention by Soult and Ney after he was made prisoner at that battle, stopped at Pinhal. He was on his parole, and when asked by some of our officers, whom he knew, "where he was going?" replied, "I am going to pass some time with my friend Marshal Ney!"

He did pass some time with him, and was an eye witness to all that went on in his camp, but where such confidence was shown to any British officer, much less one of such high character and honour as Colonel Napier, it is needless to say that it was not forfeited. The colonel (now general) is a brother of the historian of the Peninsular War.

Napier, after having stayed with his friend, Ney, for some weeks, returned on his way to England, when *en passant* he found the ridge of Busaco was about to be contested, and the gallant colonel, although not on duty, or in any way connected with the army, being' in fact on his *parole*, wished to be a looker-on. It so happened that he was wounded, while standing near Lord Wellington. His name was returned, and the French official paper the *Moniteur*, made some remarks upon the colonel breaking his parole. It was, however, soon explained by the gallant officer, and, in return, the Paris papers did not let pass an occasion which afforded them amusement, and they quaintly remarked "that a man who was so fond of French fire, after what he had got of it before,—ought to live in France!"

After a good deal of delay and vacillation, it appeared that Massena had at last seriously resolved on his enterprise. He had, under his immediate command, nearly one hundred and twenty thousand bayonets and sabres, but from this force some deductions most be made, by which it would appear that at the utmost he did not bring more than sixty thousand fighting men across the Coa. Finally he passed that river, and our army retired towards the hanks of the Mondego,—and Lord Wellington was obliged to give battle. But this obligation did not emanate from him,—quite the contrary.

It was necessary that he should do something, and the thing was forced upon him by the refractory spirit of the Portuguese councils. If then he was to fight, for the first time, with an army of Portuguese to back him, he judged that the ridge of Busaco was a good spot to try them, and he accordingly resolved to take his stand there. This ridge of mountain extends for about eight miles, and near its termination, and on a high point, stands a convent, inhabited by monks and friars. The face of the mountain is rugged, filled with dells and dykes, and the intervening space between its base and the top is one mass of rock and heath.

On the 22nd September, the Portuguese brigade of Park destroyed the bridges on the Criz, and fell back upon Crawford's division. The French, however, soon perfected their arrangements, constructed new bridges in place of the ones destroyed, and finally drove in all the outposts, cavalry as well as infantry. On the 24th, two days after, the augmentation of the enemy's force was visible.

On the 25th the light division was attacked, and Crawford, with his usual impetuosity, wanted to fight. Lord Wellington, however, having arrived at the moment, took the command in person, and set matters to right; and the division of Crawford, after escaping great danger, was freed from further annoyance. Nevertheless, there was some sharp fighting and many lives lost before the light division occupied the ground allotted for it; but the troops of Ney soon crowned the heights in Crawford's front, and it was manifest that his object was to carry that point. While Marshal Ney was thus striving, Reynier turned to the left and moved towards Saint Antonio de Cantara, nearly opposite to where the division of Picton were standing: and a very formidable French force was in array and ready to attack the hill, which at this time, was barely half occupied by our troops,—but Massena was absent, and no attack took place.

The French counted more than forty thousand, and there can be little doubt that if they attacked on the 25th, instead of the 27th, a far different account would have been given of the contest; but the Prince of Esling was a man of slow habits, and neglected to profit by occasions. In place of being with his two corps, he was many miles distant, and the wishes of Ney and Reynier to attack on the 25th were unheeded.

One day made a material difference in the line of defence of the British general During the 26th all the different corps were placed in the stations they should occupy, and the entire ridge of Busaco was fully manned on the 26th; during the evening we could perceive the enemy occupying their different stations in out front, and the light troops of both armies were warmly engaged along the entire of the line.

At night we lay down to rest; each man with his firelock m his grasp, remained at his post, anxiously waiting the arrival of the morrow, which was destined to be the last that many amongst us were to behold.

We had no fires, and the death-like stillness that reigned throughout our army was only interrupted by the occasional challenge of an advanced sentry, or a random shot fired at some imaginary foe.

Some of us sat together chatting over the past, or guessing at the future; it was impossible not to regard the scene below us with feelings of awe. An army of sixty thousand warriors, just returned from their victories in Germany, covered with trophies, and commanded by officers inferior to none, lay within cannon shot of us; their demeanour, too, argued a confidence in themselves which characterizes the French soldier above any other in the world; more than a thousand fires illumined their camp, and we could perceive them in groups, either sitting round their blaze, or performing their ordinary avocations with that *sang-froid* which alone belongs to men accustomed to danger.

Our attitude, though less brilliant, was nevertheless an imposing one. We occupied an immense ridge studded with rocks, the very look of which was enough to inspire an enemy with respect A numerous artillery out-topped these natural defences. A line of fifty thousand infantry, twenty-five thousand of them British, were stationed on the summit of this terrific ridge, and the stem appearance of discipline which our bivouac presented, must have impressed the enemy with an idea that its occupants were men of no ordinary stamp.

Circumstanced as I have described, the two armies lay, anxiously counting the hours that kept them asunder. The night at length passed over, but long before the dawn of day the warlike preparations of the enemy were to be heard. The trumpets sounded for the horsemen to prepare for the fight, and the roll of the drums and shrill notes of the fife gave notice to the infantry that the hour had arrived when its claim to being the best in Europe was to be disputed.

On our side all was still as the grave. Lord Wellington lay amongst his soldiers, under no other covering than his cloak, and as he passed through the ranks of the different battalions, already formed, his presence and manner gave that confidence to his companions which had a magical effect. All was now ready on our part; the men stood to their arms; and as each soldier took his place in the line, his quiet demeanour, and orderly, but determined appearance, was a strong contrast to the bustle and noise which prevailed amongst our opposite neighbours; but those preparations were of short continuance, and some straggling shots along the brow of the mountain gave warning that we were about to commence the battle of Busaco.

CHAPTER 6

Battle of Busaco

This battle, fought on the 27th September, 1810, though one in which the losses of the French and of the British and Portuguese army, commanded by Lord Wellington, were not of that magnitude to give it a first-rate place on the battle list, the loss of the French being not more than about five thousand (if so much), including four generals, *viz*. General Gnain d'Orge killed. Generals Foy and Merle wounded, and General Simon made prisoner, while that of the allied army was under two thousand, amongst which number not one general officer had fallen; the total loss of the two armies, counting about one hundred thousand combatants, was under seven thousand: this same battle of Busaco was, nevertheless, one of the most serious ever fought in the Peninsula, and for this reason—it was the first in which the Portuguese levies were brought under fire, and upon their conduct in this their maiden effort against their veteran opponents, depended the fate of Portugal, and the Peninsula also.

Such being the case, it must ever be classed as a very important event, and one that should be recorded by the historian with great care and fidelity, yet, strange to say, there is not, that I have read, at least, any faithful report of this battle in print. In vain do we turn to Colonel Napier's splendid history of the war in the Peninsula, in expectation of finding a correct account, but no such account is to be there found. In the fifth volume of his book, he gives the authority of Colonel Waller, an officer on the staff of the Second Division, and it would appear that Colonel Napier, never doubting (and who could doubt so circumstantial a detail as that given by Colonel Waller?) this account, published ms description of the part the Third Division took in the battle in conformity with Colonel Waller's report.

Colonel Napier was not with the Third Division on the morning in question—he was far away to the left, fighting with his own corps; it was not possible for him to see what was taking place with Piton's troops, and he naturally looked for information to those persons who were on the spot, and who, from their rank and station, ought to be counted upon as good authority as to what they related; but how does the matter stand in the pre sent instance? Not one syllable advanced by Colonel Waller in his carefully-written account furnished by him to Colonel Napier, touching the operations of Picton's division, but more particularly to the brigade of General Lightburne, is correct Colonel Waller says,—

> More undaunted courage never was displayed by French troops than on this occasion; it could not have been surpassed, for their columns advanced in despite of a tremendous fire of grape and musketry from our troops in position in the rocks, and overcoming all opposition, although repeatedly charged by Lightburne's brigade, or rather by the whole of Picton's division, they advanced, and fairly drove the British right wing from the rocky part of the position, &c.

Now, most unquestionably, this is a very strong and positive assertion, and one that makes it a delicate point to contradict, the more so as Colonel Waller adds, "being an eye-witness," &c.; but what are the facts? So far from the brigade of Lightburne being ever attacked, much less charged, that brigade never fired one shot throughout the battle! There was nothing in their front to attack them, and, consequently, so far from charging as Colonel Waller so vividly describes their having done, they remained inactive spectators of what was taking place on their right, and were obliged reluctantly to look on at the contest with their companions, consisting of the brigades of Mackinnon and d'Chaplemonde, and the division of Reynier.

As to the showers of "grape" which Colonel Waller speaks of, it is just as incorrect as the clashing of bayonets; there were no French troops (after the sharp-shooters had moved to their left) in front of the point held by Lightburne's brigade, and the moment it became manifest that the real attack was more to our right, and nearly in front of the brigade of Mackinnon, the guns were limbered up and brought into line where the French columns were descried mounting the hill. It would thus appear, if what I say be correct, and if it be not, it is easy to contradict me, that those awful attacks of the French, and those determined charges made by Lightburne's brigade, as described by Colonel Waller, had no foundation whatever.[1]

I have thought it necessary to be thus explicit in my remarks upon this very strange and erroneous document of Colonel Waller's; and in what I am going to relate as to the part the third division took in this battle, I shall keep as close as I possibly can to what I know to be the fact.

The haze was so thick that little could be seen at any great distance, but the fire of the light troops along the face of the hill put it beyond doubt that a battle would take place. Lord Wellington was close up with the brigade of Lightburne, and from the bustle amongst his staff, it was manifest that the point held by Picton's division was about to be attacked. Two guns belonging to Captain Lane's troop of artillery were ordered upon the left of the 88th Regiment, and immediately opened their fire, while the Portuguese battery, under the German major, Aranchild, passed at a trot towards the Saint Antonio Pass, in front of the 74th British.

A rolling fire of musketry, and some discharges of cannon, in the direction of Saint Antonio, announced what was taking place in that quarter, and the face of the hill immediately in front of the brigade of Lightburne, and to the left of the 88th Regiment, was beginning to show that the efforts of the enemy were about to be directed against this portion of the ground held by the Third Division.

The fog cleared away, and a bright sun enabled us to see what was passing before us. A vast crowd of *tirailleurs* were pressing onward with great ardour, and their fire, as well as their numbers, was so superior to that of our advance, that some men of the brigade of Lightburne, as also a few of the 88th Regiment, were killed while standing in line; a colour-sergeant named Macnamara was shot through the head close beside myself and Ensign Owgan. Colonel King, commanding the 5th Regiment, which was one of those

---

1. Appendix, No. 2.

belonging to Lightburne's brigade, oppressed by a desultory fire he was unable to reply to without disturbing the formation of his battalion, brought his regiment a little out of its range, while Colonel Alexander Wallace, of the 88th, took a file of men, from each company of his regiment, and placing them under the command of Captain George Bury and Lieutenant William Mackie, ordered them to advance to the aid of our people, who were overmatched and roughly handled at the moment.

Our artillery still continued to discharge showers of grape and canister at half range, but the French light troops, fighting at open distance heeded it not, and continued to multiply in great force. Nevertheless, in place of coming up direct in front of the 88th, they edged off to their left, out of sight of that corps, and far away from Lightburne's brigade, and from the nature of the ground, they could be neither seen or their exact object defined; as they went to their left, our advance inclined to the right, making a corresponding movement; but though nothing certain could be known, as we soon lost sight of both parties, the roll of musketry never ceased, and many of Bury's and Mackie's men returned wounded.

Those two officers greatly distinguished themselves, and Bury, though badly wounded, refused to quit the field. A soldier of Bury's company, of the name of Pollard, was shot through the shoulder, but seeing his captain wounded and continue at the head of his men, threw off his knapsack, and fought beside his officer; but this brave fellow's career of glory was short, a bullet penetrated the plate of his cap, passed through his brain, and he fell dead at Bury's feet These were the sort of materials the 88th were formed of, and these were the sort of men that were unnoticed by their general!

Lord Wellington was no longer to be seen, and Wallace and his regiment standing alone without orders, had to act for themselves. The colonel sent his captain of grenadiers (Dunne) to the right, where the rocks were highest, to ascertain how matters stood, for he did not wish, at his own peril, to quit the ground he had been ordered to occupy without some strong reason for so doing. All this time the brigade of Lightburne, as also the 88th, were standing at ordered arms.

In a few moments, Dunne returned almost breathless; he said the rocks were filling fast with Frenchmen, that a heavy column was coming up the hill beyond the rocks, and that the four companies of the 45th were about to be attacked. Wallace asked if he thought half the 88th would be able to do the business? "You will want every man," was the reply.

Wallace, with a steady but cheerful countenance, turned to his men, and looking them full in the face, said, "Now, Connaught Rangers, mind what you are going to do; pay attention to what I have so often told you, and when I bring you face to face with those French rascals, drive them down the hill—don't give the false touch, but push home to the muzzle! I have nothing more to say, and if I had, it would be of no use, for in a *minit* or two there'll be such an infernal noise about your ears, that you won't be able to hear yourselves."

This address went home to the hearts of us all, but there was no cheering; a steady but determined calm had taken the place of any lighter feeling, and it seemed as if the men had made up their minds to go to their work unruffled or too much excited.

Wallace then threw the battalion from line into column, right in front, and moved on our side of the rocky point at a quick pace; on reaching the rocks, he soon found it manifest that Dunne's report was not exaggerated; a number of Frenchmen were in possession of this cluster, and so soon as we approached within range, we were made to appreciate the effects of their fire, for our column was raked from front to rear. The moment was critical, but Wallace, without being in the least taken aback, filed out the grenadiers and First battalion companies, commanded by Captains Dunne and Dansey, and ordered them to storm the rocks, while he took the Fifth battalion company, commanded by Captain Oates, also out of the column, and ordered that officer to attack the rocks at the opposite side as that assailed by Dunne and Dansey. This done, Wallace placed himself at the head of the remainder of the 88th, and pressed on to meet the French column.

At this moment the four companies of the 45th, commanded by Major Gwynne, a little to the left of the 88th, and in front of that regiment, commenced their fire, but it in no way arrested the advance of the French column, as it, with much order and regularity, mounted the hill, which at this point is rather flat. But here, again, another awkward circumstance occurred. A battalion of the Fifth

Portuguese Infantry, under Colonel Douglas, posted on a rising ground, on our right, and a little in our rear, in place of advancing with us, opened a distant and ill-directed fire, and one which would exactly cross the path of the 88th, as that corps was moving onward to meet the French column, which consisted of three splendid regiments, *viz.*, the 2nd Light Infantry, the 36th, and the 70th of the line.

Wallace, seeing the loss and confusion that would infallibly ensue, sent Lieutenant John Fitzpatrick, an officer of tried gallantry, with orders to point out to this regiment the error into which it had fallen; but Fitzpatrick had only time to take off his hat, and call out "*Vamous commarades*," when he received two bullets,—one from the Portuguese, which passed through his back, and the other in his left leg from the French, which broke the bone, and caused a severe fracture; yet this regiment continued to fire away, regardless of the consequences, and a battalion of militia, which was immediately in rear of the 8th Portuguese, took to their heels the moment the first volley was discharged by their own countrymen!

Wallace threw himself from his horse, and placing himself at the head of the 45th and 88th, with Gwynne, of the 45th, on the one side of him, and Captain Seton of the 88th, at the other, ran forward at a chaining pace into the midst of the terrible flame in his front All was now confusion and uproar, smoke, fire, and bullets, officers and soldiers, French drummers and French drums knocked down in every direction; British, French, and Portuguese mixed together; while in the midst of all was to be seen Wallace, fighting,—like his ancestor of old!—at the head of his devoted followers, and calling out to his soldiers to "press forward!" Never was defeat more complete, and it was a proud moment for Wallace and Gwynne when they saw their gallant comrades breaking down and trampling under their feet this splendid division, composed of some of the best troops the world could boast of. The leading regiment, the 36th, one of Napoleon's favourite battalions, (see note end of chapter) was nearly destroyed; upwards of two hundred soldiers, and their old colonel, covered with orders, lay dead in a small space, and the face of the hill was strewed with dead and wounded, which showed evident marks of the rapid execution done at this point; for Wallace never slackened his fire while a Frenchman was within his reach.

He followed them down the edge of the hill, and then he formed his men in line, waiting for any orders he might receive, or for any fresh body that might attack him. Our gallant companions, the 45th, had an equal share in the glory of this short but murderous fight; they suffered severely, and the 88th lost nine officers and one hundred and thirty-five men. The 8th Portuguese also suffered, but in a less degree than the other two regiments, because their advance was not so rapid, but that regiment never gave way, nor was it ever broken; indeed there was nothing to break it, because the French were all in front of the 45th and 88th, and if they had broken the Portuguese they must have first broken the two British regiments, which it is well known they did not!

The regiment of militia in their rear ran away most manfully; and if they were able to continue for any length of time the pace at which they commenced their flight, they might, I should say, have nearly reached Coimbra before all matters had been finally settled between up and the French. Two of their officers stood firm, and reported themselves in person to Wallace on the field of battle; so there could be no mistake about them, no more than there was about the rest of their regiment

Meanwhile, Captains Dunne, Dansey, and Oates, had a severe struggle with the French troops that occupied the rocks. Dunne's serjeant (Brazil) killed a Frenchman by a push of his *halbert*, who had nearly overpowered his captain. Dansey was slightly wounded in four places, but it was said at the time that he killed three Frenchmen,—for he used a firelock. Oates suffered less, as the men opposed to him were chiefly composed of those that fled from Dunne and Dansey. Dunne's company of grenadiers, which at the onset counted about sixty, lost either two or three-and-thirty, and Dansey's and Oates' companies also suffered, but not to the same amount.

The French troops that defended those rocks were composed of some of the 4th Regiment and the Irish Brigade; but though several of the latter were left wounded in the rocks, we could not discover one Irishman amongst them. Lord Wellington, surrounded by his staff and some general officers, was a close observer of this attack. He was standing on a rising ground in rear of the 88th Regiment, and so close to that corps that Colonel Napier, of the

50th,—who was on leave of absence,—was wounded in the face by a musket shot, quite close to Lord Wellington. His Lordship passed the warmest encomiums on the troops engaged, and noticed the conduct of Captain Dansey in his despatch.

It has been said, and I believe truly, that Marshal Beresford, who was colonel of the 88th, expressed some uneasiness when he saw his regiment about to plunge into this unequal contest; but when they were mixed with Reynier's division, and putting them to flight down the hill. Lord Wellington, tapping Beresford on the shoulder, said to him, "Well, Beresford, look at them now!"

While these events which I have described were taking place, Picton in person took the command against the other division of Reynier's corps, and had a sharp dispute with it at the pass of Saint Antonio; but General Mackinnon, who led on the troops, never allowed it to make any head. A shower of balls from Arentschildt's battery deranged its deployment, and a few volleys from the 74th British and the Portuguese brigade of d'Champlemond, totally routed this column before it reached the top of the ridge.

As has been seen, the second column of Reynier's corps was met by Picton in person at Saint Antonio; but this attack was feeble in comparison with the one directed against Wallace, and, besides, Picton's force was vastly superior to that commanded by Wallace, while the troops opposed to him were little, if anything, more numerous. Picton had at this point five companies of the 45th, under Major Smyth, all the light companies of the third division, one company of the 60th Rifles, the 74th British and the Portuguese brigade of d'Champlemond, besides Arentschildt's battery of guns. It is not, therefore, to be wondered at that Reynier made little or no impression on Picton's right

The Fifth Division, commanded by General Leith, was in movement towards the contested point, and reached it in time either to take the fugitives in flank or to drive back any fresh body destined to support their defeated comrades. It made great efforts to join Picton when he was attacked, but the advance was so rapid, the defeat so signal, and the distance—two miles, across a rugged mountain—so great, that Leith and his gallant division could only effect in part what they intended. The arrival of this force was, however, fully appreciated; for although the brigade of Lightburne, belonging to Picton's division, had not fired a shot, or been at all molested, and although the 74th Regiment was nearly at liberty, still, had another attack with fresh troops been made, Leith might have stood in Picton's shoes on the extreme right, while the latter could in a short time concentrate all his battalions, and either fight beside Leith or turn with vigour against any effort that might be made against his centre or left But it would seem that no reserve was in hand—at all events none was thrown into the fight; and Massena gave up without a second trial that in which he lost many men and much glory!

While Picton, Mackinnon, Wallace, and d'Champlemond, and Leith's division, were occupied as I have described, the light division, under the gallant Robert Crawford, maintained a severe struggle against a large proportion of Ney's corps. Those French troops were driven down the hill with great loss, and the general of division, Simon, who headed and led the attack, was taken prisoner by the 52nd Regiment, and between two and three hundred unwounded men shared the fate of their general. The leading brigade of Leith's division put to flight some of the enemy who kept a hold of a rocky point on Picton's right, and had Picton been aware of their being there he might have cut off their retreat, while Leith attacked them in front and flank; but their numbers were scanty, and they might not have been aware of the fate of their companions, otherwise they would, in all probability, have got out of Leith's clutches before his arrival, for their remaining in the rocks could be of no possible avail; and their force was too weak to hazard any serious attack on Picton's right.

Indeed, they were routed by a battalion or two of Leith's division; and the entire British loss at this point did not count above forty or fifty. And thus ended a battle of which so many accounts have been given: all at variance with each other—and none more so than what I have just written.

It has been said that Picton directed the attack of the 45th, under Major Gwynne, the 88th, under Wallace, and the 8th Portuguese, under Douglas. Not one syllable of this is true. The conception of this attack, its brilliant execution, which ended in the total overthrow of Reynier's column, all belong to Colonel Alexander Wallace, of the 88th Regiment. At the time it was made Generals Picton and Mackinnon had their hands full at the pass of Saint Antonio, and were, in effect, as distant from Wallace as if they had been on the Rock of Lisbon; neither was General Lightburne to be seen. The nearest officer of rank to Wallace was Lord Wellington, who saw all that was passing, and never interfered *pro* or *con*, which is a tolerably strong proof that his lordship thought no alteration for the better could be made, and Wallace had scarcely reformed his line, a little in front, and below the contested ground, when Lord Wellington, accompanied by Marshal Beresford and a number of other officers, galloped up, and passing round the left of our line, rode up to Wallace, and seizing him warmly by the hand, said—

"Wallace, I never witnessed a more gallant charge than that made just now by your regiment!"

Wallace took off his hat—but his heart was too full to speak. It was a proud moment for him; his fondest hopes had been realized, and the trouble be had taken to bring the 88th to the splendid state of perfection in which that corps then was, had been repaid in the space of a few minutes by his gallant soldiers, many of whom shed tears of joy. Marshal Beresford addressed several of the soldiers by name, who had served under him when he commanded the regiment; and Picton, who at this time came up, expressed his satisfaction. Lord Wellington then took leave of us; and Beresford, shaking the officers by the hand, rode away with his lordship, accompanied by the officers about him. We were once more left to ourselves; the arms were piled, the wounded of all nations collected and carried to the rear, and in a short time the dead were left without a stitch of clothes to cover their bodies. All firing had ceased, except a few shots low down the hill on our right; and shortly after the picquets were placed in front a double allowance of spirits was served out to Wallace's men.

We had now leisure to walk about, and talk to each other on the events of the morning, and look at the French soldiers in our front. They appeared as leisurely employed cooking their rations as if nothing serious had occurred to them, which caused much amusement to our men, some of whom remarked that they left a few behind them that had got a "belly-full" already. The rocks which had been forced by the three companies of the 88th presented a curious and melancholy sight; one side of their base strewed with our brave fellows, almost all of them shot through the head, while in many of the niches were to be seen dead Frenchmen, in the position they had fought; while on the other side, and on the projecting crags, lay numbers who in an effort to escape the fury of our men were dashed to pieces in their fall!

Day at length began to close, and night found the two armies occupying the ground they held on the preceding evening; our army, as then, in utter darkness, that of the enemy more brilliant than the preceding night, which brought to our recollection the remark of a celebrated general, when he saw bonfires through France after a signal defeat which the troops of that nation had sustained.—"Gad!" said the general, "those Frenchmen are like flint-stones—the more you beat them the more fire they make!"

Captain Seton, Ensign Owgan, and myself, with one hundred of the Connaught Rangers, formed the picquet in advance of that regiment, and immediately facing: the outposts of the enemy in our front The sentries of each, as is customary in civilized armies; although within half-shot range of each other, never fire except upon occasions of necessity. Towards midnight, Seton, a good and steady officer, went in front, for the third time, to see that the sentinels which he himself had posted were on the alert. He found all right; but upon his return to the main body he missed his way, and happening in the dark to get too close to a French sharpshooter, he was immediately challenged, but not thinking it prudent to make any noise, in the shape of reply or otherwise, he held his peace.

Not so with the Frenchman, who uttered a loud cry to alarm his companions, and discharged the contents of his musket at Seton; the ball passed through his hat, but did no other injury, and he might have rejoiced at his escape, had the matter ended here; but the cry of the sentinel and the discharge of his musket alarmed the others, and one general volley from the line of outposts of both armies warned Seton that his best and safest evolution would be to sprawl flat on his face amongst the heath, with which the hill was copiously garnished.

He did so, and as soon as the tumult had in a great degree abated, he got up on his hands and knees, and essayed to gain the ground which no doubt he regretted he had ever quit. He was nearing the picquet fast, when the rustling in the heath, increased by the awkward position in which he moved, put us on the *qui vive*. Owgan, who was a dead shot with a rifle, and who on this day carried one, called out, in a low but clear tone, "I see you, and if you don't answer, you'll be a dead man in a second;" and he cocked his rifle, showing he meant to make good his promise.

Whether it was that Seton knew the temperament of the last speaker, or that the recollection of what he was near receiving caused by his obstinate taciturnity with the French soldier, is uncertain, but in this instance he completely changed his plan of tactics, and replied in a low and scarcely audible tone, "Owgan! don't fire—it's me." So soon as he recovered his natural and more comfortable position—for he was still "all-fours"—we congratulated him on his lucky escape, and I placed my canteen of brandy to his mouth; it did not require much pressing to prevail upon him to take a hearty swig, which indeed he stood much in need of.

The night passed over without further adventure or annoyance, and in the morning the picquets on both sides were relieved. The dead were buried without much ceremony, and the soldiers occupied themselves cleaning their arms, arranging their accoutrements, and cooking their rations. The enemy showed no great disposition to renew his attack, and a few of us obtained leave to go down to the village of Busaco, in order to visit some of our officers, who were so badly wounded as to forbid their being removed further to the rear.

Amongst the number was the gallant Major Silver, of the 88th. He had been shot through the body, and though he did not think himself in danger, as he suffered no pain, it was manifest to the medical men he could not live many hours.

He gave orders to his servant to leave him for a short time, and attend to his horses; the man did so, but on his return, in about a quarter of an hour, he found poor Silver lying on his right side as if he was asleep—but he was dead! Silver was one of the best soldiers in the army, and was thanked by Colonel Donkin, who commanded the brigade at the battle of Talavera, for his distinguished bravery in that action. He was laid in a deep grave, in the uniform he had fought and died in.

A curious, and, as it turned out, a laughable circumstance, took place in this village about this time. A commissary, who had about a year before joined the division as a clerk, and was esteemed by all a good sort of fellow; became promoted, made money—a matter of course—rapidly, and, in the opinion of many, began not only to forget himself but some of his old acquaintances also; it was even hinted that he gave one or two the "cut direct." Amongst those who felt most indignant was a young officer of the 88th, of the name of Heppenstal, a fellow who would have thought as little of shooting the said commissary as he would of eating one of his ration biscuits. Some angry words had passed between them while the third division was stationed at Pinhal, and it would seem from what just now followed, that neither had forgotten the circumstance.

Heppenstal had rode down to the village, and hung the reins of his horse's bridle on a hook of the door of a house he had entered; the horse was quite out of the way of the street, but the commissary, it would seem, preferred the footpath, and riding furiously between the horse's head and the wall, broke the reins, and was about to pass on when Heppenstal rushed out, and caught hold of the broken reins; the head-stall came off, leaving in Heppenstal's hands a very dangerous missile, which he made use of on the instant against the commissary.

The bit of the bridle came in contact with the commissary's teeth, leaving him minus one or two; but he still kept his seat, and brandished a huge horsewhip at Heppenstal: a rushlight would have been of as much service to him, for Heppenstal, a powerful man, and to whom danger was as nought, seized him by the right foot, and with one jerk emptied the saddle; the poor man fell on his face in the dust, and was not only made to "bite the bridle," but the "dust" also. By no means satisfied with the castigation he had given, Heppenstal rushed upon his fallan foe like an enraged tiger, and endeavoured to wrest the whip from his hand; but though the commissary lost his seat, he retained his presence of mind, and well knowing what he had to expect if the whip once got into his opponent's hands, held it with a death-like grasp.

Powerful as Heppenstal was, he could not disentangle the whip, but he dragged the commissary a great distance along the street, and as the unfortunate man defended himself on his back, his uniform coat was torn to fritters. At last some officers and soldiers interposed, and succeeded in getting Heppenstal away, and thus relieved the unfortunate commissary from his disagreeable posture, and also from his disagreeable neighbour. Had the prize sought for, the whip, been gained, I am not prepared to say that the commissary would have served out rations for some time, and from the pertinacity with which he held it, I should say he was of my opinion. Heppenstal was killed shortly after, and died gloriously. I know not what became of the commissary.

The day after the action, some English troops passed through the town of Alcobaça, on their route to join the army; and this circumstance, coupled with our victory, led the inhabitants to suppose they, as well as their property, were perfectly safe; and the idea of removing the one or the other never once occurred to them. Their surprise and confusion was in consequence increased tenfold, when they beheld our troops enter the town. Alcobaça was at that time a beautiful rich village, notwithstanding that it supported a magnificent convent, and several hundred priests and friars.

Those gentlemen, although rigid in their mode of living at times, know as well as any other class of people how to live, and having ample means of making out life at their disposal, it is not to be wondered at that the convent contained that which was far from unacceptable to us, namely quantities of provisions.

On our arrival in the town, the inhabitants, terrified at the possibility of being captured by the French, fled, leaving, in many instances, their houses in such haste, as not to allow themselves time to take away anything, not even their silver forks and spoons, a luxury which almost the poorest family in Portugal enjoys.

Those and other articles offered a strong temptation to our men to do that which they should not, *i. e,* possess themselves of whatever they found in those uninhabited mansions. Their doing so, to be sure, was a slight breach of discipline; but it was argued by the "friends of the measure," that Lord Wellington having directed the country parts, as well as the towns, to be laid waste, in order to distress the enemy as much as possible, the Portuguese were highly culpable in neither taking away their property nor destroying it.

It would be almost superfluous to add, that an argument of so sound a nature, and delivered in the nick of time, had its due force; it in fact bore down all opposition, and those whose consciences at first felt anything like a qualm, in a little time became more at ease, so that by the time the houses had been about half-sacked, there was not one who, so far from thinking it improper to do what he had done, would not have considered himself much to blame had he pursued a different line of conduct.

The priests, more cautious, or, perhaps, better informed, removed their valuables; but in all their hurry they did not forget that hospitality for which they were proverbial. They left some of their brethren behind, who had a dinner prepared for our officers, and when their longer stay was useless to us, and might be attended with danger to themselves, they opened their different stores, and with a generous liberality, invited us to take whatever we wished for. Poor men!

Their doing so showed more their goodness of heart than their knowledge of the world. Had they been a little longer acquainted with the lads that were now about to stand in their places, they would not have thought such *congè* necessary. As soon as those good men left the dwelling in which they had passed so many tranquil years, we began to avail ourselves of the permission granted us, and which decency forbade our taking advantage of sooner. Every nook was searched with anatomical precision; not even a corner cupboard was allowed to escape the scrutiny of the present inmates of the convent, who certainly were as unlike the former in their demeanour as in their costume.

In taking a survey of the different commodities with which this place was supplied, I had the good fortune, or, as it afterwards turned out, the bad fortune, to stumble upon several firkins of Irish butter. Unquestionably I never felt happier, because it was a luxury I had not tasted for months; but my servant, by a good-natured officiousness, so loaded my poor, half-starved, jaded mule with, not only butter, but everything else he could lay his paw upon, that, unable to sustain the shameful burden which had been imposed upon him, he fell exhausted in endeavouring to scramble through a quagmire, and I lost not only the cargo with which he was laden, but the animal himself: however, I had the consolation to know that few of the articles cost me anything, and he himself was a sort of windfall, having been found by my servant on the retreat.

The army continued its march upon Torres Vedras with little interruption from the enemy, and early in October we occupied our entrenched camp. This formidable position had its right at Alhandra, on the Tagus; its left rested on the part of the sea where the river Zizandra empties itself; and along its centre was a chain of redoubts, armed with cannon of different calibre; between these forts was a double and, in some instances, triple row of breastworks for the infantry, and the position might be considered faultless.

On the night of the 29th, the French army made that flank movement which obliged Lord Wellington to retire, and which is so well known as to render any detail from me unnecessary; and on that night we took our leave of the mountain of Busaco, and commenced our march to the Lines of Torres Vedras.

Remarks on the Battle

Never was a battle more differently described by those who have written upon it, and it is not an easy task for a reader who was not actually present, particularly with Picton's division, to come to a satisfactory conclusion as to who is right or who is wrong. My own opinion is, that he who has most evidence in his favour from those who from their observation on the spot are likely to know more of the matter than those who were far distant, has a fair claim to credence. As to Colonel Waller's account, that must be put out of the question altogether; it has been flatly contradicted by Sir Henry King, who commanded the 5th Infantry, which was one of the regiments belonging to Lightburne's, and Colonel King was second in command of that brigade; and if necessary, Sir Henry could be supported by the voices of all his soldiers who may be now living.

It has been positively asserted, and as pertinaciously adhered to, that the right of Picton's division was forced back; that the 8th Portuguese, under Douglas, were broken; and, in fine, that had it not been for the Fifth Division, the Third would have been routed. Lord Wellington does not say so in his dispatch, and Picton, in his letter to his lordship, of 3rd November, 1810, positively says such was not the case! But supposing, for argument sake, that Douglas's regiment was broken, surely Lord Wellington must have seen it, and it would have been easy to have sent Lightburne's brigade, who were near them and quite unoccupied, to the support of Douglas; or, the 88th, hardly as they had been handled, could have sent a few companies to this point

Independent of all this, if Picton's troops were in the peril they are represented to have been at this moment, is it likely that Lord Wellington would have frittered away such precious time in complimenting Colonel Wallace and his regiment, while almost the very ground he was standing on was in danger? Or is it likely that Picton would have been quite at his ease with the 88th Regiment, riding about at his leisure, while any portion of his division was in danger of defeat? His own character as a general might have been lost by such neglect on his part, and the character of the battle at this point quite changed. Indeed, it is not possible for anyone who was present to reconcile these accounts with what they themselves remember to have seen.

Much stress has been laid on the attack of Leith's division, and I have no reason to doubt that those who support this opinion do no more than give this gallant division their due merit; but nevertheless the dispatch of Lord Wellington, and the positive contradiction of Picton, have great weight with me as regards the overthrow of the Third Division. One thing is however tolerably clear as regards Leith's division and the attack of Wallace. If Colonel Napier has given the former more importance than it merits—and I by no means presume to say he has—he most certainly has not fallen into the same error with the latter; but he is not to be blamed, as he conceived he wrote upon unquestionable authority.

Howbeit, the matter stands as regards Lightburne's brigade and the attack of Wallace precisely as I have said; the late Sir Thomas Picton has contradicted the defeat of the right of his division, and Colonel Napier's brilliant account of the part the light division took in this battle, is no doubt perfectly correct, as is, indeed, everything he writes in his splendid *History of the Peninsular War*, when he writes from his own knowledge or from better information than that received by him from Colonel Waller.

I have before said that, immediately after the defeat of the French column by the 45th and 88th, Lord Wellington remained some time with Colonel Wallace and his regiment, and I think it must be clear to any person that had this attack, said to have been made so close to where his lordship was—not many yards from us—that not only Lord Wellington but the soldiers and officers must have heard a shot or two; but not the sound of one ever reached our ears;

I must therefore conclude, if the attack ever was made, it was confined to the use of the bayonet; for, beyond all question, no firing could have taken place so near us without its being distinctly heard. may, however, be wrong, and will not say, like Colonel Waller, that this charge did or did not take place—I only say, that I think it was morally impossible that such a contest so near us could have occurred without our hearing it I believe there has been more contradiction, more mis-statements, and more correspondence on this battle, than any that took place in the Peninsula.

There are one or two points, however, on which there can be no difference of opinion; but they are material ones, nevertheless. The first relates to Lightburne's brigade; the second to Colonel Napier's account of the attack made by the French column; but more particularly the order in which this column was in, and its fitness or unfitness for battle. If, as Colonel Napier says, they "were quite spent with their previous efforts," it would be well to know what those "previous exertions" were; and if those men were in the exhausted state they are described to have been, the 45th and 88th, although those two battalions routed four times their own numbers, did not merit the praise they received from Lord Wellington, or what I have said about them; but the fact is, as I have before stated, the column opposed to Wallace and Gwynne were composed of some of the best troops of the French army; and so far from being a "confused mass," as Colonel Napier has said, they made their gallant attack in the most perfect order, and made it like men resolved to conquer. Their soldiers, posted in the rocks, where they had been for some time before they were attacked and forced by the three companies of the 88th, fought to the last, and scarcely a man of those brave veterans escaped unhurt; and, to sum up all, the four companies of the 45th and 88th Regiments, of whom so little is said, lost about four times as many men as the entire Fifth Division!

The loss of Leith's troops in this affair of theirs was two officers, and between forty and fifty soldiers. Picton's loss was, British, twenty-two officers, and three hundred and nineteen soldiers; while the Portuguese belonging to his division lost fifteen officers and two hundred and fifty men—making a total of thirty-seven officers, and five hundred and sixty-nine non-commissioned and privates. This in itself is strong evidence as to the nature of the contest in which the two divisions were engaged, but I think it necessary to give the authorities to bear me out in what I have written, which will be found in the appendix to the present volume.

Note.—In the *Memoirs of the Empress Josephine*, page 217, this self-same 36th regiment is mentioned as being amongst the most highly-favoured by Napoleon, and the following incident is narrated concerning it, and two others:—"One day, Bonaparte having particularly remarked the excellent order of two regiments of the line and one of light infantry, called the officers in front, from the colonel to the corporal, and expressed, in very flattering terms, his satisfaction with the appearance of the men. This distinction excited no jealousy, for all had received, or expected, commendation; but in the evening, a number of the soldiers of the favoured regiments—the 36th, 57th, and 10th, assembled at a public-house a little way out of Boulogne, which was also a favourite resort of the grenadiers of the guard.

"At first, everything went on in an amicable way, until certain couplets, composed on the events of the morning, happened to be recited by some of the inhabitants, who had mixed with the military. The grenadiers for a time maintained an ominous silence, but finally protested against such verses being sung in their presence; the line interposed in their turn; a quarrel arose, first of words afterwards some blows were exchanged. On this they instantly separated, each quietly passing a challenge to his nearest opponent.

"At four o'clock next morning, above two hundred grenadiers of the guard separately stole out to the place of meeting, where had assembled, in like manner, an equal number of the three regiments. To it they went, sword in hand, without a word of explanation, and for more than an hour continued the combat with fearful obstinacy. They would probably have been massacred to a man, had not General St. Hilaire, obtaining late information of this sanguinary quarrel, galloped to the spot with a regiment of cavalry. In the conflict, the guards lost ten, and the line thirteen men; but the wounded on both sides were much more numerous." This extract shows the description of troops that were opposed to the 45th and 88th, and which advanced, not "in a confused mass," but with the utmost order and determination.

Chapter 7

Retreat of Massena's Army From Portugal

The astonishment of the French general was great, when he beheld the reception prepared for him; and his friend the Duke d'Abrantes must have been lowered in his estimation not a little, because it is well known that, contrary to the advice of several able officers, Massena was overruled by Junot, who assured him those heights could be easily carried.

After numerous reconnaissances, the French Marshal came to the resolution of renouncing any hope of success from an assault; and his army formed a line blockade, with its right at Otta, its centre at Alenquer, and its left at Villa Franca. But it must have been a matter of deep regret to him to have learned, when too late, that by this useless advance of his, he exposed upwards of three thousand of his wounded, in the battle of Busaco, left at Coimbra, to be massacred by the Portuguese militia and peasantry.

For the space of a month the French army remained inactive in their wretched cantonments, their supply of provisions growing every day more scanty; their horses, reduced to the necessity of subsisting on the vine twigs, died by hundreds; and the soldiers, pining from disease, became discontented and discouraged. In consequence, the desertions increased with their increasing wants, and it appeared very evident that matters could not long continue in the state they were the beginning of November.

Although our situation was, in every respect, better than that of the enemy, we were far from comfortable. Our huts, from want of any good materials to construct them, were but a weak defence against the heavy rains which fell at this time. We had no straw to serve for thatch, and the heath, which we were obliged to use as a substitute, though it looked well enough when in frill leaf and blossom, and was a delightful shelter in fine weather, became a wretched protection against the torrents that soon after inundated us.

The inside of our habitation presented an appearance as varied as it was uncomfortable; at one end might be seen a couple of officers, with their cloaks thrown about them, snoring on a truss of straw, while over their heads hung their blankets, which served as a kind of inner wall, and for a time stopped the flood that deluged the parts of the hut not so defended; but this, by degrees, becoming completely saturated with rain, not only lost its original appearance, but what was worse, its original usefulness; for the water, dripping down from the edges, gradually made its way towards the centre of the blanket, and thus, by degrees, it assumed a shape not unlike the parachute of a balloon, until at length being overpowered with its own weight, and, either giving way at the point or bottom, or breaking its hold from the twigs which feebly held it at top, overwhelmed those it was intended to protect, and in the space of a minute more effectually drenched them than the heaviest fall of rain would have accomplished in several hours.

In another corner lay someone else, who, for want of a better, substituted a sheet or an old tablecloth as a temporary defence; but this was even more disastrous than the blanket, for from the nature of its texture, and the imperfect manner in which it was from necessity pitched, it made but a poor stand; it soon performed the functions of a filtering machine, and with equal effect, though less force, was to the full as unserviceable as the blanket. Others more stout and convivial, sat up smoking cigars and drinking brandy punch, waiting for the signal to proceed to our alarm-post, a duty which the army performed every morning two hours before day. This was by no means a pleasant task; scrambling up a hill of mud, and standing shivering for a couple of hours in the dark and wet was exceedingly uncomfortable; but I don't remember to have heard one single murmur; we all saw the necessity of such a line of conduct, and we obeyed it with cheerfulness.

Reinforcements continued to arrive from home, and the Marquis de la Romana joined us with ten thousand Spaniards, but Lord Wellington nevertheless continued to strengthen our position. A second line of defence was established in rear of the one we occupied; its right on the river Tagus, and its left at Ericeira; an intrenched camp was also formed near Fort St Julien, at the mouth of the Tagus, so that in the event of any disaster occurring to the army which might render its embarkation necessary, this camp would effectually cover our movement. Its distance from Lisbon was sufficient to avoid the inconveniences which would arise from an operation of the kind performed in the vicinity of a great city; and had we met with the greatest reverse we could not be more guarded in our conduct: but there is a difference between caution and fear, and apprehension of danger is not to be termed pusillanimity.

Yet much as all these precautions occupied the mind of his lordship, they were as nought compared to the strife he was engaged in with the opposition in the Portuguese ministry, and the civil—anything but civil to him—authority!

On the 14th of November Massena broke up his camp, and on that night his army was in full march upon Santarem; ours made a corresponding movement, and the head-quarters were on the 18th established at Cartaxo.

It was the general opinion in the army, that a battle in the neighbourhood of Santarem would be the result of those manoeuvres, and this opinion was strengthened by Lord Wellington making a reconnaissance on the 19th; but although those expectations were disappointed, the situation of the troops was much improved, and their comforts increased. Our division occupied the town of Torres Vedras, while the other corps were in the villages of Alenquer, Azambujo, and Alcoentre. The French army foraged the country between Santarem and the river Zezere. Santarem was much strengthened, and the two armies were thus circumstanced in November, 1810.

Our fatigues being for a time at an end, we occupied ourselves in such pursuits as each of us fancied. We had no unnecessary drilling, nor were we tormented with that greatest of all bores to an officer at any time, but particularly on service, uniformity of dress. The consequence was that every duty was performed with cheerfulness; the army was in the highest state of discipline; and those gentlemen who had, or fancied they had, a taste for leading the fashion, had now a fine opportunity of bringing their talents into play.

With such latitude it is not to be wondered at that our appearance was not quite as uniform as some general officers would approve of: but Lord Wellington was a most indulgent commander; he never harassed us with reviews, or petty annoyances, which so far from promoting discipline, or doing good in any way, has a contrary effect. A corporal's guard frequently did the duty at headquarters; and every officer who chose to purchase a horse might ride on a march. Provided we brought our men into the field well appointed, and with sixty rounds of good ammunition each, he never looked to see whether their trousers were black, blue, or grey; and as to ourselves, we might be rigged out in all the colours of the rainbow if we fancied it.

The consequence was, that scarcely any two officers were dressed alike! Some with grey braided coats, others with brown; some again liked blue; while many from choice, or perhaps necessity, stuck to the "old red rag."

Overalls, of all things, were in vogue, and the comical appearance of a number of infantry officers loaded with leather bottoms to their pantaloons, and huge chains suspended from the side buttons, like a parcel of troopers, was amusing enough. Some had such a penchant for leather, that their pantaloons were covered with it from bottom to top; and it often occurred to me, while surveying the well-leathered trousers, of those modern heroes, that, notwithstanding the great change in military tactics, since in olden time the "town was threatened with a siege," they still clung to the forcible opinion delivered by the currier on that ever memorable occasion.

Quantities of hair, a regular *brutus*, a pair of *mustachioes*, and screw brass spurs, were essential to a first rate Count, for so were our dandies designated. The "cut down" hat, exactly a span in height, was another rage; this burlesque on a *chapeau* was usually out-topped by some extraordinary-looking feather; while again, others wore their hats without any feather at all—and indeed this was the most rational thing they did. In the paroxism of a wish to be singularly singular, a friend of mine shaved all the hair off the crown of his head, and he was decidedly the most *outré*-looking man amongst us, and consequently the happiest I myself had a hankering to be a *Count,* and had I half as much money to spare as time, I would not have been outdone by any man in the army, so I hit upon the expedient of cutting my hat down a couple of inches lower than anyone else: this I thought would be better than nothing.

Lieutenant Heppenstal, of the 88th Regiment, was nearly falling a sacrifice to the richness of his dress. He belonged to the light troops of our army at the battle of Busaco, and was warmly engaged with the advance of the enemy. He was a man of the most determined bravery and gigantic strength, and more than once became personally engaged with the French riflemen. At one time, carried away by his daring impetuosity, he pursued his success so far as to be nearly mixed with the enemy; a number of Portuguese Caçadores coming up at this moment, mistook him for a French general officer, and attempted to make him a prisoner; a scuffle ensued, in which he lost the skirts of his frock-coat; and it was not until an explanation took place, that he was enabled to join his regiment in this laughable trim—his beautiful gold-tagged frock being converted into a regular spencer.

Poor Heppenstal! It was his first appearance under fire, and it was not difficult for those who witnessed his too gallant *début,* to foresee that his career of glory would be short He carried a rifle, and his unerring aim brought down many a man on the morning I am speaking of; but he did not long survive the praises so justly bestowed on him; and it will soon be my painful duty to record his death.

Dress, however, with its attractions, by no means engrossed all our thoughts; some were fond of shooting, and those whose tastes lay that way, had plenty of sport, as the country abounded in game; others took to horse-racing, and here was a fine opportunity for the lovers of the turf and of dress, to display their knowledge in both. Jockeys, adorned with all colours, were to be seen on the course, and the harlequin-like appearance of these equestrians was far from unpleasing. Some of the races were admirably contested, and afforded us as much gratification as those of Epsom and Doncaster do to the visitants of those receptacles of rank and fashion.

There were a few who applied themselves to learning the Portuguese language, but these instances were rare, and seldom attended with much success, and for this reason—that we had no native society sufficiently agreeable to compensate for the purgatorial punishment we were obliged to endure when approaching the Portuguese females. The best dressed *gigot à la Française* never more profusely savoured of garlick than did the breaths of those fair ones; and in many instances a few straggling *piolhos* might be seen traversing the greasy foreheads of those odorous *senhoras*; and as to the men, there was nothing to induce us to have any intercourse with them.

Great inconvenience in making ourselves understood was in consequence often felt, and a laughable circumstance of this sort took place between a friend of mine and a shoemaker, in the village of Rio Mayor. He left his boots, his only pair, to be mended, and understood they were to be put in serviceable condition for a *crusado novo,* less than three shillings of our money. Next day, on entering the shop, the man made two or three efforts to make the officer comprehend how well the work had been done; but it was all to no purpose, for my friend, not understanding one worn of what was said, conceived the fellow wanted to impose a higher price upon him, and got into a violent rage. An Irish soldier, belonging to the 88th Regiment, of the name of Larracy, a shoemaker, who had been working for the Portuguese, a common indulgence allowed to the tradesmen of the army, came up to his officer, and thus accosted him.—

"Ah! your honour, I see you can't talk to him, but lave him to me; I've been working in his shop these three weeks, and, saving your presence, there isn't a bigger rascal in all Ireland; but I can spake as well as himself now, and I'm up to his ways."

Larracy thus became interpreter and mediatory and it would be difficult to say in which character he best acquitted himself. Possessing no knowledge whatever of the language, notwithstanding his repeated assurances that he could talk it *nately,* he brought that happy talent for invention, for which the Irish most undeniably stand unrivalled, into play. Seizing one of the boots he approached his employer, and suiting the word to the action, addressed him in the following words:—

"*Si, senhor!*[1] *Quanto* the munnee, for the solee, the heelee, and the nailee?"

The astonishment portrayed in the countenance of the Portuguese baffles all description; he surveyed Larracy from head to foot, and with much gravity of manner replied, "*Eu nào entendo-o que vós me dizeis.*" [2]

"And sure I'm telling him so," rejoined Larracy.

"What does the fellow say?" demanded my friend—

"What does he say?—What does he say, is it? He says he put a fine pair of welts to your boots, sir; (and it's true for him!) and that your honour will have to give him a dollar (about two shillings more than was demanded by the Portuguese!) but just only lave him to me, and give me the dollar, and if I don't bate him down in the price, never believe a word that I'll tell your honour again; and I'll carry home your boots for you, and bring you the account in rotation, (by which he meant in writing,) and the change of the dollar."—

"Oh! never mind, you are an honest fellow, Larracy, and keep the change for your trouble; but you may tell your employer it is the last job he shall ever do for me."—

"Och! sure I told your honour he was a blackguard," grinned Larracy, escorting his officer to the door, and putting the dollar in his pocket.

Every day the army assumed a more imposing attitude, and early in December, our brigade advanced as far as Tagarro, where General Picton established his head quarters. The enemy was not inactive. The Ninth Corps stationed at Sabugal, made a movement upon Castello Branco and Punhete, and General Drouet, penetrating the pass of Marcella formed a junction with the Prince of Esling, whose army, by this reinforcement, notwithstanding its previous losses, counted seventy thousand men and upwards.

With such a force at his disposal, it was but natural to suppose Massena would have felt anxious to revenge the disgrace of his defeat at Busaco, and his subsequent blunder in advancing to the lines of Lisbon; but the contrary was the case, and the "favourite Child of Victory," (as the Emperor Napoleon used to style him,) seemed to

---

1. Yes, sir.
2. I do not understand a word you are saying to me.

have lost his former impetuosity, and the laurels which the hero of Rivoli and Aspern had so hardly won, were unquestionably on the eve of being torn from his brow by the general, whom the *Moniteur,* a few months before, had given a friendly hint, that the French imperial army were not an army of Sepoys! Indeed, ever since the fall of Almeida, Massena did little to sustain the high reputation he hid earned; he displayed neither the qualities of a Marcellus or a Fabius, and he disappointed us as much as he did his master.

He might have cantoned his army on the Mondego and Douro, in the neighbourhood of Lamego, Vizeu, and Coimbra, where their situation would have been far better than cooped up in unhealthy half-burnt villages, such as those they occupied near the lines of Torres Vedras, and his superior cavalry would have given him the option of choosing his own field of battle or declining ours.

During this time of comparative inactivity, there were few lives lost. On our side, Captain Fenwick, an officer of first-rate merit, was killed at Obidos in an affair of outposts, and the French lost a general of high promise, of the name of Saint Croix, in the neighbourhood of Villa Franca. This officer was making a reconnaissance, when a round shot from one of our gun-boats, that were stationed in the Tagus, cut him in two. His loss was much lamented in the French army, and no person in ours felt any gratification in hearing of the death of a fine young man, so prematurely and ingloriously cut off.

He was little more than one-and-twenty, yet he commanded Massena's advance-guard in the passage of the Danube in 1809, and was his greatest favourite; it was he who anticipated our movement on Sarda—after the battle of the 27th of September at Busaco. About this time the Duke d'Abrantes received a wound in his face from one of our riflemen, while reconnoitring our post at Rio Mayor; and we had to lament the death of the Marquis de la Romana. He had passed the greater part of his life in France, but was one of the staunchest supporters of his country's cause.

When the alliance between France and Spain was closest, the Marquis co-operated in the general system of war established by Napoleon against England, and he commanded a division of troops destined to act in the north of Europe; but the moment the situation in which his country was placed was made known to him, he did not hesitate upon the part he was to act in the great drama about to be performed. A favourable opportunity occurring, he embarked his troops on board some English transports, and landed in Spain in the year 1808. From this period, up to the moment of his death, he promoted, as much as in him lay, the great cause for which we were fighting—not the liberty of Spain alone, but of Europe. His death was most sudden; he had but just left his house, when he was seized with an apoplectic fit, and he died immediately.

The day before his death he sent General Mendizabel to the relief of Olivenza and Badajoz, at this time invested by Marshal Mortier. The Spanish general arrived too late to be of any use to the former, and he lost almost all his army in endeavouring to relieve the latter.

Posting his army on the right bank of the Guadiana, under the guns of St Christoval, which was but a poor point *d'appui,* considering the description of troops General Mendizabel commanded, and those which were about to assail him, he thought himself perfectly secure. A few hours, however, undeceived him. On the following morning he was attacked in his position, and his army giving way at the first discharge, were totally overthrown, the fugitives either saving themselves under the guns of Badajoz, or taking flight towards Elvas, gained the latter fortress in the course of the day. Badajoz was forthwith invested, and in less than three weeks fell.

While in the other parts of the Peninsula much activity prevailed, with us all was quiet; and although the season was advancing towards spring, there was no appearance of our commencing the offensive, and conjectures innumerable were the consequence. Promotion, that great planet whose influence more or less affected us all, was perpetually on the *tapis.*

There were some among us of a desponding cast; they would say, "Have we not lost Almeida, Rodrigo, and now, though last not least, Badaioz? And should we be obliged to evacuate the Peninsula, goodbye to promotion."

Others there were who held a different opinion, and, resting their hopes on some fortunate "turn-up," expected ere long to have the enviable title of captain attached to their name. To this class I belonged, and as it was the most numerous in the army, it was of consequence the most clamorous on this head.

The life of a subaltern, in what Miss MacTab would call a marching regiment, where many of us, and I myself for one, had little except our pay, is a perpetual scene of irritating calculation from the 24th of one month to the 24th of the next No matter under what circumstances, or in what quarter of the globe the subaltern is placed, his first thought points towards that powerful magnet the twenty-fourth—his next to promotion.

The 24th has scarcely passed, when the same routine is pursued, every hour increasing in interest according to the immediate wants of the calculator; and time rolls on, either rapidly or slowly, in the exact ratio with the strength or weakness of his purse. The moment he receives his pay he discharges his bills, and by the time he has cot about half way into the first week of the next month, he has little occasion for a knowledge of Cocker to enable him to calculate his money.

The period generally reckoned on by a subaltern to get his company, in a good fighting regiment—that is to say, one that has the good luck to be in the thick and thin of what is going on, for all regiments fight alike for that matter, was from five to six years. The "extra shilling" was rarely heard of, and never thought of but with disgust.

It was during the time of those conflicting opinions, that an old German officer thought fit to put in his claim. He conjectured that an opportunity of witnessing the decapitation of his captain was not likely to occur, and fearing, if he let the present moment pass, he might be a subaltern for the residue of his life, resolved to memorialise. I was favoured with the rough draft, and upon perusing it, was at a loss whether most to admire the simplicity with which it was drawn up, or the forcible pithiness with which the veteran detailed his services; and as it was unlike any memorial I ever saw, or, indeed, ever heard of before, I shall give it *verbatim*; it ran thus:—

To the Commander-In-Chief.
The memorial of Kroppf Hoffinger,
Sheweth,
That when your memorialist was seven years a lieutenant, you gave him an extra shilling.
On the 16th of last September he was fourteen years a lieu-

tenant, and he hopes you will give him another extra shilling. Your memorialist has seen some service, having been present in fifteen general engagements, sixty-four skirmishes, and thirteen flying camps; and he farther takes the liberty of hinting that he is the oldest subaltern in the world.

CHAPTER 8

Battle of Fuentes d'Onore

The retreat of the French army from Portugal commenced on the night of the 5th of March 1811, and was marked by acts more suited to a horde of barbarians than a European army. On the fact being ascertained at our head-quarters, we were put in their track, which, when once found, it would have been a difficult matter to lose; the whole country through which they passed being a vast extent of burning ruins. Not a town, not a village, and rarely a cottage escaped the general conflagration. The beautiful town of Leyria was left a heap of ruins; Pombal shared the same fate, and the magnificent convent of Alcobaça was burned to the ground; two of the finest organs in Europe were destroyed by this wanton act, and a century will be insufficient to repair the evils which a few months inflicted on this unfortunate country.

Some marauders, who left their respective columns to explore those parts of the country, which from their mountainous and rocky situation were impassable for an army encumbered with baggage and cannon, surprised the unfortunate peasantry in those retreats which they had hitherto considered secure, and not only plundered them of their little remnant of provisions, but massacred all those who attempted to defend their property. The whole country, consequently, with but few exceptions, fell a prey to the fugitives of this ill-fitted expedition, who, in their turn, suffered from the system of retaliation which was practised by the people whenever an opportunity offered itself.

Scenes of the most revolting nature were the natural attendants on such a barbarous mode of warfare, and scarcely a league was traversed by our army, in its advance, without our eyes being shocked by some frightful spectacle. The French army were doubtless much exasperated against the Portuguese nation, in consequence of the manner in which they destroyed what would have contributed to the comforts of the former, who had been half-starved for six months in consequence of this conduct on the part of the people, and now, after so many privations, having a long retreat before them, with a scanty allowance of provisions in their haversacks, at is more to be lamented than wondered at, that the march of the French troops was accompanied by many circumstances which were disgraceful to them.

On the 9th of March our advanced-guard came up with the rear of the enemy, commanded by Marshal Ney, in the neighbourhood of Pombal; the light division was warmly engaged, and some charges of cavalry took place on the high ground near the castle; but the infantry of our division (the third) arrived too late to support the light, and no decisive result was the consequence. Massena continued his retreat that night and next day; but on the 11th we found him posted on a rising ground near the village of Redinha; our army formed in line on the plain, and an action of some consequence was expected; but the French marshal was so pressed in front, while his left was vigorously attacked, that it was not without sustaining a severe loss he effected his passage across the river Redinha.

On the 15th we surprised their covering division while in the act of cooking near the village of Foz d'Arouce; they retreated in the greatest hurry, leaving several camp kettles full of meat behind them. As we approached the town, the road leading to it was covered with a number of horses, mules, and asses, all maimed; but the most disgusting sight was 'about fifty of the asses floundering in the mud, some with their throats half cut, while others were barbarously houghed, or otherwise injured. What the object of this proceeding meant I never could guess; the poor brutes could have been of no use to us, or indeed anyone else, as I believe they were unable to have travelled another league; the meagre appearance of these creatures, with their back-bones and hips protruding through their hides, and their mangled and bleeding throats, produced a general feeling of disgust and commiseration.

The village of Foz d'Arouce was warmly contested, and more

than once taken and retaken. Night put a stop to this affair, in which we sustained a loss of about four hundred men; the enemy lost nearly a thousand *hors de combat;* and, as usual, taking advantage of the night, and the numerous incidents which a retreating army possesses through such a country as Portugal—and commanded by an officer of such experience and ability as Marshal Ney—continued their retreat upon Guarda, having destroyed the bridge on the river Ceira as they retired.

The army did not lose any officer of rank in the affair of Foz d'Arouce, but the service sustained a loss in Lieutenant Heppenstal—a young man, who, had he lived, would have been an ornament to a profession for which Nature seemed to have destined him. He was known to be one of the bravest men in the army, but on this occasion his usual spirits deserted him. He moved along silent, inattentive, and abstracted—a brisk firing in our front soon roused all his wonted energy, and he advanced with his men apparently cheerful as ever; turning to a brother officer he said, "You will laugh at what I am going to say; you know I am not afraid to die, but I have a certain feeling that my race is nearly run."

"You jest," said his friend.

"No, I don't," was his reply; they shook hands, the light troops advanced, and in a few minutes the brave Heppenstal was a corpse. His presentiment was too just, and though I had heard of instances of the kind before, this was the first that came under my immediate observation. I ran up to the spot where he lay; he was bleeding profusely; his breast was penetrated by two bullets, and a third passed through his forehead. His death was singular, and it appeared as if he was resolved to fulfil the destiny that he had marked out for himself.

Our light troops were gradually retreating on their reinforcements, and were within a few paces of the columns of infantry; his men repeatedly called out to him to retire with the rest, but he, either not hearing, or not attending to what they said, remained, with his back against a pine-tree, dealing out death at every shot Pressed as we were for time, we dug him a deep grave at the foot of the tree where he so gallantly lost his life, and we laid him in it without form or ceremony.

Nothing particular occurred after the action of Foz d'Arouce, until our arrival at Guarda; as usual, we met with groups of murdered peasantry and of French soldiers. At the entrance of a cave, amidst these rocky mountains, lay an old man, a woman, and two young men, all dead. This cave, no doubt, had served them as an asylum the preceding winter, and appearances warranted the supposition that these poor creatures, in a vain effort to save their little store of provisions, fell victims to the ferocity of their murderers. The clothes of the two young peasants were torn to atoms, and bore ample testimony that they did not lose their lives without a struggle to preserve them; the hands of one were dreadfully mangled, as if in a last effort to save his life he had grasped the sword which ultimately dispatched him; beside him lay his companion, his brother, perhaps, covered with wounds; and a little to the right was the old man.

He lay on his back with his breast bare; two large gashes were over his heart, and the back part of his head was beaten to pieces. Near him lay an old rusty bayonet fixed on a pole, which formerly served as a goad for oxen, and one of his hands grasped a bunch of hair, torn, no doubt, from the head of the assassin; the old woman was in all probability strangled, as no wound appeared on her body.

At some distance from this spot were two French soldiers of the 4th of the line,—their appearance was frightful. They had been wounded by our advance, and their companions either being too much occupied in providing for their own safety to think of them, or, their situation being too hopeless to entertain an idea of their surviving, they were abandoned to the fury of the peasants, who invariably dodged on the flanks or in the rear of our troops. These poor wretches were surrounded by half a dozen Portuguese, who, after having plundered them, were taking that horrible vengeance too common during this contest On the approach of our men they dispersed, but, as we passed on, we could perceive them returning like vultures that have been scared away from their prey for the moment, but who return to it again with redoubled voraciousness. Both the Frenchmen were alive, and entreated us to put an end to their sufferings. I thought it would have been humane to do so, but Napoleon and Jaffa flashed across me, and I turned away from the spot.

During the entire of those operations, which lasted two or three and twenty days, the events which took place, save those I mention, are not worth recording. The light division, so celebrated even at this early period of the war, was ever in advance; it had almost all the fighting as well as the fag; while ours (the Third) had plenty of fag but scarcely any fighting. The army, however, soon afterwards styled us "the fighting envision," a title we never forfeited, for from our first formation as a division until the peace of 1814, that is to say five years, during which period we fought six general battles, stormed two towns, and were engaged m numberless minor combats, we never sustained a reverse.

On the 30th of March, General Picton arrived before Guarda, his approach to that town was not only unperceived, but seemed unexpected, having advanced to within two gunshots of the town without meeting a *vidette*. Such conduct on the part of the French general was not only culpable in the extreme, but showed the greatest presumption and confidence, because, had we a brigade of guns with us, and a few hundred cavalry, the five thousand men that occupied Guarda would have been forced to lay down their arms.[1]

Fortunately for them, we had neither the one nor the other; and instead of being in a condition to attack the town, we had the mortification to witness the French getting out of it, bag and baggage, as quick as they could. The scene of confusion that the streets presented was great; infantry, artillery, and baggage, men, women, and children, all mixed pell-mell together, hurrying to the high road leading to Sabugal. Our cavalry came up shortly after the enemy had evacuated the place, but too late to do much good. Some prisoners and baggage, and a few head of cattle, were captured; and we took up our quarters in the town for the night.

On the 3rd of April we again, and for the last time in Portugal, encountered the enemy at Sabugal. The light division had a gallant affair with the corps of General Reynier, and, though greatly outnumbered, they not only succeeded in forcing the position, but captured a howitzer and several prisoners; the Third Division soon after reached the ground, and its leading battalions, especially the

---

1. It may be asked why we had not one, or both. I cannot say why we had not. The fault lay somewhere, hut whether in the general of division, or the commander-in-chief, I cannot pretend to say.

5th Regiment, had deployed, and, having thrown in a heavy fire, were advancing with the bayonet, when a violent hail-storm came on, and completely hid the two armies from each other. Reynier hurried his divisions off the field, and this unlooked-for event snatched a brilliant exploit from us, as the total overthrow of this corps would have been in all probability the result

The French suffered severely, but they never fought better; so rapidly did they fire, that instead of returning their ramrods, they stuck them in the ground for expedition, and continued to fight, until overpowered by our men, who are certainly better at close fighting than long shot

The enemy fought their howitzer well, and almost all the gunners lay dead about it: a young artillery officer was the first I took notice of; his uniform was still on him, an unusual thing; he wore a blue frock-coat; across his shoulder hung his cartouche-box; and the middle of his forehead was pierced by a musket ball. His features, which, were beautiful, showed, nevertheless, a painful distortion, and it was evident that the shock which deprived him of life, though momentary, was one of excruciating agony—beside him lay one of the gunners, whose appearance was altogether different from that of his officer. A round shot had taken off his thigh a few inches below the groin, and his death, though not as instantaneous, seemed to be void of pain. The bare stump exhibited a shocking sight,—the muscles, arteries, and flesh, all hanging in frightful confusion, presented the eye with a horrid sample of the effects of those means made use of by man for his own destruction; the ramrod of the gun was near him; his back rested against one of the wheels; and there was that placid look in his countenance which would lead you to think he had sat himself down to rest

The wounded having been all removed, and the enemy continuing their retreat, we bivouacked on the ground they had occupied at the commencement of the action, and the next day we went into cantonments. The French recrossed the Agueda, and Portugal was, with the exception of Almeida, freed from their presence, after having occupied it for nearly eight months, and having inflicted on the inhabitants every misery it is possible to conceive.

Four weeks had scarcely elapsed when we were again called into action. On the 2nd of May, Marshal Massena passed the river

Agueda at Rodrigo, and moved upon Almeida, in order to supply it with provisions. He had left a garrison of three thousand men in that fortress, commanded by General Brennier, in whom he placed much confidence. The French Marshal stationed his army on the river Azava, in the neighbourhood of Carpio, Espeja, and Gallegos; and next day (the 3rd) made a movement on Almeida. Lord Wellington made a corresponding movement, and our army occupied a fine line of battle; its right at Nava d'Aver, the centre at Fuentes d'Onore, and the left resting on the ruins of the Fort de la Conception; in our front ran the little stream of Onore. General Pack's brigade of Portuguese invested Almeida.'

This position, though a desirable one in many respects, was not faultless; there were parts of it of difficult access; from the Fort of Conception, on our extreme left, to our centre at Fuentes d'Onore, was mostly a rugged ravine, but the ground between Fuentes d'Onore and Posobello, and between Posobello and Nava d'Aver, was a continued flat, and afforded a fine field for the French cavalry to manoeuvre upon; they were much superior to ours in number, and thither it was supposed the enemy would direct his efforts, but the contrary was the case.

Without waiting to ascertain the strength or weakness of the position, Marshal Massena, with that impetuosity which had formerly characterised him, ordered the village of Fuentes d'Onore to be carried; and to make his success certain, the entire of the Sixth Corps was employed in the attack. The town was at this time occupied by some of our First Division, consisting of the Highland regiments, supported by others of the line, and the light companies of the First and Third Division, commanded by Major Dick, of the 42nd Highlanders, and Colonel Williams, of the 60th. The village was taken and retaken several times, and night found both armies occupying a part each.

Massena perceiving that the obstacles opposed to his carrying this point, which he considered the key of our position, were too great for him to surmount, employed himself the entire of the 4th in reconnoitring our line, and in making preparations for the battle which was to take place the following day. On our side we were not inactive: the avenues leading to Posobello and Fuentes were barricaded in the best manner the moment would allow; temporary defences were constructed at the heads of the different streets, and trenches dug here and there, as a protection against the impetuous attacks expected from the cavalry of General Mont Brun. We lay down to rest perfectly assured that every necessary precaution had been taken by our general; and as to the result of the battle, we looked upon that as certain, a series of engagements with the enemy having taught us to estimate our own prowess; and being a good deal overcome with the heat of the weather, we lay down to rest, and slept soundly.

Day had scarcely dawned, when the roar of artillery and musketry announced the attack of Fuentes d'Onore and Posobello. Five thousand men filled the latter village, and after a desperate conflict carried it with the bayonet General Mont Brun, at the head of the French cavalry, vigorously attacked the right of our army; but he was received with much steadiness by our Seventh Division, which, though it fought in line, repulsed the efforts made to break it, and drove back the cavalry in confusion. The light troops, immediately in front of the First and Third Divisions, were in like manner charged by bodies of the enemy's horse, but by manoeuvres well executed, in proper time, these attacks were rendered as fruitless as the main one against the right of our army.

The officer who commanded this advance, either too much elated with his success, or holding the efforts of the enemy in too light a point of view, unfortunately extended his men once more to the distance at which light troops usually fight; the consequence was fatal. The enemy, though defeated in his principal attack, was still powerful as a minor antagonist; and seeing the impossibility of success against the main body, redoubled his efforts against those which were detached; accordingly he charged with impetuosity the troops most exposed, amongst whom were those I have been describing: the bugle sounded to close, but whether to the centre, right, or left, I know not; certain it is, however, that the men attempted to close to the right, when to the centre would have been more desirable, and before they could complete their movement, the French cavalry were mixed with them.

Our division was posted on the high ground just above this plain; a small rugged ravine separated us from our comrades; but although the distance between us was short, we were, in effect, as far from them as if we were placed upon the rock of Lisbon: we felt much for their situation, but could not afford them the least assistance, and we saw them rode down and cut to pieces, without being able to rescue them, or even discharge one musket in their defence.

Our heavy horse and the 16th Light Dragoons executed some brilliant charges, in each of which they overthrew the French cavalry. An officer of our staff, who led on one of those attacks, unhorsed, and made prisoner Colonel La Motte, of the 16th French Chasseurs; but Don Julian Sanchez, the guerilla chief, impelled more by valour than prudence, attacked with his guerillas a first-rate French regiment; the consequence was the total overthrow of the Spanish hero; and as I believe this was the first attempt this species of troops ever made at a regular charge against a French regiment, so I hope, for their own sakes, it was their last

All the avenues leading to the town of Fuentes d'Onore were in a moment filled with French troops; it was occupied by our 71st and 79th Highlanders, the 83rd, the light companies of the First and Third Divisions, and some German and Portuguese battalions, supported by the 24th, 45th, 74th, and 88th British regiments, and the 9th and 21st Portuguese.

The Ninth Corps, which formed the centre of the French army, advanced with the characteristic impetuosity of their nation, and forcing down the barriers, which we had hastily constructed as a temporary defence, came rushing on, and torrent-like, threatened to overwhelm all that opposed them. Every street, and every angle of a street, were the different theatres for the combatants; inch by inch was gained and lost in turn.

Whenever the enemy were forced back, fresh troops, and fresh energy on the part of their officers impelled them on again, and towards midday, the town presented a shocking sight; our Highlanders lay dead in heaps, while the other regiments, though less remarkable in dress, were scarcely so in the numbers of their slain; the French grenadiers, with their immense caps and gaudy plumes, in piles of twenty and thirty together—some dead, others wounded, with barely strength sufficient to move; their exhausted state, and the weight of their cumbrous appointments, making it impossible for them to crawl out of the range of the dreadful fire of grape and round shot which the enemy poured into the town: great numbers perished in this way, and many were pressed to death in the streets.

It was now half-past twelve o'clock, and although the French troops which formed this attack had been several times reinforced, ours never had; nevertheless the town was still in dispute. Massena, aware of its importance, and mortified at the pertinacity with which it was defended, ordered a fresh column of the ninth corps to reinforce those already engaged. Such a series of attacks, constantly supported by fresh troops, required exertions more than human to withstand; every effort was made to sustain the post, but efforts, no matter how great, must have their limits. Our soldiers had been engaged in this unequal contest for upwards of eight hours, the heat was moreover excessive, and their ammunition was nearly expended.

The Highlanders were driven to the churchyard at the top of the village, and were fighting with the French grenadiers across the tombstones and graves; while the Ninth French Light Infantry had penetrated as far as the chapel, distant but a few yards from our line, and were preparing to *debouche* upon our centre. Wallace with his regiment, the 88th, was in reserve on the high ground which overlooked the churchyard, and he was attentively looking on at the combat which raged below, when Sir Edward Pakenham galloped up to him, and said, "Do you see that, Wallace?"

"I do," replied the colonel, "and I would rather drive the French out of the town than cover a retreat across the Coa."

"Perhaps," said Sir Edward, "his lordship don't think it tenable."

Wallace answering said, "I shall take it with my regiment, and keep it too."

"Will you?" was the reply, "I'll go and tell Lord Wellington so; see, here he comes."

In a moment or two Pakenham returned at a gallop, and, waving his hat, called out, "He says you may go—come along, Wallace."

At this moment General Mackinnon came up, and placing himself beside Wallace and Pakenham, led the attack of the 88th Regiment, which soon changed the state of affairs. This battalion advanced with fixed bayonets in column of sections, left in front, in double quick time, their firelocks at the trail. As it passed down the road leading to the chapel, it was warmly cheered by the troops that lay at each side of the wall, but the soldiers made no reply to this greeting—they, were placed in a situation of great distinction, and they felt it; they were going to fight, not only under the eye of their own army and general, but also in the view of every soldier in the French army; but although their feelings were wrought up to the highest pitch of enthusiasm, not one hurrah responded to the shouts that welcomed their advance,—there was no noise or talking in the ranks, the men stepped together at a smart trot, as if on a parade, headed by their brave colonel.

It so happened that the command of the company which led this attack devolved upon me. When we came within sight of the French Ninth Regiment, which were drawn up at the corner of the chapel, waiting for us, I turned round to look at the men of my company, they gave me a cheer that a lapse of many years has not made me forget, and I thought that that moment was the proudest of my life. The soldiers did not look as men usually do going into close fight—pale; the trot down the road had heightened their complexions, and they were the picture of everything that a chosen body of troops ought to be.

The enemy were not idle spectators of this movement; they witnessed its commencement, and the regularity with which the advance was conducted made them fearful of the result. A battery of eight-pounders advanced at a gallop to an olive-grove on the opposite bank of the river, hoping by the effects of its fire to annihilate the 88th Regiment, or, at all events, embarrass its movements as much as possible; but this battalion continued to press on, joined by its exhausted comrades, and the battery did little execution.

On reaching the head of the village, the 88th Regiment was vigorously opposed by the Ninth Regiment, supported by some hundred of the Imperial Guard, but it soon closed in with them, and, aided by the brave fellows that had so gallantly fought in the town all the morning, drove the enemy through the different streets at the point of the bayonet, and at length forced them into the river that separated the two armies. Several of our men fell on the French side of the water.

About one hundred and fifty of the grenadiers of the Veteran Guard, in their flight, ran down a street that had been barricaded by us the day before, and which was one of the few that escaped the fury of the morning's assault; but their disappointment was great, upon arriving at the bottom, to find themselves shut in;—mistakes of this kind will sometimes occur, and when they do, the result is easily imagined,—troops advancing to assault a town, uncertain of success, or flushed with victory, have no great time to deliberate as to what they will do; the thing is generally done in half the time the deliberation would occupy. In the present instance, every man was put to death; but our soldiers, as soon as they had leisure, paid the enemy that respect which is due to brave men. This part of the attack was led by Lieutenant George Johnston, of the 88th Regiment.

CHAPTER 9

General Brennier's Escape From Almeida

As soon as the town of Fuentes d'Onore was completely cleared of the enemy, we sheltered ourselves in the best manner we could behind the walls, and at the angles of the different streets; but this was a task not easy to be accomplished, the French batteries continued to fire with such effect: nevertheless, Sir Edward Pakenham remained on horseback, riding through the streets with that daring bravery for which he was remarkable. If he stood still for a moment, the ground about him was ploughed up with round shot

About this time, Colonel Cameron, of the 79th Highlanders, fell, as did also Captain Irwin, of the 88th Regiment; the death of the latter officer was singular. He had been many years in the army, but this was his first appearance in action. He was shortsighted, and the firing having in some degree slackened, he was anxious to take a view of the scene that was passing: he put his head above the wall behind which his men were stationed, but had scarcely placed his glass to his eye, when a bullet struck him in the forehead—he sprang from the earth and fell dead.

General MacKinnon and a group of mounted officers were behind the chapel wall, which was the highest point in the village, and consequently much exposed to the enemy's view. This ill-built wall was but a feeble defence against round shot, and it was knocked down in several places, and some wide gaps were made in it. The general stood at one of these breaches giving his directions; he attracted the enemy's notice, and they redoubled their fire on this point. Salvos of artillery astounded our ears, at each of which some part of the old wall was knocked about us; at one of these discharges, five or six feet of it was beaten down, and several men were crushed. Colonel Wallace, of the 88th, was covered with the rubbish, his hat was knocked off, and we thought he was killed, but fortunately he escaped unhurt.

By two o'clock the town was comparatively tranquil. The cannonading on the right of the line had ceased, but the enemy continued to fire on the town; this proceeding was attended with little loss to us, and was fatal to many of their wounded, who lay in a helpless state in the different streets, and could not be moved from their situation without great peril to our men—and they were torn to pieces by the shot of their own army. Several of these poor wretches were saved by the humane exertions of our soldiers, but still it was not possible to attend to all; and, consequently, the havoc made was great.

Towards evening the firing ceased altogether, and it was a gratifying sight to behold the soldiers of both armies, who but a few hours before were massacring each other, mutually assisting to remove the wounded to their respective sides of the river. The town too, as was usual in such cases, was not passed unnoticed; it contained little, it is true, yet even that little was better than nothing; and it was laughable to see the scrupulous observation of *etiquette* practised by our men, when any windfall, such as a chest of bread or bacon, happened to fall to the lot of a group of individuals in their foraging excursions. The following was the method taken to divide the spoil, and as no national distinction was thought of, the French as well as the British shared in whatever was acquired.

An old experienced stager or two, took upon themselves the responsibility of making a division of the plunder according to the number that were present at the capture. This done one of the party was placed with his back to the booty; when one of those who had partitioned it called out with an audible voice—"Who is to have this?" at the same time pointing to the parcel about to be transferred, while he, that was appealed to, without hesitation particularized some one of the number, who immediately seized on his portion, put it into his haversack, and proceeded in search of fresh adventures.

We had now leisure to walk through the town, and observe

the effects of the morning's affray. The two armies lost about eight thousand men, and as the chief of this loss was sustained by the troops engaged in the town, the streets were much crowded with the dead and wounded. French and British lay in heaps together, and it would be difficult to say which were most numerous; some of the houses were also crowded with dead Frenchmen, who either crawled there after being wounded, in order to escape the incessant fire which cleared the streets, or who, in a vain effort to save their lives, were overpowered by our men in their last place of refuge; and several were thrust halfway up the large Spanish chimneys.

General Mackinnon, who directed the attack of the 88th Regiment, and accompanied it in its advance, ordered it to retire to the position it had previously occupied, and as he was unwilling to attract the notice of the enemy too much, he desired that this operation should be performed by companies. My company, or at least the one I commanded, was the first to quit the town. As I approached the spot where Sir Edward Pakenham was on horseback, he said—"Where are you going, sir?" not at the moment recognizing the regiment I told him that General Mackinnon had desired me to retire, but of course if he wished me to stay I would.

"Oh no," said he, "the 88th have done enough for this day; but the regiment that replaces you would do well to bring a keg of ammunition, each man, in addition to his sixty rounds, for, while I have life, the town shall not be taken," He was in a violent perspiration and covered with dust, his left hand bound round with his pocket handkerchief as if he had been wounded—he was ever in the hottest of the fire, and if the whole fate of the battle depended upon his own personal exertions, he could not have fought with more devotion.

Lord Wellington caused the village of Fuentes d'Onore to be occupied by five thousand fresh troops. The Light Division was selected for this service, and it passed us about five o'clock on the evening of the 5th. General Crawford took the command of this post, and every precaution was resorted to, to strengthen the town; temporary walls were thrown up at the bottom of the streets, carts and doors were put into requisition to barricade every pass, but, as it turned out, those observances were unnecessary; for Marshal Massena, giving up all idea of success, declined any further contest.

Thus was the object of his movement frustrated—a battle lost, and Almeida left to its fate.

Our wounded were removed to Villa Formosa, and Lord Wellington decided upon diminishing his front. By this movement we lost our communication with Sabugal, but we effectually covered Almeida, and still possessed the pass of Castello Bom. At half-past nine o'clock at night, the regiments which had so bravely defended Fuentes d'Onore passed us as we were about to lie down to rest; they were much fatigued, and we were struck with their diminished appearance; the 79th Highlanders, in particular, attracted our notice. We asked them what their loss had been; they said, thirteen officers, including their colonel, Cameron, and more than three hundred rank and file: and the soldiers were nearly correct in their estimate.

The next day, the 6th, we had no fighting; each army kept its position, and Villa Formosa continued to be the receptacle for the wounded. This village is beautifully situated on a craggy hill, at the foot of which runs the little stream of Onore. Its healthful and tranquil situation, added to its proximity to the scene of action, rendered it a most desirable place for our wounded; the perfume of several groves of fruit-trees was a delightful contrast to the smell that was accumulating on the plain below; and the change of scene, added to a strong desire to see a brother officer, who had been wounded in the action of the 5th, led me thither.

On reaching the village, I had little difficulty in finding out the hospitals, as every house might be considered one, but it was some time before I discovered that which I wished for; at last I found it. It consisted of four rooms; in it were pent up twelve officers, all badly wounded. The largest room was twelve feet by eight; and this apartment had for its occupants four officers. Next the door, on a bundle of straw, lay two of the 79th Highlanders, one of them shot through the spine. He told me he had been wounded in the streets of Fuentes on the 5th, and that although he had felt a good deal of pain before, he was now perfectly easy, and free from suffering. I was but ill skilled in surgery, but, nevertheless, I disliked the account he gave of himself. I passed on to my friend; he was sitting on a table, his back resting against a wall. A musket-ball had penetrated his right breast, and passing through his lungs came out at his back, and he owed his life to the great skill and attention of Doctors Stewart and Bell, of the Third Division.

The quantity of blood taken from him was astonishing; three, and sometimes four times a day, they would bleed him, and his recovery was one of those extraordinary instances seldom witnessed. In an inner room was a young officer shot through the head— his was a hopeless case. He was quite delirious, and obliged to be held down by two men—his strength was astonishing, and more than once, while I remained, he succeeded in escaping from the grasp of his attendants. The Scotch officer's servant soon after came in, and stooping down, inquired of his master how he felt, but received no reply; he had half turned on his face; the man took hold of his master's hand, it was still warm, but the pulse had ceased—he was dead. The suddenness of this young man's death sensibly affected his companions; and I took leave of my friend and companion, Owgan, fully impressed with the idea that I should never see him again.

I was on my return to the army, when my attention was arrested by an extraordinary degree of bustle, and a kind of half-stifled moaning, in the yard of a *quinta,* or nobleman's house. I looked through the grating, and saw about two hundred wounded soldiers waiting to have their limbs amputated, while others were arriving every moment. It would be difficult to convey an idea of the frightful appearance of these men; they had been wounded, on the 5th, and this was the 7th; their limbs were swollen to an enormous size.

Some were sitting upright against a wall, under the shade of a number of chestnut-trees, and many of these were wounded in the head as well as limbs; the ghastly countenances of these poor fellows presented a dismal sight The streams of gore, which had trickled down their cheeks, were quite hardened with the sun, and gave their faces a glazed and copper-coloured hue,—their eyes were sunk and fixed, and what between the effects of the sun, of exhaustion, and despair, they resembled more a group of bronze figures than anything human,—there they sat, silent and statue-like, waiting for their turn to be carried to the amputating-tables. At the other side of the yard lay several whose state was too helpless for them to sit up; a feeble cry from them occasionally, to those who were passing, for a drink of water, was all they uttered.

A little farther on, in an inner court, were the surgeons. They were stripped to their shirts and bloody;—curiosity led me forward; a number of doors, placed on barrels, served as temporary tables, and on these lay the different subjects upon whom the surgeons were operating; to the right and left were arms and legs, flung here and there, without distinction, and the ground was dyed with blood.

Doctor Bell was going to take off the thigh of a soldier of the 50th, and he requested I would hold down the man for him; he was one of the best-hearted men I ever met with, but, such is the force of habit, he seemed insensible to the scene that was passing around him, and with much composure was eating almonds out of his waistcoat-pockets, which he offered to share with me, but, if I got the universe for it, I could not have swallowed a morsel of anything. The operation upon the man of the 50th was the most shocking sight I ever witnessed; it lasted nearly half an hour, but his life was saved.

Turning out of this place towards the street, I passed hastily on. Near the gate an assistant-surgeon was taking off the leg of an old German serjeant of the 60th. The doctor was evidently a young practitioner, and Bell, our staff-surgeon, took much trouble in instructing him. It is a tolerably general received opinion, that when the saw passes through the marrow, the patient suffers most pain, but such is not the case. The first cut, and taking up the arteries is the worst. While the old German was undergoing the operation, he seemed insensible of pain when the saw was at work; now and then he would exclaim in broken English, as if wearied—"Oh! mine Got, is she off still?" but he, as well as all those I noticed, felt much when the knife was first introduced, and all thought that red-hot iron was applied to them when the arteries were taken up.

The young doctor seemed much pleased when he had the serjeant fairly out of his hands, and it would be difficult to decide whether he or his patient was most happy; but, from everything I could observe, I was of opinion that the doctor made his *début* on the old German's stump. I offered up a few words—prayers they could not be called—that, if ever it fell to my lot to lose any of my members, the young fellow who essayed on the serjeant should not be the person to operate on me.

Outside of this place was an immense pit to receive the dead from the general hospital, which was close by. Twelve or fifteen bodies were flung in at a time, and covered with a layer of earth, and so on, in succession, until the pit was filled. Flocks of vultures already began to hover over this spot, and Villa Formosa was now beginning to be as disagreeable as it was the contrary a few days before. This was my first and last visit to an amputating-hospital, and I advise young gentlemen, such as I was then, to avoid going near a place of the kind, unless obliged to do so—mine was an accidental visit.

When I reached my regiment I found everything as I left it, except that each hour made our position more disagreeable, from the increasing putridity of the dead men and horses with which the plain was covered. Three days of extreme heat make a serious alteration in a field of battle; the bodies which but a short time before possessed life, and were animated by the finest feelings, were now stretched naked and unnoticed, except by the birds of prey; not, indeed, a lump of cold inanimate clay, but a moving mass of corruption. Some of the bodies were swelled to an enormous size, and upon these the vultures had already commenced their attacks, fancying, perhaps, like other two-footed animals, that the largest was best.

Those birds of ill omen flocked about us in quantities, but although I have frequently attempted to get a shot at them, I never was able to do so. We used first to observe them at an immense height; by degrees they lowered themselves, soaring round as they approached their prey; and when it was ascertained by their advanced scouts that all was safe, they pounced down and stalked on to the different carcases they intended to devour. At a distance, when they were seated, they resembled a number of grey-headed men.

Massena, renouncing all hope of gaining any advantage by a fresh attack upon our position, recrossed the river Agueda with his army, and left the Governor of Almeida to shift for himself. On the 8th and 9th we heard several explosions in that direction, but although we guessed that the governor was destroying some of the magazines previous to his surrender, it never for a moment occurred to us that he meditated what he afterwards executed with too much success.

On the morning of the 11th we heard, with the greatest astonishment, that the garrison, after having successfully passed through our lines that encompassed the place, had escaped, with trifling loss, by the pass of San-Felizes, and succeeded in reaching the French lines on the Agueda. This was certainly the most extraordinary event that took place during the campaign, and the regiments that formed the blockade afforded amusement for several days to our men; the soldiers used to say that the regiment nearest the town was asleep, and that the others were watching them.

It appeared that on the 7th, Massena sent orders to Greneral Brennier to blow up the fortifications of Almeida; after having done which, he directed him to put himself at the head of his troops, and open a passage for himself through our lines, which having effected, he was to march on Barba-del-Puerco in the first instance, and afterwards make a rapid movement upon the bridge of San-Felizes, where he would find a corps ready to act with him if necessary. General Brennier obeyed these directions with much exactness: he loaded the mines with powder; spiked the cannon, and otherwise injured them by firing balls from one gun into another: he rendered the ammunition and provisions useless, and on the 10th he disclosed his intentions to the officers most in his confidence.

He made no secret of the dangers attendant on the enterprise they were about to embark in; and having informed them of the measures he had taken to insure its success, asked if they were willing to stand by him—he added that the watchword was to be *Buonaparte Bayard*. The mention of this in itself would have sufficed to rally all around him, had there been any backwardness on the part of the officers; but all seemed devoted to the general and the enterprise. He then conducted them to the ramparts, from whence be pointed out the direction he meant to follow in his march. He observed that the stars should serve as their compass, and having hastily collected the garrison, he left the place at eleven o'clock at night.

Several of the mines in the ramparts exploded about the time the advance of the column reached the British outposts, but they not expecting such an attack, and being greatly outnumbered, were unable to offer any effectual resistance, and a passage was in consequence made for the leading battalion which opened the march. The rear of this little band suffered some loss, but Brennier succeeded in his enterprise, and was lauded to the skies for his chivalrous exploit.

The command of the army of Portugal was now transferred to Marshal Marmont, Duke of Ragusa. Massena returned to France in ill-health and ill-humour, in consequence of the bad success of his combinations, since his elevation to the command of this army, which, it was confidently stated, was to drive the English from the Peninsula. With the qualifications of our new antagonist we were unacquainted, except that having been for a considerable time *aide-de-camp* to the Emperor Napoleon, we looked upon him as something out of the common way—a kind of "*rara avis*" however, we found him out before we parted with him.

For six days we had not seen our baggage, and were in consequence without a change of linen; we lay among dirty straw for those six days.

I had no nightcap, and my socks scarcely deserved the name. But this was not all; those who had beards—at this epoch I had not—suffered them to grow to a hideous length, and their faces were so altered as to be scarcely recognizable even by themselves. They might be compared to old Madame Rendau, who not having consulted her glass since her husband's death, on seeing her own face in the mirror of another lady, exclaimed, "Who is this!"

We all agreed that it would be delightful to bathe ourselves in the river, and half a dozen of us walked to the banks of the Duos Casas. Having washed ourselves, we had a hankering for clean linen; and as none of us could be brought to the opinion of the Irishman, who said it was a charming thing when he turned his shirt, we proceeded to wash ours, and as this was the first appearance of any of us in the character of a *blanchisseur*, we all acquitted ourselves badly, but I worst of all.

In an unguarded moment, I flung my unfortunate shirt a little farther than the other's did, and, not being quite as light as the day it came out of the fold, it sunk to the bottom, and I never saw it afterwards. I soon discovered the cause of my mishap; a small whirlpool (which at the moment, appeared in my eyes little inferior to

Charybdis,) carried it into its vortex, and left; me shivering and shaking like a solitary heron watching for a fish by the bank of a river.

This accident, however, happened at rather a lucky time; our men had ransacked the French knapsacks with tolerable effect, and as soon as my mishap was known to the men of the company, I was not long wanting the means to supply my loss; at another time this might not have been a matter of easy accomplishment, because it is well known in the army, that the men in my regiment were never remarkable for carrying too great a kit.

The soldiers, as was their custom, made a display of the different articles they had picked up: some had watches, others rings, and almost all money. There cannot be a stronger contrast between the soldiers of any two nations, than between those of France and England: the former, cautious, temperate, and frugal, ever with something valuable about him; the latter the most unthinking, least cautious, and intemperate animal in existence, with seldom a farthing in his pocket, although his pay is three times greater than the others. A French soldier was quite a prize to one of our fellows, and the produce of the plunder gained, served him for drink for a week, and sometimes for a fortnight!

I knew a soldier once make a capture of thirteen hundred dollars, which having squandered, this same man, in less than a year afterwards, was tried for his life, for a highway robbery, and he would have been hanged, had not a Portuguese woman proved an alibi in his favour; the booty taken by him (for I am convinced the woman swore falsely to save his life) amounted to six *vintens*, or about eight-pence sterling! Under similar circumstances, a French soldier would have hoarded up his treasure, and, on his return home, dressed like a gentleman, and gone to all the dancing-houses in his neighbourhood.

On the 12th, we left the position we had occupied for eight days, and returned to our old quarters at Nave d'Aver. As we passed over the ground between that village and Posobello, we traversed a part of the field of battle which we had not before viewed, except at a distance too great to distinguish distinctly the objects with which it was covered; this was the ground upon which the 7th division, and the troops that were forced from Posobello, had fought

It was strewed with horses and soldiers.

In general, the bodies of both were, in part, devoured by the eagles and vultures; but there was one figure amongst them that remained untouched, as if it was too horrible even for them to approach. This man, who in his lifetime must have been of enormous size, presented the human figure under a frightful aspect; he was swollen to the size of a horse, and I cannot account for this extraordinary enlargement of his frame—which was not partial, but general. This giant arrested our attention for several minutes, and we stopped to survey him distinctly; the flesh was quite green, except the face, which was black—he had been shot through the head perhaps. It would be difficult to convey a description of the frightful spectacle this man offered to our view, and the recollection of him haunted me for a week afterwards.

Chapter 10

Olivenza Surrenders

We occupied our old quarters at Nave d'Aver, and were well received by the inhabitants, who preferred taking a quiet view of the combats of the 3rd and 5th to taking a part in both or either; their plan of operations was of a far different sort, and although unattended with any danger to themselves, was fraught with the most disastrous consequences to their foes, which is, no matter what may be urged against it, the very essence of the art of war.

It may, perhaps, be asked what their method was? or why I, a mere subaltern, should take upon myself the censorship of the art of war? My answer to the former shall be plain and I hope conclusive. To the latter, that having served during part of the year 1809, the entire of 1810-11-12, and part of 1813, in the third division (commonly designated the fighting division) of the Peninsular army, and the division never having, during the period alluded to, squibbed off as much as one cartridge without my being in every place,—I had opportunities of gaining, and I think I did gain, a little insight into military tactics. If, however, the view I have taken of the subject upon which I am speaking, be an erroneous one, I fear my readers will come to the conclusion that I have lost some time which might have been better employed—or to speak more plainly, that I have mistaken my profession. Marshal Saxe used to say, that a mule which had made twenty campaigns under Caesar would still be but a mule.

I have digressed thus far before touching on a subject, that, no doubt (although I have not seen any work of the kind) has been written upon, and upon which much diversity of opinion did exist at one time in England; whether it still exists or not I shall not pretend to say, not having been in the United Kingdom for some years, but certain it is that a very general opinion was prevalent that the war in the Peninsula was carried on, on the part of the peasantry, in a spirit bordering more on a crusade, than the ordinary exertions of a brave people struggling for liberty, and that those heroes fought more like a parcel of devils incarnate than mortal men.

Indeed, the engravings struck off at Lisbon in commemoration of those days, certainly represented them as a gigantic, ferocious people, while the few British that were thrown into the background, looked like so many dwarfs who were afraid to come to close quarters with the French. I have ever combated this mistaken opinion, nor does the recollection of the hundreds of those heroes that I have seen marched to the different depots, handcuffed like a gang of criminals, weaken the view I have taken of the voluntary part the Peninsular people took in the contest In a word, their plan was this:

The moment our troops had completely routed a body of the enemy's infantry, strewing the ground with dead and wounded, disorganized a park of artillery, or unhorsed some squadrons of dragoons, then, and then only, would these gallant fellows sally forth from their lurking places, and first taking the precaution to put a stop to any sort of parley from their unfortunate victims by knocking them on the head, completely rifle them of everything they possessed.

On the contrary, if our troops met with any reverse, as in the case of Don Julian Sanchez and his ragged band, our allies would take advantage of every incident of ground, and make one of those rapid retrograde movements, sufficient to baffle the evolutions of the most redoubtable *legère* regiments in the French army. This I say is the true harassing system, and the one suited to the genius of the Peninsular nations. It weakens your enemy, and is attended with no risk to yourselves or your friends, which is the same thing; for in England many think that the Portuguese and Spaniards did as much, if not more, during the Peninsular contest, than the British army.

I remember once, upon my return home in the year 1813, getting myself closely cross-examined by an old lawyer, because I said I thought the Portuguese troops inferior to the French, still more to the British. "Inferior to the British, sir, I have read Lord Wellington's last dispatch, and he says the Portuguese fought as well as the British, and I suppose you won't contradict him?"

I saw it was vain to convince this pugnacious old man of the necessity for saying these complimentary things, and we parted mutually dissatisfied with each other, he taking me, no doubt, for a forward young puppy, and I looking upon him as a monstrous old bore.

After the affair of Pombal, General Beresford was detached with the second division to the province of Alemtejo. He passed the Tagus at Villa Velha, and reached Portalegre on the 20th of March. On the 24th he advanced to Campo Mayor; this town was occupied by three thousand French troops, under the command of General Latour Maubourg. On perceiving the advanced guard of General Beresford's army, he quitted the town and established his troops on the heights in his rear. The 13th Regiment of Light Dragoons gallantly charged the cavalry of Latour Maubourg and overthrew them at the first onset, but the French infantry which were posted behind their cavalry, formed into square, and not only protected their own horse, but drove back ours with considerable loss. The bravery of the infantry saved their cavalry from total defeat and disgrace, and gave them time to reform and advance again to the combat.

The infantry, with that promptitude which characterises French troops, took advantage of this change in their favour, and continued their march upon Badajoz, repeatedly performing this fine manoeuvre, and at last succeeded in reaching the Guadiana unbroken, and unquestionably with the honours of the day on their side. They neither lost cannon nor baggage, and not more than twenty prisoners fell into our hands. The conduct of the 13th Light Dragoons in this affair was particularly dashing.

General Beresford quartered his army in the neighbourhood of Elvas, and made preparations to act on the left bank of the Guadiana. On the 4th of April he passed that river with little opposition. He reconnoitred Olivenza, and was informed by his spies that the garrison consisted of only five hundred infantry. This was, doubtless, an oversight on the part of the Duke of Dalmatia, because a town of such extent required a force of at least three thousand men.

No time was lost in investing it; the first parallel was completed on the 12th of April; on the 15th the batteries opened, and on the same day Olivenza surrendered, but the power of the enemy was still unshaken; the surprise of a single garrison, though a distinguished evidence of what might be done by our troops, was trivial in the scale of a war to be conducted against the whole power of France.

Matters remained thus in this quarter, and Lord Wellington, after the battle of Fuentes d'Onore, and the retreat of the army of Portugal across the Agueda, employed himself in giving directions for the repairs of the injury inflicted by Brennier upon Almeida previous to his evacuation of that fortress. The troops had recovered from their fatigues and were fresh again, and ready for anything, when accounts reached us from the Alemtejo that General Beresford was carrying on the siege of Badajoz, in which operation he was likely to be disturbed by Marshal Soult, who was on his march from Seville. Our division broke up from its cantonments on the 16th of May, and Lord Wellington, who rode at a rapid pace, reached Elvas in three days. There he received the report of the battle of Albuera.

The weather was fine, and we continued our route without any forced marches, taking the old beaten track through Castello Branco, Niza, and Portalegre. Our march was uninterrupted by any particular incident; we had no enemy near us, and were therefore left to ourselves.

The French army have the character of being the best marchers in Europe, and I know from experience that no men, to use a phrase of the "Fancy," understand better than they do, how to "hit and get away;" nevertheless, I would say, that an army composed exclusively of Irishmen would outmarch any French army, as much as I know they would outfight them.

The quality which carries a Frenchman through, and enables him to overcome obstacles truly formidable in themselves, is his gaiety, and his facility of accommodating not only his demeanour but his stomach also, to circumstances as they require it. An Irishman is to the full as gay as a Frenchman; if he does not possess his *piquant* wit,— and I don't say that he does not,— he has in a paramount degree the rich humour of his own country, which is nowhere else to be found. He can live on as little nourishment as a Frenchman; give him his pipe of tobacco, and he will march for two days without food and without grumbling—give him, in addition, a little spirits and a biscuit, and he will work for a week.

This will not be a task so easy of accomplishment to the English soldier; early habits have given him a relish for good eating, and plenty of it too: if he has not a regular allowance of solid food, it is certain he will not do his work well for any great length of time. But an Irish fellow has been accustomed all his life to be what an Englishman would consider half-starved; therefore quantity or quality is no great consideration with him; his stomach is like a corner cupboard—you might throw anything into it. Neither do you find elsewhere the lively thought, the cheerful song, or pleasant story to be met only in an Irish regiment.

We had a few Englishmen in my corps, and I do not remember ever to have heard one of them attempt a joke. But there are those who think an Irish regiment more difficult to manage than that of any other nation. Never was there a more erroneous idea. The English soldier is to the full as drunken as the Irish, and not half so pleasant in his liquor.

These opinions are, however, mere matter of fancy. Some of our best regiments were English, and one, to please me, decidedly the finest in the Peninsular army, the 43rd, was principally composed of Englishmen. Then there was that first-rate battle regiment, the 45th, a parcel of Nottingham weavers, whose sedentary habits would lead you to suppose they could not be prime marchers, but the contrary was the fact, and they marched to the full as well as my own corps, which were all Irish save three or four.

But if it come to a hard tug, and that we had neither rations nor shoes, then, indeed, the Connaught Rangers would be in their element, and outmarch almost any battalion in the service; and for this plain reason, that scarcely one of them wore many pairs of shoes prior to the date of his enlistment, and as to the rations, (the most part of them at all events) a dozen times had been in all probability the outside of their acquaintance with such a delicacy.

But the grand secret, in a good marching, good fighting, or loyal regiment, one not given to a habit of deserting, is being well commanded; because the finest body of men may be ruined, the efforts of the bravest regiment paralysed, and the best disposed corps become marauders and deserters, from having an inefficient man at their head.

At a period later than the one I am touching upon, my regiment was placed in a situation where the greatest facilities were afforded, and the strongest temptation made use of, to induce the men to desert. Several regiments lost from one to three hundred men each! but notwithstanding that we were stationed on the bank of a river, within a few hours' sail of the American territory—notwithstanding that the river was crowded with their trading vessels, and that more than one third of the battalion were allowed daily to work on board those ships, which were hourly arriving and departing,—and notwithstanding that we had no possible means of preventing the desertion of the entire regiment in a night if they chose it—we never lost one man.

This is a fact that I take the greatest pride in recording of my old comrades, and a point that in my opinion is worthy the attention of officers at the head of regiments. It may not be amiss to add that the men, generally speaking, were in debt in consequence of the arrival of a detachment from Ireland; the company I paid owed about fifty pounds, and the other companies averaged the same amount Everything depends on a good commanding officer; I do not mean one too fond of quackery—quite the contrary. Too much training is as bad as too little; we had no fuss with our men—no chocolate breakfast, and we had but few, as compared with others, on the sick list. We generally turned out half as strong again as other regiments; but ours was no rule to go by, because the soldiers were too hardy to be overcome by any ordinary fatigue, and too goodhumoured, if they were, to let the officers know it. Poor Joe Kelly used to call us the united Irishmen.

Colonel Alexander Wallace, who commanded us for so many years, and under whom the regiment repeatedly covered itself with glory, was the very man we wanted. Although a Scotsman himself, he was intimately acquainted with the sort of men he had under him, and he dealt with them, and addressed their feelings, in a way that was peculiar to himself, and suited to them. In action he was the same as on parade, and in either case he was as he should be.

If we were placed (as we often were) in any critical situation, he would explain to the soldiers what he expected them to do; if in danger of being charged by cavalry, he would say, "Mind the square; you know I often told you that if ever you had to form it from line, in face of an enemy, you'd be in a d——d ugly way, and have plenty of noise about you; mind the tellings off, and don't give the false touch to your right or left hand man; for by G—d, if you are once broken, you'll be running here and there like a parcel of frightened pullets!"

But Colonel Wallace was out of his place as a mere commander of a regiment; he was eminently calculated to head a division, because he not only possessed that intrepidity of mind which would brave any danger, but genius to discover the means of overcoming it. It was by his foresight that our brave companions, the 45th, were sustained in their unequal contest with Reignier's division at Busaco; and Lord Wellington, who saw and fully appreciated the manoeuvre, rode up to the 88th Regiment, and seizing Colonel Wallace by the hand, said—"Upon my honour, Wallace, I never witnessed a more gallant charge than that just now made by your regiment"

The dead and wounded of the 2nd, 4th, 36th, and Irish brigade, (four French regiments which were opposed to the 88th singly,) lay thick on the face of the hill, and their numbers gave ample testimony that we deserved the praises bestowed upon us by our general. The 45th also came in for their share of praise, and no battalion ever merited it better than they did,—at one time they were engaged with nearly ten times their own number. It was the fashion with some to think that the 88th were a parcel of wild, rattling rascals, ready for a row, but loosely officered. The direct contrary was the fact

Perhaps in the whole British army there was not one regiment so severely drilled. If a man coughed in the ranks, he was punished; if the sling of the firelock, for an instant, left the hollow of the shoulder when it should not, he was punished; and if he moved his knapsack when standing at ease, he was punished, more or less, of course, according to the offence.

The consequence of this system, exclusively Colonel Wallace's, was that the men never had the appearance of being fatigued upon a march, and when they halted, you did not see them thrusting their firelocks against their packs to support them. Poor Bob Hardyman, of the 45th, said, the reason the Connaught Rangers carried their packs better than any other regiment was, "that they never had anything in them!" and, to speak candidly, we never had more than was necessary, and in truth it was very little that satisfied our fellows.

A writer of celebrity so strongly bears me out in what I have been saying, that I shall take leave to quote a few lines of his opinion of my old corps.

> Our division continued to march in pursuit of the enemy till near dark, when we took up our quarters in some villages and farmhouses. In one of these latter, where I was proceeding to quarter some of my company, I found a party of the light company of the 88th, or Connaught Rangers, who, after the pursuit of the enemy, had brought up there for the night. They were all tolerably fresh, as may be supposed, and were seated round the fire cutting their jokes, as they contemplated with greedy looks the culinary process which was taking place in a large cauldron depending from the roof of a kitchen chimney. The first salutation I received on entering was, "Plase your honour, you will be after taking some of our supper; we have got a couple of geese boiled in wine!'
> This invitation, however my curiosity might have disposed me to taste of so novel a dish, I could not accept; but I left a party of my soldiers to assist them in discussing the banquet, which I have no doubt was highly palatable. This 88th, although from their name one would suppose them to be a rollicking set, was a very good regiment, and in excellent order. They had always a soldier-like look, and they carried their packs well, which, trifling as the circumstance may appear, is a sure sign of a good service regiment [1]

At drill our manoeuvres were chiefly confined to line marching, *echelon* movements, and formation of the square in every possible way; and in all these we excelled. Colonel Wallace was very unlike an old major, who having once got his battalion into square, totally

---

1. *Twelve years' Military Adventure*, vol. 2 p. 330.

forgot how to get it out of it. Having tried several ways, each time more effectually clubbing the sections, he thus addressed his officers and soldiers:—

> Gentlemen! I can clearly discern that there is a something wanting, and I strongly recommend you, when you reach your barracks, to peruse Dundas!—Men, you may go home.

And he thus dismissed them.

I never remember our having as much as one adjutant's drill; all was done by the commanding officer himself. Our adjutant was left ill at Lisbon, and he that acted was more of a good penman (an essential point) than a drill. I forget now how the circumstance of our having been sent an adjutant from the Guards occurred; but one of their serjeant-majors did reach us in the capacity of adjutant: on his arrival at head-quarters he dined with the colonel, who invited him to attend parade the next morning. We were under arms at ten, and never once ordered arms until two! Not a man fell out of the ranks, not a man coughed, and not a man moved his pack.

When the drill was over, "Well," said Colonel Wallace, "what do you think of the state of the battalion?"

"Very steady indeed, sir," replied the Guardsman. He left us that night, and we never saw him afterwards. No one knew where he went, but it was conjectured that he was unused to the mode of discipline he had just witnessed, and that he was unwilling to embark in an undertaking that most unquestionably would be no sinecure. I was not sorry for this, because I always had, and have, an aversion to adjutants raised from the ranks. An adjutant is, properly speaking, the mouth-piece of his commanding officer, and should be a gentleman capable of writing a good official letter; and surely this cannot be expected or looked for in a man raised from the station of a private soldier.

I knew two persons of this description: one commenced an official letter, and concluded with stating that his wife and children were quite hearty. The other, one evening in a large company, hearing an argument carried on as to the different merits of Virgil and Homer, said,

> *They might be fine fellows for aught he either knew or cared, but*

that he would lay a bet neither of them ever smelt powder and he would, without doubt, have won his wager.

On the 22nd of May, our division reached Niza. Any person who has ever had the misfortune to remain an hour in that filthy place, must, no doubt, remember the squalid appearance of its inhabitants; perhaps the world does not contain a more wretched race than those beings. The Portuguese nation are at best rather a dirty race, but Niza as compared with other towns, is like a filthy puddle, in comparison to a clear stream. It is one of those antiquated, fortified, and neglected towns, which, like Aronches, Portalegre, and Campo Mayor, was once of some importance.

At present, it is remarkable but for two things—the dirt of its inhabitants, and the number of storks that inhabit an old Moorish castle which stands in the centre of the town. Notwithstanding the countless number of these birds, and the voracious attacks which they make upon frogs, toads, serpents, and other reptiles, (I wish they would attack the people!) the ditches were filled with the latter. Several of the soldiers were stung by vipers and centipedes, and although I escaped both, I was frightfully bitten by fleas.

On the 24th of May, we reached Campo Mayor, and here I became acquainted with Maurice Quill. It would be quite idle in me to attempt giving any very detailed account of a character so well known; one who, whenever he opened his mouth, was sure to raise a laugh, and often before he had time to speak; and he by whom I was introduced (Dr. O'Reily) was little, if anything, inferior to Quill in either eccentricity or humour.

The first question Quill asked O'Reily was, if we all slept soundly the night Brennier got away from Almeida.

O'Reily replied, "that some of our army certainly slept sounder than was desirable; but that in their affair at Albuera, they did seem to have had their eyes perfectly open, not only during the action, but after it;"—at this moment, a couple of hundred of those troops that had been broken by the Polish horse, having escaped from the enemy, passed us.

During our conversation, O'Reily, as was customary with him, became quite abstracted, and apparently absorbed in his own reflections, and upon our turning round, we discovered him in one of Mendoza's attitudes!

"What are you squaring at?" demanded Maurice.

"My good friend Quill," replied O'Reily, "I have long felt the difficulty of coming to a satisfactory conclusion as to the probability of science being eventually able to overcome savage strength. There is much, sir, to be said on both sides of the question, and I have great doubts concerning the battle about to be decided."

"What battle? why sure we are not going to fight another so soon?" said Quill.

"The fight to which I allude, sir," said O'Reily, with Quixote-like gravity—for he paused between every word—"is the one pending between Crib and the black man Molineux; it will be a contest of science against brute strength"—and he threw himself into one of the finest defensive attitudes I ever saw; "there," said he, "there is the true science for you; nevertheless, it might be overcome by savage strength, and there is the rub, sir. I have devoted much time in endeavouring to come to a satisfactory conclusion on this point, but hitherto without effect; so I must await the issue of this fearful encounter; and my dear Quill, having said so much on the subject, allow me to wish you a very good morning."

It was evident, that although Quill was no novice, O'Reily had taken "a rise out of him," and it afforded us matter of amusement for many a day after.

We remained in Campo Mayor until the 27th May, (in order to allow the stores and battering train from Elvas to arrive) on which day we passed the Guadiana at a ford, distant from San Christoval about three cannon-shots: we received no interruption in our passage of the river, and the operation was performed without loss. The 28th, 29th, and 30th, were taken up in marking out our camp, and constructing huts; and as the weather was beautiful, and our camp abundantly supplied by the peasantry, we passed a very agreeable time of it.

The river ran within a few yards of us; its marshy banks being thickly covered with plantations of olives, afforded a delightful shade to us when we either went to fish or bathe. Its breadth at this point might be about sixty *toises*, and it is well stocked with fine mullet. We had several expert fishermen amongst us, and they contrived not only to supply their own tables with fish, but also to increase the comforts of their friends.

CHAPTER 11

Second Siege of Badajoz

Badajoz was laid siege to for the second tithe on the 30th of May 1811; on that day, the investment of the town on the left bank of the Guadiana was completed, as was also that of the fort of San Christoval on the right bank; and the trenches before both were opened that night.

This was my first siege, and the novelty of the thing compensated me in some degree for the sleepless nights I used to pass at its commencement; but habit soon reconciled me, and I could sleep soundly in a battery for a couple of hours at a time. Nothing astonished me so much as the noise made by the engineers; I expected that their loud talking would bring the enemy's attention towards the sound of our pick-axes, and that all the cannon in the town would be turned against us, and in short I thought every moment would be my last. I scarcely ventured to breathe until we had completed a respectable first parallel, and when it was fairly finished, just as morning began to dawn, I felt inexpressibly relieved. The Seventh Division was equally fortunate before San Christoval.

As soon as the enemy had a distinct view of what we had been doing, he opened a battery or two against us with, however, but little effect, and I began to think a siege was not that tremendous thing I had been taught to expect; but at this moment a thirty-two pound shot passed through a mound of earth in front of that part of the parallel in which I was standing, (which was but imperfectly finished) and taking two poor fellows of the 83rd (who were carrying a hand-barrow) across their bellies, cut them in two, and whirled their remnants through the air. I had never before so close a view of the execution a round shot was capable of performing, and it was of essential service to me during this and my other sieges. It was full a week afterwards before I held myself as upright as before.

On the 2nd of June, our batteries opened against the Castle and San Christoval; the communication between the latter and Badajoz was covered by a *tête du pont*, that protected the Roman bridge, which terminates at the Elvas gate. Our fire on the left bank commenced with a good deal of brilliancy, but the brass guns were inadequate to the task they had to perform, and after being a short time at work, became so hot as to be useless.

The artillerymen were occupied for several hours throwing buckets of water over their barrels, in order the sooner to render them fit for work. The cannon of the enemy were, it is true, of the same description, but their train was more numerous; and besides they could, without much trouble, disarm such of their batteries as were not opposed to ours, and thus, by a continual interchange of guns, overpower our fire, while we were obliged to work with the same set: this they did, and with considerable effect too, and our casualties increased in proportion.

The touch-poles of several of the cannon melted away, and became so large, that they were unserviceable; others were rendered useless by being plugged up with the enemy's shot; and by ten o'clock each morning, our line of batteries presented a very disorganized appearance; sandbags, gabions, and fascines, knocked here and there; guns flung off their carriages, and carriages beaten down under their guns.

The boarded platforms of the batteries, damp with the blood of our artillery-men, or the headless trunks of our devoted engineers, bore testimony to the murderous fire opposed to us, but nevertheless everything went on with alacrity and spirit; the damage done to the embrasures was speedily repaired, and many a fine fellow lost his life endeavouring to vie with the men of the engineers in braving dangers, unknown to any but those who have been placed in a similar situation.

It was on a morning such as I am talking of, that Colonel Fletcher, chief officer of engineers, came into the battery where I was employed; he wished to observe some work that had been thrown up by the enemy near the foot of the castle the preceding night. The battery was more than usually full of workmen repairing the effects of the morning's fire, and the efforts of the enemy against this part of our works were excessively animated.

A number of men had fallen and were falling, but Colonel Fletcher, apparently disregarding the circumstance, walked out to the right of the battery, and taking his stand upon the level ground, put his glass to his eye, and commenced his observations with much composure. Shot and shell flew thickly about him, and one of the former tore up the ground by his side and covered him with clay; but not in the least regarding this, he remained, steadily observing the enemy. When at length he had satisfied himself, he quietly put up his glass, and turning to a man of my party who was sitting on the outside of an embrasure, pegging in a fascine, said, "My fine fellow, you are too much exposed; get inside the embrasure, and you will do your work nearly as well."

"I'm almost finished, colonel," replied the soldier, "and it isn't worthwhile to move now; those fellows can't hit me, for they've been trying it these fifteen minutes."

They were the last words he ever spoke! He had scarcely uttered the last syllable, when a round shot cut him in two, and knocked half of his body across the breech of the gun. The name of this soldier was Edmund Man; he was an Englishman, although he belonged to the 88th Regiment. When he fell, the French cannoniers, as was usual with them, set up a shout, denoting how well satisfied they were with their practice!

On the right bank of the river, the operations against San Christoval proceeded more rapidly than those against the castle, and the loss was proportionable to that sustained by the troops employed on the left of the Guadiana. Amongst the officers who fell, was Lieutenant Hunt, of the artillery; he was a young man of much promise, and had distinguished himself by his zeal in the batteries.

One evening while we were occupied in the usual way in the trenches, a number of us stood talking together; several shells fell in the works, and we were on the alert a good deal in order to escape from them. A shell on a fine night at a distance is a pretty sight enough, but I, for one, never liked too near a view of it We were on this night kept tolerably busy in avoiding those that fell amongst us; one, however, took us by surprise, and before we could escape, fell in the middle of the trench; every one made the best of his way to the nearest *traverse*, and the confusion was much increased by some of the sappers passing at the moment with a parcel of gabions on their backs.

Colonel Trench of the 74th, in getting away ran against one of these men, and not only threw him down, but fell headlong over him, and sticking fast in one of the gabions was unable to move. As soon as the shell exploded, we all sallied forth from our respective nooks, and relieved Colonel Trench from his awkward position.

"Well," said Colonel King, of the 5th, "I often saw a gabion in a trench, but this is the first time I ever saw a Trench in a gabion"

Considering the time and place, the pun was not a bad one, and made us all laugh heartily, in which Colonel Trench good humouredly joined.

Not long after this, a round shot carried away the arm of a soldier of the 94th. Doctor O'Reily, of my corps, happening to be the nearest medical man, was awoke out of a sound sleep by his orderly serjeant, and having examined the stump, amputated the fractured part. O'Reily was one of the most eccentric, and at the same time one of the pleasantest fellows in the world. He delighted in saying extraordinary things in extraordinary places, and it was amusing to those who knew him well, to see his countenance, after saying something out of the common way before a stranger.

In the present instance, after having wrapt his boat-cloak about him, and settled himself in the same position he had been in before he performed the operation on the 94th man, he, with the most profound gravity of manner, asked the serjeant if he recollected the state in which he had found him?

"Indeed, sir," replied the orderly, with a broad grin, "your honour was fast asleep, snorin mighty loud."

"Well then, sir, if you return here in five minutes, in all human probability you will find me in precisely the same situation," and he immediately fell asleep, or feigned to do so.

On the evening of the 5th, I was sent in advance with a covering party of forty men; we were placed some distance in front of the works, and as usual received directions to beware of a surprise. Our batteries were all armed, and a sortie from the garrison was not improbable; the night was unusually dark, and except an occasional shell from our mortars, the striking of the clocks in the town, or the challenge of the French sentinels along the battlements of the castle, everything was still.

A man of a fanciful disposition, or indeed of an ordinary way of thinking, is seldom placed in a situation more likely to cause him to give free scope to his imagination, than when lying before an enemy on a dark night; every sound, the very rustling of a leaf, gives him cause for speculation; figures will appear, or seem to appear in different shapes; sometimes the branch of a tree passes for a tremendous fellow with extended arms, and the waving of a bush is mistaken for a party crouching on their hands and knees.

The certainty that several batteries may be opened upon you at "sight" without "advice" being given of it, or that some hundreds of chosen troops may rush upon you with fixed bayonets, is an unpleasant idea, and the knowledge that those fellows are paid by the governor according to the way they do their work, tends but little to tranquillize you, or give you a turn for sleep.

Expecting both, or either of these things, it is not to be wondered at, that a man should be a little on what the French call the *qui vive*, and I don't know why it was, but I could not divest myself of the idea that an attack upon our lines was meditated. I cast a look at my men as they lay on the ground, and saw that each held his firelock in his grasp, and was as he should be; half an hour passed away in this manner, but no sound gave warning that my suspicions were well founded. The noise of the workmen in the trenches lessened by degrees, and as the hour of midnight approached, there was, comparatively speaking, a death-like silence.

I went forward a short distance, but it was a short distance, for in truth—to say the least of it—I was a little "hipped." I even wished the enemy would throw a shot or two against our works to give a fillip to my thoughts. Heavens! how I envied the soldiers, who slept like so many tops, and snored at least as loud as Dennis Brulgruddery, when he awoke the congregation of Parson Snufflebags—I went forward again, but had not proceeded more than about one hundred paces when I heard voices whispering in my front, and upon observing more minutely in the direction from whence the sounds proceeded, I saw distinctly two men. The uniform of one was dark; the other wore a large cloak, and I could hear his sabre clinking by his side as he approached me.

At the instant I do not know what sum I would have considered too great to have purchased my ransom, and placed me once more at the head of my men. I need scarcely say that I regretted the step I had taken, but it was too late. The figures continued to advance towards the spot where I was crouched, and were already within a few paces of me: I did not know what to do, I dreaded remaining stationary, and I was ashamed to run away—there was not a moment to be lost, and I made up my mind to sell my life dearly. I sprang up with my drawn sabre in my hand, and called out as loud as I was able (and it was but a so-so-effort), "Who goes there?"—My delight was great to find in place of two Frenchmen (the advance, as I expected, of several hundred).

Captain Patten, of the Engineers, attended by a serjeant of his corps; he held a dark lantern under his cloak, and told me he had been on his way to reconnoitre the breach in the castle-wall, but that he thought it as well to return to the first covering party he should meet with, in order to get a file of men which he proposed taking with him to within a short distance of the breach. I was just then in that frame of mind, from my own little adventure, to approve highly of his precaution, and I gave him a couple of what our fellows (the Connaught Rangers) used to call, lads that weren't easy, or, to speak without a metaphor, two fellows that would walk into the mouth of a cannon if they were bid to do it.

Previous to this I had passed an uneasy night, but I was now filled with much anxiety for the fate of Captain Patten, and my own two men. They had left me about a quarter of an hour, when a few musket-shots from the bastion nearest the breach, announced that the reconnaissance had not been made unnoticed by the enemy; and shortly after, the return of my soldiers confirmed the fact.

It appeared, that upon arriving within pistol-shot of the wall. Captain Patten motioned to the men to lie down, while he crept forward to the breach; he had succeeded in ascertaining its state, and was about to return to the. soldiers, when some inequality in the ground caused him to stumble a little, and the noise attracted the notice of the nearest sentinel, whose fire gave the alarm to the others—one of those shots struck Captain Patten in the back, a little below the shoulder, and he survived its effects but a few hours. Thus fell a fine young man, an ornament to that branch of the service to which he belonged, and a branch, which in point of men of highly cultivated scientific information, as well as the most chivalrous bravery, may challenge the world to show its superior.

The fire against the castle was continued on the following day, the 6th, with much effect, and the batteries in front of San Christoval had not only overcome the fire of that outwork, but towards midday the breach was judged assailable. At nine o'clock at night, one hundred men of the seventh division, commanded by Major Macintosh, of the 85th Regiment, advanced to the assault; the forlorn-hope, consisting of six volunteers, and led on by Ensign Joseph Dyas, of the 51st Regiment, who solicited this honour, headed the attack. The troops advanced with much order, although opposed to a heavy fire. Arrived upon the glacis they speedily descended the ditch, and the forlorn-hope, accompanied by an officer of engineers, pressed on to the breach.

They had scarcely arrived at its foot, when the officer of engineers was mortally wounded, and Ensign Dyas was in consequence the only person to direct the men at the breach; for the main body, including the commanding officer, attempted to mount what appeared to them to be the breach, but which was in reality nothing more than an embrasure which had been a good deal injured by the fire of our batteries. Some of the most foremost succeeded in planting ladders against its rugged face, but their efforts were baffled by the exertions of the French engineers, who, notwithstanding our fire of grape and musketry, contrived to clear away the rubbish from the base of the wall; and the ladders were in consequence not of a sufficient length to enable the men to make a lodgement.

A quarter of an hour had now elapsed, during which time several fruitless attempts had been made to enter the fort; and Major Macintosh, with his few remaining men, succeeded with difficulty in reaching their own lines, which they had left but a short time before with feelings of a very different description. None of the party could give any account of Ensign Dyas—indeed, how could they? for the storming party had never seen the forlorn-hope, from the moment they descended the ditch! As is common in such cases, there were many who said they believed that he, individually, was the last living man in the ditch, and it was a generally received opinion that Dyas had fallen.

Major Macintosh, in company with a few friends, was sitting in his tent talking over the failure of the attack, and regretting, amongst others, the loss of this officer, when to his amazement he entered the tent, not only alive, but unhurt. This brave young man, after having lost the greater part of his men, and finding himself unsupported by the storming party, at length quitted the ditch, but not until he heard the enemy entering it by the sally-port.

Notwithstanding that we had occupation sufficient within our lines to employ men of ordinary minds, still our fellows—or, as they familiarly called themselves, "the boys,"—found leisure to stroll a little beyond the limits allowed to the soldiers for their recreation. Perhaps in the whole British army, or in the army of any other nation, there were not a set of "boys" who knew better than ours did, how to find out which way the land lay; to see what "was going," or to take share of it, whether it was freely offered to them or attempted to be withheld; their name too, "The Rangers," implied—or they took it in that sense, I believe—their right to make little excursions, which, perhaps, another corps would not think of; and as they never had a turn for desertion, they were not as closely watched as might be necessary with other men; and their officers were never uneasy about then), because they were aware they knew how to take care of themselves.

Under all these circumstances, it is not to be wondered at that the country about our camp became a spot of some interest to the "boys." Lord Wellington might, and no doubt did reconnoitre Badajoz well, but not one whit better than the aforesaid gentlemen did the neighbouring country.

Not far from the river's edge, and distant about half a league from our lines, stood a snug cottage, at the rear of which was a plantation of olives, and at one side, under the brow of a little hillock, might be seen ten or a dozen beehives. Our fellows having tasted some of the bitters of a siege, were resolved to have a trial of the sweets, and this congregation of hives, carried by a *coup-de-main*, appeared in their eyes a set-off against the slow process of an operation such as they were engaged in.

An attack was immediately resolved on, and as immediately put into execution; one of a party of three, a *nate* boy volunteered his services, not only to reconnoitre the cottage, but to take a hive off by way of sample, that is, if such was found to be practicable; the other two lay at hand, and were ready to act as circumstances might require. A fellow named Roger Gafney was the individual who distinguished himself on this occasion; he passed by the rear of the cottage, rendering the caution of the Spaniard of no avail by this flank movement; and taking up one of the hives, rammed it into a sack, which he had borrowed for the occasion from his captain's batman. Success had crowned his efforts thus far, and he was carrying off his prize, when upon turning round the clump of olive-trees, he encountered some officers in their undress, who were coursing. "Hallo! what have you in the sack?" said one of them.

Roger, at a glance, saw the awkward situation in which he was placed, and that nothing but stratagem could save him. Not in the least abashed, he replied to the question with the same freedom it had been put; thinking, or seeming to think, that those by whom he was addressed, were, like himself, on the look-out "What have I, is it?—a bee-hive!"

"A bee-hive! where did you get it?"

"You mane to say where did I find it; why then, avich, I found it where it wasn't lost, and if it's honey yees are after, don't be standing here talking to me, but make haste, or by my soul they'll not lave yees a taste, at all, at all."

"Who? where?" were the rapid interrogatories put to Roger.

"Why over there fore'nents [1] you." replied he, pointing to a grove of trees in the very opposite direction of the place where the hives stood.

Away galloped the officers to detect the delinquents, and away scampered Roger, lightening himself of his load, which he was reluctantly obliged to leave behind him; and, it is scarcely necessary to say, that on the return of the disappointed officers, they did not find Roger Gafney waiting to receive them. Upon his return to his companions, he was asked why he left the hive behind him; "Why then, sure," said he, "I thought it better to lose the honey, and save my bacon."

On the 7th, 8th, and 9th, the fire against San Christoval was continued with increased vigour, and on the latter day it was re-

---

1. Opposite.

solved that the attack of it should be a second time made that night A superior number of troops to those which failed on the 6th, but still inferior to the garrison of the fort, were selected for the attack, and the command given to Major MacGeechy, an English officer in the service of Portugal, who volunteered this duty—Dyas again leading the forlorn-hope.

As before, the troops advanced under the fire of every gun that could be brought to bear upon them, and with much spirit descended the ditch. A little disorder amongst the men who carried the ladders, caused some delay, but the detachment pressed on to the breach without waiting for the reorganization of the ladder-men. The soldiers posted on the glacis, by their determined fire, notwithstanding their exposed situation, forced the enemy to waver, and if ever there was a chance of success, it was at this moment Dyas and his companions did as much as men could do, but in vain.

Their efforts were heroic, though unavailing; the spot was strewed with the dead and dying—the breach was covered with Frenchmen, and the glacis and ditch covered with our dead and disabled soldiers. Major MacGeechy fell pierced with bullets, and almost all the party shared his fate. Ensign Dyas was struck by a pellet, in the forehead [2] and fell upon his face, but, undismayed by this, he sprang up and rallied his few remaining followers, but in vain. This heroic intrepidity deserved a better fate, but his efforts were paralysed by the obstacles opposed to him, and Dyas was at length reluctantly obliged to abandon an enterprise, on the issue of which he had a second time chivalrously, though unsuccessfully, staked his life.

As before, he was the last to leave the ditch, and with much difficulty reached our lines: his mode of escape was as curious as it was novel. One of the ladders that could not be placed upright, still hung from the glacis on the *pallisadoes*; this he sprang up, and in an instant he was upon the glacis, where he flung himself upon his face. The Frenchmen upon the walls seeing him fall at the moment of their fire, shouted out "*Il est tué, en voila le dernier!*" Dyas,

---

2. A small bullet, larger than a swan drop: four of them were inclosed in a piece of wood, three inches long, and at the top was placed the musket-ball. Upon being discharged the wood burst, and this shrapnel in miniature did considerable execution.

perfectly collected, saw that his only chance of escape was by remaining quiet for a short time, which he did, and then seizing a favourable moment when the garrison were thrown off their guard by the silence that prevailed, he jumped up and reached our batteries in safety: he and nineteen privates were all that escaped out of two hundred, which was the original strength of the storming-party and forlorn-hope.

The failure of these two attacks led to many remarks, not only in our own army, but also in that of the enemy. It was our first attempt in the Peninsula to storm a place, and its success or failure was, without doubt, a matter that in a great measure involved the character, not only of the soldiers engaged, but of the two armies generally—it was in fact a national concern. Our fellows knew that if the thing were practicable, success was sure to follow; but the French thought differently, and notwithstanding the defeats they had sustained in the different affairs which preceded this unfortunate event, they considered themselves the same invincible heroes who had conquered on the fields of Marengo and Austerlitz; and this little affair set them quite at ease with themselves.

This is a dangerous idea to let a Frenchman get hold of, for though naturally brave, they are, as a nation, or even individually, the most gasconading race on earth—the Yankees always excepted; I shall, therefore, enter a little into the causes of this reverse.

The evening upon which the first assault was made, (the 6th of June,) the storming party consisted of but one hundred men, whilst the garrison of the fort amounted to one hundred and fifty. Dyas at the head of six chosen men, (and accompanied by an officer of engineers, whose name I forget, and who was mortally wounded while he was in conversation with Dyas,) led the advance. The situation of the fort, the bastions that had been disabled by our fire, as also the breach, were well known to both these officers; but the remainder of the party including the commanding-officer. Major Macintosh, it would appear were ignorant upon points of such vital importance. The consequence was fatal. The handful of men that formed the forlorn-hope, led on by their brave young commander, jumped into the ditch, and proceeded along the curtain to the breach, but unfortunately the remainder of the party allowed themselves to be occupied before a dismantled bastion, which they mistook for the real breach. The ladders were lowered into the ditch and raised against this part of the wall; and while the soldiers were endeavouring to place them upright, they were cut off almost to a man. Dyas, finding himself unsupported, ran back from the breach, and having reached the spot where his companions had been so uselessly, yet fatally employed, found it occupied only by the dead and wounded.

Thus far it was evident that the attack had failed, but it was also proved that the failure was owing to the misconception which the troops had of the real breach, because that portion of the storming party that had the ladders stopped short at a place where they should not Dyas, although little acquainted with engineering, or not even having had a trial of the ladders, which were but twelve feet long, at once pronounced the breach impracticable. He was immediately ordered to the tent of General Houston, who directed the operations on the right bank of the Guadiana, and there he was closely questioned in the presence of the chief engineer, (I believe it was Colonel Squires): in answer to a question put to him respecting the depth of the ditch, he said, that he conceived it to be twelve feet, and he, one of the most active men in the army, judged of its depth from the great shock he felt when he jumped down.

He was not credited; and the engineer smiling, said that "Certain allowances should be made for young beginners;" this was too much for Dyas, but the brave fellow modestly observed that he considered the estimate he had made of the depth of the ditch to be tolerably correct,—and from this moment he made up his mind to head the next attack.

When the breach was again deemed practicable, on the 9th, three days after the first attack and failure, Ensign Dyas waited upon General Houston, and requested his leave once more to lead the advance. The general said, "No, you have already done enough, and it would be unfair that you should again bear the brunt of this business."

"Why, general," said Dyas, "there seem to be some doubts of the practicability of this business on the last night of our attack; and, although I myself don't think that the breach is even now practicable, I request you will allow; me to lead the party."

The general still refused, when Dyas thus addressed him, "General Houston, I hope you will not refuse my request, because I am determined, if you order the fort to be stormed forty times, to lead the advance so long as I have life." The general, fully appreciating the earnestness of this brave and high-minded young man, at length acquiesced; and Major MacGreechy having volunteered to command the storming party, he and Dyas made the necessary arrangements to reconnoitre the fort that evening.

They made a detour by the edge of the river, and succeeded in reaching unperceived to within a short distance of the fort. Under cover of some reeds, they carefully examined the breach, which, to Major MacGeechy, appeared a practicable one; but Dyas, better informed from experience, combated all the arguments of his companion, and desired him to watch attentively the effect of the next salvo from our batteries; he did so, and appeared satisfied with the result, "Because the wall," he remarked to Dyas, "gave way very freely."

"Yes," replied Dyas, "but did you observe how the stones fell instead of rolling; rely on it if there were any rubbish about the base or face of it, the stones would roll and not fall." The observation was not lost on Major MacGeechy, but it having been decided that the attack was to be made that night, both the leader of the forlorn-hope and the commander of the storming party, at once made up their minds for the trial.

At ten o'clock at night, two hundred men moved forward to the assault, Dyas leading the advance. He made a circuit until he came exactly opposite to the breach, instead of entering the ditch as before: a sheep-path, which he remembered in the evening while he and Major MacGeechy made their observations, served to guide them to the part of the glacis in front of the breach. Arrived at this spot the detachment descended the ditch, and found themselves at the foot of the breach; but here an unlooked-for event stopped their further progress, and would have been in itself sufficient to have caused the failure of the attack. The ladders were entrusted to a party composed of a foreign corps in our pay, called "the Chasseurs Britanniques." These men, the moment they reached the glacis, glad to rid themselves of their load, flung the ladders into the ditch, instead of sliding them between the *palisadoes*; they fell across them, and so stuck fast, and being made of heavy green wood, it was next to impossible to move, much less place them upright against the breach, and almost all the storming party were massacred in the attempt.

Placed in a situation so frightful, it required a man of the most determined character to continue the attack. Every officer of the detachment had fallen, Major MacGeechy one of the first; and at this moment Dyas and about five-and-twenty men were all that remained of the two hundred. Undismayed by these circumstances, the soldiers persevered, and Dyas, although wounded and bleeding, succeeded in disentangling one ladder, and placing it against what was considered to be the breach; it was speedily mounted, but upon arriving at the top of the ladder, instead of the breach, it was found to be a stone wall that had been constructed in the night, and which completely cut of all communication between the ditch and the bastion, so that when the men reached the top of this wall, they were, in effect, as far from the breach as if they had been in their own batteries. From this faithful detail it is evident that the soldiers did as much as possible to ensure success, and that the failure was owing to a combination of untoward circumstances over which the troops had no control. Nineteen men were all that escaped.

On the night of the 8th of June, (the one previous to the second assault,) Ensign Dyas being on duty in the trenches, an order arrived to send an officer and fifteen men to a hollow spot in front of our lines, between San Christoval and the *tête du pont,* close to the Roman bridge which communicated with the Elvas gate. I know not how it happened, but Dyas was selected for this arduous duty. The object of this movement was for the purpose of observing if any and what communication or reinforcement would be sent to the fort. The detachment was to be recalled before day.

The night was unusually still, and every sound was distinctly heard, but nothing could be ascertained except that one piece of ordnance (a howitzer, I believe,) had passed over to the fort. Day at last began to dawn, yet no order had been received for the withdrawal of the party so stationed; their situation was most critical—within point blank shot of the fort in their rear. Dyas ordered his men to lie flat on their faces, though he every moment expected his situation would be discovered, and a rush made at him; nevertheless, unintimidated by his perilous posture, he dispatched a trusty man to the trenches, with orders to make known to the officer commanding, the information he had been enabled to collect, and to know what was to be the final duty of the party.

"Now, mind," said Dyas, "if we are to be recalled, do you raise your cap on your firelock above the battery No. 1; if we are to remain, you know what your duty is."

"By J——, and plase your honour, I do; and recall or no recall, I'll be back with you in five minutes, dead or alive," replied the poor fellow, who, I need not add, (after his speech,) was an Hibernian.

"Do as you are ordered, sir," said Dyas, "we have not a moment to lose."

A few minutes (a long time under such circumstances) only elapsed before the signal agreed upon was made; the cap was hoisted, and Dyas knew that he and his party were to retire. He addressed a few words to his men, and told them that their safety depended on their adhering strictly to his directions. He then started them singly to different parts of the lines, and singular as it may appear, although it was now clear daylight, not one man was hit. What a fine fellow at the head of a regiment would this Dyas be! He possessed all the requisites necessary to make a first-rate officer,—bravery, tact, and head!

It may, perhaps, be asked by persons unacquainted with these details, what became of Ensign Dyas; and they no doubt will say what a lucky young man he was to gain promotion in so short a time; but such was not the case, although he was duly recommended by Lord Wellington. This was no doubt an oversight, as it afterwards appeared, but the consequences have been of material injury to Ensign, now Captain, Dyas. This officer, like most brave men, was too modest to press his claim, and after having served through the entire of the Peninsular war, and afterwards at the memorable battle of Waterloo, he, in the year 1820—ten years after his gallant conduct—was, by a mere chance, promoted to a company, in consequence of the representation of Colonel Gurwood (another, but more lucky, forlorn-hope man) to Sir Henry Torrens.

Colonel Gurwood was a perfect stranger (except by character) to Dyas, and was with his regiment, the 10th Hussars, at Hampton Court, where Sir Henry Torrens inspected the 51st Regiment

Colonel Ponsonby and Lord Wiltshire, (not one of whom Dyas had ever seen,) also interested themselves in his behalf; and immediately on Sir Henry Torrens arriving in London, he overhauled the documents connected with the affair of San Christoval, and finding all that had been reported to him to be perfectly correct, he drew the attention of His Royal Highness the Duke of York to the claims of Lieutenant Dyas.

His Royal Highness, with that consideration for which he was remarkable, immediately caused Lieutenant Dyas to be Gazetted to a company in the 1st Ceylon Regiment. Captain Dyas lost no time in waiting upon Sir Henry Torrens and His Royal Highness the Duke of York. The Duke received him with his accustomed affability, and after regretting that his promotion had been so long overlooked, asked him what leave of absence he would require before he joined his regiment Captain Dyas said, "Six months, if His Royal Highness did not think it too long."

"Perhaps," replied the Duke, "you would prefer two years."

Captain Dyas was overpowered by this considerate condescension on the part of the Duke, and after having thanked him, took a respectful leave; but the number of campaigns he had served in, had materially injured his health, and he was obliged to retire on the half-pay of his company.

CHAPTER 12

Affair of El Bodon

At eleven o'clock at night, on the 9th of June, 1811, the siege of Badajoz virtually ceased. From the moment the second attack against San Christoval was repulsed, Lord Wellington resolved to make the best of a bad business, and he converted the siege into a blockade. On the 10th, the battering train and stores were removed from the trenches, and by the 13th our works were clear. The town was closely blockaded until the 17th, on which day we broke up from before the place, and crossing the Guadiana by the ford above San Christoval, reached the banks of the Caya, in the neighbourhood of Aronches, a little after noon.

Soult was aware of this movement, but whether he was apprehensive of its being a feint to draw him into a separate action before he was joined by the army of Portugal, or that the battle of Albuera had made him cautious of again coming in contact with the British troops, without a great superiority in numbers on his side, is best known to himself; but this much is certain, that although the road to Badajoz from Fuente-del-Maestro, by the village of Albuera, was open to him, he never once attempted to molest us.

It appeared from the different reports of our spies, that the whole disposable force, not only of the army of the South, but likewise that of Portugal, were in march against us; and Lord Wellington accordingly took up a defensive position near Elvas, with his advance at Campo Mayor, consisting of the third and seventh divisions of infantry, while Blake's corps of Spaniards recrossed the Guadiana near Mertola.

The Dukes of Dalmatia and Ragusa formed their junction at Badajoz on the 28th, and the two Marshals dined there together on that day; great praise was bestowed upon General Phillipon for his fine defence of the place, and, as a matter of course, much bombastic stuff was trumpeted forth in the papers about the valour displayed by the Imperial soldiers on the occasion. Our losses were rated at more than four times their real amount; and though no blame was attached by the enemy to our troops, the engineers were attacked with a severity that I have reason to think was unjust. One writer speaking on the subject says,—

> But in spite of the valour of the assailants, they were repulsed; because, contrary to the rules of the art, they had not taken the precaution of being masters of the ditch, in order to prevent the entrance of the besieged into it. This blunder on the part of the English engineers had not escaped the observation of the French Governor, Phillipon. As soon as it was night, he sent miners into the ditch, to clean the foot of the breach, and thus render it impracticable. When the English came, they not only could not reach the steep breach by climbing, but their ladders also proved too short, on account of the height to which the miners had raised the new parapet

And the same writer again observes,—

> Had the engineers followed the rules of fortification with as much ability as his lordship displayed in the application of the principles of the higher branches of tactics, Badajoz would, no doubt, have surrendered about the 14th or 15th of June. It scarcely would be believed, were it not expressly mentioned in the official reports, that in the beginning of the nineteenth century, troops should have been sent to the assault with ladders after the breach had been judged practicable.

I shall leave it to the gentlemen of the engineers to answer these remarks; but for myself, I cannot conceive how it would be possible for us to make ourselves "masters of the ditch," while there was a French garrison in the fort ! What the general feeling on this subject may be, I profess myself ignorant of; the situation of troops so posted would, I have no doubt, be one of high distinction ; but I am quite certain, that I know at the least one individual who would not give a pin's point to be amongst the number so honoured, and that individual is the writer of these *Adventures*.

As far as I have been able to collect the facts, and I have received my information from good, I might say, the best authority, our defeat before San Christoval arose from three causes; first, the want of knowledge displayed by the officer commanding the first attack of the real situation of the breach, and owing to the unfortunate circumstance of the engineer being killed at the onset; secondly, the shortness of the ladders, and the smallness of the storming party each night; and thirdly, the conduct of the men who were entrusted with the charge of the ladders—a foreign corps it is true; but why employ troops of this description upon a service so desperate?

There is no duty which a British soldier performs before an enemy that he does with so much reluctance—a retreat always excepted—as working in trenches.

Although essentially necessary to the accomplishment of the most gallant achievement a soldier can aspire to—the storming a breach—it is an inglorious calling; one full of danger, attended with great labour, and, what is even worse, with a deal of annoyance; and for this reason, that the soldiers are not only taken quite out of their natural line of action, but they are, if not entirely, at least partially, commanded by officers, those of the engineers, whose habits are totally different from what they have been accustomed to.

No two animals ever differed more completely in their propensities than the British engineer and the British infantry soldier; the latter delights in an open field, and a fair "stand-up-fight," where he meets his man or men (for numbers, when it comes to a hand to hand business, are of little weight with the British soldier); if he falls there, he does so, in the opinion of his comrades, with credit to himself; but a life lost in the trenches is looked upon as one thrown away and lost ingloriously.

The engineer, on the contrary, braves all the dangers of a siege with a cheerful countenance, he even courts them, and no mole ever took greater delight in burrowing through a sand-hill, than an engineer does in mining a covert-way, or blowing up a counter-scarp: not so with the infantry soldier, who is obliged to stand to be shot at, with a pick-axe or shovel in his hand, instead of his firelock and bayonet If, then, this is a trying situation, as it unquestionably is for a soldier, where death by round-shot and shell in the works is comparatively less than it is at the moment of the assault of a breach, how much more care should there be taken in the selection of the ladder men, than appears to have been the case at San Christoval?

Beyond all question or doubt, the advance of a column to escalade should be preceded by a force consisting of the best description of troops, commanded by a field-officer of tried valour, and seconded by others, though of inferior rank, equal to their superior in this essential qualification. In point of qualification it ought even to supersede, if possible, those of the forlorn-hope!

What caused the great loss in the second attack of San Christoval? The misconduct of the men who carried the ladders; because, had these even been long enough, which they were not, the immense loss of time, and the consequent loss of lives which took place before they could be brought up to the face of the breach, in consequence of the gross misconduct of the men that carried them, was in itself enough to cause the failure of the enterprise.

On the 22nd of June, the two French marshals moved a large body of troops towards Elvas and Campo Mayor, in order to cover their reconnaissance of the position of our army. Some skirmishing between the cavalry took place, but nothing serious was the result, and the loss in killed and wounded trifling. A squadron of our 11th Light Dragoons, mistaking a French hussar regiment for a Spanish corps, were surrounded and captured.

Our army at this time counted about sixty-six thousand men, of which number only six thousand were cavalry. The combined French army exceeded us by about ten thousand, and in the arm of horse they were upwards of three thousand our superiors. Notwithstanding this disproportion of force, Lord Wellington had made able dispositions to beat the French marshals in detail, and there is little or no doubt but that he would have succeeded, had Marmont been acting in concert with a man as presumptuous as himself; but Soult was too good a judge not to see the sort of adversary he was opposed to, and it was not possible to entrap him. Albuera taught him a lesson,

After the reconnaissance of the 22nd, and after supplies had been thrown into Badajoz, the enemy took up the quarters he had occupied previous to the junction of the armies of Portugal and the South;—the army of Soult in the neighbourhood of Seville, that of Marmont at Placentia. The Seventh and Third Division of our army occupied Campo Mayor, and having got ourselves and our appointments into good order, we began to have all the annoyances of garrison duty, which was not lessened by the presence of three or four general officers.

The mounting of guard, the salute, and all the minutiae of our profession, were attended to with a painful particularity; and poor old General Sontag was near falling a sacrifice to his zeal on this particular point of duty. This officer was by birth either a German or Prussian, I don't know which, but, from his costume, I should myself say that he was a disciple of the Grand Frederick: be was a great Martinet, and had all the Appearance of one brought up in the school of that celebrated warrior, and might have passed, and deservedly so, for aught I know to the contrary, for one who had served in the "Seven Years' War." His dress was singular, though plain: he usually wore a cocked hat and jacket, tight blue pantaloons, and brown top hunting-boots.

One day, when it came to my tour of duty, General Sontag was the senior officer on the parade. Mounted on a spirited horse, he took his station in front to receive the "salute;" when the band of my regiment, much more celebrated for its harshness and noise than its sweetness, struck up as discordant a jumble of sounds as ever proceeded from the same number of wind instruments; the animal, a German horse, and no doubt with a good ear for music, took fright, and standing upright on his hinder legs, commenced pawing and snorting in a manner that astounded every one present, the old general alone excepted; he continued immoveably steady in his saddle, from which a less skilful or an inexperienced rider must inevitably have been flung, and sawed his horse's mouth with such effect, as to compel him to resume his former and more natural position; but, unfortunately at this moment, the drum-major, who justly estimated the cause of the refractory movements of the brute, made a flourish with his mace, as a token for the band—music I can't call it—to desist, and so terrified the animal, that he made a sudden plunge to get away, but was so firmly held by the grip of his rider, that his feet came from under him, and both the general and his charger were prostrate on the ground in a second.

It was an alarming, as well as a ludicrous exhibition: for a moment the general was unable to disentangle his foot from one of the stirrups, and when he got rid, after much exertion, of this incumbrance, he lost not only his hat, but his wig also; providentially he sustained no injury, and everyone was glad of it. He was a man much esteemed in his brigade, and had, perhaps, the largest nose in the world! he was humorously styled by some Marshal (Nez) Ney! His nose hung in two huge flaps under his cheek-bone, and their colour and size were like two red mogul plums. Joe Kelly said that he would be a capital gardener, "because he always had his fruit under his eye!"

A few weeks terminated our sojourn here, and the day of our leaving it was a delightful one to us all.

We marched to the northern frontier, which we considered as our own natural element; for in this quarter we witnessed nothing but reverses, and our division had no opportunity of keeping up its established name.

The country between the river Coa and the Agueda was filled with troops. The Third division occupied Aldea de Ponte, Albergaria, and the neighbouring villages. Gallegos, Espeja, Carpio, El Bodon, and Pastores, were likewise occupied; and Ciudad Rodrigo might be said to be invested; the garrison were, at all events, much circumscribed in the extent of country for their foragers, but, nevertheless, they made some successful excursions to the nearest villages, such as Pastores and El Bodon. The 11th Light Dragoons, stationed at the latter, were considerably annoyed by the nocturnal visits of the garrison; and independent of the difficulty which a cavalry outpost has to contend with against an experienced infantry, thoroughly acquainted with the country in which they are acting, the 11th had but lately joined the army from England, and could not be said to be accustomed to the climate, or to have gained a sufficient knowledge of the French troops, or of out-post duty, to enable them to cope with their veteran antagonists.

The towns had been almost all robbed of bread and wine, the sheepfolds entered, and the spoil carried off, before the cavalry could be got together from their distant stabling, and be in a state to act. A regiment of infantry was, therefore, thought necessary to co-operate with the cavalry, and mine (the 88th) was the one selected; and it was a good choice, for the men had a natural turn for independent acting, and I never saw that set of fellows who would so soon make themselves acquainted with a country, or a good large town either.

General Picton, no matter what his other faults might be, (and who is there amongst us without one?) knew well what he was about when he sent "the Rangers of Connaught" to support the 11th; he was aware that before many hours after their arrival in their quarters, they would be tolerably well acquainted with the resources of the country about them; and that though now and then, perhaps, in a case of emergency, they might enlist an odd sheep or goat into their own corps, they would not allow another to do it. The general was right, and thought it better that a few sheep should be lost, than an entire pen of them carried off in triumph, and our dragoons (the worst of it!) bearded to the edge (almost) of their sabres.

We were not long unemployed. On the tenth night after our arrival the enemy made a formidable attack on our advance at the village of Pastores. The advanced sentry, Jack Walsh, passed the word to the next, who communicated with the picket, and in an instant every man was on his legs. Walsh waited quietly until the French officer who headed the advance approached to within a few paces of where he was standing, when he deliberately took aim at him, and shot him dead. The remainder retired for a moment, panic struck, no doubt, at the fate of their leader; they, however, rallied—for they were not only brave, but, what is almost as great a stimulus, hungry—and they forced our advance to give way: but Colonel Alexander Wallace placing himself at the head of his men, drove back this band of cormorants, and they never molested us afterwards.

Notwithstanding that we were thus placed with respect to Rodrigo, the army of Portugal maintained its position; the army of the North, commanded by Count Dorsenne, remained in its cantonments on the Douro, and Rodrigo was thus abandoned to its own resources.

Lord Wellington was not an idle spectator of this supineness on the part of the two French generals. As early as the month of August, he directed that a large number of the tradesmen of our army, with a proportion of officers, should be attached to the Engineers, in which branch we were deficient in point of numbers; and these men in less than six weeks gained much useful information, and besides, made a quantity of fascines and gabions sufficient for the intended operations. By the 5th of September the town of Ciudad Rodrigo was completely blockaded, and we were employed in making arrangements for its siege, when the two Generals, Dorsenne and Marmont, made theirs to drive us back on Portugal.

On the 22nd of September they formed their junction at Tamames, which is about three leagues distant from Rodrigo. Their united force amounted to sixty thousand men, including six thousand horse; ours to not quite fifty thousand, including the force necessary to observe the garrison. We could not, therefore, taking it for granted, as a matter of course, that we wished to maintain the blockade, have brought forty thousand bayonets and sabres into the field, with an inferiority too in cavalry of two thousand! This, in a country so well calculated for the operations of that arm, at once decided Lord Wellington, and he raised the blockade on the 24th.

Previous to these movements, an intrenched camp had been formed at Fuente-Guinaldo, and this point was fixed Upon for the union of our army. General Graham occupied the line of the Azava with a numerous advanced guard; General Picton, with the third division, was posted in the vicinity of El Bodon; while General Robert Craufurd, with the light division, occupied the opposite bank of the Agueda. The Fourth Division, under the command of General Cole, was at Fuente-Guinaldo; and the other divisions of our army (the northern) were in cantonments close by, ready to act as might be deemed necessary.

Early on the morning of the 25th, the French army were in motion; the cavalry, under General Montbrun, supported by several battalions of infantry, advanced upon the position held by our third division; but the over zeal of Montbrun, and the impetuosity of his cavalry, would not allow them to keep pace with the infantry, who were in consequence completely distanced at the onset, and never regained their place during the day.

The ground occupied by the Third Division was of considerable extent, and might, to an ordinary observer, appear to be such as to place that corps in some peril of being defeated in detail: for instance, the 5th Regiment, supported by the 77th, two weak battalions, barely reckoning seven hundred men, were considerably to the left, and in advance of El Bodon, and were distant upwards of one mile from the 45th, 74th, and 88th; while the 83rd and 94th British, and the 9th and 21st Portuguese were little, if anything, closer to those two battalions; some squadrons of the First German Hussars and 11th Light Dragoons supported the advance, and a brigade of nine pounders, drawn by mules, and served by Portuguese gunners, under the command of a German major, named Arentschild, crowned the causeway occupied by the 5th and 77th.

These dispositions were barely completed, when Montbrun, at the head of his veteran host, came thundering over the plain at a sweeping pace; ten of his squadrons dashed across the ravine that separated them from Arentschild's battery, which opened a frightful fire of grape and canister at point blank distance, but although the havoc made by those guns was great, it in no way damped the ardour of the French horse; they panted for glory, and nothing of this kind could check their impetuosity: once fairly over the ravine, they speedily mounted the face of the causeway, and desperately, but heroically charged the battery. Nothing could resist the torrent,—the battery was captured, and the cannoniers massacred at their guns.

In an instant, the 5th, commanded by the gallant Major Ridge, formed line, threw in an effective running fire, steadily ascended the height, charged the astonished French dragoons, and having repulsed and poured a volley into the latter, as they rushed down the opposite face of the hill, recaptured the guns, with which, joined by the 77th, they deliberately retired across the open plain after a long and determined stand against the enemy's cavalry and artillery, and only retreating when the approach of a strong body of French infantry rendered such a movement imperative.

Flushed with his first success, Montbrun, at the head of his victorious squadrons, now thought to ride through the 5th and 77th, but this handful of heroes threw themselves into square, and received the attack with unflinching steadiness. Nothing but the greatest discipline, the most undaunted bravery, and a firm reliance on their officers, could have saved these devoted soldiers from total annihilation; they were attacked with a fury unexampled on three faces of the square—the French horsemen rode upon their bayonets, but unshaken by the desperate position in which they were placed, they poured in their fire with such quickness and precision, that the cavalry retired in disorder.

To reunite the 5th and 77th with the other corps of the third division, was a task of no easy accomplishment, because that division was of necessity much extended, and the French cavalry were so numerous, that they were enabled to traverse the plain upon which the 5th and 77th were about to manoeuvre; nevertheless these two regiments joined the 83rd British and the 9th and 21st Portuguese, the whole being now directed by General Colville. The brigade of guns, also made good their retrograde movement, with the loss, however, of half their gunners, who were cut down on the hill.

While this was taking place on the left, the regiments of the right brigade were posted on a height, parallel to that occupied by the 5th and 77th; we had a clear, and painful view of all that was passing,—and we shuddered for our companions; the glittering of the countless sabres that were about to assail them, and the blaze of light which the reflection of the sun threw across the brazen helmets of the French horsemen, might be likened to the flash of lightning that preceded the thunder of Arentschild's artillery,—but we could do nothing.

A few seconds passed away, we saw the smoke of the musketry,—it did not recede, and we were assured that the attack had failed; in a moment or two more we could discern the brave 5th and 77th following their beaten adversaries, and a spontaneous shout of joy burst from the brigade. What would we have given at that moment to have been near them? They were not only our companions in arms, but our intimate friends (I mean the 5th, for the 77th had but just joined the army, and were comparatively strangers to us.) But we were now menaced ourselves.

From the great space that intervened between the regiments that had been engaged and those that had hitherto been unoccupied, it was not easy, taking into account the mass of French cavalry that covered the plain, to reunite the Third Division. Lord Wellington, it is true, was on the spot, but the spot was a large one, with but few troops to cover it, and had the French cavalry done their duty on that day, I doubt much if the Third Division would not have ceased to exist!

Meanwhile the time was passing away without the enemy undertaking anything serious; but the 5th and 77th, and the other troops under General Colville, seeing the danger of their position, and profiting by the inaction of the French troopers, who seemed to be paralyzed after their failure, made one of the most memorable retreats on record, across the plain, surrounded by three times their own number of horse, and exposed to the fire of a battery of eight pounders; but the 40th, 74th, and 88th had not yet been able to disentangle themselves from the rugged ground and vineyards to the rear of El Bodon, and their junction with the remainder of the division might be said to be at this moment (three o'clock) rather problematical, because the French light horse, and Polish lancers, not meeting with a force of our cavalry sufficient to stop their progress, spread themselves over the face of the country, capturing our baggage and stores, and threatening to prevent the junction of the right brigade with the other two.

While the French might be said to have the undisputed possession of the entire field of battle, over which they were pouring an immense mass of dragoons, followed by infantry and artillery, the regiments of our division which were in column, continued their retrograde movement upon Fuente-Guinaldo; the 45th and 74th had by this time cleared the rugged ground and enclosures, and were in march to join the remainder of the column, but the 88th were most unaccountably left in a vineyard, which was enclosed by a loose stone wall.

In the hurry of the moment they might, and I believe would, have been forgotten, had not the soldiers, who became impatient upon hearing the clashing of weapons outside the enclosure, burst down several openings in the wall, by which means they not only saw the danger of the position in which their comrades were placed, but also the hopelessness of their own, if they did not speedily break down the walls that incarcerated them; for our 1st Hussars and 11th Light Dragoons were giving way before the overpowering weight of the enemy's horse, while the bulk of the Third Division were marching in a line, parallel to the enclosure occupied by the 88th;

so it was manifest, that if this regiment did not at the instant break from its prison, a few moments would have decided its fate, and left the Third Division minus the Connaught Rangers.

Each moment that we remained was of consequence, and the delay of five minutes would have been fatal; we were without orders, and were at a loss how to act; but nothing tends more to bring the energies of men into action than their seeing clearly the danger that they are placed in, and the consciousness that their only means of escaping it depends upon their firm reliance on themselves.

Some officers called out to have the wall broken down, and in a second, several openings were made in it; every officer made the greatest efforts to supply, by his own particular dispositions, such as were on the whole necessary; but an operation of so delicate a nature, made in the face of a powerful antagonist, could not be performed with as much order and regularity as was desirable.

From the great coolness of the men, and the intelligence and gallantry of the officers, the regiment was at last extricated from its dangerous position, but it was far, very far from being safe yet; and had the French dragoons, at the close of the day, shown the same determination they did at its commencement, not one man of the 88th would have escaped, because from the isolated situation of that regiment, and the nature of its movement, it might have been cut off by companies, in the attempt to complete its formation outside the enclosure, as every company was obliged to act as an independent body, and as may be supposed, some confusion was unavoidable.

We had scarcely cleared the enclosure, when we witnessed a series of petty combats between our horse and that of the enemy, some of whom had posted themselves directly between us and our intrenched camp at Fuente-Guinaldo; immediately in our front, some of Lord Wellington's staff were personally engaged with the French troopers; and one of them, either Captain Burgh, or the young Prince of Orange, owed his life to the excellence of his horse. Lieutenant King, of the 11th Dragoons, lost one arm by a sabre cut; Prior, of the same regiment, had all his front teeth knocked out by a musket shot, and Mrs. Howley, the black cymbal-man's wife of the 88th, was captured by a lancer.

The fate of the officers I have mentioned was deplored, but the loss of Mrs. Howley was a source of grief to the entire division. The officers so maimed might be replaced by others, but perhaps in the entire army such another woman, take her for all and all, as Mrs. Howley could not be found. The 88th at length took its place in the column at quarter distance, and the Third Division continued its retrograde movement.

Montbrun, at the head of fifteen squadrons of light horse, pressed closely on our right flank, and made every demonstration of attacking us, with the view of engaging our attention until the arrival of his infantry and artillery, of which latter only one battery was in the field; but General Picton saw the critical situation in which he was placed, and that nothing but the most rapid, and at the same time most regular movement upon Guinaldo could save his division from being cut off to a man.

For six miles across a perfect flat, without the slightest protection from any incident of ground, without artillery, and I might say without cavalry, (for what were four or five squadrons to twenty or thirty?) did the Third Division continue its march, during the whole of which the enemy's cavalry never quitted them; a park of six guns advanced with the cavalry, and taking the Third Division in flank and rear, poured in a frightful fire of round-shot, grape, and canister; many men fell in this way, and those whose wounds rendered them unable to march were obliged to be abandoned to the enemy,

This was a trying and pitiable situation for troops to be placed in, but it in no way shook the courage or confidence of the soldiers; so far from being dispirited or cast down, the men were cheerful and gay; the soldiers of my corps (the 88th) telling their officers, that if the French dared to charge, every officer should have a *nate* horse to ride upon. General Picton conducted himself with his accustomed coolness; he remained on the left flank of the column, and repeatedly cautioned the different battalions to mind the quarter distance and the "tellings off."

"Your safety," added he, "my credit, and the honour of the army, is at stake: all rests with you at this moment." We had reached to within a mile of our entrenched camp, when Montbrun, impatient lest we should escape from his grasp, ordered his troopers to bring up their right shoulders, and incline towards our column: the movement was not exactly bringing his squadrons into line, but it was the next thing to it, and at this time they were within half pistol-shot of us. Picton took off his hat, and holding it over his eyes, as a shade from the sun, looked sternly, but anxiously at the French; the clatter of the horses, and the clanking of the scabbards were so great, when the right half squadron moved up, that many thought it the forerunner of a general charge; some mounted officer called out, "Had we not better form square ?"

"No," replied Picton; "it is but a ruse to frighten us, but it won't do."

At this moment a cloud of dust was discernible in the direction of Guinaldo; it was a cheering sight; it covered the Third Dragoon Guards, who came up at a slinging trot to our relief; when this fine regiment approached to within a short distance of us, they dismounted, tightened their girths, and prepared for battle; but the French horse slackened their pace, and in half an hour more, we were safe within our lines. The light division, which were also critically circumstanced on this memorable day, joined us in the morning, and thus the whole army was reunited.

CHAPTER 13

Retreat of the French Army

The Duke of Ragusa and the Count Dorsenne employed themselves the whole of the day (the 26th of September) in reconnoitring the ground we occupied, and everything announced that a battle would be fought the next day, (which had it taken place, would have been the anniversary of the battle of Busaco, gained by us the preceding year,) but Lord Wellington observing a considerable body of troops moved upon his left, apparently with the intention of turning it, withdrew from his entrenched camp in the course of the night, to the neighbourhood of Alfayates, leaving the fourth division, commanded by General Cole, at Aldea-de-Ponte.

At break of day on the 27th, the French army were in motion, but their surprise seemed great on finding our lines unoccupied Marmont pushed his advance upon the village of Aldea-de-Ponte, and a gallant affair for our fourth division took place there. The two regiments of Fusiliers particularly distinguished themselves, and repulsed the enemy at the point of the bayonet. Night put an end to this affair, which cost us a couple of hundred men. and nearly double that number fell on the side of the French.

The enemy being but ill supplied with provisions, and the country in which they now were (Portugal) being quite unsuited to their operations, as well as unable to supply their wants, the French Marshal, having provisioned Rodrigo, which was the object sought for when he formed his junction with the army of the north, resolved upon retracing his steps, which he did on the following day, the 28th.

Both Marshal Marmont and the Count Dorsenne wrote accounts of their operations to Berthier, the War Minister, which were amusing enough. They both accuse Lord Wellington of having posted his men badly, and of committing all kinds of blunders; but still they admit that, with sixty thousand men under their command, they were unable to disorganize a single battalion, or take one piece of cannon. Dorsenne says:

> Could we have foreseen that this General (*meaning Lord Wellington*) would have been guilty of such a fault, we might have taken part of the English by separate combats; but our infantry only arrived at night.

And he thus concludes as bombastic a dispatch as ever came from under the hand of a French marshal or count, "Were the moment fixed for the catastrophe of the English arrived, we should have followed the enemy up to the lines of Lisbon. Whenever the Emperor shall think the proper moment arrived for driving the English definitively from the Peninsula, His Majesty will not find in any other army more zeal and devotion."

What stuff is all this! Every person knew well that Marmont had not more than ten days' provisions for his army, and that it could not subsist in Portugal, which had been so completely exhausted by its occupation by Massena the preceding year; besides, double the number of the united force of Dorsenne and the Duke of Ragusa, would have been inadequate to the task of forcing the lines of Lisbon; but I never knew a Frenchman who would stop at a good bounce if it suited his purpose.

Lord Wellington issued a most flattering order to the troops engaged on the 25th, and so delighted was he with the conduct of the 5th and 77th, that he held them up as an example to the army. On the 29th, we went into cantonments, our division occupying Aldea-de-Ponte; and until our arrival there, I had no idea the loss of men and horses on the 27th had been so great The ground was thickly covered with both, and immense numbers of vultures had already established themselves in the neighbourhood. These birds, the sure harbinger of a disputed field, crowded around us in vast flocks; whether this was owing, to the lateness of the season, or to a scantiness in the supply of their accustomed food, I know not; but the voracity of these birds, and consequently their boldness, was beyond anything I had ever before witnessed. In many instances they would throw off their ordinary wariness, and strut before the carcase they were devouring, as if they supposed we were about to dispute their pretensions to it; but it is astonishing what birds of this description will do when really pressed by hunger.

Fuente-Guinaldo was occupied by our light division, who made that town agreeable both to themselves, and also to their brothers in arms, not only by their hospitality, but by the attraction of their theatrical performances, which were got up in a style quite astonishing, considering the place, and the difficulties which they must have found in supplying themselves with suitable costume; but the light division had an *esprit du corps* among them, whether in the field or quarters that must be seen to be understood.

Their *dramatis persona* were admirable, and Captain Kent of the Rifles, by his great abilities, rendered every performance in which he took a part doubly attractive. The Third Division, although unable to cope with the light, in this species of amusement, got up races, which, though inferior to those of the former year at Torres Vedras, were far from bad; amongst the jockeys was one, an officer in the Portuguese service, who, though an excellent horseman, was, without exception, the ugliest man in the division, or perhaps, in the army. Major Leckie, of the 45th, took the greatest dislike to him on this account, and gave him the name of "Ugly Mug,"—by which cognomen he was after known.

Just as the horses were about to start for a tolerably heavy stake, I went up to Leckie, who was one of the most knowing men on our turf. "Well, Leckie," said I, "who's the winning jockey today?"

"Why look," replied he, "I've laid it on thick, myself, upon Wilde's horse, Albuquerke, and tortured as I am with this infernal attack of gout, (to which he was a great martyr,) I have hobbled out to witness the race; but, my dear fellow, I don't care one rush who wins, provided Mug loses."

However, Mug won his race easily, and poor Leckie went home quite out of sorts; whether from the effect of his favourite horse losing, or "Mug's" winning, or that the exertion was too much for him, I know not, but upon his return to Aldea-de-Ponte, he was seized with a violent attack of gout; towards midnight he was a little more composed, and had just sunk into a gentle slumber, when he was awoke by a young ensign who had lately joined, and who occupied an apartment in the house where Leckie was quartered.

This officer played a little on the violin, and had a very good voice; he began to practise both, and commenced singing the little air in Paul and Virginia of

> *Tell her I love her while the clouds drop rain,*
> *Or while there's water in the pathless main;*

but whether from being imperfect in the song, or that those particular lines struck his fancy, he never got beyond than. Leckie became very fidgety —every scrape of the violin touched his heart, but in a far different manner from that in which it seemed to affect the performer; a quarter of an hour passed on, and the same lines were repeated; at last the accompaniment grew fainter and fainter, until it died away altogether.

Leckie became composed: "Well!" exclaimed he, "that young fellow is at rest for the night, and so I hope shall I," and he was beginning to settle himself in a more easy posture, when the same sounds re-assailed him—this was too bad! He sprang out of bed,— the perspiration rolling in large drops down his forehead; he rushed to the door of the ensign's apartment, which he forced at one push, and in a second was standing before the astonished musician in his shirt.

The fatal words, "Tell her I love her," had just been uttered, and he was preparing to add, "while the clouds drop rain," when Leckie exclaimed, "By God! Sir, I'll tell her anything you wish, if you'll only allow me to sleep for half an hour."

It would be impossible to convey an idea of the confusion of the young man, upon finding his commanding officer before him at such a time and upon such an occasion—he made a thousand apologies; and poor Leckie, who was one of the pleasantest fellows in the world, in spite of his pain, could not avoid laughing at the occurrence, which amused him to the hour of his death.

Matters being in the state I have described in the month of October, 1811, and as there was no likelihood of any active operations taking place, we began to make ourselves as comfortable as the wretched village of Aldea-de-Ponte would admit of. Any person acquainted with a Portuguese cottage, will readily acknowledge that a good chimney is not its fort; we therefore turned all the skill our masons possessed, to the construction of fireplaces that would not smoke, and it required all their knowledge in the arcana of their profession to succeed even in part; however they did succeed, partially, I must admit, but it was easy to satisfy us, and we made up for the badness of our fire-places, by stocking them abundantly with wood, of which article there was no lack; but we had barely sufficient straw to keep our horses and mules alive, much less afford ourselves a bed. In the entire village, I believe, there were not a dozen mattresses.

Provisions were but ill supplied us, and we were reduced to subsist upon half allowance of bad biscuit; as to money, we had scarcely a *sou*, for although there was plenty of specie in Lisbon for our use, the want of animals to convey it to the army, left us as ill off as if there had not been a dollar in the chest of the paymaster-general: so that between smokey houses, no beds, little to eat, and less money; we were in anything but what might be termed "good winter quarters."

This state of privation was sadly annoying to the soldiers, and the men of my corps, or, as I am more in the habit of calling them, "the boys," were much perplexed as to what they would do. Several desertions had taken place in the army, but our fellows did not like that at all-at-all.

"Why, then, by my sowl," said Owen Mackguekin, of the Grenadiers, "I think misther Strahan, the commissary, is grately to blame to keep us poor boys without mate to ate, when those pizanos have plenty of good sheep and goats; and sure if they'd ate them themselves, a man wouldn't say anything; but they'll neither ate them, nor give us lave to do so, and sure a'tanny rate, *bacallôo* and *azete* is good enough for them."

I need scarcely remark, that an argument so full of sound sense, was not likely to be thrown away upon the hearers of Owen Mackguekin. From this moment our fellows determined to be their own commissaries.

For some weeks there had been a general defalcation amongst the different neighbouring flocks; and the Portuguese shepherds, confounded to know what had become of them, armed themselves, and kept watch with a degree of vigilance that they were heretofore unaccustomed to. Wolves, they remarked, were not sufficiently numerous in that part of the country to effect such havoc, even in the depth of winter; but, said they, it is impossible at this early stage of the season that it could be them; and they were right, for it would be difficult to point out one regiment that did not take something in the shape of tithe from the sheep-holders.

One night in November, 1811, three of the "boys" walked out of their quarters with nothing at all—but their bayonets; Mackguekin headed them. The sheep-fold they assailed was defended by five armed Portuguese; but what did the "boys" care for that? After nearly sending the unfortunate men to the other world, they very deliberately tied their arms and legs together to keep them aisy, as they afterwards said, and then performing the same office to three sheep, they left their owners to look after the remainder.

As may be supposed, this affair made a great noise; the provost-marshal was directed to search, with the utmost care, the quarters and premises of all the regiments; but the fellow instinctively, I believe, turned towards those of my corps, and here, I am sorry to confess, he found that which he wanted, namely, the three sheep, part of them in a camp-kettle on the fire, and the remainder in an outhouse. This was enough, The three men were identified by the Portuguese, tried, flogged, and had to pay for the sheep, which (the worst of it!) they had not the pleasure of even tasting; but this example by no means put a stop to the evil.

The sheep-folds were plundered, the shepherds pummelled, and our fellows flogged without mercy. General Picton at length issued orders, directing the rolls of the regiment to be called over by an officer of each company at different periods during the night; and by this measure the evil was remedied; but we did not get credit for even this. That pleasantest of all pleasant fellows, Bob Hardyman, of the 45th, used to say, in jest, that instead of the officers going round the quarters, we entrusted the duty to a serjeant; and, according to Bob's account, the manner of his performing the duty was as follows:—

Arrived at the door, he gave a gentle tap, when voices from within, called out, "Who's there?"

Ser. "It's me, boys!"

Sol.. "And who are you?"

Ser. "Why then blur 'an ouns, boys, don't yees know my voice?"

Sol. "Och! and to be sure we do now."

Ser. "Well, boys, yees know what I'me come about"
Sol. "Sure we do, serjeant"
Ser. "Well, boys, are yees all within?"
Sol. "Within, is it I to be sure we are; why, where else would we be?"
Ser "That's right, boys! but boys, take care, are yees all in bed?"
Sol. "In bed! sure we are, and all asleep too!!"
Ser. "Och! that's right, honies, it's myself that's proud to find yees grown so regular!"

And having thus performed his duty, he wished them good night. But poor Bob Hardyman was one of those sort of fellows that could say a thing, (and make you laugh at it too, although at your own expense,) that if another person attempted, he would get his teeth knocked down his throat; he verified a saying in his own county, (Galway,) that one man in that country might steal a horse with impunity, when another darn't look over the hedge where he was grazing.

At Aldea-de-Ponte, the head-quarters of our division, all was quiet; and although our allowance of provisions was scanty, and our supply of money scarcely sufficient to procure us salt and rice for our soup, the division, nevertheless, was in high order; we had a good deal of drill, and regular examination's of the men's kits, a very necessary precaution with all regiments and with my corps as well as another. At an inspection of this kind by General Mackinnon, he found fault,—and deservedly so, I must confess—with the scanty manner in which some of the men of my company were supplied.

The general was too much the gentleman to row, or call names, but it was, clear from his manner that he was far from satisfied with the wardrobe displayed by these fellows; indeed, if he was, it would have been easy to please him! At last coming to a "boy" of the name of Darby Rooney, whose knapsack was what a Frenchman would term *vide,* or—to speak more intelligibly, one that contained nothing whatever but his watch-coat, a piece of pipe-clay, and button-brush! he seemed thunder-struck, as well he might, for I believe "he ne'er had looked upon its like before!" With more asperity of manner than I ever observed him to make use of, he asked "Darby" to whose squad he belonged. Darby Rooney understood about as much English as enabled him to get over a parade tolerably, but a conversation such as the general was about to hold with him was beyond his capacity, and he began to feel a little confused at the prospect of a *tête-à-tête* with his general; "*Squidha—squodha—cad-dershe-vourneen?*" [1] said he, turning to the orderly-serjeant, Pat Gafney, who did not himself speak the English language quite as correctly as Liudley Murray.

"Whist, ye Boston," [2] said Gafney, "and don't make a baste of yourself before the General." "Why," said General Mackinnon, "I believe he don't understand me."

"No, sir," replied Gafney, "he don't know what your honour manes."

The general passed on, taking it for granted that the man had never heard of a squad, and making some gentlemanlike observations on the utility of such partitions of a company, expressed himself satisfied with the fine appearance of the regiment, and our inspection ended with credit to us, this solitary instance excepted. This was, however, enough. Ill-nature and scandal seldom lack arguments. They are ever ready to take a hint, and it is unnecessary that a report should be as true as the gospel to form a foundation for their belief of it. An hour had not elapsed when the entire division were made acquainted (through some of our friends!) with the story. Groups of officers might be seen together (God forgive them!) laughing at our expense.

"Well!" cried one, "did you hear what happened with the Connaughts today?"

"No," replied a second, "but I'll bet twenty dollars I guess; another sheep or goat found in their quarters?"

"No. But when General Mackinnon inspected them just now, there was not one man in the regiment who knew what a squad was!"

"I would have sworn it," replied a third.

An old crone of a major, now joined the group, and shaking his head, said, "Ah! they are a sad set!" Poor idiot! The 88th was a more really efficient regiment than almost any two corps in the third division.

---

1. What does he say, Honey?
2. Hold your tongue, you booby.

But to return to the war. The partial successes which the guerrillas obtained over detached bodies, and in some instances over regular columns of the enemy, gave them great confidence in themselves, and they carried their effrontery so far, that in many instances they captured the oxen belonging to the garrison of Rodrigo close to the glacis of that fortress. On the 15th of October, Don Julian Sanchez, who had waited the night before in ambush near Ciudad-Rodrigo, surprised General Reynaud, the governor, when he was coming out for a ride, and took him prisoner; while the brave and enterprising Empecinado attacked the garrison of Calatayad, and took four hundred prisoners; and Espos y Mina destroyed, in the neighbourhood of Ayorbe, a French detachment of eleven hundred men,

Although all hostile movements in the neighbourhood of Ciudad-Rodrigo had ceased, and both British and French in its vicinity were in a state of comparative repose, in the other parts of the Peninsula much activity prevailed. On the first of October, the second division of our army, commanded by General Hill, resumed its position on the left of the Tagus, with the view of covering the province of Alentejo against any attempts that might be made to disturb its tranquillity by the garrison of Badajoz. The Fifth French corps, under the command of General Girard, was posted at Estramadura; while General Drouet, with the Ninth corps, kept up a line of communication between Girard's corps and Badajoz.

The Spanish General, Castanos, was busily employed in the organization of a considerable corps between the Guadiana and the Tagus; these demonstrations caused some uneasiness to Marshal Soult, who accordingly gave directions to General Girard to make a movement upon Merida, and to use every means in his power to disperse this force of Spaniards before it should be in a situation to act on the offensive. General Girard followed those orders with success, and forced the Spanish General into Portugal; but General Hill was by no means an idle spectator of the movement made by the French general, and he anxiously watched for an opportunity to punish him for his apparent disregard of the presence of a British division. General Hill was at Portalegre, distant but a few marches from the French, nevertheless they continued to pillage the country with as much security as if there was no enemy within reach of them. After several marches, made with the greatest precaution, on the 27th of October, the English general established himself in the village of Alcascar, close to the town of Arroyo-de-Molinos, the head-quarters of General Girard!

At two o'clock on the morning of the 28th, the British division was in motion, and under cover of a thick fog attacked the French troops as they were about to *debouche* from their position; nothing could exceed their consternation at this unexpected attack; their column made but a feeble resistance, and out of three thousand men of which the division consisted, it lost upwards of two thousand, together with the General of Brigade, Bron, and Colonel the Duke of Aremberg.

CHAPTER 14

Third Division at the Siege of Ciudad Rodrigo

The joke about Darby Rooney's wardrobe, and the conversation that took place between him and General Mackinnon, was circulated throughout the army, and I believe there was not one regiment unacquainted with the circumstance; indeed, so general was its circulation, that it reached the head-quarters of Lord Wellington himself, and if report spoke truly (which it don't always do,) it caused his lordship to laugh heartily.

I have myself,—before, and since I wrote the story,—often been asked if it was really a fact that we had no squads in the companies of my regiment, and I have invariably answered that we had not, and that every iota told by Bob Hardyman was true, for I think Bob's description of the Connaught Rangers altogether too rich to be contradicted or even altered; but were I myself to give a "full and true account" of the "boys," I would set them down as a parcel of lads that took the world easy, or, as they themselves would say—aisy, with a proper share of that nonchalance which is only to be acquired on service-real service; but I cannot bring myself to think them, as many did, a parcel of devils, neither will I by any manner of means try to pass them off for so many saints! but the fact is, (and I have before said so,) that there was not one regiment in the Peninsular army more severely—perhaps so severely—drilled as mine was; but I also say, without the slightest fear of contradiction, that the officers never tormented themselves or their men with too much fuss.

We approached their quarters as seldom as we possibly could—I mean as seldom as was necessary—and thereby kept up that distance between officers and privates, so essential to discipline; this we considered the proper line of conduct to chalk out, and we ever acted up to it We were amused to see some regiments whose commanding officers obliged every subaltern to parade his men at bedtime in their blankets! Why, they looked like so many hobgoblins! but if such an observance were necessary as far as concerned the soldiers, surely a serjeant ought to be able to do this much.

The serjeants in the British army are better paid than the subalterns of any other European power, and if they are incapable of performing the regimental drudgery, it comes to this—that they either receive too much pay, or do too little duty. Upon this conviction we ever acted; we made our serjeants do the duty usually performed by officers in other regiments, and we found our account in it.

Our argument was one that must be, I should conceive, obvious to the meanest capacity,—it was this: if the serjeants were proper attentive persons, as they should be from the rate of their pay, they were just as capable as commissioned officers to fulfil such duties as I have mentioned; if, on the contrary, they were idle inefficient fellows, the best method to make them acquainted with their duty was by accustoming them to perform it.

Practice, they say, makes perfect, and sure enough we kept our fellows to it. There may be some few who would combat this line of reasoning, but my reply to those gentlemen is, that a certain emulation ought to exist amongst the non-commissioned officers in every battalion; otherwise, how will that *esprit du corps* so essential to the well-being of a crack regiment, be kept up? It cannot be done.

Old General Hamilton used to say, that a soldier without pride was not worth his salt—and old General Hamilton was right; however, should there be persons sceptical enough to combat my position, backed as I think it is by so good an. authority, "come on and fight—if I have no fence, there is the better chance of victory." But what is any regiment the better for too much quackery? Decidedly not one whit It is the cant to say that it is not only the better for it, but that it is an ingredient essential to its very existence. I know this; but have I found it so? Certainly not. Does it make a regiment more healthy, march better, fight better, or more staunch to its colours? I have never found that it did.

Does it make the men more content with their lot, or the officers with theirs? Or—and here is a point of some consideration—does it raise the non-commissioned officers in the estimation of the soldiers, or in their estimation of themselves? I think not, and there's the rub; for I should be sorry to have it supposed that my anxiety to make the minor duties of a battalion be performed by serjeants, was meant as a cloak for the subalterns to shy their work. Heaven knows, and so do my brother subs—at least such of them as are in the land of the living—that such is not my motive; but there are some curmudgeons at the head of regiments who are never at rest unless they have their unfortunate subs thrusting their noses into every nook, no matter how filthy.

If a selection of good serjeants and corporals be made by the officer at the head of a regiment, and if that officer will only allow those individuals to do their duty, there is not the least doubt but that they will do it—I peril myself upon the assertion, and I bet a sovereign that the "Guards" agree with me.

I well remember some of those regiments, circumstanced as I have described, during the Peninsular War; those poor fellows were much to be pitied, for they were not only obliged to fag, but to dress also, with as much scrupulous exactness as the time and place would admit of. What folly! but was Lord Wellington to blame for this? Unquestionably not. He never troubled his head about such trifles, and had the commanding officers of corps followed the example set them (of not paying too much respect to minutiae) by the commander-in-chief, the situation of the junior officers in the army would have been far different from what it was.

Another custom prevailed in many regiments, which was attempted to be got up in mine, but we crushed it in its infancy; it was the sending a surgeon or his assistant to ascertain the state of an officer's health, should he think himself not well enough to attend an early drill.

We had in my old corps, amongst other "characters," one that, at the period I am writing about, was well known in the army to be as jovial a fellow as ever put his foot under a mess-table; his name was Fairfield; and though there were few who could sing as good a song, there was not in the whole British army a worse duty officer; indeed, it was next to impossible to catch hold of him for any duty whatever, and so well known was his dislike to all military etiquette, that the officer next to him on the roster, the moment Fairfield's name appeared for guards-mounting or court-martial, considered himself as the person meant, and he was right nine times out of ten.

The frequent absence of Fairfield from drill, at a time too when the regiment was in expectation of being inspected by the general of division, obliged the officer commanding to send the surgeon to ascertain the nature of his malady, which from its long continuance (on occasions of duty!) strongly savoured of a chronic complaint. The doctor found the invalid traversing his chamber rather lightly clad for an indisposed person; he was singing one of Moore's melodies, and accompanying himself with his violin, which instrument he touched with great taste. The doctor told him the nature of his visit, and offered to feel his pulse, but Fairfield turned from him, repeating the lines of Shakspeare, "Canst thou minister," &c. &c.

"Well," replied the surgeon, "I am sorry for it, but I cannot avoid reporting you fit for duty."

"I'm sorry you cannot," rejoined Fairfield; "but my complaint is best known to myself! and I feel that were I to rise as early as is necessary, I should be lost to the service in a month."

"Why," said the doctor, "Major Thompson says you have been lost to it ever since he first knew you, and that is now something about six years;" and he took his leave for the purpose of making his report

The major's orderly was soon at Fairfield's quarters, with a message to say that his presence was required by his commanding officer. Fairfield was immediately in attendance.

"Mr. Fairfield," said the major, "your constant habit of being absent from early drill has obliged me to send the surgeon to ascertain the state of your health, and he reports that you are perfectly well, and I must say that your appearance is anything but that of an invalid—how is this?"

"Don't mind him, sir," replied Fairfield; "I am, thank God! very well now, but when the bugle sounded this morning at four o'clock, a cold shivering came over me—I think it was a touch of ague! and besides, Doctor Gregg is too short a time in the Connaught Rangers to know my habit"

"Is he?" rejoined the old major, "he must be d——d stupid then; but that is a charge you surely can't make against me; I have been now about nineteen years in the regiment, during six of which I have had the pleasure of knowing you, and you will allow me to tell you, that I am not only well acquainted with 'your habit,' but to request you will, from this moment, change it,"—and with this gentle rebuke he good humouredly dismissed him. He was an excellent duty officer ever after.

There are many who will, perhaps, say that the commanding officer should have been more rigid, and at the very least have placed the offender under arrest, but this is a false notion. An officer at the head of a regiment is often obliged—or at least ought often—to shut his eyes against little irregularities, and a gentle rebuke is sometimes better than a harsher mode of proceeding; and not only the interior economy, but the interior harmony of a corps is better insured by this means. If the officers are happy, the soldiers are sure to be so; and if officers and privates are content with their lot, all must go right.

A soldier of the 88th (while that corps was stationed in Lower Canada, in 1814,) was once asked by a Yankee, "Why it was that the men of his corps never deserted when so fine an opportunity was afforded them to do so?"

"Why thin," replied Paddy, "iv you want to know the raison that we don't desart, I'll tell it to you nately. We have no complaint to make against our officers, and we can't be more happy than we are. Our officers and we give and take with each other, and there's the ins and outs of it" And there is the "ins" and "outs" of it: this is the grand secret.

A regiment is a piece of mechanism, and requires as much care as any other machine, whose parts are obliged to act in unison to keep it going as it ought If a screw or two be loose, a skilful hand will easily right them without injuring the machine; but if it falls into the hands of a self-sufficient, ignorant bungler, it is sure to be injured, if not destroyed altogether; and as certain as the daylight, if it is ever placed in a situation where it must, from necessity, be allowed to act for itself—where the main spring cannot control the lesser ones, much less the great body of the machine—it will be worse than useless—worse than a log—not only in the way, but not to be depended upon!

It must not, however, be supposed, that these observations are meant to favour a too little regard to that system of discipline which is so essential to be observed in the army, and without which any army—but particularly a British one—would be inefficient; they are written by one who, although he never did, or, in all human probability, ever will, attain a higher rank than these "Reminiscences" avow him to hold, has had, nevertheless, some experience; and if anything he writes now, or may write hereafter, conduces to the amusement—he is not vain enough to say information—of his military readers, he will be more than repaid for his trouble.

Extremes should be avoided, and too much familiarity is as bad as too much severity. I once heard of a commanding officer of a first-rate regiment, who was in the habit of allowing the junior officers of his corps to make too free with him; he at length found it necessary to send his adjutant to inquire the reason why a young ensign, who was in the habit of absenting himself from parade, did so on one of those days which was allotted as a garrison parade? The adjutant informed the ensign, that the colonel awaited his reply. "Shall I say you are unwell?" demanded he.

"Oh! no," replied the ensign, "I'll settle the matter with the commanding officer myself." The hour of dinner approached, yet no communication was received from the ensign. Passing from his quarters to the mess-room, the commanding officer met the ensign, and was about to accost him, when the latter turned his head aside, and declined recognising his colonel, who, upon arriving at the mess-room, was so dejected as to attract the notice of all the officers. Upon being asked why he was so out of spirits, the colonel, "good easy man," told a "round unvarnished tale," and in conclusion, added, "I thought nothing of his not answering my message! but I cannot express how much I am hurt at the idea of his cutting me as he did when I wished to speak with him!"

This was *un peu trop fort;* and had the regiment in question been much longer under the command of the good-natured personage I have described, there is little doubt but that it would have become rather relaxed in its discipline.

The different movements amongst the contending armies in the end of the 1811, caused it to be presumed that the campaign the following year would open with much spirit; and so it did, although earlier than was anticipated. On the 27th of December, the division of General Hill left its cantonments in the vicinity of Portalegre, in the expectation of surprising the French at Merida. The advanced guard of the British fell in with a party of French marauders, who, having collected, formed a square, and owing to the nature of the ground, (which was uneven,) and to the rapidity of their march, succeeded in re-entering Merida before they could be attacked by the English infantry. The French general did not await the arrival of General Hill, but retreated upon Lerena, at which place he was sustained by the Fifth Corps, under the command of the Count D'Erlon.

General Hill reached Almandralejo on the 2nd of January, 1812, and made a reconnoissance as far as Los Santos. A brilliant affair of cavalry took place in the environs of this town, and Lieutenant-Colonel Abercromby, who commanded our detachment, completely overthrew the French horse, although they were much superior in numbers. This advantage made Marshal Soult apprehensive of a more serious attack; and he concentrated the forces of Victor and Laval; but General Hill, satisfied with having created an alarm in the French army of the south, retired to his former quarters on the frontiers of Portugal.

The advance of General Hill was but a feint to deceive the enemy; it was made with the view of making Marshal Marmont believe that our forces on the left of the Tagus were much more numerous than they really were; thereby inducing him not to harbour any apprehensions respecting Ciudad-Rodrigo, the possession of which, Lord Wellington had resolved on. Marmont's security was besides increased by the facility with which the blockade of that fortress had been raised three months before, through the bare junction of four divisions with the army of the Count Dorsenne; a manoeuvre which might be repeated at any time with an equal probability of success. He not only quartered his army in very extensive cantonments, but also detached General Montbrun, with three divisions, to co-operate with Marshal Suchet in the kingdom of Valencia.

Intimately acquainted with these details, Lord Wellington redoubled his efforts in the arrangement of all that was necessary to carry on the siege of Ciudad Rodrigo with vigour. The Third Division, which was one of those destined to take a part in the attack, broke up from its cantonments on the morning of the 4th of January, 1812. Carpio, Espeja, and Pastores, were occupied by our troops, and the greatest activity prevailed throughout every department, but more especially in that of the engineers.

All the cars in the country were put into requisition for the purpose of conveying fascines, gabions, and the different materials necessary, to the Convent de la Carida, distant a league and half from Rodrigo: the guns were at Gallegos, and everything was in that state of preparation which announced that a vigorous attack was about to be made in the depth of a severe winter, against a fortress that had withstood for twenty-five days all the efforts of Marshal Massena, in the summer of 1810, when it was only occupied by a weak garrison of Spaniards; yet. nevertheless, everyone felt confident, and the soldiers burned with impatience to wipe away the blot of the former year in the unfortunate siege of San Christoval and Badajoz.

The attack of Ciudad-Rodrigo, although sudden in its development, was, nevertheless, one of long contemplation; and the result, which was so rapid as to baffle all the calculations of the French marshal, proved to the world that the British army were not only not inferior to the French in their engineer department, but that it excelled them in that arm as decidedly as it did in every other.

I have before mentioned that we had not an effective corps of engineers; I mean in point of numbers: to remedy this defect, a proportion of the most intelligent officers and soldiers of the infantry were selected during the autumn months, and placed under the direction of Colonel Fletcher, the chief engineer: they were soon taught how to make fascines and gabions, and what was of equal consequence—how to use them. They likewise learned the manner of working by sap, and by this means, that branch of our army which was before the weakest, had now become very efficient.

The morning of the 4th of January was dreadfully inauspicious. The order for marching arrived at three o'clock, and we were under arms at five. The rain fell in torrents, and the village of Aldea de-Ponte, which the brigade of General Mackinnon occupied, was a sea of filth; the snow on the surrounding hills drifted down with the flood, and nearly choked up the roads, and the appearance of the morning was anything but a favourable omen for us who had a march of nine leagues to make ere we reached the town of Robleada, on the river Agueda, which was destined to be our resting-place for the night.

At half-past six the brigade was in motion, and I scarcely remember a more disagreeable day; the rain which had fallen in the morning was succeeded by snow and sleet, and some soldiers, who sunk from cold and fatigue, fell down exhausted, soon became insensible, and perished; yet, strange to say, an Irishwoman of my regiment was delivered of a child upon the road, and continued the march with her infant in her arms.

Notwithstanding the severity of the day, it was impossible to avoid occasionally smiling at the *outré* appearance of some of the officers. The total disregard which the commander-in-chief paid to uniformity of dress, is well known, and there were many on this day who were obliged to acknowledge that they showed more taste than judgment in their selection.

Captain Adair, of my corps, nearly fell a victim to the choice he had made, on this our first day of opening the campaign of 1812. He wore a pair of boots that fitted him with a degree of exactness that would not disgrace a "Hoby;" the heels were high, and the toes sharply pointed; his pantaloons were of blue web; his frock-coat and waistcoat were tastefully and fashionably chosen, the former light blue richly frogged with lace, the latter of green velvet with large silver Spanish buttons, but he forgot the most essential part of all—and that was his boat cloak.

For the first ten or twelve miles he rode, but the cold was so intense that he was obliged to dismount, and unquestionably his dress was but ill calculated for walking. The rain with which his pantaloons were saturated, was by this time nearly frozen (for the day had begun to change,) and he became so dreadfully chafed that he was necessitated to give up the march, and we left him at a village half way from Robleada, resembling more one of those which composed "the army of martyrs," than that commanded by Lord Wellington. I myself was nearly in as bad a state, but being a few years younger, and more serviceably clad, I made an effort to get on.

We had by this time (eight o'clock at night proceeded a considerable way in the dark, and, as may be supposed, it was a difficult matter to keep the men together as compactly as could be wished. Whenever an opportunity occurred, a jaded soldier or two of my regiment used to look in on our Spanish friends, and if they found them at supper, they could not bring themselves to refuse an offer to "take share of what was going," and, to say the truth, this was no more than might be expected from a set of fellows who belonged to a country so proverbial for its hospitality to strangers as theirs (Ireland) was! besides this, the men of the Connaught Rangers had a way of making themselves "at home" that was peculiar to them, and for which—whatever else might be denied them!—they got full credit. Bob Hardyman used to say, "they had a taking way with them."

Passing a hamlet a short distance from Robleda, we saw a number of Spaniards, women as well as men, outside the door of a good-looking house; much altercation was apparently taking place, at length a soldier (named Ody Brophy,) rushed out with half a flitch of bacon under his arm; a scuffle ensued, and Lieutenant D'Arcy, to whose company the soldier belonged, ran up to inquire the cause of the outcry, but it was soon too manifest to be misunderstood; the war-whoop was raised against our man, who, on his part, as stoutly defended himself, not by words alone but by blows, which had nearly silenced his opponents, when he was seized by my friend D'Arcy.

Piccaroon, Ladrone, and other approbrious epithets were poured with much volubility against him, but he, with the greatest *sang-froid,* turned to his officer and said, "Be aisy now, and don't be vexing yourself with them, or the likes of them. Wasn't it for you I was making a bargain? and didn't I offer the value of it? Don't I see the way you're lost with the hunger, and the divil a bit iv rations you'll get ate tonight. Och! you cratur, iv your poor mother—that's dead! was to see you after such a condition, it's she that id beleev'd iv herself for letting you away from her at all-at-all."

"Well," said D'Arcy, (softened no doubt, and who would not at such a speech?) "what did you offer for it?"

"What did I offer for it, is it? Fait, then, I offered enough, but they made such a noise that I don't think they heard me, for, upon my sowl, I hardly heard myself with the uproar they made; and sure I told them iv I hadn't money enough to pay for it (and it was true for me I had'nt, unless I got it dog cheap!) you had; but they don't like a bone in my skin, or in yours either, and that is the raison they are afther offinding me afther such a manner. And didn't one of the women get my left thumb into her mouth, and grunch it like a bit of mate? Look at it," said he, in conclusion, at the same time thrusting his bleeding hand nearly into D'Arcy's face, "fait and iv your honour hadn't come up, it's my belief she would have bit it clane off at the knuckle."

This speech, delivered with a rapidity and force that was sufficient to overwhelm the most practised rhetorician, carried away everything along with it, like chaff before a whirlwind, and D'Arcy made all matters smooth by paying the price demanded (two dollars;) and the piece of bacon was carried away by Ody, who was a townsman of D'Arcy's, and who repeatedly assured him "he would do more than that to sarve him."

It was impossible to avoid paying a tribute of praise to Ody Brophy for the tact with which he avoided the storm with which he was threatened; and upon this occasion he proved himself as good a pilot as ever guided a vessel, and to the full equal to one I once heard of in the harbour of Cork.

A captain of a man-of-war, newly appointed to a ship on the Irish station, took the precaution, "in beating out" of harbour, to apprise the pilot that he was totally unacquainted with the coast, and therefore he must rely on the pilot's local knowledge for the safety of his ship.

"You are perfectly sure, pilot," said the captain, "you are well acquainted with the coast?"

"Do I know my own name, sir."

"Well, mind, I warn you not to approach too near the shore."

"Now make yourself aisy, sir, in troth you may go to bed iv you plaise."

"Then shall we stand on?"

"Why,—what else would we do?"

"Yes. but there may be hidden dangers, which you know nothing about."

"Dangers? I'd like to see the dangers dare hide themselves from Mich,—sure, don't I tell you I know every rock on the coast," (here the ship strikes), "and that's one of 'em."

CHAPTER 15

Progress of the Siege

The brigade reached Robleada at nine o'clock at night, and our quarters there, which at any time would have been considered good, appeared to us, after our wretched billets at Aldea-de-Ponte, and the fatigue of a harassing march, sumptuous. The villages in Spain, like those of France, are well supplied with beds, and the house allotted to me, D'Arcy, and Captain Peshall, was far from deficient in those essentials. A loud knocking at the door of the cottage announced the arrival of Peshall, who, like some others, had been "thrown out" on the march, and who sought for his billet in the best manner he could.

He was a man who might boast of as well-stocked a canteen as any other captain in the army; and upon this occasion it made a proud display. The fire-place was abundantly supplied with wood, and at each side of the chimney there was a profusion of that kind of furniture which I ever considered as indispensable to complete the garniture of a well-regulated cuisine, no matter whether in a cottage, or *château*—I mean hams, sausages, and flitches of well cured bacon. While I contemplated all the luxuries with which I was surrounded, I felt exceedingly happy, and I am inclined to think that the evening of the 4th of January 1812 was, if not one of the pleasantest of my life, unquestionably one of the most rational I ever passed.

Our baggage had by this time arrived, and having got on dry clothes, we began to attack the contents of Peshall's canteen, which was ever at the service of his friends; it contained, among other good things, a Lamego ham, and a cold roast leg of mountain mutton, "morsels which may take rank, notwithstanding their Spartan plainness, with the most disguised of foreign manufacture." It is scarcely necessary to add, that we did ample justice to the viands placed before us, and having taken a sufficient libation of brandy punch, in which the Spaniard joined us, we began to turn, not only our thoughts, but our eyes also towards our beds; but it was soon manifest, from divers demonstrations on. the part of our hostess, that she intended putting D'Arcy, and me, on what is called in Ireland the "Shaugarawn," or, in plain English, that she had made up her mind to give one bed to Peshall, and that the other should be occupied by herself and her husband.

We arose early the following morning, the 5th, and the brigade reached the small village of Attalaya, distant three leagues from Rodrigo, a little before noon. That fortress was completely invested on the evening of the 7th, and dispositions were made to commence operations against it on the night following.

Ciudad Rodrigo stands upon an eminence, on the right bank of the river Agueda, and is difficult of access; it had been since its occupation by the French, much strengthened by the construction of a redoubt on the hill called St, Francisco; some old convents in the suburbs were also turned into defences, and these places no longer presented their original peaceful appearance, but were, in fact, very respectable outworks, and tended much to our annoyance and loss at the commencement of the siege.

To be safe against a *coup-de-main*, Rodrigo would require a force of from five to six thousand troops, and its present garrison did not reckon anything like three thousand bayonets; it was therefore manifest that, notwithstanding the unfavourable time of the year, it must fall if not speedily succoured, yet it would seem that Marshal Marmont took no measures to make a diversion in its favour. Strongly impressed with this state of the matter, Lord Wellington saw the advantage he would have over his opponent, by acting with as little delay as possible; his situation, which could not be better, would, by the nature of things, change by losing time, and he resolved to open the trenches on the night of the 8th, but it was necessary to carry the redoubt of St. Francisco in the first instance.

Protected by a strong escort. Lord Wellington carefully reconnoitred the town on the 8th; and shortly after dark, three hundred men of the light division, headed by Colonel Colborn of the 52nd, were formed for the attack of St. Francisco. They were followed by a working party, composed also of men of the light division. The storming party, led on by Colonel Colborn, advanced under cover of the night, and were not discovered until they had reached to within a few yards of the redoubt, and our troops rushed on with such impetuosity, that the outwork was carried, and the soldiers that defended it put to the sword, before the garrison of Rodrigo thought it in danger; and profiting by the panic with which the enemy were seized, Colonel Colborn caused the works of the redoubt to be razed, completed the first parallel, and rendered our future approaches secure.

The duty in the trenches was carried on by the First, Third, Fourth, and Light Divisions, each taking its separate tour every twenty-four hours; we had no tents or huts of any description; and the ground was covered with snow, nevertheless the soldiers were cheerful, and everything went on well. The fortified convents in the suburbs were respectively carried, and each sortie made by the garrison was immediately repulsed; in some instances our men pursued them to the very glacis, and many a fine fellow, carried away by his enthusiasm, died at the muzzles of their cannon.

Every exertion was made to forward the works, so fully were all impressed with its necessity; but not- withstanding the animated exertions of the engineers, and the ready co-operation of the infantry, their progress was at times unavoidably slower than was anticipated. In some instances the soil was so unfavourable, it was next to an impossibility to make head against it; instead of clay or gravel, we frequently met with a vein of rock, and invariably when this occurred, our losses were severe, for the pick-axes coming in contact with the stone, caused a fire to issue that plainly told the enemy where we were, and, as a matter of course, they redoubled their efforts on these points; nevertheless, on the 14th, in the afternoon, we were enabled to open our fire from twenty-two pieces of cannon superior to those which armed our batteries at Badajoz the year before, inasmuch as the former guns were of brass, while those which we now used were of metal. On this night we established the second parallel, distant only one hundred and fifty yards from the body of the place.

On the 15th the second parallel was in a forward state, and the approach by sap to the glacis was considerably advanced; the effect also of our fire was such as made us perceive a material alteration in the enemy's mode of replying to it; and it was apparent, that although but seven days before the place, our labours were soon likely to be brought to a termination. The cannonade of the enemy, however, if not as great as at first, was more effective, and our casualties more numerous, and their guns and mortars were directed with a scientific precision that did credit to the men who served them. On the 18th, a battery of seven thirty-two pounders opened its fire, and from this height the walls of the Fausse Braye were distinguishable, while the guns in the first parallel overpowered the several bastions against which they were directed; indeed, every hour proved the visible superiority of our fire over that of the enemy, which at times seemed to be altogether extinguished, and whenever it shone forth with anything like brilliancy, it was but momentary, and might be well likened to some spark of combustible matter, issuing from the interior of a nearly consumed ruin.

The battery which opened on the 15th had almost effected a breach opposite to the suburb of St Francisco, and it was manifest that the one which assailed the Fausse Braye, although later in its construction, was to the full as effective as its companion. Wherever danger was greatest, there were our engineers, and it was painful to see their devotedness; on horseback or on foot, under cover or exposed to fire, was to them the same, and their example was followed by the soldiers with an enthusiasm unequalled; in short, it was plain that a few hours would suffice to decide the fate of Ciudad Rodrigo. At this period (the 18th), the fourth division occupied and performed the duty in the trenches. Early on the morning of the 19th, the third division (although not for duty that day,) received orders to march to the Convent de la Carida,[1] and as Lord Wellington was not in the habit of giving us unnecessary marches,

---

1. "On the 19th of January the Light Division was ordered to assault out of its turn. At first it was reported they were to take both breaches, but as the Third Division were also throwing up earthy their General remonstrated."—(*Sketch of the Storming of Ciudad Rodrigo, by an Officer engaged*).
Answer by the Author,—This is a mistake. The Third Division, like the Light, was ordered to assault "out of its turn;" it did not arrive before Rodrigo until the afternoon of the 19th, neither did it throw up earth on that day, nor was any remonstrance made—indeed, it could not—on the part of its general on that score.

we concluded that he intended us the honour of forming one of the corps destined to carry the place.

On our march we perceived our old friends and companions, the light division, debouching from their cantonments, and the joy expressed by our men when they saw them, is not to be described: we were long acquainted, and like horses accustomed to the same harness, we pulled well together. At two o'clock in the afternoon we left La Carida, and passing to the rear of the first parallel, formed in column about two gunshots distant from the main breach. The fourth division still occupied the works, and it was the general opinion that ours (the third) were to be in reserve. The number of Spaniards, Portuguese, and soldiers' wives in the character of suttlers, was immense, and the neighbourhood, which but a few days before was only to empty plain, now presented the appearance of a vast camp.

Wretches of the poorest description hovered round us, in hopes of gelling a morsel of food, or of plundering some dead or wounded soldier: their cadaverous countenances expressed a living picture of the greatest want; and it required all our precaution to prevent these miscreants from robbing us the instant we turned our backs from our scanty store of baggage or provisions.

Our bivouack, as may be supposed, presented an animated appearance: groups of soldiers cooking in one place; in another, some dozens collected together, listening to accounts brought from the works by some of their companions whom curiosity had led thither; others relating their past battle to any of the young soldiers who had not as yet come hand to hand with a Frenchman; others dancing and singing; officers' servants preparing dinner for their masters, and officers themselves, dressed in whatever wav best suited their taste or convenience, mixed with the men, without any distinguishing mark of uniform to denote their rank; the only thing uniform to be discovered amongst a group of between four and five thousand, was good conduct and confidence in themselves and their general.

It was now five o'clock in the afternoon, and darkness was approaching fast, yet no order had arrived intimating that we were to take a part in the contest about to be decided; we were in this state of suspense, when our attention was attracted by the sound of music: we all stood up, and pressed forward to a ridge, a little in our front, and which separated us from the cause of our movement, but it would be impossible for me to convey an adequate idea of our feelings, when we beheld the 43rd Regiment, preceded by their band, going to storm the left breach; they were in the highest spirits, but without the slightest appearance of levity in their demeanour,—on the contrary, there was a cast of determined severity thrown over their countenances, that expressed in legible characters that they knew the sort of service they were about to perform, and had made up their minds to the issue.

They had no knapsacks—their firelocks were slung over their shoulders—their shirt collars were open, and there was an indescribable something about them that at one and the same moment impressed the lookers-on with admiration and awe. In passing us, each officer and soldier stepped out of the ranks for an instant, as he recognised a friend, to press his hand; many for the last time: yet, notwithstanding this animating scene, there was no shouting or huzzaing, no boisterous bravadoing, no unbecoming language; in short, everyone seemed to be impressed with the seriousness of the affair entrusted to his charge, and any interhange of words was to this effect: "Well, lads, mind what you're about tonight;" or, "We'll meet in the town by and by;" and other little familiar phrases, all expressive of confidence. The regiment at length passed us, and we stood gazing after it as long as the rear platoon continued in sight: the music grew fainter every moment, until at last it died away altogether; they had no drums, and there was a melting sweetness in the sounds that touched the heart.

The first syllable uttered after this scene was, "And are we to be left behind?" The interrogatory was scarcely put when the word "Stand to your arms," answered it; the order was promptly obeyed, and a breathless silence prevailed, when our commanding officer, in a few words, announced to us that Lord Wellington had directed our division to carry the grand breach. The soldiers listened to the communication with silent earnestness, and immediately began to disencumber themselves of their knapsacks, which were placed in order by companies, and a guard set over them; each man then began to arrange himself for the combat in such manner as his fancy or the moment would admit of,—some by lowering their cartridge-boxes, others by turning theirs to the front, in order that they might the more conveniently make use of them; others unclasping their stocks or opening their shirt collars, and others oiling their bayonets; and more taking leave of their wives and children.

This last was an affecting sight, but not so much so as might be expected, because the women, from long habit, were accustomed to scenes of danger, and the order for their husbands to march against the enemy was in their eyes tantamount to a victory, and as the soldier seldom returned without plunder of some sort, the painful suspense which his absence caused was made up by the gaiety which his return was certain to be productive of; or, if unfortunately he happened to fall, his place was sure to be supplied by some one of the company to which he belonged, so that the women of our army had little cause of alarm on this head. The worst that could happen to them was the chance of being in a state of widowhood for a week.

It was by this time half-past six o'clock, the evening was piercingly cold, and the frost was crisp on the grass; there was a keenness in the air that braced our nerves at least as high as concert pitch. We stood quietly to our arms, and told our companies off by files, sections, and sub-divisions; the serjeants called over the rolls, not a man was absent

It appears it was the wish of General Mackinnon to confer a mark of distinction upon the 88th Regiment, and as it was one of the last acts of his life, I shall mention it He sent for Major Thompson, who commanded the battalion, and told him it was his wish to have the forlorn hope of the grand breach led on by a subaltern of the 88th Regiment, adding at the same time, that, in the event of his surviving, he should be recommended for a company. The major acknowledged this mark of the general's favour, and left him folding up some letters he had been writing to his friends in England—this was about twenty minutes before the attack of the breaches. Major Thompson, having called his officers together, briefly told them the wishes of their general; he was about to proceed, when Lieutenant William Mackie (then senior lieutenant) immediately stepped forward, and dropping his sword said, "Major Thompson, I am ready for that service."[2]

---

2. Appendix, No. 3.

For once in his life poor old Thompson was affected; Mackie was his own townsman, they had fought together for many years, and when he took hold of his hand and pronounced the words, "God bless you, my boy," his eye filled, his lip quivered, and there was a faltering in his voice which was evidently perceptible to himself, for he instantly resumed his former composure, drew himself up, and gave the word, "Gentlemen, fall in," and at this moment Generals Picton and Mackinnon, accompanied by their respective staff, made their appearance amongst us.

Long harangues are not necessary to British soldiers, and on this occasion but few words were made use of; Picton said something animating to the different regiments as he passed them, and those of my readers who recollect his deliberate and strong utterance will say with me, that his mode of speaking was indeed very impressive. The address to each was nearly the same, but that delivered by him to the 88th was so characteristic of the general, and so applicable to the men he spoke to, that I shall give it, word for word; it was this—

> Rangers of Connaught! it is not my intention to expend any powder this evening. We'll do this business with the could iron.

I before said the soldiers were silent—so they were, but the man who could be silent after such an address, made in such a way, and in such a place, had better have stayed at home. It may be asked what did they do? Why, what would they do, or would anyone do but give the loudest hurrah he was able.

CHAPTER 16

Storm of Ciudad Rodrigo

The burst of enthusiasm caused by Picton's address to the Connaught Rangers had scarcely ceased, when the signal gun announced that the attack was to commence. Generals Picton and Mackinnon dismounted from their horses, and placing themselves at the head of the right brigade, the troops rapidly entered the trenches by sections right in front; the storming party under the command of Major Russell Manners, of the 74th, heading it, while the forlorn-hope, commanded by Lieutenant William Mackie, of the 88th, and composed of twenty volunteers from the Connaught Rangers, led the van, followed closely by the 45th, 88th, and 74th British, and the 9th, and 21st Portuguese; the 77th and 83rd British belonging to the left brigade, brought up the rear, and completed the dispositions.

While these arrangements were effecting opposite the grand breach, the 5th and 94th, belonging to the left brigade of the third division, were directed to clear the ramparts and Fausse Braye wall, and the 2nd Regiment of Portuguese Caçadores, commanded by an Irish colonel of the name of O'Toole, was to escalade the curtain to the left of the lesser breach, which was attacked by the light division under the command of General Robert Craufurd.

The 43rd Light Infantry, heading the light division, were followed by the 95th and 52nd British, and the 3rd and 7th Portuguese Caçadores; the storming party, led by Major G. Napier of the 52nd, and the forlorn-hope by Lieutenant Gurwood of the same regiment, preceded the entire. It wanted ten minutes to seven o'clock when these dispositions were completed—the moon occasionally, as the clouds which overcast it passed away, shed a faint ray of light upon the battlements of the fortress, and presented to our view the glittering of the enemy's bayonets as their soldiers stood arrayed upon the ramparts and breach awaiting our attack; yet, nevertheless, their batteries were silent, and might warrant the supposition to an unobservant spectator that the defence would be but feeble.

The two divisions, arrayed as I have described, got clear of the covert way at the same moment, and each advanced to the attack of their respective points with the utmost regularity. The obstacles which presented themselves to both were nearly the same, but every difficulty, no matter how great, merged into insignificance when placed in the scale of the prize about to be contested. The soldiers were full of ardour, but altogether devoid of that blustering and bravadoing which is truly unworthy of men at such a moment; and it would be difficult to convey an adequate idea of the enthusiastic bravery which animated the troops.

A cloud that had for some time before obscured the moon, which was at its full, disappeared altogether, and the countenances of the soldiers were for the first time, since Picton addressed them, visible—they presented a material change. In place of that joyous animation which his fervid and impressive address called forth, a look of severity bordering on ferocity, had taken its place; and although ferocity is by no means one of the characteristics of the British soldier, there was, most unquestionably, a savage expression in the faces of the men, that I had never before witnessed. Such is the difference between the storm of a breach and the fighting a pitched battle.

Once clear of the covert way, and fairly on the plain that separated it from the fortress, the enemy had a full view of all that was passing; their batteries, charged to the muzzle with case-shot, opened a murderous fire upon the columns as they advanced, but nothing could shake the intrepid bravery of the troops. The light division soon descended the ditch, and gained, although not without a serious struggle, the top of the narrow and difficult breach allotted to them;—their gallant general, Robert Craufurd, fell at the head of the 43rd, and his second in command, General Vandeleur, was severely wounded, but there were not wanting others to supply their place; yet these losses, trying as they were to the feelings of the soldiers, in no way damped their ardour, and the brave Light Division carried the left breach at the point of the bayonet. Once established upon the ramparts, they made all the dispositions necessary to ensure their own conquest, as also to render every assistance in their power to the Third Division in their attack. They cleared the rampart which separated the lesser from the grand breach, and relieved Picton's division from any anxiety it might have as to its safety on its left flank.

The right brigade, consisting of the 45th, 88th, and 74th, forming the van of the Third Division, upon reaching the ditch, to its astonishment, found Major Ridge and Colonel Campbell at the head of the 5th and 94th, mounting the Fausse Braye wall; these two regiments, after having performed their task of silencing the fire of the French troops upon the ramparts, with a noble emulation resolved to precede their comrades in the attack of the grand breach—both parties greeted each other with a cheer, only to be understood by those who have been placed in a similar situation: yet the enemy were in no way daunted by the shout raised by our soldiers—they crowded the breach, and defended it with a bravery that would have made any but troops accustomed to conquer, waver.

But the "fighting division" were not the men to be easily turned from their purpose; the breach was speedily mounted, yet, nevertheless, a serious affray took place ere it was gained. A considerable mass of infantry crowned its summit, while in the rear and at each side were stationed then, so placed that they could render every assistance to their comrades at the breach without ant great risk to themselves; besides this, two guns of heavy calibre, separated from the breach by a ditch of considerable depth and width, enfiladed it, and as soon as the French infantry were forced from the summit, these guns opened their fire on our troops.

The head of the column had scarcely gained the top, when a discharge of grape cleared the ranks of the three leading battalions, and caused a momentary wavering; at the same instant a frightful explosion near the gun to the left of the breach, which shook the bastion to its foundation, completed the disorder. Mackinnon, at the head of his brigade, was blown into the air.

His *aide-de-camp*, Lieutenant Beresford of the 88th, shared the same fate, and every man on the breach at the moment of the explosion perished. This was unavoidable, because those of the advance being either killed or wounded, were necessarily flung back upon the troops that followed close upon their footsteps, and there was not a sufficient space for the men who were ready to sustain those placed *hors de combat,* to rally.

For an instant all was confusion; the blaze of light caused by the explosion, resembled a huge meteor, and presented to our sight the havoc which the enemy's fire had caused in our ranks; while from afar, the astonished Spaniard viewed for an instant, with horror and dismay, the soldiers of the two nations grappling with each other on the top of the rugged breach which trembled beneath their feet, while the fire of the French artillery played upon our columns with irresistible fury, sweeping from the spot the living and the dead.

Amongst the latter was Captain Robert Hardyman, and Lieutenant Pearce, of the 45th, and many more whose names I cannot recollect. Others were so stunned by the shock, or wounded by the stones which were hurled forth by the explosion, that they were insensible to their situation; of this number I was one, for being close to the magazine when it blew up, I was quite overpowered, and I owed my life to the serjeant-major of my regiment, Thorp, who saved me from being trampled to death by our soldiers in their advance, ere I could recover strength sufficient to move forward, or protect myself.

The French, animated by this accidental success, hastened once more to the breach which they had abandoned, but the leading regiments of Picton's division, which had been disorganized for the moment by the explosion, rallied, and soon regained its summit, when another discharge from the two flank guns swept away the foremost of those battalions.

There was at this time but one officer alive upon the breach, (Major Thomson, of the 74th, acting engineer;) he called out to those next to him to seize the gun to the left, which had been so fatal to his companions—but this was a desperate service. The gun was completely cut off from the breach by a deep trench, and soldiers, encumbered with their firelocks, could not pass it in sufficient time to anticipate the next discharge—yet to deliberate was certain death.

The French cannoneers, five in number, stood to, and served their gun with as much *sang froid* as if on a parade, and the light which their torches threw forth, showed to our men the peril they would have to encounter if they dared to attack a gun so defended—but this was of no avail. Men going to storm a breach, generally make up their minds that there is no great probability of their ever returning from it to tell their adventures to their friends; and whether they die at the bottom or top of it, or at the muzzle, or upon the breech of a cannon, is to them pretty nearly the same!

The first who reached the top after the last discharge, were three of the 88th. Serjeant Pat Brazill—the brave Brazill of the grenadier company, who saved his captain's life at Busaco,[1]—called out to his two companions, Swan and Kelly, to unscrew their bayonets and follow him; the three men passed the trench in a moment, and engaged the French cannoneers hand to hand—a terrific but short combat was the consequence.

Swan was the first, and was met by the two gunners on the right of the gun, but, no way daunted, he engaged them, and plunged his bayonet into the breast of one; he was about to repeat the blow upon the other, but before he could disentangle the weapon from his bleeding adversary, the second Frenchman closed upon him, and by a *coup de sabre,* severed his left arm from his body a little above the elbow; he fell from the shock, and was on the eve of being massacred, when Kelly, after having scrambled under the gun, rushed onward to succour his comrade. He bayoneted two Frenchmen on the spot; and at this instant Brazill came up—three of the five gunners lay lifeless, while Swan, resting against an ammunition chest, was bleeding to death.

It was now equal numbers, two against two, but Brazill in his over anxiety to engage, was near losing his life at the onset; in making a lunge at the man next to him, his foot slipped upon the bloody platform, and he fell forward against his antagonist, but as both rolled under the gun, Brazill felt the socket of his bayonet

---

1. "Captain Dunne fought with his sabre, while Captain Dansey made use of a firelock and bayonet; he received three wounds, and Captain Dunne owed his life to a serjeant of his company named Brazill, who, seeing his officer in danger of being overpowered, scrambled to his assistance, and making a thrust of his *halbert* at the Frenchman, transfixed him against the rock on which he was standing."—*Reminiscences of a Subaltern.*

strike hard against the buttons of the Frenchman's coat The remaining gunner, in attempting to escape under the carriage from Kelly, was killed by some soldiers of the 5th, who just now reached the top of the breach, and seeing the serious dispute at the gun, pressed forward to the assistance of the three men of the Connaught Rangers.

While this was taking place on the left, the head of the column mounted the breach, and regardless of the cries of their wounded companions, whom they indiscriminately trampled to death, pressed forward in one irregular but heroic mass, and putting every man to death who opposed their progress, forced the enemy from the ramparts at the bayonet's point Yet the garrison still rallied, and defended the several streets with the most unflinching bravery; nor was it until the musketry of the light division was heard in the direction of the Plaza Major, that they gave up the contest! but from this moment all regular resistance ceased, and they fled in disorder to the citadel.

There were, nevertheless, several minor combats in the streets, and in many instances the inhabitants fired from the windows, but whether their efforts were directed against us or the French, is a point that I do not feel myself competent to decide; be this as it may, many lives were lost on both sides by this circumstance, for the Spaniards firing without much attention to regularity, killed or wounded indiscriminately all who came within their range. This led many to suppose that the defence of the town would be prolonged, and that the houses, as at Buenos Ayres, would be defended; but although this idea had the good effect of keeping our men more compactly united than would otherwise have been the case, it was an erroneous opinion, as the French never attempted the defence of a single house.

During a contest of such a nature, kept up in the night, as may be supposed, much was of necessity left to the guidance of the subordinate officers, if not to the soldiers themselves. Each affray in the streets was conducted in the best manner the moment would admit of, and decided more by personal valour than discipline, and in some instances officers as well as privates had to combat with the imperial troops. In one of these encounters, Lieutenant George Faris of the 88th, by an accident so likely to occur in an affair of this kind, separated a little too far from a dozen or so of his regiment, found himself opposed to a French soldier who apparently was similarly placed;—it was a curious coincidence, and it would seem as if each felt that he individually was the representative of the country to which he belonged; and had the fate of the two nations hung upon the issue of the combat I am about to describe, it could not have been more heroically contested.

The Frenchman fired at, and wounded Faris in the thigh, and made a desperate push with his bayonet at his body, but Faris parried the thrust, and the bayonet only lodged in his leg; he saw at a glance the peril of his situation, and that nothing short of a miracle could save him;—the odds against him were too great, and if he continued a scientific fight he must inevitably be vanquished; he sprang forward, and seizing hold of the Frenchman by the collar, a struggle of a most nervous kind took place; in their mutual efforts to gain an advantage, they lost their caps, and as they were men of nearly equal strength, it was doubtful what the issue would be.

They were so entangled with each other, their weapons were of no avail, but Faris at length disengaged himself from the grasp which held him, and he was able to use his sabre; he pushed the Frenchman from him, and ere he could recover himself he laid his head open nearly to the chin; his sword blade, a heavy, soft, ill-made Portuguese one, was doubled up with the force of the blow, and retained some pieces of the scull and clotted hair! At this moment I reached the spot with about twenty men, composed of different regiments, all being by this time mixed *pell mell* with each other. I ran up to Faris,—he was nearly exhausted, but he was safe. The French grenadier lay upon the pavement, while Faris, though tottering from fatigue, held his sword firmly in his grasp, and it was crimson to the hilt The appearance of the two combatants was frightful!—one lying dead on the ground, the other faint from agitation and loss of blood; but the soldiers loudly applauded him, and the feeling uppermost with them was, that our man had the best of it! It was a shocking sight, but it would be rather a hazardous experiment to begin moralizing at such a moment and in such a place.

Those of the garrison who escaped death were made prisoners, and the necessary guards being placed, and everything secured, the troops not selected for duty commenced a very diligent search for those articles which they most fancied, and which they considered themselves entitled to by "right of conquest" I believe on a service such as the present, there is a sort of tacit acknowledgment of this "right;" but be this as it may, a good deal of property most indubitably changed owners on the night of the 19th of January, 1812.

The conduct of the soldiers too, within the last hour, had undergone a complete change; before, it was all order and regularity,—now, it was nothing but licentiousness and confusion—subordination was at an end; plunder and blood was the order of the day, and many an officer on this night was compelled to show that he carried a sabre.

The doors of the houses in a large Spanish town are remarkable for their strength, and resemble those of a prison more than anything else; their locks are of huge dimensions, and it is a most difficult task to force them. The mode adopted by the men of my regiment (the 88th) in this dilemma, was as effective as it was novel; the muzzles of a couple of muskets were applied to each side of the key-hole, while a third soldier, fulfilling the functions of an officer, deliberately gave the word, "make ready"—"present"—"fire!" and in an instant the ponderous lock gave way before the combined operations of the three individuals, and doors that rarely opened to the knock of a stranger in Rodrigo, now flew off their hinges to receive the Rangers of Connaught.

The failure of forcing open the houses in the unfortunate assault of Buenos Ayres, no doubt taught our fellows a lesson by which they profited on the present occasion; and had the South American army understood the art of war as well as the heroes of the Peninsula, so many valuable lives would not have been lost in endeavouring to force open doors strong enough to defy the powers of a battering-ram!

The chapels and chandler's houses were the first captured, in both of which was found a most essential ingredient in the shape of large wax candles; these, the soldiers lighted, and commenced their perambulations in search of plunder, and the glare of light which they threw across the faces of the men as they earned them through the streets, displayed their countenances, which were of that cast that might well terrify the unfortunate inhabitants. Many of the soldiers with their faces scorched by the explosion of the magazine at the grand breach; others with their lips blackened from biting off the ends of their cartridges, more covered with blood, and all looking ferocious, presented a combination sufficient to appal the stoutest heart

Scenes of the greatest outrage now took place, and it was pitiable to see groups of the inhabitants half naked in the streets—the females clinging to the officers for protection—while their respective houses were undergoing the strictest scrutiny. Some of the soldiers turned to the wine and spirit houses, where having drunk sufficiently, they again sallied out in quest of more plunder; others got so intoxicated, that they lay in a helpless state in different parts of the town, and lost what they had previously gained, either by the hands of any passing Spaniard, who could venture unobserved to stoop down, or by those of their own companions, who in their wandering surveys happened to recognize a comrade lying with half-a-dozen silk gowns, or some such thing, wrapt about him.

Others wished to attack the different stores, and as there is something marvellously attractive in the very name of a brandy one, it is not to be wondered at that .many of our heroes turned not only their thoughts, but their steps also, in the direction in which these houses lay; and from the unsparing hand with which they supplied themselves, it might be imagined they intended to change their habits of life and turn spirit venders, and that too in the wholesale line!

It was astonishing to see with what rapidity and accuracy these fellows traversed the different parts of the town, and found out the shops and storehouses. A stranger would have supposed they were natives of the place, and it was not until the following morning I discovered the cause of what was to me before incomprehensible.

In all military movements in a country which an army is not thoroughly acquainted with, (and why not in a large town?) there are no more useful appendages than good guides. Lord Wellington was most particular on this point, and had attached to his army a corps of this description. I suppose it was this knowledge of tactics which suggested to the soldiers the necessity of so wise a precaution; accordingly, every group of individuals was preceded by a Spaniard, who, upon learning the species of plunder wished for by his employers, instantly conducted them to the most favourable ground for their operations.

By this means the houses were unfurnished with less confusion than can be supposed, and had it not been for the state of intoxication that some of the young soldiers—mere tyros in the art of sacking a town—had indulged themselves in, it is inconceivable with what facility the city of Ciudad Rodrigo would have been eased of its superfluities; and the *conducteur* himself was not always an idle spectator. Many of these fellows realized something considerable from their more wealthy neighbours, and being also right well paid by the soldiers, who were liberal enough, they found themselves in the morning in far better circumstances than they had been the preceding night, so that, all things considered, there were about as many cheerful faces as sad ones; but although the inhabitants were, by this sort of transfer, put more on an equality with each other, the town itself was greatly impoverished.

Many things of value were destroyed, but in the hurry so natural to the occasion, many also escaped; besides, our men were as yet young hands in the *arcana* of plundering a town in that *au fait* manner with which a French army would have done a business of the sort, but they, most unquestionably, made up for their want of tact, by the great inclination they showed to profit by any occasion that offered itself for their improvement.

By some mistake a large spirit store, situated in the Plaza Mayor, took fire, and the flames spreading with incredible fury, despite of the exertions of the troops, the building was totally destroyed; but in this instance, like many others which we are obliged to struggle against through life, there was a something that neutralized the disappointment which the loss of so much brandy occasioned the soldiers: the light which shone forth from the building was of material service to them, inasmuch as it tended to facilitate their movements in their excursions for plunder; the heat also was far from disagreeable, for the night was piercingly cold, yet, nevertheless, the soldiers exerted themselves to the utmost to put a stop to this calamity. General Picton was to be seen in the midst of them, encouraging them by his example and presence to make still greater efforts; but all would not do, and floor after floor fell in, until at last it was nothing but a burning heap of ruins.

Some houses were altogether saved from plunder by the interference of the officers, for in several instances the women ran out into the streets, and seizing hold of three or four of us would force us away to their houses, and by this stroke of political hospitality saved their property. A good supper was then provided, and while all outside was noise and pillage, affairs within went on agreeably enough. These instances, were, however, but few.

In the house where I and four other officers remained, we fared remarkably well, and were passing the night greatly to our satisfaction when we were aroused by a noise, like a crash of something heavy falling in the apartment above us. As may be supposed, we did not remain long without seeking to ascertain the cause of this disturbance; the whole party sprang up at once—the family of the house secreting themselves behind the different pieces of furniture, while we, *sabre a la main,* and some with lights, advanced towards the apartment from whence the noise proceeded; but all was silent within. Captain Seton, of my corps, proposed that the door should be forced, but he had scarcely pronounced the words, when a voice from within called out, not in Spanish, or French, but in plain English, with a rich Irish brogue, "Oh, Jasus, is it you, Captain?"

On entering we found a man of the Connaught Rangers, belonging to Seton's company, standing before us, so disfigured by soot and filth, that it was impossible to recognize his uniform, much less his face—his voice was the only thing recognisable about him, and that only to his captain; and had it not been for that, he might have passed for one just arrived from the infernal regions, and it may be questioned whether or not the place he had quitted might not be so denominated. It appeared, from the account he gave of himself, that he had been upon a plundering excursion in one of the adjoining houses, the roof of which, like most of those in Rodrigo, was flat, and wishing to have a distinct view of all that was passing in the streets, he took up his position upon the top of the house he had entered, and not paying due attention to where he put his foot, he contrived to get it into the chimney of the house we occupied, and ere he could resume his centre of gravity he tumbled headlong down the chimney, and caused us all the uneasiness I have been describing.

His *tout ensemble* was as extraordinary as his adventure; he had eighteen or twenty pairs of shoes round his waist, and amongst other things a case of trepanning instruments, which he immediately offered as a present to his captain! Had the grate of this fireplace been what is called in England the "Rumford grate," this poor fellow must have been irretrievably lost to the service, because it is manifest, encumbered as he was, he would have stuck fast, and must inevitably have been suffocated before assistance could be afforded him; but, fortunately for him, the chimney was of sufficient dimensions to admit an elephant to pass down it, and, in truth, one not so constructed would have been altogether too confined for him.

Morning at length began to dawn, and with it the horrors of the previous night's assault were visible. The troops not on guard were directed to quit the town, but this was not a command they obeyed with the same cheerfulness or expedition which they evinced when ordered to enter it; in their eyes it had many attractions still, and, besides, the soldiers had become so unwieldy from the immense burdens they carried, it was scarcely possible for many of them to stir, much less march: however, by degrees the evacuation of the fortress took place, and towards noon it was effected altogether.

The breaches presented a horrid spectacle. The one forced by the light division was narrower than the other, and the dead lying in a smaller compass, looked more numerous than they really were. I walked along the ramparts towards the grand breach, and was examining the effects our fire had produced on the different defences and the buildings in their immediate vicinity, but I had not proceeded far when I was shocked at beholding about a hundred and thirty or forty wounded Frenchmen lying under one of the bastions and some short distance up a narrow street adjoining it I descended, and learned that these men had been performing some particular duty in a magazine, which through accident blew up, and these miserable beings were so burnt, that I fear, notwithstanding the considerate attention which was paid to them by our medical officers, none of their lives were preserved.

Their uniforms were barely distinguishable, and their swollen heads and limbs gave them a gigantic appearance that was truly terrific; added to this, the gunpowder had so blackened their faces that they looked more like a number of huge negroes than soldiers of an European army. Many of our men hastened to the spot, and with that compassion which truly brave men always feel, rendered them every assistance in their power; some were carried on doors, others in blankets, to the hospitals, and these poor creatures showed by their gestures, for they could not articulate, how truly they appreciated our tender care of them.

At length I reached the grand breach—it was covered with many officers and soldiers; of the former, amongst others, was my old friend Hardyman of the 45th, and Lieutenant William Pearse of the same regiment; there were also two of the 5th, whose names I forget, and others whose faces were familiar to me. Hardyman, the once cheerful, gay Bob Hardyman, lay on his back; half of his head was carried away by one of those discharges of grape from the flank guns at the breach, which were so destructive to us in our advance; his face was perfect, and even in death presented its wonted cheerfulness.

Poor fellow! he died without pain, and regretted by all who knew him; his gaiety of spirit never for an instant forsook him; up to the moment of the assault he was the same pleasant Bob Hardyman, who delighted every one by his anecdotes, and none more than my old corps, although many of his jokes were at our expense. When we were within a short distance of the breach, as we met, he stopped for an instant to shake hands, "What's that you have hanging over your shoulder?" said he, as he espied a canteen of rum which I carried.

"A little rum, Bob," said I.

"Well," he replied, "I'll change my breath, and take my word for it, that in less than five minutes, some of the 'subs' will be scratching a captain's ———, for there will be wigs on the green."

He took a mouthful of rum, and taking me by the hand squeezed it affectionately, and in ten minutes afterwards he was a corpse!

The appearance of Pearse was quite different from his companion; ten or a dozen grape-shot pierced his breast, and he lay or rather sat beside his friend like one asleep, and his appearance was that of a man upwards of sixty, though his years did not number twenty-five. Hardyman was stripped to his trousers, but Pearse had his uniform on, his epaulettes alone had been plundered. I did not see the body of General Mackinnon, but the place where he fell was easily distinguishable, the vast chasm which the spot presented resembled an excavation in the midst of a quarry.

The limbs of those who lost their lives by that fatal explosion, thrown here and there, presented a melancholy picture of the remnants of those brave men whose hearts, but a few short hours before, beat high in the hope of conquest It was that kind of scene which arrested the attention of the soldier, and riveted him to the spot; and there were few who, even in the moment of exultation, did not feel deeply as they surveyed the mangled remains of their comrades.

I next turned to the captured gun, so chivalrously taken by the three men of the 88th. The five cannoneers lying across the carriage, or between the spokes of the wheels, showed how bravely they had defended it—yet they lay like men whose death had not been caused by violence—they were naked and bloodless, and the puncture of the bayonet left so small a mark over their hearts, it was discernible only to those who examined the bodies closely.

The details I have given of the capture of Rodrigo will, I believe, be found to be tolerably correct; I have in no way placed any one corps, much less division, above its companions—where all fought well, and did their utmost to conquer, I think such a comparison would be improper; but were I inclined to do so, I should give the preference to the Portuguese, under O'Toole, and for the reason that they surpassed the expectations we had of their success, because they were not a British corps. But I can in no way agree with the officer who wrote the *Sketch of the Storming of Ciudad Rodrigo*, where he says, "Without doing injustice to the gallant Third Division, I fear that the attack of the great breach would have failed, had the small breach not been carried."

The Third Division, upwards of three thousand strong, and composed of as good troops as any in the world, were certainly a match for one thousand one hundred or one thousand two hundred Frenchmen, which at most defended a practicable and wide breach. The same writer observes, "When the Third Division gained the top of the ramparts, they were in a manner enclosed and hemmed in, and had nowhere to go, while the enemy continued to fire upon them from some old ruined houses, only twenty yards distant.

I am confident a plan would convince any person, that the Light Division extricated the Third Division from their disagreeable situation." The Light Division would, no doubt, as far as they could, have "extricated" the Third Division if they required it, but they did not, because that corps carried all before them after, without doubt, a most serious strife; but their success was never for an instant doubtful, although it was unavoidably protracted. The explosion upon the breach necessarily caused some confusion and delay; how could it be otherwise?

But from the time the brigade of Mackinnon passed the Fausse Braye, until the Third Divison had overcome all obstacles, half an hour did not elapse, and certainly, all things considered, this was not an unreasonable lapse of time. The same writer, in speaking of the dispositions made previous to the attack, says, "The Third Division had relieved the first as usual in the morning, but it did not return as usual to its quarters. If the Governor had kept a sharp look-out, he must have been expecting the assault; but 'I guess' he was no great things."

The Third Division did not occupy the trenches until a short time previous to the assault, nor did they relieve the first division on that day. (See note end of chapter.) Then again he observes, "Neither were there any officers among the dead, or else they were carried away." So late as nine o'clock on the morning of the 20th, there were those I have mentioned, but whether they were there or not, is surely of little consequence.

I turned away from the breach, and scrambled over its rugged face, and the dead which covered it On reaching the *bivouack* we had occupied the preceding evening, I learned, with surprise, that our women had been engaged in a contest, if not as dangerous as ours, at least one of no trivial sort. The men left as a guard over the baggage, on hearing the first shot at the trenches, could not withstand the inclination they felt to join their companions; and although this act was creditable to the bravery of the individuals that composed the baggage-guard, it was nigh being fatal to those who survived, or, at least, to such as had anything to lose except their lives, for the wretches that infested our camp, attempted to plunder it of all that it possessed, but the women, with a bravery that would not have disgraced those of ancient Rome, defended the post with such valour, that those miscreants were obliged to desist, and our baggage was saved in consequence.

We were about to resume our arms when General Picton approached us. Some of the soldiers who were more than usually elevated in spirits, on his passing them, called out, "Well, General, we gave you a cheer last night: it's your turn now!"

The general, smiling, took off his hat, and said, "Here then, you drunken set of brave rascals, hurrah! we'll soon be at Badajoz!" A shout of confidence followed: we slung our firelocks, the bands played, and we commenced our march for the village of Atalaya in the highest spirits, and in a short time lost sight of a place, the capture of which appeared to us like a dream.

Note. It has been repeatedly asserted that the reason why the Third Division, under Picton, were allowed the honour of storming the great breach was on the score of that division being working in the trenches before the great breach on the day of the assault, namely, the 19th of January. This assertion was made some years ago in a work entitled *Sketch of the Storming of Ciudad Rodrigo, by an officer engaged*. This work was, I believe, written by Captain Cooke of the 43rd Regiment, and was contradicted by me when I read it; but since then a pamphlet, written and published by the late Colonel Gurwood, has asserted the same, and the name and authority of the Duke of Wellington are given in support of the assertion; nevertheless Captain Cooke, Colonel Gurwood, and the Duke of Wellington are in error.

Colonel Gurwood says in his pamphlet,

> The Light Division halted short of the besieging ground, occupied by the third division doing duty in the trenches, and being ordered to assault the great breach, the lesser breach having been allotted to the Light Division. After the receipt of the order, by General Crawford, for the Light Division to storm the lesser breach, that officer remonstrated with Lord Wellington, and claimed for it, as it had broken ground, the honour of assaulting the great breach from the trenches. Lord Wellington told General Crawford that he could not insult the Third Division by turning them out of the trenches to make room for the light division; and that as to privileges, he had experience in sieges, and knew of none but obedience to orders. The Duke of Wellington mentioned this to me many years afterwards, when speaking of General Crawford.

If, as Colonel Gurwood states in his pamphlet, the Third Division were "doing duty in the trenches" on the 19th of January, the day of the assault, the colonel must be in error in page 29 (which he is not) where he says:—

> The Light Division were in the trenches three times during the siege, *viz.*, the 8th, the 12th, and the 17th, being relieved alternately by the Frst, Fourth, and Third Divisions, &c. &c. On the night of the 17th I was on duty on the midnight relief, &c. &c. At the end of the four hours (four a. m. of the 18th,) while anxiously waiting the hour of relief from the striking of the clock of the cathedral, &c. &c.

Now the Light Division, according to the order of relief as set down by Colonel Gurwood, and he is perfectly right, was relieved on the 18th (about midday) by the First Division; the First Division in like manner was relieved by the Fourth Division (about midday) on the 19th, and consequently were in the trenches at work the entire day of the 19th, and would have continued there at work until midday of the 20th had not the Light Division and the Third Division carried the place by storm on the evening of the 19th.

It is therefore an error—and a very grave one too—to assert that the Third Division was throwing up earth in the trenches on the 19th; and I am surprised that officers who write on military matters, and who are so well aware of the jealousy that is felt by soldiers on these points, are not more correct in what they state.

Chapter 17

Army Rest in Cantonments

The fortress of Ciudad Rodrigo fell on the eleventh day after its investment; and taking into account the season of the year, the difficulty of the means to carry on the operations, and the masterly manner in which Lord Wellington baffled the vigilance of the Duke of Ragusa, the capture of Rodrigo must ever rank as one of the most finished military exploits upon record, and a *chef d'œuvre* of the art of war.

Our loss was equal to that of the enemy; it amounted to about one thousand *hors de combat,* together with three generals; of the garrison but seventeen hundred were made prisoners, the rest being put to the sword. Yet, notwithstanding the off-hand manner in which the place was laid siege to, and the slashing style it was carried by the bayonet, there were many people—I must say unreasonable ones—who found fault with Wellington for his mode of attack, as also for his inactivity after his victory. One writer, [1]—a Frenchman of course—says, "he," (meaning Lord Wellington,) "might have easily carried off the French advanced guard, which, on the 22nd, made its appearance near Tamames. The enterprise was favoured by the occupation of Ciudad Rodrigo, as the detachment entrusted with the operation would have had a safe retreat under the cannon of the town.

"Fifteen thousand choice men ought to have been placed in ambush on the road to Salamanca. A corps of four or five thousand light troops should have marched against the French, with orders to fall back at their approach. These light troops, when near the ambush, would have hastened their retreat, in apparent confu-

---
1. General Sarrazin

sion, which would have induced the French to be more eager in the pursuit. The concealed soldiers, then rushing from the ambush, would have fallen upon the rear of the French column, and infallibly destroyed it. It is by manoeuvres like the one here described that the forces of an enemy are ruined, without experiencing the enormous losses occasioned by sieges and battles." [2]

All this may be very true, and, had Lord Wellington done what Monsieur Sarrazin says he could and should have done, he, most unquestionably, would have done more than he did; but as it was, bungler as he is,—for it is well known that every man in France is ready to take his oath that he is so, and, to the shame of our own country, there are not wanting those who are willing to leash-in in the general cry raised against this great man by the fellows he has trounced from the heights of Lisbon to the walls of Paris,—he did as much in eleven days, in the depth of a severe winter, with twenty thousand men, as the hero of Rivoli and Esling and the conqueror of Suwarrow was able to accomplish in twenty-five days, in summer, with forty thousand French veterans against a Spanish garrison! It is clear, however, that Marshal Marmont was a little puzzled at what had taken place.

On the 16th of January he wrote to Berthier: "I had collected five divisions, for the purpose of throwing supplies into Ciudad Rodrigo, but this force is now inadequate to the object I am, therefore, under the necessity of recalling two divisions from the army of the north. I shall then have above sixty thousand men, with whom I shall march against the enemy. You may expect events as fortunate as glorious for the French army."

But in spite of these flattering promises, he was obliged to write to Prince Berthier on the 20th:

On the 16th the English batteries opened their fire at a great distance. On the 19th the place was taken by storm, and fell into the power of the enemy. There is something so incomprehensible in this event, that I allow myself no observation. I am not provided with the requisite information.

This speaks a volume, and renders it quite unnecessary to say more on the subject

---

2. Bobadil was nothing to this fellow.

Lord Wellington has been also censured for allowing generals to place themselves at the head of the columns that attacked Rodrigo.

"A general officer," says Monsieur Sarrazin, "is extremely valuable, especially when he is skilled in his profession. General Crawford possessed the qualities for a commander-in-chief; whilst, at the head of a storming column, his thin person and diminutive size rendered him inferior to a grenadier."

This is a just remark, because, beyond all doubt, the commanding officer of a battalion is as likely, if not more so, than a general, to lead his men through a breach. Neither at Rodrigo nor Badajoz did General Picton head his division, and their success in both was as complete as if he had; and why not? a general is supposed to direct, a colonel to lead; and if any proof were wanting to prove the truth of this assertion, the success of the Third Division at both Rodrigo and Badajoz, the latter "one of the most astonishing exploits mentioned in history," ought to suffice.

The two officers who led the forlorn-hope at each breach escaped unhurt; but although fortune favoured both equally in the field, the results which followed were widely different And here I wish I could lay down my pen; but justice must be done to the living as well as the dead. Lieutenant Gurwood of the 52nd, who led the forlorn-hope of Crawford's division, obtained a company, and in the course of a few years, in consequence, rose to the rank of lieutenant-colonel; while the brave Lieutenant William Mackie of the 88th, who so gallantly volunteered, and so bravely led on the forlorn-hope of the Third Division, notwithstanding the promise of General Mackinnon, which ought to, have been held sacred, was altogether passed over by General Picton; his name was not even, mentioned, nor did he gain promotion for his conduct.

But this was only the commencement of a series of slights which I regret being obliged to say the 88th met with for the four years and a-half that General Picton commanded the third division, during which long period—it is worthy of remark—not one officer of that regiment was ever promoted through his recommendation!

No officer ever better merited promotion than Lieutenant Mackie, and none was ever worse treated. He volunteered the forlorn-hope in the handsomest manner—led it on in the most gallant style—and what was his reward for such conduct? He was passed over without so much as being noticed by his general, for conduct that gained his fellow forlorn-hope companion an immediate step, which placed him high up amongst the lieutenant-colonels in the army, while Mackie remained—after a lapse of twenty years—a captain! [3]

> I know a man, of whom 'tis truly said,
> He bravely twice a storming party led,
> And volunteered both times—now here's the rub,
> The gallant fellow still remains a sub[4]

These four pithy lines have relation to Ensign Dyas of the 51st Regiment; but Dyas, unlucky as he was, was more fortunate than Mackie, because his bravery was officially proclaimed to the world in Lord Wellington's account of the two attacks of San Christoval, and His Royal Highness, the late lamented Duke of York, made every possible reparation in his power, the moment the mistake—for it was a mistake—was made known to him, and had he continued in the service, there can be no doubt that his lost rank would have been made up.

It was once remarked by the French general, Brennier, that too much was exacted from the subalterns of the British army, and more than the Emperor Napoleon, all powerful as he was, would venture to attempt with his; but if General Brennier heard that the senior lieutenant of a distinguished regiment,—and one, too, who had greatly signalized himself on other occasions,—had successfully led a forlorn-hope, which service he had volunteered, and that the general under whom he served did not so much as notice this officer for such conduct—if, I say, General Brennier knew this, I should be monstrously curious to hear what he would say touching the conduct of such a general!

When Mackie volunteered to lead the advance, those who witnessed the manner in which he did it will, I think, bear me out when I say that glory, and not emolument was his object He was at the moment the senior lieutenant, and he might reasonably

---

3. Gained a brevet step in 1831, after being nineteen years a captain, which rank he obtained in his regular turn!
4. Johnny Newcombe, p. 77.

look for speedy promotion without thrusting his head amongst a forlorn-hope party to gain it; he looked forward with that pride, which cannot be styled vanity, to see, if he survived, his name enrolled amongst the list of those who merited praise, or, if he fell, it would be a consolation to him in his last moments to think that his friends and relatives knew that he did so while serving his king and country in one of the most perilous situations in which a man can be placed.

If, on the other hand, promotion should be—as it was—given to his fellow forlorn-hope companion, he certainly had a right to expect the same; but twenty years of his life have passed—his rank has been lost to him, and his fame, if not blasted,—that it could not be!—has been denied its just and hardly-earned reward.

Now this gallant conduct of Mr. Mackie was known to General Picton who, being,—at least his biographer says so,—"a strict disciplinarian," and had "a strong sense of justice," it will naturally be supposed that on such an occasion as the present, the general would have given a proof of his "sense of justice." But what is the real fact?

Let the division order issued by Picton on the 20th of January—the day after the assault—speak for itself. It gives a much truer insight into the character of the general than his biographer has been able to accomplish in the eight hundred and thirty-five pages he has written on the subject

DIVISION ORDER BY LIEUTENANT GENERAL PICTON.

Zamarra, 20th of January, 1818.

By the gallant manner in which the breach was last night carried by storm, the Third Division has added much credit to its military reputation, and has rendered itself the most conspicuous corps in the British army.

Lieutenant-Colonel Campbell, commanding the right Brigade and 94th Regiment, Lieutenant-Colonel Donkin, commanding 77th, and Major Ridge, the second battalion, 5th Regiment, are peculiarly entitled to the thanks of the lieutenant-general, as having led and carried the breach; as is Major Manners, 74th Regiment, who volunteered the storming party, and Captain Milne, of the 45th Regiment, for the able support of the attack, &c.

I have given these two extracts from this division-order of General Picton, and if the reader can find either good taste or "a strong sense of justice" in either, it is more than I can. It was not good taste to say that Picton's division was "the most conspicuous corps in the British army," particularly as the light division, who also fought on this night, and carried the other breach, was ever considered in the army to be as "conspicuous" as any other. This, I say, was not good taste.

Lieutenant William Mackie, volunteered and successfully led the forlorn-hope. Major R. Manners, volunteered and successfully led the storming party, which Mackie preceded with his forlorn-hope. Manners was noticed in the division order, and was in consequence promoted. Mackie was not noticed, and consequently not promoted. Did this neglect of Mackie shew "a strong sense of justice?"

So soon as my regiment reached the village of Attalaya, its former quarters, I obtained leave to return to Rodrigo, for I was anxious to see in what situation the family were, with whom I, in common with my companions, had passed the preceding night. Upon entering the town, I found all in confusion; the troops ordered to occupy it were not any of those which had composed the storming divisions; and although the task of digging graves, and clearing away the rubbish about the breaches was not an agreeable one, they nevertheless performed it with much cheerfulness; yet, in some instances, the soldiers levied contributions upon the unfortunate inhabitants, light ones it is true, and for the reason that little remained with them to give, or more properly speaking, withhold; but the provost-marshal was so active in his vocation, that this calamity was soon put a stop to, and the miserable people, who were in many instances in a state of nudity, could without risk venture to send to their more fortunate neighbours for a supply of those articles of dress which decency required.

Upon reaching the house I had rested in the evening before, I was rejoiced to find it uninjured, and the poor people, upon once more seeing me, almost suffocated me with their caresses, and their expressions of gratitude knew no bounds for our having preserved their house from pillage.

The house occupied by myself, Captain Seton, and three or four more, was, as I before said, intruded upon by a fellow of the Connaught Rangers, who took upon himself to walk down the chimney; we had scarcely rid ourselves of him, when a loud knocking at the street door—the sure harbinger of a group of marauders—brought us once more upon our legs. We ran to the window to ascertain the cause, but had scarcely reached the balcony when some drunken fellows, from the opposite side of the street, discharged their muskets at us. The woodwork was shattered about our ears, but fortunately no one was hurt, and when we made good our retreat, which was certainly a rapid one, and that all was safe, Seton began humming, sweetly but faintly, the little French air, "*Ah! Quel plaisir d'être soldat.*"

The knocking at the door continued, and was immediately followed by a discharge of musketry, such as I have before described, against that part of the panel nearest the keyhole. I was the first that reached the spot, and by the light of a huge wax candle, that had been thrust through the dismantled panel, with pleasure, though not surprise, I found the man who held it to be, not only a Connaught Ranger, but one of my own company, his name was Noonan.

"Noonan," said I, "you cannot come in here."

"Can't I, sir," said he.

"No, you cannot," said I.

"And why can't I, sir?" replied he.

"Because," I replied, "I have promised to protect the family of this house, and I will do so at all risks."

"Oh! then blur-an-ouns, is it talking of risks you are when Pat Noonan is next or nigh your honour? but how will I palaver these Englishmen of the light division, that's forty times worse than ourselves, (iv that be possible!) afther a dhrop iv. dhrink?"

Repeated knocks at the door, and loud execrations, put a stop to any further dialogue between me and Pat Noonan, and proved but too truly that the account he gave of his associates was not exaggerated. A violent altercation, of which I could not distinguish a word, now took place; in a few moments afterwards all was silent, and after a lapse of a minute or so, Noonan thrust in his head again and said, "You may make yourself aisy now, for they won't throuble the house anymore."

"Why, what did you say to them?"

"What did I say to them is it? I touid them a big lie anyhow—I tould them your honour was the docthur iv the regiment, and that you were just afther cuttin the leg iv a poor cratur, and that you were going to sarve four more afther the same fashion. I knew as soon as they'd hear-tell iv your cuttin off the leg.iv the 'boy,' that they'd go away—and it was thrue for me they did!"

"Noonan," I replied, "you are an honest fellow, and I won't forget your behaviour."

"Honest is it? fait and sure, the Connaught Rangers is all honest for that matters, only our General (God prosper him!) tells us another story."

I barricaded the door in the best manner I could, and we all got round the fire once more; the merits of different officers and soldiers, as well as divers bowls of brandy punch, were freely discussed, and it was late before we retired to rest for the night; but previous to doing so, I went once more to the balcony, in order to ascertain how matters went on in the street, and to my astonishment found that Noonan was standing sentinel at the door; who, at my recommendation, was made a serjeant next day.

Having satisfied myself that my *patrona* and her daughters had escaped molestation, I took my leave of them, and once more visited the large breach. On my way thither, I saw the French garrison preparing to march, under an escort of Portuguese troops, to the fortress of Almeida; they were a fine-looking body of men, and seemed right well pleased to get off so quietly; they counted about eighteen hundred, and were all that escaped unhurt of the garrison.

At the breach there were still several wounded men, who had not been removed to the hospitals; amongst them was a fellow of my own corps, of the name of Doogan; he was badly wounded in the thigh, the bone of which was so shattered as to protrude through the skin; near him lay a French soldier, shot through the body, quite frantic from pain, and in the agonies of death. The moment Doogan observed me, he called out most lustily, "Och! for the love of Jasus, Mr. Grattan, don't lave me here near this villain that's afther curbing me to no end."

I observed to Doogan that the poor fellow was in a much worse state than even himself, and that I doubted whether he would be alive in five minutes. At this moment the eyes of the Frenchman met mine, "*Oh! monsieur,*" exclaimed he, "*je meurs pour une goutte d'eau!* Oh, *mon Dieu! mon Dieu!*"

"Now," ejaculated Doogan, addressing me, "will you believe me, (that never tould a lie in my life!) another time? Did you hear him then, how he got on with his *mon dew?*" I caused Doogan to be carried to an hospital; but the French soldier died as we endeavoured to place him in a blanket.

I quitted the breach, and took a parting glance at the town; the smell from the still burning houses, the groups of dead and wounded, and the broken fragments of different weapons, marked strongly the character of the preceding night's dispute; and even at this late hour, there were many drunken marauders endeavouring to regain, by some fresh act of atrocity, an equivalent for the plunder their brutal state of intoxication had caused them to lose by the hands of their own companions, who robbed indiscriminately man, woman, or child, friend or foe, the dead or the dying! Then, again, were to be seen groups of deserters from our army, who, having taken shelter in Rodrigo during the winter, were now either dragged from their hiding places by their merciless comrades, or given up by the Spaniards, in whose houses they had sought shelter, to the first officer or soldier who would be troubled, at the moment, with the responsibility of taking charge of them.

In the midst of a group of a dozen men, deserters from different regiments, stood two of the Connaught Rangers. No matter what their other faults might be, desertion was not a species of delinquency they were addicted to; and as the fate of one of these men—indeed both of them, for that matter—was a little tragical, I purpose giving it a nook in my adventures. The two culprits to whom I have made allusion were as different in their characters as persons; one of them (Mangin) a quiet, well-disposed man, short in stature, a native of England, and, as a matter of course, a heavy feeder, one that could but ill put up with "short allowance," and in consequence left the army when food became as scarce as it did in the winter of 1811.

The other, a fellow of the name of Curtis, an Irishman, tall and lank, and, like the rest of the "boys" from that part of the world, was mighty aisy about what he ate, provided he got a reasonable supply of drink; but as neither the one nor the other were "convenient" during the period in question, they both left an advanced post one fine night, and resolved to try the difference between the French commissariat and ours. This was their justification of themselves to me, and I believe, for I was not present at it, the *summum bonum* upon which the basis of their defence at their trial rested.

There were also six Germans of the 60th Rifles in the group, but they seemed so unnerved by their unexpected capture, that they were unable to say anything for themselves. I, most unquestionably, felt much for these poor wretches; I bore strong in my own recollection what I had myself suffered from an empty stomach; and the old adage, which I had often heard repeated, "that hunger will break through a stone wall," was in the present instance, I thought, fully illustrated; for these men, without any other aid than a craving for food, made their way with greater ease into the strong fortress of Rodrigo than we were able to do, backed, as we were, by the fire of several powerful batteries.

Towards evening I reached the village which my regiment occupied. An altered scene presented itself. The soldiers busied in arranging their different articles of plunder; many of them clad in the robes of some priest, while others wore gowns of the most costly silk or velvet; others, again, nearly naked; some without pantaloons, having been plundered, while drunk, of so essential a part of their dress; but all, or almost all, were occupied in laying out for sale their different articles of plunder, in that order which was essential to their being disposed of to the crowds of Spaniards which had already assembled to be the purchasers; and if one could judge by their looks, they most unquestionably committed a breach in their creed, by "coveting their neighbours' goods;" and had the scene which now presented itself to our sight been one caused by an event the most joyous, much less by the calamity that had befallen the unfortunate inhabitants of Rodrigo, to say nothing of the human blood that had been spilt ere that event had taken place, the scene could not have been more gay.

Brawny-shouldered Castilians, carrying pig-skins of wine on their backs, which they sold to our soldiers for a trifling sum; bolero-dancers, rattling their castanets like the clappers of so many mills; our fellows drinking like fishes, while their less fortunate companions at Rodrigo—either hastily flung into an ill-formed grave, writhing under the knife of the surgeon, or in the agonies of death—were unthought of, or unfelt for. *Sic transit gloria mundi!* The soldiers were allowed three days *congè* for the disposal of their booty; but long before the time had expired, they had scarcely a rag to dispose of, or a *real* of the produce in their pockets.

While this "shilloo" was carried on throughout the division, the officers had little to do except amuse themselves; the country abounded in game; and those who fancied field sports, had no lack of opportunities to indulge themselves in such pursuits. Taking advantage of this state of things, I rode over to the hospital near La Corrida, with the view of seeing an officer of my regiment, of the name of Flack, who had been desperately wounded by a round shot, two days before the storming of the place. The nature of the wound, as well as its cause, was extraordinary; and being greatly interested for the fate of a brother officer, I took an early opportunity to inquire after him.

I found him stretched upon a miserable truss of straw; at his feet lay his faithful little spaniel bitch, Fidèle, beside him stood a huge earthen jar, or, as the Spaniards call it, *panella* of water, while at his head sat, in a dejected posture, his servant Larry Fegan; he had been, for many years, Flack's bat-man, servant-man, and he might now be termed his right-hand man. He was a perfect prototype of Teague O'Connor, of whose history, as well as his roaster, Johnny Newcome, there are few, I should hope, of my readers ignorant The moment I entered the room, Larry put his finger to his nose, and pointing to his master, gave me to understand that I was not to speak to him; but poor Flack was so rejoiced to see me, that he commenced talking, and he would, I believe, have continued while he had a puff of breath left, had I not declared I would leave him if he did not desist.

It was now Larry's turn; and he began to recount, with much minuteness, his master's adventure; and from everything I could learn, it was evident that Flack had exposed himself very foolishly, and to very little purpose. It appeared that a man of his company having been killed while at work in an advanced battery, he wished to pay a just tribute to his gallantry, and going out, accompanied by three soldiers, in front of the works, commenced preparing a grave for this soldier, who, it seems, had much distinguished himself.

The enemy no sooner perceived this hardihood of behaviour, than they opened a fire against the party; their first discharge was sufficient to disperse it, and Lieutenant Flack fell, struck by a round shot in the thigh, which carried away the flesh from nearly the groin to the knee, while, at the same instant, four musket balls passed through different parts of his body. He was carried out of the works in an insensible state, and the surgeons judged it expedient to take the thigh out of the socket, a delicate operation, to which he objected.

The foregoing is the substance of Larry Fegan's "detail," I shall give the continuation in his own phraseology.

"The docthur," said Larry, in winding up his narrative, "came here yesterday with his 'God save all here,' and turning to me said, 'Your masther, it's like, isn't dead yet?'

"'You may say that with your own ugly mouth,' says I (to myself), for I was aloath to offind him, seeing how complately my poor masther's life was in his hands. 'No, sir,' says I, 'he's as alive as your honour.'

"'Had he much himmorige [5] since I saw him?' says he.

"Now when he got on about the himmorige, I knew what he was at, and that he only wanted to thry iv I gave my masther too much to ate; so says I, quite bould (because I followed his directions about the ateing), 'the devil receave the himmorige he tasted, iv I except the little dhrop iv gruel your honour ordered me to give him;' and upon the same, its what the baste began to laff in my face."

Larry was about to continue his narration, when the arrival of the staff-surgeon of the Fourth Division, accompanied by different surgeons and their assistants, put a stop to any further colloquy.

It was the general opinion amongst the medical officers that he could, not survive the effects of the shock forty-eight hours; he nevertheless made a most rapid recovery, and although he was, by some mistake, reported dead, and gazetted as so, he was in a few months nearly as well as before he was wounded.

---

5. Larry, no doubt, mistook the doctor's words as well as their meaning. I suppose he said hemorrhage.

The entrance of the medical gentlemen was the signal for my departure. They commenced the operation of unbandaging the mangled thigh of my poor friend, around which there appeared to me to be about as many folds of wrapping as usually envelope the body of an Egyptian mummy; but before I left the hospital altogether, I was assured by one of the medical men, that there was every prospect of Flack's recovery.

A few days sufficed for the reorganisation of the soldiers after they had disposed of their hard-earned plunder, and we were once more ready and willing for any fresh enterprise, no matter how difficult or dangerous. Badajoz was talked of, but nothing certain was known, and the quiet which reigned throughout all our departments was such, as not to warrant the least suspicion that any immediate attack against that fortress was contemplated by the commander-in-chief.

On the sixth day after our arrival at Atalaya, we were again in motion; the village of Albergaria was allotted for our quarters, and a court-martial was ordered to assemble for the trial of the deserters from our army found in Rodrigo. The men of the 60th, and the two men of the 88th (Mangin and Curtis) were amongst the number. The court held its sitting—the prisoners were arraigned, found guilty, and sentenced to be shot! All were bad characters, save one, and that one was Mangin. He received: testimonials from the captain of his company, (Captain Seton—ever the soldier's friend,) highly creditable to him, and Lord Wellington, with his accustomed love of justice, resolved that his pardon should be promulgated at the time of the reading the proceedings and sentence of the court-martial. Three days after the trial, it was made known to the prisoners, and the army generally, that they were to die the following morning.

At eight o'clock the division was under arms, and formed in a hollow square of small dimensions; in the centre of it was the provost-marshal, accompanied by his followers, with pick-axes, spades, shovels, and all the necessary etceteras for marking out and forming the graves into which the unfortunate delinquents were to be deposited as soon as they received the last and most imposing of military honours—that of being shot to death! In a few moments afterwards, the rolling of muffled drums—the usual accompaniment of the death-march—was heard; and the soldiers who guarded the prisoners were soon in sight The division observed a death-like silence as the prisoners defiled round the inside of the square; every eye was turned towards them; but Mangin, from his well-known good character, was an object of general solicitude.

The solitary sound of the muffled drums at last died away into silence—the guard drew up in the centre of the square, and the prisoners had, for the last time, a view of their companions from whom they had deserted, and of their colours which they had forsaken; but if their countenances were a just index of their minds, they seemed to repent greatly the act they had committed! The three men of the 60th were in their shirts, as was also Mangin of the 88th, but Curtis wore the "old red rag," most likely from necessity, having, in all human probability, no shirt to die in; a circumstance by no means rare with the soldiers of the Peninsula army.

The necessary preliminaries, such as reading the crime, and finding the sentence, had finished, when the adjutant-general announced the pardon granted to Mangin, who was immediately conducted away, and placed at a short distance in rear of the division; the rest staggered onward to the spot where their graves had been dug, and having been placed on their knees, their legs hanging over the edge of the grave, a bandage was tied over their eyes; the provost-marshal then, with a party of twenty musketeers, their firelocks cocked, and at the recover, silently moved in front of the prisoners until he reached to within five paces of them, and then giving two motions of his hand—the one to present, the other to fire—the four, men fell into the pit prepared to receive them.

The three Germans were dead—indeed they were nearly so before they were fired at! And if the state of their nerves was a criterion to go by, a moderate sized pop-gun would have been sufficiently destructive to have finished their earthly career; but Curtis sprang up, and with one of his jaws shattered, and hanging down upon his breast, presented a horrid spectacle. Everyone seemed to be electrified, the provost-marshal excepted; he, I suppose, was well accustomed to such sights, for without any ceremony, he walked up to Curtis, and with the most perfect composure levelled a huge instrument (in size between a horse-pistol and blunderbuss) at his head, which blew it nearly off his shoulders, and he fell upon the bodies of the Germans without moving a muscle.

This ceremony over, the division defiled round the grave, and as each company passed it, the word "eyes right," was given by the officer in command, by which means every man had a clear view of the corpses as they lay in a heap. This is a good and wholesome practice, for nothing so much awakes in the mind of the soldier, endowed with proper feeling, the dishonour of committing an action which is almost certain to bring him to a disgraceful end, while it deters the bad man from doing that which will cost him all that he has to lose,—for such persons have no character,—his life. It was ten o'clock before the parade broke up, and we returned to our quarters, leaving to the provost-marshal and his guard the task of filling up the grave. Several Portuguese peasants crowded near the fatal spot, and so soon as all danger was passed, they flocked to witness the interment, making, all the time, divers appeals to the Virgin Mary; but whether these wore intended for the preservation of the souls departed, or their own bodies corporate, I neither knew nor enquired.

Mangin, the man who had received his pardon, was still in a state of stupor; after the lapse of an hour or so, his captain went to see him; but the shock he had received was too severe; he had not nerve to bear up against it; he replied in an incoherent manner, soon fell asleep and awoke an idiot! Every effort that could be made by the medical men, and every assurance of favour from his captain, proved vain—he became a palpable, irreclaimable idiot, and shortly afterwards died of convulsions.

The consternation with which the capture of Rodrigo had filled the French army, made it paramountly necessary for Lord Wellington to mask with the greatest caution his intended operation against Badajoz, but it nevertheless began to be whispered that such was his design: indeed it required but little knowledge of the man, or of the splendid troops he commanded—now in that state of efficiency which no British army ever surpassed, and impressed with a feeling of their own decided superiority over those boasted and hitherto invincible legions, which the testimony of countless victories was sufficient to attest—to feel assured that such a general and such an army could not remain inactive, while it might be truly, and without bombast, said, that the fate of Europe depended in a great measure upon their exertions.

But how was this to be effected? Not by remaining inactive in Portugal; but to advance into the heart of Spain, with such a fortress as Badajoz, (occupied by an enemy,) in their rear, would be next to madness; it therefore was palpably manifest that Badajoz must fall, or the British army and its general lose their character.

Of all this Lord Wellington was aware, and he adopted his measures accordingly. A powerful battering train, composed of guns supplied by the vessels of war in the Tagus, were embarked on board ships of heavy tonnage at Lisbon; those ships put to sea to avoid suspicion, and when out of sight of the port, reshipped the guns into vessels of a smaller size, which carried them up the Tagus. By this means, the entire train, with the necessary stores, were landed in a part of the country where animals could, without difficulty, be procured to drag them to the banks of the Guadiana, and by this, finished ruse on the part of Lord Wellington, the enemy were ignorant of the formidableness of his means of attack.

At Elvas, only three leagues distant from Badajoz, the engineers were directed to cause a vast supply of fascines and gabions to be prepared, but this created no suspicion, because that fortress was an extensive one, and it might well be supposed that these materials were destined for its use. Those preparations were followed by others—if not as imposing in their aspect, of equal necessity to the success of the enterprise, and more complex in their execution—the forming of magazines at so difficult a season of the year, sufficient to supply an army of fifty thousand men with food; but all was completed early in the month of March.

Lulled into security by the apparent supineness of his adversary, and also by the extensive works he had constructed for the defence of Badajoz, Soult had, or thought he had, little to apprehend for its safety. General Lacy, Engineer-in-chief to the army of the South, was intrusted with the superintendence of the dispositions necessary for its defence, and this officer reported to the French Marshal that the place was amply garrisoned with chosen troops, amounting to five thousand men and upwards,—that it contained provisions for two months, and that the guns and mortars placed in battery, counted above two hundred pieces of ordnance of large calibre, in the best possible state, with a proportionate supply of ball and powder.

The garrison was moreover commanded by General Count Phillipon, considered to be one of the best engineers in the imperial army, and whose two recent successful defences had inspired the greatest confidence amongst his troops. Thus circumstanced, it may be fairly said, that never was a place in a better state, better supplied, and better provided with the requisite number of troops. All this took place in the middle of February, and towards the end of that month it was known in the army that Badajoz was to be attacked.

CHAPTER 18

Preparations Against Badajoz

The soldiers were full of ardour; they anxiously counted the hours as they passed; and when at length, on the 8th of March, the order arrived for the advance of the army to the Alemtejo, their joy was indescribable. Badajoz had ever been looked upon by them as unfriendly to our troops, and they contemplated with delight the prospect of having it in their power to retaliate upon the inhabitants their treatment of our men. On the 9th, the army was in movement; the light division opened the march, followed by the third and fourth; they crossed the Tagus by a bridge of boats, thrown over that river at Villa Velha, and pressed rapidly forward towards Elvas.

One division of infantry and a brigade of cavalry remained on the Agueda. On the 14th, the light and third divisions were concentrated in the neighbourhood of Elvas; they were joined by the fourth division on the following day, while the remainder of the army, under Hill and Graham, were pushed forward to Llerena, Merida, and Almendralejo, to observe the motions of the Duke of Dalmatia, who by this time was informed of the preparations, though not to their full extent, that had been formed against Badajoz.

The city of Badajoz, which had already been the theatre of two sieges, arising out of the first of which one of the most sanguinary battles of modern times, considering the numbers engaged, was fought; subsequently the scene of a great reverse to our troops, and now about to be the grave of several thousands of the flower of the British army, is a considerable town in Spanish Estremadura.

The great efforts that were made on the part of the English

general to possess himself of it, as likewise the obstinate pertinacity with which it was defended by the enemy, which, taking into account the losses on both sides, including the battle of Albuera, cost the armies of the two nations a loss of between twenty-five and thirty thousand veteran soldiers, sufficiently mark it to the reader as a place worthy of his notice. It stands on a point of land at the union of the rivulet of the Rivellas with the Guadiana, the former a tributary stream, meandering round the south-east of the fortress, and passing close to the ravelin called San Roque, which forms a sort of *tête-du-pont* to a bridge that protects the entrance to the gate named *El puerto del Talavera,* and covering a reservoir and sluice on the Rivellas which finally empties itself into the Guadiana. A bold and rocky height, one hundred feet above the level of the river, at this point upwards of two hundred and fifty *toises* in breadth, is out-topped by an old Moorish castle which stands above the other works, and overlooks the junction of the Rivellas with the Guadiana, lording it, in a manner, over the entire.

The fortifications of the castle consist of a wall without ditch or counterscarp; but the curtains and bastions are regular, and their height upwards of thirty-five feet; in many parts the wall is nearer forty than thirty-five feet high, owing in some measure to the inequality of the ground, but principally in consequence of a trench having been sunk (where the soil, which is very rocky, would admit of it) since the former siege. Besides this, there were two outworks on the left of the Guadiana, one called La Picurina, within two hundred and fifty *toises* of the body of the place, and standing on the right bank of the Rivellas; the other, a fort named Pardaleras, distant only half that space from the walls of the town, and situated between the lower Guadiana and the fort of Picurina.

On the right bank of the river is the hill and fort of San Christoval—so memorable, and so disastrous to our arms in the siege of the former year—to which outwork had been added another, built on the site where our batteries stood when that fort was so gallantly, yet so fatally attacked by the Seventh Division: this new work was called Moncœur; and there was another fort at the head of the Roman bridge, standing a gunshot below San Christoval, but feeble, being commanded on every side. Those works formed the exterior defence of Badajoz, and were, as well as the town itself, in the most efficient state.

On the 16th of March, everything being in readiness, a pontoon bridge was thrown across the Guadiana; fifteen thousand men broke up from their bivouac at Elvas, and advanced towards the river; the enemy disputed the ground, and here—even here, with only a handful of cavalry opposed to us—the French horsemen had actually the best of it, and kept us at bay during a march of three hours. At length we gained the river's edge—passed the bridge—drove back the enemy's outposts, and completed the investment. The following day, the 17th, Lord Wellington, accompanied by his engineers, carefully reconnoitred the place. He found its aspect materially changed; the parapets of the castle had been considerably raised, the outworks of Pardaleras and Picurina much strengthened, and a great portion of the ditch filled by the inundation of the Rivellas, which was easy of accomplishment by means of the sluice at San Roque.

The point of attack which his lordship decided upon, notwithstanding the advantages which were on the side of the enemy, was quite at variance with that of the preceding year, so it must be naturally presumed that the former was found to be faulty. Then, the outworks were by no means so formidable as now on the side about to be assailed, while, on the other side, the scene of the former attack, little progress had been made towards its amelioration. At the same time the siege was undertaken in 1811, it was urged by the Engineers that the fortifications on the side of the castle were confined to a single wall; that the interior of the castle was commanded by the fort of San Christoval on the right bank of the river; and that, once in possession of the fort, we could as completely command the castle as it did the remainder of the works of the fortress, or, in other words, that all resistance on the part of the enemy must be futile. The attack against San Christoval the preceding year failed, it is true, but why it failed has been already told.

From what I have written, it will be seen that the town of Badajoz was deemed a prize worthy of contention; that Lord Wellington had left nothing undone, as far as in him lay, to ensure success, and that the enemy, on his part, had been far from inactive. Our battering train, as compared with the former siege, was formidable indeed, but nevertheless the entire number of guns did not exceed forty—of the best description, no doubt, being metal guns of the largest calibre—while the batteries, on the enemy's side, counted more than three times that number, without taking into account the cannon he had at his disposal to succour his batteries, as they might require such aid, by placing his guns *en barbette,* or in any other way that might best suit his purpose.

To reduce a town so circumstanced, supposing every requisite means existed, would have occupied more time than could, under existing circumstances, be spared; because the Duke of Dalmatia might readily assemble forty thousand men, while the Duke of Ragusa, with an equal force, could co-operate with him; and if, by a protracted affair, Badajoz was not carried before the junction of those two armies, it was clear that we must give it up altogether, or encounter an army more than double our own numbers, and in a country, too, decidedly favourable for cavalry, in which arm the French had a vast superiority. Lord Wellington, therefore, resolved to hazard the trial, which, all things considered, offered a fair chance of success, and decided, after a minute examination of its defences, to attack Badajoz on the side of the fort of Picurina, from which point the part of the wall that embraced the bastions of Santa Maria and La Trinidad could be seen across the inundation.

The evening of the 17th of March had scarcely closed, when three thousand men broke ground before La Picurina, at the distance of one hundred and fifty yards. The night was unusually dark, the wind was high, and the rain fell in torrents—all of which favoured the enterprise. The soldiers, accustomed to fatigues, and knowing by experience, if for nothing but their own safety, the necessity of getting on rapidly with their work, exerted themselves to their utmost, and when the grey dawn of morning made its appearance, the enemy beheld, with surprise, through the mist that surrounded them, the first parallel of our works completed, without their having anticipated it, or having thrown one shot in the direction of our workmen; but as the fog cleared away, it was too palpable to be misunderstood, that, despite of the sagacity of General Count Phillipon and his devoted garrison, a line of circumvallation had been cut close to one of the best of his outworks, without his having the remotest idea of the attempt.

The different alarm-bells in the town rang a loud peal, and in less than half an hour a tremendous cannonade was opened upon us, from the guns of the fort, as well as the town itself. Some men were killed, and several wounded, but, excepting this, no loss was sustained; the works were uninjured, their progress unimpeded, and this, our first attempt, for the third time, was crowned with that unlooked-for success which was a good omen for the future.

The entire of the 18th, the rain continued to fall, and the trenches were already nearly knee-deep with water, but by the great exertions of the engineers, and the persevering resolution of the soldiers, the works were pushed on with extraordinary vigour, the earth not being as yet sufficiently saturated to lose its consistency. On the night of the 18th, it rained still more heavily; nevertheless some guns were dragged through the slough by the soldiers into the batteries marked out to act against La Picurina, and the following morning the works were m that forward state as to cause the French governor much alarm for the fate of this outwork.

Towards midday on the 19th, a dense vapour, issuing from the Guadiana and Rivellas, caused by the heavy rains that had fallen, made Phillipon consider the moment a favourable one to make a rush into our works; he accordingly placed two thousand chosen troops at the different gates and sally-ports with fixed bayonets, ready to storm the batteries at a given signal. At this time our soldiers were working in the trenches, nearly up to their hips in water; the covering party were too distant to afford immediate relief if required to do so, because they were kept out of the wet ground as far as was consistent with the safety of our lines; and the soldiers. that composed the working party were in a helpless and defenceless state, their arms and appointments being thrown aside.

I happened to be in the works on this day, and having a little more experience than the officer who commanded the party, I observed with distrust the bustle which was apparent, not only in the fort of Picurina, but also along the ramparts of the town. Without waiting the formality of telling the commanding officer what I thought, I,, on the instant, ordered the men to throw by their spades and shovels, put on their appointments, and load their firelocks. This did not occupy more than three minutes, and in a few seconds afterwards the entire trenches to our right were filled with Frenchmen, the workmen massacred, and the works materially damaged; while at the same moment, several hundred men attempted to throw themselves into the battery we occupied: but the workmen were armed and ready to receive them; they had just been placed—I must say it, for it is the truth—by me, in a posture not only to save their own lives, but the battery also.

The Frenchmen advanced with that impetuous burst so well known to those who have witnessed it, and so difficult to stand before by any. They had a double motive to urge them on on this occasion, honour had a forcible auxiliary in the shape of a dollar, which they were to receive for every pick-axe or shovel they carried out of our trenches, and well as I know the French character, it is difficult for me to say which of the two, honour or avarice, most predominated upon the present occasion; I shall only say that it is my firm conviction—and I judge from the spirit of the attack, that both had their share in stimulating those heroic and veteran plunderers to seek for a footing within our trenches, for I never saw a set of fellows that sought with greater avidity than they did, the spades and shovels that were thrown aside by our men. Lieutenant D'Arcy of the 88th and Lieutenant White of the 45th pursued them almost to the glacis of the town; and had the movement been foreseen, there can be little hazard in saying, that, with a sufficient supply of ladders at the moment, the fort of Picurina could have been carried by the workmen alone, so great was their enthusiasm, with a less loss of lives than it cost us (after six days labour) on the 25th!

The sortie had been well repulsed at this point, but higher up, on the right, we were not so fortunate: the workmen were surprised, and, in addition to the injury inflicted upon the works, a great loss of men and officers was sustained before the covering party reached the spot. General Picton soon after arrived in the battery where I was stationed, and seemed to be much alarmed for its safety, not knowing, in the confusion of the moment, which was great, that the enemy had attacked it, and had been driven back; but when he learned from me, that the workmen alone had achieved this act, he was lavish in his praise of them, and spoke to myself—for him—in flattering terms; but there was an austerity of demeanour, which, even while he gave praise,—a thing he seldom did of the Connaught Rangers at least!—kept a fast hold of him, and the caustic sententiousness with which he spoke rather chilled than animated.

He was on foot, but his *aide-de-camp*, Captain Cuthbert of the fusiliers, was mounted, and while in the act of giving directions to some of the troops, (for by this time the whole of the besieging force, attracted by the cannonade, was in motion towards the works,) he was struck in the hip by a round shot, which killed his horse on the spot, leaving him dreadfully mangled and bleeding to death. This officer was a serious loss to Picton, and was much regretted by the division; he possessed all the requisites for a staff-officer, without that silly arrogance—the sure sign of an empty mind, as well as head—which we sometimes meet with amongst the gentlemen who composed the *état major* of our army.

We lost in this affair about two hundred men, many of whom were cut down in the works, and several in the depots far in the rear, by a body of the enemy's light cavalry that galloped out of the town at the moment the sortie commenced. Absurd as this may read, it is nevertheless true: the garrison of Badajoz, cooped up within its walls, without a foot of ground that they could call their own beyond the glacis, and, in a manner, begirt by an army of fifty thousand men, were—by their admirable arrangement of their forces, or by the superlative neglect of our people, enabled to ride through our lines—unopposed by a single dragoon!—from right to left! Brilliant, however, as was this exploit, it was of no such service to the garrison : their loss exceeded four hundred men, and the capture of a few dozen spades and shovels but ill repaid them for so great a sacrifice of lives, at any time valuable, but in their present position, doubly so.

The sortie being at length repulsed, and order once more restored, the works in the trenches were continued under a torrent of rain and fire of artillery. Lieutenant White, of the 40th, who had been much distinguished in the batteries, was struck by a shell, (without a fuse,) on the head, which killed him on the spot; he was reading a book at the moment, and Lieutenant Cotton, of the 88th, who was sitting beside him, was so covered with his blood, that it was thought at first he had been frightfully wounded.

Up to this time the fall of rain had been so violent as to threaten the total failure of the operation; it had never ceased since the 17th, and the trenches were a perfect river; the soldiers were working up to their knees in water, and the fatigue and hardships they endured were great indeed, but there was no complaint—not even a murmur to be heard! and Lord Wellington might be seen in the midst of his soldiers, sometimes with his beard unshaven.

Those,—ignorant people I admit, and quite unworthy of any rational persons taking the trouble to reply to their fooleries—who have the presumption to call Lord Wellington "a General of Fortune," had they seen him, as thousands of his companions have, at this same siege, worn down with fatigue of body and mind, giving himself up wholly to an operation of such momentous consequence, not to his own country alone, but to Europe generally,—had those persons, I say, seen him then, it is to be hoped, for their own sakes at least—for such creatures can have no national feeling—that they would not give their tongues the license they do. Poor ignorant idiots! The fame of this great man—this first of generals—is too firmly established to be blighted by their slanders, and will, despite of factious renegades, be handed down to posterity, so long as an Englishman—worthy of the name—shall be found on the face of the earth.

The next day, the 22nd, the pontoon bridge over the Guadiana was carried away by the floods which the late rains had caused in the river, and the stream became so rapid that the flying bridges could not be made use of, and, in short, all supplies from the other side were cut off. In the trenches, matters were in as bad a state, for the earth no longer retained its consistency, and it was impossible to get it into any shape. On the 24th, however, the weather happily settled fine, and much progress was made towards forwarding the works; but this, and the following day, were perhaps two of the most dreadful recorded in the annals of sieges. The soldiers laboured with a degree of hardihood, bordering on desperation, while the engineers braved every danger with as much composure as if they either set no value upon their lives, or thought their bodies impregnable to shot or shell.

In proportion as our works advanced, the enemy redoubled his fire, and the attempt made by us to drag the heavy guns through the mud, or to form magazines for the gunpowder, was almost certain death; but not content with the destruction which his fire carried throughout our ranks, Phillipon brought to his aid a battery from San Christoval, which he placed close to the edge of the river; the fire of this battery completely enfiladed our works, and rendered it difficult and hazardous for the workmen to keep their ground. Half a battalion was ordered down to the water's edge, and the effect of their fire against these guns was soon appreciated by the soldiers in the batteries; the cannonade of the enemy lost its effect, their fire became irregular, their shot passed over our heads, and finally they were compelled to limber up their park of artillery, and retrace their steps, at a gallop, up the Christoval height.

Nevertheless, this battery did an incalculable hurt to us; many men were struck down by its fire, but, above all, our engineers suffered the most. This was a loss that could be but ill spared, for we were so scantily supplied with this description of force, that it was found necessary to substitute officers of the infantry to act as such during the siege. These officers were very zealous in the performance of the dangerous duties they had to fulfil: some had a tolerable knowledge of the theory, but none, if I except Major Thompson of the 74th, and one or two that had served at Rodrigo, knew anything of the practical part; they strove, however, by great intrepidity, to make up for their other defects; they exposed themselves to every danger, with a bravery bordering on foolhardihood, and consequently, under such a fire as we were exposed to, scarcely one escaped death.

Lieutenant Fairtlough of the 5th, and Rammage of the 74th, both acting engineers, were cut asunder by a round shot from the San Christoval battery; others, whose names I forget, shared the same fate, and several were wounded.

Towards three o'clock in the afternoon our works had been materially advanced, several small magazines were in progress, the batteries destined to act against La Picurina were armed, and the losses which we sustained amongst our engineers repaired by the arrival of others to replace their fallen companions. It was at this time, while I was seriously occupied with thirty men, in covering with boards and sand- bags a magazine which had been, with great labour, formed during the forenoon, that a shell of huge dimensions exploded at the entrance of it.

There were, at the moment, above a dozen or so of the staff

corps and engineers, with some of the line, placing a quantity of gunpowder in the vault which had been prepared to receive it. The roof of the magazine was, in defiance of the dreadful fire which was incessant upon this point, crowned by a few soldiers of the party under my command; some kegs of gunpowder, which were at the entrance of the cave, unfortunately blew up, destroying all at that side of the magazine, and hurling the planks which were but in part secured upon its top, together with the men that were upon them, into the air, caused us a great loss of lives and labour, but fortunately the great store of powder which was inside, escaped.

The planks were shivered to pieces, and the brave fellows who occupied them, either blown into atoms, or so dreadfully wounded as to cause their immediate death; some had their uniforms burned to a cinder, while others were coiled up in a heap, without the vestige of anything left to denote that they were human beings.

An 88th soldier, of the name of Cooney, barber to the company he belonged to, escaped the effects of the explosion, unhurt, except a slight scratch in the face, caused by a splinter from a rock that had been rent in pieces by the blowing up of the magazine; he was an old and ugly man, but yet so vain of his personal appearance, as to be nearly in despair at the idea, as he said, "of his good looks being spoiled."

While he was in the midst of his lamentation, a round shot struck his head and carried it off his shoulders, when one of his companions exclaimed, with that humour which none but an Irishman could possess at such a time, "Well! upon my sowl, he was always an ugly-looking cratur, but now he's the very devil!"

All the men laughed, and said, "It was thrue for him he was."

In his coat pocket was found his soap and razor, which were instantly drawn lots for, but to whose "lot" they fell I know not. Those—ill-timed, some will say—jokes, may appear to many, out of place, but they are not so nevertheless; it is much better that soldiers while enduring fatigues, and braving dangers such as those I am describing, should have a light and cheerful bearing, and it is plain that he who passes his joke in this manner against his fallen comrade stands a fair chance of being similarly placed himself, without any risk of his taking offence at it. It is this gaiety of demeanour—this steel-hardiness in moments of peril—that makes soldiers, in the true acceptation of the word, what they ought to be.

No matter what a man's feelings may really be, he should, and must stifle them, because it is well known—at least to those who have seen service—how readily the opinions of a few act upon the great mass of the multitude; and if soldiers were to indulge themselves in mourning over the dead bodies of their fallen companions, it would act like a contagion, and it would be difficult to say how the great body might be infected by it.

The Duke of Wellington was never known to pay attention to the reports carried to him of the fall of any of his officers: no more was Nelson. At Trafalgar, when his ship, the *Victory*, was along side of the Spanish *Santissima Trinidada*, one of the first discharges from that mountain of floating timber killed eight men on the quarterdeck. Nelson quietly turned round to his captain, and said, "This is too good to last long."

Yet Nelson was a man of such humanity, and tenderness of feeling, that he was never known to remain on board of his ship when a sailor was to be punished; and at Waterloo, it is affirmed by French officers, and more than hinted at in the bulletin detailing that battle, that the cry of "*Sauve qui peut!*" raised by a few obscure individuals, was the cause of its loss to the French army. However, averse as I am to such conduct, I will not—although not a "Waterloo man"—go the length that my French acquaintances have done, because I verily believe that, at the time the cry of "*Sauve qui peut!*" was raised at Waterloo, it was just about the same service to the Imperial army as the warning given by a Lisbon *femme de chambre* when she has discharged the contents of a certain machine, that shall be nameless, upon the head of some ill-fated passenger—or, to speak more plainly, when the advice came too late.

The French cannoniers were loud in cheering when they discovered the effects of their fire upon Cooney's sconce; our men cheered in turn, and continued to crown the top of the already half-dismantled magazine, but as last as they mounted it, they were swept off its face by the overwhelming fire from the town: yet notwithstanding the great loss of lives that had already taken place, and the almost certain death which awaited all who attempted to remain on the magazine, it was never for five minutes unoccupied, and by four o'clock in the afternoon it might be said to be perfectly finished.

Baffled in his endeavours to stop our progress, Phillipon was determined to make it cost us as dear as he could. Twelve additional guns were brought from the unemployed batteries and placed along the curtain *en barbette*. These, at half-range distance, without the means on our side to reply to them, were fired with a fearful precision; it was next to impossible to stand under it, but the soldiers, on this day, surpassed all their former efforts. The fire of three score pieces of artillery was employed in vain against them; the works were repaired so soon as injured, and everything warranted the opinion, that, should the night prove fine, our batteries would open the following day.

Captain Mulcaster, of the Engineers, by his heroic conduct, stimulated the soldiers wonderfully; no danger could unnerve him, or prevent his exposing himself to the hottest of the French fire, and for a time he escaped unhurt, but at length, while standing on a rising ground, in front of the battery No. 1, a twenty- four pound shot struck him in the neck, and carried away his head and part of his back and shoulders. The headless trunk was knocked several yards from the spot, but was speedily carried to the engineer camp by some of the brave men who, but a few short moments before, looked upon what was now an inanimate lump of clay, with that admiration naturally inspired by one of the finest, as well as the most intrepid young men in the army; for he had endeared himself to the soldiers as much by his kind manner to them, as by his total disregard of danger to himself.

It is well known that infantry soldiers had a great dislike to being placed under the control of the engineer officers, who exacted, or at least they thought so, too much from them, but Captain Mulcaster had a manner, peculiar to himself, that gained him the good will of all.

Major Thomson of the 88th, soon after fell. He was observing a party of the enemy who were rowing a *bateau* across the inundation of the Rivellas with a reinforcement of men intended to succour the troops that occupied the ravelin of San Roque. This operation, although embracing but a small portion of the garrison, was one of a very delicate nature, inasmuch as the distance between our works, and the inundation, was so short as to enable us to command with musketry its entire span; but the Governor, ever ready in strategy, provided against even this chance of his plans for defence being marred.

He caused to be constructed a large *bateau*, or, perhaps, more properly speaking, a raft. The side of it which faced our lines was raised by light poles to the height of four feet, through which were intertwined wattles of osier; by this means, a support sufficiently strong, without being too cumbrous to impede the movement of the raft, was completed, and the inside was carefully padded with hay, or such light matter, as was a sufficient defence against musketry without any danger of the machine's losing its centre of gravity.

To stop as much as possible this operation, several hundred riflemen were placed in advance, and so soon as the machine was discovered in motion on the water, a heavy fire was opened; a corresponding demonstration was made by the enemy, sustained by several batteries, and those mutual efforts were always productive of a heavy loss of lives on both sides, but particularly on ours, because the enemy's line of musketry commanded us at a distance of three hundred and fifty yards, and up to this time we had not one gun to answer their powerful salvos.

Major Thomson, who was in command of the riflemen, was in conversation with an *aide-de-camp* belonging to the staff of Marshal Beresford at the moment he fell; a musket ball struck him in the right temple, and passing through the brain, killed him on the spot. He had been but just Gazetted to his majority, by purchase, and had served with the army from the campaign in Holland in 1794, to the moment of his death, without ever having been absent from his regiment in any of the battles in which it had been engaged, a few of which have been recorded by me. Captain Seton, an officer of precisely the same standing and services, succeeded him in the command of the 88th, and led his regiment up the ladders on the night of the storming of Badajoz, but he gained no promotion, except in his regular turn I and he was the only commanding officer of a battalion in the third division that did not get a brevet step.

Near the spot where Thomson fell, an officer of his regiment named North met his death, and, as it was one of great singularity, I shall notice it out of the many that occurred on this fatal day. He was struck in the cheek by a round-shot; the under part of his face and a portion of his throat were carried away, leaving the upper part perfect, which hung down in a hideous flap like a deformed mask. He was carried to the hospital, where I saw him two days afterwards, not only alive but sitting upright against a wall; he was perfectly sane, and recognized my voice; he endeavoured to speak to me, but the effort he made inexpressibly shocked me.

The voice, in place of issuing from its natural channel, the mouth, but mouth there was none, came spectre-like from the chest, and more resembled the howling of some wild animal than the voice of man. He did not survive the night, and died after a violent effort of nature to sustain life, which he had done for more than fifty hours, giving a proof of the awful capability of suffering that exists in our frame, and faithfully bearing out the writer who says that "many are the shapes of death, and many are the ways that lead to his grim cave—all dreadful."

The evening of a day—never to be forgotten by those who witnessed it—at length began to close; the shades of night soon rendered our lines invisible to the enemy, and under its cover, the men who had been at work for so many hours were withdrawn to the camp; two thousand fresh soldiers replaced them and carried on the duty in the trenches until the dawn of morning, at which time they presented a formidable appearance. Two batteries of thirty-two pounders were unmasked at the distance of one hundred and fifty yards from La Picurina, and ere the sun was clearly distinguishable on the horizon, a violent cannonade commenced against that outwork. It was replied to with vigour, not only from the fort itself, but the batteries of the town also.

On this day I was attached to the engineers; but the fatigues I had undergone the preceding one, caused me to sleep soundly, and in truth I had great need of repose, so it was late ere I proceeded to the engineer camp to report myself to Colonel Fletcher, the commanding officer. On my way thither I was much amused by a dialogue which took place between a soldier of the light division, one of the 43rd I think, an Englishman, and a young man who afterwards turned out to be a commissary's clerk—for many of those men who afterwards made such sums of money, and some of them who became so intolerably presuming as to cut their old acquaintances, came out to the Peninsula in this character.

The young clerk was attached to the light division, and wished to know from the soldier (whom he recognized by his uniform as belonging to it) whither he was to bend his steps in order to find it. I shall give the conversation word for word, as nearly as I can now recollect after so great a lapse of time.

Com. "Pray, my good fellow, don't you belong to the light division?"

Sol. "No, sir, I belong to *the* division."

Com. "Why what division is that? I never heard of it before."

Sol. "Have you been long with the army, sir?"

Com. "I have only this morning joined it"

Sol. "I thought so!"

Com. "Why what has that to do with my question?"

Sol. "As you seem to be but a young hand—or as we call it in this here army—a green horn—I'll just tell you all about it. This here army is composed of seven divisions, and I'll tell you all about 'em and their names—at least the names that we, soldiers, have given them. Ours is called the division, because as how we think ourselves the crack one. Then there's the First Division; those we call the gentlemen, because they are made up of Guardsmen and Germans, and His Majesty (God bless him!) is fond of his body-guard, and likes to have good care taken of them; and the Germans he likes as well as the Guards, because they say his own mother was a German bred and born.

These chaps have the snuggest berth in the army. The Second Division is a corps of observation like, we never see 'em, though we sometimes hear about 'em. The Third is the fighting division—and the Fourth would fight if they were axed! The Fifth come up to a town after we have taken it, and are useful enough. The Sixth are scattered over the country, here and there, and the Seventh are trying to get them together; and this is the way the army is divided in this here Island."

"Why truly, my friend," replied the commissary, "your description is amusing enough; but as I have nothing to do with the fighting merits of the army, it does not concern me. In a word, I am a commissary, and wish to know where I am to find your division, to which I am attached."

"A commissary are you? Why then bless your stars that you did not join the division when the brave Bob Crawfurd—black Bob we used to call him—commanded it, it was he as knowed how to whop a thieving commissary! Why look ye, sir, I knowed him once myself to throw one of them 'ere chaps neck and shoulders out of a winder, and it is said, though I don't know it for sartin, that he whopped another in such prime style, the poor cratur ever after looked so promiscuously.[1] I may say, when he met Bob, that he quitted the division, and went—if all as was said of him be true—to the devil, and when he went to him, it must have been a great release to the poor soul, for black Bob was worse than the devil himself for sarving out a commissary."

The young man took his departure in the direction of the light division camp, and if his looks were a criterion to go by, he, most unquestionably, was not of the number that mourned Crawfurd's death.

Towards evening the fire against La Picurina was so effective, that Lord Wellington resolved to storm it after dark.

---

1. I suppose the soldier meant "confused."

CHAPTER 19

Badajoz Taken

At about three o'clock in the afternoon of the 25th of March, almost all its batteries on the side of our lines were disorganized, its palisades beaten down, and the fort itself, having more the semblance of a wreck than a fortification of any pretensions, presented to the eye nothing but a heap of ruins; but never was there a more fallacious appearance: the work although dismantled of its cannon, its parapets crumbling to pieces at each successive discharge from our guns, and its garrison diminished, without a chance of being succoured, was still much more formidable than appeared to the eye of a superficial observer.

It had yet many means of resistance at its disposal. The gorge, protected by three rows of palisades, was still unhurt; and although several feet of the scarp had been thrown down by the fire from our battering-park, it was, notwithstanding, of a height sufficient to inspire its garrison with a well-grounded confidence as to the result of any effort of ours against it; it was defended by three hundred of the *élite* of Phillipon's force, under the command of a colonel of Soult's staff, named Gaspard Thiery, who volunteered his services on the occasion. On this day a deserter came over to us from the fort, and gave an exact account of how it was circumstanced.

Colonel Fletcher, the chief engineer, having carefully examined the damage created by our fire, disregarding the perfect state of many of the defences, and being well aware that expedition was of paramount import to our final success, advised that the fort should be attacked after nightfall. Five hundred men of Picton's division, who on this day did the duty in the trenches, were ordered to hold themselves in readiness for the assault—eight o'clock was the hour named. At seven the men were arrayed in order, and divided into three detachments of equal proportions; the right column was intrusted to Major Shawe of the 74th; the centre to Captain Powis of the 83rd; and the left to Major Rudd of the 77th—all, officers as well as privates, belonging to the third division.

And here I am forced to digress so far as to say, that the officer of the light division who wrote the *Sketch of the Storming of Badajoz*, is in error when he says that a part of his corps formed any of those that carried the fort of La Picurina. If such was the case, it is not—at least that I have read—so recorded, except by himself! I was on the spot—was personally acquainted with the greater part of the officers, and, I might add—privates; I did not see one man of the light division amongst the troops destined for the attack, nor do I think—so far as my recollection directs me—that Lord Wellington, in his account of that affair, says that the light division bore any part in it The third division, although never defeated, cannot spare any portion of their hard-earned fame to another; and the gallant light division stand in no need of an auxiliary to commemorate their imperishable deeds in the Peninsula.

At half-past seven o'clock the storming party, consisting of fifteen officers and five hundred privates, stood to their arms. General Kempt, who commanded in the trenches, explained to them the duty they had to perform; he did so in his usual clear manner, and everyone knew the part he was to fulfil. All now waited with anxiety for the expected signal, which was to be the fire of one gun from No. 4 battery. The evening was settled and calm; no rain had fallen since the 23rd; the rustling of a leaf might be heard; and the silence of the moment was uninterrupted, except by the French sentinels, as they challenged while pacing the battlements of the outwork; the answers of their comrades, although in a lower tone of voice, were distinguishable, "*Tout va bien dans le fort de la Picurina,*" was heard by the very men who only awaited the signal from a gun to prove, that the *réponse*, although true to the letter, might soon be falsified.

The great cathedral bell of the city at length tolled the hour of eight, and its last sounds had scarcely died away when the signal from the battery summoned the men to their perilous task; the three detachments sprang out of the works at the same moment, and ran forwards to the glacis; but the great noise which the evolution unavoidably created gave warning to the enemy, already on the alert, and a violent fire of musketry opened upon the assailing columns.

One hundred men fell before they reached the outwork; but the rest, undismayed by the loss, and unshaken in their purpose, threw themselves into the ditch, or against the palisades at the gorge. The sappers, armed with axes and crow-bars, attempted to cut away or force down this defence; but the palisades were of such thickness, and so firmly placed in the ground, that before any impression could be made against even the front row, nearly all the men who had crowded to this point were struck dead. Meanwhile, those in charge of the ladders flung them into the ditch, and those below soon placed them upright against the wall; but in some instances they were not of a sufficient length to reach the top of the parapet.

The time was passing rapidly, and had been awfully occupied by the enemy; while as yet our troops had not made any progress that could warrant a hope of success. More than two-thirds of the officers and privates were killed or wounded; two out of the three that commanded detachments had fallen; and Major Shawe, of the 74th, was the only one unhurt. All his ladders were too short—his men, either in the ditch or on the glacis, unable to advance, unwilling to retire, and not knowing what to do, became bewildered—the French cheered vehemently, and each discharge swept away many officers and privates.

Shawe's situation, which had always been one of peril, now became desperate; he called out to his next senior officer (Captain Oates, of the 88th), and said, "Oates, what are we to do?" but at the instant he was struck in the neck by a bullet, and fell bathed in blood. It immediately occurred to Oates, who now took the command, that although the ladders were too short to mount the wall, they were long enough to go across the ditch! He at once formed the desperate resolution of throwing three of them over the fosse, by which a sort of bridge was constructed; he led the way, followed by the few of his brave soldiers who were unhurt, and, forcing their passage through an embrasure that had been but bolstered up in the hurry of the moment, carried—after a brief, desperate, but decisive conflict—the point allotted to him.

Sixty grenadiers of the Italian Guard were the first encountered by Oates and his party; they supplicated for mercy, but, either by accident or design, one of them discharged his firelock, and the ball struck Oates in the thigh; he fell, and his men, who had before been greatly excited, now became furious when they beheld their commanding officer weltering in his blood. Every man of the Italian Guard was put to death on the spot.

Meanwhile Captain Powis's detachment had made great progress, and finally entered the fort by the salient angle. It has been said, and, for aught I know to the contrary, with truth, that it was the first which established itself in the outwork; but this is of little import in the detail, or to the reader. All the troop engaged acted with the same spirit and devotion, and each vied with his comrade to keep up the character of the "fighting division."

Almost the entire of the privates and non-commissioned officers were killed or wounded; and of fifteen officers, which constituted the number of those engaged, not one escaped unhurt! Major Rudd's detachment, as also the one commanded by Captain Powis, were composed of soldiers belonging to the different regiments of Picton's division; but that commanded by Major Shawe were, to a man, Connaught Rangers. Of the garrison, but few escaped; the commandant, and about eighty, were made prisoners; the rest, in endeavouring to escape under the guns of the fortress, or to shelter themselves in San Roque, were either bayoneted or drowned in the Rivellas; but this was not owing to any mismanagement on the part of Count Phillipon.

He, with that thorough knowledge of his duty which marked his conduct throughout the siege, had, early in the business, ordered a body of chosen troops to *débouche* from San Roque, and to hold themselves in readiness to sustain the fort; but the movement was foreseen. A strong column, which had been placed in reserve, under the command of Captain Lindsey, of the 88th, met this reinforcement at the moment they were about to sustain their defeated companions at La Picurina. Not expecting to be thus attacked, these troops became panic-struck, soon fled in disorder, and running, without heed, in every direction, choked up the only passage of escape that was open for the fugitives from the outwork, and by a well-meant, but ill-executed evolution, did more harm than good.

So soon as the result of this last effort to succour the fort was apparent to Phillipon, he caused a violent cannonade to be opened against it, but it was not of long duration; and our engineers, profiting by the quiet which reigned throughout the enemy's batteries, pushed for- ward the second parallel with great success. A corps of sappers, under my command, were charged with the work of dismantling the fort, and before day we had nearly completed its destruction.

Amongst the officers who fell on this evening, independent of those immediately belonging to the storming party, were two who were much regretted: the major of our brigade, Captain Wilde, of the 87th, and Lieutenant George Johnston, of the 88th. This latter officer was not on duty in the works; but when it was made known to him that his Captain (Oates) was to take a part in the fray, he ran down to join his friend, and—with his arm in a sling, and an unhealed wound which he received on the breast at Rodrigo—fell, with many others, in endeavouring to force the gorge of the fort. It was he who so much distinguished himself at the battle of Fuentes d'Onore, when his regiment (the 88th) overthrew the French Imperial Guard.

Thus terminated the siege and storming of La Picurina, after a lapse of eight nights and nine days of unprecedented labour and peril. It might be said that its capture opened to us the gates of Badajoz, or at all events put the key of that fortress into our hands; it nevertheless cost us some trouble before we could make use of the key so gained.

Never, from the commencement of the war until its termination, was there a more gallant exploit than the storming of this outwork; and it may be well here to analyze the description of force by which so difficult an affair was achieved, as likewise the rank of the officers who conducted the attack. I know it is the fashion with some to think, or say, at all events, that in an affair of the kind, a body of chosen, or, as the phrase goes, "picked" men should be employed, and none others. Now what is meant by "picked men?" Why, neither more nor less than stout-looking fellows. This is folly— perfect folly.

There may be some, sticklers for this, their hobby, who will say, "Oh no! not stout big fellows, but men of good character." Greater folly again.

Others may say, "Well, at all events, such duties ought to be performed by grenadiers or light infantry, and under the command of a general officer." This is greater folly than both the others put together. Such opinions are, and I speak from experience, fallacious. It is well known that a man of six feet is not more capable of enduring fatigue than a short stout-built fellow of five feet six; and, if the heart be in the right place, the little man will be as efficient in the breach as his gigantic comrade.

As to good characters, we have, all of us seen the most profligate fellows in a regiment the like heroes at the muzzle of a gun; and as to grenadiers and light infantry, experience has shown that they have been defeated, although headed by generals, when, as in the case of La Picurina, the men who happened to be on duty of Picton's division, commanded by a major and two captains, achieved an exploit that stands unrivalled in the Peninsular campaigns.

The three officers who commanded detachments gained a step in consequence; but the brave Captain Oates,—who so chivalrously planted his ladders across the ditch, and who succeeded to the command of Major Shawe's detachment after that officer was wounded,—so far from being recommended for a brevet-step, although he was a captain of nine years' standing, was not even noticed by General Picton (the general of his division) for his gallant conduct!

From this period until the 30th, a heavy fire was kept up against the works of the place; but it would be uninteresting to the reader to enter into a detail of all the *minutiæ* of our operations during this time. On the night of the 29th the enemy attacked the troops posted on the right bank of the Guadiana, but their efforts were vain, and they were repulsed with loss.

While these events were taking place before Badajoz, the remainder of the army, under Generals Hill and Graham, were pushed in advance on the Seville road; Hill occupied Merida with two divisions; while Graham, stationed at Santa Martha, observed the movements of the French Andalusian army under Drouet.

On the 30th of March, two breaching-batteries armed with twenty-six guns of heavy calibre, and of the very best description, opened their fire to batter down the face of the two bastions already named; and, notwithstanding every effort which the powerful resources of the enemy enabled him to command, it was abundantly manifest that a few days would suffice to finish the labours of the army before Badajoz.

All this time Soult was making the greatest exertions to get together a sufficient force for the succour of the garrison; but he miscalculated the time necessary for such an effort; and the fine defence of Count Phillipon the preceding year, together with the efficient state of the place, inspired him with a confidence that was fatal. So late as the 1st of April he was at Seville, seven days' march from Villa Franca, and nine from Badajoz!

He had early apprized Marmont of the events that were passing; but that marshal, instead of seriously occupying himself in making use of the means at his disposal to succour his friend, allowed himself to be occupied in a petty warfare against the militia of Portugal, and when he had trifled a few days in this manner, he recrossed the Agueda, after having frittered away five precious days in folly, and left the city of Badajoz, which was of such vital importance, and the army of his brother marshal, to their fate. Thus, with a force of little more than forty thousand men (including the army of observation,) Lord Wellington took the place, as it were, in presence of two French armies, amounting together to upwards of eighty thousand of the veterans of France. This was pretty well for a *sepoy* general, as the *Moniteur* styled him, or, as the renegades in England called him,—a lucky general.

The breaching-batteries, which opened their fire on the 30th, were effective beyond our expectations against the works, and the sappers had made considerable progress towards completing a good covert-way for the troops to debouche from in their attack of the breaches. On the 25th, thirty-two sappers were placed under my command, but on the night of the 4th of April, their numbers were reduced to seven. I lost some of the bravest men I ever commanded; but, considering the perils they encountered, it is only surprising how any escaped: we were frequently obliged to run the flying-sap so close to the battlements of the town, that the noise of the pick-axes was heard on the ramparts, and, upon such occasions, the party were almost invariably cut off to a man.

But it was then that the courage of the brave fellows under my orders showed itself superior to any reverse, and what was wanted in force, was made up by the most heroic bravery of individuals. There were three men of my own regiment, Williamson, Bray, and Macgowan, and I feel happy in being able to mention the names of those heroes: when a fire, so destructive as to sweep away all our gabions, took place, those men would run forward with a fresh supply, and, under a fire in which it was almost impossible to live, place them in order, for the rest of the party to shelter themselves, while they threw up a sufficiency of earth to render them proof against musketry. This dangerous duty was carried on for eleven successive nights, that is to say, from the 25th of March to the 5th of April,

On this day, the batteries of the enemy were nearly crippled, and their replies to our fire scarcely audible; the spirits of the soldiers, which no fatigue could damp, rose to a frightful height—I say frightful, because it was not of that sort which alone denoted exultation at the prospect of their achieving an exploit which was about to hold them up to the admiration of the world, there was a certain something in their bearing that told plainly they had suffered fatigues, which, though they did not complain of, and had seen their comrades and officers slain while fighting beside them without repining,—they smarted under the one, and felt acutely for the other, yet smothered both, so long as their minds and bodies were employed: now, however, that they had a momentary licence to think every fine feeling vanished, and plunder and revenge took their place.

Their labours, up to this period, although unremitting, and carried on with a cheerfulness that was astonishing; hardly promised the success which they looked for; and the change which the last twenty-four hours had wrought in their favour, caused a material alteration in their demeanour; they hailed the present prospect as the mariner does the disappearance of a heavy cloud after a storm, which discovers to his view the clear horizon. In a word, the capture of Badajoz had long been their idol; many causes led to this wish on their part; the two previous unsuccessful sieges, and the failure of the attack against San Christoval in the latter; but, above all, the well-known hostility of its inhabitants to the British army, and perhaps might be added, a desire for plunder, which the sacking of Rodrigo had given them a taste for. Badajoz was, therefore denounced as a place to be made an example of; and, most unquestionably, no city, Jerusalem excepted, was ever more strictly visited to the letter than was this ill-fated town.

The soldiers had, from some cause or other, perhaps from the disabled appearance of the bastions near the breaches, conceived the idea that the storm was to take place on the night of the 5th: they accordingly began to make such arrangements as they fancied suitable to the occasion; some by a distribution of their little effects amongst their immediate friends, others bequeathed their arrears of pay to those whom they fancied, or upon receiving a similar pledge from any soldier who felt disposed to make a like barter. Their minds being thus made up for an event which was destined to be the grave of so many, they awaited, with ill-suppressed impatience, in groups, for the order which was to summon them to the assault; a little rain had fallen, and there is something, even in a shower, extremely composing to the spirits. A quiet calm settles over the mind; every straggling thought is called in; bygone scenes revisit the mind; and it is not long before this stagnant gloom of the intellect is dispersed by a mental monsoon.

The demeanour of the soldiers on this evening faithfully exemplified what I have just written: a quiet but desperate calm had taken the place of that gayness and buoyancy of spirits which they possessed so short a time before, and nothing now was observably in their manner but a tiger-like expression of anxiety to seize upon their prey, which they considered as already within their grasp.

Towards five o'clock in the afternoon, all doubts were at an end, in consequence of some officers arriving in the camp from the trenches: they reported that Lord Wellington had decided upon breaching the curtain that connected the bastion of La Trinidad and Santa Maria, and as this operation would necessarily occupy several hours' fire, it was impossible that the assault could take place before the following day, the 6th, and the inactivity that reigned in the engineer camp, which contained the scaling-ladders, was corroborative of the intelligence. For once I saw the men dejected; yet it was not the dejection of fear, but of disappointment.

Some of the most impetuous broke out into violent and unbecoming language; others abused the engineers; and many threw the blame of the delay upon the generals who commanded in the trenches; but all, even the most turbulent, admitted that the delay must be necessary to our success, or Lord Wellington would not allow it.

The night at length passed over, and the dawn of morning ushered in a day pregnant with events that will be recorded in our history as amongst the most brilliant that grace its annals. The batteries against the curtain soon reduced it to a heap of ruins; and the certainty that the trial would be made the same evening, re-established good humour amongst the soldiers. It was known, early in the day, that the breaches were allotted to the Light and Fourth divisions; to the Fifth, the task of escalading the town on the side of the fort of Pardeleras; and to Picton, with his invincible Third, to carry the castle by escalading its stupendous walls, upwards of thirty feet high. The Portuguese brigade, under General Power, were to divert the enemy's attention on the side of San Christoval; while three hundred men, taken from the guard in the trenches, were to carry the outwork of San Roque.

To ensure the success of an enterprise, upon which so much was at stake, twenty thousand men were to be brought into action as I have described; by five o'clock, all the ladders were portioned out to those destined to mount them. The time fixed for the assemblage of the troops was eight; that of the attack ten. The day passed over heavily, and hour after hour was counted, each succeeding one seeming to double the length of the one that preceded it; but, true as the needle to the pole, the long-expected moment arrived, and the clear, but deep note of the town clock was now heard throughout our lines, as it tolled the hour of eight, and ere its last vibration had ceased, the vast mass of assailants were in battle array.

A thick and dusky vapour, issuing from the Guadiana and Rivellas, hung above the heads of the hostile forces, and hid alike, by its heavy veil, each from the view of its opponent; the batteries on both sides were silent, as if they reserved their efforts for the approaching struggle; and, except the gentle noise which the rippling of the Guadiana created, or the croaking of the countless frogs that filled the marshes on each side of its banks, everything was as still as if the night was to be one of quiet repose; and a passing stranger, unacquainted with the previous events, might easily have supposed that our army were no otherwise occupied than in the ordinary routine of an evening parade; but Phillipon, profiting by this cessation, retrenched and barricaded the breaches in a manner hereafter to be described.

So soon as each division had formed on its ground in open column of companies, the arms were piled, and the officers and soldiers either walked about in groups of five or six together, or sat down under an olive tree, to observe, at their ease, the arrangements of the different brigades which were to take a part in the contest. Then, again, might be seen some writing to their friends—a hasty scroll no doubt, and, in my opinion, an ill-timed one. It is a bad time, at the moment of entering a breach, to write to a man's father or mother, much less his wife, to tell them so; and, besides, it has an unseasonable appearance in the eyes of the soldiers, who are decidedly the most competent judges of what their officers should be, or, at least, what they would wish them to be, which is tantamount, at such a crisis.

There is a solemnity of feeling which accompanies the expectation of every great event in our lives, and the man who can be altogether dead to such feeling is little, if anything, better than a brute. The present moment was one that was well calculated to fill every bosom throughout the army; for, mixed with expectation, hope, and suspense, it was rendered still more touching to the heart, by the music of some of the regiments, which played at the head of each battalion, as the soldiers sauntered about to beguile the last hour many of them were destined to live.

The band of my corps, the 88th, all Irish, played several airs which exclusively belong to their country, and it is impossible to describe the effect it had upon us all; such an air as "Savourneen Deelish" is sufficient, at any time, to inspire a feeling of melancholy, but on an occasion like the present, it acted powerfully on the feelings of the men: they thought of their distant homes—of their friends, and of bygone days.

It was Easter Sunday; and the contrast which their present position presented to what it would have been, were they in their native land, afforded ample food for the occupation of their minds; but they were not allowed time for much longer reflection. The approach of General Kempt, accompanied by his staff, was the signal for the formation of the column of attack; and almost immediately the men were ordered to stand to their arms. Little, if any, directions were given; indeed, they were unnecessary,—because the men, from long service, were so conversant with the duty they had to perform, that it would have been but a waste of words and time, to say what was required of them.

All was now in readiness. It was twenty-five minutes past nine: the soldiers, unincumbered with their knapsacks—their stocks off—their shirt-collars unbuttoned—their trowsers tucked up to the knee—their tattered jackets, so worn out, as to render the regiment they belonged to barely recognizable—their huge whiskers, and bronzed faces, which several hard-fought campaigns had changed from their natural hue—but, above all, their self-confidence, devoid of boast or bravado, gave them the appearance of what they, in reality, were—an invincible host.

The division now moved forward in one solid mass,—the 45th leading, followed closely by the 88th and 74th; the brigade of Portuguese, consisting of the 9th and 21st Regiments of the line, under Colonel de Champlemond, were next; while the 5th, 77th, 83rd, and 94th, under Colonel Campbell, brought up the rear. Their advance was undisturbed until they reached the Rivellas; but at this spot, some fire-balls, which the enemy threw out, caused a great light, and the third division, three thousand strong, was to be seen from the ramparts of the castle.

The soldiers, finding they were discovered, raised a shout of defiance, which was responded to by the garrison, and in a moment afterwards, every gun that could be brought to bear against them was in action; but, no way daunted by the havoc made in his ranks, Picton, who just then joined his soldiers, forded the Rivellas, knee-deep, and soon gained the foot of the castle wall, and here he saw the work that was cut out for him, for he no longer fought in darkness.

The vast quantity of combustible matter, which out-topped this stupendous defence, was in a blaze, and the flames which issued forth on every side, lighted, not only the ramparts and ditch, but the plain that intervened between them and the Rivellas.

A host of veterans crowned the wall, all armed in a manner as imposing as novel; each man had beside him eight loaded fire-locks; while at intervals, and proportionably distributed, were pikes of an enormous length, with crooks attached to them, for the purpose of grappling with the ladders; the top of the wall was covered with rocks of ponderous size, only requiring a slight push to hurl them upon the heads of our soldiers; and there was a sufficiency of hand-grenades and small shells at the disposal of the men that defended this point to have destroyed the entire of the besieging army; while on the flanks of each curtain, batteries, charged to the muzzle with grape and case shot, either swept away entire sections, or disorganized the ladders as they were about to be placed, and an incessant storm of musketry, at the distance of fifteen yards, completed the resources the enemy brought into play, which, as may be seen were of vast formidableness.

To oppose this mass of warriors, and heterogeneous congregation of missiles, Picton had nothing to depend upon for success but his tried and invincible old soldiers—he relied firmly upon their devoted courage, and he was not disappointed. The terrible aspect of the rugged wall, thirty feet in height, in no way intimidated them; and, under a frightful fire of small arms and artillery, the ponderous ladders were dragged into the ditch, and, with a degree of hardihood that angered well for the issue, were planted against the lofty battlements that domineered above his soldier's heads: but this was only the commencement of one of the most terrific struggles recorded during this hard-fought night.

Each ladder, so soon as placed upright, was speedily mounted, and crowded from the top round to the bottom one; but those who escaped the pike-thrusts, were shattered to atoms by the heavy cross-fire from the bastions, and the soldiers who occupied them, impaled upon the bayonets of their comrades in the ditch, died at the foot of those ladders which they had carried such a distance, and with so much labour.

An hour had now passed over—no impression had been made upon the castle, and the affair began to have a very doubtful appearance, for, already, more than half of the Third Division had been cut off. General Kempt, commanding the right brigade, fell, wounded, early in the night; and the 88th Regiment alone, the strongest in the division, lost more than half their officers and men, and the other regiments were scarcely in a better condition. Picton, seeing the frightful situation in which he was placed, became uneasy; but the good will with which his brave companions exposed and laid down their lives reassured him; he called out to his men—told them they had never been defeated, and that now was the moment to conquer or die.

Picton, although not loved by his soldiers, was respected by them; and his appeal, as well as his unshaken front, did wonders in changing the desperate state of the division. Major Ridge, of the 5th, by his personal exertions, caused two ladders to be placed upright, and he, himself, led the way to the top of one, while Canch, a grenadier officer of the 5th, mounted the other; a few men, at last, got footing on the top of the wall; at the same time. Lieutenant William Mackie of the 88th—he who led the forlorn hope at Rodrigo,—(unnoticed!—still a lieutenant!!)—and Mr. Richard Martin (son of the member for Galway, who acted as a volunteer with the 88th during the siege) succeeding in mounting another. Mackie—ever foremost in the fight—soon established his men on the battlements, himself unhurt; but Martin fell desperately wounded.

A general rush to the ladders now took place, and the dead and wounded, that lay in the ditch, were indiscriminately trampled upon, for humanity was nowhere to be found. A frightful butchery followed this success; and the shouts of our soldiery, mingled with the cries of the Frenchmen, supplicating for mercy, or in the agonies of death, were heard at a great distance. But few prisoners were made; and the division occupied, with much regularity, the different points allotted to each regiment. Meanwhile the ravelin of San Roque was carried by the gorge, by a detachment drawn from the trenches, under the command of Major Wilson of the 48th, and the engineers were directed to blow up the dam and sluice that caused the inundation of the Rivellas, by which means the passage of that river, between La Picurina and the breaches could be more easily effected. One entire regiment of Germans, called the regiment of Hesse d'Armstadt, that defended the ravelin, were put to death.

While all this was taking place at the castle and San Roque, a fearful scene was acting at the breaches. The Light and Fourth divisions, ten thousand strong, advanced to the glacis undiscovered—a general silence pervading the whole, as the spirits of the men settled into that deep sobriety which denotes much determination of purpose; but at this spot their footsteps were heard; and, "perhaps since the invention of gunpowder," [1] its effects were never more powerfully brought into action.

In a moment the different materials, which the enemy had arranged in the neighbourhood of the breaches, were lighted up—darkness was converted into light—torches blazed along the battlements—and a spectator, at a short distance from the walls, could distinguish the features of the contending parties. A battery of mortars, doubly loaded with grenades; and a blaze of musketry, unlike anything hitherto witnessed by the oldest soldier, opened a murderous fire against the two divisions; but, unshaken by its effects, they pressed onward, and jumped into the ditch. The Fourth Division, destined to carry the breach to the right, met with a frightful catastrophe at the onset.

The leading platoons, consisting of the fusilier brigade, sprang into that part of the ditch that had been filled by the inundation of the Rivellas, and were seen no more; but the bubbles that rose on the surface of the water were a terrible assurance of the struggles which those devoted soldiers—the men of Albuera—ineffectually made to extricate themselves from the deadly grasp of each other, and from so unworthy an end.

Warned by the fate of their companions, the remainder turned to the left, and following the footsteps of the light division, pressed onwards in one mingled mass to the breaches of the curtain and La Trinidad. Arrived here, they encountered a series of obstacles that it was impossible to surmount, and which I find great difficulty in describing. Planks, of a sufficient length and breadth to embrace the entire face of the breaches, studded with spikes a foot long, were to be surmounted ere they reached the top of the breach; yet some there were—the brave Colonel Macleod, of the 43rd, amongst the number—who succeeded so far, but on gaining the top, *chevaux de fries*, formed of long sword-blades firmly fixed in the trunks of trees of a great size, and chained, boom-like, across the breach, were still to be passed; while at each side, and behind the *chevaux de frise*,

---

1. Colonel Jones's sieges.

trenches were cut, sufficiently extensive for the accommodation of three thousand men, who stood in an amphitheatrical manner—each tier above the other—and armed with eight muskets each, like their companions at the castle, awaited the attack so soon as the planks on the face, and the *chevaux de frise* on the top of the breach were surmounted; but they might have waited until doomsday for that event, because it was morally impossible.

The vast glare of light caused by the different explosions, and the fire of cannon and musketry, gave to the breaches the appearance of a volcano vomiting forth fire in the midst of the army: the ground shook—meteors shone forth in every direction—and when for a moment the roar of battle ceased, it was succeeded by cries of agony, or the furious exultation of the imperial soldiers. To stand before such a storm of fire, much less endeavour to overcome a barrier so impregnable, required men whose minds, as well as frames, were cast in a mould not human; but, nevertheless, so it was.

The gallant Light and Fourth Divisions boldly braved every danger, and with a goodwill, rarely to be found, prolonged a struggle, the very failure of which, taking into account the nature of the obstacles opposed to them, and their immense losses, was sufficient to immortalize them.

At length, after a dreadful sacrifice of lives—all the generals, and most of the colonels, being either killed or wounded—they were driven from the breaches, while the Frenchmen, securely entrenched behind them, might be seen waving their caps in token of defiance. This was too galling for men who had never known defeat—and they ran back headlong to the attack, and destruction. But for what end? To judge from the past, when their numbers were more numerous, they had failed; they were now reduced to less than half, while the resources of the enemy were unimpaired; and the prospect before them was hideous.

Their former efforts, when they were in their full vigour, had not been productive of any good result, and they felt that those they had made were stronger than those which were yet to come; but experience and feeling were alike unheeded—hope, more powerful than either, urged them on, "and like an unlucky gamester, every fresh reverse but increased their eagerness to continue the game."

Again did they attempt to pass this terrible gulf of steel and flame—and again were they driven back—cut down—annihilated. Hundreds of brave soldiers lay in piles upon each other, weltering in blood, and trodden down by their own companions. The 43rd left twenty-two officers and three hundred men on the breach; four companies of the 52nd were blown to atoms by an explosion; and the 95th, as indeed every other regiment engaged, suffered in proportion.

Our batteries, from whence a clear view of all that was passing could be distinguished, maddened by the havoc at the breaches, poured in a torrent of shot; and, in the excitement of the moment, killed friends as well as foes. Finally, the remnant of the two divisions retired; and with a valour, bordering upon desperation, prepared for a third trial; but the success of Picton's attack was by this time whispered amongst them, and the evacuation of the breaches soon after confirmed the rumour.

While the attack of the castle and breaches was in progress, the Fifth Division, under General Leith, maintained a fierce and dangerous struggle on the south side of the city and the Pardeleras fort; but the resistance at those points was feeble, as compared with the other two.

In some instances, the French troops deserted the walls before they were carried; and it is worthy of remark, that while the 38th Regiment were mounting the ladders, the imperial soldiers were scrambling down them at the reverse side—in many instances treading upon the fingers of our own men! The few men of Leith's division, thus established on the ramparts, boldly pressed on in the hope of causing a change in favour of the men at the breaches; but the multitude that had fled before this handful of troops became reassured when they beheld the scantiness of their numbers, and, returning to the fight, forced them up a street leading to the ramparts.

Leith's men became panic-struck by this unexpected burst, and retraced their steps in confusion; many were killed ere they reached the wall; and some, infected by the contagion of the moment, jumped over the battlements, and were dashed to pieces in their fall. One, an officer, bearing the flag of his regiment, fearing it might be captured, flung himself from the wall, and falling into a part of the ditch that was filled with the slime of the river, escaped unhurt

At this critical moment General Walker reached the spot with a fresh body of troops, and driving back the French with ruinous disorder, established his men at this point; and from that moment, the fate of Badajoz was sealed. The enemy fled in every direction towards the bridge leading to San Christoval; and the remnant of the ill-fated Light and Fourth Divisions with difficulty entered the town by the breaches, although unopposed.

It was now half-past two o'clock in the morning, and the fighting had continued, without cessation, from ten the preceding night. More than three hundred and fifty officers and four thousand men had fallen on our side; yet the enemy's loss was but small in proportion; because, with the exception of the castle, where the Third Ddivision got fairly amongst them, the French with that tact for which they are so remarkable, got away the moment they found themselves outmatched.

Shortly after the last attack at the breaches had failed, and long after the castle had been carried, (although it was not generally known at the time,) I was occupied, with Major Thompson of the 74th, (acting-engineer,) in placing some casks of gunpowder under the dam of the Rivellas, in front of San Roque; when, while leaning on his shoulder, I was struck by a musket-bullet in the left breast; I staggered back, but did not fall, and Thompson, bandaging my breast and shoulder with his handkerchief, caused me to be removed inside the ravelin; but the firing continued with such violence upon this point, that it was long before I could venture out of it.

At length, nearly exhausted from loss of blood, and fearing that I might be unable to reach the camp if I delayed much longer, I quitted it, accompanied by two sappers of my own corps, (Bray and Macgowan,) who supported me as I walked towards the trenches. Bray was wounded in the leg while he tried to cover me from the enemy's fire; but this brave fellow soon recovered, and afterwards greatly distinguished himself in the battle of the Pyrenees, by killing a French colonel at the head of his battalion.

By this time the attack of Badajoz was, in effect, finished. Some irregular firing was still to be heard as the fugitives hurried from street to street towards the Roman bridge leading to San Christoval, but all resistance might be said to have ceased. An attempt to retake the castle was made in vain; but the brave Colonel Ridge of the 5th, who had so distinguished himself, lost his life by almost one of the last shots that was fired in this fruitless effort to recover a place which had cost the army the hearts'-blood of the Third Division; and the dawn of the morning of the 7th of April showed to the rest of the army, like a speck in the horizon, the shattered remnant of Picton's invincible soldiers, as they stood in a lone group upon the ramparts of a spot that, by its isolated situation, towering height, and vast strength, seemed not to appertain to the rest of the fortifications, and which the enemy, with their entire disposable force, were unable to take from the few brave men who now stood triumphant upon its lofty battlements.

Nevertheless, triumphant and stern as was their attitude, it was not without its alloy, for more than five-sixths of their officers and comrades either lay dead at their feet, or badly wounded in the ditch below them.

All their Generals, Picton amongst the number, and almost all their colonels, were either killed or wounded; and as they stood to receive the praises of their commander, and the cheers of their equally brave, but unfortunate companions in arms, their diminished front and haggard appearance told, with terrible truth, the nature of the conflict in which they had been engaged. Yet those soldiers—the companions of Lord Wellington in six campaigns, and victorious in more than a hundred combats, and, in saying this, I make no distinction between any of the Peninsular heroes—have no medal to mark their deeds! They stand,—if not a degraded,—that they could not be,—an unrewarded tribe, while the Waterloo army,—nine-tenths of whom never saw a shot fired before that battle,—are honoured with a medal, and two years' of service over the heads of these very men.

The limits of this chapter will not allow the writer of it to enter more in detail upon the different features of the storming of Badajoz. Many brave officers greatly distinguished themselves, and some few escaped as by a miracle; but those matters, as also the sacking of the city, shall be the subject of the next Early on the morning of the 7th of April, Phillipon and his garrison, which had taken refuge in San Christoval, hoisted the white flag in token of submission, and from that moment the beautiful and rich town of Badajoz became a scene of plunder and devastation.

CHAPTER 20

Calamities of War

Badajoz, one of the richest and most beautiful towns in the south of Spain, whose inhabitants had witnessed its siege in silent terror for one and twenty days, and who had been shocked by the frightful massacre that had just taken place at its walls, was now about to be plunged into all the horrors that are, unfortunately, unavoidable upon an enterprise such as a town taken by storm. Scarcely had Count Phillipon and his garrison commenced their march towards Elvas, when the work of pillage commenced. Some—many indeed—of the good soldiers turned to the ditch of the castle and to the breaches to assist and carry off their wounded companions; but hundreds were neglected in the general and absorbing thirst for plunder.

The appearance of the castle was that of a vast wreck: the various ladders lying shattered at the base of its walls, the broken piles of arms, and the brave men that lay as they had fallen—many holding their firelocks in their grasp—marked strongly the terrible contest in which they had been engaged, and presented to the eye of a spectator ample food for reflection. It was not possible to look at those brave men, all of them dead or frightfully maimed, without recollecting what they had been but a few short hours before; yet those feelings, fortunately perhaps, do not predominate with soldiers, and those sights, far from exciting reflections of a grave nature, more usually call forth some jocular remark, such as, "that he will have no further occasion to draw rations;" or—"that he has stuck his spoon in the wall and left off messing,"—such is the force of habit.

At the breaches, the light and Fourth Division soldiers lay in heaps upon each other—a still warm group; and many of those veterans from whom the vital spark had not yet fled, expired in the arms of the few of their companions who sought to remove them to a place better suited to their miserable condition. But war, whatever its numerous attractions to a young mind may be, is but ill calculated to inspire it with those softer feelings so essential to soothe us in the moment of our distress; it must not, therefore, be wondered at, that a wish for plunder and enjoyment took the place of humanity, and that hundreds of gallant men were left to perish from neglect.

A military writer,[1] whose book has been the theme of admiration by all who have read it,—and I hope, for their own sakes, that there are few who have not,—in speaking of this epoch, says, that three days after the fall of the town he rode towards the Guadiana, and that in passing the verge of the camp of the Fifth Division, he was surprised and shocked to find two soldiers standing at the door of a small shed; they made signs to him, and upon examination he found that each had lost a leg! The surgeon had dressed their wounds on the night of the assault, and although their melancholy and destitute situation was known to hundreds of their companions, who had promised them relief, they were actually famishing within three hundred yards of their own regiment.

Before six o'clock in the morning of the 7th of April, all organisation amongst the assaulting columns had ceased, and a scene of plunder and cruelty, that it would be difficult to find a parallel for, took its place. The army, so fine and effective on the preceding day, was now transformed into a vast band of brigands, and the rich and beautiful city of Badajoz presented the turbulent aspect that must result from the concourse of numerous and warlike multitudes nearly strangers to each other, or known only by the same of the nation to which they belonged. The horde of vagabonds, Spaniards as well as Portuguese, women as well as men—that now eagerly sought for admission to plunder, nearly augmented the number of brigands to what the assailing army had reckoned the night before; and it may be fairly said that twenty thousand people—armed with full powers to act as they thought fit, and all, or almost all, armed with weapons which could be turned, at the pleasure or caprice

---

1. Captain Kincaid.

of the bearer, for the purpose of enforcing any wish he sought to gratify—were let loose upon the ill-fated inhabitants of this devoted city.

These people were under no restraint—had no person to control them, and in a short time got into such an awful state of intoxication that they lost all control over their own actions. What a frightful picture is this of a town carried by storm!—it is true, nevertheless, and unfortunately for the sake of humanity, it is considered necessary; because if such latitude was not allowed to the soldiery, I believe that few fortresses would be carried by assault; the alternative is not, however, the less painful. If the reader can for a moment fancy a fine city, containing an immense population, amongst which may be reckoned a proportion of the most beautiful women that Andalusia, or perhaps the world could boast of,—if he can fancy that population, and those females, left to the mercy of twenty thousand infuriated and licentious soldiers for two days and two nights,—if, I say, he can fancy this, he can well imagine the horrors that were acted within the walls of Badajoz.

In the first burst, all the wine and spirit stores were forced open and ransacked from top to bottom; and it required but a short time for the men to get into that fearful state that was alike dangerous to all—officers or soldiers, or the inhabitants of the city. Casks of the choicest wines and brandy were dragged into the streets, and when the men had drunk as much as they fancied, the heads of the vessels were stove in, or the casks otherwise so broken that the liquor ran about in streams.

In the town were a number of animals that belonged to the garrison, several hundred sheep, numerous oxen, as likewise many horses; these were amongst the first taken possession of; and the wealthy occupier of many a house was glad to be allowed the employment of conducting them to our camp, as, by doing so, he got away from a place where his life was not worth a minute's purchase; but terrible as was this scene, it was not possible to avoid occasionally laughing, for the *conducteur* was generally not only obliged to drive a herd of cattle, but also to carry the bales of plunder taken by his employers—perhaps from his own house—and the stately gravity with which the Spaniard went through his work, dressed in short breeches, frilled shirt, and a hat and plumes that might vie with our eighth Henry, followed, as he was, by our ragamuffin soldiers with fixed bayonets, presented a scene that would puzzle even Mr. Cruikshank himself to justly delineate. The plunder so captured was deposited in our camp, and placed under a guard chiefly composed of the soldiers' wives.

The shops were rifled, first by one group, who despoiled them of their most costly articles, then by another, who thought themselves rich in capturing what had been rejected by their predecessors; then another, and another still, until every vestige of property was swept away. A few hours were sufficient for this; night was fast drawing near, and then a scene took place that has seldom fallen to the lot of any writer to describe. Every insult, every infamy that human invention could torture into practice was committed. Age as well as youth was alike unrespected, and perhaps not one house, or one female, in this vast town, escaped injury: but war is a terrible engine, and, when once set in movement, it is not possible to calculate when or where it will stop.

Happy are those countries that have not been visited by its scourge; and grateful ought the nation to be that can boast of having had such an army and such a man as the Duke of Wellington, who, by his great genius as a general and steel-hardiness as a man—because nothing but the latter quality, in which, perhaps, he surpasses all ancient or modern heroes, could have enabled him or his army to remain in the Peninsula one day after the invasion of Portugal by the Prince of Esling, in 1810, have kept the British empire free from such a calamity. For the latter, everything that a sovereign and a nation could do has been done; but, the former—as a body—have met with nothing but—neglect.

The day of the eighth of April was also a fearful one for the inhabitants; the soldiers became reckless, and drank to such an excess, that no person's life, no matter of what rank, or station, or sex, was safe. If they entered a house that had not been emptied of all its furniture or wine, they proceeded to destroy it; or, if it happened to be empty, which was generally the case, they commenced firing at the doors and windows, and not unfrequently at the inmates, or at each other! They would then sally forth into the streets, and fire at the different church-bells in the steeples, or the pigeons that inhabited the old Moorish turrets of the castle—even the owls were frighted from this place of refuge, and, by their discordant screams, announced to their hearers the great revolution that had taken place near their once peaceful abodes.

The soldiers then fired upon their own comrades, and many men were killed, in endeavouring to carry away some species of plunder, by the hands of those who, but a few hours before, would have risked their own lives to protect those they now so wantonly sported with: then would they turn upon the already too deeply injured females, and tear from them the trinkets that adorned their necks, fingers, or ears!

And, finally, they would strip them of their wearing apparel. Some, 'tis said there were—ruffians of the lowest grade, no doubt—who cut the ear-rings out of the ears of the females who bore them, when they discovered a band of marauders approaching the unfortunate beings that were subjected to such brutal treatment, and whom they feared might anticipate them in their infamy; for here, as in all such disgraceful scenes, "might made right;" and the conduct of the soldiers during the sacking of Badajoz, is a sufficient proof, if such proof be wanting, of the dangers attendant upon anything where the multitude are allowed to think and act for themselves.

Hundreds of those fellows took possession of the best warehouses, and for a time fulfilled the functions of merchants; those, in their turn, were ejected by a stronger party, who, after a fearful strife and loss of lives, displaced them, and occupied their position, and those again were conquered by others, and others more powerful I and thus was Badajoz circumstanced on the morning of the 8th of April, 1812. It presented a fearful picture of the horrors that are inevitable upon a city carried by assault; and although it is painful to relate these disgraceful fads, it is essential nevertheless. All writers, no matter how insignificant they may be,—and I am willing to place myself at the bottom of the list of those persons,—should, in any detail which may lay claim to historical facts, be extremely cautious that they in no way mislead their readers; and in anything that I have ever written, or may hereafter write, I shall not deviate from this principle. I feel as much pride as any man can feel in having taken a part in actions that must ever shed lustre upon my country; but no false feeling of delicacy shall ever prevent me from speaking the truth—no matter whether it touches the conduct of one man or ten thousand!

To put a stop to such a frightful scene, it was necessary to use some forbearance, as likewise a portion of severity. In the first instance, parties from those regiments that had least participated in the combat were ordered into the town to collect the hordes of stragglers that filled its streets with crimes too horrible to detail; but the evil had spread to such an extent that this measure was inadequate to the end proposed, and in many instances the parties so sent became infected by the contagion, and in place of remedying the disorder, increased it, by joining once more in revels they had for a time quitted.

At length a brigade of troops was marched into the city, and were directed to stand by their arms while any of the marauders remained; the provost-marshals attached to each division were directed to use that authority with which they are of necessity invested. Gibbets and triangles were in consequence erected, and many men were flogged, but, although the contrary has been said, none were hanged—yet hundreds deserved it

A few hours, so employed, were sufficient to purge the town of the infamous gang of robbers that still lurked about its streets, and those ruffians—chiefly Spaniards or Portuguese, not in any way attached to the army—were infinitely more dangerous than our fellows, bad as they were. Murder—except indeed in a paroxysm of drunkenness, and in many cases, I regret to say, it did occur in this way,—never entered their thoughts, but the miscreants here referred to would commit the foulest deed for less than a dollar.

Towards evening tranquillity began to return, and, protected as they now were by a body of troops, untainted by the disease which had spread like a contagion, the unfortunate inhabitants took advantage of the quiet that reigned: yet it was a fearful quiet, and might be likened to a ship at sea, which after having been plundered and dismasted by pirates, is left floating on the ocean without a morsel of food to supply the wants of its crew, or a stitch of canvass to cover its naked masts; by degrees, however, some clothing, such as decency required, was procured for the females, by the return of their friends to the town; and many a father and mother rejoiced to find their children, who were still dearer to them than ever from the dangers they had escaped, alive, although it was impossible to hide from them the fact that they had been seriously and grossly injured.

But there were also many who were denied even this sad consolation, for numbers of the towns-people had fallen in the confusion that prevailed, some of our officers also were killed in this way, and it has been said, I believe truly, that one or two, one a colonel commanding a regiment, lost their lives by the hands of their own men.

These calamities are, however, the unavoidable attendants on war; and a great victory, gratifying as it unquestionably is to the general who achieves it, is not without its alloy, and brings forcibly to my recollection the fine reply of the Duke of Wellington after the battle of Waterloo, to a lady of great literary celebrity in Paris. This lady was amongst the many French who were at a ball given at the time the allied armies occupied Paris in 1815. She was most pointed in her attentions to the duke, and devoted almost her entire conversation to him in preference to the two Emperors, the King of Prussia, or the other distinguished allied generals.

"My lord," said she, in the course of conversation, "do you not think the gaining a great battle a delightful thing?"

"*Ne pensez vous pas, qu'une grande victoire est la plus agréable de toutes choses?*"

"Madam," replied the Duke, with a degree of coldness bordering on austerity, "I look upon it as the greatest calamity—except losing one!"

"*Je la regarde, Madame, comme le plus grand malheur—excepte une defaite!*"

It was a fine saying and worthy of him who uttered it.

The plunder with which our camp was now filled was so considerable, and of so varied a description, that numerous as were the purchasers, and different their wants, they all had, nevertheless, an opportunity of suiting themselves to their taste; still the sale had not commenced in form, although, like other markets, "some private sales were effected." From the door of my tent I had a partial view of what was taking place; but for the present, I shall leave the *marché*, and describe how I, myself, was circumstanced from the period I reached my tent, wounded, on the morning of the 7th.

The two faithful soldiers, Bray and McGowan, that conducted me there, on entering, found my truss of straw, or bed, if the reader will so allow me to designate it, occupied by Mrs. Nelly Carsons, the wife of my bâtman, who, I suppose, by the way of banishing care, had taken to drinking divers potations of rum to such an excess, that she lay down in my bed, thinking, perhaps, that I was not likely again to be its occupant; or, more probably, not giving it a thought at all. McGowan attempted to wake her, but in vain! a battery of a dozen guns might have been fired close to her ear without danger of disturbing her repose.

"Why then, sir," said he, "sure the bed's big enough for yees both, and these are no times to stand on saramony with another man's wife,—and she'll keep you nate and warm, for, be the powers, you're kilt with the cold and the loss ov blood."

I was in no mood to stand on ceremony, or, indeed, to stand at all; and I will venture to say that no man ever entered a bed occupied by the wife of another with a clearer conscience. I allowed myself to be placed beside my partner, without any further persuasion; and the two soldiers left us to ourselves, and returned to the town. Weakness from loss of blood soon caused me to fall asleep, but it was a sleep of short duration. I awoke, and saw the awkward dilemma in which I was placed. I was unable to move, and was completely at the mercy of Mistress Carsons, or any freak or gambol she might think fit to play.

I, in fact, lay like an infant The fire of small arms, the screams of the soldiers' wives, and the universal buzz throughout the camp, acted powerfully upon my nervous and worn-out frame; but having a clear conscience, and mine was certainly a clear one as far as regarded my bed-fellow at least,—Somnus conquered Mars,—at least he did so in my case, for I soon fell into another doze, in which I might have remained very comfortable had not my companion awoke sooner than I wished; discharging a huge grunt, and putting her hand upon my leg, she exclaimed, "Arrah I Dan, jewel, what makes you so stiff this morning?"

It required but few words from me to undeceive her. Tea and chocolate were soon in readiness, and having tasted some of the former, I sat up in my bed waiting the arrival of the first surgeon to dress my wound. My bâtman, Dan Carsons, shortly afterwards made his appearance; he led up to the door of my tent three sheep whose soft fleeces would not have disgraced the pen of Monsieur le Baron Torneaux, who sent to the mountains of Caucasus for a supply of rare sheep for the purpose of improving the French shawl manufactory. He had, moreover, a pig-skin of enormous size filled with right good wine which the Spaniards call *la tinta de la Mancha*: "And sure," said he, "I hard of your being kilt, and I brought you this (pointing to the pig-skin of wine), thinking what a nate bolster it I'd be for you while you slept at your aise;" and, without waiting for my reply, he thrust the pig-skin under my head.

"And look," said he, shewing me a spigot at the mouth of my bolster, "when you're thirsty at all at all, you see nothing is more pleasant or aisy than to clap this into your mouth, and sure won't it be mate and dhrink for you too?"

"Oh! Jasus!" responded Nelly, "he's kilt out and out; see, Dan, how the blood is in strames about the blankets."

A little learning is a dangerous thing,

so—under certain circumstances—is a little laughing I and Dan Carsons and his wife made me laugh so immoderately, that a violent discharge of blood from my wound nearly put an end to my career in this world. Had it not been for the arrival of Dr. Grant, the staff-surgeon of the division, who just now made his appearance, I doubt much if any of my readers would ever have had the pleasure of reading these my reminiscences. But I must have done with myself, Dan Carsons, and his wife Nelly; and resume my narrative of the sale of the plunder with which our camp was, to use a mercantile phrase, glutted.

Early on the morning of the 9th of April, a great concourse of Spaniards had already thronged our lines; the neighbouring villages poured in their quota of persons seeking to be the purchasers of the booty captured by our men, and each succeeding hour increased the supply for their wants, numerous and varied as they were, and our camp presented the appearance of a vast market. The scene after the taking of Rodrigo was nothing in comparison to the present, because the resources of Badajoz might be said to be in the ratio of five to one as compared with her sister fortress, and, besides, our fellows were, in an equal proportion, more dexterous than they had been in their maiden effort to relieve Rodrigo of its valuables. It may, therefore, be well supposed, and the reader may safely take my word for it, that the transfer of property was, on the present occasion, considerable.

Some men realized upwards of one thousand dollars (about 250/.), others less, but all, or almost all, gained handsomely by an enterprise in which they had displayed such unheard-of acts of devotion and bravery; and it is only to be lamented that they tarnished laurels so nobly won by traits of barbarity for which it would be difficult to find a parallel in the annals of any army. But such atrocities are ever the attendants upon anything where those, hitherto dependent upon their superiors—whose station in society enables them to be the most competent judges of what is proper— are allowed to think and act for themselves; and a licentious army, although not by the half so bad as a licentious mob, is nevertheless a terrible scourge.

The sale of the different commodities went on rapidly, notwithstanding we had no auctioneers; there was no "king's duty," but, most undeniably, if the Spaniards paid no "king's duty," they paid the piper! While the divers articles were carried away by the purchasers, the wounded were removed to the hospitals and camp, and the lamentations of the women for their dead or wounded husbands was a striking contrast to the scene of gaiety which almost everywhere prevailed.

Mr. Richard Martin, since a member of parliament, whom I before mentioned as having been a volunteer with the 88th, and as badly wounded while gallantly mounting one of the ladders against the castle wall, had with him his own private servant: it was not possible to persuade, this man that his master had not lost his senses, and his lamentations for the fate that had befallen him were of the most extravagant sort.

He would sit on a rising ground, that overlooked the town, and wringing his hands in an agony of grief exclaim, "Och! Jasus, so I was once more back in sweet Connamara, sure the divil himself wouldn't tempt me to lave it, but sure it was he—and none other!—that tempted my poor dear masthur to quit his twinty thousand good acres, with no one to lay claim to them at all at all; and now see how he's kilt with the rest, shriving to get the hoult ov a dirty spot that doesn't cover more ground than he'd give to a dacent boy for a potato-garden. Och! murther, murther!"

Martin's servant had decidedly good "ground" for his lamentations, because I believe, since the days of knight-errantry, never was there a parallel to his conduct. He came out as an amateur, but fulfilled the functions of a soldier, taking his tour of duty in the trenches, six hours out of the twenty-four; he was one of the foremost in the assault, and declined receiving a commission, which was offered him by the Duke of Wellington for his gallant conduct;— but he was unnoticed by General Picton, and what I now write of him is, I believe,, the first intimation the public, or perhaps many of his acquaintances, have of his conduct at Badajoz.

In any other army except the British, a thing of the sort would be blazoned forth, and the man who had so distinguished himself lauded, and deservedly so, by the general in command of the troops to which such a hero was attached; but it was not so, shamefully not so, with us: it was, however, only in keeping with the treatment— the chilling treatment—the 88th experienced for nearly four years of their services in the Peninsula. These observations, which I regret being obliged to make, lead me on to others, touching the gallant behaviour of some who fell unnoticed, and others who survive unrewarded.

Lieutenant Whitelaw, of the 88th, led the advance of the ladders; he lost his life in so doing, but his name nowhere appears, except in the list of killed! Lieutenant William Mackie, the neglected and discountenanced leader of the forlorn-hope at Rodrigo—was most conspicuous during the assault of the castle of Badajoz, and was one of the first—if not the very first, to enter it; yet no mention is made of him.

Captain Seton, commanding the regiment, and commanding such a fine fighting regiment as the 88th, on such an occasion too, got no rank—except in his turn. Lieutenant Macpherson, of the 45th, was the first to mount the round tower, upon the top of which floated the tri-coloured flag; he got a company, but the rest I have mentioned—all 88th men, were never even noticed; and although it would not be possible to reward every act of bravery in an army like the British, or in a regiment like the Connaught Rangers, it is, nevertheless, chilling to those who have deserved it, and enough to damp any ardour in those who may follow in their footsteps, to know that such facts as I write have taken place.

In the space of three short months, the following officers of the 88th were passed over,—their services unrewarded,—and they were not even noticed by their general. The first of these was Major Thomson, commanding the battalion at the storming of Rodrigo; the second, Lieutenant William Mackie, leading the forlorn-hope; the Third, Lieutenant Whitelaw, leading the advance of the ladders at Badajoz; the fourth, Captain Oates, in the attack of La Picurina; and the fifth, Captain Seton, commanding the regiment on the night of the storming of Badajoz.

Surely a change should be made in the system, or how can a regiment, much less an army, be supposed to work with goodwill? When, in after-times, the details of these eventful epochs shall be read, if any person was bold enough to state that such a series of slights had been put upon the brave men who bore so conspicuous a share in their accomplishment, would he not be looked upon as a fool or madman? Undoubtedly he would; but as the writer of this work conceives himself to be neither the one nor the other, he gives them to the army and the world, and he challenges any person to disprove one scintilla of what he says. There are many still alive who have taken a part in those memorable combats; and the writer feels confident that they will bear him out in what he asserts.

Towards the evening of the 9th, our camp was nearly emptied of all its saleable commodities, and the following morning was occupied in getting rid of the many Spaniards who still hovered about us, endeavouring to get a bargain of some of the unsold articles. By noon, all traffic had ceased, and the men began to arrange themselves for a fresh combat with Marshal Soult, who was advancing towards Badajoz. The appearance and demeanour of the soldiery in no way warranted the idea that they had been occupied as they were for the last three weeks, but more especially for the last three days. They were the same orderly set of men they had been before the attack on the town, and were just as eager to fight Soult as they were to storm Badajoz: the only change visible was their thinned ranks. In my regiment alone, out of seven hundred and fifty privates, four hundred and thirty-four had fallen; and of the officers, who, at the commencement of the siege counted twenty-four, but five remained unhurt!

The wounded by this time were all brought to the different hospitals; and those of the dead, which had not been drowned in the ditch near the breaches, or at the Ravelin of San Roque, were buried; and but few paces were to be found that did not show traces of the grave-digger's hand. The men of the Connaught Rangers, or, as they called themselves, "the Boys," had, nevertheless, their joke, and the merits and demerits of the enterprise were regularly canvassed by them.

The following conversation, which I am about to relate, will give the reader a slight insight into the view they took of the matter. Ten or a dozen of "the boys" had got together near my tent, where I still lay wounded, and after they had made themselves tolerably comfortable over a large camp-kettle of spiced wine, one of them—a man of my own company—named Paddy Aisy, having fairly discussed the merits of the contents of the camp-kettle, began to give his opinion of our late operations.

"Well!" said he, "now ids all past and gone, and wasn't it the divil's own dthroll business, the taking that same place; and wasn't Long-nose (meaning the. Duke of Wellington) a quare lad to sthrive to get into it, seeing how it was definded! But what else could he do, afther all? didn't he recave ordhers to do it; and didn't he say to us all, 'Boys,' says he, 'ids myself that's sorry to throuble yees upon this dirty arrand; but we must do it, for all that; and iv yees can get into it, by hook or by crook, be the powers, id 'ill be the making ov yees all—and ov me too!' and didn't he spake the thruth?

"'Sure,' says he, 'did I ever tell yees a lie, or spake a word to yees that wasn't as thrue as the Gospil? and, iv yees folly my direction, there's nothin can bate yees?' And sure, afther we got in, was he like the rest, sthriving to put us out before we divarted ourselves?

"Not he, faith. It was be that spoke to the 'boys' dacently, 'Well, boys,' says he, when he met myself and a few more aising a house ov a thrifle, 'well, boys,' says he *(for he knew the* button,) 'God bless your work! ids myself that's proud to think how complately yees tuck the concate out ov the Frinch 88th, in the castel last night'

"'Why, Sir,' says I (forgettin to call him my Lord,) 'the divil a *Frinch* Connaught Ranger ever was born that the Irish Connaught Rangers isn't able to take the concate out ov;' and ids what he said upon the same, splitting his sides with laffin, that it was thrue for me there wasn't; and blur-an-ouns, boys, aint he the man to stand by? Don't he take the rough and the smooth with us, and wouldn't it be a pitty not to give him his dew? don't he expose himself to the wet and the could with us, lie out on the grass at night, like any other baste? and ain't he afthur kicking the French before him, just as we'd kick an old football? Be the powers, whin I see him commin next or nigh me, my heart gets so big that my body isn't big enough to hould it, and it jumps up clane into my throat—to get room! And don't think that I'm romancin, when I tell yees how he said we tuck the concate out ov the Frinch 88th; he said every word ov it, and more too—iv I could repate it in his own words."

"Why," replied Corney Fagan, "what you say is parfectly thrue; we ought to stand by him,—and didn't we? Sure yees remember how Misther Mackie ran up the laddher as nimble as a cat, and poor Misther Martin thought to do the same, till he was kilt! and didn't Captain Seton owe his life to his being so thin that the French couldn't hit him? and whin we have such a man to direct us, and such officers to lade us on, why, what else can we do but folly them through thick and thin?"

The sound of the drum for roll-call put a stop to any further colloquy; but rude as was the dialect, and homely the language, much might be gathered from it. It gave to the hearer the unsophisticated opinion of those men, whose deeds, in a great measure, tended to settle the European contest What was uttered by those few obscure individuals, in their own rude phraseology, was the opinion of the entire army; and they who would strive to efface those impressions, which were imprinted upon the hearts of the Peninsular soldiery might as well try to efface the sun from the heavens.

While we were occupied as I have described at Badajoz, Soult was busied in collecting a force sufficient to ensure the safety of that city. On the 1st of April, placing himself at the head of 25,000 men, he broke up from Seville; on the 8th he arrived at Villa-Franca, only two marches distant from Badajoz, but yet two days after its capture. Mortified beyond measure at this unlooked-for misfortune, he wished to press onward, and, by a brilliant success, wipe away the disgrace; but he was in no condition to act as his zeal prompted him, because his own force was inadequate to the task;

and Marmont, instead of co-operating with him, frittered away his time before Rodrigo and Almeida, or in the dispersion of a few thousand wretched Portuguese militia.

The bulk of our covering army being thus under no apprehension of molestation, passed the Guadiana, and established itself on the right bank of that river. Soult retired back upon Seville, and Marmont, closely pressed by our horse, retired upon Salamanca. Thus terminated our operations before Badajoz, which, as may be seen, were of no common description. Four thousand prisoners, a considerable quantity of ammunition, with one hundred and seventy-two pieces of cannon, and one hundred thousand shot, were found in the place. Our loss exceeded five thousand men; and although no officer of a higher rank than colonel was killed, it is a singular circumstance that every general was wounded on the night of the assault.

Picton, Colville, Kempt, Walker, and Bowes, all heading either brigades or divisions, were wounded; yet the men, notwithstanding, went through their work well; which proves what I have always said, and said from long experience, and an intimate knowledge of the materials which compose our army, that troops storming a breach are as well, if not better, when left to their own officers. A soldier of the old Peninsular army (but where can we again expect to see, during our sojourn in this world, such a specimen of what a true British soldier should be?) was ever ready to lay down his life when opposed to the enemy—and what more can any man do? But the countless gallant exploits that have been achieved by our army in Portugal and Spain, without the aid of generals, are sufficient to illustrate the truth of what I have frequently repeated.

All writers who have written upon the taking of Badajoz, whether French or English, agree that it was one of the best connected, one of the most gallant, as well as one of the most bloody, exploits recorded in history. So secret were the arrangements of Lord Wellington before he invested the place, and so prompt and straightforward his operations after he had taken that step, that we are at a loss whether most to admire his strategy or daring. Even Soult himself, the most celebrated of Napoleon's captains, was under no apprehension for the safety of this fortress. Count Phillipon's fine defence of it the preceding year, a garrison of six thousand men, and the formation of numerous outworks, appeared to be a sufficient guarantee for his confidence.

The place was, moreover, amply provisioned for three months; and all these causes, if to be combated by another sort of man than he who was at the head of the British army, would have been sufficient to insure the safety of the place; but, as it was, they only made its loss the more certain, because Soult, with that presumption which scarcely any Frenchman can divest himself of, relied too firmly on his own dispositions, and the quality of his soldiers, while he held those of his antagonist, as well as the sort of troops which be commanded, at too cheap a rate: his mortification must, therefore, have been at the greatest height, when he found himself out-generalled by the one and out-fought by the other.

General Lery, chief engineer of Soult's army, and who superintended the arrangements for the defence of Badajoz, was so utterly confounded upon hearing of its fall, that he wrote to General Kellerman respecting its capture.

> "The conquest of Badajoz," said he, "costs me eight engineers. I am not yet acquainted with the details of that fatal event. Never was there a place in a better state, better supplied, and better provided with the requisite number of troops. There is in that event a marked fatality. I confess my .inability to account for its bad defence. Very extensive works have been constructed: all our calculations have been disappointed; and Lord Wellington, with his Anglo-Portuguese troops, has taken the place, as it were, in the presence of two armies, amounting together to about eighty thousand men. In short, I think the capture of Badajoz a very extraordinary event"—(and he was right)—"and I should be much at a loss to account for it in a clear and distinct manner."

Now this is plain speaking, and says more in praise of our men than any British writer could do; but the air of mystery which Monsieur Lery strives to throw over the affair is amusing enough. No person can deny that the French are good troops, and that at this same siege they fought well; and there cannot be a shadow of doubt,—at least there is none on my mind,—but that they would have been successful, had not our men fought better than they did; and thus may the mystery be solved.

Note.—Attack and Capture of Badajoz, 6th April, 1812, taken from the Journal of Lieutenant Parr Kingsmill, 88th Regiment.

The French were collecting an overpowering force at one of the gates of this citadel, apparently with an intention of charging and driving us from the ramparts. They had already opened a most galling fire of musketry from this dark gateway, which was warmly returned by our soldiers, whose impetuosity could no longer be restrained, and they charged through the gateway led on by my gallant friend Lieutenant Davern, of the 88th Regiment, and were received by a shower of balls; but the massive gate being closed, little impression was made. A second and Third charge was likewise made without effect, when a number of light infantry of the 74th and 88th Regiments assisted each other in climbing up on the archway over the gate, and opened such a destructive and unexpected fire down on the French, who thought themselves quite secure on the other side, that a general panic seized them and they fled with the utmost precipitation and confusion, followed rapidly by our men, who now dashed through, the gateway without opposition. A great many gallant fellows fell at this trying moment.

(Signed)   P. Kingsmill,]   Lieut. 88th Regiment.

From United Service Journal, 3rd vol. 1837.

CHAPTER 21

Movements of Marshal Marmont

On the 10th of April, 1812, the heroes of Badajoz took a last farewell of the scene of their glory and the graves of their fallen companions, and marched towards the banks of the Coa and Agueda, where, but a few months before, they had given proofs of their invincible valour. Indeed it might be said, without any great stretch of historical truth, that every inch of ground upon which they trod was a silent evidence of their right to be its occupant—so far, at least, as right of conquest goes.

Ill as I was, in common with many others, who, like myself, lay wounded, and were unable to accompany our friends, I arose from my truss of straw to take a parting look at the remnant of my regiment as it mustered on the parade; but, in place of upwards of seven hundred gallant soldiers, and four-and-twenty officers, of the former there were not three hundred, and of the latter but five!

At any time, when in the full enjoyment of health and vigour, this sad diminution would have affected me; but in my then frame of mind it acted powerfully upon my nerves. I asked myself, where are the rest? I suppose I spoke louder than I intended; for my man, Dan Carsons, ran out of his tent to inquire "who I was looking after?"

"Dan," I replied, "I am looking for the men that are absent from parade; where are they?"

"Kilt, sir," replied Dan, "and the greater part of them buried at the fut of the ould castle forenent ye."

"Their bodies are there, Dan, but where are they themselves?"

"Och, Jasus!" cried Dan to his wife, "he's out of his sinces! Nelly! run and fetch the pigskin of wine; you know how it sarved him last night when he was raving."

Nelly brought the remnant of the Tinto-de-la-Mancha, and a few mouthsfull of it raised my spirits considerably, but the fever with which I was attacked was increasing rapidly.

The drums of the division beat a ruffle; the officers took their stations; the bands played; the soldiers cheered, and, in less than half an hour, the spot which, since the 17th of the preceding month, had been a scene of the greatest excitement, was now a lone and deserted waste, having no other occupants than disabled or dying officers and soldiers, or the corpses of those who had fallen in the strife. The contrast was indeed great, and of that cast that made the most unreflecting think, and the reflecting feel. The sound of the drums died away; the division was no longer visible, except by the glittering of their firelocks: at length we lost sight of even this; and we were left alone, like so many outcasts, to make the best of our way to the hospitals in Badajoz.

It is a task of more difficulty than may appear to the reader, to describe the feelings that a separation, such as I have told of, caused in our breasts. Five-sixths of our old companions—dear to us from the intimate terms upon which we had lived together, fought together, and, I might say, died together, for three years, were parted from us, most of them forever!—the others gone to a distant part of the theatre of war, while we, enervated and worn down, either by loss of limb, or by loss of strength and vigour, were left to seek shelter under the roofs of those very people who had been so barbarously maltreated by our own soldiers.

Nevertheless every one betook himself to the method he thought best suited to the occasion. Some caused themselves to be conveyed in wagons; others rode on horseback; and many, from a disinclination to bear the jolting of the carts, or the uneasy posture of sitting astride a horse, hobbled on towards the dismantled walls of the fortress. As we continued our walk, we met, at almost every step, heaps of newly turned-up earth, beneath which lay the bodies of some of our companions; and a little farther in advance was the olive-tree, at the foot of which so many officers of the Third Division had been buried. At length we reached the ravelin of San Roque.

The Talavera gate was opened for our admission; it was guarded by a few ill-looking, ill-fed, and ill-appointed Spanish soldiers. As we entered, each man we passed saluted us with respect; but the contrast between these men, who were now our protectors, and the soldiers we had but a short time before commanded, was great indeed; and the circumstance, trifling as it may appear, affected us proportionably. We walked on towards our wretched billets; and, as we passed through the streets that led to them, we saw nothing but the terrible traces of what had taken place.

Piles of dismantled furniture lay scattered here and there; houses, disfigured by our batteries, in a ruined state; the streets unoccupied, except by vagabonds of the lowest grade, who prowled about in search of plunder; while at the windows of some houses were to be seen a few females in disordered dresses; but their appearance was of that caste that served rather to increase the gloom which overhung the city. Nevertheless, as the wounded men and officers passed, they waved their handkerchiefs and saluted us with a *viva;* but it was pitiable to witness the wretched state to which the unfortunate inhabitants had been reduced.

Upon reaching the house allotted to me, I was met at the door by an old woman, who showed me my apartment. It was scantily garnished with furniture, most of which was broken: the bed was on the tiles, but that was rather an advantage than the contrary, because the heat was excessive. I stood in no need of any refreshment; my man, Dan, having been so active during the *bouleversement,* that be supplied my cellar as well as larder; and it was fortunate that he did so: for the inhabitants of the house, as I afterwards learned, were without a morsel of food, or a stitch of clothing, having been plundered of everything.

I lay down upon my mattress, soon fell asleep, and, in less than an hour, awoke in a high fever. Dan wished that I should attack the pig-skin of the Tinta-de-la-Mancha, but I positively refused to do so: "Why then, sir," said he, "hasn't it been the making ov yee?"

"You mean the killing of me, Dan. Go and seek for a surgeon."

He went, and soon returned with a young man, in the uniform of the staff surgeons of our army; but, from his youthful appearance, and the unworkmanlike manner he went about dressing my wound, I opine he was but an hospital mate. My man Dan was decidedly of my opinion; for after the doctor had examined my breast, and applied some dressing to it, he was about to retire, when Dan said, with an air of authority, "You're not going to be afthur going, without looking at his hinder part?" meaning my back.

The doctor took the hint, and, turning me on my face, found a large piece of the cloth of my coat, which had been carried in by the ball, protruding through the wound. The doctor looked confounded; Dan looked ferocious, and, though he spoke with respect to the medical man, I plainly saw the storm which was gathering. I feared that he was about to make use of the *forliter in re,* in preference to the *suaviter in modo;* so I dismissed the doctor, upon an assurance that he would visit me the following morning.

After a lapse of three days, all the wounded capable of being removed were ordered to Elvas. Spring wagons, carts drawn by oxen, mules harnessed with pack-saddles, and in default of them, asses prepared in like manner, were put in requisition, for the purpose of freeing Badajoz of as many of the disabled men who crowded the hospitals, as possible. I was among the number, but so ill was I, as to have no recollection of how I was transported, except that a wagon stopped at my door, and, after some hours, finding myself in the streets of Elvas. From the wagon I was placed in a car, and it was night before my man Dan, with all his tact, was enabled to procure me a billet During a space of fifteen days I lay in a state of great pain, accompanied by fever, but after that I soon recovered my strength, and being allowed the option of either joining the second battalion of my regiment, to which I then belonged, quartered at home, or going back to the army, I preferred the latter.

On the 25th of April, the troops that had carried on the siege were at Alfyates, on the Portuguese frontier, the army of the Duke of Raguza having retired before them. That general had repassed the Agueda on the 23rd, and was in full march towards the Tormes. Drouet was at Fuente Ovejuna, near Cordova, and Soult back again at Seville.

The situation of the Imperial army, the want of union amongst their generals, and the panic with which both had been Infected by the fall of Badajoz, afforded Lord Wellington a fine opportunity of profiting by the disease which had infected all—marshal, general, and soldier! He accordingly sent orders to General Hill to take advantage of the confusion that prevailed in the enemy's councils—

to march with the necessary number of troops to the bridge of Almarez, on the Tagus, and to destroy the fortifications which the French had, at great pains and expense, erected at that point.

It was not until the middle of May that General Hill was enabled to arrange his troops in that order which was necessary to guarantee his success, and the difficulties to be surmounted were so great, that the general did not reach the point of attack before the 19th. The fort named "Napoleon" was the first carried at the point of the bayonet; the castle of Mirabeta shared the same fate; both were scaled with ladders, and the troops, under a destructive fire, passed through the works, driving the enemy before them in such disorder, that many, in a vain effort to escape to the fort of Ragusa, on the opposite bank of the river, were lost in the stream, and the panic communicating to the troops in the latter fort, which ought to have sustained the rest, increased the confusion, and all crowded in one disordered mass to the nearest point of safety, abandoning those works, which, if well defended, were capable of resisting three times the number of those that assailed them. Thus were thirteen pieces of artillery and three hundred prisoners taken; three formidable forts rendered useless, and the command of the passage of the Tagus by Almarez lost to the enemy. It is not easy to account for this dastardly conduct of the French commandant, who, it is said, was afterwards tried at Talavera and shot by the sentence of a court-martial.

It may appear to the reader, acquainted with the position of those formidable forts,—doubly formidable from their distance from the scene of action,—to have been an enterprise that might be termed rash, but he must take into account the *morale* of the troops that attacked, and those that defended the pass. It is true that a fort strongly fortified and secure against a *coup-de-main,* and a fort of that nature that guns could not be brought to bear against, was a hazardous trial. Almarez is forty leagues from Badajoz—it required a march of eight days to reach;—Hill's forces did not count more than ten thousand, while the French General Drouet, at the head of twenty thousand veteran troops, could have, in a march of four days, by occupying Torremancha and Cauras, placed himself between Hill and Badajoz. Had the latter general remained one day longer on the Tagus, his corps would have been destroyed, but, aware of his critical situation, he lost not a moment in retracing his steps. He dismantled the forts, destroyed the bridge, retired upon Truxillo, and finally reached his original position before the success of his enterprise was known in the Imperial army.

The capture of these forts created much perplexity in the councils of the French marshals. Soult ordered Drouet to advance towards Medilen, while Marmont directed a corps to move to the left bank of the Tagus, to co-operate with Soult's troops in the reconstruction of the bridge. So occupied I shall leave the two marshals, and return back to Elvas.

Such officers and soldiers as were able and willing to join the army were directed to hold themselves in readiness to do so; such as were obliged to go to Lisbon, and finally to England, were similarly placed; and such as were to remain, namely, the disabled, from loss of limb, or a worn-out constitution in the service, had no choice, left them but to rest quietly where they were, and take their chance for the first casual "turn-up" that might release them from their unpleasant situation. Amongst the first class I was one; four days were allowed us to make our arrangements, and to say the truth, as far as regarded myself at least, as many hours would have sufficed.

My friends, Darcy and Adair, were my companions on my route to the army; and, punctual at the appointed hour, we left Elvas at six o'clock on the morning of the 3rd of June, without any incumbrance, such as a detachment to look after. We had no escort except our three servants, and Dan's wife Nelly; and it is needless to say that they were perfectly competent to take care of themselves, without causing us one moment's uneasiness, either on their account or our own; and never did any three officers in the service of His Britannic Majesty, or in the service of any other sovereign, set out on a route to join their companions with a more fervent intention of making the time pass as agreeably as possible.

Our route towards Salamanca, near which city the army was stationed, lay through the old line of march, and we were obliged; unfortunately, once more to encounter that place of dirt and wretchedness, Niza. No matter what change had taken place either amongst ourselves or the different towns through which we passed, Niza was still the same; positively dirt,—comparatively dirt,—superlatively dirt!—dirt! dirt! dirt! The ditches were filled with reptiles, the houses with bugs and fleas, and Adair, who was already blind of one eye, had the other nearly darkened by the bite of a huge centipede. We poulticed his eye with rye bread and cold water, and in the morning carried him, with a wry face, to his saddle.

Once clear of Niza, we traversed the country towards the Spanish frontier; at length we got clear of Portugal, and once more reached the village of Fuentes d'Onor; every house, I might almost say every face, was familiar to me. The heaps of embanked earth which denoted the places where many of our old companions had been interred, were covered with grass, which grew luxuriantly over the graves of the men who had once stood there victorious, but who were now lifeless clay. We traversed the churchyard, where so many of the Imperial Guard and our Highlanders had fallen; and we marked well the street where three hundred of the former had been put to death by the 88th Regiment. Many of the doors still retained the marks of the contest; and the chimneys, up which the Guard had sought shelter, bore the traces of what had taken place. The torn apertures in the large twigged chimneys, broken down by the Guard in attempting to get up them, were in the same state we had left them,—untouched—unmended. Even the children could trace, with accuracy, the footsteps of those fallen heroes.

We walked on to the chapel wall, where the 79th had suffered so severely, and through which the French had forced their passage, under a torrent of shot, against the bayonets of the brave Highlanders. The chapel door was riddled through and through with bullets, and the walls bore the marks of the round shot fired from the French batteries. Several mounds of earth, covered as they were with herbage, still pointed out the grave of someone who had fallen; yet, to a passing stranger, the inequality of the ground would scarcely have been noticed, so little attention bad been paid to the arrangement of the graves, which were dug in the hurry of the moment; but with us it was different.

We could point out every spot, and lay our finger on the place where a grave ought to be found; but even in this sad duty we were disappointed, because a drove of wild pigs, from the adjoining forests, a day or two after the battle, and before the inhabitants had ventured to return to the town, found their way to the scene of action, and rooted up many of the graves—devouring all that came in their way. Many bodies were thus torn up, and the places that contained them, as a matter of course, were levelled, and arranged as they had been before the battle.

It so happened that the house I was quartered in for the night, was one of those in which some of the Imperial Guard had sought shelter. I asked my patron why he had not mended the broken chimney. His reply was, that he preferred the inconvenience of the smoke, which the aperture caused, for the pleasure he derived from viewing the grave, as he termed it, of the base French who had so scandalously ravaged his country. I cannot say that I much admired this feeling, the more so, as I well remembered the dastardly part the inhabitants had taken in the defence of the town, and I could not but feel that their detestation of the French might have been better shown on the day of trial, than by a posthumous recollection of it

Captain Kincaid, of the Rifles, in his amusing book, says something about the difference between Spain and Portugal, and likens the leaving the latter, and getting into the former, as a step from the coal-hole to the drawing-room. No doubt it is, but I am of opinion that the Portuguese, with all their dirt, are more in character than their neighbours; they suit the action to the object—the collecting of vermin: they suit their dress—a garb of filth—to the same purpose; but it is too ridiculous to see a Castilian, with his broad-brimmed hat, out-topped with a plume of feathers, leathern belt with a huge knife, and oftentimes a sword stuck in it, officiating as a master of the ceremonies in those obsequies to the dead!

Can anyone for a moment reconcile it to himself as at all consistent, to see a huge cavalier, dressed as I have described, and caparisoned *à la Henri Quatre,* superintending the picking away vermin from his children, and often submitting to the same ordeal himself? The thing is preposterous, and deserves to be scouted. The Portuguese are a filthy race, no doubt, but they have one merit, and it is the only one I can give them—namely,—that they feel and seem to know themselves to be a dirty race, and do not pretend to what their neighbours do, by any affectation of false pride in a matter in which both are equally involved—dirt

Of the relative merits of each nation, as to bravery, I profess myself to be ignorant; but I am certain that our newspaper writers have devoted too great a space in recording the merits of both. I never saw a Spanish battalion exposed to fire: the Portuguese I have seen, and I can say nothing in their favour, notwithstanding all that has been written in their praise; but in the matter at issue between the Spanish nation, the Portuguese, and myself, namely—filth, I decidedly give my voice in favour of the Portuguese, and for this reason, that they are more in keeping, and presume nothing; while their neighbours would wish to make you suppose them the very acme of perfection. If you ask a Portuguese shopkeeper for a thing he may not have, he will tell you that he has it not; but will add, with a shrug of his shoulders, "You can get it at Lisbon."

Ask a Spaniard the same question, and if he cannot accommodate you, he will refer you to Madrid; but he will add, "*Donde esta Madrid, calle il mundo;*" the plain English of which modest sentiment is, "Where Madrid is, let the world be silent"

From Fuentes d'Onor we reached Rodrigo, which we had left only five months before. The breaches were repaired, the trenches levelled, and were it not for the different spots that had been assigned to many of our fallen companions, which we found untouched, there, was no trace of those works which had caused us so much time and labour to construct But those places, well known to us, brought back to our recollection the ground upon which we had stood a short time before under circumstances so different; and the change that had taken place during the short interval,—the thousands that had fallen in the two sieges,—and the difference of our attitude as compared to what it was when we before trod the spot we were then standing upon, afforded ample food for reflection.

From the period of our investment of Rodrigo to the capture of Badajoz, that is to say, twenty-six days, we lost, in my regiment alone, twenty-five officers and five-hundred and fifty-six men; and it cannot be wondered at, that we, who were alive and in health, should have a feeling of regret for our less fortunate companions, as also a feeling of thankfulness for our own escape.

There may be some who will think that such ideas are out of place, but, in my opinion, they are not so. No truly brave man ever looked upon the graves of his fallen companions without a feeling of regret A man falling in the heat of battle is quite a different thing, because there all are alike, and subject to the same chance; and it is, moreover, wrong to mourn over the death of a comrade while the strife is going on; but the strife once ended, then will the feelings be brought into play, and the man who is incapable of a pang of regret for his fallen companion is unworthy of the name of a British soldier.

My man, Dan, had scarcely arranged my billet, ere I bent my steps to the house where I had slept on the night of the storming of the town. I had scarcely made my appearance at the portal, when the old lady to whom the house belonged, recognised my voice. She ran forward to meet and welcome me,—her daughters accompanied her, and it was in vain that I said I had a billet in a distant part of the town. The excuse would not be taken, and I was forced, absolutely forced, to have my baggage conveyed to the house where I had so short a time before entered under far different circumstances. The old lady asked how long I was to remain at Rodrigo. I replied, for that night only.

"*J'en suis fâché*" she replied in French, which language she spoke tolerably well,— "*mais j'essayerai de faire votre séjour ici plus agréable qu'elle ne l'etait la dernière fois;*"—and she immediately sent an invitation to her friends to assemble at her house the same evening.

Profiting by the confusion, which of necessity took place in arrangements for the *soirée,* I left the house and took a survey of the town and breaches. The houses which were destroyed in the Great Square by the fire which had taken place on the night of the assault, as also those near the breaches, remained in the same ruined state we had left them; but excepting this, and a few gabions which outtopped the large breach, whose reconstruction had not been quite completed, we could find nothing to denote the toil and labour we had sustained during our operations.

An hour sufficed for me to make my "reminiscence" of past events: it was eight o'clock before Darcy and Adair joined me, and when we reached my billet, we found the saloon filled by a large and varied company.

Upon entering the room, all eyes were turned towards us, for the good hostess had said a thousand kind things in my praise, and the height and imposing look of Darcy were in themselves sufficient to cause a stare; but the elegance of Adair's manners, who had passed the greater part of his life on the Continent,— his perfect knowledge of the Portuguese, Spanish, Italian, and French languages, captivated all. And although he was some fifteen or twenty years our senior, he decidedly bore away the palm; and in less than an hour after our *entré,* he made, to my own knowledge, five conquests; while Darcy and myself could boast of but two each! I never felt so humiliated,—and from that moment, I resolved that if ever I had a son, I would make him a linguist.

It is not possible to describe the advantage one man possesses over another in society by a knowledge of languages; but if he can tack to that, a knowledge of music, with anything at all bordering on pretensions to good looks, —or what is, in the long run, of more consequence—good manners—(but where will the man be found possessing the former qualities, without having attained the latter?)—then goodbye to any man who is bold enough to enter the lists against him. He may do so, no doubt,—rank and fortune are formidable antagonists to encounter—but no matter, in nine cases out of ten the young accomplished man will have it all his own way; that is, if he is as he should be, a gentleman, a gentleman by birth, and a gentleman in the full acceptation of the word. Let him have these qualifications, and I will forfeit my existence that he will put an extinguisher upon those dolts who enter the army without any other claims except fortune and connexion.

The ball was opened by Avandano de Alcantaro, a young Portuguese captain, belonging to the garrison of Almeida, and Señora Dolares de Inza, a Spanish lady, a relative of the governor. The dance was the *bolero*, of which I had heard so much, but had never seen danced before. All eyes were turned towards the spot which the youthful couple occupied. I was an attentive spectator. Avandano danced well, and kept his elbows—a material point by the way—in that position which no *bolero* dancer should depart from, (I obtained this information at Madrid,) not to raise them higher than his ear; but he danced mechanically, like one that had been taught, and had his lesson by rule more than by heart.

Although he moved his arms with much grace, and kept the proper measure with his feet, there was nothing inspiring in his mode of dance, or in the manner he used his castanettes. His partner, on the contrary, had all the fire of the true Andalusian breed.

Her movements, though not perhaps as correct as his, were spirited, and drew down thunders of applause from the spectators; and each plaudit, as was natural, caused her to increase her exertions. She danced beautifully, and every one expressed by their approbation the gratification they felt by her display; but the dance had scarcely ended when she fainted away, in consequence, no doubt, of the exertions she had made.

She soon recovered, and would have once more joined the dance, had not her friends dissuaded her from so foolish an act, and she was reluctantly obliged to be a spectator for the remainder of the night Waltzing was continued to a late hour; but there was no lady hardy enough to attempt the bolero after the success of Señora Dolares in this most difficult and graceful dance. The company at length retired to their different homes: I bade an affectionate good-night to my hostess and her daughters; and, long before they were awake in the morning, I was several miles on the road leading to Salamanca.

On the opening of the campaign of 1812, Lord Wellington found himself formally invested with the chief command of the allied armies; a command, by the way, not exactly as real as onerous. After the fall of Badajoz, the head-quarters were established at Funeda, which town the first division reached in the end of April; and from that period until the beginning of June, every effort that could be made to reorganise and recruit the army was exerted. On the 13th, it arrived upon the banks of the Agueda, which river it passed the same day, and on the 16th it was within two gunshots of Salamanca. The following day, the 17th, my two companions, Darcy and Adair, and myself, joined our old regiment on the heights of San Christoval.

Upon the approach of the British army, the Duke of Ragusa retired, leaving, nevertheless, a garrison of one thousand troop in three forts, which had been constructed around some convents. He halted five leagues from Salamanca, when, having collected several divisions, he again advanced to succour the forts. Lord Wellington invested the town with the sixth division, and, with the remainder of the army, awaited, upon the heights of San Christoval, the development of the enemy's movement.

On the following day, Marmont made a reconnaissance, by

which he found that at all points the post occupied by the British army was of that nature that forbade his attempting to force it After some outpost fighting, in which a brigade of the first division, directed by General Graham, gained an advantage, the French army once more retired to the village of Cabere Velossa, where, by signals agreed upon, the situation of the forts was hourly made known to it.

The batteries against the forts opened their fire on the 17th, but so imperfect were the means of attack, and so languid their fire, that it was six days before the breach against one called Saneayatons was deemed practicable. At nine o'clock at night, on the 23rd, the brigade of General Bowes attacked the outwork; the general headed his troops, and fell wounded at the onset; but the moment his wound was dressed, he again returned to his men, and fell, with many of his soldiers, in a vain attempt to carry the fort.

Marmont was intimately acquainted with the events that were passing. The signals from the forts informed him they could hold out but five days longer; and in this distressing state of affairs he made up his mind, in a moment of despair, to pass over to the left bank of the Tonnes—but for what end? An army which proposed him battle on the right bank of the river could with as much ease fight him on the opposite side; but he, too late, found out the error he had committed, in leaving a garrison of one thousand men, which he could so ill spare, in forts incapable of any very long resistance; and, by a well-meant effort to correct the error, had well nigh sacrificed his army in their passage of the river, because Lord Wellington, weighing well the troops of his adversary, and foreseeing what he was likely to try, changed his front, brought forward his left wing, and with the right of the army, under Graham, was in battle array on the left of the Tormes, at two o'clock on the morning of the 24th inst, at the moment Marmont was effecting the passage of that river at Alla de Tormes. Finding himself so opposed, Marmont hastily retraced his steps, and retired upon Huerta, where he remained until the 27th, and then retreated towards the Douro.

It was asked at the time—has since been asked—and will perhaps be asked in after times, why did not Lord Wellington attack an army so ill placed by its General? It would ill become me, a subaltern, and one who, in anything he writes, endeavours only to amuse his readers, to enter into an argument that can be discussed with more propriety by those persons who write an account of the Peninsular war, than by one who only writes his own reminiscences, which can never be supposed, or are meant, to be anything more than a few facts collected together from memory, and which, not having been known, or perhaps not thought worthy of insertion by those who have preceded him, are given to the public in the hope that they may not be thought uninteresting.

It would be, nevertheless, wrong not to give the opinions of those who it is to be presumed were, or at all events thought themselves, competent to criticise the conduct of the two commanders. Sarrazin, in his *memoir*, says:

> Why did not his Lordship attack him on the 24th of June, when the French General had so foolishly ventured to the left bank of the Tonnes? To say that his Lordship was besieging the forts of Salamanca is an idle answer. Eight hundred men might have been kept in check by an equal number, nay, by the population of Salamanca alone," (this I much doubt,) "and the whole allied army might have been employed against the French, whose unpardonable fault of crossing and recrossing the Tormes, as it were, under the cannon of the allies, was left unpunished!

It is not for me to decide the point, but unquestionably, the feeling in the army was, that a battle should have been fought at this time.

Meanwhile a fresh supply of shot reached our batteries, and on the 27th, their effect was so powerful, that one of the magazines in the principal fort blew up, and the fire communicating with a quantity of mod which had been incautiously placed near the magazine, the whole fort was soon one vast fire, and a general attack by our troops taking place at the moment, completed the disorder which naturally prevailed. The three forts were thus taken, and our loss, which was estimated by the enemy at thirteen hundred, did not much exceed one-third of that number; and Salamanca was freed from the enemy.

As soon as the garrison of the forts were made prisoners, they were marched through the streets leading from the outworks, to that part of the town that had been allotted for their reception; but it was painful to witness the degradation which these men were obliged to endure at the hands of the excited population. Women of the lowest grade insulted them, and some there were base enough to spit in their faces; yet the French soldiers bore all these insults with composure,—I might say, with truth,—gentlemanly demeanour; but it is not possible for me to express the disgust I felt at seeing brave men so treated by a base rabble, who, but a few hours before, were on the most friendly terms with these very men.

At one time, when I saw such an indignity as mud thrown at them, and a likelihood of something more serious taking place, I expressed myself in strong terms against the ruffians who so acted; and whether it was that I spoke Spanish well enough to be understood, or that I suited the action to the word, by knocking down two fellows who were the ringleaders, I know not; but from that moment the prisoners were allowed to move on quietly.

Thus fell the forts of Salamanca, and with them the hopes of the Imperial Army, so far as regarded their being able to keep the line of the former by so powerful a support; the more particularly, as the Duke of Ragusa was forced to await the junction of the army of the north, as it was called, under the Count Dorsine. On the 28th, he accordingly retrograded towards the Douro, and on the following day rested at Trahujos. Lord Wellington followed the enemy's movement, who, on the 2nd of July, passed the Douro at Tordesillas, which point was sufficiently formidable to embarrass a general who might be desirous of forcing it. The line of the Douro is unexceptionable; it possesses all the requisites which a retreating army could wish for,—uneven banks, narrow fords, and abundance of woods, sufficient to mask the operations of a large body of troops; and Marmont did all that a general could do to render any effort to force it more than hazardous.

On the evening of the 3rd, Picton's division was abreast of the ford of Pollos; some cavalry tried the depth of the river, which was deemed fordable; but the attitude of the enemy on the opposite bank was so imposing, that the idea of forcing the passage was given up. From the 3rd until the 12th of July, the two armies remained in presence of each other, encamped on each side of a river which at times is a formidable sheet of water, but which was then little more than an insignificant stream. Nevertheless, although both armies kept their guards on their respective sides of the water, and that the movements of each were cautiously watched, not one life was lost, nor one shot fired by either army.

Indeed so different from hostility was the conduct of both nations, that the French and British lived upon the most amicable terms. If we wanted wood for the construction of huts, our men were allowed to pass without molestation to the French side of the river to cut it. Each day the soldiers of both armies used to bathe together in the same stream, and an exchange of rations, such as biscuit and rum, between the French and our men, was by no means uncommon. A stop was, however, soon to be put to this friendly intercourse; and it having been known in both armies that something was about to be attempted by Marmont, on the evening of the 12th of July, we shook hands with our *vis à vis* neighbours, and parted the best friends.

It is a remarkable fact that the part of the river of which I am speaking was occupied, on our side, by our Third Division; on the French side by the Seventh Division. The French officers said to us on parting, "We have met, and have been for some time friends. We are about to separate, and may meet as enemies. As 'friends' we received each other warmly—as 'enemies' we shall do the same." In ten days afterwards the British Third and the French Seventh Divisions were opposed to each other at the battle of Salamanca,— and the Seventh French were destroyed by the British Third: but I am now about describing one of the most memorable battles ever fought by the British army—the battle of Salamanca.

CHAPTER 22

Complete Defeat of the French Army

The situation and position of the hostile armies have been described in the last chapter; it left them on the banks of the Douro: and the probability, nay the certainty, that a collision was about to take place between them was manifest to the lowest soldier of both. This collision did take place in a few days afterwards; and as the battle about to be recorded stands in one of the first, if not the very first, classes of those memorable combats in which the British army contended, it may not be unacceptable to the reader to detail with some minuteness the actual strength of the two armies, as likewise the end proposed by each commander.

But to do so I must go back a little. I have before stated that every effort that could be made to place the army of Lord Wellington in that state to ensure the success of an advance into the heart of Spain, had been attended to; its arrival at Salamanca, and the success of its operations before the forts of that city have been described; and it now only remains, before detailing the great events which followed, to briefly mention the views of his opponent.

They were based upon one principle, and one only—namely, to take the field with an army that, after weeks of consideration and calculation, was deemed competent, not only to keep Lord Wellington at bay, but to take advantage of any fault he might commit, and to profit by it on the moment. The French general had no one to control him; because, since the opening of the campaign in May, he had no communication with France; his acts were his own—unshackled, unrestricted. It is, therefore, plain that he courted the meeting which subsequently took place on the plains of Salamanca; but it is nevertheless due to him, and but fair to state, that if he was not commanded, he could not be said to command any troops except those placed under his immediate orders; for the French generals at the head of detached corps, from the want of a competent chief, were each invested with power to act according to their own particular discretion; and thus the machinery of the French army became dislocated and disjointed beyond the possibility of cure.

Of all this the Marshal Duke of Ragusa was aware; he weighed well the force, and the description of force, he had in hand; he was not ignorant of the numbers as well as the quality of the troops of his opponent; therefore upon his head must be attached the disgrace of the total failure of the campaign, which he opened with the idea that its conclusion would be the total overthrow of the Anglo-Portuguese army; and it is now only left to state the number of soldiers that filled the ranks of both armies. It was this:—

The army of Lord Wellington counted fifty thousand men—horse, foot, and artillery; but they were composed of different nations; some without discipline, or order; others without that *esprit* necessary to encounter even the French riflemen; and all—twenty thousand British veterans excepted—unable to withstand a regular attack from a French column. Thus then the brunt of the battle was to be sustained by those twenty thousand British. So it seemed, and so it was. The artillery counted fifty guns, and the cavalry three thousand sabres, or thereabouts, two thousand of which were British. This was the amount and description of force that Lord Wellington had in hand to stem the torrent which was directed against him.

The French marshal, if he could not boast of the same number of infantry, had nevertheless under his command forty-two thousand veteran Frenchmen. His cavalry, it is true, were, at the commencement of the campaign, inferior in number to that of the Allied army; but numbers, in comparison to the quality of the troops is as nought! He had two thousand French horsemen; yet he, with great care, and at the risk of his popularity with the army, caused a thousand horses to be seized and taken from those of his officers who were not entitled to have them (their full value being paid to the owners): and thus reinforced, his horsemen were equal in number to those commanded by the British general. The artillery consisted of twelve brigades of six guns each; and while he seemed in doubt as to the plan he would adopt, General Bonnet, with an entire division, joined him from the Asturias, and thus reinforced, he decided upon crossing the Douro.

The line of the Douro has been already described. Its passage in presence of an army in a condition for battle is difficult; and it requires much circumspection on the part of the general to hazard it in the face of on enemy. The French marshal employed the days of the 13th, 14th, 15th, and 16th of July in a series of evolutions we had hitherto been unaccustomed to witness; and, in fine, on the morning of the 17th, after having made a night-march of thirteen Spanish leagues, his army was in battle array on the plain to the right of Nava del Rey, and immediately facing the ford of Tordesillas, while the bulk of our army was in full movement upon Toro, distant several leagues from the 4th and Light Divisions and the two brigades of heavy horse. The village of Tordesillas de la Orden was in their front

Marmont finding how well the passage of the Douro bad been masked by his night-march, and seeing the small number of troops that were at hand to oppose his movement, ordered his masses forward in the hope of crushing them. The 4th and Light Divisions, covered by Bock's heavy dragoons, retired upon the rising ground behind the villages. At this point various charges were made by the cavalry of both armies; and it was not until after a retreat of three hours, under a burning sun and a torrent of shot, that the two divisions reached the heights of the Guarena. The soldiers, famishing with thirst, their tongues cleaving to their mouths, and fainting with fatigue, pushed headlong towards the river; and before they had drank sufficiently to satisfy their burning thirst, the heights above them were crowned with forty pieces of cannon at half-range. Great was the confusion caused by the cannonade; and it was not without suffering some loss that they effected their retreat to the opposite bank. In less than an hour they joined the 1st and 3rd divisions, and the entire continued the retrograde movement.

The French then advanced in two columns of twenty-five thousand men each; the intervening space between them might be reckoned at two miles. The right wing commanded by Clausel, the left by Marmont in. person. Clausel had scarcely arrived before the point occupied by the 4th Division, when, seeing the smallness of their force, he conceived the idea of making a sudden rush, in the hope of cutting them off.

His troops had scarcely formed when he pushed onward at the head of two divisions of infantry and the brigade of dragoons commanded by General Carrie; but, Cole, placing himself at the head of the 27th and 40th Regiments, received him with steadiness, and drove the French infantry back in disorder. Meanwhile Carrie, seeing some open spaces in Cole's line, caused by their movement against Clausel's infantry, thought, to profit by this disorder, and galloping forward at the head of his troopers, sabred many men; but at this moment the cavalry sent to sustain Cole met them, and after a severe but short conflict, totally overthrew the brigade of Carrie, who was himself numbered amongst the prisoners.

The defeat of Clausel and Carrie checked in a great degree the ardour of the French marshal. The following day he rested; and on the 19th threw back his right wing, and moving forward with the left of his army menaced the right of the British; but Lord Wellington, anticipating the movement, was prepared. for him, and offered battle on the plain of Yelosa. This was refused on the part of the French general; and from this until the 20th, the two armies manoeuvred within half cannon-shot of each other, the British retiring as it had advanced—moving, not directly rearward, but rather in a line parallel with the march of. the French. The columns were in movement in an open country, fairly in the view of each other, and their respective attitudes were of that novel sort that it would be difficult to find the like recorded in the history of any two armies. At times the French and British were within musket-shot of each other, the soldiers of both in momentary expectation of being engaged, yet not one shot was fired by either.

On the 20th, the British army reached the strong position of San Christoval, on the right bank of the Tormes, distant a league from Salamanca, the French general likewise resting for the night upon the heights of Aldea Rubea, holding the ford of Alba on the Tormes. Towards midday on the 21st the French passed the river in two compact bodies, and, screened by the woody nature of the country, established themselves upon a new line of operations, threatening, in a manner, the communication of the British with Rodrigo.

This manoeuvre—a bold one it may well be called—under the camion of an army that had proffered battle but a few days before on a plain of vast extent, was enough to puzzle a man less capable of command than he who was at the head of the Allied army; but, unruffled in his temper by such vacillating conduct, and keeping a steady eye upon his opponent, the British General diligently followed his track. He passed his army, the Third Division under Packenham excepted, across the Tormes, and taking hold of one of two isolated spots called Arapilles, he resolved to rest the right of his army upon this point while his left leaned upon the Tormes river at Santha Martha, and, in the event of a battle taking place, to stand the issue on the ground I have described.

The Third Division still held the position of San Christoval on the right bank, but was in readiness to pass over the river by the bridge of Salamanca, in the event of a battle. taking place. The British general thus threw down the gauntlet for the second time; and whether it was. the impetuous spirit of the French soldiers, or the temper of their leader, or both combined, wrought a change in either, it is not easy to say; but one thing is certain, that from this moment Marmont made up his mind to try the issue of a battle.

In front of the Arapilles hill, which was the *point d'appui* for our right, stood another of the same name of greater altitude, distant five hundred yards from the one we possessed. This mound commanded the one occupied by us, and, after some severe contention, was finally held by the French; and it was evident from the earnest manner in which they sought to gain the possession of it, that it was destined to be the support of the left of their army, as the other was clearly marked out, by the previous events, to be intended for our right.

All doubts as to a battle not taking place were now hushed; and the soldiers of both armies were' aware that the result was to decide to whom Madrid belonged. The die was cast; neither were inclined to back out of it, or to gainsay what they had in a manner pledged themselves to fulfil; and the evening of the 21st July, 1812, closed upon the heads of many a man who was destined never again to behold the setting of that sun. Nevertheless, the Third Division under Packenham had not been recalled; on the contrary, they were busy in throwing up breastworks, and by other means adding to the strength of the position they occupied.

This division, though encamped on a height of considerable altitude, had received strict orders to intrench themselves; the earth was thrown up, the works were *pallisadoed*, and in fine they were so well secured, that they had no fear of an attack or surprise. It is this precaution that marks the great general. Lord Wellington had no idea of being taken aback by any change in Marmont's plans during the night: on the contrary he was convinced that he was serious in his desire to give battle; but to guard against any and every chance was but right.

Marmont might have again, on the night of the 21st, passed the river, and brought his army in battle array before a handful of men, and cut them off piecemeal before his movement could have been arrested by the British general. The thing was not probable—barely possible; but where possibilities, much less probabilities, exist, it is essential that the mind of the commander should be awake, and instead of brooding over what is likely to take place the following day, look to what may take place in the night It was a remark of that eminent general, Kleber, that to be surprised was much more disgraceful than to be defeated: he said, "the bravest man may be beaten; but whoever suffers himself to be surprised is unworthy of being an officer."

At Trafalgar, when Collingwood was leading on the centre ships of attack, Nelson attentively watched him—saw what was right,—and then looked about him to see what was wrong! He observed that the ships of the combined French and Spanish fleets had the hoops round their masts painted yellow, while the British—five ships excepted, which carried yellow hoops also—were black. Judging that some mistake might occur in the heat of the action, he made a signal to the yellow-hooped ships. It was seen and acknowledged. "Paint your hoops black" was the order.

In less than an hour afterwards, one of the ships, which had changed the colour of her hoops from yellow to black, was engaged with a Spanish seventy-four. In the confusion, a British ship fired a broadside into her companion—the smoke cleared away—

her masts were seen—the sailors called out—"She is one of us—she has black hoops, don't fire again;" and the ship was saved from another broadside, which would in all probability have sent her to the bottom.

This circumstance, which, when the order was given, might have seemed to many as trifling, while other events of more consequence were taking place, and, to the common eye, of greater import, was by no means so trifling as might at first have appeared It is trifles like these that have oftentimes decided the fate, not only of a battle, but an empire.

The evening of the 21st of July was calm, and appeared settled, but persons well versed in those symptoms in the horizon which were unobserved by others, (who were unacquainted with their meaning, or so intensely occupied with the anticipations of the events which the morrow was to produce that they did not remark them,) pronounced that a hurricane was not distant Packenham's division was occupied, as I have before said, in entrenching themselves, when about ten at night a torrent of rain fell in the trenches, and so completely filled them with water, that the soldiers were obliged to desist from their labour. Later in the night a storm arose, and the wind howled in long and bitter gusts.

This was succeeded by peals of thunder and flashes of lightning, so loud and vivid, that the horses of the cavalry, which were ready saddled, took alarm, and forcing the pickets which held them, ran away affrighted in every direction. The thunder rolled in rattling peals, the lightning darted through the black and almost suffocating atmosphere, and presented to the view of the soldiers of the two armies the horses as they ran about from regiment to regiment, or allowed themselves to be led back to their bivouac by the troopers to whom they belonged. The vivid flashes of lightning, which seemed to rest upon the grass, for a few moments wholly illuminated the plain, and the succeeding flashes occurred with such rapidity, that a constant blaze filled the space occupied by both armies.

It was long before the horses could be secured, and some in the confusion ran away amongst the enemy's line, and were lost. By midnight the storm began to abate, and towards morning it was evidently going farther: the lightning flashed at a distance through the horizon; the rain fell in torrents, and the soldiers of both armies were drenched to the skin before the hurricane had abated.

Towards five o'clock the storm was partially over, and by six, the dusky vapour which had before veiled the sun disappeared, and showed the two armies standing in the array they had been placed the evening before. All doubts were now set at rest as to which side of the river the battle would be fought The entire army of Marmont remained on the left bank, and Packenham was ordered to move across the Tormes with the Third Division, by the bridge of Salamanca, with as much speed as possible; but it was one o'clock before it reached the station allotted to it—the extreme right of the British.

At half-past one o'clock the two armies were within gunshot or each other; the British, placed as follows, awaited with calmness the orders of their General. The Third Division, under Packenham, were on the right of the line, but hid by the heights in their front, and unseen by Marmont; two squadrons of the 14th Light Dragoons, and a brigade of Portuguese horse, commanded by General D'Urban, supported them. Next to the Third Division stood the Fifth, led on by Leith; next to the Fifth, and at the head of the village of Arapilles, were placed the Fourth and Seventh Divisions; beyond them, and a little in the rear, was the Sixth Division, under General Clinton; and to the left of all was the Light Division commanded by Colonel Barnard.

The First Division, composed of the Guards and Germans, were in reserve; and the cavalry, under Sir Stapleton Cotton, was behind the Third and Fifth Divisions, ready to act as circumstances might require. The guns attached to each brigade were up with the infantry; the park in reserve was behind the cavalry of Cotton, while in the rear of all, and nearly *hors de combat,* might be seen the Spanish army, commanded by Don Carlos D'Espana. Thus stood affairs, on the side of the British, at half-past one o'clock.

The French army, composed of seven divisions of infantry, amounting to forty-two thousand men, four thousand cavalry, and seventy pieces of artillery, occupied a fine line of battle behind a ridge, whose right, supported by the Arapilles height held by them, overlooked the one upon which the left of our army rested. The Fifth Division occupied this point; the 122nd Regiment, belonging to Bonnet's division, with a brigade of guns, crowned the

Arapilles; the Seventh Division supported the 122nd Regiment; the Second Division was in reserve behind the Seventh; the Sixth were at the head of the wood, protected by twenty pieces of artillery; and Boyer's dragoons occupied the open space in front of the wood to the left of all.

There was some irregularity in the arrangement of these troops, and the Duke of Ragusa essayed in person to remedy the evil. He marched with the Third and Fourth Divisions to the head of the wood occupied by Boyer, and it was then he conceived the idea of extending his left, which afterwards proved so fatal to him. On our side all was arranged for defence; the bustle which was evident in the ranks of the enemy, caused no change in our dispositions. Lord Wellington having surveyed what was passing, and judging that something was meant by it, gave his glass to one of his *aide-de-camps*, while he himself sat down to eat a few mouthfuls of cold beef. He had scarcely commenced when his *aide-de-camp* said, "The enemy are in motion, my Lord!"

"Very well; observe what they are doing," was the reply.

A minute or so elapsed, when the *aide-de-camp* said, "I think they are extending to the left."

"The devil they are!" said his Lordship, springing upon his feet,—"give me the glass, quickly." He took it, and for a short space continued observing the motions of the enemy with earnest attention.

"Come!" he exclaimed, "I think this will do at last,—ride off instantly, and tell Clinton and Leith to return as rapidly as possible to their former ground."

In a moment afterwards Lord Wellington was on horseback, and all his staff in motion. The soldiers stood to their arms—the colours were uncased—bayonets fixed—the order to prime and load passed, and in five minutes after the false movement of Marmont was discovered, our army, which so short a time before stood on the defensive, was arrayed for the attack! It was twenty minutes past four when these dispositions were completed; and here it may not be amiss to tell the reader the nature of the movement made by the French general, which so materially altered his position, as likewise that of his antagonist—and in doing so I shall be as brief as I can.

It has been already seen that both armies were so circumstanced as to almost preclude the possibility of a battle not taking place. Marmont coveted it—Wellington did not seek to decline it—both had the confidence of their soldiers—and both, as to numbers, might be said to be on an equality. When I speak of "numbers," I include the Portuguese troops. Military men know what was the real value of these soldiers! At two o'clock in the afternoon Marmont was the aggressor; he held the higher hand; yet at four, in two short hours afterwards, the relative situation of both was altogether changed. The natural question will be—How was this? It occurred just as I am about to describe.

The two armies took their ground under the impression that the French would attack, the British defend. All this was plain; but Marmont had no sooner mounted his horse and taken a survey of the field of battle, than he conceived the idea—like Melas at Marengo—of extending his line, and that by marching his seventh division to a distance to his left, he might cause an alarm in the breast of the British general for the safety of his communication with the Rodrigo road, and in a manner circumvent his movements.

Lord Wellington, at a glance, saw all that was passing in the mind of his antagonist—he saw the error he had committed; and calculating that his Third Division, distant but three quarters of a league from the French Fourth, would reach them before the Seventh French Division could retrace their steps and be in a position fitted for fighting, he decided upon attacking the left before this division, commanded by Thomier, could regain its ground, or at all events be in an efficient state to resist the attack of his invincible old Third.

The result proved the soundness of the calculation, because, although Thomiers got into his place in the fight, he did so before his men had foreseen or expected it, and their total overthrow was in itself sufficient to cause the loss of this great battle. The soldiers had but just resumed their arms, when Lord Wellington, at the head of his staff appeared amongst them. The officers had not taken their places in the column, but were in a group together in front of it.

As Lord Wellington rode up to Packenham, every eye was turned towards him. He looked paler than usual, but notwithstanding the sudden change he had just made in the disposition of his army, he was quite unruffled in his manner, and as calm as if the battle about to be fought was nothing more than an ordinary assemblage of the troops for a field-day. His words were few, and his orders brief. Tapping Packenham on the shoulder, he said, "Edward, move on with the Third Division—take the heights in your front,—and drive everything before you."

"I will, my Lord," was the laconic reply of the gallant Sir Edward. Lord Wellington galloped on to the next division, gave, I suppose, orders to the same effect; and in less than half an hour the battle commenced.

The British divisions were scarcely incorporated when fifty pieces of artillery crowned the ridge occupied by the French. A heavy fire was soon opened from this park at half range, and as the Fourth and Fifth Divisions advanced, they were assailed by a very formidable fire; but as yet the French infantry, posted behind the ridge were not visible; Cole's troops advanced to the left of the Arapilles height, while Pack, with his brigade of Portuguese, two thousand strong, pressed onward to attain it The Fifth Division, under Leith, advanced by the right of Cole's troops; and at this moment the French Seventh Division were seen hurrying back to occupy the ground they had so short a time before quitted, while the Third and Fourth French Divisions were arranging themselves to receive the attack of Cole and Leith.

When all was in readiness, Packenham departed at the head of ten battalions and two brigades of guns, to force the left of the enemy. Three battalions, the 45th, 74th, and 88th, under Colonel Alexander Wallace, of the 88th, composed the first line; the 9th and 21st, Portuguese of the line, under the Portuguese Colonel, De Champlimond, formed the second line; while two battalions of the 5th, the 77th, 83rd, and 94th, British, under the command of Colonel Campbell, were in reserve. Such was the disposition of the Third Division. In addition. General D'Urban, with six squadrons, had orders to make head against Beyer's dragoons; and that the Third Division might not be molested in its operation, Le Marchant's three regiments of heavy cavalry were placed in reserve in the rear of it. It now only remains to relate what actually happened.

No sooner was Packenham in motion towards the heights, than

the ridge he was about to assail was crowned with twenty pieces of cannon, while in the rear of this battery were seen Thomiers' division endeavouring to regain its place in the combat. A flat space, one thousand yards in breadth, was to be crossed before Packenham could reach the heights. The French batteries opened a heavy fire, while the two brigades of artillery, commanded by Captain Douglas, posted on a rising ground behind the Third Division, replied to them with much warmth. Packenham's men might thus be said to be within two fires; that of their own guns firing over their heads, while the French balls passed through their ranks, ploughing up the ground in every direction; but the veteran troops which composed the Third Division were not to be shaken even by this.

Wallace's three regiments advanced in open column until within two hundred and fifty yards of the ridge held by the French infantry. Thomiers' column, five thousand strong, had by this time reached their ground, while in their front, the face of the hill had been hastily garnished with riflemen. All were impatient to engage, and the calm but stern advance of Wallace's brigade was received with beating of drums and loud cheers from the French, whose light troops hoping to take advantage of the time which the deploying from column into line would take, ran down the face of the hill in a state of great excitement; but Packenham, who was naturally of a boiling spirit and hasty temper, was on this day perfectly cool.

He told Wallace to form line from open column without halting, and thus the different companies, by throwing forward their right shoulders were in line without the slow manoeuvre of a deployment. Astonished at the rapidity of the movement, the French riflemen commenced an irregular and hurried fire, and even at this early stage of the battle a looker-on could, from the difference in the demeanour of the troops of the two nations, form a tolerably correct opinion of what would be the result.

Regardless of the fire of the riflemen, and the showers of grape and canister, Packenham, at the head of Wallace's brigade, continued to press onward; his centre suffered, but still advanced; his left and right being less oppressed by the weight of the fire, continued to advance at a more rapid pace, and as his wings inclined forward and outstripped the centre, his right brigade assumed the form of a crescent. The manoeuvre was a bold, as well as a novel one, and the appearance of the brigade imposing and unique, because it so happened that all the British officers were in front of their men—a rare occurrence.

The French officers were also in front; but their relative duties were widely different: the latter, encouraging their men into the heat of the battle; the former keeping their devoted soldiers back!—what a splendid national contrast! Amongst the mounted officers was Sir Edward Packenham and his staff, Wallace of the 88th, commanding the brigade, and his gallant *aide-de-camp*, Mackie, (at last a captain—in his regular turn!) Majors Murphy, and Seton of the 88th, Colonels Forbes and Greenwell of the 45th, Colonel Trench of the 74th, and several others whose names I cannot now remember.

In spite of the fire of Thomier's *tirailleurs*, they continued at the head of the right brigade, while the soldiers, with their firelocks on the rest, followed close upon the heels of their officers, like troops accustomed to conquer. They speedily got footing upon the brow of the hill, but before they had time to take breath, Thomier's entire division, with drums beating and uttering loud shouts, ran forward to meet them, and belching forth a torrent of bullets from five thousand muskets, brought down almost the entire of Wallace's first rank, and more than half of his officers.

The brigade staggered back from the force of the shock, but before the smoke had altogether cleared away, Wallace, looking full in the faces of his soldiers, pointed to the French column, and leading the shattered brigade up the hill, without a moment's hesitation, brought them face to face before the French had time to witness the terrible effect of their murderous fire.

Astounded by the unshaken determination of Wallace's soldiers, Thomier's division wavered: nevertheless they opened a heavy discharge of musketry, but it was unlike the former,—it was irregular and ill directed, the men acted without concert or method, find many fired in the air. At length their fire ceased altogether, and the three regiments, for the first time, cheered! The effect was electric; Thomier's troops were seized with a panic, and as Wallace closed upon them, his men could distinctly remark their bearing. Their *mustachioed* faces, one and all, presented the same ghastly hue, a horrid family likeness throughout: and as they stood to receive the shock they were about to be assailed with, they reeled to and fro like men intoxicated.

The French officers did all that was possible, by voice, gesture, and example, to rouse their men to a proper sense of their situation, but in vain. One, the colonel of the leading regiment (the 22nd), seizing a firelock, and beckoning to his men to follow, ran forward a few paces and shot Major Murphy dead in front of the 88th: however, his career soon closed: a bullet, the first that had been fired from our ranks, pierced his head: he flung up his arms, fell forward, and expired.

The brigade, which till this time cheerfully bore up against the heavy fire they had been exposed to without returning a shot, were now impatient, and the 88th greatly excited: for Murphy, dead and bleeding, with one foot hanging in the stirrup-iron, was dragged by his affrighted horse along the front of his regiment. The soldiers became exasperated, and asked to be let forward. Packenham, seeing that the proper moment had arrived, called out to Wallace "to let them loose."

The three regiments ran onward, and the mighty phalanx, which but a moment before was so formidable, loosened and fell in pieces before fifteen hundred invincible British soldiers fighting in a line of only two deep.

Wallace, seeing the terrible confusion that prevailed in the enemy's column, pressed on with his brigade, calling to his soldiers "to push on to the muzzle." A vast number were killed in this charge of bayonets, but the men, wearied by their exertions, the intolerable heat of the weather, and famishing from thirst, were nearly run to a standstill.

Immediately on our left, the Fifth Division were discharging volleys against the French Fourth: and Pack's brigade could be seen mounting the Arapiles height, but disregarding everything except the complete destruction of the column before him: Packenham followed it with the brigade of Wallace, supported by the reserves of his division. The battle at this point would have been decided on the moment, had the Heavy Horse, under Le Marchant, been near enough to sustain him.

The confusion of the enemy was so great, that they became

mixed pell-mell together without any regard to order or regularity: and it was manifest that nothing short of a miracle could save Thomier's from total destruction. Sir Edward continued to press on at the head of Wallace's brigade, but Thomier's troops outran him. Had Le Marchant been aware of this state of the combat, or been near enough to profit by it, Packenham would have settled the business by six o'clock instead of seven. An hour at any time, during a battle, is a serious lapse of time; but in this action every minute was of vital import.

Day was rapidly drawing to a close; the Tormes was close behind the army of Marmont; ruin stared him in the face; in a word, his left wing was doubled up—lost; and Packenham could have turned to the support of the Fourth and Fifth Divisions, had our cavalry been on the spot ready to back Wallace at the moment he pierced the column. This, beyond doubt, was the moment by which to profit, that the enemy might not have time to recollect himself; but while Le Marchant was preparing to take a part in the combat, Thomier, with admirable presence of mind, remedied the terrible confusion of his division, and calling up a fresh brigade to his support, once more led his men into the fight, assumed the offensive, and Packenham was now about to be assailed in turn.

This was the most critical moment of the battle at this point. Boyer's horsemen stood before us, inclining towards our right, which was flanked by two squadrons of the 14th Dragoons and two regiments of Portuguese cavalry; but we had little dependence on the Portuguese, and it behoved us to look to ourselves.

Led on by the ardour of conquest, we had followed the column until we at length found ourselves in an open plain, intersected with cork trees, opposed by a multitude who, reinforced, again rallied and turned upon us with fury. Packenham and Wallace rode along the line from wing to wing, almost from rank to rank, and fulfilled the functions of adjutants, in assisting the officers to re-organize the tellings-off of their men for square. Meanwhile the first battalion of the 5th drove back some squadrons of Boyer's dragoons; the other six regiments were fast approaching the point held by Wallace, but the attitude of the French cavalry in our front and upon our right flank caused some uneasiness.

The peals of musketry along the centre still, continued without intermission; the smoke was so thick that nothing to our left was distinguishable; some men of the Fifth Division got intermingled with ours; the dry grass was set on fire by the numerous cartridge-papers that strewed the field of battle; the air was scorching; and the smoke, rolling onward in huge volumes, nearly suffocated us. A loud cheering was heard in our rear; the brigade half turned round, supposing themselves about to be attacked by the French cavalry. Wallace called out to his men to mind the tellings-off for square. A few seconds passed—the trampling of horses was heard—the smoke cleared away, and the heavy brigade of Le Marchant was seen coming forward in line at a canter. "Open right and left" was an order quickly obeyed; the line opened, the cavalry passed through the intervals, and, forming rapidly in our front, prepared for their work.

The French column, which a moment before held so imposing an attitude, became startled at this unexpected sight. A victorious and highly-excited infantry pressing close upon them: a splendid brigade of three regiments of cavalry ready to burst through their ill-arranged and beaten column, while no appearance of succour was at hand to protect them, was enough to appall the boldest intrepidity. The plain was filled with the vast multitude: retreat was impossible: and the troopers came still pouring in to join their comrades, already prepared for the attack. Hastily, yet with much regularity, all things considered, they attempted to get into square: but Le Marchant's brigade galloped forward before the evolution was half completed. The column hesitated, wavered, tottered, and then stood still!

The motion of the countless bayonets as they clashed together might be likened to a forest about to be assailed by a tempest, whose first warnings announce the ravage it is about to inflict. Thomier's division vomited forth a dreadful volley of fire as the horsemen thundered across the flat! Le Marchant was killed, and fell downright in the midst of the French bayonets: but his brigade pierced through the vast mass, killing or trampling down all before them. The conflict was severe, and the troopers fell thick and fast: but their long heavy swords cut through bone as well as flesh. The groans of the dying, the cries of the wounded, the roar of the cannon, and the piteous moans of the mangled horses, as they ran away affrighted from the terrible scene, or lying with shattered limbs, unable to move, in the midst of the burning grass, was enough to unman men not placed as we were: but upon us it had a different effect, and our cheers were heard far from the spot where this fearful scene was acting.

Such as got away from the sabres of the horsemen sought safety amongst the ranks of our infantry; and scrambling under the horses, ran to us for protection: like men, who, having escaped the first shock of a wreck, will cling to any broken spar, no matter how little to be depended upon. Hundreds of beings, frightfully disfigured, in whom the human face and form were almost obliterated—black with dust, worn down with fatigue, and covered with sabre-cuts and blood—threw themselves amongst us for safety.

Not a man was bayoneted—not one even molested or plundered; and the invincible old Third Division on this day surpassed themselves; for they not only defeated their terrible enemies in a fair stand-up fight, but actually covered their retreat, and protected them at a moment when, without such aid, their total annihilation was certain. Under similar circumstances would the French have acted so? I fear not. The men who murdered Ponsonby at Waterloo, when he was alone and unprotected, would have shown but little courtesy to the Third Division, placed in a similar way.

Nine pieces of artillery, two eagles, and five thousand prisoners were captured at this point; still the battle raged with unabated fury on our left, immediately in front of the fifth division. Leith fell wounded as he led on his men, but his division carried the point in dispute, and drove the enemy before them up the hill.

While those events were taking place on the right, the Fourth Division, which formed the centre of the army, met with a serious opposition. The more distant Arapilles, occupied by the French 122nd, whose numbers did not count more than four hundred, supported by a few pieces of cannon, was left to the Portuguese brigade of General Pack, amounting to two thousand bayonets. With fatal, though well-founded reliance—their former conduct taken into the scale—Cole's division advanced into the plain, confident that all was right with Pack's troops, and a terrible struggle between them and Bonnet's corps took place. It was, however, but of short duration. Bonnet's soldiers were driven back in confusion;

and up to this moment all had gone on well.

The three British divisions engaged, overthrew every obstacle, and the battle might be said to be won, had Pack's formidable brigade—formidable in numbers at least—fulfilled their part; but these men totally failed in their effort to take the height occupied only by a few hundred Frenchmen, and thus gave the park of artillery that was posted with them full liberty to turn its efforts against the rear and flank of Cole's soldiers. Nothing could be worse than the state in which the Fourth Division was now placed; and the battle, which ought to have been, and had been in a manner, won, was still in doubt.

Bonnet, seeing the turn which Pack's failure had wrought in his favour, re-formed his men, and advanced against Cole, while the fire from the battery and small arms on the Arapilles height completed the confusion. Cole fell wounded; half of his division were cut off; the remainder in full retreat; and Bonnet's troops pressing on in a compact body, made it manifest that a material change had taken place in the battle, and that ere it was gained some ugly up-hill work was yet to be done.

Marshal Beresford, who arrived at the moment, galloped up at the head of a brigade of the Fifth Division, which he took out of the second line, and, for a moment covered the retreat of Cole's troops; but this force—composed of Portuguese—was insufficient to arrest the progress of the enemy, who advanced in the full confidence of an assured victory; and at this critical moment Beresford was carried off the field wounded. Bonnet's troops advanced, loudly cheering, while the entire of Cole's division and Spry's brigade of Portuguese were routed.

Our centre was thus endangered. Boyer's dragoons, after the overthrow of the French left, countermarched and moved rapidly to the support of Bonnet; they were close in the track of his infantry; and the fate of the battle was still uncertain. The fugitives of the Seventh and Fourth French divisions ran to the succour of Bonnet, and by the time they had joined him his force had indeed assumed a formidable aspect: and thus reinforced, it stood in an attitude far different from what it would have done had Pack's brigade succeeded in its attack.

Lord Wellington, who saw what had taken place by the failure of Pack's troops, ordered up the Sixth Division to the support of the Fourth: and the battle, although it was half-past eight o'clock at night, recommenced with the same fury as at the onset

Clinton's division, consisting of six thousand bayonets, rapidly advanced to assert its place in the combat, and relieve the fourth from the awkward predicament in which it was placed, and essayed to gain what was lost by the failure of Pack's troops in their feeble effort to wrest the Arapilles height from a few brave Frenchmen: but they were received by Bonnet's troops at the point of the bayonet, and the fire opened against them seemed to be threefold more heavy than that sustained by the Third and Fifth Divisions. It was nearly dark: and the great glare of light caused by the thunder of the artillery, the continued blaze of the musketry, and the burning grass, gave to the face of the hill a novel and terrific appearance: it was one vast sheet of flame: and Clinton's men, looked as if they were attacking a burning mountain, the crater of which was defended by a barrier of shining steel.

But nothing could stop the intrepid valour of the sixth division, as they advanced with a desperate resolution to carry the hill. The troops posted on the face of it to arrest their advance were trampled down and destroyed at the first charge, and each reserve sent forward to extricate them met with the same fate. Still Bonnet's reserves having attained their place in the fight, and the fugitives from Thomier's division joining them at the moment, prolonged the battle until dark.

Those men, besmeared with blood, dust, and clay, half naked, and some carrying only broken weapons, fought with a fury not to be surpassed: but their impetuosity was at length calmed by the bayonets of Clinton's troops, and they no longer fought for victory but for safety. After a frightful struggle, they were driven from their last hold in confusion: and a general and overwhelming charge, which the nature of the ground enabled Clinton to make, carried this ill-formed mass of desperate soldiers before him, as a shattered wreck borne along by the force of some mighty current .

The mingled mass of fugitives fled to the woods and to the river for safety; and under cover of the night succeeded in gaining the pass of Alba over the Tonnes. It was now ten o'clock at night: the battle was ended. At this point it had been confined to a small space, and the ground, trampled and stained deep, gave ample evidence of the havoc that had taken place. Lord Wellington, overcome as he was with fatigue, placed himself at the head of the 1st and light divisions and a brigade of cavalry, and following closely the retreating footsteps of the enemy, with those troops who had not fired a shot during the conflict, left the remnant of his victorious army to sleep upon the field of battle they had so hardly won.

CHAPTER 23

Disgraceful Conduct of the Portuguese Dragoons

No battle since that of Marengo, in 1800, which opened the gates of Vienna to the First Consul of France, has been fought, whose consequences ought to be more duly appreciated than the battle of Salamanca.

While the north of Europe attracted the notice of the world by the gigantic efforts made by the French Emperor to conquer and to crush Russia, all eyes were at the same time turned towards the Peninsula, in the hope, though not exactly in the expectation, of seeing a stand made there, which might mar the designs of one who it would appear was determined at all hazards to lay prostrate at his feet the civilized world from the port of Archangel to the Bay of Cadiz.

Philosophers, historians, and statesmen were all on the tiptoe of expectation to witness an event which, while it puzzled many as to its probable result, made nine-tenths of Europe turn pale for the consequences. Independent of any other reasons—and there were many of much heavier weight in the scale—curiosity prompted many to reason as to the probability of one extraordinary, but certainly great man, being able to wield two armies with success in climes so many hundred leagues distant from each other, at one and the same moment. A war carried on on such a vast scale has not been recorded in modern times at least; and it may not come amiss to the reader if I touch on the consequences that might have followed the defeat of the British army on the plains of Salamanca, as also the results that actually followed that splendid victory.

Had that battle been lost, the disasters of the French army before Moscow would have been of little account in the scale of the south, and the Imperial Eagles would have soared with the same splendour, from Madrid to Cadiz, or perhaps to Lisbon, as if no event of importance had occurred beyond the Vistula. Portugal would have been then open to invasion—the siege of Cadiz continued—the lines of Lisbon once more invested—and what then?—why, the probable withdrawal of the British army from the Peninsula. Portugal would be thus conquered—Spain laid prostrate—England in utter dismay,—and one hundred and fifty thousand veteran French troops marched across the Pyrenees to take a part in the combats of Leipsic and Lutzen.

These would have been the results of a defeat at Salamanca; and who is the man bold enough to say what the results in the north of Europe would have been, had such an augmentation of force—which would have been certain—joined Napoleon in the end of 1812, or even in the spring of 1813? As it was he gained the battle of Lutzen with a "green army." Had he been backed by one hundred and fifty thousand veteran troops from Spain, it requires no conjuror to tell what the upshot would have been; These are the consequences which would have followed a defeat at Salamanca.

The gaining that battle placed matters on a different footing; Portugal had nothing to dread—Soult was forced to raise the siege of Cadiz—Madrid was evacuated, and Castille and Andalusia were freed from the presence of a French force: but, above all, no reinforcement of any account durst leave Spain to succour the French army in the north of Europe; and the European struggle was brought to a favourable result, and England saved from invasion—perhaps conquest! But those services of the Peninsular army are forgotten, and unrewarded.

The battle of Salamanca has been attempted to be described by me in the preceding Chapter. I say "attempted," because it is not possible for me, possessing the limited means I have at my disposal, to give a full account of this important battle; and one which was held in such high estimation by Lord Wellington himself, that he selected it in preference to all his other victories as that most fitting to be fought over in "sham fight," on the plains of St. Denys, in the presence of the three crowned heads who occupied Paris after the second abdication of the Emperor Napoleon, in 1815.

It was not only a hard-fought battle—a battle of points—but it was a parade battle in the fullest acceptation of the word. It was unlike those that had preceded it, where the bravery, and the bravery only, of the British soldier was to be called into the scale, and nothing else left to him but to defend the ground he occupied "to the death." But on this day the British soldier proved that he was as quick in movement as the redoubtable Imperial Veteran, and that he was able to foil him with his own weapon—rapidity of motion.

At ten o'clock at night, Lord Wellington at the head of twelve thousand infantry, and two thousand horsemen, was in pursuit of the routed and discomfited army of Marmont, while the bulk of his own soldiers lay on the field of battle. The results of that battle were—prisoners, one hundred and thirty officers, seven thousand five hundred men, two eagles, and fourteen guns. The field of battle was heaped with the slain, and the total loss of the enemy may be estimated at seventeen thousand: it has been reckoned by some writers as exceeding twenty thousand; but I apprehend I am nearer the mark, and that seventeen thousand was the outside.

The dead and wounded on the side of the British and Portuguese (for the grand Spanish army, commanded by Don Carlos de Espana, lost but four!) were nearly five thousand; but the greater number of the Portuguese either fell in their feeble attempt against the Arapilles height, or by the shot that passed over the first line, composed of British, which fell at random amongst the Portuguese placed in the rear.

I have already said, that at one period the battle was in doubt, and that it was prolonged until nearly ten at night; but what caused the delay, the doubt— the total annihilation of Marmont's fifty thousand men?—The failure of Pack's Portuguese brigade. Their failure caused the prolongation of the battle to ten at night, when there was a fair prospect of its successful termination at eight. Had it been finished at that hour, how was it possible for Marmont to escape in broad day with one man of his army, pursued as he was by three superb divisions that had not pulled a trigger in the battle? The thing was morally impossible.

Some there were who said, in the excitement of the moment,

that Lord Wellington was to blame, because he placed too much confidence in the Portuguese under Pack. Perhaps he was—indeed the result proved that he was wrong in his estimate of this brigade; but how could he suppose that a body of two thousand men, opposed at most to four hundred—seeing the battle at all points going in their favour—and commanded, too, by such a battle-general as Pack—would allow themselves, in the view, and within hail of their gallant and victorious comrades, the British, to be beaten by a handful of men that did not count more than one-fifth of their number? Yet so it was.

The fate of this momentous battle was kept in doubt, and what was, if possible, worse, prolonged for two hours; the total annihilation of the army of Portugal which must have followed, averted, and the British general actually robbed of the fairest field he ever had of destroying, to a man, one of the most formidable and carefully-organised French armies he was ever opposed to.

I am aware that many may diner from these my opinions, but I speak from experience; and notwithstanding all that has been said and written of the Portuguese troops, I still hold the opinion that they are utterly incompetent to stand unsupported, and countenanced by British troops, with any chance of success, before even half their own numbers of Frenchmen; and if the front line of British at Salamanca had been worsted, every man of the Portuguese army would have been routed. The victory was nevertheless a glorious one, and was as much owing to the presumption of the French marshal, as to the bravery of the British troops, and the wise combinations of their general; because the inconsistency of the Duke of Ragusa was palpable in seizing on the line of communication of an army that had offered battle but two days before on the plains of Velosa.

This confirms the maxim which has oftentimes been repeated, that those principles should never be departed from which the art of war prescribes; and that circumspection should be invariably attended to which obliges all commanders never to swerve from rules which, even when everything favours such meditated projects, the surest way is never so far to despise an enemy as to suppose him incapable of resistance.

Good or ill fortune is decided in a moment—chance never

resigns its rights; nevertheless, in this very battle, the failure of Pack was nigh being fatal to the British: yet it must be acknowledged that the description of the British troops that fought at Salamanca, and the qualities of the general who commanded them, considered, no great doubts could be entertained of the issue of the battle, notwithstanding the unlooked-for failure of the Portuguese under Pack. Of forty British battalions, twenty-two only were in action, and carried the victory; and it may be said, without any great metaphorical stretch, or much alteration in the words of Frederick King of Prussia, that the world rested not more securely on the shoulders of Atlas, than England on such an army and such a general.

No one ought to be surprised that the victory was not more complete, and the French closer pursued: both were impossible. The attack against the French line was unavoidably delayed until five; it never would have taken place but for the false movement of Marmont's seventh division, and the unlooked-for failure of Pack's Portuguese brigade prolonged the battle until it was too late to profit by its results. Night had set in; the wooded country near the Tormes favoured the French in their flight; and to all these circumstances is attributable the escape of a single man of the French army of Portugal.

The battle, though short, was one continued effort; and although the desperate fighting of Clinton's men re-established it towards its close, it was not possible for a single division, no matter how brave, to undo altogether what had been effected by Pack's failure. The time lost could not be recalled, and Lord Wellington saw, without being able to control it, two-thirds of the French army scrambling, in a manner, from his grasp. Besides this, the Spaniard who commanded the troops that garrison Alba, gave up that post without any cause whatever, and thus left the pass open to the French, and Lord Wellington was not even made acquainted with his having done so.

The troops that had gained the victory lay buried in sleep until two o'clock of the morning following, when the arrival of the mules carrying rum aroused them from their slumber, but the parties sent out in search of water had not yet reached the field. The soldiers, with parching lips, their tongues cleaving to their mouths from thirst, their limbs benumbed with cold, and their bodies enfeebled by a long abstinence from food, and the exertion of the former day, ran to the casks, and each man drank a fearful quantity. This for a short time satisfied them, but a burning thirst followed this rash proceeding, and before any water arrived, we were more in need of it than at the close of the battle.

The inhabitants of Salamanca, who had a clear view of what was passing, hastened to the spot, to afford all the relief in their power. Several cars, most of them loaded with provisions, reached the field of battle before morning; and it is but due to those people to state, that their attentions were unremitting, and of the most disinterested kind, for they sought no emolument.

They brought fruit, and even quantities of water, well knowing how distant from us, and how scantily the country near the field of battle was provided with so necessary a relief to men who had not tasted a drop for so many hours, under a burning sun, and oppressed with the fatigue they had endured during the fight

The soldiers, thus refreshed, forgot all their toil, and proceeded to examine those parts of the field where each battalion had been most engaged. The men of Wallace's brigade naturally turned their attention to the hill they had won, and to the flat space behind it, where Le Marchant's horse had so gallantly seconded them: at both they found ample food for reflection—for a horrible massacre had taken place there!

Hundreds of human beings lying dead, or what is worse, mutilated in a frightful manner—horses mangled by shot or shell, running here and there in disorder, or lying in a helpless state, still endeavouring to eat a mouthful of grass around the spot which it was evident they would never leave. These beautiful animals, unconscious of the cause of their agony, looked at us as we passed them, and their sufferings touched the heart of many a veteran, who never knew what it was to feel a tear moisten his cheek: but a field of battle, after a battle, is not easy of description; it is a fearful sight, even for those who are the victors.

Men looking after their tried old friends and companions—women and children seeking for their husbands or fathers—looking for those whom destiny had decreed that they should never again behold, except as lifeless corpses, or as objects more to be shunned than sought after, is a frightful but too true a sketch of a battlefield.

Those who but a short time before were in the prime of life and vigour, now lying dead—rode down—trampled into atoms, with not a vestige of face recognisable, is a melancholy feature in war, and a trying sight to witness, much less describe; nevertheless, many of the brave men who have taken a part in those battles—who have shared in all those dangers, and some who have volunteered their services on occasions when, without such gallant men, matters might have taken a different turn—when in place of a victory being proclaimed, a defeat would perhaps have been announced—are passed over unnoticed and unrewarded!

During the battle there were many circumstances which, if related in their places at the period they occurred, would have broken in upon the narrative, but may be told with more propriety now.

When the Third Division under Packenham had crossed the flat, and were moving against the crest of the hill occupied by Thomier's *tirailleurs*, a number of Caçadores commanded by Major Haddock were in advance of us. The moment the French fire opened, these troops which had been placed to cover our advance, lay down on their faces, not for the purpose of taking aim with more accuracy, but in order to save their own sconces from the French fire. Haddock dismounted from his horse and began belabouring with the flat side of his sabre the dastardly troops he had the misfortune to command, but in vain; all sense of shame had fled after the first discharge of grape and musketry, and poor Haddock might as well have attempted to move the great cathedral of Salamanca as the soldiers of his Majesty the King of Portugal.

At the time the colonel of the 22nd French regiment stepped out of the ranks and shot Major Murphy dead at the head of his regiment, the 88th, a number of officers were beside Murphy. It is not easy at such a moment to be certain who is the person singled out. The two officers who carried the colours of the regiment, and who were immediately in the rear of the mounted officers, thought that the shot was intended for either of them. Lieutenant Moriarty, carrying the regimental flag, called out, "That fellow is aiming at me!"

"I hope so," replied Lieutenant D'Arcy, who carried the other colour, with great coolness—"I hope so, for I thought he had me covered."

He was not much mistaken: the ball that killed Murphy, after passing through him, struck the staff of the flag carried by D'Arcy, and also carried away the button and part of the strap of his epaulette! This fact is not told as an extraordinary occurrence, that the ball which killed one man should strike the coat of him who happened to stand in his rear, for such casualties were by no means uncommon with us; but I mention it as a strong proof of the great coolness of the British line in their advance against the enemy's column;

The staff of the wounded pole and its companion, have been, with good taste and true soldier-like feeling, preserved by Colonel O'Malley, who commanded the 88th, and he was, by special permission, allowed to affix on the old poles—the silent evidence of many a hard-fought day—the new colours that have been presented to the 88th. It was a happy thought, and I doubt not but there are many officers at the head of regiments, who, when they hear of it, will feel regret at not having done the like. On the wounded pole there is engraved, on a plate of silver, the day, and the manner in which it was so mutilated, and when the "Connaught Rangers" again take the field against the enemies of their country, if the sight of those bits of stick don't inspire them with a proper recollection of the former deeds of the regiment— the sooner they go back to their native homes the better.

It may be asked why I dwell so much on the poles that carry the colours? I do so, first, because I think that the touch—the very sight of those "bits of stick" is sufficient to inspire men who have never before fought beside them, with a feeling that they ought to look up to them, and if they cannot add to their lustre, at least never to forsake or allow them to fall into the hands of the enemy. But I turn to the poles in preference to the colours, because the former stand firm on their own deeds!—they may be lopped down—cut smaller—shaved to a shred!—but still, there they are, the very same identical poles that were present in every battle which the silk that out-tops them ought to mention! One battle (the battle of the Pyrenees) has been withheld from the 88th; and it is a singular fact that a part of that regiment (see note following) was in a most particular manner distinguished on the very day for which it is, in a manner, disgraced: for most unquestionably, if it be an honour to a regiment to receive a badge for a battle, it is a disgrace to them if one is withheld from them on the day they have been under fire with the enemy.

Note—On the 28th July, 1813, when the Third and Fourth British divisions occupied a post in the Pyrenees, the latter was warmly engaged, and every regiment belonging to it charged with the bayonet; but the Third Division was unmolested, although menaced, until about five o'clock in the afternoon. At this time a considerable body of the enemy's *tirailleurs* pressed forward to that part of the ridge occupied by the Third Division, and immediately in front of the 88th Regiment, the light infantry company of which, commanded by Captain Robert Nickle, was ordered to drive back this force: he did so in the most gallant manner; but the enemy could ill brook such a defeat, the more annoying, as it was witnessed by our Third Division, as also by a considerable portion of one of the enemy's *corps d'armée*.

A reinforcement commanded by an officer of distinction, rushed forward to redeem the tarnished honour of their nation. The detachment of the 88th lay behind a low ditch, and waited until the French approached to within a few yards of them; they came on in gallant style, headed by their brave commanding officer, who was most conspicuous, being several paces in front of his men.

The soldiers of the two armies, posted at a distance, and lookers on at this national trial, shouted with joy as they beheld their respective comrades on the eve of engaging with each other. But this feeling on the part of the French was of but short duration, for at the first fire their detachment turned tail, and were what they themselves would term "*culbutés*," leaving their brave commandant, with many others, mortally wounded behind. Captain Robert Nickle ran up to his bleeding opponent, and rendered him every assistance in his power.

He then advanced alone, with his handkerchief tied on the point of his sword, which he held up as a token of amity, and, thus reassured, some of the French soldiers returned without their arms, and carried away their officer with them. They were delighted with the considerate conduct of Captain Nickle, and embraced our men on parting.

Perhaps, for so much, there never was a more gallant exploit; and it may be better conceived than expressed what the feelings of the bystanders must have been. It may also be asked, what favour was granted to the brave 88th for their distinguished behaviour, or what mark of distinction was conferred on the chivalrous Captain Robert Nickle. He was not even noticed, and the 88th is the only regiment of the brigade to which they belonged that is not allowed to bear the badge of this battle (termed Pyrenees) on their colours!!!

When the cavalry of Le Marchant passed through Wallace's brigade in their advance against Thomier's column, Captain William Mackie of the 88th, the discountenanced leader of the forlorn-hope at Rodrigo, who acted as *aide-de-camp* to Colonel Alexander Wallace, was missing. In the confusion that prevailed it was thought he had fallen. No one could give any account of him; but in a short lapse of time, after the cavalry had charged, he returned covered with dust and blood, his horse tottering from fatigue, and nothing left of his sabre—but the hilt! He joined the cavalry so soon as the fighting amongst the infantry had ceased, and those who knew the temperament of the man were not surprised at it: wherever glory and danger were to be met, there was Mackie to be found, and nothing—not even the chilling slights he had experienced—could damp his daring spirit

At the first dawn of the morning of the 23rd of July, Lord Wellington continued the pursuit of the defeated army of Marmont. He placed himself at the head of the light division, which opened the march, followed by the heavy German cavalry under General Bock, and Anson's brigade of light horse. Those two superb brigades of dragoons had only joined the army the night before. The first division of infantry, composed of the Guards and German Legion, followed the cavalry, and Lord Wellington at the head of thirteen thousand men that had not pulled a trigger, or unsheathed a sabre in the battle, followed the enemy's track; but the retreat was so quick, that Marmont's head-quarters were thirty miles from Salamanca the day after the battle.

Nevertheless, the corps that covered the retreat, consisting of three battalions of infantry and five regiments of cavalry, were attained near the village of Lerena. The infantry formed themselves into a square, the cavalry were posted on the flanks for its support, but the panic with which all were infected by the defeat of the preceding day had taken such a fast hold of them, that the French horse in advance could not be prevailed upon to show a front. This threw those that were at hand to support them into disorder: confusion was communicated to the remainder, and the field of battle was precipitately abandoned by the cavalry, who, in the most unaccountable manner, left their companions, the infantry, to their fate.

The cavalry having thus fled, Bock, with his German Horse, galloped at the square, and breaking through it, slew or took prisoners the entire; and the contest ended in one dreadful massacre of the French infantry. Nevertheless, many of the troopers fell; for one regiment in particular, the 105th French, bravely stood their ground, but the ponderous weight of the heavy cavalry broke down all resistance; and arms lopped off, heads cloven to the spine, or gashes across the breast and shoulders, showed to those who afterwards passed the spot, the fearful encounter that had taken place; and from this moment nothing more of the Army of Portugal was to be seen.

If anything was wanting to prove what I have before said of the certainty of the total annihilation of this army on the 22nd at Salamanca—had that battle not been prolonged until dark by the failure of the Portuguese under Pack—the overthrow of the rear-guard on the following day, after such a lapse of time, when the spirits of the enemy had a reasonable time to recruit and refresh themselves, is a sufficient evidence of the manner in which they would have behaved on the field of battle in the midst of their routed companions—in the hearing of the shouts of their victorious opponents—opposed to that invincible infantry, which no fire, poured in as it was from the formidable masses that it broke through, could shake—under the edges of those sabres that cut in piecemeal their best organised squares! Behaving as this rear-guard did on the day after the battle, when the rout had ceased, and was converted into a regular retreat—acting thus, I ask, is not the conclusion I have come to as to what might, or rather ought, to have been the results of the battle of Salamanca, a fair estimate?

The overthrow of the rear-guard, which covered the flight of the army of the Duke of Ragusa, and the rapid manner in which Clausel made good his retreat from the heights of La Serena, where that army for the last time made any show of a stand against the British troops that had defeated him on the plains of Salamanca, finished the campaign, so far, at least, as regarded the army of Portugal.

The leading regiments followed the enemy's track as far as Flores de Avila, which town, distant ten leagues from Salamanca, had been evacuated by them two days after the battle. The cavalry and artillery of the northern army met them on their retreat near Arevela; but nothing—not even this reinforcement—could inspire them with confidence; and the mass of fugitives hastily followed the road leading to Valladolid. The good generalship displayed by Clausel, and the steady front he showed when in the presence of a victorious army, raised him considerably, and justly so, in the estimation of his own troops; but all his skill would have been of no avail had the battle not been unavoidably prolonged until dark.

The British general continued the pursuit; but for what end? The moment for crushing that army was lost at Salamanca; and he might, with as much chance of success, have attempted to catch the tail of a comet as the tail of the army that fled before him. The failure of Pack ruined all. One flitting hour, lost by that failure, was productive of the disastrous results which followed—but of them hereafter. War, with all its terrible accompaniments, is a fearful-sounding thing; yet it is, nevertheless, a complicated and delicate web, the meshes of which require to be as delicately handled as if they were composed of the finest materials. The least false touch may destroy all its arrangement; and that which cost so much time and labour to render perfect, may be undone by falling into hands unable to appreciate its texture.

But to speak without any metaphorical aid, so it is with soldiers going into battle. Their commander makes his arrangements—allots to each corps, brigade, or division, the part they have to take in the accomplishment of his end—the defeat of his foe. If any one part give way, the whole machinery becomes unhinged—broken up; and the repairing of it oftentimes costs more than the original outlay; or, more properly speaking, than the cost of the repair is worth, and the end sought for—is lost!

So it was at Salamanca. The failure of Pack's brigade caused the loss of half the Fourth Division; and the bloody conflict which the Sixth, under Clinton, were engaged in to save not only Cole's troops, but the general issue of the battle, never would have taken place had the Portuguese done their duty. But the fate of a battle often hangs, as it were, by a hair. At Marengo, when the day was, to all appearance, lost to the army of the First Consul, Dessaix arrived on the field. It was two o'clock. Napoleon asked his opinion,—"What do you think of it?" said the First Consul.

Dessaix replied, with the bluntness of a soldier, "By G—d, it is lost!—but," said he, at the same time taking out his watch, "it is only two o'clock, and we have time enough left to gain a battle yet."

Dessaix's division gained the battle of Marengo—Clinton's decided Salamanca.

The march of the British army continued without interruption. Those divisions which followed the enemy were enthusiastically welcomed as they passed through the different towns and villages on the Valladolid road; the inhabitants flocking in vast numbers with a supply of wine, fruit, bread, and vegetables, which were all bought up by the soldiers. Arrived at Valladolid, and finding himself as far as ever from being able to overtake the army of Marmont, Lord Wellington made a full stop. Giving the army one day's rest for the purpose of allowing the stragglers to come up, he, on the 1st of August, turned off abruptly towards the grand Madrid road; while Hill, with the second corps, reached Zafra.

Marmont being thus disposed of for the present, and Lord Wellington having formed the resolution of marching to the Spanish capital, every road leading to it was occupied, and thronged by cavalry, infantry, and artillery, baggage and commissariat mules, stores of all descriptions, the reserve park guns, and the followers of the camp, such as suttlers, Portuguese servants, and women who followed the soldiers. These, when assembled together, formed one vast mass of between sixty thousand and seventy thousand souls. The sight was an imposing one; the weather was beautifully fine, and the advance of the army as it moved onward towards the capital was one scene of uninterrupted rejoicing.

Never was the general feeling in Spain so much in favour of the

British nation, the British army, and the Hero who commanded it, as on the present occasion. The news of the great victory gained by the British army only a few days before, under the walls of Salamanca, which was witnessed by thousands upon thousands of Spaniards, was spread afar; and the different routes which the army traversed were crowded almost to suffocation by the Spanish people, who vied with each other to gain a passing view of the men who had so distinguished themselves, and to supply them with every assistance in their power.

Every face was cheerful; and at the termination of each day's march, our bivouacs, or the villages we occupied, were crowded with Spanish girls and young men, who either brought wine, lemonade, or fruit; the evening was wound up by *boleros* and *fandangos*; and, in short, our march to Madrid more resembled a triumphal procession—which, in point of fact, it really was—than the ordinary advance of an army prepared for battle.

Meanwhile the King of Spain hastily endeavoured to make arrangements to stop the torrent which threatened his capital. He had advanced upon Blasko Sancho on the 25th of July; but there hearing of the fate that had befallen his favourite general at Salamanca, he retraced his steps, and gaining the passes of the Guadarama, retired towards the palace of the Escurial. He collected all the disposable force that could be taken from the capital; but his army, chiefly composed of *Jurementados*, (Spaniards that entered into King Joseph's service,) counted not quite fifteen thousand bayonets and sabres—a force as to number, without taking into account its *morale*, not of that formidableness very likely to disconcert the grand designs of Lord Wellington. In short, the army continued its march towards the Spanish capital without molestation.

On the 6th of August the head-quarters were at Cuellar; on the 7th, at the ancient town of Segovia, so celebrated in Spanish romance; and on the 8th the divisions destined to march upon Madrid were concentrated at Saint Ildefonso.

Saint Ildefonso is beautifully situated. The magnificent waterworks, the elegant taste with which the gardens and pleasure-grounds are laid out, and the vast concourse of people who thronged them on the day of our arrival, gave to it the appearance, in our eyes at least, of the most enchanting spot on the face of the globe. At each of the principal walks, bands of music played inspiring airs; and at half-past six in the evening the water-works were in full play.

These works, situated at the base of a lofty blue mountain, cast up water to an immense height; and one in particular seemed to us to be much superior to anything we afterwards witnessed at either Versailles or St. Cloud. To me it certainly seems so; but I, in common with many others, may be wrong: for, in truth, we were so charmed with the novelty of the scene we then witnessed, and the vast contrast it presented to' the scenes we had for such a length of time not only witnessed, but taken an active part in, that all due allowance ought to be made—if we are wrong—for our prepossession in favour of this spot.

At eight o'clock Lord Wellington, surrounded by a number of generals of different nations, a splendid staff, and many grandees of Spain, entered the gardens. All the bands, at one and the same moment, played "See the Conquering Hero comes," the singers joined in chorus, and the vast multitude rent the air with acclamations. The females, disregarding all form or etiquette, broke through the crowd to get a nearer view of his Lordship, and many embraced him as he passed down the different alleys of the gardens.

The groups of singers continued to sing; this was succeeded by *bolero* dancing, *fandango* dancing, and waltzing; and all was wound up by one of the most intoxicating and delightful nights of pleasure that we had ever witnessed, and, if I mistake not greatly, that was ever acted on the same spot. It was late before we retired to rest—and indeed we had need of repose: our minds as well as bodies required it; and when the shrill note of the bugle, the following morning (for that matter, it was the same morning) aroused us from our sleep, all that had passed seemed but as a dream.

The causeway lending to Madrid is broad and well arranged: as we reached each league-stone, we counted with anxiety the distance we had yet to pace ere we arrived at the capital of Spain. The mountains which overhang the Guadarama passes are bold and lofty: these passes, easy of defence, and requiring but a small force, were abandoned without a musket-shot being fired for their protection; and, in fine, on the 11th, Lord Wellington was near the village of Majalahonde, distant but one march from the capital.

Thirty thousand infantry were encamped half a league in its rear; the different brigades of horse and artillery attached to the infantry were at hand—in short all was in readiness, but the advanced guard of cavalry, unfortunately intrusted to the brigade of Portuguese of D' Urban, was in front of all. Behind them, at the distance of a mile, were the two regiments of heavy German horse, while the splendid "*parc*" of horse artillery, commanded by Captain Macdonald, was ready to support D' Urban.

The greatest part of the day had passed over without any event taking place between the advanced posts; some slight skirmishing with the enemy's lancers and D'Urban's cavalry left matters as they were at the commencement The army was preparing its arrangements for the night's repose and the march of the following day, when the thunder of Macdonald's artillery aroused us in an instant from our occupations.

It was soon manifest that the enemy's advance had attacked the Portuguese cavalry; and the vast cloud of dust that came rolling onward towards the village, where the German horse were placed in reserve, told but too plainly that the Portuguese were routed, and the Germans about to be cut off. The infantry betook themselves to their arms, and in a few moments the entire were in readiness to march to the scene of action, for so in fact it was.

The Portuguese dragoons fled at the first onset, without waiting to exchange one sabre-cut with the French; and so rapid was their flight,—for they rode through the village where the reserve of Germans were posted to support them,—that not more than half of the Germans were mounted: many men thus fell before they could defend themselves, and their colonel was cut down while in the act of shaving himself; but his brave soldiers, forming themselves together in the best manner the time would admit of, closed with drawn sabres upon the French lancers, which turned the stream, broke the mad fury of the attack, and drove back the lancers in confusion.

Up to this time the combat was one scene of desperation. An irregular and furious crowd might be seen mixed together, fighting without order or regularity, and from the confusion that prevailed, it was not possible to see distinctly to which side the victory belonged; but at a distance, far from the scene of action, the burnished helmets of the Portuguese troopers were distinguishable as they fled from the post they had deserted, and from their brave companions, the Germans, whom they left to be massacred. The din of arms, the clashing of swords, and the thunder of the cannon, mingled with shouts from every side, completed the confusion.

In the hurry of the moment, some tents belonging to the 74th Regiment took fire, the flames soon communicated with those of the next regiment, and the camp was enveloped with smoke: but this was soon overcome; and by the time we approached near the point in dispute, the French cavalry had been driven off the field, but not before many of the Germans had fallen.

Two guns of Macdonald's brigade had also been taken; and upon the whole, it was one of the most disgraceful and unlooked-for events that had taken place during the campaign. To be beaten at any time was bad enough, but to be beaten, by a handful of lancers, on the eve of our entering Madrid, almost in view of the city, was worse than all. But what caused our defeat—our disgrace—under the eyes of the people of Madrid? The placing undue reliance on the Portuguese troops.

CHAPTER 24

The British Army Approach Madrid

Order having been at length restored, and the French pushed back again to their former ground, the German horse took the advance and the night passed over quietly, but in the disgraceful encounter, which I have related in my last chapter, two guns of Macdonald's troop, which were upset during the clamour, fell into the enemy's hands.

As we passed over the ground which had been the object of dispute the preceding evening, we beheld many of the brave Germans lying dead and naked. Every wound was in the breast, and at the skirts of the village lay the two captured guns; their carriages were broken, and they could not in consequence be removed; the French had set fire to the wheels, which were still smoking.

In less than two hours we reached the heights which command Madrid; the soldiers ran forward to catch a glimpse of the countless steeples that were distinguishable through the haze, and their joy was at its height when they beheld a city that had cost them so much toil and hard fighting to gain the possession of. Ten thousand voices, at one and the same moment, vociferated "Madrid! Madrid!"

The enthusiasm of the army was still further increased by the thousands upon thousands of Spaniards that came from the town to accompany us in our entry; for miles leading to the capital the roads were crowded, almost to suffocation, by people of all ranks, who seemed to be actuated by one simultaneous burst of patriotism, and it was with difficulty that the march was conducted with that order which we were in the habit of observing. The nearer we approached the city the greater was the difficulty of getting on, for the people forced themselves into the midst of our ranks, and joined hand in hand with the soldiers.

Wine was offered and accepted, though not to the extent the Spaniards wished, but the soldiers were too well-disciplined, and felt too proud of the station they held in the estimation of the people, and in the estimation of themselves, to allow anything bordering on excess to follow the latitude they thus had. There was nothing like intoxication, not the slightest irregularity, and the appearance of the officers, almost all of whom were mounted, and the respect with which they were accosted by the soldiers when occasion required it, was so strongly contrasted with the loose discipline of the French army, to say nothing of the bands of half-naked creatures that com posed the army of their own nation, that it may be fairly said no troops ever entered any capital with all the requisites necessary to ensure them a cordial as well as a respectful reception, as the British army did on the present occasion.

At length we entered that part of the town near which the palace stands, but the obstacles which impeded our march, great as they were before, now became tenfold greater. Nothing could stop the populace, which at this period nearly embraced all that Madrid contained, from mixing themselves amongst us. The officers were nearly forced from their horses in the embraces of the females, and some there were who actually lost their seats if not their hearts.

Old or young, ugly or well-looking, shared the same fate; and one in particular, an old friend of my own, and a remarkably plain-looking personage, was nearly suffocated in the embraces of half a dozen fair Castilians. When he recovered himself and was able to speak, he turned to me and said,—"How infernally fond these Madrid women must be of kissing, when they have nearly hugged to death such an ill-looking fellow as me."

I would mention his name, but as he is still alive he might not like the joke second-hand. We soon reached the Convent of St. Domingo, near the Plaza Major, which was destined for our quarters, and for a time took leave of these people who had so cordially welcomed us to their capital. The soldiers, thus quartered, were left to arrange their barracks, while the officers, who were billeted in those parts of the city adjoining the barrack, proceeded to occupy the houses allotted to them, and to partake of the hospitality of their patrons.

Evening had scarcely closed when every house was illuminated. The vast glare of light which the huge wax candles and torches, placed outside each balcony, threw out, so completely lighted the town, that night seemed to be converted into day, and the whole population of Madrid might be said to fill the streets. Nothing could exceed the popular feeling in favour of the British, and although the ancient palace of the Retiro was garrisoned by two thousand five hundred French troops, with a park of artillery at its disposal, sufficient to batter down the city, the gaiety was continued as if no enemy was within several leagues of the place. The illuminations lasted for three nights, during which not the slightest irregularity or misunderstanding took place.

On the morning of the 13th of August, the general commanding the fortress of La Chine having refused to give it up, orders were given to carry it by storm. The 3rd, or "fighting division," as ours was called, was selected by Lord Wellington for this duty. At eight o'clock in the morning all the ladders were in readiness, and the division commanded by Sir Edward Packenham defiled under the walls of the botanic gardens.

The sappers had succeeded in opening several breaches in the wall, and the fire of the riflemen in the interior of the gardens announced that the attack of the outposts had commenced. One hundred thousand people of all ranks, ages; and sex crowded the street, houses, and housetops to witness the contest. No sooner was the first gun fired, which was the signal for attack, than an universal shout was raised by this vast multitude of spectators, and it would be very difficult indeed, if not quite impossible, to describe this animated scene. The soldiers, infected by the example thus set them, cheered in turn, and it was several minutes before any word of command could be heard from the Babel-like tumult that prevailed. Little or no orders were given—they were unnecessary.

The men were directed to carry the fort at the bayonet's point, and this was all that was said or that was necessary to be said. The troops were then put in motion, and this was the signal for another burst of enthusiasm from the Spaniards, several of whom joined our ranks. The *vivas* now became so tremendous that nothing else could be heard, and the leading platoons had made some progress through the shrubberies before the order to halt was known; owing to this a few men were killed and wounded, and those old and tried soldiers lost their lives or were disabled in a mere *bagatelle*, for the French general commanding in the fort displayed the white flag in token of submission the moment he saw the Third Division in movement towards the Retiro.

The fall of this place was of vast importance to us. In it was found a large supply of provisions, as well as one hundred and eighty-nine pieces of cannon, including a complete battering train. There was likewise a great quantity of powder and ball, and some clothing, as likewise twenty thousand stand of arms. The garrison, consisting of three thousand veteran soldiers, were made prisoners and sent to Lisbon, and the fort was converted into a state prison for disaffected or suspected Spaniards.

All the *partisans* of King Joseph were loud in their denunciations against the French Governor for not having defended the fort to the last extremity, and, by way of enforcing their argument, added that there was a sufficient number of guns in the Retiro to have battered Madrid to the ground; this indeed the governor hinted he would do should he be molested,—but what man of common sense would pay attention to such a threat? Was it to be supposed that a handful of soldiers, no matter how brave, could defend a place of such extent, that twelve thousand men for its garrison would be nearer the mark than three thousand—which was the outside of their number—in presence of fifteen thousand troops that had beaten all before them from the lines of Lisbon to the heights of Salamanca?

The town, it is true, might have been battered down—but for what end? The general who could be guilty of so wanton an act would deserve, if he escaped, to be hanged by his sovereign for destroying his capital, and if he fell into the hands of the Spaniards—as he would to a moral certainty have done—he would have been torn to pieces or perhaps reserved for a more cruel and lingering death. No, no—the man was right in what he did, and the only fault he committed was not surrendering sooner, for the people of Madrid were so incensed at the injury done to the botanic gardens, during their occupation by our troops, that it required a strong British escort; to save the Governor and his soldiers from being murdered on the Prado.

There was no blame to be attached to the general. He could do no more than simulate a defence. The fault of leaving him and his garrison at Madrid rested not with him, but was a great error in King Joseph; three thousand good troops could not be so easily thrown away, and notwithstanding the fulminations of General Sarrazin, who is no doubt a very competent judge in matters of the kind, I am of opinion that in this instance he is wrong when he accuses the general of cowardice in not defending his post to the last extremity.[1]

Thus ended our operations for the present, and we had leisure to make our observations upon Madrid, and avail ourselves of the hospitality of such of our patrons as were disposed to show us attention.

Madrid stands in a flat uninteresting country, devoid of scenery; fields of tillage encompass the city up to the mud wall that surrounds it, and the rivulet that meanders round it is in summer so insignificant as to be barely able to supply the few baths on its banks with a sufficiency of water; nevertheless this side of the town, which is next the Grand Park, and the regal cottage called Casa del Campo, is far from uninteresting, and as the Park, which abounds with game of all sorts, was open to the British officers, we had abundance of sport when we wished to avail ourselves of it.

The streets are wide, and the principal ones, generally speaking, clean, but by far that part of the town possessing the greatest interest is the great street called Puerto del Sol: some centuries ago it was the eastern gate of the town, but as the city became enlarged from time to time, it is now, like the University College of Dublin, in the heart of the metropolis, instead of at the verge of it. Half a dozen or so of the principal streets empty, in a manner, their population into this gangway, where the Exchange is held, and all public business carried on, so that any one desirous of hearing the news of the day, the price of the funds, or any other topic discussed, has but to station himself here and his curiosity will be satisfied, as almost the entire of the population of Madrid pass and repass under his

---

1. "Lord Wellington granted him the honours of war, of which he was certainly unworthy. It is allowable to profit by the cowardice of another, but it is painful to see a brave man honour a *poltroon* whom he despises."—General Sarrazin.

eye during the day. Merchants, dealers, higglers, charcoal venders, fellows with lemonade on their backs, girls with *pamellas* of water incessantly crying out "*Quien quiere aqua?*" all congregate to this focus where everything is to be known.

Next to the Puerto del Sol must be placed the *Prado* or public walk, which is decidedly the most agreeable lounge that Madrid can boast of; but as the promenade never commences before five in the evening, while, on the contrary, the bustle of the Puerto lasts during the forenoon, it must have from me the precedence though not the preference. By five o'clock, as I before said, the walk begins to be frequented, the great heat having by this time subsided, and the *siesta* over. At seven it is crowded almost to suffocation, and groups of singers with guitars slung across their shoulders enliven the scene.

At each side of the walk are tables at which sit groups of people enjoying the scene, but you rarely see men and women seated at the same table; indeed, it would seem as if the men totally shunned the company of the fairer sex, and engrossed themselves more with the news of the day than the gaiety of the *Prado*. Much has been said of the jealousy of the Spaniards, and in England it is a generally received opinion that they are a jealous race, but I never found them such,—quite the contrary. In Madrid a married woman may go to any house she pleases, or where and with whom she wishes. They might have been a different people when Spanish romances and Spanish plays—old ones I mean—were written, but if the manners and habits of the people were then truly narrated, I can with truth say that no nation in the world has undergone a more wholesome, thorough, and radical reform than Spain.

In some instances we experienced much hospitality from the people, but those occurrences were rare; for the Spaniards are naturally a lofty and distant people, and most unquestionably our officers did not endeavour by any act on their part to do away with this reserve, and in fact after a sojourn of nearly three months in the Spanish capital they knew nearly as little of its inhabitants as they did of the citizens of Pekin.

This is a fatal error, and I fear one that it will be difficult to counteract, for it is not easy to correct national habits and national prejudices; but if the officers of the British army were to reflect upon the effect their conduct must have on the people of a different nation, and if they could be made to understand how different, how far different, their reception in foreign countries would be if they unbent themselves a little, and conformed themselves to the modes of those nations amongst whom they were sent by their sovereign; but, above all, if they knew how much the British nation would be raised in the estimation of foreign countries by a different line of conduct than that pursued by our officers in Spain and Portugal, they would at once come to the resolution of changing their tone, and they would by so doing get themselves not only respected and regarded, but the British nation as much beloved as it is respected.

It is a singular fact, and I look upon it as a degrading one, that the French officers while at Madrid made, in the ratio of five to one, more conquests than we did! How is this to be accounted for? The British officer has the advantage of appearance: his exterior is far before that of a Frenchman; his fortune, generally speaking, is ten times as great; but what of all this if the one accommodates himself to the manners, nay the whims, of those he is thrown amongst, while the other, disregarding all forms, sticks to his national habits, struts about, and not only despises, but lets it be seen that he despises, all he meets, save those of his own nation.

What a fatal error! The British army under Lord Wellington have immortalized themselves in Portugal and Spain; the people of those nations know, and have witnessed, their prowess in arms, but the British army—although they have emancipated those two countries—have made but few friends in either.

While we thus continued to pass our time in gaiety and idleness, other divisions of the army had moved onwards towards Burgos, which was strongly held by a chosen garrison under the command of an experienced and skilful general of the name of Dubreton. The means at the disposal of Lord Wellington to effect its reduction were not of that magnitude to warrant a confident hope that the enterprise would be as successful as the two former sieges of Rodrigo and Badajoz; but so much was at stake on the issue of the thing that it was resolved to hazard the trial.

Meanwhile we continued at Madrid, and either enjoying the amusement of the theatres, the luxuries of the hotel called El Fonte d'Oro, the hospitality of the good citizens, or the gay but noisy scenes at the Calle de Baimos, we passed our time as agreeably as men could do considering the scanty amount of pay which was issued to us, for from the difficulty of getting a supply of animals sufficient to bring up specie from Lisbon, where there was an abundance, the army was at this period five months in arrear of pay, and except for the commissaries and some paymasters who cashed our bills (at seven shillings the dollar!) many of us would have been' in a sad plight.

Those who were enabled to raise money at this enormous percentage got on well enough, but others, who were limited in their resources, were obliged, per force, to be lookers on at all that was passing.

My regiment (the 88th) established a mess at an hotel kept by a Spanish woman who had been married to a Frenchman, but who made his escape with King Joseph. We paid her a dollar a day each for our dinner and a bottle of wine. Our paymaster, Rogers, was a good man and discharged our bill weekly, and although we all considered the price high, no one complained, thinking it better to have the certainty of having right good cheer while we were in the land of the living, than the chance of never touching a *sou* of our arrear of pay which we thus mortgaged, by a sort of post-obit, to our worthy *pagador*.

An event was now about to take place that engrossed much of the conversation of all Madrid, and created amongst the army no little curiosity. It was the condemnation to death, by the garrotte, of a Spanish priest named Diego Lopez. This ill-fated man, it appears, had been, for some time previously to his arrest, in the pay of King Joseph; he acted as a spy, and gave circumstantial information of all that was passing in our army.

Accurately acquainted with his proceedings, the police agents narrowly watched his motions. For some days he had been missing from his lodgings in the Calle de Barrio Nuevo. No enquiry was made after him by the police, they being too conversant in their calling to raise any suspicion in his breast by a step that they knew would be abortive; but his return was eagerly looked for, carefully watched, and his apprehension made more certain. At length he did return.

It was midnight when he reached the barrier at the Toledo gate, where a police agent was stationed. He was asked but few questions and was allowed to pass, and mounted as he was on a jaded horse fatigued by a long journey, it was not difficult for the agent to keep near enough to him to track him unobserved to his dwelling. The trampling of his horse was soon recognized by an old woman who kept watch for his return.

A light was placed at the window as a beacon that all was safe within, and he was about to dismount when he was seized by three police agents who hurried him away to the *bureau* of the director, while another entered his house for the purpose of seizing his papers. He underwent an immediate examination, but nothing could be elicited from him to criminate himself, and no papers, excepting commonplace ones, were found at his lodgings. He was then stripped of his clothes, and another suit given him in their stead. Every part of his dress was examined, the linings carefully parted, his clothes in fact cut into shreds, when, at last, after a scrutiny of an hour, was found, folded up, in a button, covered with cloth, which corresponded with the rest, a note from King Joseph to some person in Madrid, briefly detailing the information he had received from Lopez, and asking his advice as to the plans to be pursued.

No more was required, or indeed necessary, to confirm his guilt, and the next day he was by the orders of Don Carlos de Espanaga, Governor of Madrid, hurried before a military tribunal summoned together to try him. The only evidence brought forward against him was the concealed note; and nothing could induce him to betray the name of his confederate. The trial was, therefore, of but short duration, and when called upon by the president to make his defence, he calmly stood forward, and looking his judges full in the face, prepared to address them.

Every eye was fixed upon him, and it would be difficult to look upon a man of a more imposing figure. In stature he was about five feet eleven inches, and his make was in proportion to his height; his lank black hair lay flat on his forehead, and hung behind over the cape of his coat in loose but neglected masses; his face bore the marks of care, and his fine dark eye was sunk and wan,—he was, in short, the outline of a once fine, but now broken-down man. Having wiped away the drop of sweat that covered his forehead caused by the heat of the weather, the crowded state of the court, and, no doubt, the agitation of his mind, he spoke as follows:—

> It is now something more than two years since I first attached myself to the service of his Majesty King Joseph: during that period I have served him faithfully, and with the utmost diligence. I have rendered him some service, and he will be, I doubt not, sorry when he learns my fate. I have said that I served His Majesty faithfully: the expression is too weak—I but lived for him; and the only regret I feel in now laying down my life, while endeavouring to promote his interests, is, that I have not been able to succeed in this, my last mission, which is the only one I ever failed in. Gentlemen, I have done.

He then bowed to the court, and resumed his former place.

During the delivery of this short but impressive speech, the court and spectators were silent When it was concluded, a buzz of admiration and pity burst forth from almost every person present, and there were many who would, if they dared, have expressed their sentiments more fully, but the strong guard which occupied the hall was sufficient to maintain order; and though no lives were lost, many arrests took place.

When order was restored, the chief of police conducted the prisoner, under a strong escort, back to his dungeon; and the court being cleared, the president asked the opinion of the members as to the guilt of Lopez. They were unanimous—indeed there could be but one opinion, and by that his life became the forfeit. The sentence pronounced against him was, that he should suffer death by strangulation, on the following day, at two o'clock; and the Plaza Major, or Great Square, where a vast market is daily held, was the spot decided upon as most fitting for the execution.

This decision was soon known throughout Madrid; and so greatly does the bent of man lean towards sights and scenes of horror, that, notwithstanding the individual was a priest, and one belonging to a nation proverbial for its superstition, the catastrophe that was about to befall him, so far from calling forth commiseration, was hailed with joy by the populace of the city, who counted with impatience each hour as it tediously followed the one that preceded it, until the moment arrived which was to gratify their curiosity.

It was thought necessary to augment some of the British Guards in the neighbourhood of the *Plaza*; and the barrack occupied by the 88th being close to it, I, as the next subaltern for duty, was ordered to repair there to take charge of thirty soldiers, lest any rioting should take place during the night. It was five o'clock in the afternoon when I reached the square on my way to the barrack. It was already much crowded with people of all classes; some led by curiosity to see if any and what preparations had been made towards erecting the platform upon which the garrotte was to be fixed; others bargaining for and cheapening seats either at the windows of the shopkeepers, or on the tops of the market stalls; others calling out a sort of programme of the offences, &c., for which Lopez was to suffer; and, though last not least in the list, a host of beggars, who assailed the bystanders with entreaties for charity in the name of the soul about to depart!

In this appeal they had a powerful auxiliary; and many who would not give the one-fourth part of a *real* to ensure the safety of the unfortunate Lopez, in the world to come, "came down handsomely," in the hope that they, at some future period, might get value for their money!

The arrival of several carts carrying planks for the formation of the platform, the presence of a large body of police, and the appearance of the workmen entering the square, dissipated anything like apprehension of a disappointment. This circumstance, or announcement, had an instant and powerful effect on the price of seats—the same as the intelligence of a great victory would have on the funds in London."*Omnium* was above par," and "much business was effected." Every person seemed pleased with the bargain he had made, and I myself was among the number.

I paid, by way of deposit, half a dollar to ensure my place; the remaining half to be handed down the following morning. All being settled, so far as related to myself, I left the square to look after my guard. I found all quiet in the quarters of our barrack, and towards nightfall I again returned to the *Plaza*. It was quite deserted, except by the workmen, who were busily employed in marking out and completing the rude platform for the scaffold, in which they had made considerable progress. Its height from the ground was about four feet; the square or area was fourteen by twenty; and from the quantity of materials, and their grossness, it might be supposed that it was meant to sustain, at one and the same moment, half the population of Madrid. But it yet wanted that terrible instrument of death—the iron clasp, to complete its structure.

The night passed over quietly and uninterrupted, except by the arrival of the peasants with their usual supply of fish, fruit, and vegetables, to the marketplace, where the execution was to take place the following day. It was not until two o'clock in the morning that I quitted the guard-house to take a little repose; but before doing so, I turned once more into the square. The men employed in erecting the scaffold were working by torchlight, surrounded by a crowd of peasants who had arrived from the country with provisions.

The look of horror which was depicted in their countenances when they learned that a *padré* was to be strangled, was a striking contrast to the ferocious exultation expressed by the mob of Madrid; but such is, I believe, the difference in all countries. Scenes of the worst sort, which are in a manner indigenous to the inhabitants of a vast city, are unknown to the lower orders, who are too far removed from its vicinity to be contaminated by its excesses, its crimes, and its familiarity with scenes of horror; and much as I approved the justness of the sentence pronounced upon the culprit, I could not but admire the native simplicity with which the country people gave vent to their sorrow for the fate that awaited him.

It was three o'clock before I lay down to rest, but I slept little. I had never seen a man strangled, and there was a novelty in the thing that awakened my curiosity. I had seen men die in many shapes and under distressing circumstances, but there was a certain something so repulsive to my ideas of death in the word "strangling," that I could not rest I fancied myself amongst a parcel of Turks. The din of hammers, and the creaking of wagons, put sleep out of the question. I took up a volume of Gil Blas, and attempted to read and laugh, but in vain: I could do neither the one nor the other—the *garrotte* was still in perspective, and nothing could banish it from my thoughts.

At length the stillness which prevailed terribly told that all was prepared, and I went once more to the spot. I found it deserted by the workmen, who had done their part, and these preparations now wanted nothing to complete them but the presence of the man who was to die by the pressure of the clasp, which hung from a beam of wood placed in the centre of the platform.

I have before described the height and dimensions of this platform: at each side of it was a flight of four steps; one for the criminal, the other for the two executioners. In the centre was a beam, to which was attached a chair or stool; through the beam a clasp was introduced, and behind was a screw, or sort of vice, which at one turn crushes the neck. Having so far satisfied my curiosity, I once more returned to my post, and awaited with impatience for the coming of the hour destined for the arrival of the priests.

So early as ten o'clock the square was thronged with Spanish troops, and the platform upon which the scaffold stood, surrounded by a strong guard. Vast multitudes already began to congregate towards the spot, in order to take possession of the places they had paid for, or to secure those which would give them an opportunity of witnessing the execution. All business was at a standstill, and every idea, except that connected with the coming event, seemed to be extinct.

By midday, the square, the market-sheds in its centre, and the houses which formed it, were filled nearly to suffocation; and the other streets leading from the prison to the *Plaza* were thronged with people of all ranks. At length the shouts raised in the streets nearest the prison announced the removal of the criminal, and the huzzas from that quarter were rapidly taken up as they passed onward towards the square: they increased by degrees, and, like a vast torrent which is formed by tributary streams, each stream contributed its quota to the current, until at length it reached the vast vortex, the Plaza Major. At this place the shouts were so deafening, that for some minutes it was impossible to ask a question, much less hear one. At length the head of the cavalcade was in sight, and a death- like silence followed the tumult that had preceded it. The soldiers stationed in the square, as also those that surrounded the platform, resumed their firelocks; the words "*Los armas a l'ombro*" was quickly obeyed, and the entire procession was soon within the precincts of the *Plaza*.

The convict, Lopez, dressed in black with a loose cloak covering his shoulders, was on horseback, attended by two priests, also mounted, one at each side of him. He wore a hat of large dimensions turned up in the front, and his demeanour was the same as at his trial—firm, collected, and calm. Arrived at the foot of the scaffold, he dismounted with ease, and throwing a rapid glance, first at the vast crowd, and then at the *garrotte* itself, he ascended the flight of steps leading to it.

The two priests followed, but did not speak to him, his wish being that they should not. He then, without flurry or agitation, took off his hat and cloak, and handed them to the assistant executioner, to whom he said something. He wished to address the people, but was prevented by the officer commanding the Spanish troops. He bowed obedience, and instantly took his seat upon the stool under the clasp. His arms were then bound with cords, and the iron collar passed through the stake and placed upon his throat.

This scene had a strong effect upon the multitude: the quiet but determined self-possession of the man; his extraordinary resolution, devoid of any bravado, was enough to check any indecent ebullition of patriotism: but the sight of that terrible collar seemed to awaken feelings, and to call forth that sympathy which, a few moments before, was nowhere to be found. Women, who, to their shame be it told, waved their handkerchiefs with joy upon his arrival at the scaffold, now might be seen covering their eyes to hide from their view the horrid sight, or to wipe away the tears that traced their cheeks.

All was now in readiness: the executioner stood behind, holding the screw with both hands; at each side was a confessor, and behind one was the assistant executioner, with a square piece of cloth in his hand: one of the priests road from a book, while the other held the hand of Lopez. This ceremony occupied but a few moments; and when the priest had finished reading, he stooped clown to kiss the cheek of the ill- fated Lopez. He then closed the book; the man behind him threw the cloth over the culprit's face; the executioner turned the screw—and Lopez was dead! The two priests hurried down the steps, and, in their confusion and fright, ran headlong under the horses of the cavalry which were posted round the scaffold. One of them, a corpulent man—as indeed most priests are—was dreadfully lacerated, but the other escaped uninjured.

During the entire of this scene, the vast crowd preserved the most profound silence; but the sight they had just witnessed was succeeded by another of a more disgusting nature. The assistant executioner removed the cloth from the face of the dead man: it was perfectly black; the eye-balls were forced from their sockets; the throat was pressed quite flat, and the mouth, with the tongue hanging down on the chin, was dragged under the right ear.

The troops then defiled out of the square, the multitude dispersed, and by six o'clock in the evening, not more than twenty persons were near the scaffold upon which the dead priest was still bound. The body was at length put into a cart, the platform was removed, and the spot which so short a time before was the theatre of this tragedy, now bore no evidence of the horrid scene that had been acted upon it

The day but one after this event, it was publicly announced that, in honour of the British army, the Plaza de los Toros, which had been shut for many years, was to be opened, and bull-fights exhibited upon a scale of grandeur and magnificence hitherto unrivalled.

Chapter 25

Lord Wellington in the Plaza de los Toros

The execution of the priest Lopez, narrated in the last chapter, was followed by many arrests. In eight days no fewer than one hundred and forty-nine persons were thrown into prison; some on good grounds, others on trivial circumstances, and many on the charge alone of having held employment under the late government. The consequence of this ill-judged severity was, that all those who escaped arrest in the first burst of tyranny practised by the local authorities, fled from Madrid, and scarcely a family was to be found who had not to lament the loss of some individual belonging to it, either by flight or imprisonment; and had the siege of Burgos been successful, and the French troops driven to Pampeluna, which would have been the natural result, a tragical scene would have been enacted, not only at Madrid, but throughout the whole of Spain. Yet all the time nothing but forgiveness for the past, and promises for the future, were to be heard of—except the daily and nightly imprisonments that took place!

Two evenings after the execution of Lopez, I met a number of Spaniards at the house of my *patron*, Don Miguel d'Inza, who had himself been an engineer in the employment of the late King Charles IV: different topics, as a matter of course, were discussed; the sieges of Rodrigo and Badajoz, the battle of Salamanca, and the triumphant entry of our troops into the capital of Spain. Most of the party seemed well inclined towards us, and towards the king we pro- claimed, Ferdinand VII.; but there was little confidence amongst the party themselves, and there was some who would, if they dared, have spoken in favour of the French.

One old *Donna*, in particular, was rather severe in her observations on the dress of the British officers, and remarked, that not one in fifty of them could speak French. Whether it was that she was piqued at my paying much attention to a lady who sat near her, or that she wished to display her wit at my expense, I being nearer to her than any other Englishman, I can't say, but she turned round, and asked if I spoke the French language. I replied, that I understood it tolerably, but that I spoke it but indifferently.

"I thought so," was her reply; "I knew by that young fellow's appearance he was a booby (*sot*)" said she, addressing one of her friends. This she spoke in the very worst French that ever came from the mouth of a Bastan peasant. I was determined to have my revenge. I mustered up all my resolution, made a rapid *repasser* of all I had ever learned of French grammar, and took the first opportunity that presented itself to attack her. In a word, I completely out-talked her, out-spoke her, and out-crowed her in the estimation of her friends; and she who had been so short a time before the "leader of the opposition," was mum for the remainder of the evening.

Harmony was once more restored, and we were beginning to forget the bickerings that party feeling had introduced amongst us, when a violent knocking at the door from the street threw the company into consternation and dismay. Everyone looked confounded; some were for barring the door, others wished to escape, but this was easier said than done, for in front stood the police agents (for it was them, and none other), and in the rear—if rear it could be cabled—was nothing but a pile of buildings, to the full as lofty as the house we inhabited. "What is to be done?" was a demand much easier made than answered; though in fact the proper and only reply to be made was—"Open the door, and see who the gentlemen are looking after."

Several persons, who had nothing to dread, loudly called out for this proceeding, but it was far from palatable to the majority of the company. It was idle, however, to talk, and, in time, the massive door was heard to creak on its rusty hinges. At the same moment, six ill-looking fellows entered the saloon, and having taken a hasty but scrutinizing survey of the company, seized the son-in-law of my patron, and rudely carried him away.

Saturio de Padilla was the name of this gentleman, and his only crime was that of holding the situation of Juiz de Fora, under the government of King Joseph. Nothing could be more unjust or impolitic than this arrest: it was, however, idle to reason so with the police agents; Saturio was taken off to the fort of La China, and thrown into a dungeon, without bed, or any other comfort which a gentleman of his rank might have expected.

At an early hour the following morning I was awoke by his father-in-law, the venerable Don Miguel de Inza; he begged of me to allow my servant to convey some bedding to him, which I not only consented to do, but, at the entreaties of his daughter, Donna Maria Ignatia de Inza, (whose sister was married to Padilla, and who, by the way, was one of the most beautiful women in Madrid,) went to the prison myself. All entreaties to allow us to see the prisoner were vain, and, had it not been for the kindness of Colonel Manners of the 74th, who was the Governor of the fort, we should not have been allowed to send even a change of linen to this gentleman.

A week passed away, and no tidings were heard of Padilla; and his friends, fearing that he might be made away with, became extremely uneasy. Without mentioning my intention, I waited upon Colonel Manners, who was much interested in his behalf, when I told him the circumstances; and, owing to his intercession, I had the happiness of seeing my friend, Don Saturio, at liberty the day but one following.

I need scarcely say that this exploit of mine, for so my Spanish friends termed it, raised me considerably in the estimation of the ladies, and all of them, my old formidable antagonist not excepted, were lavish in their praises of my conduct. Nothing but balls, concerts, and parties to the theatre and the Prado, were thought of, until the announcement in the newspapers, and the never-ceasing cries of *affiche* venders in the streets, that the bullfights were to take place, put a stop to all thoughts on any other but this, to a Spaniard at least, momentous affair.

This national amusement is of so old a standing; and has been so often related in novels and romances, that a description of it may, in the present day, be thought ill-timed; but, as many of my readers may have never thrown their eyes over such works—which, to say the truth, give but an imperfect outline of these combats—I shall, as far as my recollection will permit, detail the particulars of the day's fighting I witnessed at the Plaza de los Toros; as also the manner in which those animals are bred and trained, before it can be ascertained by their owners how far they will justify the expectations held by them of their probable success in their debut before a Madrid audience, or, more correctly speaking, before the eyes of the bulk of the population of that city.

So soon as those bulls which, from their pedigree, are thought to be worthy of entering the public lists for fame, attain the age of one year, they are collected together by the breeder, who invites his friends, to be present at the trial. The fate of the bull is decided in a short time; he is either destined for the plough, the butcher, or the matador. To attain the chance of dying so honourable a death as by the hands of the latter, he must attack a horseman, armed with a long spear, twice, bearing its point on his neck or shoulder, before his pretensions to figure at the amphitheatre can be admitted; and it is really astonishing that animals so young possess such daring; but such is the fact, nevertheless.

The bull who thus "passes muster," is destined for the long Toledo blade of the matador; those who hang back, for the ploughman's *rivo* stick, or the butcher's knife. Poor devils!—if they knew but all, it is—as regards the two latter at least—but "hang choice" between them; and, for that matter, they have a better life than he that falls to the lot of the ploughman. We soldiers of the Peninsula used to say, "a short life and a merry one;" so say, or think, I suppose, the pugnacious bulls, and so say I; so said the veterans who went out to this same Spain, to fight for the Spanish queen; so say the young men who have never "smelt powder," and have gone out likewise; so say the old pensioned soldiers, and so say the raw recruits.

All, one and all, are carried on by the destiny marked out for them; and, though we sometimes make "bulls," we, nevertheless, follow our destiny as they do. But, as I am going to write a chapter on "bulls," or bullfights at least, I must go on regularly, lest I should write a page of bulls!

Those animals destined for the amphitheatre on the day I am speaking of, were conducted from the wilds they were brought up in, and, amidst a number of oxen and cows, were, on the evening previous to the display of the following day, within a league of Madrid. It was deemed necessary to confine them as short a time as possible, in order that their spirit might not be broken. There was something extremely exciting in this scene; for a number of gentlemen on horseback, armed with spears, went out to witness the shutting-in of the bulls. They were followed by the greater part of the mob of Madrid, and the bulls became so wild at the novel scene, that two of the most savage rushed among the crowd, and killed an old man, a shoemaker, and dreadfully wounded two women.

Yet this, so far from being a warning to the rest, seemed to stimulate others to the risk which they madly courted. I saw one fellow, certainly in a state of intoxication, run forward and take a bull by the horns. He was tossed in the air, and fairly caught again by the infuriated brute, who had him placed in a sitting position on his head. Some of the boldest among the vast crowd ran forward to extricate him, which was effected by means of cloaks thrown over the bull's face. The man, to the astonishment of all, escaped unhurt, and was about to attack the bull again, but was restrained by his friends.

My man servant, Dan Carsons, whom I have more than once introduced to the notice of my readers, was on the spot, and, seeing the foolhardiness of the Spaniard, attempted to expostulate with him, but Dan either speaking the Castilian language imperfectly, or the fellow being so drunk that he could not or would not take his council, turned away, and was about to break from his friends, when Dan quickly walked up to him, and, seizing him by the collar, thus addressed him:—

"Will ye be quiet now; can't you be aisy, and don't be afthur frettin' your poor ould mother there? Sed what a takin' she's in at your manner of misconducting yourself; you ought to know bether, before so many jontlemen, how to bemane yourself; and that baste of a bull gave you enough already to put a start in your poor ould mother."

The number of bulls destined for the sports of the morrow was nine; these were shut into a small courtyard, divided by partitions, with a sluice-gate attached to each; by this means the bulls were got one by one into their respective cells, where they were lodged for the night.

A *dia de los toros*, or bull day, at Madrid, is an event of such importance that all business is at a standstill; young and old, female as well as male, are, one and all, engrossed by this all-powerful amusement; and, as the hour approaches for the opening of the amphitheatre, the streets of the city are nearly impassable from the vast and dense mass which throng them, all bending their steps towards the Plaza de los Toros. The spirits, too, of the multitude are wound up to the highest pitch of enthusiasm, and it is by no means safe to walk the suburbs on these occasions.

So early as ten in the morning the doors of the amphitheatre were thrown open for the admittance of those who had tickets of admission, to witness the final arrangement of the bulls previous to their appearance on the stage.

This part of the ceremony consists in arranging a bunch of ribbons, called the *devisa*, tied to a piece of barbed iron, which is fastened in the neck of the bull. This is meant to distinguish the breed of the animal, something like the colours worn by our jockeys at the different racecourses, which denote to whom such and such a horse belongs.

The clearing of the amphitheatre, where a vast number of people remain up to the last moment, is considered a part of the exhibition, and is termed *el despejo*. Some hundreds of soldiers are on duty to perform this ceremony; they enter at one of the two great gates in a solid body, and, debouching to the right and left, perform a variety of evolutions, which, while it attracts and amuses the multitude, gains the object in view—their dispersion.

The arena is thus cleared by this *ruse militaire*; a splendid band of music, playing inspiring national airs, heightens the effect; every countenance is gay; and the ground once cleared, the gates are shut. The soldiers then perform a few evolutions, which are meant as a sort of peace-offering to those who have been ejected from the circus, and immediately afterwards retire behind the *palisadoes*.

To accomplish what I have described, occupied three hours and a half, that is to say, from ten o'clock, until half-past one. At that hour all was in readiness; nine magnificent bulls were prepared for the fight; and the *picadors, banderilleros*, and matadors, were equally ready and equally anxious to enter the lists with their formidable antagonists. The amphitheatre was filled almost to suffocation; all the rank and beauty of Madrid were here congregated together, and the arrival of Lord Wellington was looked for with breathless expectation. The hour named for the commencement of the combats was two; it now wanted twenty minutes of the time, and every minute was counted over in awful suspense until the arrival of the commander-in-chief of the British army should be announced.

True to his appointment. Lord Wellington reached the Plaza de los Toros at two o'clock precisely. A shout of approbation from without announced the fact, and his appearance in the royal box was hailed by a thunder of applause. He wore the uniform of a Spanish general, and was attended by a numerous staff of British, Spanish, and Portuguese officers. The whole assembly stood up to greet him on his arrival, and the different bands of bull-fighters, according to their precedence in rank, passed before him in turn. They were as follows:—

First, the *banderilleros*, in number, twenty, dressed in scarlet and blue cloaks, silk breeches and stockings, their hair dubbed like the soldiers of Napoleon's guard, advanced in a line across the arena, and made their bow in front of the box occupied by Lord Wellington. These were followed by the two matadors, attended by their assistants; then came the *picadors* on horseback, wearing brown jackets trimmed with silver lace, and adorned with a profusion of silver buttons. Their pantaloons were of buffalo leather, extremely wide and stuffed with a quantity of cotton, which resists the bull's horns; their hats were large, tied under the chin, and turned up in the front, a plume of feathers out-topped the hat, and their appearance altogether was of a very imposing nature.

A pike, six feet in length, with a spike at the end not more than three inches long, was all they had to defend themselves against the desperate fury of the ball. So soon as this part of the ceremony finished, the trumpets sounded, the two large gates were again thrown open, and the three classes of combatants quitted the arena; the horsemen by the gate to the right, those on foot by the one opposite to it

The amphitheatre of Madrid, perhaps the finest ill the world, is capable of accommodating several thousand spectators, the seats in the pit and gallery rise one above the other, like our opera-house. The gallery is flanked on each side by boxes, where those who wish to take a more distant view of the combat can sit with ease and safety; but the greater portion of the spectators, young ladies as well as gentlemen, prefer, like our play-going critics, the lower seats, as being best suited to give them a nearer view of those terrific, but certainly most exciting, encounters.

This tier, protected by a strong palisade, or fence, six feet in height, with a space twenty feet wide between it and the first tier, is considered a sufficient defence against most bulls; but, to guard against accident, there are several doors which open from this space into the circus, as a high-mettled bull will not be stopped in his pursuit by this barrier. We looked upon this as an exaggeration, and did hot credit it, but the sequel of the day's fighting proved that we were in error, and that the precaution was one of absolute necessity.

The ceremony of giving the key of the *toril*, or bull's cell, having been finished, the trumpets again sounded, the doors were flung open, and the two *picadores* entered the arena by separate gates; their attendants on foot, unarmed, and unprotected, except by a cloak which is rolled in a coil round the left arm, followed close after the horses, and the interest which these preparations excited was so intense, that a pin might have been heard had it fallen in any part of the amphitheatre. But when the door of the bull's den was thrown open, and the animal himself, like a roused tiger, burst into the arena, a shout arose that resembled more a thunderclap than the voices of human beings, and there were some who feared that the building would fall, so great was the shock.

The bull, unused as he was to such a scene, was no way shook or daunted; he threw a rapid and ferocious glance at the vast crowd, but in a second one of the horsemen caught his eye. Rushing onward with desperation, he was met by his cool and scientific adversary, but, although the point of the lance was well directed and took effect in the bull's neck, it was not of sufficient weight to throw him back, and he turned on the *picador* before he was again in an attitude to receive him.

Seeing the advantage he had thus gained, the bull seemed resolved to make the most of it, and, by one desperate effort, raised horse and rider from the ground; but the force of his attack was so great, that he fell forward, and the spearman, his horse, and the infuriated bull tumbled in one mingled group in the centre of the arena, which was covered with the blood of the horse. The sight was a terrific one. The horse in the agonies of death, his bowels literally torn out, lay on the man; the bull stood over both, trampling and goring the dying; horse; the *banderilleros* in vain exerted themselves by loud shouts and waving their flags to attract the attention of the bull, while the spectators in the pit, boxes, and gallery, rent the air with thunders of applause. At length the men with the flags succeeded in drawing off the bull, who was met by the other *picador*, and the cavalier who had sustained defeat, extricated himself from under the dead horse, and remounted a fresh one.

The courage of the bull remained unbroken, but his impetuosity was checked; and he paused for a moment to take breath. He then made a rush at the other horseman, but was cleverly met by his spear and fairly turned off. This defeat but increased his fury, and he attacked the spearmen five successive times; in four of them he was worsted, but his last effort against his first opponent was crowned with success. The spear of the *picador* snapped in two, half of the shaft remained in his hand, and he and his horse were left to the mercy of the bull, who galloped forward and killed the horse on the spot; the *picador* had one of his legs broken.

The trumpets sounded, the other horseman retired, and the disabled man was carried from the bloody arena amidst the shouts of the spectators, while the bull remained sole master of the battlefield, awaiting with impatience any fresh attack that might be directed against him. The trumpets again sounded, and the *banderilleros* entered the circus.

The *banderilla* is a piece of cane two feet long, at the end of which is a barbed dart and small flag; it is ornamented with festooned ribbons of varied and gay colours. The men hold one of these in each hand, and the group of fighters encompass the bull in a circle. He may make choice of any one of the number, and the man so selected and attacked is bound to meet him. The fighter so marked out, runs headlong at the bull, and, stopping for an instant to await the attack and measure his distance, plunges the two darts into the neck of the bull, making a vault or kind of summerset over the head of the animal.

The man who fails to accomplish this is in a perilous state, and has nothing to depend on for safety but great swiftness, great presence of mind, and great activity; for the bull follows him .with extraordinary speed, and at one time was so near one of the flag-men that his horns touched him as he vaulted over the *palisadoes*. There were many who said the man owed his safety to having placed his feet on the bull's head; but, although he was certainly very close to him, I will not take upon myself to say whether he did so or not

At the close of this part of the fight six men advanced with darts prepared with a sort of firework inside, something like what are called "Roman candles." These darts are so arranged that, by the pressure attendant on forcing them into the bull's neck, they attain a sufficient force to reach the combustible matter inside the cane, which explodes in regular order.

The poor animal becomes more or less stupefied; his former efforts against the pike and flagmen were sufficient in themselves to weaken his strength and subdue his courage; but this last mode of attack did more than all the rest put together. Worn down by fatigue, harassed by so many different and formidable opponents, his neck streaming with blood, and pierced by numerous darts which still adhered to him, his faculties impaired by the stunning noise of the fireworks, his head enveloped in one continued blaze, was enough to damp the courage of any beast, no matter how brave or ferocious; but on him it seemed to have but little effect—except from the fatigue of his own exertions. His courage was still the same; and when the trumpets sounded for the Third time, and the flagmen left the arena, the gallant brute looked about undismayed as before.

He was not long kept in suspense. The matador entered, flung off his cloak, and approached the bull with a quick step and fearless bearing; in his left hand he held a short pole, upon which was rolled a narrow piece of cloth, which hung like a flag at the end of it, and in his right a sword of great length and breadth. The moment he placed himself before the bull he held out the flag, which, in a great degree, screened him from his view, but the high mettled animal rushed forward, and was near killing him at the first onset.

A shout from the audience inspired both the matador and the

bull; the latter made another and last effort against the matador— the rush was fatal— he tumbled on the sword, which, passing through his body, came out at the hip—and he fell dead at the feet of the victor.

The uproarious applause which followed might be termed awful. The amphitheatre shook as if an earthquake had visited us. Four mules, beautifully harnessed, with a bar and crook attached to the traces, entered at a gallop; the crook was fixed to the bull's neck, the mules passed across the arena at a rapid pace, the gates were thrown open, mules, drivers, and bull disappeared in a twinkling; the trumpets again sounded, and a fresh bull bounded into the middle of the arena.

CHAPTER 26

The Retreat From Burgos

It is not my wish, to dwell with too much minuteness on the different features that marked the day's fighting with which I concluded the last chapter. Many of my readers were, no doubt, present on the day I speak of; to them it would be irksome; but as, in all human probability, nine-tenths of those who may perchance throw their eyes over what I have written, or what I now write, never saw a Spanish bull-fight, much less a day's fighting where nine bulls were killed, I must for their gratification—not to say one word in defence of the amusement it affords myself to give my own memory a jog after so many years having passed over my head since I witnessed those scenes—go a little into detail, and this I will do as briefly as is consistent with the object I have in view.

The bull that now occupied the arena was to the full equal in courage and swiftness with the one that preceded him, but the horsemen to whom he was opposed were better mounted, and had learned experience from their contest with his comrade. His attacks were, therefore, less fatal; neither horse nor man sustained any serious injury, and he was killed by the matador after a. gallant struggle against the different bands of fighters, as well as missiles, he was obliged to encounter.

The same detail might be given of the next five bulls, who all fought gallantly, and excited the same feeling amongst the spectators as the two first; but the eighth and ninth bulls created a strong sensation, though the cause was as different as night is from day. The eighth bull, the most active of any that had yet appeared, the moment he entered the arena, took a hasty glance at the horsemen—it was, however, but a glance—and in a trice bounded over one of the gates, upwards of five feet in height! It would be impossible to give a description, a just one at least, of the astonishment, not to say indignation, of the Spanish part of the company.

Cries of "shoot him—tear him to pieces," were vociferated from thousands of throats; but those in "office" did their duty without paying attention to public clamour, and drove the bull back again into the arena. It was in vain—for fight he would not with the horsemen. He ran round the circus, and crouched on his belly, looking fearfully around at the vast multitude. It was then decided that two dogs of a ferocious breed should be let loose at him—but this also proved fruitless; his activity was such that they could not catch him, and it was too evident, even to the most thorough-going amateur, that fighting was not his forte. Nothing could exceed the mortification of the lookers-on.

It would seem as if the honour of all Spain had been tarnished, and had the fate of the nation depended on the trial of the unfortunate brute they could not have felt much more. The disastrous battle of Ocana, in which the Spanish General, Venegas, was defeated by Sebastiani, who killed, wounded, or made prisoners some 24,000 or 25,000 men, [1] and by which Spain was nearly conquered, did not make a greater impression on the good people of Madrid than the want of "pluck" in one of their favourite bulls.

Some excuse might be made for the one,—the troops might have been badly fed, badly commanded, or over-matched—there, there was a loop-hole, some chance of glossing over the disgrace of defeat,—but what could be said now? Nothing—absolutely nothing. The bull was in proper "trim," brought to the "mark" as he should be, fairly pitted against his antagonists—and yet he would not fight!

An old man who sat next me cried out in an agony of despair, "The character of the nation is lost!" another said, "We have degenerated; what will be said after this defeat?" The clamour throughout all parts of the amphitheatre was at its height—nothing could be heard except execrations against the bull and his breeder, whose name was told me about fifty times over, but I cannot now take upon me to say who he was, nor is it, I believe, of much consequence to the reader,—in fine, other dogs were brought in, and

---

1. See note at the end of this chapter.

the bull at length made some fight with them, but the president of the ceremony put a stop to the combat by ordering two file of soldiers to advance and shoot the bull on the instant When he fell, a general shout of bitter execration followed his remains as they were dragged out of the circus.

It is a true, though trite observation, that after a storm comes a calm. So it was in the present instance. The gates were scarcely closed upon the delinquent bull, when the sound of trumpets announced the entry of the next and last; and if the Spaniards had suffered mortification before, they were amply recompensed by the splendid animal that now entered the arena. The moment he got footing, he attacked the first horseman he saw, killed the horse in almost a second, and then turned to the other, who shared the same fate.

The two *picadores* lay under the dead horses, and the field of battle was fairly won. The bull had no enemy to encounter; he ran about with the utmost fury, when the uproarious shouts in the lower tier of seats attracted him. Looking ferociously at the crowd that caused the tumult, he sprang over the outer fence, which was thickly lined with people, and disabled nineteen persons. The consternation was great, but had he killed half those in the Plaza de los Toros he would have been held in higher estimation than his predecessor who so disgracefully fled from his opponents. The arrangements were so excellent, that he was soon got into the arena again, and he died gallantly, like his companion, who first entered the lists, by the hands of the matador.

Thus ended the day's fighting, and a tremendous day's sport it was. Nine bulls were killed, seven horses shared the same fate, and one of the fighters was dreadfully injured. More than twenty people were hurt by the last bull; but fortunately, and indeed miraculously, no person was killed.

Thus the "casualties" of the day may be summed up as follows:— Killed, nine bulls, seven horses: total, sixteen; wounded, twenty-three men and women; grand total of killed and wounded, thirty-nine. I have not thought it necessary to enumerate the particulars of each combat, as it would be tedious to the reader.

The first encounter, which I have already described, is sufficient to put the reader in possession of all the rest: the limits of these volumes do not afford scope for more than has been said—too much, perhaps, for the casual reader—too little, no doubt, for the thorough-going bullfighter. I would wish to please both it I could, or indeed to please anybody, but the task is not so easy as many imagine, and I shall wind up my narrative by stating, that the animals are small but well-proportioned, formed by nature for great activity and muscular power, and trained from their infancy to attacks the most daring.

The bullfights once over, the execution of the Priest Lopez forgotten, and the probability of our soon leaving Madrid taking place, were not things to be passed over lightly by the ladies of that city; and no matter what may be said or written of their being "a grave people," I saw, during my sojourn amongst them, no symptoms of "gravity," except when they thought we were about to leave their capital. It was palpably evident that something should be done to drive away the gloom that had in a great measure already begun to take a fast hold of our friends; and the officers of the Light Division, aided by some of the other regiments in the garrison, resolved to treat the inhabitants with a specimen of their dramatic powers.

The play selected was the "Revenge," and "Zanga" was well personated by Captain Kent of the Rifles; but whether it was that the other characters were ill cast, or that the tragedy was too dull for the Spaniards to relish, it is a positive fact, that long before the second act was ended, the audience were heartily tired of the play; and, notwithstanding the fine acting of Kent, the play would have never been allowed to proceed had not the performers been British officers, and the object, the relief of the poor of the capital.

The "Mayor of Garrett" followed, and this amusing farce was a set-off against the "Revenge," and put the audience quite at ease; for from the moment "Zanga" (or *El Preto,* as they styled him) appeared, there was one universal buzz of disapprobation. It is not possible for me to say why they were so averse to the play; it might have been their dislike to the Moors; but be this as it may, I would advise my friends in the army never to try the same play before a Madrid audience—that is, which is a hundred to one—should they ever have the same opportunity we had. This was the first and last play ever attempted by us to be got up at Madrid.

The season was on the wane, summer was almost over, and

it was well known that Lord Wellington meditated an attack on the town of Burgos; nevertheless all was tranquillity and gaiety with the troops at Madrid, and many of the sick and wounded from Salamanca reached us. Amongst the number was my friend and companion, Frederick Meade of the 88th: he had been badly wounded in the action of the 22nd, and, with his arm in a sling, his wounds still unhealed, and his frame worn down by fatigue and exhaustion, his commanding officer was surprised to see him again so soon with his regiment; but various rumours were afloat as to the advance of the Madrid army upon Burgos, and Meade was not the kind of person likely to be absent from his corps when anything like active service was to be performed by it.

Endowed with qualities which few young men in the army could boast of, he soon made his way into the very best society that the capital of Spain could be said to possess. A finished gentleman in the fullest acceptation of the word; young, handsome, speaking the Castilian language well, the French fluently, a first-rate musician, endowed by nature with a fine voice, which had been well cultivated, it is not surprising that he soon became a general favourite. In a word, wherever he went he was the magnet of attraction, and when we quitted Madrid it would have required a train of vehicles much more numerous than would have suited our order of march, to convey those ladies who were, and would like to be more closely, attached to him.

Poor fellow! he was greatly to blame, but it was not his fault; if the ladies of Madrid liked his face, or his voice, how could he help that? My man, Dan Carsons —and here I must say a word of apology to my friend Meade for coupling their names together— told me when we were on the eve of quitting Madrid, "that he (Carsons) didn't know how the devil he could get away at all at all, without taking three women, besides his wife "Nelly,' with him."

The accounts of our wounded and sick friends, left at Salamanca, were of a varied description; some had died, others were in a bad state, and many had suffered amputation; amongst the latter was Lieutenant William Nickle, who lost his leg while volunteering the duty of another officer, who should have been on the baggage-guard at Salamanca; but poor Nickle, who was in (command of the Light Infantry company, could not bear to see them going into battle without being at their head, and he lost his leg but gained the esteem of his brother soldiers in consequence.

Captain Adair was wounded just in the same spot, the cap of the knee, as Nickle, and they were both put into one room. For several days the surgeons delayed the operation upon Nickle, hoping that his constitution and youth would bring him through, but it was a vain hope. The limb by degrees became numb, and mortification was making rapid strides, when at length it was resolved to take off the leg high above the knee. Adair, circumstanced precisely as his companion, with this difference only—and it is no small difference notwithstanding—that he was some twenty years his senior, listened with horror to the determination of the surgeons to commence operations upon his friend.

His feelings on the occasion might be likened to those cast away at sea, when lots are drawn to ascertain who is to be the first victim. It, as has been seen, was decided that Nickle was the first, but poor, Adair ("Robin" we called him) looked more like a criminal going to execution, while he observed the hangman commencing his vocation by arranging the noose round the neck of his fellow-companion who was about to precede him.

The surgeons, seeing the state of agitation which not only their presence, but that which they were about to do, caused Adair, with great humanity—and humanity is not their *forte*—examined his knee and told him he had nothing to fear, as amputation would not be necessary. Adair, though advanced in years, was what we, in the Peninsular army, used to dub a "Count" Although a perfect gentleman, he had a dash of puppyism attached to him, which no circumstance, no matter how grave, could get the better of.

Whether it was that he felt revived by the reprieve he had just got, or that he was indignant at the insinuation of the surgeons, I know not, but it is most certain that he turned on them with great wrath. "Gentlemen," said Robin, "it is not for myself that I feel—it is for my friend Nickle." He then called for his servant-man, whose name was Walton, and ordered him to remove him to another chamber. Walton obeyed, and poor Adair was spared the sight of the operation upon Nickle. Had he witnessed it, I firmly believe he would not have been a living man in forty-eight hours afterwards.

In taking off Nickle's thigh, by some mismanagement the bandages and tourniquet gave way, and he lost so much blood that his life was in danger, but he recovered and gained his rank of Captain. He has been dead some years, and in him his regiment lost a young man of tried gallantry, and the army one of its most promising officers. He lost his leg by volunteering the duty of another, and never gained promotion by it: so much for volunteering extra duties!

I have known many do the same who were never rewarded or even noticed, and unless the system in our army be greatly ameliorated, I would advise young men to be content with doing their duty and nothing more.

So far all went on gaily at Madrid; but Lord Wellington was deeply occupied with matters of a different nature, although he joined in the amusements that took place. The capture of Burgos was what he aimed at, and his stay at Madrid was but a cloak to cover his real intentions. On the 1st of September he quitted the capital, and took upon himself the direction of that part of the army which he had deckled was to march upon Burgos. He crossed the Douro on the 6th, and arrived at Valladolid on the same day, and from thence he followed the enemy on their retreat to Burgos.

On the 16th he was, with a portion of his army, before that fortress, which he soon invested and laid siege to. The result of: that siege, its failure, and the circumstances which led to it, have nothing to do with my adventures; they are the property of Colonel Napier—the only writer that, I believe, can be held up as a standard to refer to on the Peninsular War.

We are to bring forward to the public eye, and the eye of posterity, too, the character of the Peninsular soldiers, whether they be showed up as men who were able to conquer the choicest legions of France, or whether they would sell the most essential part of their dress for a glass of brandy. No matter: they would, and have done both.

Perfection is nowhere to be found; and if the British soldier equalled the Frenchman in habits of sobriety and caution, there could be no possible comparison between them: but the retreat from Madrid and Burgos, which I am about to relate, will give the reader a clearer insight into what I have just now written: and I will here say, without the least fear of contradiction, that the French soldier as far surpasses the British soldier in the essential qualities requisite for general operations, as the latter excels the Frenchman in a pitched battle. Let two armies of the two nations be placed in circumstances the same, in advance or retreat.

The supply of provisions may be scanty or abundant,—no matter which. Both: armies, for argument sake, we will say are placed in the same position as to food: it may be asked what, then, is this great difference between the soldiers of two nations who have been opposed to each other for so many campaigns, and who ought to have profited by the better system followed by either? It is this: the British soldier is not so moderate in his appetites as his neighbour, and he wants the head, which the other possesses, to control him.

Then, again, there can be no comparison between our army and the French as to the facility of cooking. And why? Because their method is the best. In the French army, every company carries the kettles requisite for their mess, and every soldier carries, according to circumstances, a certain number of days' provisions—say ten or twelve days.

Can this be done in the British Army? Certainly not. Because the temperament of the soldiers of the two nations is widely different. The one is frugal in the extreme, always hoarding up what he has gained; and looking forward to amass more. Give to a British regiment ten days', nay five days' bread at a time, and, as may be necessary, five days' rations of spirits; at the end of the second day—not the fifth, to which period it ought to last—what quantity will be forthcoming? Not one half ounce of bread, or half pint of spirits—half pint did I say! not one thimbleful, nay, less than that, not one drop!

Should the ration be limited to bread, and in all armies, even the moist temperate, a large advance of spirits ought to be avoided, the danger would be the same in any British army, because the soldiers would barter their bread for spirits or wine, and would become equally inefficient, as if they had been supplied with both by our commissaries. Added to this, what means had the soldiers of the Peninsular army to compete with the French in celerity of cooking? None. The latter carried their cooking utensils on their backs, while the camp-kettles for our troops were often leagues distant when the meat arrived.

This was the state of our army when the retreat from Burgos, on the one side, and Madrid on the other, commenced, and it will be seen in the following pages how that retreat was conducted, and how the subordinate officers of the army were blamed for not performing a duty which was impossible; and for this reason was it impossible, that the means did not rest with them. Our system was altogether faulty, and no exertions of the junior, or even senior, officers could remedy it. Lord Wellington at length discovered this, and in his next campaign profited by the example which the enemy showed him, and which ought to have been followed long before.

On the 20th of October, 1812, the siege of Burgos was raised, and the troops before it retired towards the Douro, while the portion of the Army which occupied Madrid made arrangements to join him when the proper time should arrive. Accordingly the fort of La China was mined, the battering train found there removed, and all the necessary arrangements for retreat were completed.

On the 31st of October, the array quitted Madrid, and bivouacked in the Royal Park near the palace; no disaster occurred, and, was it not for the loss of one life, the evacuation of the capital might be termed bloodless. The person I allude to was. a young man attached to the ordnance department: he was a storekeeper, and had the management of some part of the placing the gunpowder in the Fort of La China.

This unfortunate fellow, and he was an unfortunate fellow, as the sequel will prove, was a man of cadaverous aspect, was always prowling about the magazines with such an air of dejection, that it might have been supposed he anticipated the fate he was destined for, namely, being blown up by the very powder he had the charge of.

He was better known in the division by the soubriquet of "Guy Fawkes," than his own proper name, which I now forget. "Fawkes," if history is to be credited, was an ill-looking man, but if he surpassed in ugliness the person of whom I am now writing, he must have been plain indeed. Poor "Fawkes," for so I will call him, not thinking that the different trains were well arranged at La China, ventured in after the match had been lighted by himself; he calculated, or thought so at least, with much exactness, the precise time the first explosion would take place, but he, like many of us, reckoned without his host, and, in short, before he could quit the building, the mine exploded, and he was blown into atoms.

One of his legs was thrown out towards the botanic gardens; the foot was perfect, and to it was attached a large brass spur which was bent in its fall. The soldiers were shocked when they beheld the mangled leg, but the long spur, bent as it was, caused some merriment. My servant, Dan Carsons, who always had his joke ready, said "he was spurred on to do a mighty foolish action."

"Well! and iv he was," replied Paddy Lowry, "wasn't it bent on the occasion, and how could the poor creature help that?" On this day our commanding-officer, Colonel Alexander Wallace, was attacked with fever and ague, and was, in consequence, sent to Salamanca.

The conflagration of La China continued all night, and story after story fell in until it became a heap of ruins. The following day, the 1st of November, the advance of the French entered Madrid, and on that day our army commenced its retreat upon Rodrigo and Portugal. On the side of Burgos matters were in the same state.

The attack against the citadel having failed in default of means to carry it on, the army before it broke up on the 20th of October, and by the admirable arrangements of Lord Wellington, who took the command in person, gained two marches on the enemy before he was aware of it. Nevertheless a vigorous pursuit took place, and the Burgos army was closely pressed, until it reached the heights of San Christoval, where it was joined by the troops that had occupied Madrid.

Up to this time no serious disaster had occurred, although from the heavy rains that had fallen, which rendered the roads nearly impassable, and the scanty supply of rations which the troops received, it was feared that, if Soult pressed on vigorously, our army would shortly become much disorganized; but the marshal took six days, that is to say, from the 10th to the 16th of November, to examine the ground occupied by the British General. On the 14th, our army was in battle array close to the spot where we had fought the battle of Salamanca the July before, but Soult, although at the head of 90,000 soldiers, and two hundred pieces of cannon, declined the offer, and confined his operations to the sending a brigade or two on the line of our communication with Rodrigo.

On the 17th, Lord Wellington commenced his march for the frontiers of Portugal, and from that moment he was closely pursued by Marshal Soult; the rain fell in torrents, without almost any intermission; the roads could no longer be so called, they were perfect quagmires; the small streams became rivers, and the rivers were scarcely fordable at any point. In some instances the soldiers were obliged to carry their ammunition boxes strapped on their shoulders to preserve them while passing a ford which on our advance was barely ankle deep. The baggage and camp-kettles had left us; the former we never saw until we reached Rodrigo, and the latter rarely reached us until two o'clock in the morning, when the men, from fatigue, could make but little use of them.

The wretched cattle had to be slaughtered, as our rations seldom arrived at their destination before the camp-kettles, and when both arrived, there was not one fire in our *bivouac* sufficient to boil a mess. Officers as well as soldiers had no covering except the canopy of heaven; we had not one tent, and the army never slept in a village. We thus lay in the open country; our clothes saturated with rain, half the men and officers without shoes, nothing to eat, or, at all events, no means of cooking it. What then could be much worse than the situation in which the army was placed? But this was not the worst, because, from the nature of the retreat, and the pursuit, neither the cavalry nor artillery horses could be supplied with forage.

The retreat each day generally began at four in the morning, in the dead dark of night; towards eight the army had gained perhaps six miles, perhaps not five, start of the enemy. At ten they were at our heels. The rear, as a matter of necessity, for the preservation of the whole, was then obliged to face about, and show a front, to enable the remainder to proceed on their retreat. The position taken up was, as a matter of course, according to the urgency of the moment, sometimes in a vast tract of ploughed land, where the troops were drawn up ankle deep in mud. In this position, those who were not fighting were obliged to remain in their tattered uniforms, worn to rags after two years' service, scarcely a good pair of shoes or trowsers on any, and the greater part without the former.

The ague had also attacked the bulk of the army, and as the soldiers picked up the acorns that fell from the oak trees (which, by the way, is the property of the pigs in Spain, but who, fortunately for themselves, had not as yet appeared in the woods we just now traversed,) many were unable to eat them, so much were they enfeebled by the disorder.

Yet under all these privations, the soldiers, at least the "Connaught Rangers," never lost their gaiety. Without shoes they fancied themselves "at home," and there were few, I believe, who would not have wished themselves there in reality. Without food they were nearly at home, and without a good coat to their backs equally so!

My man, Dan Carsons, came up to me, and with a broad grin, said, "By gor, Sir, this same place" (at the time we were, and had been for hours before, standing in a wet ploughed field,) "puts me greatly in mind iv Madrid."

"Of Madrid! why, Dan, no two places can be more unlike."

"By Jasus, Sir, the're as like as two paise, only that we want the houses, and the fires, and the mate, and the dhrink, and the women! But, excepting that, don't the jaws to the boys with the ague, when they rattle so, put your honour greatly in mind iv the castonetts?"

Dan's joke was not quite so palatable as it might have proved at a more fitting opportunity, or in a more fitting place, for at that moment I felt a queer sort of motion about my own jaws, which in less than an hour proved itself to be a confirmed attack of ague. On this night the rain never ceased; the rations could not be cooked, having arrived too late, and the army had no food except biscuit.

What I have related took place on the 16th. The following day matters became worse, the rain continued to come down in torrents, and in the passage of one river, out of ten that we forded, a woman and three children were lost, as likewise some baggage mules, which the women of the army, in defiance of the order against it, still contrived to smuggle into the line of retreat. The rations arrived alive (I mean the meat), as usual after midnight, but no kettles reached us for an hour after the poor famished brutes had been knocked on the head.

Each man obtained his portion of the quivering flesh, but before any fires could be relighted, the order for march arrived, and the men received their meat dripping with water, but little, if anything, warmer than when it was delivered over to them by the butcher. The soldiers drenched with wet, greatly fatigued, nearly naked, and more than half asleep, were obliged either to throw away the meat, or put it with their biscuit into their haversacks, which from constant use, without any means of cleaning them, more resembled a beggarman's wallet, than any part of the appointments of a soldier.

In a short time, the wet meat completely destroyed the bread, which became perfect paste, and the blood which oozed from the undressed beef, little better than carrion, gave so bad a taste to the bread, that many could not eat it; those who did were in general attacked with violent pains in their bowels, and the want of salt brought on dysentery. A number of cavalry and artillery horses died on this night, and fatigue and sickness had already obliged several men and officers to remain behind, so that our ranks were now beginning to show that we had commenced, in downright earnest, a most calamitous retreat.

Lord Wellington wished for a battle, if he could fight one on advantageous terms, before his army became disorganized; but this was not to the interest of the French army; and the Duke of Dalmatia, who could at any time make choice of his own field from his vast superiority in horsemen, was too experienced a tactician to be led into so fatal an error as that of fighting. Experience had shown him that a retreat, such as the one I am describing, would cost him little trouble to inflict as great a loss upon our army as if he gained the advantage in a battle, and that it would be a bloodless victory to him; whereas, if a general action took place, and the entire of the two armies were thrown into the fight, he could not expect to get off with a loss of less than six or eight thousand men, with the chance, perhaps the probability, of being defeated.

No marshal in the French army knew the good and the bad qualities of the soldiers he now followed better, few so well, as Soult He had pursued them to Corunna, and fought them at Albuera. Knowing then, as he did, their imperfection in retreat, and their superlative perfection in a pitched battle, it would have been strange had he risked by a battle what it was, as clear as the noonday, he would gain without one, namely, the loss to us of several thousand men and horses, who, if they did not fall into his hands, or die on the retreat, were sure to be lost to our ranks in consequence of its effects.

The game was in his hands, and if he lost it by bad play, the fault would be his, and his only; he did not do so, but played a safe game, and when battle was offered him near Salamanca, he reneged. He finessed well, and though he did not drive us before him at the point of the bayonet, his flank movement on the Rodrigo line, by a side wipe, effected his purpose just as well for him.

A circumstance occurred on this day, that so strongly marks the difference between the British soldiers and the soldiers of any other nation on such a retreat as we were engaged in, that I cannot avoid noticing it. I have already said that we had no means of cooking our meat, and that the soldiers and officers, for all shared the same privations alike, carried their meat raw, or nearly raw; consequently it was not an additional supply of "raw material" that we so much needed as the means of dressing what we had.

Nevertheless, towards noon, while a portion of the army was engaged in a warm skirmish with the enemy's advance, which lay through a vast forest of oak, some hundreds of swine, nearly in a wild state, were discovered feeding upon the acorns which had fallen from the trees the autumn before. No flag of truce ever sent from the advance post of one army to the advance of another had a more decisive effect.

Our soldiers immediately opened, a murderous fire upon the pigs, who suffered severely on the occasion, being closely pursued on the route, which they followed with that stupid—and for them, on this occasion, fatal—pertinacity which the pig tribe are so proverbial for, namely, going to the rear when they ought to go straight forward. Had this herd of swine deviated from the old beaten track of pigs in general— had they, in short, gone forward instead of rearward—many valuable lives, in the eyes of the owners at least, would have been saved, because they would have soon reached the French advance, and our fellows, once more placed *vis à vis* with the riflemen of the *grande nation,* would have left off the pursuit—if for nothing else, but to save their bacon!

This *rencontre,* one of the most curious that came within my knowledge during my Peninsular campaigns, or indeed during my sojourn in this world, led to consequences the most comic as well as tragic Colonel O'Shea, who commanded the cavalry of the French advance ordered to support the *tirailleurs*, was astounded when he saw the direction which the British fire took.

He could not be mistaken; the fire of the advance of his own soldiers had slackened—ceased. It immediately occurred to him that some corps must have got in rear of our advance, and he galloped up to the *tirailleurs* to ascertain the real state of affairs. He was soon undeceived; but when he learned the cause of the retrograde movement on the part of our men, he could not avoid—and who could?—laughing heartily.

Meanwhile the discomfited and routed pigs fled, and soon got out of the clutches of the advanced guard. The bulk of the fugitives took the road to their right, but here they were again wrong. Had those ill-fated animals known anything of the "rules of the road," they would have kept to the left. On the right they were encountered by a nearly famished brigade, that had received no rations at all the preceding twenty-four hours; and when they were, as has been seen, so roughly handled by men whose haversacks were amply stocked with meat, what chance had they—I ask the question fearlessly—of any mercy from a body of famished, ferocious fellows?

The question I have just put is easily answered. They had none to expect, and none did they receive. Neither age nor sex was spared; and put of this fine herd of swine, scarcely one in one hundred escaped unhurt No victory was ever more complete; and the grunting and squeaking of the wounded pigs and hogs throughout the forest was a sad contrast with the merriment of the soldiers, who toasted, on the points of their bayonets—intended for other and more noble game—the mangled fragments of their former companions.

The line of retreat had been well considered by Lord Wellington. Several brigades of infantry and a division of cavalry, perfectly competent to the task, had been placed on this part of the country which I have described. He had nothing to fear, and the generals commanding divisions or brigades were equally confident; in short, there was nothing left undone to guard against any surprise, and, in fact, there was nothing to apprehend on this side. Day was drawing to its close, and the Third Division, commanded by Sir Edward Packenham, was about to retire from the ground it had held during several hours in face of the enemy, when a warm fire of musketry on our left led us to suppose we were outflanked.

The officers of the staff galloped in the direction from whence the firing proceeded Sir Edward did the same, but it was some time before they reached the scene of action. In the meantime, the different regiments were so arranged as to be ready either to advance or retreat, as circumstances might require; and the French corps in our front made demonstrations of a similar kind. In this state of suspense we remained for nearly an hour, when at last Sir Edward returned with the news that the firing was caused by a fresh attack on the pigs that had escaped the first brunt of the attack against them. He ordered the different advance posts to be placed, which he superintended in person; the soldiers then prepared to fell timber for fires, and some ran to an uninhabited village—they were all uninhabited on the line of our march, for that matter—for the purpose of getting dry wood, that is to say, the doors and roofs of the houses, to enable us to light up the green timber, which was the only fuel we could command. The soldiers and officers of all ranks were nearly exhausted from cold and wet; and had the village in question belonged to the king of England, much less to a parcel of Spanish peasants, it would have shared the same fate as the one in question.

The party from the village soon arrived, Both bringing doors, others articles of different kinds of household furniture, such as chairs, tables, and bedsteads; but nothing in the shape of food was to be found. No doubt, had it been day, something might be got at, but warmth was what we stood in need of more than food. Several of us still carried the parboiled beef of the night before, and when the fires were lighted we made a shift to roast it either on our swords, bayonets, or bits of sticks, which we formed into respectable skewers.

This operation finished, the fire around which each group sat or stood, in order of companies, their arms regularly piled behind them, was replenished with green and dry timber, according to our supply of each or both. The soldiers then placed their knapsacks round the outer part of the circle, and having given the best place to their officers inside the circle, all lay down together, or at their own choice, with their feet towards the heat of the fire. Some arranged in this manner, others did not lie down at all; and those who had captured a door, propped it up as a defence against the rains and winds.

There were others who got a blanket and fixed it with branches of trees and stones against some uneven spot, and lay down in the mud. It was, in fact, all mud and wet; and in whatever manner we accommodated ourselves, according to circumstances, whether walking, standing, or sleeping, it was of little difference. No matter what mood any of us might have been disposed to follow, the imperative had the call; and, as has been seen, we could not decline it. *Verbum sat sapienti.*

Thus ended the operations of this day; officers and soldiers were placed exactly, or nearly, as I have described. Many were so feeble as not to be capable of the least exertion; others, on the contrary, were hale and stout, and I, myself, was amongst the number of the latter. I had lain sometime with my feet near the fire, but I dreaded an attack of ague, and I walked about to keep my body warm, which was but thinly clad. I had not been long on my legs, and I was at the moment standing near the small tent where Sir Edward Packenham lay in his wet clothes, when a rush of pigs,—the remnant, I suppose, of those that had escaped in the day,—disorganized several piles of arms.

The soldiers stood up, and every man seized his firelock. A Portuguese regiment near us, thinking the enemy were at their heels, began to fire right and left, without knowing what they fired at. Sir Edward Packenham ran out of his tent, and while in the act of mounting his horse, and giving directions to his orderly dragoon, the man was shot dead by the side of the general It required some time before the confusion that prevailed could be remedied; but the soldiers never for a moment lost their presence of mind, and the Third Division was formed with astonishing celerity in battle array.

The error into which the Portuguese had fallen was, with some difficulty, remedied, and, except a few men who were wounded, nothing serious happened. The pigs, who were the cause of all, escaped without any loss, but whether they ever found their way back to their original owners I know not. Trifling as the affair was, with troops less accustomed and less ready to face an enemy than those that composed the Third Division, it might have had a different result.

The rations and camp-kettles soon after arrived, but it was late before the bullocks were slain, skinned, and delivered to the men; and the retreat commenced before any provisions could be cooked. This was the worst night we had passed since we crossed the Tormes.

Many of the young soldiers and worn-out veterans could no longer march, and were abandoned to their fate; many died during the night, and the artillery and cavalry horses perished in vast numbers, the infantry, however, was still formidable and efficient. The heroes of Rodrigo, Badajoz, and Salamanca, were the same men in spirit; but it cannot be denied that the privations they had suffered in a great degree undermined their stamina. It is true the marches were short, but the long halts, under an almost constant torrent of rain, were worse than can be conceived; and under any other general except Lord Wellington, it would be hard to say what the result might have been.

The officers, placed on a par with the soldiers, like them obliged to march on foot, many without shoes, and all with scanty and bad clothing, obliged to lie out in an open country without shelter of any kind, with no means, generally, of cooking their food, how can it be wondered at that they were not able to cope with their more hardy companions, the soldiers, in the actual essentials necessary to carry them onward, much less fulfil those duties which were afterwards—during a halt for the night—expected from them?

I shall touch but lightly on this matter now, it shall be the subject of my next chapter; but I will put one plain question to any officer who was present in the retreat from Burgos and Madrid—it is this. What duty could a subaltern officer perform more than he did perform during that retreat? Lord Wellington, in his circular letter to officers commanding regiments —after the retreat had been effected—says much as to the duties officers should attend to. He was perfectly right in so writing.

But what duty did the officers neglect on that occasion? Did the subaltern officers offer any impediment to the cooking? I think not was there any deficiency of wood to cook? The fires around which we endeavoured to warm ourselves, and dry our tattered uniforms, is an answer to the question. Was there any want of water to cook the provisions when they reached us? The ground that we lay upon, surrounded by dikes of water, settles that point Where, then, did the error rest? I will explain presently.

The march was continued the following morning. The troops commenced the retreat some hours before day. Towards ten o'clock the enemy's advance were at the heels of the rear-guard, which, as before, disputed the ground. A rapid stream on the Rodrigo side of the village of San Munoz was to be passed before the rear could be considered safe. Many regiments had already forded the river, but one entire brigade was missing, and the haze was so great that it was difficult to distinguish any object clearly.

Packenham's division was already on the left bank of the stream, while the brigade of nine pounders, commanded by that admirable officer, Captain Douglas, opened its fire on the French advance. This, for a moment, arrested their progress; but O'Shea, at the head of fifteen hundred dragoons, passed between the French infantry and the river, and, disregarding the fire of our artillery, overtook the brigade before it had passed the ford. The confusion at this point was great, some men were sabred; but the fire of Douglas's guns caused the French dragoons many casualties, and they galloped back to their former ground.

The safety of the brigade which was missing was thus insured; but Sir Edward Paget, who had gone in quest of it, and knowing nothing of what had taken place at the river's edge, was taken prisoner by O'Shea. We thus lost our second in command, as also many men; and the cavalry and artillery horses had become so enfeebled for want of forage, that it was manifest our retreat, if vigorously followed by Soult, would, as a matter of necessity, have been protected by the infantry alone; but Soult either could not or would not press us, and the remainder of the day passed over languidly.

A heavy cannonade on both sides was the principal feature in the operations of the day, and, as we were now within one march of the fortress of Rodrigo, the French marshal appeared to be satisfied with the loss inflicted upon us. It is not possible for me to say what his motives were for discontinuing a pursuit which had been productive of so great a disorganization in our army. His own, perhaps, were nearly as ill off; but it is most certain, that, had he followed our footsteps for three days longer with the same energy he had done on the preceding ones (for the country was still open), our artillery and cavalry must have suffered serious loss.

Note.—Amongst the trophies captured by the French at the battle of Ocana, were the astounding number of thirteen thousand eight hundred and seventy-seven guitars; twelve thousand seven hundred and fifty-two being in cases, and one thousand one hundred and twenty-five without cases; being nearly in the ratio of two guitars to each combatant!

CHAPTER 27

Jokes of the Connaught Rangers

Notwithstanding the attitude of Packenham's troops, and the excellent arrangement of the park of artillery under Douglas, the troopers of O'Shea still menaced the ford. A brigade of French guns ascended the heights, and opened their fire upon the Third Division, but they were replied to with vigour by Douglas, who, on this day, surpassed himself; and the decided superiority which his fire had over that of the enemy was so palpable, that, after a short trial, the French left the heights.

Day was drawing to its close, and our march, as usual, commenced soon after dark. The entire day had been one of drizzling wet, but, towards evening, the run came down in torrents; the army had to march two leagues ere they reached the point marked out for them on the line of retreat, and, it would be difficult to describe the wretched state of the troops.

The cavalry half dismounted; the artillery without the requisite number of horses to draw the ammunition-cars, much less the guns; the infantry without shoes, or nearly so; and the roads, even in the broad day nearly impassable, made the march of this night one of great loss. When a halt occurred, which was often unavoidable, in consequence of the guide mistaking the way, or by means of the narrowness of a part of the road, or the difficulty of ascertaining the pass of a river, those in the rear fell down asleep, and it was next to impossible to awaken them, so much were they exhausted; it then became incumbent on every man who was awake to rouse those in his front, who impeded the line of march, not only of the individual himself, but of the army in general.

Nevertheless, many were obliged to stay behind, and were abandoned to their fate. None but the stout and hale could bear up against the inclemency of the weather and the want of food; but the worst of all was the wretched state of the horses of the cavalry and artillery: these poor animals, when they reached the place marked out for our resting for the night, had not one morsel to eat, for it was absolutely impossible to forage for them at such an hour and under such circumstances, and the consequence was that many died from cold and famine, either in the harness of the artillery or under the saddles of the dragoons.

It was nine o'clock this night of the retreat before we reached the ground where we were to rest; and we had scarcely lit our fires when the bullocks and kettles arrived. This circumstance—a rare one—put us in good spirits, and, by the time we had eaten our first meal that day, we became more gay, and the "boys" of the 88th had their joke about the slaughter of the pigs by the Fourth Division, of which I have made some slight mention in the last chapter. That I might have said more on the subject I am aware, for it was a subject that much might be said upon; but, had I done so, my readers, perhaps, would consider me a bore.

However, the Connaught Rangers would have, and had, their joke at the expense of the defunct pip. Jack Richardson, of the light infantry company, said, "The poor craturs must be blind intirely when they run into the mouth of the Fourth Division."

"No," replied my man, Dan Carsons, "they weren't blind all out, but perhaps they had a stye in their eye!" This sally of Dan was loudly applauded; and this kind of gaiety of spirit never forsook the men of the 88th under any circumstances. It was well for themselves, and for the service also; for I believe no regiment in the Peninsula had more uphill work to contend against than the ill-fated 88th. No matter!—all that is past and gone now; and those who survive, and recollect the events that took place during their stay in the Third Division, are now changing positions; they had up-hill work then—now they are going down the hill. It is, nevertheless, a galling reflection to those who bravely earned notice and promotion, to find themselves passed over, while others, of regiments in the same division, and under the same general, and placed in circumstances the same, and sometimes-less hazardous, have been lauded and promoted, while those of the 88th were not even noticed!

But I am digressing. After Carsons' pun we soon fell asleep; and were again on our legs at four in the morning; but our appearance was greatly changed for the worse: several soldiers had died during the night from exhaustion and cold; and those who had shoes on them were soon stripped of so essential a necessary; and many a young fellow was too happy to be allowed to stand in a "dead man's shoes."

Others were so crippled as to be scarcely able to stand to their arms. Ague and dysentery had, more or less, affected us all; and the men's feet were so swollen, that they threw away their shoes in preference to wearing them. The cavalry presented a miserable sight: the horses nearly starved to death, and all, or almost all, with sore backs, caused by the friction of' the saddles from the effects of the heavy rains that fell almost without any intermission. The artillery was even worse than the cavalry: out of every team of eight horses scarcely four were left; and, had the pursuit been carried on with vigour for two marches beyond Rodrigo, it would not require much knowledge on military points, or much foresight in common understanding, to predict what the result would have been.

As it was, the artillery and cavalry were nearly placed out of the fight The infantry—the acknowledged best infantry in Europe—were still formidable and efficient, as compared with the other two arms; and had there been any thing like a good, even a tolerable, arrangement in their supply of provisions, or—which was of more vital consequence—their means of cooking them, all would have been right; but the reverse was the fact.

Owing to the faulty arrangements of those who should have looked to it, the supply of rations never arrived in due time; and it is idle to say that such could not have been the case, for the army was not engaged in a rapid retreat—quite the contrary; therefore, it was easy to ascertain whereabouts the troops would halt for the night, and the mules carrying the provisions for each division might have dodged about the environs destined for the occupation of each corps.

All this was easy, because it would be worse than childish to argue, in defence of the neglect, that the army was in retreat. To be sure it was: but after a certain time—after dark—what was to molest it?—what disaster had it to look to? None, except the bad arrangement of its own superiors, who neglected to do what was necessary and easy of accomplishment—namely, the supplying the troops with food.

The French fire generally ceased before five o'clock in the afternoon; it was then dark: could the army of Soult make any way—in short, dare he; attempt it after that hour? It was well known he could not Then why were not arrangements made for the comfort, the keeping life in the soldiers? No, retreat was ever made in the face of an enemy where, the marches were shorter or the halts more frequent. The army met with no disaster from the enemy—all rested with our own officers,—not the subordinate) ones, but the chiefs.

In the memorable letter which Lord Wellingtons addressed to the army after this retreat, he takes notice of the celerity with which the French soldiers cooked in comparison with ours. Now, why should this not be the case in the campaign alluded to? The, British soldiers had no more the means of competing, with the Frenchmen in celerity of cooking then, than the French nation have now in competing with our Leeds and Manchester manufactories; and for this reason, that they had not the means of so doing.

Had the generals under the command of Lord Wellington paid as much attention to the minor duties of the army as he did to the principal ones—had they followed the example of the French, in the arrangements of their divisions—had they, in short, provided their men with the means of cooking, as the French did,— the letter from his lordship, to which I have made allusion, would never have been published; and no letter ever gave, and justly so, more annoyance to the officers of the army.

Was it possible, or was it fair to suppose, that that great man, whose mind was not only occupied with the deliverance of the Peninsula, but the deliverance of Europe into the bargain, could turn his thoughts into every little minutia? Was he to attend to the arrangement of camp-kettles, stew-pots, and ammunition? What had he, or what ought he to have had, to do with such minor duties? It was the business of those in command of divisions and brigades—a subaltern with *nous,* for that matter, would have done it—to have looked to the evil.

So much for the generals, the camp-kettles, and the porridge-pots. The retreat on this day was less severe than any of the preceding ones; but the bad food of the troops, and the misery and fatigue they had undergone, occasioned a great number of sick; the soldiers and officers were attacked with dysentery, and scarcely half the men of each regiment were free from this disorder. Subsistence was nowhere to be found, for the army traversed a wilderness. The towns and villages were deserted—no peasant came to us to sell provisions; in short, all the people forsook their homes, and, quitting the line of march occupied by the hostile armies, fled in every direction.

No corps was allowed to enter a village—all were obliged to lie in the open country; and although this seemed, and was, a rigorous measure, it was one of absolute necessity—because, had the army been placed under cover, however desirable, the inevitable result would have been the complete disorganization of the whole.

Scarcely any provisions were to be found, but an abundance of wine could have been easily procured from the different wine-caves in each village. The troops, once let loose in this kind of way, could not be restrained, and all discipline would have been at an end; therefore, no one ought to be surprised that Lord Wellington forbade the occupation of a town. He did his part in the grand scale, but those who acted under him were deficient in every way.

Sometimes the troops were bivouacked in a muddy swamp, when dry ground, in comparison at least, was nigh. The consequence of all this bungling was fatal: the troops became ill and inefficient; they became discontented; and, to wind up all, the junior officers of the army were blamed for those things over which they had as much control as they had over the action's of the Dey of Algiers or the Great Mogul. The officers divided the misery of the retreat with their men; and it is well known that many of them had scarcely a covering to their backs.

Scarcely a subaltern in the army had a dollar in his pocket, the troops being four months in arrear of pay; but, even supposing he had money in abundance, what use could he make of it? There was nothing to be had for love or money—we had no money, and few of us were inclined to make love; but even if we were, there was no one (the worst of it) to make love to.

It has been said by a celebrated warrior, that to false the great superstructure of an army, it must be remembered the belly is the foundation. There are few, I believe, that will deny this axiom; yet, with the truth of this staring us in the face, our infantry, the main spring of the army, were left without food, or the means of cooking it, during one of the most inclement seasons that troops in such a climate ever witnessed. Happily, the army was not further pressed; but, if it had, it must have been totally disorganized. In default of food at home, the men must have looked elsewhere; and, it is scarcely necessary to add, that a marauding system would not have suited a British army at any time, much less when vigorously pursued by an enemy. As it was, it took six months to reorganise the troops, so as to enable them again to take the field.

Such was the end of a campaign, the commencement of which augured the most fortunate results. The men who composed this fine army—which, at Rodrigo, Badajos, and Salamanca, carried all before them—were now greatly changed for the worse. Scarcely a man had shoes; not that they were not amply supplied with them before the retreat commenced, but the state of the roads, if roads they could be called, was such, that so soon as a shoe fell off or stuck in the mud, in place of picking it up again, the man who had thus lost one kicked its fellow-companion after it. Yet the infantry was efficient, and able to do any duty. No excesses were committed, for Lord Wellington having taken the precaution of keeping the army away from the different villages, no man had an opportunity of obtaining wine or spirits, and thus drunkenness and insubordination were not added to the list of our misfortunes.

But the cavalry and artillery were in a wretched state indeed. The artillery of the Third, Sixth, and Seventh Divisions, the Heavy Cavalry, together with the: 7th and 12th Light Dragoons, were nearly a wreck; and the artillery of the Third Division lost seventy horses between Salamanca and Rodrigo. It was next to impossible that the artillery and cavalry could have made, if vigorously pursued, three marches beyond the latter place. What force, then, was to arrest the enemy in his pursuit?—The infantry, and the infantry alone; yet this main-prop of the army was, by mismanagement, left without the means of nourishment!

Had not the infantry, by their firmness in bearing up against all the evils they had to surmount—such as bad clothing, no tents to shelter them from the heavy rains that fell, and no means of dressing their food—presented the front they did, the army must have been lost before it could have reached Gallegos; and, if equal zeal had been exhibited by the general officers in providing for the wants of their troops, as was shown by the subordinate officers in the maintenance of discipline amongst them, the letter of Lord Wellington would never have been written.

Blame and praise, if properly employed, make a great change in the actions of a young man—so they do if improperly employed; and this letter of Lord Wellington, directed chiefly against the junior officers of his army, had a bad effect; Those officers asked each other, and asked themselves, how or in what manner they were to blame for the privations the army endured on the retreat? The answer uniformly was—in no way whatever.

The junior officers had nothing to do with it at all. Their business was to keep their men together, and, if possible, to keep up with their men on the march, and this was the most difficult duty they had to perform; for many, very many, of these officers were young lads, badly clothed, with scarcely a shoe or boot to their feet, some, attacked with dysentery, others with ague, and more with a burning fever raging through their system, had scarcely strength left to hobble on in company with their more hardy comrades, the soldiers.

Nothing but a high sense of honour could have borne them on; and there were many who would have remained behind, and run all rides as to the manner in which they would be treated as prisoners, were it not for this feeling. The different bivouacks each morning presented a sad spectacle—worn-out veterans, or young lads, unable to move, were abandoned to their fate. Some were thrown across the backs of the commissariat mules, and conveyed to the rear; but this was rare, for the drivers were obliged to make all haste to reach their destination, and the frames of the men, worn down by sickness, unhealed wounds, or old ones breaking out afresh, were unable to bear the jolting of the mules, and these men generally preferred taking their chance on the line of march, to submitting to such an uneasy mode of conveyance.

Thus ended the year 1812, and thus ended our retreat upon

Portugal. The details I have given of that retreat have not been the least exaggerated. It had, nevertheless, but little effect on my regiment, the 88th, for we scarcely lost a man by fatigue or sickness. The "boys of Connaught" were not much put out of their way by the want of shoes, a good coat to their backs, or a full allowance of rations: they took all those wants *aisy!* In short, it was astonishing to see the effective state of the regiment, as compared with others, when we reached our cantonments.

Since I commenced these pages, I have endeavoured to impress my readers with the idea—and I hope I have succeeded—that the 88th were none of those hum-drum set of fellows that ought to be classed with other regiments: they, in fact, had a way of their own! There are many who will agree—cordially on this point at least—with me; but their reading and mine, of the text, may be widely different, nevertheless.

The 88th was a regiment whose spirit it was scarcely possible to break, and the many curious incident's which occurred during this retreat, afforded them ample food for that ready humour for which they were proverbial, and for which they got full credit, but, nevertheless, they still are in arrear, and they owe a debt to themselves which they must pay off,—no matter what the price may be. It was well for them that they had food for their humour, for they had little for their stomachs; but that did not cause them much uneasiness.

The state in which some of the officers were placed was quite pitiable. Many were obliged to throw off their boots, their feet having become so swollen that they could not bear them. Those so circumstanced were necessitated to look to the soldiers for a new fit-out; but where could that be found? The men themselves, not caring much whether they had or had not shoes, left those they had worn in the muddy roads, and it would not be an easy matter to find on this same retreat a second pair with any man. However, by hook or by crook, those who wanted shoes were supplied; yet, though the soldiers might be termed the shoemakers of their officers, they never got the upper-hand of them!

To describe the state of the officers would be impossible; for myself, I can truly say, I was in rags. I wore a frock-coat, made out of a dress belonging to a priest that was captured by my man Dan

Carsons, at Badajos. I wore it during our sojourn at Madrid: it was lined with silk, and might be termed a good turnout there; but, as it turned out on the retreat, it was the worst description of clothing I, or rather my man Dan, could have pitched on. Every copse I passed, and they were many, took a slice off my Madrid frock, and, by the time I had undergone three marches, it was reduced to a spencer!

My feet never quitted the shoes in which they were placed from the moment of the retreat until its close. I knew too well their value, and, if I once got my feet out of them (no easy matter), I knew right well it would take some days to get them back again, they were so swollen; and, even if I were dead, much less crippled, there were many to be found anxious to stand in my shoes—to boot!

There were others, and many others, as badly off as I was. My friend, Meade, was obliged to leave his shoes behind him. He tried to walk barefooted for a while, but it was impossible. The gravel so lacerated his feet that he could not move, and he was obliged to make some shift to get a pair in place of those he had abandoned. Captain Graham, of the 21st Portuguese, a lieutenant in my regiment, was so worn out with fatigue, bare-backed, and barefooted, that, on one night of the retreat, having been fortunate enough to get a loaf of bread, he joined me and my companion Meade; but, so unable was he to eat of the food he brought to share with us, that he fell down on the ground and never tasted a morsel of it. It is, therefore, tolerably clear to any man possessing common understanding, that the junior officers of the army, from the neglect of their superiors, were not in a state to do more than they did.

During the retreat, a supply of money reached the army; but it was of no use, except to encumber the officers paying companies. I received, as paying a company, seven hundred and twenty dollars; some of the money was in pieces of eight, but the bulk was in dollars, and I was obliged to carry all. I was over-weighted. It was not, on this race, "weight forage," but weight for character! and the "young ones," if good, had an additional weight placed on them!

The army was still four months in arrear of pay, and a young ensign, who had just joined, hearing of an issue of money, although he was paid up, and two months in advance of the issue now made, went to the paymaster, and demanded some dollars.

"On what account, sir?" was the reply.

"On my account, sir; for I have not a farthing in my pocket, and, as I am told there is an 'issue,' I have called upon you."

Now, the paymaster was a pleasant fellow, and would have his joke, so he asked the poor ensign if the "issue" he spoke of was "in his leg?"

The lad was a ready boy, and seeing that the *pagador* was inclined to be witty at his expense, told him that he had not as yet put an issue in either of his legs, but that, if the retreat continued much longer, he feared he would have to do so, as they were much puffed, and, as he had drank nothing but water, he apprehended an attack of dropsy.

"In that case," replied the paymaster, "you must be tapped."

"Very true, sir," rejoined the ensign; "but I now should like to 'bleed' you!"

The paymaster laughed, and so did the ensign, for he saw that he had made a hit, and he was resolved to profit by it if he could.

"I will give you a bill on London, sir, at sixty-one days, for any sum you may choose to advance me."

"The date is too long, sir," replied the paymaster. "I am not in the habit of cashing bills that have so many days to run before they are payable."

"But, sir," replied the ensign, "you ought to recollect that this is the month of November, and those self-same sixty-one days are the shortest in the year!"

The paymaster was delighted at the wit of the young man: he advanced him, without bill, note, or acknowledgment, one hundred dollars, which would, I have no doubt, been punctually accounted for, had the ensign lived; but he, poor fellow! paid the debt of nature—the great debt—before we reached Portugal, and, consequently, before he could pay his friend; and the paymaster died in Lisbon shortly afterwards. It is a pity that they could not have been both placed in the same grave. The commencement of their acquaintance was a grave one, and their exit from this world—though buried some leagues distant from each other—was equally grave. The paymaster was a regular "dust,"—so was the ensign,—and I have been obliged, in putting the sod over each, to go from "dust to dust!"

The retreat still continued, but the army was unmolested, and, at length, after an absence of so many days, we once more got sight of our baggage. The poor animals that carried it were in a bad state; but they were even better than our cavalry or artillery horses, Of the former, three-fourths of the men were dismounted; and the latter could, with difficulty, show three horses, in place of eight, to a gun.

On this night, I think it was the 26th of November, (that is to say, four weeks, less by two days, since we left Madrid), I enjoyed what I never expected to see again—a hearty meal. A knot of us got together under a tent belonging to Captain Robert Nickle, whose batman was one of the first to arrive with his baggage, and he kept open house for as many as the tent could accommodate. In the centre was placed a huge *pannella* of chocolate, which was garnished by a couple of large loaves of Spanish bread.

The contents of the *pannella*, as also the dimensions of the loaves, were soon altered in appearance, and so, indeed, were we. Our stomachs, which before were as lank as half-starved greyhounds, now became plump and full, and, moreover, some fragments were left even after the servants were fed, and abundantly fed.

A dog belonging to Nickle, that had been absent with the baggage, and which had been on as short rations as his master, also got a bellyful, and soon after came into the tent, but his owner was so changed in appearance and dress, that the dog did not at first recognise him; which proves the old adage to be correct, that "a man is sometimes so changed that his own dog don't know him."

The army continued its retrograde movement unassailed, and, by the 30th of November, was established in its different stations; but here the real effects of the retreat began to be felt The soldiers, while in action, or in a state of activity, had not time to get ill! So long as the mind and body are occupied, everything, in comparison, goes on well; but after a storm a calm succeeds, and that calm is sometimes as bad, and even worse, than the storm that has preceded it. So it was in the present instance. More than half the men were attacked with some complaint; but fever and dysentery, from over-work and bad treatment, were most prevalent, and the number of bayonets which we counted at the conclusion of the retreat, was considerably diminished before we were settled in our winter quarters.

Many men, whose frames were as robust as their minds were ardent, began to sink under the accumulation of the miseries they had endured during the retreat. The continued and unsparing exposure of their bodies under such heavy rains as had fallen, and their being obliged to lie out, without any covering, for so many nights during so inclement a season, now began to be felt, and made visible ravages amongst our ranks. The oldest and most hardy soldiers, as well as the youngest, sank alike under diseases, and it was heart-breaking to see our ranks thinned, not only of the hardy old stock, but of the promising young suckers also. But, so it was! The men died by tens—twenties—thirties—and, in the course of a short time, every battalion was reduced to the half of its original strength.

> Yet this army has met with no disaster; it has suffered no privations which but trifling attention on the part of the officers" [What officers?] "could not have prevented, and for which there existed no reason whatever in the nature of the service; nor has it suffered any hardships, excepting those resulting from the necessity of being exposed to the inclemencies of the weather at a moment when they were most severe. Yet, the necessity for retreat existing, none was ever made in which the troops made such short marches; none on which they made such long and repeated halts, and none in which the retreating armies were so little pressed on their rear by the enemy.
>
> We must look, therefore, for the existing evils, and for the situation in which we now find the army, to some cause besides those resulting from the operations in which we have been engaged. I have no hesitation in attributing those evils to the habitual inattention of the officers of regiments to their duty, as prescribed by the standing regulations of the service, and by the orders of this army.

These last lines are Lord Wellington's own words; but how they are applicable to the officers of regiments I never could understand. What had the officers of regiments to do with "such long and repeated halts?" Those same "halts" were what destroyed the frames of both men and officers: for, during the time of those "halts," the men were standing under arms, drenched with rain, neither making a movement in advance, or to the rear, or exchanging one shot with the enemy. Surely the officers of regiments had nothing to do with that! If the troops had such opportunity of repose, they might as well have been allowed time to cook their meat when it reached them, instead of being marched off their ground some hours before day!

Lord Wellington, in his letter, farther says—

> In regard to the food of soldiers, I have frequently observed and lamented, in the last campaign, the facility and celerity with which the French soldiers cooked, in comparison with our army. The cause of this disadvantage is the same with that of every other description,—the want of attention of the officers to the orders of the army, and to the conduct of their men; and their consequent want of authority over their conduct

Now, it is plain that the French army were much more expert in cooking than we were. The French nation is proverbial for its proficiency in the art of cooking, and here the merits of the two nations might be left to stand upon the authority of gastronomic writers, without the interference of a military one; but, as the food with which each army was supplied, did not require much insight in the arcana of cooking, it only remains for me to show why our army was so far behind the French in "the facility and celerity" of cooking. It was this,—the army of France had a better method than we had.

Their soldiers were obliged to carry their camp-kettles on their backs, and, consequently, had them always on the spot where they were required. Not so with our army. Our cumbrous camp-kettles were carried by mules, and, at the moment they were wanted, they were, perhaps, leagues distant from the division they belonged to. Thus, then, it is plain that, while we were waiting for the means of cooking our food, the French had theirs not only cooked, but eaten. Who was to blame for that? Was it the junior officers? Certainly not. They had nothing to do with it; it all rested with the superiors.

Reader! only conceive, for a moment, what support Lord Wellington must have had, to be under the necessity of taking the trouble and the labour of writing such a letter to officers commanding regiments. Where were his generals? One represented as his right arm—another his left arm—the next his special adviser, &c. Where were all those members of his body corporate? Was there none amongst them able to take such a weight off his mind? If there was one, why did he not do it? But the letter of Lord Wellington goes further, he says—

> The commanding officers of regiments must likewise enforce the orders of the army, regarding the constant real inspection of the soldiers' arms, ammunition, accoutrements, and necessaries, in order to prevent, at all times, the shameful waste of ammunition, and the sale of that article, and of the soldiers' necessaries. With this view, both should be inspected daily.

Now, these orders are much about the same that the officer at the head of a regiment would issue to his captains or officers commanding companies, and it comes to this, that Lord Wellington was obliged to fulfil the functions, not only of commander-in-chief, but also that of general of brigade, or colonel of a regiment!

What I have now written is not assertion without proof, for I quote Lord Wellington's own words, and by that letter the merits of his subordinate officers should be judged, in preference to the overstrained encomiums of their admirers. Let every man—no matter what his rank may be—have his deserts; but, to lay the blame of the misfortunes of the retreat upon the junior officers of the army, was the greatest injustice. At the time that memorable letter was written, the terrible effects of the retreat had only commenced to be felt. In less than a month afterwards the hospitals were overstocked, and many officers were taken ill. I, for once, was amongst the number on the sick-list A bad unhealed wound, which I received in the breast on the night of the storming of Badajoz, now began to revisit me. A high fever was the consequence, but I was at length relieved by the taking away three pieces from one of my ribs. The reader is not to suppose from this confession, that I was a married man at the time this operation was performed; but I had, nevertheless, a "rib," though not a wife; and as to the "pieces" which I lost, it would be but a useless task to look after them now.

The serjeant-major's wife, a fine, fat, well-looking woman,

amongst many others, was taken ill, and visited with a bad fever. She was the sister of my man, Dan Carsons, and had kept close with the regiment from the time of its first landing in the Peninsula to the time I am now speaking of. She acted in many a useful capacity towards the officers. She supplied us with wine and bread, and every other comfort she could afford us; and was, in fact, a necessary appendage to the officers, for she was one of the best foragers I ever saw in the 88th regiment; and the army knows—the Peninsular army, I mean—that we had some good ones.

But this poor woman lost two fine mules during our retrograde movement, as also the cargoes with which they were laden, amounting to a good round sum, which, at the lowest estimate, I must value to be worth three hundred dollars. This loss affected her. She had left no stone unturned to realize it, and this untoward event brought on a violent fit of illness. The fatigue she had undergone, no doubt, aided the cause of her disorder; but, be this as it may, she became quite delirious. While in her bed, she could not be made to understand that the army was not in full retreat "Where," she would exclaim, "are my mules?"

My man, Dan, was in constant attendance upon his sister, and was, as a matter of course, continually intoxicated! If she got better, he would say that he took a little "dhrop more than usual," for joy; if she relapsed, he did the same "to dhrown grief." So that, between Dan's "joy" and Dan's " grief," to say nothing of my own helpless state, I was anything but well off.

At length the poor woman became quite insane, but she still looked up to Dan as her sheet-anchor; nevertheless, Dan always paid her that respect which he conceived due to the wife of the serjeant-major, and always called her Misthress O'Neil; she, on the contrary, forgetting the station she held, always called her brother "Dan,"

"Och, then." said she, "Dan, what do the Frinch mane at all—where do they mane to dhrive us to?—an't my mules gone, and our baggage gone, and still we're on the rethrate? Haven't they taken all from us, even our necessaries?—where do they mane to send us to?"

"By god! Misthress O'Neil," replied Dan, with a broad grin, "I think they mane to send us all to pot?"

CHAPTER 28

Wolves

Dan Carson's prognostication, which closed the last chanter, was not fulfilled, although a retreat on Portugal was necessary.

Once clear of the Spanish frontier, we arrived, by easy marches, at the different towns and villages appointed for our occupation, while the French army retraced their steps, and, it is to be presumed, followed the course we had taken, though not exactly the same route.

The village of Leomil was the one allotted to the 88th, and was also the head-quarters of Sir John Keane (the general of brigade) and his staff. This town, distant about five leagues from the city of Lamego, and two from Moimenta de Beira, was by no means a bad resting-place for men who had for so many days, and in such inclement weather, inhabited no town, or slept, if sleep it could be called, under any covering, except their tattered uniforms; but the transition was too sudden, and it is not difficult for the reader to see what the consequence was.

An abundant supply of money, a great plenty of wine, meat, and poultry, were things not to be lightly treated by a parcel of men in a state of nakedness and starvation. In a word, all were bought up greedily, and as greedily devoured. But the frames of the soldiers had undergone a great change; their stomachs were much weakened by the bad diet they had heretofore tasted, and the disordered state of their bowels was such, that in five cases out of six the soldiers were attacked with some complaint or other. The officers suffered little, because they had a greater command over themselves; but I knew an instance of a man of the company I commanded (his name was Travers) eating, for one week, independent of his rations, the head of an ox, daily!

Reader, do not laugh at this. It is a true but melancholy picture, not a laughable one, of what a half-starved man will do when opportunity favours. The result, as may have been foreseen was fatal. A violent inflammation of the bowels took place, and the poor fellow died in the most excruciating agonies. No remedy of our doctors could relieve him; they did all they could, but in vain. It has often since occurred to me that had our medical people been as conversant with the use of oxygen gas as those of the present day, they might, by a timely application, have extracted the head of the ox-again from his stomach. They had recourse to the stomach-pump, but, alas! there was no succour (sucker.)

To persons like me, of a serious habit, the catastrophe of this ill-fated man afforded as much food for the reflection as the heads of the oxen he had eaten afforded food for his carnivorous maw. I, and many others like me, reasoned with the soldiers upon the undue liberty this poor fellow had taken with his stomach, but we might as well have attempted to arrest the progress of a ship in full sail, with a fair wind and all her sails bent The men were "bent" on eating and drinking; nothing could stop them; and, in less than six weeks from the I speak of, more than one-half were on the sick-list.

The 88th, at this period, was commanded by Major Macgregor: he did all he could to check this terrible evil; but the junior officers, being more intermixed with the soldiers, had a better opportunity of controlling them and they thus fulfilled the minor as well as the major parts of the duty. I was however, soon relieved (if relief it could be called,) from any trouble on this score. My old wound bore out again, and a large abscess had formed on my left breast, but, by care and attention, I was in a few days as well as ever.

This wound, which to me was a bore, must not be so to my readers, and I will not "bore" them with any further details on the subject. It nevertheless revisited me twice afterwards; once in Canada in 1814, and again, in Paris in 1815. The aperture might be as large,, each time, as an augur-hole; but my readers are not to "augur" from this, that I mean (as Colonel Trench, of the 74th, used to say when the same story was too often told) to give them the "real screw !"

The country in the neighbourhood of Leomil, and between that town and Moimenta de Beira, is in the highest degree grand; it moreover abounded in game, and officers who were fond of their gun, or of coursing, had ample opportunities of enjoying both. There was, however, one drawback which was an unpleasant one, and that was the vast number of wolves that infested the mountains. These fierce animals were so terrific, when pressed by hunger, that in one instance they seized the head of a sheep, which was in a house, having made their way under the door. The owner, bearing the cries of the animal, rushed to its assistance, and, catching hold of the hind legs, dragged it back, but the head and a part of the neck were carried away by the wolves.

Another instance of their ferocity soon after occurred. A young child, who had wandered into the street of a small village earlier than usual, was carried off and devoured by these animals; but this in no way damped the ardour of our sportsmen. With a double-barrelled gun on his shoulder, no one feared danger, though he might guard against it; and I never knew an instance of any one being attacked by a wolf, although we saw many in our sporting excursions.

Our cantonments, by this time, the first week in February, had undergone so great a change for the better, that they might be really termed comfortable. Chimneys had been constructed, and we were as well off as any set of men who could put up with fair winter quarters. We contrived to get up a sort of ball court, and we all, men and officers, amused ourselves at this' game. The Irish, I believe, stand unrivalled as handball players, and this healthful exercise afforded the officers and soldiers much amusement. Sir John Keane often looked on, and I believe, though I will not say so positively, joined in the game. He, however, approved of the means the officers of the 88th took to amuse their men, and it is attributable to those trifles, that the soldiers of the "Connaught Rangers" were so devoted to their officers and their colours. Nothing, as has been seen, could shake their devotion to either.

This line of conduct on the part of the officers had a magical effect. Those soldiers who were present at head-quarters never wished to leave it, although severely drilled; and those who were in the rear either in depot or hospital, thought the hour would never arrive until they had again the happiness of being with their regiment. The consequence was, that on the day of battle the "Connaught Rangers" appeared nearly double the number of any other regiment in the division.

From the time we were first settled in our present quarters we established an evening club, which was superintended by Mistress O'Neil, who was by this time re-established in health. We wished to have a regular mess, but that was not possible, as the difficulty and expense of purchasing materials would have been too great; so we were necessitated to content ourselves with our evening club, which was a source of great amusement and conviviality.

It brought us together each evening after our requisite duties to the soldiers had been gone through; and we had no sort of gambling: whilst our favourite game, was always played at a low rate, and each night was wound up by a supper of such materials as could be procured. Our commanding-officer, Major Macgregor, gave up his best room for our use, and, all things considered, our club was most comfortable, and tended to keep up that feeling of harmony and action for which the "Connaught Rangers" were so remarkable during the Peninsular War. In 1809, after the battle of Talavera, the 88th, while quartered at Campo Mayor, established a mess.

This circumstance, trifling as it may appear, was nevertheless attended with a good deal of trouble and a heavy expense. I do not remember that any other regiment in the army did the same. In 1812, after the battle of Salamanca, the 88th established a splendid mess, for which the officers paid a high rate. During both these periods the 88th was commanded by Colonel Alexander Wallace, whose name I have repeatedly mentioned in these pages for his distinguished conduct.

Now the object of all this must be clear to any military man: it had but one object, and one only—the keeping up a gentlemanly and social feeling amongst the corps; and when, as has been seen, such feelings did exist, will any man give credit to the calumnies that have been attempted to be fastened upon the "Connaught Rangers" by the biographer of the late Sir Thomas Picton?

Sir John Keane was to dine with the regiment on St. Patrick's day. Even at this early period I was their caterer, although in a far different way from that in which I am now employed: then I catered for their stomachs—their *faim*; now I cater for their honour—their fame! At an early hour on the 15th of March, mounted on a good mule, with fifty dollars in my pocket, I left my regiment on the route to the city of Viseu, with a *carte blanche* to do the best I could in the purchase of provisions.

I was followed by my man Dan, who had for his assistant, or co-adjutor, as be styled him, my bâtman, Jack Green, as handy a "boy" as ever "listed" in the ranks of the "Connaught Rangers." The mule they took charge of was little inferior to the one I rode, but their pace was of necessity slower, as he was encumbered not only with a pair of panniers, destined to carry the prog for our St. Patrick's dinner, but also with the weight of Dan and Jack, who arranged themselves in the best manner they could astride his back. Viseu is five leagues from Leomil, but, as I knew the country tolerably well, I struck out of the high road, and, crossing the mountains, reached the town some hours before my servants.

Here I unexpectedly met with a young officer of the regiment, of the name of Mills, who was on his way up to join the army, but, being taken ill with an attack of ague, was obliged to remain at Viseu. Nothing could exceed his good-natured attention, and, through his means, both myself and party were made very comfortable, and by the time my two trusty servants arrived, good beds and a remarkable good dinner were prepared for all.

The appearance of Dan Carsons and Jack Green astounded the servants, as likewise the men who composed the detachment commanded by Mr. Mills. There was something imposing in their demeanour as well as dress, to say nothing of their large whiskers, velvet waistcoats, bedecked with immense silver Spanish buttons (God knows how got,) and forage caps of no ordinary value, which at one period might have graced, the head of some general or colonel in the French Imperial Army.

Although their appearance was imposing, the reader may rest assured that it would be, no easy matter to impose on them. Dan, after saluting his officer and, I might add, host, turned to the "greenhorns," and desired them to look to the mules, and see that they were well fed; and "My boy," said he,, turning to Mills's bâtman, "iv you're short iv forrage, wait until afther night falls, and we can go out and stale a thrifle for the bastes." But he was informed that there was an abundance provided, and, in short, that there was nothing wanting.

He then came up to me, and said, "Now, sir, that we are aisy about ourselves and the poor bastes, would you allow me to go down the town for about half an hour, for I've a mighty great notion of paying a visit to a girl that was civil to me in this same town, before we were on the rethrate to the lines, last autumn was a twelvemonth; she wouldn't come then, but I think I'll do something with her this time in spite of her ould father."

I told Dan that he should have the *congé* he asked, but that he ought to recollect he had a wife. "To be sure I do," replied Dan, "but does she always remimber she has a husband?" Seeing that Dan was bent on making a conquest, I acquiesced, and he left me. The young soldiers were too happy in being allowed to take care of our mules, who fared as well as ourselves, and, to say the truth, we all fared well. The merits of several *canadas* of spiced mulled wine were discussed ere we retired to rest, and at an early hour next morning I proceeded to the market

Viseu is a good town, one of the best in Portugal, and the shops are abundantly supplied with such commodities as would suit the taste of a general buyer. Brazil sugar, nearly as white as snow, green tea at a cheap price, cloths of every description, and a rich assortment of Braganza shawls, so much prized in England, were severally named to us, as we passed the different shops; but Dan, who was, or at least made himself, spokesman on the occasion, shrugged up his shoulders and replied to each, "No, *senor*, me no care the chocolate, nor the suggera, nor the shawla; me care the *peché*." An old man, the proprietor of the shop before which we stood, addressed me in tolerable good English and said he had what we wanted. As he said this he cast a look of reproach upon Dan, which I did not at the moment understand; but I entered into conversation with him before I entered his shop, and found him to be a well-informed pleasant old fellow.

As I was about to cross his threshold, my man seized my arm, saying, with a significant nod, "Don't go next or nigh him; he's an ould blackguard, and only wants to thrick us out of our money!"

I told Dan, if he cheated us it was our own faults, as our eyes were as open as his shop door, and there could be no great harm in going in.

"Why, Sir," rejoined Dan, "isn't it fish you want, and is it into an ould grocer's shop you'd go to be afther looking for it? I tell you, again, some of us will be sorry iv we have anything to say to that ould vilhain, and I've a mighty strong idea that we'll make a kettle of fish ov it before we part." Despite of Dan's remonstrance I entered the shop; but, in place of the fish I sought for (good mullet and trout,) nothing was to be seen but dried Newfoundland ling. I explained to the old shopkeeper the description of fish I wanted, and that, although his stock was very good in its kind, we had abundance of it at the head-quarters of my regiment.

While we were in conversation, Dan got behind the counter of the shop, and when I turned round to take leave of the old man, and proceed to the market, I observed my servant in deep conversation with one of his daughters. The old grocer was enraged, and, jumping up on the counter, struck a blow at Dan that nearly floored him; but Dan gave him a "counter" hit that balanced matters by putting the pugnacious old fellow into his own scale.

I felt greatly irritated at seeing my servant so unworthily treated, and with much heat demanded of the Portuguese why he presumed to act so towards a British soldier. But the mystery was soon unravelled. The daughter of the Portuguese shopkeeper was the selfsame "girl" who was so "civil" to Dan on the "rethrate," by which means he had, somehow or other, contrived to make the old man a grandfather before he expected it. To remonstrate further would have been futile, so I conducted my man out of the house, and having condoled with the Portuguese on the "untoward event," wished him and his daughter a very good morning.

When we got outside the door, Dan turned to me and said, "Well, sir, you see I was right about that ould thief, but you wouldn't listen to me, and now you see that I knew the ins-and-outs of it."

I made no remark—it would have been useless to do so; and we soon reached the market-place. There I found an abundance of what I most wished for—fish. I purchased a number of fine mullet, some hens and fowls, and a variety of other matters which 1 thought requisite to garnish our table the following day, and I dispatched my two trusty servants on their route some hours before

I departed myself.

Being mounted on a superb mule, I did not mind much what road 1 took, but struck across the mountains above Leomil, bordering on Moimenta de Beira. Before I reached the passes I so well knew, it became dark, and I lost my way. On reaching a small village, I was informed by the peasants that I was still two leagues from Leomil, had a bad and difficult country to traverse before I could reach the road, and that the mountains were infested with wolves. I was aware that the latter part of their report was but too true; and when they told me the name of their village, near which I had shot before, I was convinced that my knowledge of the country by night was not quite as perfect as in broad day. The peasants endeavoured to make me remain where I was for the night; but notwithstanding their offers of hospitality, I preferred taking my chance with the wolves to the certainty of being half-devoured by fleas, a commodity with which, I well knew, their houses were amply stocked.

I therefore determined to proceed, as I was anxious to reach home; and I had no great fear of an attack, as I was well mounted, with a case of pistols in my holsters, and my sabre at my side. I left the reins loose on the neck of my mule, who, with wonderful sagacity, made her way through the different passes. We had nearly reached the high road without meeting any obstacle, save the different glens we were obliged to pass, when all of a sudden the mule became alarmed, and bounding to the right and left made it difficult for me to keep my saddle. The distant cry of wolves soon, however, explained the cause of her uneasiness; and although I pressed on at as rapid a pace as the nature of the country would admit of, I found that the pack were palpably gaining on me.

I was within a few yards of the high road, when three ringleaders of the pack came close to me. Two of them attacked my mule behind, while the other made a spring at her throat, and the remainder were coming rapidly into the field of battle, for so in fact it was. I discharged one of my pistols at the foremost, but whether I wounded him or no I cannot say; for, to speak candidly, I looked with more anxiety to secure a safe retreat than the honour of a splendid victory; and I can affirm, without the slightest qualm of conscience, that mine on this night was never surpassed—in rapidity, at least—in either ancient or modern times.

Moreau was celebrated for his retreat through the Black Forest—Wellington for his to the lines of Torres Vedras—but what was the disparity of numbers in either case to what I had to contend against? Neither of those great men had more than three to one opposed to him, while I had—if I may judge from the howling of the reserve, and the daring of the advance—fifteen to two! for my mule must have her share in the exploit, because had it not been for her I firmly believe I should have never had an opportunity of relating what took place on the night I speak of. In a word, never was mortal man nearer being devoured.

The rest of the story is easily told. At length I reached the high road leading to Leomil. I gave my mule a touch of the rowels of my spurs, which might have been dispensed with, for she, poor thing, was to the full as anxious as myself to quicken our pace. In less than half an hour I reached the head-quarters of the "Connaught Rangers," and no man, I will venture to say, ever rejoined his corps with greater pleasure than I did mine on that occasion.

On arriving at my billet I inquired if my man Dan had safely brought his cargo to port, and having received an answer in the affirmative from himself, I ordered him to provide me something to eat. He told me all was ready, that he had a stewed *galphinia* (by which he meant a pullet, but which turned out to be an old hen, and might have been, from her hardness, the mother of many clutches of chickens,) a piece of ham, and six *quartellos* of mulled wine. The latter part of the bill of fare appeared so strongly contrasted with the first, that I asked Dan why he had so badly "sized' his company."

"Why, sir," he replied, "you know that Jack Green is the man that always manages the dhrink, and I the dinner; so says I to Jack, 'see that there's nothin wantin, for you know that our masther will be could whin he comes home—and that we're could ourselves. So,' says I, 'Jack, see that you have enough iv wine; and, sure,' says I, 'it's a'most Pathrick's mornin, and mightn't we as well d'hroun our shamorick now as thin?'

"'By God,' says Jack, 'I agree with you intirely,' and upon the same he put down the *pannilla* with the wine, and whin I tould him just now how you were all but ate by the wolves,—'Och!

murther,' says he, 'I'll put down more!'

"'Don't' do that,' says I, 'until you ear more from me.' So, sir, shall I let him have his own way this time."

It was manifest, notwithstanding Dan's elaborate explanation, that both he and Jack Green had determined to make a hole in my pig-skin of wine; and, as it was totally under their control, I thought it better to acquiesce with a good grace, and make a merit of necessity. I told Dan that I wished them to make themselves comfortable, and I have little doubt that they did so, as he told me at parting—after having given me a fair share of the mulled wine—that they would do so, "in honour iv the day." I soon went to bed, soon fell asleep, and at an early hour next morning awoke, and bent my steps towards our club-room, for the purpose of having a *tête-à-tête* with Mistress O'Neil on the subject of our dinner. I found all things right, the fish cool and fresh, the hams safe and sound, the turkeys in proper trim; but I observed in place of the three turkeys which I bought, that five were in the kitchen. I asked my bâtman. Jack Green, how this addition took place?

"Why, you see, sir," said Jack, "I thought when we bought the first three, that the other two we left looked mighty lonely after them, so I bought them also, and I got them at less than half the price you paid for the rest" I am not prepared to say that there was not "fowl-play" on this occasion, but as Jack accounted scrupulously to the vintner for the money he was entrusted with, I asked no questions. The hour for dinner at length arrived, and the dinner was a good one; and I say it was such, although I was the person who provided it.

The fish was excellent, the fowl of the best quality, and to anyone who has ever had the good fortune to taste a Lamego ham, it would be but superfluous to descant on the merits of so delicious a morsel. For the beef and mutton I can't say much, but the wine was of the best quality. I had taken particular care on this essential point, and went to a convent where my friend Graham, with his Portuguese regiment, were quartered, and, through his interest, prevailed on the priests to send us some of their own best. In saying this I need not say more in praise of the wine, as it is well known those gentlemen never kept, for their own use, one drop of any wine that was not of the best quality.

The dinner went off well, the attendance was good, and we were all as happy as any corps could wish to be; but our doctor O'Reily being a little "*Bacchi plenus*," mistaking a veranda for the door, walked out of it and fell, uninjured, about fifteen feet! The spot in which he happened to fall, fortunately was a soft one, and he himself, being a little moist, escaped as by a miracle, without any mishap.

Next morning I examined the spot, and was struck with astonishment at the exactness of the impression his features had left. Had he sat to have his likeness taken, and underwent the troublesome process of having his face daubed over with paste, it could not have been more perfect, and thus in a second of time, without any trouble to himself, he performed what would have cost him a full half hour at least with a great deal of annoyance into the bargain, had he regularly allowed a sculptor to take his bust He had no doubt taken his wine without measure, and it is clear that the wine, or the effects of it had taken his "measure," and made him "measure" his length on the heap of mud upon which he fortunately fell, and it was in this instance "measure for measure."

Major Macgregor, who commanded the 88th up to this period, now left us on leave, and was succeeded in the command by one of the most gentlemanlike officers, and best soldiers in the British Army—Captain Robert Nickle. Sir John Keane, as I have before said, commanded the brigade, Sir Edward Packenham the division; and from the period of our arriving at our quarters at Leomil, until our leaving it on our advance towards Vittoria, we had not one single syllable of annoyance with either our brigadier or major-general, nor do I believe we had as much as one court-martial in the battalion: and this embraced a period of more than six months.

A general court-martial was ordered to assemble at Lamego for the trial of some officers and soldiers, and I amongst others of the 88th was called upon to attend, but it so happened that none of us were required, and our stay at Lamego was a mere lounge. We were admirably billeted; the house in which I was quartered belonged to a Padre, and, as a matter of course, was excellent in accommodation of every kind. The old man, like all priests, was fond of good eating, good drinking, and was possessed of a quantity of plate. My quarter was therefore deemed the best rendezvous for our party, which consisted of six, myself included.

The old priest was a kind-hearted and good man, but very fond of his bottle, and violently passionate when heated by wine. He either dined with us or passed a portion of each evening in our company during my stay at Lamego; and upon one of those days we had a few friends to dine with us,—Hay, of the Staff, Hemming and O'Reily, of the 44th, Nickle and Mahon, of the 88th, and some others. The *Padre* on this occasion made a proud display of his place, all of which he gave in charge to me, and I made a transfer of the "trust-property" to my man servant, Dan Carsons, and my bâtman. Jack Green. We passed a most delightful evening. Nickle sang some of his best songs, and two or three glees were well executed. The old priest, whose voice was a decided bass, gave us some fine specimens of his musical powers, and Anna, a beautiful Spanish girl, who was under the protection of Hay, sang several songs, accompanying herself on the guitar, which so delighted the priest that he not only became intoxicated with music, but what was worse, with wine; and he had just taken a sufficient quantity to make him extremely cautious; he therefore left the room for the purpose of looking over his plate, and we were making merry in his absence, when of a sudden the door was flung open, and the Padre rushed into the room in a storm of rage. He thus addressed us:—"*Senhores! eu tenho perdido a minha prata! e estou roubado! De seis garfos e cinco colheres—mas eu nao penso qu'l sirga algum dos senhores (a Deos nao agrade!), mas eu suponho um dos vossos moços, e principalmente hum de'elles, que se chama Joao, que as tira guardado, sem duvida, pois he muito desestrado!*"

Now, it was clear from this harangue that the priest thought he had lost some of his plate, and his pointed language against Joao showed too plainly that he was the person suspected. [1]

It is merely necessary to say again that this same Jack, or as

---

[1] As many of my readers may not be sufficiently acquainted with the Portuguese language to understand fully the meaning of what the *Padre* said, I will enlighten them on this knotty point, and give the pith and marrow of his speech. It was thus:—"Gentlemen, I have lost some plate! I have been regularly robbed! Six forks and five spoons are gone; but do not for a moment suppose that I think any of you were the culprits (God forbid that I should!) but I suspect some of those lads in the kitchen, and one in particular, called Jack! He has, without doubt, mislaid them; and I am aware, from experience of him, that he is very unhandy!"

the priest loftily denominated him, Joao, was my own confidential man, Jack Green. From the time I first joined the Connaught Rangers to the present, I had six servants or batmen killed in action, and most unquestionably if what the priest now charged my present man with was true, he did not deserve to be in the land of the living. I, however doubted the charge; but before sifting it too closely I attempted to reason with the priest, but he was too much intoxicated, and in too great a passion to listen to reason.

It was in vain that I requested he would tranquillize himself; in vain that I told him the spoons and forks should be forthcoming; that he had no cause of alarm, but it was all to no purpose; his rage rather increased than diminished, and no words of mine could, in the slightest degree, pacify him. His shirt collar was open (which was a fortunate circumstance, as otherwise, I do think he would have been suffocated), and he was in a state that more resembled a devil incarnate than a teacher of the gospel. He was, moreover, greatly intoxicated, and was in that ungovernable state that much perplexed us all as to what we should do with him.

The little Spanish girl laughed at him, and rattled her "castanets" in his ears, which nearly set him out of his senses; but again turning to me, as I tried in vain to soothe him, "*Vos falais muito bien, Senhor, e miuto politicamente, porem que' s'que issò me fas, qundo ainda eu noa tenho mais a minha prata?*" [2]

"Go," said Nickle to me, in his own quiet way, "and see what all this means. There must be some mistake." I was about to leave the room when the eye of the priest caught me. It was fortunate for me it was not his hand! "*Principalmente um!*" said he, as he raised his finger considerably beyond his eyebrows. This motion was like the evolution of a fugleman in front of a regiment, who gives the time to those who are to follow his motions. Yet annoyed as I was at the slur attempted to be cast upon my servant, I made no reply, but proceeded to the kitchen to inquire into the affair. The first person I encountered was my man Dan, who was in the act of delivering over to my charge the plate that he and Jack Green had been entrusted with. I asked the cause of the uproar with the priest, and how it was that he said his spoons and forks had been missing?

---

2. "You speak very well, Sir, and with much politeness, but how does all that benefit me while as yet I am deficient of my spoons and forks?"

"Missin is it?" said Dan; "why thin, to tell you the plain truth, the priest is too fond ov 'missing,' and too fond of his d'hrop; and i'dst these girls that puts him all asthray—and his things too; and whin he upbraided Jack in the regard iv the spoons.

"'Sir,' says Jack, 'they're all here, and I'll count thim out to your reverince.'

"'You may put them in your ——,' says the ould thief iv a priest! But Jack knew betther how to bemean himself to his clargy than the priest did to him, and upon the same he asked his blessing, and ids't what the ould vilhain tould him that he might go and be d—d!"

This was enough for me. I had satisfied myself that all was as it should be, as far at least as regarded the *gorfos* and *colheres,* and I returned to my friends, and to my great satisfaction and relief found the *Padre* fast asleep in his chair. We did not disturb him; and after passing a most agreeable night, left the old man to dream about his imaginary loss.

Chapter 29

Adventures on the Road

To those who have never seen service, or been present with the Peninsular army for a series of years, it would be rather a difficult task to make them comprehend the feelings of an officer upon his regiment being ordered home. There are many, no doubt, who would say it was a lucky "turn up;" but there are many, I know, who would have a contrary opinion. Years of hard fighting, fatigues, and privations, that we now wonder at, had, nevertheless, a charm, that, in one way or another, bound us together, though it severed some; and, all things considered, I am of opinion that our days in the Peninsula were amongst the happiest of our lives.

Nothing tends so much to enjoyment in this life as variety,—I mean at a certain age,—when the mind is free from the care of domestic anxiety; you then have no one to think of but yourself. If you lose a friend in battle, you say—"It might have been my own lot; I am sorry for him, but perhaps my own turn will come next" So it is, no doubt, in private life; but then it wants the stirring impetus which carries the soldier through all dangers and difficulties, unshackled as he is, or ought to be; for no soldier should have a wife, much less a family!

With feelings such as I have described, or attempted to describe, I was on the eve of quitting the First battalion of the Connaught Rangers, but, before doing so, I resolved to spend a few days with my old friend and companion, Captain Graham. He was attached to the 21st Portuguese regiment, quartered in a large convent halfway between Leomil and Lamesso; and here, for the first time, I had a full specimen of the manners and habits of the priesthood of Portugal. I had, it is true, met them occasionally before, and always found them pleasant, agreeable companions; but I had little idea of the depraved state they lived in, until I became, in a manner, an inmate of the convent where my friend was quartered.

Dinner was about to be announced, when some five or six priests entered, each carrying under his arm a small pig-skin of wine. They were all merry, gay lads, and looked as if they had—which I have no doubt of—tasted the contents of their *fardau*. All were agreeable men; they talked upon all subjects; but the fair sex "had the call." My friend asked where the others were who had promised to come. He was told they were on duty; but what that "duty" was, I could not exactly define. Be this as it may, dinner was scarcely over when three monks entered the apartment. One, who seemed to be the provider, was loaded with an enormous pig-skin of wine, which he carried on his back; and, so soon as the door was flung open, he, with some difficulty, placed it in a corner, and then, with his two companions, joined our festive board.

Now, at the time I am speaking of, I was a very young lad. I had, nevertheless, seen something of the world; I had mixed in society, high and low; I had read books—some of them moral; some the contrary; but in all that I had ever seen, read, or heard of, I never could suppose that, amongst any set of men—much less priests—so great a scene of blackguardism could be amalgamated together as I witnessed on this night Songs of the most indecent kind were sang, attitudes of the most indelicate nature were resorted to, in order to give effect to those songs: but still the fellows were so pleasant, that, if you could forget they were priests, it would have been well enough; but it is disgraceful to see men in this calling adopt the manners and habits of the most profligate; by which means, they not only disgrace themselves, but the religion they profess.

It was, as well as I remember,—for then I could not be exact as to the hour,—about four o'clock in the morning when a summons reached the "high priest" that "mass" was to be performed, and the "Host" carried to the dwelling of some person who was dying. The evening's, or rather morning's, work, was thus interrupted, and all those on duty were obliged to scamper off. However, those who were not on the muster-roll remained; and we were about to begin the morning) when a serjeant of Graham's regiment entered, and told him—he being on duty—that the "Host" was about to pass, and that the guard was already drawn out to pay it those honours which were exacted from them.

It may be here necessary to remark, that, in Portugal, the troops not only " present arms" to the "Host," but fall down on their knees as it passes. This order was strictly enforced by Lord Wellington, so far as regarded the British troops, with the exception of kneeling. I was once on duty, when a procession passed, and the man who was at the head of it, fulfilling, I suppose, the functions of some saint, was neither more nor less than the blacksmith who shod my mules! I, as a matter of course, presented arms with my guard, but the fellow laughed so immoderately, that he was near being unhorsed.

When Graham turned out his guard to receive the "Host," and his quondam friends, the "Headsman" was so intoxicated as he passed, that he nearly fell downright on the troops that were arrayed to pay him due honour. This picture of the Romish priesthood in Portugal, may be supposed by many to be an exaggerated one; but it is no such thing. What I have written is true, and those men I met with in this convent, were, most indubitably, the gayest set of drunken fellows I ever associated with before or since. I left the convent the next day; my head was confused from the liberal potations of wine which I drank, but the priests were as steady as rocks, and, ere we all parted, they gave me a friendly invitation to pass a week with them; but I had not time to do so, and I never saw them again,—nor is it likely I ever shall.

I took leave of my old regiment, and, with two hundred and sixty-five dollars in my pocket, bent my way towards Lisbon. My old friend, D'Arcy, accompanied me, and my man, Dan Carsons, took charge of our baggage-mule, which carried our kits. This, indeed, was a sort of sinecure to him; for, to say the truth, we were not overstocked with much extras. Little occurred worthy of notice until we reached Lisbon, and there we met with our companion, Simon Fairfield, so well known to the army.[1] Maurice Quill was also there, and, as they were both, like ourselves, waiting for a passage home by the first fleet that was to leave the Tagus for England, we thought we could not do better than "club" together.

---

1. Fairfield was better known in the army by his Christian name, and was almost invariably called "Sim," or, as Joe Kelly called him—"Simmy."

It was a rare circumstance to meet two such characters, and our time passed away agreeably in learning those anecdotes which have been told of both. Much has been related of Quill, but Fairfield was immeasurably his superior on some points. In the first place, he sang beautifully, while Maurice could not sing at all; and, if Quill possessed that extraordinary humour, which it is so well known he did, poor Simon Fairfield was an overmatch for him as a punster.

Our stay in Lisbon was but short, as, in a few days after our arrival, the fleet was in readiness to sail for Portsmouth. But, short as our sojourn was, it was of sufficient length to nearly empty our purses. That sink of profligacy and nest of sharpers, the San Carlos gambling-house, was the constant resort of all the idlers in Lisbon; and, in a few days, I and my friends were completely eased of all our loose cash. But we had one resource left, and, in the shape of a horse each, which was the same thing as ready money, we determined to try our luck once more at the gambling table. Accordingly, the horses were sent to the fair, were sold, and brought a "fair" price. Mine fetched one hundred and twenty-five dollars; those belonging to Hill, D'Arcy, and Adair, all of my corps, were also disposed of at a "fair" value. Poor "*Fair*"field had no horse or mule. He had an old jackass,—his companion for years,—which brought to the general fund only fifteen dollars. A sort of council of war was now held as to the line of operations we should follow, and it was unanimously agreed that D'Arcy, being a good judge of the game, should be the purse-bearer, and play according to his own judgment to any amount he might think proper, for the profit or loss of the entire party.

Matters were so far arranged, and we were ready and panting with anxiety to have another trial with the bankers of the San Carlos tables, when Hill, a young man of sound sense, hinted that, to prevent any mistake, and not to leave all on the "hazard of the die," we should deposit a certain number of dollars each for the purchase of our sea stock. This hint was so replete with rationality that we all acquiesced, and fifteen dollars *"par tête"* was regularly pouched by Hill, who was understood to be our caterer. He laid in a capital stock of wine, brandy, fowls, and meat,—and, so far, all went on right The wine and brandy he purchased from the far-famed Signor Cavizoli; but, if he paid high for them, they were of excellent quality.

Meanwhile D'Arcy, who conducted his department in the capacity of Chancellor of the Exchequer, was regular in his attendance at the gaming-table. He marked with much circumspection the gains and losses of the numbers on his cards, for and against the banker; but his caution was of no avail. In the first night's play one hundred dollars had been scooped from him by the Portuguese banker, leaving a surplus of about seventy-five more at his disposal. As this was our last stake, and as the fleet was to sail the following day, (I wish it had sailed ten days sooner,) we all went to San Carlos to witness the luck of D'Arcy. Before him lay seventy-five dollars, and before him sat the banker, ready and willing to relieve him of their weight.

For the first half hour he played with some success, but afterwards the tide of luck was against him. Not one of the party interfered *pro* or *con*. Again he made a rally, and, like a ship at sea who has weathered the storm and begins to right herself, he went on, as it were, sailing before the wind. But, in a moment of exultation, and having, as he thought, calculated to a nicety the certainty of success, he staked the entire of our stock in trade on the turn of the card. He was right,—the card turned up in his favour,—and he was a winner of three hundred dollars and upwards.

I looked on quietly, and expected to see him take the money or double the card, (which means "double or quit,") thereby insuring his stake, at the worst, or doubling it in the event of success.

What, then, was our astonishment and dismay when we saw him "cock" the card, and heard him, in a loud tone, addressing the dealer of the pack in the single monosyllable, "Cock." Now, the meaning of the word "cock," and "cocking" the card, that is to say, turning up one of the corners of it, implies, that you will have, if you gain, three times the stake on the table, but, if you lose, you lose all. So it was with D'Arcy; the wrong card turned up, and we, one and all, turned out, went home to our beds, sailed for Portsmouth next day, and I never wagered a shilling at a gaming table since. Perhaps it was the best "turn up " I ever had.

Our passage home was pleasant and short No incident worth relating occurred; and, in twelve days after we left Lisbon, we found ourselves off Spithead. The number of Jews which crowded the vessel was astonishing. They all sought for gold, but amongst us, it was a scarce commodity. One solitary guinea was all I possessed, and I believe I could say as much as any of my companions. For this guinea I received, from a Jew, thirty shillings; and it was then that I really began to lament the loss of my "specie" in Lisbon.

It was, however, of no use to repine. We had, after a good deal of peril, arrived once more on our native shore. We saw ourselves, on landing, hailed by our own people, and, though last, not least, had an order on the agent for seven months' pay! We were all splendidly dressed, with braided coats, handsome forage caps, rich velvet waistcoats, appended to which were a profusion of large silver Spanish buttons,—some wore gold ones,—and our pantaloons bore the weight of as much embroidery as, poor Fairfield once said, would furnish a good sideboard of plate! Thanks to the old German tailor in Lisbon, (I forget his name,) for this.

If he charged high, he gave everything of the best quality; but, as we landed, and saw the garrison of Portsmouth in their white breeches and black gaiters, and their officers in red coats, long boots, and white shoulder belts, we must have appeared to them, as they did to us, like men who formed a part of an army of different nations.

We experienced much difficulty in the removal of Adair from the ship. He had been badly wounded in the knee at Salamanca, and we were obliged to construct slings to enable us to lower him into the boat. We at length succeeded, and got him on shore; and once landed, we were assailed by the different waiters and attendants belonging to their respective hotels, to give "their house the preference." Poor fellows! they little knew the scantiness of our purses, or they would not have been so obsequious.

We, however, pitched upon one, the "George," and, as a matter of course, ordered a good dinner, good wines, and everything befitting the heroes of the Peninsula. It was nevertheless necessary to put our heads together, and see if we had the wherewithal to pay for what we had ordered, and pay for our seats up to London. We consulted, put our remnant of cash on the table, and found ourselves wanting in the scale! Hill, an Englishman, and his family known to the hotel-keeper, said he would manage the matter.

"I fear it will be up-"Hill" work," said Sim. He accordingly spoke with our host, told him of our lackage of cash, and settled all by giving an order on our agent, McDonald, of Pall Mall, for the amount of our bill. The landlord even offered to advance us any sum we might require, but we refused his offer, having no need of it, yet we were not the less obliged by his good nature and confidence Next day we started for London, where we took up our abode with our friend "Mrs. Tait," of the "Hungerford;" Fairfield "roosting" at his old perch, the "Northumberland."

The evening of the day of our arrival, there was to be a grand fête at Vauxhall. I had never been there, and expecting to meet, as we did, a great crowd, we thought our Peninsula dress would attract too much notice, so Hill wrote a note to his tailor, requesting he would send his foreman to us, and, if possible, let Hill and myself have a dress-suit,—that is to say, black coat, vest, and trowsers, in time for the gala. In less than half an hour, not the foreman, but Mr. ———, himself, in *propria persona*, was with us. He came fully prepared with all those essentials so necessary in his profession, such as parchment measures, scissors, &c., &c.

The process of measurement having been gone through, we were asked at what hour we wished the clothes. We answered, at six that evening, if possible, (it was then eleven). You shall have them at four, was the reply; and at four, to the minute almost, we had them, and shortly afterwards set off for Vauxhall. I had expected to see, and also to hear, a great deal.

When I say "hear," I mean as regarded the musical part of the entertainment; but I was greatly disappointed in this branch of the fete. The orchestra was not good, and the fire-works only a shade above mediocrity; however they were less annoying than the "fireworks" we had been in the habit of seeing in Spain, and the novelty of the scene amused me much. The gardens were crowded by people of rank, but the groups of drunken sailors, and women of not the most unexceptionable character, was a strong contrast to what I afterwards saw at the Tivoli Gardens in Paris.

While traversing the dark walks, Miss Burney's novel was brought forcibly to my recollection; but I saw no Evelina there. However, the songs of Taylor and Mrs. Bland were well sung in the style which belonged to each, and were not only loudly applauded, but loudly *encored*, Taylor's "Grand Panorama of London," was received with bursts of applause; and Mrs. Bland's "Oh! no, Mr. Jeremy," was equally successful.

Six of us retired to one of those arcades, (I forget the name that appertained to them,) and asked for something to eat a slice of ham, to which was added bread and butter, was brought up, and as quickly dispatched. I had before heard of a "Vauxhall slice," but never witnessed it till then. To be plain, there was not two ounces of meat sent to us for our consumption. We had often been on short rations, but never paid so dearly for them before. The charge was five shillings each, to which I must add, by way of addenda, a glass of brandy-punch.

Upon our return home, we found Adair waiting for us, and in the act of dressing a couple of lobsters for supper. He prided himself upon his culinary knowledge in this branch, and would by no means allow the interference of any cook, no matter how *au fait* at her or his vocation. On the table stood the tin conjurer, as it is called, and at the head of the table sat (for he could not stand,) Adair, who was the real conjurer. Both conjurers were formed of the same, or nearly the same metal. The one of "tin" was of metal, and Adair a man of "mettle." They might thus be termed brothers, not quite as closely allied as the "Siamese twins," but nearly akin. So soon as "Adair" had scooped the meat from his second lobster, he thought the dish not capacious enough for his friends. He rang the bell and called for another.

"Sir," replied the waiter, "lobsters are very scarce and very high in price now, and we have but one left in the house."

"Scarce and dear! what does the fellow mean?" said Adair, turning to me.

"Pray, sir," said he, addressing the attendant, "what do you call dear?"

"Half-a-guinea each lobster, sir."

"Then bring me one more; I am a perfect glutton when I get lobsters:—quick—quick!"

The waiter disappeared, but did not return so soon as Adair expected, and he rang the bell in a furious manner, The waiter was soon on his legs, and brought up a remarkably well-featured lobster.

"Pray, sir, what has kept you away so long?" demanded Robin, (we always called Adair "Robin,") "I and you, it would appear, have changed places."

"How so, sir?" said the man, with the greatest respect

"Because, I not you, am the waiter!"

The pun was completely thrown away upon our attendant, whose name was Kain.

"Remove that table," said Adair. The man essayed to do so, but was unable to move the table; and—for once in my life—perpetrated a pun. I turned round to Adair, and said, It is manifest that Cain (Kain) is not Abel (able).

"Robin" was much pleased with the pun; but whether it was the high price of the lobsters, or the high flavour of them that stuck in his throat, I cannot now recall to my recollection, but I should say the former; for he turned round to me and said, "*Le prix de ces omares est cher.*"

The waiter, not understanding one syllable of French, and but few correct ones of his vernacular tongue, addressed Adair, and said, "Do you want him, sir?"

"Want who?" demanded Adair. "Why, sir, were you not asking for the priest from St Omers that put up here last night, and is in the next room just now?"

"By all means," cried Adair, anticipating some fun. "Request his Reverence to favour us with his company."

The invitation was promptly accepted, for we had scarcely done justice to Adair's splendidly dressed dish of lobster, and were preparing to wash it down with something stronger than water, when the priest was announced by the waiter. Adair, one of the most finished gentlemen, received him with much politeness, and while he explained the waiter's mistake expressed the pleasure which that mistake had procured for us, but it was manifest that any apology was quite needless. The priest turned his eye in the direction of the wine and brandy, which was on the table, and then towards Adair.

He was what Lord Byron would call a "broth of a boy," and moreover he was an Irishman. So far as I could make out from him his father had been hanged during the rebellion of 1798 in Ireland, but whether his father was hanged or not, was "not" of any consequence to us, as it was evident the priest was resolved to "hang" on us,—and a most agreeable companion he turned out to be, though not "turned off" as his poor father had been; for when he turned out from us he did so with a warm stomach and into a warm bed. His case was as unlike his father's as night is from day, and I dare venture to say he thought so, though he could scarcely know night from day when he left us, and no doubt saw double.

We were all Irish and "cottoned" together, but there wasn't much "fustion" about us; and Fairfield was in great spirits, and in good voice. He sang several songs which delighted the priest and us all, and he then entered into a discussion with the priest, not only on political matters but religious ones also. This, latter, astounded us, for it was generally supposed that Fairfield had studied about as much on theological matters as he had on military ones, or, to speak plainly, that he had not given the one or the other a single thought But Fairfield was a very extraordinary person, and a man possessed of much more ballast than his friends gave him credit for; indeed, poor fellow, as I shall have to relate, he carried so much ballast that he was swamped at last!

His knowledge of the scriptures was so imperfect that it would be ridiculous, a perfect burlesque, to say he knew anything about them at all; but he had so much tact, and threw in his remarks so aptly, that to one unacquainted with him, he might have passed for a person well versed in religious matters. He was a man of considerable talent, and his ear for music so wonderfully perfect, that he could from memory,—for he was too idle to study—play a long and difficult overture on the violin; he had, perhaps, one of the sweetest voices ever possessed by man, and its flexibility was equal to that of almost the best public singer; had he managed his time as well as he did his voice, he would have been an acquisition to any regiment, or any society, no matter how elevated,—for he was, indeed, a most agreeable companion. His irresistible passion for a play upon words was unbounded, and an anecdote was told of him during a time on ship-board that is so strong a proof of this propensity, that I cannot forbear mentioning it.

He was on board a Liverpool packet on his passage to Dublin; when off the Welsh coast a violent storm came on, and it was expected that the vessel would founder on the rocks, and the passengers, one and all, betook themselves to prayer. Fairfield knelt down with the rest, but he could not at the moment—I doubt if he ever could—remember one solitary prayer; he was thus obliged to try back to his catechism, but here again he was at fault; and he never got beyond the sentence, "What is your name?"

These words he repeated so often that an old gentleman next to him, and who, at the moment, was wrapt up in thought, supposed he was the person addressed, turned round and said in a grave and tremulous voice—"My name is Thomas Wood, sir."

"It is, is it?" replied Fairfield, "I wish you would not inierrapt me just now, I was thinking of another person."

A large woman, who knelt at the other side of the elderly gentleman, and who was scarcely able to articulate from sea sickness and fright, thought perhaps it was she Fairfield was thinking of, and like most persons who suppose themselves on the eve of drowning.—ready to catch at everything—immediately told Fairfield her name was Toomey. "By the Lord, madam," said "Sim," "'tis nothing to me what your name is!"

The poor old gentlewoman was quite discomfitted, cast down, and chop-fallen; she looked up to Fairfield as one who might have joined her in prayer and given her religious consolation; or, if the worst came to the worst, and that the vessel should be knocked in pieces on the rocks, he might be the means of saving her; for he was a stout and remarkably fat person, and it is well known,—perhaps the old lady was acquainted with the fact—that fat men make the best swimmers.

Never was a woman more completely out in her calculation, for "Sim" could neither pray nor swim, and had matters concluded unfavourably—making it a sort of a "make-shift" affair, Fairfield would have been much more likely to seize on his fat companion, and made a sort of "buoy" of her to buoy up not only his hopes, but his body also, and "Sim" was the very sort of boy that would not have had many qualms about doing what I have described. Fortunately, however, the storm abated, and the ship got safely into port Fairfield, though not cast down, or cast away as has been seen, said if he escaped he would reform his former life, but those promises, so made, are fine, and are, I fear, but seldom kept; and I can affirm with the greatest truth that "Sim" was not an exception to the general rule.

It was late at night before any of us thought of our beds, though we had arranged to leave London early the following morning, Adair for Kent, and Darcy and In for Dublin. My servant, Dan Carsons, though disabled by a wound in his left arm was still my right hand man, and arranged our baggage which was on a more extensive scale than when we left the regiment on our route to Lisbon.

Though many years absent from Ireland, the priest of St Omers recollected the most minute circumstances connected with that country, and entered into an amusing detail in contrasting the Romish priesthood in France with their brethren in Ireland; and most certainly his account of the scanty provision made for the former appeared to us so far out of the range of probability, that, though from politeness we could not contrast, or doubt his assertion, we most certainly did not believe one word of it At the time I write of, 1813, I had little idea I should so soon afterwards form one of those who were to be the occupants, as conquerors, of Paris. While in France, I enquired into the circumstances relative to the priesthood of that country, and I found that, in no one way, had the priest exaggerated. The following is the outline given us by our friend from St Omers:—

"A parish priest," said he, "is paid twenty pounds a-year, and is allowed to take only five pence for marrying a couple, and two pence half-penny for christening a child. If he charges more than he is entitled to by the "code," he is liable to a punishment of fine and imprisonment This has only reference to his fees and dues; but his general conduct is most rigorously looked after. In France, no priest durst introduce any topic relating to the conduct of government, or enter into any political discussion whatever. On being convicted of such offence, he is liable to be imprisoned for five years; and, if the offence be repeated, he is certain to be transported for life. Now," continued the priest, "In Ireland, a priest thinks himself poor if he has not at least two hundred pounds a-year, and I know many that make their parish worth three times that sum; so you see that Ireland is a better country for a priest than France;" and so it most certainly is.

I did all I could to persuade our companion to join our party for Dublin the next day, but he was immoveable in his determination not to visit his native soil, so I did not press him. I took leave of him and Adair, and it was the last time I ever saw either. I never heard what became of the priest, and poor Adair died shortly after his arrival in England, in consequence of the effects of his wound received at the battle of Salamanca. At an early hour the following morning, I took my place on the top of the Liverpool coach, and, with a light heart, viewed the beautiful country we passed over. The contrast it presented to that which I had but a few weeks before left, was great indeed, and I felt a pride when I reflected that I, humble as I was, was one of those who had fought and bled not only for my country's honour,—but my country's safety.

My servant, Dan Carsons, sat behind, and kept all the outside passengers near him, either in astonishment at the tales he recounted as to what he had seen, or in roars of laughter at some of his adventures, which he told without any scrupulous qualms as to whether they were true or not. He had made himself so agreeable to those behind, that, at the first stage, where we changed horses, some of the front passengers requested he would take his place with them; but there was no vacant seat, and no one seemed disposed to resign his place, so I thought the best plan was for me to go behind, which, I said, I preferred to the front; and my man, "Dan," was installed beside the driver. The laughter in front was, if possible, louder than it had been before in the rear, and when "Dan" had become tired of recounting his Peninsular reminiscences) he began to criticize the team of horses which drew the coach, and which the driver seemed to prize very highly.

"Well now, Pat," said coachee, "what do you think of this ere set of osses; did you ever see the likes of 'em in Spain?"

They were four light chestnuts. "I never did, Mr. Coachman," replied Dan, "but I don't like their colour. I never knew iv a chestnut horse that wasn't blind or lame."

"A good oss never had a bad colour," was coachee's answer, but the words were scarcely uttered when the off leader made a stumble.

"By my conscience," said Dan, "that may be thrue,—but there's a cull among them." Now a cull in the Irish acceptation of the word, means a bad one, and "Dan" was right, for in a few minutes afterwards the same horse made another *faux-pas*, and dropped as if he was shot. "Dan" immediately roared out, "I say, Misthur Coachman, I see you have an Irish horse amongst your set!"

"Which do you mean, Pat?" was the answer.

"Why, the one that fell just now to be sure; he must be an Irish horse,—because he's so fond of taking a drop!"

The ill-fated horse received a severe castigation for his mistake, which went nigh to upset the coach; but, even had such been the case, I doubt if the driver would have been more annoyed than he was by the humorous sallies of "Dan" against chestnut horses, and the driver's want of knowledge in horse flesh.

We reached Liverpool without any other adventure, and next day sailed for Dublin. In those days which I write of we did not use steam, and a three-day passage from Liverpool to Dublin was quite a common thing, and it was the practice then to lay in a sea stock for a voyage of four or five days. This was a matter of easy accomplishment, and, having laid in a fair supply of edibles, &c., we set sail, and on the third day arrived in Dublin. After remaining in the capital one day, I parted from my old companion, D'Arcy, and took the first coach for the Kildare road, while D'Arcy brought himself to an anchor in the Ennis mail. Our leave of absence was for three months, and, before the expiration of that time, the second battalion of the regiment was expected in Ireland, so we did not calculate on a long separation, nor were we mistaken.

It would be tedious and uninteresting to give any minute detail of my reception amongst my family and friends. Those sort of adventures read well in novels, but I do not think my readers will be displeased with me for leaving them out. As a matter of course all my acquaintances got round me, and I had to recount all my four years' adventures in the Peninsula, and, while I was so employed in the drawing-room, my man "Dan" fulfilled his part in the kitchen, and, I have little doubt, did much more justice to the matter than I did

Ireland, at this period, presented a scene of great gaiety; the prices of every article were high, but money was plentiful. Every country town could boast of its ballroom, and public assemblies were quite common. In each county there were several packs of hounds, and almost every respectable farmer was well mounted; indeed, many of their horses were worth upwards of one hundred pounds sterling each. After one of these hunting or market days, it was a service of danger to be on the high road.

A dozen or more of these farmers, styled by the lower classes "gentlemen farmers," after having discussed the merits of several tumblers of punch, would sally out of the tavern in which they had been so agreeably occupied, mount their horses, and run races on the high roads, galloping without heed, to and fro, to the imminent risk of their own lives, as well as the lives of those persons they might meet or overtake on the highway.

Some of these men, having made and drunk divers tumblers of punch, would make the last "tumbler" himself by either breaking his own or his horse's neck, in attempting to jump over a turnpike-gate ! It was a common saying at this time, "If I leap the gate, will I be free of the 'pike?'"

"The invariable answer was, "You will, and more power to your elbow!"

If the gate was cleared, as it generally was, a burst of applause followed; if, on the contrary, the man broke his neck,—by no means a rare occurrence,—a pleasant "wake" and " big funeral," made amends for the loss of the defunct farmer. This is the manner the Irish farmers spent their time and their money during the war.

My leave was now about to expire, so, taking leave of my friends, I joined the second battalion which w:as stationed at Fermoy, The army of the Peninsula had by this time, the spring of 1814, established itself within the French frontier, and reinforcements were in readiness to be sent from Cork to join their companions in the south of France, but, as will be seen in the next chapter, there was no need of this augmentation of force.

CHAPTER 30

The Connaught Rangers Embark for Canada

After six years' of terrible war, the army of the Peninsula at length found a stop put to its victorious career, and the inhabitants of the city of Thoulouse were the last who heard a hostile shot fired against their countrymen. From the commencement of this wonderful struggle, in August, 1808, to April, 1814, more battles had been fought (all of them won,) than England could boast of for nearly a century; and the triumphant march of the army of Wellington was uninterrupted by one defeat until the subjection of their brave opponents was complete, which forbad further hostile advance upon the French territory.

It would be a work of supererogation to bring events before the reader which have been so often and so well told. Suffice it to say that upon the news of the abdication of the Emperor Napoleon having reached the head-quarters of the Dukes of Dalmatia and Wellington, the armies of the different nations which formed portions of those troops were so arranged as to be ready to return to their respective countries or destinations. Those of Spain returned to Spain, and those of Portugal returned to Portugal. The British infantry embarked at Bordeaux, some for America, some for England; and the cavalry, marching through France, took shipping at Boulogne.

The separation of those troops from each other, after so long an intercourse, and an uninterrupted series of victories, was a trying moment. There were, no doubt, many at least, about to return to their native country and to their friends; but they were also about to leave behind them, probably for ever, those countries in which they had passed the most eventful years of their lives, and to be separated from friends whose claim to the tide could not be doubted—because such friendships as those I speak of were not formed by interested motives, and were consequently the more sincere and lasting.

They left also behind them the bones of forty thousand of their companions, who had fallen, either by disease or by the sword, in the tremendous but glorious contest they had been all engaged in,—a contest which not only decided the fate of the Peninsula, but the very existence of England was the stake played for, or rather fought for, in this terrible game; the loss of one single point would not only have rendered the game desperate, but lost it altogether. The players on both sides were nearly equal in skill, and, if Wellington could not boast of the same evenness and perfection of some of the materials he had in hand, as compared with his opponents, he most undeniably held a few trumps that always decided the game in his favour. Sixty thousand Anglo-Portuguese, under their great leader, accomplished more on the southern frontier of France than did half a million of the Allies on the side of Germany.

These are heart-stirring facts, and the recollection of them, even after so long a lapse of time, causes the pulse to quicken, and the heart to beat high; for it can never be too often repeated, or too well remembered, by those of the Peninsular army who are now living, that it was the imperishable deeds of that army that saved their country. But it is idle to talk so. As well might a frail and shattered bark contend against an overwhelming billow, as a single voice, like mine, hope for success in the attempt to place the survivors of that army in the position they had every expectation, and had every right to expect, their country would have done. But, on the other hand, if they stood forward, as a body, and calmly, but firmly, put forward their just claim, how could it be refused?

They see other armies of their own countrymen decorated with medals and rank, while they are passed over and discountenanced,—in short, forgotten!

Their great leader now left them; but he did not do so without his marked expressions of what he thought of the past, and his promises for the future. His general order contained the following words:—

> Although circumstances may alter the relations in which he has stood towards them for some years, so much to his satisfaction, he assures them he will never cease to feel the warmest interest in their welfare and honour, and that he will be at all times happy to be of any service to those to whose conduct, discipline, and gallantry their country is so much indebted.

How these promises have been kept is too well known, and it is difficult to say whether that he ever made them, or never kept them, is to be regretted most. However, the Duke of Wellington, no doubt, does not put the same construction on his words, and on his acts, that others do; and it will be the task of the historian and posterity to deal with a matter which can be better judged of by unbiased feelings than by the parties interested. That the Duke of Wellington is one of the most remarkable, and perhaps the greatest man of the present age, few will deny; but that he has neglected the interests and feelings of his Peninsular army, as a body, is beyond all question; and, were he in his grave tomorrow, hundreds of voices, that are now silent, would echo what I write.

All the necessary preparations being made, the armies of the three nations parted, and proceeded on the different routes pointed out for them to follow. The breaking up of this splendid army of veterans, that for six years slept on the field of battle they had invariably won, was a trying moment. Many a bronzed face, that had braved every danger unmoved, was now moistened with a tear; but the proud consciousness that so long as their country required their services, and that nothing, save death, had separated them, until at last they stood triumphant on the threshold of the invaders' country, stifled every other feeling. In fine, the commands of the great man that had so often assembled them at his beck, now separated them,—and forever.

Several of the most effective regiments were ordered to embark for Canada, and as the war between England and America was at its height, the battalions destined for American service were restricted to a certain number of soldiers' wives. The English, Irish, and Scotch were sent to England, and proper attention paid to their wants and comforts. They had also on board the transports that were to convey them to England their own countrymen and their own countrywomen, amongst whom were many personally known to them, having served in the same brigade or division. But the poor faithful Spanish and Portuguese women, hundreds of whom had married or attached themselves to our soldiers, and who had accompanied them through all their fatigues and dangers, were from stern necessity obliged to be abandoned to their fate.

This was also a trying moment: many of these poor creatures, the Portuguese in particular, had lived with our men for years, and had borne them children. They were fond and attached beings, and had been useful in many ways, and under many circumstances, not only to their husbands, but to the corps they belonged to generally. Some had amassed money, (Heaven knows how!) but others were without a sixpence to support them on their long journey to their own country, and most of them were nearly naked. The prospect before them was hideous, and their lamentations were proportionate, for many, though they had a country to return to, had neither friends to welcome them nor a home to shelter them: for in this war of extermination, life, as well as property was lost

The soldiers were seven months in arrear of pay, and the officers were as badly off; nevertheless subscriptions were raised, and a fund, small no doubt in proportion to their wants, enabled relief to be portioned amongst all. This partial and insufficient aid did not, nor could not, however, lessen the real bitterness of the scene, for many of those devoted beings,—now outcasts, about to traverse hundreds of miles ere they reached their homes, if homes they found any—had followed their husbands through the hottest of the battlefield; had staunched their wounds with their tattered garments, or moistened their parched lips, when without such care death would have been certain, or who, when such aid was not required, devoted days and nights in rendering those attentions, which only they who have witnessed them can justly appreciate.

Yet these faithful and heroic women were now, after those trials, to be seen standing on the beach, while they witnessed with bursting hearts the filling of those sails, and the crowding of those ships, that were to separate them forever from those to whom they had looked for protection and support.

In this list there was one female, a lady,—I call her so, for her rank and prospects entitled her to the appellation I have given her,—who was as much to be pitied as the rest, though her circumstances were widely different She was a beautiful woman, only daughter of the wealthy Juiz de Fora of Campo Major. During the autumn of 1809, when a portion of the Peninsular army, after the battle of Talavera, was quartered in that town, this girl,—for so she was then,—fell in love with the drum-major of the 88th Regiment. His name was Thorp. As in most cases of the sort, both parties had made up their minds to the consequences. The girl was determined to elope with Thorp, and Thorp was equally resolved to carry her off; but this required measures as well as means.

Touching the latter, Thorp was amply supplied, for he was pay-sergeant of a company, and, moreover, received constant remittances from his father, who was a man of respectability in Lancashire. In a word, Thorp was a gentleman, and lived and died a hero! As to the lady, her tale is easily told. Her father, Senor Joze Alfonzo Cherito, Juiz de Fora of Campo Major, was a man possessing large estates, and having but one child, and that child a daughter, he naturally looked forward to a suitable match for her. Now as poor Thorp could not boast of those qualities or attributes which the worthy Juiz de Fora had very naturally anticipated, when his daughter had made up her mind to espouse Thorp, his rage and disappointment may be easily imagined when he learned that she had left his *quinta*, taking all her jewels with her.

The regiment was to march the following morning, and as all mode of conveyance in the shape of cars or mules, for the wounded or sick, was under the "surveillance" of the worthy magistrate, he apprehended no difficulty in tracing his runaway daughter,—but he was mistaken. The cars were examined, the baggage-mules were overhauled, the commissariat mules, carrying ammunition, biscuit, and rum, were looked at,—but amongst all these no trace of the fugitive could be found. What, then, was to be done?

There was but one other chance of finding the girl, and this was a survey of the officers' horses, as the officers rode at the head or in rear of the column; but the Juiz de Fora, although a functionary of high note and high authority in his own calling, and amongst his own neighbours, did not much relish an inspection, though freely granted, which would place him amongst a thousand shining British bayonets. However he did accept the invitation, and was allowed to make the inspection,—but he discovered no trace of his daughter.

"Are you satisfied?" said the colonel.

"I am satisfied that my daughter is not with your regiment, sir; yet I am anything but satisfied as to her fate!" replied the old man.

The band played a quick march; Thorp, as drum-major, flourished his cane, the daughter of the Juiz de Fora, in her new and disguised character of cymbal-boy, with her face blacked, and regimental jacket, banged the Turkish cymbals, and Thorp, who as drum-major was destined to make a noise in the world, was for obvious reasons silent on this occasion. The regiment reached Monte Forte the same day, and the *Padre* of that town performed the marriage ceremony in due form.

In detailing the history of the elopement and marriage of Jacintha Cherito with Drum-Major Thorp, I have given but a short outline of a very romantic, and as it was nigh turning out, a tragical affair. But were I to sit down quietly, and write of all the intrigues that were set in motion, or of all the attempts that were made to assassinate this girl, and also her husband, what I could truly write would be fitting for the pages of a romance. Thorp's history shall be told in a few words. It was this:—

He joined the 88th Regiment on its return from South America in 1807. He was quite a lad, and being rather too young to be placed in the ranks, was handed over to the drum-major. He soon became so great a proficient that, on the regiment embarking for Portugal, at the end of 1808, he was raised to the rank of drum-major, in the room of his preceptor, who was invalided. In those days our drum-majors wore hats pretty much the same as those now worn by field-marshals; indeed, the only difference between them was that the hat then worn by the former was not only of a more imposing and capacious size, but more copiously garnished with white feathers round the brim than those of the latter now are.

The coat, too, a weight in itself, from the quantity of silver lace with which it was bedizened, was an object sufficient to attract attention and respect from the multitude that witnessed the debarkation of the regiment at Lisbon. In short, Thorp was mistaken by the Portuguese for a general officer, and some went so far as to guess at his being the Earl of Moira, who, it was rumoured at the time, was about to join the army. Absurd as those opinions were,—and most absurd they assuredly were, because Thorp, neither in years nor appearance, resembled in the slightest degree the high personage he was mistaken for, Thorp felt gratified,—and where is the drum-major that would not?—at being taken for a general officer; and from that moment he made up his mind to pitch drums, drummers, and drum-sticks, not only from his hands but his thoughts also, and fight his way to the honourable privilege of carrying the pole of a colour in place of the mace of a drum-major.

His wish was soon gratified, for when his regiment, at Busaco, was running headlong with the bayonet against three of Reignier's splendid battalions, Thorp, to the amazement of Colonel Wallace, was seen at the head of the 88th, not with his "mace of office" in his hand, but with his plumed hat, waving it high over his head, as he called out, "The Connaught Rangers forever!"

During the action the sergeant-major had been killed while fighting beside Thorp, and Wallace, on the field of battle, named him as sergeant-major, in place of the one he had lost From this period up to the battle of Thoulouse, Thorp was a distinguished man; four times had he been wounded, but he was always up with his regiment in time for the next battle, often with his wounds unhealed. At the battle of Orthes, his conduct was so remarkable that his name was forwarded for an ensigncy. Thorp knew this, and at Thoulouse, the last battle fought by the Peninsular army, be was resolved to prove that his recommendation was deserved. In this action his bravery was not bravery alone,—it was rashness.

Some companies of Picton's division had been repulsed in an attack at the bridge-head, near the canal,—which attack it has been said, and in my opinion truly said, should never have been made,—when Thorp ran forward, and assisted in rallying the soldiers. The fire from the fire-arms and batteries of the French was incessant, and many officers and soldiers had fallen. There was one spot in particular that had been the scene of much slaughter to those who occupied it, and five officers, besides numbers of soldiers, had been already struck down by cannon- shot, and others wounded by musketry.

Amongst the latter was Captain Robert Nickle, one of the most distinguished officers in the army. While he was hobbling to the rear, he observed Thorp standing in the midst of those who had fallen, the rest having been withdrawn out of fire from a position that should never have been occupied, because in front of the French battery, and running in a direct line from the canal to this position was a low narrow avenue or hedge, which ended within a few yards of where our people had formed after their repulse, and this avenue served as a guide, or groove, for the enemy's range; they were now, however, more or less, under cover.

In a moment of excitement, Thorp, with his cap in his hand, stood alone on this spot, saying, "Now let us see if they can hit me!"

Nickle, who was passing at the moment, supported by two of his company,—for his arm was badly shattered, called out to Thorp to leave the spot.

"Oh, Captain Nickle," replied Thorp, "they can't hit me I think." Those were the last words he ever uttered. A round shot struck his chest, and, cutting him in two, whirled his remains in the air. Thus fell the gallant Thorp, and though his rank was humble, his chivalrous deeds were those of a hero. The day after his death the English mail brought the Gazette, in which poor Thorp's name was seen as promoted to an ensigncy in his old regiment; and though this announcement came too late for him to know it, it was a great consolation to his poor afflicted widow, and it was the means of reconciling her father to the choice she had made, and her return once more to her home was made a scene of great rejoicing; but nothing more of her was ever heard by the regiment.

It was said at the time that both Soult and Wellington were aware of the abdication of the Emperor Napoleon and the occupation of Paris by the Allies, and that the former made an offer to abandon the city of Thoulouse to its fate for a certain sum of money; and by way of completing the story, the Duke was represented to have replied, "That he would give no such sum, as he could beat Soult for half the money."

Absurd as the story was, it was credited by many, and an Irish officer remarked, "that both commanders ought to be satisfied, as both had a dead bargain of the battle." Indeed, to say the truth, it was only fit to be laughed at; for it is well known that Soult did not hear of the events at Paris until the 12th of April, and even then he only heard of them through the English general. Two soldiers, of the Connaught Rangers, had their argument on the subject also. One said Soult retreated; the other said he did not. The former said he did retreat, and retreated on the village of Aranda; the other said he only halted at a village, not Aranda, but *Penny*aranda. The argument waxed warm, when a Third soldier of the Connaughts arriving, asked the cause of the dispute, when upon hearing what it was, replied, "Why, then, arn't yees a pair of divils to be arguing so, when there's only a Penny difference between ye?"

The war in the Peninsula was now, however, ended, after having continued for nearly six years with various changes; and gloriously, in truth, was it ended by the British general and his unconquerable army. "Thus the war terminated, and with it all remembrance of the veterans' services."

Detachments belonging to the regiments sent to Canada were forthwith in readiness to embark at Cork, and the 88th to which I belonged, formed one of those. On the 14th of June, 1814, we left the barracks of Fermoy, and took up our quarters at the Royal Barracks at Cork. The soldiers belonging to all the detachments were, with few exceptions, young men lately drafted from the militia; and it required much attention and care to keep them sober or from desertion.

The old soldiers, who were only too anxious to join their former companions, never thought of desertion; but they certainly made up for their fidelity to their colours in their visits to the whiskey cribs, as they called them, with which the neighbourhood about the barracks was abundantly sprinkled. To say that much drunkenness and a reasonable portion of fighting, not only amongst themselves, but amongst the inhabitants, was a sort of pastime that was carried on with a good deal of life and a good deal of spirit, would be only saying what is too well known to need repetition; but we had no corporal punishments, as O'Hara, who commanded the 88th detachment, thought enough of that had been carried on amongst the men themselves, and, indeed, their faces told plainly that some handy-work had been in practice.

At length, on the 28th of June, we marched to Core, and two transports, the *George* and *Atlas*, were allotted for our use. After a good deal of trouble, we got the men on board, and it would be hard to say whether we experienced more trouble in getting the drunken men into the transports, or the women out of them, because, in spite of the "rules and regulations," dozens of those poor soldiers' wives continued to smuggle themselves into the hold, which proceeding was winked at by the sailors and by some of the young officers, who were not as yet seasoned to what real service meant.

Major Dunne, who was in command of the second battalion, stationed at Fermoy, superintended the embarkation in person. He was a most severe officer and a dangerous one to have anything to do with, because, as he often said, "if any one thing is undone, nothing is done;" and right well he acted up to this favourite saying, for if you committed one fault out of one hundred cases where you did right, he was down on you the same as if you had done wrong ninety-nine times out of one hundred. An instance or two will give the reader a sample; but he had one redeeming quality, and as I do believe it was his only one, it is but justice to tell it—he was as brave a soldier as ever went into battle. His severity, nevertheless, was extreme, and I shall give a specimen of it.

While in command of the second battalion on the advance of our army from the lines of Torres Vedras, the young soldiers that composed the greater portion of the regiment, could not cope with the old veterans in long marches, which at this period were harassing and severe. Many men were unable to continue on the march, and were left behind. This so exasperated Dunne, that he issued orders that no man should fall out of the ranks without the officer in command of the company producing a certificate of his inability to proceed, signed by one of the surgeons. On one occasion, a man was unavoidably left behind without the necessary certificate. Mr. Graham, who commanded the company, told the major that the man dropped down from exhaustion, and had died on the road.

"Well, sir," replied Dunne, "where is he? Produce him immediately. I don't care whether he is dead or alive, but I must have him."

Now this was very tantalizing; but there was no remedy, and Graham set off, accompanied by a serjeant and a file of soldiers, and after an hour's smart walk, found the man where he had been left, but he was quite dead. They carried him by turns until they reached the village they had left. Hungry and jaded, they arrived at the major's quarters; it was midnight, and Dunne was enjoying a sound sleep, when Graham, who had now placed the dead man on his shoulders, kicked loudly and violently at the door.

Dunne jumped out of bed, seized his sword, and running to the door, in his shirt and nightcap, kept fumbling at the latch; but in the hurry, confusion, and darkness, in place of opening the door, he contrived to double lock it, all the while screaming out to know the cause of the disturbance. But Graham, who was by no means disposed to talk, turned his back, on which lay the dead soldier, and, with one powerful effort, burst open the door, which gave way, hinges and all; while Dunne, with eyes distended, and standing with his huge cut-and-thrust sword in the middle of the floor, seemed to forbid further entrance on the part of Graham and his dead burthen. But it was too late; the great force with which Graham hurled himself against the door, brought him and his defunct companion to the ground; and Dunne, in a feeble effort to arrest their entrance, snapped his sword in two, as it came in contact with the buff belt of the dead man.

"What does this mean?" cried Dunne.

"Sir," replied Graham, "I have obeyed your orders, and have brought you the man as you desired."

"Take him away instantly," roared Dunne.

"You must excuse me if I do not," said Graham; "I have carried him far enough already, and have no wish for his company any longer. He is a Scotchman, and so are you, so you may make Scotch collops of him if you choose."

This answer was, no doubt, an improper one: but Graham, jaded and hungry, lost all control over himself; and Dunne was so sensible of his tyrannical conduct, that he durst not bring him to a court-martial; but he kept a close eye on him, and, to avoid his vengeance, Graham accepted a company in the 21st Portuguese Regiment. Poor fellow! he served all through the Peninsular war, and at its close went out, with the rank of colonel, to South America, where he, with many others, perished.

The detachment commanded by O'Hara was regularly put on

board the two transports; he commanding in the *George*, while Captain Bagwell took charge of the *Atlas*. Major Dunne having fulfilled his part, determined on returning to Cork the same evening; but, much as he was disliked, we thought it better that we should part good friends, and we asked him to dine with us.

He was pleased with this attention, which he knew he did not merit; and he was accordingly our guest on this occasion. Mrs. Broadway's hotel was our *rendezvous*, and a most excellent dinner she placed before us. Dunne seemed really happy, and we were all in high spirits. I had often told the story about Graham and the dead soldier; and a young ensign, who had just joined, thought it a capital opportunity to have a farewell thrust at the major, and he began recounting the adventure, and actually asked Dunne if it was true. The major started at the question; but he smiled—a dangerous omen—and I thought for the moment it was well for the ensign that the Atlantic was soon to be between them.

"Sir," said Dunne, "you are very forward, and extremely ill-bred—you are the rawest of the raw."

"Well, major," replied the ensign, "how could I be anything but raw when I am under (Dunne) done?"

The major, for once in his life, laughed heartily, and Fairfield, seizing the moment, said, "That when the adjutant of the first battalion got the ensign on the roaster, he would then be done brown."

The soldiers once arranged, their arms carefully placed in arm-racks, the different messes told off, and, in short, all that was necessary to be done for the men was completed; but the arrangement of the soldiers' wives was not so easy of accomplishment. The regulations allowed but four women to each hundred soldiers, and after a few of those who, from long standing and good character, were selected, the others took their chance by lot. This was the most trying task of all; however, we got through with it, put the chosen few on board, and gave the rejected ones the wherewithal to enable them to return to their homes.

The fleet of transports at this time collected at Cove exceeded one hundred; a portion of it, with troops and stores, was destined for Halifax, and the remainder for Quebec. A fifty-gun ship, two frigates, and two sloops of war accompanied the fleet for protection, which was so essential, as the seas at this period were infested with American privateers. It was calculated the fleet would not sail for a week, so we had ample time to make the necessary preparations.

Our long service in the Peninsula had taught us to be expeditious; so leaving the soldiers in charge of the young officers, we took a Cove jingle, and set off for Cork. Previous to embarkation, I had been requested by Major Dunne to act as paymaster; and as this took a deal of trouble off O'Hara's shoulders, he joined in the request, and I thus acted for the entire. A paymaster without money is like a clock without a pendulum, no tick, tick, so I paid my respects to the District Paymaster, and telling him my story, was advised by him to make out my pay-list, and draw for three months' pay for officers and soldiers. This amounted to a good round sum, as our strength consisted of fifteen officers and three hundred and fifty men.

My first care was to lay in trousers, shirts, shoes, and stockings, calculating that, after so long a voyage as we anticipated, such things would be essential on our reaching Quebec. Those things, with tobacco, soap, &c., I bought from O'Brien, of Tucky Street, and I recommend his house to those who may be similarly situated as we were. The pay-serjeants purchased a quantity of vegetables, and gave the soldiers a daily allowance of money, to make such bargains as they chose from the proprietors of the numerous "bumboats" that daily flocked round the ships.

Thus, having completed all that was necessary for the comfort of the soldiers, I naturally turned my thoughts as to what was essential for the officers. Those gentlemen, not content with the onerous duties I had to perform in the double capacity of paymaster and quartermaster, insisted that I should also take upon myself the office of caterer for the entire batch.

If there was one thing more than another at which I was *au fait*, it was this sort of employment, and I set to work with vigour, I was ably assisted by my old friend and brother colour-bearer Owgan; it was he who, in our first battle at Busaco, carried one of the colours, while I carried the other; it was he who shot the French colonel of the 9th French Legères, at Fuentes d'Onore; and it was he who, in return for the compliment he thus paid the colonel, was himself shot through the body by a grenadier of the same regiment He, poor fellow, is now no more, and he died, like many other daring souls, without any badge to denote his gallant services. He was a Cork man himself, and was of the greatest service to me in providing our sea-stock.

I requested the presence of the officers at McDowall's hotel, where we quartered ourselves; and it was there agreed that a stock purse of ten guineas each should be put into my hands; and as I, in the quality of paymaster, then held the strings of the purse, the needful was of easy access. Thus, with one hundred and fifty guineas at my disposal, Ogwan and I set to work in earnest. We wrote down a list of what we thought requisite. Four sheep were the first lot we purchased, and as pigs are a sort of animal that thrive well at sea, we set down their numbers at fifteen, of all sizes.

Those gentlemen, as the Irish call the pigs, during the war, fetched enormous prices; but at this moment there was a great depression in their value, and they were fully twenty *per cent*, below par. In short, "pigs were looking down," and so I told the butcher from whom we were about to purchase the lot of this circumstance he was as well aware at least as I was, but, with true Irish craft, he replied,—"Looking down, is it? Why the divil should they be looking down? Shure they needn't be ashamed to show their faces! Look at them, and tell me did you ever see a nater set iv pigs?"

I told him the pigs were good enough, but that he must go with the times, and sell his pigs like other people, as the war was now at an end.

"Is Boney done clane?" cried he.

"He is," said I.

"Och murther, the divil! If he had only held out till I sould the pigs, I wouldn't care." So he sold us the number we wanted at a much less price than he asked—but, of course, we were cheated.

Having in like manner completed our purchases in sheep, wine, porter, and ale, Owgan and I looked at our list, and found we had done all our business, except securing fishing-hooks and two goats. The former served us well when we reached the banks of Newfoundland, and the others gave us plenty of milk during our voyage. All being now concluded, we sailed from Cove, with a fair wind, on the first of July; but when off the Old Head of Kinsale, it blew a strong gale, which continued for three days; the fleet was greatly dispersed, and a signal was made to put into Beerhaven.

This we accordingly did, and glad we were to find ourselves once more at anchor. All except the pigs, had suffered from sea-sickness, but they, profiting by the occasion, fared sumptuously on what the soldiers were unable to eat. The country people flocked to us in great numbers, and brought us fowls, eggs, and fish in abundance. We had a large stock of the former, but as those offered to us now were so cheap, we continued to purchase more.

At length we were tormented with the numbers of cocks we had in our pens; their constant crowing was absolutely deafening, and Owgan who, like myself, was fond of cockfighting, proposed we should set apart some of the best, and have a regular "main."

We accordingly set off to Bantry, and having purchased several pairs of steel spurs, returned with those requisite implements. We fixed on the day following for our battle royal, and on that day also we had invited some officers from the shore to dine with us. Amongst others, a staff-surgeon, of the name of Crowe (a capital name, by the way, for a man at a cock-fight), formed one of the party.

I will just mention here that Captain O'Hara, who commanded the detachment, had come to us from the 52nd, and had been brought up under that admirable officer Colonel Barclay. I am not aware that the colonel was any relative of the celebrated pugilistic colonel of that name; but he most certainly possessed many of those "hard-hitting" qualities for which his namesake was so justly celebrated.

Whenever any petty dispute arose amongst the soldiers, his answer was, "God damn them, why don't they fight it out?"

His address to the 52nd at Busaco, when that regiment was about to charge the head of Ney's column, was pretty much in the same style: "Do you see those rascals coming up the hill?" said he, turning to the men. Some of the soldiers began to laugh, for they knew that something rich was coming.

"What the devil are you grinning there for, you set of fools, when in five minutes more some of us will be laughing at the wrong sides of our faces? Fix your bayonets, and come along. Knock them heels over tip, and give them a taste of the Barclay touch!" What the 52nd, 43rd, and 95th did at Busaco is too well known to need repetition.

Now, as I before said, O'Hara was bred up in the school of this fine old man, but, though my senior, he was not so long a "Connaught Ranger" as I was. He took me aside, and having told me how those kinds of disputes used to be adjusted by Barclay, asked my opinion on the subject.

"You know," he said, addressing me, "I dislike quacking with the men. I hate unnecessary fuss or trouble. What say you if we were to adopt old Barclay's plan?"

"Why what else would we do?" was my reply. "I think it a good code to follow. It will be fine healthy exercise for the men, and be an amusement to them during the passage."

"But then," said O'Hara, "I am not to know anything of the matter!"

"Leave that to me," was my reply; and that moment Owgan, who acted as adjutant, came up, and reported that two of the new hands from the militia were fighting in the forecastle.

"The very thing we were talking about !" exclaimed O'Hara; "let them fight it out, and see that all is fair."

"Oh," said Owgan, "there's no fear of foul play, for the men are all in the rigging, and Robinson, the mate, and Jerry, the Canadian sailor, are the seconds; and when I left them they were at it 'hammer and tongs.'"

"Then let them have a comfortable fight," said O'Hara; "but remember, Owgan, I am not to know anything of the matter. Do you understand me?"

"If I don't," replied Owgan, "I must be as great a jackass as any in my native town, Clonakilty; never fear! a few touches like this, and the militia boys will be quiet enough."

Owgan was right, for during our voyage of three months, we had not more than six or eight combats of this sort, and not one court-martial! This is what I have striven hard (since I first began to scribble my *Adventures*) to knock into the heads of officers commanding regiments. Let the men, I say, have their fling on those points when it amuses them. Every regiment in the service should have a boxing and cudgelling school. Old fogies at the head of regiments will start at such advice; but they are wrong, nevertheless, they may depend upon it.

The day for our dinner-party and main of cock- fighting at length arrived, and preparations were made for both on the best scale at our command. Good soup, good fish, good beef and mutton, together with Westropp's best port and sherry, were in abundance. The two feeders and "handlers" of the cocks, Serjeants Hartigan and Cooney, declared that neither "Archy" or "Gallagher" ever had a finer pen of fowl, and that all should be as it ought. Owgan and I went on shore in the jolly-boat, and brought back a sufficiency of sods to make a "pit. The "main" was to be five battles, and, as high betting was not our wish, we fought for a crown the battle, and a guinea the "main," or odd battle.

The boat conveying our friends was seen to put off from the shore, while at the helm sat Doctor Crowe. He was looking not only pale and, ill, but, as Fairfield remarked, was naturally ill-looking, and he did not by any means seem to relish the prospect of the day's sport he was invited to witness. As the boat neared the ship, the bell rang for the cocks to appear on the "pit" This had been agreed upon as the most fitting manner to prove to our friends that we were in readiness to receive them.

"This bag a pound," roared Owgan, as he pointed to Hartigan.

"Cooney, half-a-crown," cried Barney Flood, as he looked at Owgan's servant, Pat Kelly.

"You're a liar!" cried Pat "The divil himself can't beat Mr. Owgan."

The words were scarcely articulated before Kelly received a "facer" from Flood, and poor Doctor Crowe, who was the last of the party in mounting the ladder from the boat, was knocked back with great violence, and he fell into the boat, bilging out a portion of its bottom, and seriously spraining one of his ankles.

Regardless of this accident, or, most likely, not knowing it, Kelly and Flood continued to fight at the gangway; while on the quarter-deck all was uproar. In the bustle poor' Crowe was not even thought of, much less missed. So soon as he had recovered from the shock of his fall, he hobbled up the ladder, but on reaching the gangway he was quite hemmed in, for the crowd was so dense it was not possible for him to make any way except the way he came, and that was back again to the ladder. On the top round of this he took his stand, with the tiller ropes firmly held in his grasp; indeed, his safety, his life, most probably, depended on his maintaining his position, for Flood and Kelly were fighting a desperate battle, and as the crowd of spectators either advanced or retreated, Crowe might be likened to a wreck at sea, when each coming or receding wave may be either his ruin or salvation.

Meanwhile the quarter-deck was a scene of equal animation. Three battles had been decided ere Crowe was even missed, but then, and not until then, search was made for him. The fight between Kelly and Flood had by this time ended to the advantage of the latter, but he was in a feeble state, and might well exclaim, "Such another victory," &c.

O'Hara immediately went up to Crowe, and in his usual gentlemanly style apologized to him for the apparent neglect he had experienced. "But you see, my good sir," said O'Hara, "this is the way we carry on the war here."

"I do indeed, sir," replied the affrighted doctor; "you seem to keep your hands in practice."

Just then old Taylor, the "skipper," came up and reported that Kelly had fainted.

"You had better take a look at him, Doctor," he said to Crowe. "A little bleeding might sarve him."

"If I were to judge from appearances," said Crowe, "he has bled enough already. Let him be put to bed, and give him some warm gruel."

We now made our way to the quarter-deck. Two battles had yet to be fought before dinner. The cocks were in their bags, and Owgan calling out "This bag a pound," still pointing to Hartigan, when he caught Crowe's eye, who was looking with evident dismay at the scene before him.

"I think," said the doctor, addressing O'Hara, "that young officer of yours who has offered to give a pound is, I should say from his appearance, one that is extremely likely to do as he says!"

So soon as the last battle was ended we went down to the cabin, where dinner was placed on the table. The dishes were so numerous that I directed one of the servants to place the large metal tureen of soup on one of the lockers, and we sat down to commence the attack; but at this moment Smith, a young Ensign, very awkward and very absent, (it was to be wished he had been absent altogether on the present occasion!) entered the cabin, and seeing the table rather crowded, preferred taking his seat on the locker where the soup stood. This was unfortunate, for moving suddenly, by a backward motion, he tossed plump into the tureen. The soup was boiling hot, and, as a matter of course, he was most frightfully scalded; but this. was not the worst, in the agony of the moment he sprang up, but the tureen stuck as close to him as a cupping-glass. The roars of laughter became awfully great, and poor Crowe for the moment forgot his own mishap, and laughed loudest of all. His merriment was of short duration, for Smith, by a sudden and skilful jerk, rid himself of his "*fardeau*," and the tureen, or rather its contents, tumbled into the breeches of Doctor Crowe. Here was a fine business truly! Crowe was in such torture that it was advisable to put him on shore.

When he was fairly off, the laughter so long suppressed, which for decency's sake could not be discharged while he was present, now got full scope, and never was man better laughed at, and few men better scalded—though many have been laughed at, and many have been scalded. As for Smith, the cause of all, he suffered comparatively nothing. His pantaloons were of a much stronger and a much thicker texture than those worn by the doctor, and besides this, his astonishing readiness and address in ridding himself of the tureen tended greedy to save him, and though his awkward conduct cannot be too highly reprobated, his quickness and tact in saving himself is deserving of praise. The night was most agreeably spent, and next morning we received accounts that Crowe was better, though confined to his bed.

The wind still continued unfavourable, and taking advantage of the circumstance, we went on a shooting excursion up the river, and had some capital sport. Three large seals were caught, and Owgan killed at one shot four wild ducks. It was late at night when we reached the ship, and old Captain Taylor, the "skipper," was much gratified by a present of some twenty sea-gulls, which he requested, seeing that we set no great value on them.

"What do you want with them?" inquired Owgan.

"Want with them!" exclaimed Taylor. "Why they will make a most capital pie, when they are skinned and well pursed with salt"

"I should rather think," remarked O'Hara, "they will be likely to return the latter compliment to you if you eat them."

The operation of skinning both the seals and the gulls was, however, proceeded with, and was followed by a most awful smell throughout the ship. Glad to get away from this scene of flaying and pickling, we next day explored the neighbouring country, and our driver, who acted as our guide, showed us all that was remarkable and worthy of notice; but on our return the fore-springs of our jaunting-car gave way with a sharp crash, and not only flung the driver over his horse's head, but tumbled myself and Owgan into the middle of the road; however, none of us were hurt.

"Gintlemin," said our coachee, "are yees kilt? As for myself the devil's a fear in me, for I'm used to it!"

We assured him we were safe, and hastened to help him to brace up the broken springs. The fellow rummaged in the well of his car, and soon brought forth as many ropes and chains as would tow a good-sized vessel into harbour. Smith, who was an Englishman, was much amused with all he saw, and he told the driver he was only astonished the accident did not take place sooner, as he said the springs hung so low in front that he found it almost impossible to keep his seat, and he asked the reason why the machine was hung in a manner that rendered the driving-seat especially so uneasy to those who occupied it.

"Why, sir," said Pat, "in this country we always hang our cars low in front, to make the horse believe he's going down a hill!"

This answer so pleased Smith that he gave the fellow half-a-crown for his humour.

Next morning the wind was fair, and we weighed anchor. The entire fleet was put in motion, and we sailed with every prospect of a fine passage.

CHAPTER 31

Our Ship is Separated From the Fleet

It is a true though trite observation, that, after a storm a calm generally follows; and this remark is not confined to sailors only, but to landsmen likewise. In the last chapter, I narrated what befell our detachment of troops ordered to embark for Canada, and in what I then wrote I traced their progress from Cork to Cove, and from thence to Beerhaven. It now only remains to bring them to their final destination, Quebec, the best way I can, and, to say the truth, the task is not an easy one, as, from the day we left the latter harbour, to the moment of our arrival in the capital of Lower Canada, we had rarely the good fortune to enjoy the benefit of a fair wind for six consecutive hours.

Our remaining so long as we did at Beerhaven most certainly enabled us to increase our sea-stock considerably, which added greatly to our comforts during our long voyage; but the time lost, and the fair weather lost, could not be recalled; but, though, neither of those could be recalled, it was strongly urged that our naval commandant, should have been, and, as will be seen this opinion was not confined to mere gossip, but was the serious opinion of the entire fleet It is, however, but justice to observe, that our stay enabled many of the scattered ships to rally back upon us; and, amongst the number was our fellow companion, the Atlas. On the other hand, many continued their course and reached Quebec before us; but some were never heard of afterwards,—by us at least.

Our fleet, though protected by one fifty gun ship, one splendid frigate, and two brigs, was nearly dispersed on the open sea, and a portion of it captured by American privateers; and it took us three months and four days ere we found ourselves, such of us as were uncaptured at least, on *terra firma* at Quebec.

The command of this squadron was entrusted to Captain Butcher, of the *Antelope*, of fifty guns; under him was the *Newcastle* frigate, commanded by Lord George Stewart; the names of the captains of the two brigs I forget, and I am sorry for it, as, had it not been for them, some of the best transports and some of the best soldiers in the service of His Majesty might have garnished a Yankee port or a Yankee prison. And I may here observe that, for ten days, while we were at anchor at Beerhaven, the wind was perfectly fair; but Captain Butcher was absent from the fleet, and without him we could not budge an inch.

A strong remonstrance was made by the shipowners to the Admiralty, but what the result was we never heard. The cause of our commodore's absence, when his presence was so imperatively called for, was accounted for in different ways and with different versions; some said he went to Bantry to see his wife; others said he was particularly addicted and passionately fond of shooting seals.

The first excuse was only laughed at, but the latter was received with much severity of observation by the masters of the transports and merchantmen, who remarked that, in place of killing seals, he would be better employed in killing time,—by making sail However, be this as it may, on the day of his return Captain Butcher made the: signal for sailing, and in a short time the fleet, consisting of some fifty or sixty ships, were dear of the harbour and steering their course for the new world.

Many officers and men had suffered from sea sickness on the passage from Cove to Beerhaven; one in particular, Mr. Wilkinson, had been so ill that we feared he would have died from exhaustion, never having tasted a morsel of food for a week previous to; our arrival in harbour; and it would seem that he leaned to the opinion of the surgeon, for, the moment he heard the capstan at work, and the anchor heaving, he fainted on deck, and we had a strong inclination to put him on shore. This, however, he declined by means of gestures and motions of the hand,—for he was unable to articulate,—and we acquiesced in his noble resolve to die even so unworthy a death; many of the old Peninsular soldiers regretting that he had not fallen at the muzzle of a cannon or on the summit of a breach. But those regrets on their parts were futile; for poor Wilkinson had never so much as smelt powder, far less faced a cannon; and, as he truly said, the only enemy he ever knew of was the sea.

However, all our forebodings as to his fate, and his own perfect conviction that his death would be speedy,—for, so certain was he of it, that he made his will,—were perfectly groundless, and, strange to say, he was never for one hour unwell during the rest of the voyage, which was one of the most tempestuous ever witnessed by the oldest sailor in the ship. Our transport was a capital ship, the *George,* her crew was excellent, and the Captain, a sturdy bluff Yorkshireman, had been twenty years in the service, and this was his fifth trip to Quebec.

The provisions on board were of the best quality, and the sea stock abundant; and old Taylor, our captain, had a large, stock of London porter, which he said he brought out on a "spec," as he called it; but, from the liberal manner in which he helped himself, I was strongly of opinion that it was chiefly for his own use, and, at the end of the voyage, which undoubtedly was a long one, my surmise was not far from the mark, for, when we reached Quebec, scarcely a "spec" of the porter was to be seen.

A melancholy accident occurred as our ship was getting out of the harbour, and what the sailors termed "the bar." Our pilot had just finished his duty, had received his payment, and was about to descend into his boat, which was alongside, but, by some mismanagement or carelessness on his part, he lost his hold, fell into the sea, and was drowned.

One of the sailors, named Robinson, an excellent swimmer and a courageous fellow, jumped after him, but, before he could reach him, he had sunk to rise no more. The pilot boat took up Robinson, who was greatly exhausted, for the tide was rapid and high, and he swam in his clothes.

"Well," said Taylor, our skipper, "I've been at sea since I was a child, I may say, but I never saw the like of that before, and I hope I never shall again; and the poor fellow—the worst of it—they tell me, is married, and has left a wife and three children behind him; we must do something for them."

This considerate offer on the part of Taylor had been just anticipated by some of ourselves, and in a few minutes a very handsome sum was collected and given to his two. companions in the boat, to be by them presented to his widow. Robinson, who had so gallantly risked his life to save the pilot's, was taken care of by our surgeon, and he was on deck again in less than an hour.

We had how cleared the harbour, and the entire fleet was in our view; the transports and merchant vessels counted over sixty, and it was a cheering and a fine sight The day was beautiful; the breeze fresh, but scarcely a curl on the water, and the splendid *Newcastle* frigate, with canvass white as snow and steady as a piece of pasteboard, skimmed through the sea like a sword-fish. Our spirits were high, and, in the hope of a fine and speedy voyage, we set to work and made all the arrangements necessary for the regularity and comfort of the soldiers.

They were told off in messes, six men to each mess; and, for the comfort of the officers, I, as caterer, selected our cook, baker, and butcher. Our stock, both alive as well as dead, was abundant and good; and our supply of wine, porter, and ale, was equal to the long voyage before us. Having thus arranged those essential points, and put everything in proper trim, we portioned out the soldiers, and allotted to each section the duties to be performed.

On board the transport were six very tolerable ship guns, with a good supply of powder and ball; and we attached thirty-six of our old Peninsular soldiers to this department. It required but little trouble to instruct them in their duty; long habits had made those men so ready and intelligent, that an order had but to be given and it was promptly obeyed on the instant. The next thing to be looked to was a selection of men to man the rigging in case of an attempt at close fighting, which, at this period, was not uncommon with the American privateers. This was also a matter of easy accomplishment, as we had a number of fine young men from the Waterford and Cork militia, most of whom were either the sons of fishermen or had been fishermen themselves; and many of those could .mount the rigging with as much quickness as the sailors.

To this duty we allotted sixty privates, with a proportionate number of non-commissioned officers,—the entire under the command of Mr. Owgan, an officer of great bravery, and one who had been much distinguished in Spain. Our next care was the selection of sixty boarders. Those were placed under the command of Captain Walker, Mr. Watkins, and Mr. Hickson; and the arm chest of the transport having undergone a very minute ransacking, was found to contain a respectable muster of sabres .and cutlasses; they were not, it is true, in the best repair, but the qualities of the grinding-stone, a very good one by the way, were soon tested, and in a few hours those weapons that underwent the process of whetting were in that state, either for cut or thrust, that a Yankee would scarcely know whether he was run through the body or had undergone the operation of decapitation.

These dispositions being completed, nothing was left to be done but to exercise the men in their respective duties and departments; and all this was as well managed by Captain O'Hara, who commanded, and by us all, who acted more with him than under him, (for, in the Connaught Rangers, we all worked, fagged, and fought together more like affectionate brothers than those under the cold brow of austere command), that I do think never did a transport leave a port in a better trim, or with a better organised body of troops, than the one I now speak of. Indeed, the extraordinary attachment of the soldiers of the 88th to their officers and to their colours, and the gentleman-like good feeling and affection for each other, that prevailed amongst the officers themselves, obtained for them the unviable title—on this occasion at least "United Irishmen," and I will give one instance of this feeling on the part, of the soldiers.

The day after we left harbour, and when off the old head of Kinsale, the men attached to the guns were at exercise. Amongst them I noticed one who more than once fixed his eyes on me, I thought I had seen him before, yet there was scarcely a feature that I could, recall to my recollection. His nose had been nearly beaten in, he had no front teeth, and his tongue, which was nearly cleft in two, gave to his appearance anything but a favourable impression on first view, or, indeed, at any time. Nevertheless, there was a fire in his dark eye, and a soldier-like appearance in his carriage, that plainly told he was a man who had seen service.

"Who is that fellow at the gun with a nose like an ace of dubs," said I to O'Hara, who was standing beside me, "he is paying more attention to me than his work, though, for that matter, see how well he goes, through it"

"Who? he with the ramrod in his hand, standing up as stiff as a poker?" replied O'Hara, "he's a fine looking fellow though internally ugly; and, standing in his present erect position, with that huge truncheon of a ramrod in his hand, looks more like the knave than the ace of clubs!"

So soon as the drill at the guns was over, and before the men allotted to the rigging were mustered, I went up to the half-nosed soldier and asked his name. His face became nearly as scarlet as his jacket; his eyes filled up, and he could not articulate.

"What ails; you man, why don't you speak?" was the question naturally put by me.

"I see, sir," replied the poor fellow, "you don't remember me; but how can I wonder at it! I am greatly altered in appearance since I fought beside you at Salamanca; don't you remember Deady,—Bill Deady!"

" Perfectly now,! was my answer; "I recollect your voice, but your face is not as smooth as it was then, and your nose is sadly altered; in other respects you seem as well as ever and as fit to fight the Yankees as you were ever willing to have a crack at a Frenchman,—but your pension! I have you noted down as discharged, and admitted to Chelsea at a shilling a-day. How is this?"

"All true, sir," was his reply; "but, when I heard the regiment was going again on service, I threw up the pension and got leave to join; for, you know sir, I was always fond of the button." By the "button," the poor fellow meant the number of his corps. Many other instances might be quoted of the wonderful attachment of the soldiers of this regiment to their colours; or, as they themselves termed it in their own expressive way,—their "button" and this is the more strange, because no regiment in the service was worse treated than the Connaught Rangers; but, I suppose military persecution, like religious persecution, gains, rather than loses, proselytes.

"Jony,—Mr. Owgan," said our skipper, "if you wish to exercise your men in the rigging, you had better lose no time; for, so sure as my name is John Taylor, we are in for a stiff breeze and hazy weather, How is her head now, Flemming?"

This was addressed to the man at the helm. "Two points worse than when I took the wheel an hour ago," was the reply.

"I thought so! there goes the old *Antelope* like a tub; she's making a signal. Give me the telescope, Whetherhall," said Taylor, as he called his cabin boy. "Ay, there it is; a strange sail in sight! the *Newcastle* is after her. A fine beginning this, in sight of our own coast, when we should be off the banks of Newfoundland by this time. Ten days of fair wind lost at Beerhaven; what good could come of it! See 'Mother Carey's chickens' already. Never saw them yet. that we hadn't a splitting gale. Don't whistle, sir, if you please," continued the Captain, addressing Hickson, "we're bad enough as it is, and we sailors think it unlucky to whistle when the wind is not right in our teeth."

By this time, Owgan's people had got through their exercise in the rigging, and beautifully did they go up and down the ladders; old Taylor remarking—"they were as nimble as cats." An hour occupied in those evolutions was sufficient, and, by the time the arms were deposited in their respective arm racks, the dinner drum summoned the soldiers to mess.

Whether it was that our captain's caution to Hickson not to whistle, or that it was so ordained I know not, but the wind, though it continued high, became much more favourable; and, next day, we not only lost sight of land, but were steering our course at about seven knots an hour. The *Newcastle* frigate left us, and we saw no more of her again, though her signal was made to return.

This conduct on the part of Lord George Stewart was considered highly culpable; in fact, it admitted of no excuse, for, even supposing he had not seen the signal of recall, it was his duty to have returned and aided in the protection of a fleet of so much value, and of such consequence, and at a time, too, when the seas were glutted with American privateers. Some said he was on bad terms with his senior officer, Captain Butcher, others affirmed he had gone away in search of prizes; while again, it was said by his friends, he had lost the fleet, and, notwithstanding all his exertions, could not find them again.

This latter assertion was perfect folly, for never was fleet more scattered than ours, and it is next to impossible to suppose that he could not, with his splendid sailing frigate, have found some of them, had such been his object. That Captain Butcher thought so there can be little doubt, as he brought Lord George to a court martial the following year at Sheerness; but, the charges not being thought sufficiently proved, he, was acquitted.

The weather still continued fine, and our troops were regularly exercised at the guns, rigging, and the boarding; the men were healthy and in good spirits, and all went on well. Pigs, sheep, and poultry rather threw up flesh than lost it; but here, I regret to say, that the butcher's knife and the butcher's block did awful execution on the necks of many of our Beerhaven veteran cocks.

Those gallant birds, the victors in many fights, were now doomed to suffer an ignominious death; their gallant deeds forgotten, and all remembrance of their former services no more thought of than if they had never been performed by them. Yet, after all, they were as well treated, or nearly so, as the Peninsular army. The only difference between them is this,—that the cocks were killed and roasted, notwithstanding their protesting against such bad treatment; while the Peninsular army are only "roasted" by Lord Londonderry for presuming to remonstrate against the vile treatment they have met with.

It is fortunate for the survivors of that army that ours is not a country of cannibals, otherwise they would be devoured to a man; but, if we are not cannibals, we most assuredly have some vultures amongst us, who would carry away all the spoils for themselves, and leave the rest without any thing. Such unworthy treatment from any quarter is bad enough, but, from such a person as Lord Londonderry,—it is "too bad."

By this time we were six days out of harbour, and though the weather still continued good, appearances were manifest that a change was nigh; towards nightfall the wind veered round, the sky became clouded,' and though the moon was at its full, not a vestige of it was to be seen,—all was darkness. "Make all right and tight above," said old Taylor to Robinson, the mate.

"Ay, ay, sir," was the reply; and the ship which a short time before had all sail set, and was making her course gallantly through the water, might now be seen, with her top-sails reefed, her dead-lights in, her guns doubly lashed, and all those precautions taken which auger that a storm is not only expected, but prepared for.

About ten at night the wind increased with great violence, and by midnight it blew a perfect hurricane from the north-west, with such a sea as few had ever seen before.

The ship rolled badly, and all, or almost all, our bulwarks were carried away; three pigs, a goat, and all our stock of poultry, shared the same fate; and the cries of the poor goat, the squeaking of the pigs, mixed with the screams of the cocks and hens, had a melancholy effect on our spirits, which before were considerably damped by a heavy fall of rain.

The men on watch were all sent below, the hatches were fastened down, and none remained on deck save the captain and ship's crew, and the men posted at the forecastle. Those men, six in number, were on the lookout to see that no ship ran foul of us; and the constant blowing of their tin horns, added to the doleful ringing of the bell, formed a combination of sounds the most discordant and disagreeable it is possible to conceive.

Then again, every half-hour, might be heard the heavy guns of the *Antelope*, firing her signal for the ships to tack; but the fog was so heavy and the wind so high that the cannon was sometimes not heard, and the tacking of the greater portion of the fleet was at the discretion of the different captains. The consequence was, that when day broke, we could see nothing of the rest of the fleet; but the goodness of our ship, and her crew, and the admirable state of discipline in which our soldiers were, made us tolerably easy on the score of being taken by a privateer.

About ten o'clock, the fog had considerably cleared away, and we could see clearly for a couple of miles in every direction; but not the sign of a ship was visible. Several pieces of wood and some hencoops floated past us, which proved that we were not the only sufferers in the late gale. The storm had by this time considerably abated, but the sea ran mountains high, and the ship rolled far more than in the night. About this time the man at the foretop called out, "three ships in sight," and far distant on our starboard bow, we saw three sail, which our captain recognized as transports. They were steering the same course as ourselves, and like us with close-reefed topsails.

It was immediately decided that we should bear down on them, and as ours was a good sailer, and had the wind of them, in less than two hours we found ourselves alongside the *Spring*, transport, while the other two were not far distant. The *Spring* had on board one hundred artillerymen, several guns, and a large store of powder, and was destined for Halifax, She was a fine ship, and sailed well, and it was thought advisable to name her, *pro. tem*, our commodore.

The four transports now sailed in company, and kept well together, but as evening approached, a heavy fog and heavy rain set in, and, though with less wind, we were nearly as badly off as the preceding night.

The signal guns of the *Spring* were too feeble to be heard at any distance, and we tacked as we best could. All the officers and men were, more or less, sea-sick, and the pigs and ducks fared sumptuously. When morning dawned, we were close to the *Peggy Cleary*, transport She was one of the four that were together the preceding day, and had on board a detachment of the "Buffs," From her we learned the bad news of the capture of the *Spring,* the night before; but though we regretted the loss of so valuable a ship, the certainty that we had ourselves escaped, tended in a great measure to reconcile us to her loss. In less than an hour we had the satisfaction to see the *Antelope*, the two brigs, and fifteen of the fleet, but no appearance of the *Newcastle* frigate. The wind also had changed a few points in our favour, and the day was beautifully fine and warm.

This change put us all in good spirits, and we set to work arranging all our matters, which had been a good deal deranged during the gale. Besides our loss of pigs and poultry, a pipe of spruce beer was stove in; it was to have been bottled off the day of the hurricane, but fate ordained it otherwise. However, we had plenty of essence of spruce in store, and we soon made good the loss.

Next day the greater part of the fleet joined us, but we learned, with much regret, that two merchant brigs ran foul of each other in the fog of the first night, and all hands went to the bottom; but it is only to be wondered that many more did not share the same fate.

CHAPTER 32

Our Ship Visited by a Privateer

It would be tedious and uninteresting to the readier was I to detail the constant system of tacking and retacking we were obliged to have recourse to on this unusually long voyage; suffice it to say, that before we reached Newfoundland we had sailed over twice as much distance as it would have taken, with a fair wind, to have made Quebec.

Though the wind was foul, the weather was dry and fine, and we were quite free from fogs. The soldiers were all dressed in their slop-clothing, and their exercise was so admirably arranged that it was to them quite an amusement. The men dined at two, after which their ration of rum was served out on deck. The officers dined at four, and never sat at table beyond five. We then assembled on the quarter-deck, and the brass band of the second battalion, the greater portion of which we brought out with us, was in attendance, and then all the soldiers' wives made their appearance, dressed in their best frocks, the young women with their hair neatly dressed, while those of the more advanced age wore caps.

Dancing immediately commenced, and it is not necessary to add that in any Irish regiment, but above all in such a one as the "Connaught Rangers," there was no lack of good reel and jig dancers. The consequence was, that each evening brought forward some new faces, and new aspirants for applause; and it was as heartily given as it was fairly merited. The dancers were likewise a sort of privileged class, and had a separate allowance of punch allotted for their use; and this department was ably filled by our cook, Mistress Nelly McCarthy, for whom I used all my interest with our commandant to gain for her an appointment which I knew from experience she was well calculated for; and I may here add that I never saw that woman who knew better how to fill a glass—ay, and empty one, too—than did my *protégée*, Nelly.

Seven o'clock no sooner sounded than the dance ceased; the watch for the night paraded, and the rest sent below to arrange their beds. In those days I write of, the men slept together, four in each bed, there was no "ladies' cabin," or even separate beds allotted for the soldiers' wives. How they managed to get on I know not, but we never heard any complaint on this head; and as one-fourth of the men were on deck all night, their absence from bed gave the rest more room, and I have no doubt many of the unmarried men were better contented to have their room than their company.

At eight o'clock the officers had their tea, and at ten supper was laid on the table. After this, each occupied himself as he chose; some played whist, others read; and Hicks and Wilkinson, who were good musicians, played prettily together, the former on the flute, the other on the violin. Thus passed away the time, and as our play was confined to low stakes, we never had one unpleasant though much less one disagreeable word amongst us.

One night, when within a day or two's sail from Newfoundland, O'Hara, Lewis, Owgan, and myself, were engaged at a rubber of whist, when we were surprised to see Mr. Smith (he that upset the tureen of pea-soup into the lap of Doctor Crowe,) walk out of his berth and stand beside us in his shirt His eyes were wide open, but he was fast asleep. We remained silent, and anxiously waited to see what he would do; and we were not long kept in suspense. He deliberately walked over to where his sword was hanging, and drawing it out of the scabbard, rushed out of the cabin, and was on the deck in an instant, calling out, at the top of his voice, "Board, board!"

We were beside him in a second, and it was fortunate that we were, as he was in the act of springing over the side of the vessel, when Owgan caught him in his arms. When he awoke, he was greatly alarmed, but said, when at school he often, when asleep, got out of bed, and went down to the school-room.

It was decided he should be looked to; and, to prevent anything like a recurrence of the same thing, a sentry was placed at the head of the stairs leading to the deck, with positive directions to bring him down to the cabin in case he should attempt such another evolution as he had just then performed. We made him take a large glass of mulled port, for he was shivering like an aspen leaf, and we soon afterwards went to bed, and met with no further interruption from him.

The next night passed over without any disturbance from Smith, but towards morning, I saw a figure move out of the state cabin, where O'Hara and Captain Walker slept. I at once recognized Walker, who kept fumbling at one of the lockers where I had a reserve of Fermoy ale. This did not either surprise me or cause me any uneasiness, as the locker was well secured with a padlock, the key of which was in my pocket. He then walked round the cabin, and I could occasionally see him stooping, though, happily for our ale, not taking the stoop he had evidently meditated. At last he returned to his bed, and I fell asleep.

The eight o'clock drum, next morning, told us the time for dressing had arrived, and I looked on the chair beside my berth for my clothes, where my servant always left them. But no clothes were there nor could my servant give any account of them. Owgan had the same story to tell, so had Smith I and it was thought right to send for the serjeant of the watch, and ascertain from him who the sentries were at the hatchway during the night; but just at this moment O'Hara threw his eye towards Walker's berth, and there we discovered all the missing articles.

Walker was interrogated, but he had not the remotest recollection of having quitted his bed; so it was manifest that, bad as we thought ourselves with being obliged to take charge of one somnambulist, we had now the felicity of being saddled with two. One obliged to be watched lest he should, in one of his pranks, be tempted to throw himself into the sea, and the other, when suffering from the horrors of indigestion, unconsciously attacking our lockers, and, failing there, leaving us without clothes to cover our nakedness.

So soon as our morning parade and exercise was over, the events of the preceding night formed our . principal topic of conversation; and we were forming plans for our amusement with our sleep-walking friends, when old Taylor joined us. Though a rough man in manner, like most of his profession, he was a kind-hearted soul, and moreover had taken a fancy to Walker. He looked serious and discomposed, and addressed O'Hara with much earnestness on the danger that might have happened.

"You see, Captain O'Hara," said Taylor, "Captain Walker is a married man, and ought to be looked to, so ought Mr. Smith; for would it not be a sad business if they took it into their heads, some of these nights, to throw themselves into the sea?"

"What! Walker throw himself into the sea?" roared Owgan. "Who ever saw Walker look at fresh water, much less at salt water? You need not have any fears on that score; but we will have our eye to him, nevertheless; and if you are anxious about his safety, just get from below one of your barrels of strong ale, put it into your own cabin, and never fear, whether asleep or awake, you'll find he won't stay far from it."

Old Taylor at once agreed to the suggestion, and took Owgan's advice. A barrel of ale was soon got from the hold, and I took advantage of the opportunity, and got placed in one end of our cabin a vessel of Cork porter, leaving still a good supply in the hold. Before we left Cork, I purchased, amongst other things, a couple of patent cocks with keys. This I did as a precaution against our servants, but in tapping the vessel, now got up, a portion of the cock was broken, and it might be turned with any sharp instrument. However, it was not noticed, or I thought so at least, by any person except myself, and I forgot the circumstance.

We were now within, according to our reckonings one day's sail of the banks of Newfoundland. The fleet had got together wonderfully well, and we had not been annoyed by privateers for several days. The weather was clear, but the wind still foul,- and the tacking system was obliged to be followed. A few hours had wrought a great change in the temperature, and, though but the end of August, it was as cold as the month of November. One of Owgan's sharp-shooters was amusing himself in the rigging, and had not been long at the foretop, when, with a broad Irish brogue, he called out—"Land."

"What fool is that up there?" said Taylor. "Some of your Waterford fishermen, I suppose. I say, is that you, Cleary? You see land, don't you? You must have devilish good sight, then!" By this time Cleary was on deck, protesting strongly that he had seen land.

"What was it like?" said Taylor, at the same time telling Robinson, the mate, to run up to the foretop.

"It was for all the world like the hill of Howth, except that it was white."

Cleary had got so far with his story, when Robinson called out—"Three icebergs ahead."

A loud laugh assailed poor Cleary, but though mistaken as to what it was he saw, his quickness was applauded, and a glass of rum was his reward.

As we neared the icebergs, the cold became so intense that the hallyards were frozen, and we were obliged to exercise the men to keep them warm. For this purpose, we placed ropes, hurdle fashion, on the deck, and by constant running round and taking their jumps, the men regained their natural warmth. The large iceberg was a beautiful sight, and so high and broad, that the *Antelope*, and two of the transports, which passed beyond it, were lost to our view for several minutes; but there were several smaller ones scarcely visible, being little more than a foot over the water, which were as dangerous as rocks, and they were watched with great attention and some alarm by the sailors. But we escaped them all, and as we left them, and they us, the cold disappeared, and we continued to struggle on towards Newfoundland.

Towards evening, a gun fired from the *Antelope* attracted the eyes of all in the fleet; and the two brigs immediately answered the signal, which announced, "a strange sail in sight." The signal for chase was the next made, and we soon saw the brigs disentangling themselves from the rest of the fleet; but night was coming on rapidly, and we lost sight of them.

As there could be little doubt that the stranger was an enemy, the *Antelope* ordered the fleet to keep as close to her as possible, and two of her boats came alongside the nearest transports, and, as they passed, each ship was directed to keep a good look out This precaution was not necessary with us, because, on the first alarm being given, we prepared and were ready for action. No signal guns for tacking were fired, and we kept on the same course which we had at nightfall. We thus made no way towards our final destination; but, on the contrary, rather lost than gained ground; but it was unavoidable. It was ascertained that three privateers were amongst us, and, had we tacked, many of the ships would have been so far separated from the vessels of war, that their capture would have been inevitable.

Towards midnight, a heavy firing from one of the brigs announced that she was engaged. In a few minutes it ceased, and shortly after we were informed by a man-of-war's boat that one of the three privateers had been just captured close to us; and at the same time reiterating the order to be prepared, and not to allow any ship to approach too near us. This order had not been given more than an hour, when a vessel was seen on our starboard bow; she was on the same tack as ourselves, but was evidently nearing us. "Port,—port, I say," said Taylor to the man at the helm.

"Port it is—hard a port," was the reply. "Why, she's putting us a point and more out of our course," said the man.

Taylor then took up the speaking trumpet and hailed the stranger, but, no reply being made, Owgan seized a firelock, and, taking a steady aim, fired at the man at the wheel A bustle on board left little doubt but that Owgan's fire was effective; and, as he reloaded the musket, he quietly remarked that the best stopper was a nobber; and so it appeared for, in the morning we discovered that our neighbour was a privateer; that she carried fifteen guns, and had a crew consisting of one hundred and fifty men; that the sailor was shot dead by Owgan, and her intention was to have boarded us. All this was put beyond a doubt, as the American was taken the following morning by the boats of the *Antelope*. Her audacity was so great that she had penetrated so far into the middle of the fleet as to render escape impossible; and she struck her colours without firing a shot or having taken a prize.

Owgan was the only one of us who felt annoyed at the occurrence; but it was not for his having shot the steersman,—quite the contrary; but his regret was great at having been the cause of his boarders losing the opportunity of making a prize, a thing both he and they looked upon as certain. Whatever Owgan's feelings might have been on the subject, they were far from being responded to by Taylor, whose joy was ungovernable at the thought of the escape of his ship; and he justly remarked that had she been taken, the owners would have sustained a heavy loss, and he, himself, nearly beggared.

"No, no," said he, "no fighting, no fighting, Mr. Owgan. I have no wish to end my days in a Yankee prison."

The very thought of a failure on his part, and on the part of his brave companions, was enough for Owgan, who was a young man of a fiery temperament, and he immediately offered to fight old Taylor on the quarter-deck; and, to prove he was in earnest, he ran down to the cabin for his pistols.

"See now," said he, addressing Taylor, "see now, here are a pair of as good pistols as ever Bowles of Cork sent out of his shop. You may either toss up for choice or take the one you fancy most, and I'm content. Name your distance, the deck is wide enough; but, if I had my choice, I wouldn't measure as much ground with you as would sod a lark-cage!"

So far from liking, much less agreeing to the proposal, old Taylor tried to laugh and stammer out some explanation; and we all joined him, leaving poor Owgan in more than a minority,—for not one voice was with him. The skipper held out his hand, which Owgan accepted with a squeeze that made Taylor's face, naturally a ruddy one, as red as scarlet: and thus ended the affair.

The entire fleet were in high spirits when they learned that two out of the three privateers, had been captured; and, had the *Newcastle* frigate been with us, as she ought to have been, there is little doubt but that the third Yankee ship would have shared the fate of her companions.

The previous night's sailing, which, from necessity, obliged us to keep on the one tack, caused us to be as far from Newfoundland as we were twenty-four hours before, and there seemed to be no likelihood of our reaching Quebec before the winter had set in; for it' was now the first week in September, and we had not seen land since we lost sight of the Irish coast

However, the men continued healthy and our sea stock abundant; but Taylor became uneasy about our supply of water, which, upon examination, was calculated not to be more than a month's consumption at the rate we had used it. To guard against any deficiency in this essential article, it was agreed that a reduction in the supply should be adopted, and, in order to effect this, a sentry was placed at the water cask with strict orders not to allow any waste or undue consumption by either the soldiers or their wives; but in this instance, like most others we meet with throughout life, the moment it was known that there was a restriction put on the water cask, men who scarcely ever tasted it before, now had, or fancied they had, a burning thirst, and were constant applicants for a drink; and we were inundated with complaints from the soldiers.

"I'll tell you what it is," said Owgan to me and O'Hara, "This puts me in mind of the 'run' on Rogers's bank when it was thought that he would fail. For three days the bank was besieged by people bringing in his notes; and he would have failed at last, for a time at least, if it had not been for my father."

"Ay, he relieved him, I suppose," said O'Hara.

"He did, faith," replied Owgan," but not in the way you suppose—with money: he did no such thing, but he took Rogers aside; 'Rogers,' said he, 'you know I'm your friend,'

"'I do,' was the reply.

"'Will you take my advice, then? If you do, you will soon stop the 'run.''

"'That's what I'd like,' said Rogers, 'for the pace they are going at is too fast to last long. 'Tis the pace that kills.'

"'Well,' said my father, 'put up a notice that your bank will be open at six every morning instead of at ten, and put an advertisement to the same effect in the "Chronicle" this evening.'

"He did so, and after the first two hours he was troubled no more, and the bank got on better than ever. Now, let us do the same with. the water; say there's plenty below that you didn't find out at first, take the sentry off the cask, and see whether I am right or not."

We tried the experiment. The first day the consumption was a quarter less than the preceding one, the next, nearly half less, and we had an abundance for the rest of the voyage.

On this night we had rare sport with Walker and Smith. About two o'clock in the morning I felt very thirsty—not an unusual thing with me—and had stolen over to a locker where I had a good supply of bottled cider. While in the act of drawing the cork, the neck of the bottle broke, leaving it and the screw in my hand, but the remainder of the bottle fell, and in its fall stuck in my left leg.

I was severely cut, but I knew I was wrong in nibbling at the general stock; and, resolving to keep my own counsel, gathered up the pieces of the broken bottle and was retiring to my berth, when a rustle in the corner where the barrel of porter had been placed, caused me to look round, and here I beheld Walker, not asleep but wide awake, sprawling on his back: he was nearly naked, his shirt being turned up under his chin, the ale cock was in his mouth, while with his hand he turned, with the turn-screw of his gun, the broken cock, and thus supplied his wants. He motioned me to silence, and pointed to the bottle, plainly indicating that if I kept his secret he'd keep mine; but I told the story next morning at breakfast, though I knew the laugh would be at my expense.

I had not been long in bed when down marched Smith from his berth, which was an upper one. He was fast asleep, but, as before, sought for his sword, which, after his first night's ramble, had been placed out of his reach. He then walked to the fire place and quietly laid hold of the poker, and proceeded up the ladder to the deck. Here he was met by Bill Deady, who happened to be the sentry on duty. His directions were to watch quietly until Smith approached the side of the ship, and then to give him a gentle touch with his bayonet, and immediately hide himself behind the caboose or cook's house.

A shrill cry from Smith, who came rushing down the stairs, left little doubt that Deady had obeyed his orders. I never stirred or seemed to notice Smith, and the poor fellow got quietly into bed; and next day he was told how matters had been arranged to preserve his life. He was very thankful, and never walked in his sleep during the remainder of the voyage.

After the morning parade was over, I interrogated Deady as to Smith's adventure, and his account was as follows:—

"I was standing close to the ladder, when, just as the two o'clock watch was set, who should I see but Mr. Smith coming up the ladder in his shirt; he had his nightcap on, and the poker in his hand, and bad luck to me but he put a start in me, and it's not easy to do that same! 'Whist,' says he, 'Owgan, I'll go first,' and upon the same he made for the side iv the ship, and was goin t'jump into the say. Begorra, says I to myself, you'll not do that while I'm here any how; so I ran behind him and gave him a prod that made him sneeze.

"'Murther,' says he, 'I'm wounded,' and it was thrue for him he was! but I think it will sarve him well, for he was awake in a minit, and looked quite shy iv himself!"

I told Deady he acted perfectly right, and that I had little doubt Mr. Smith would remember his escape, and be quiet for the rest of the voyage.

"The rest is it!" responded Deady, "will it ever be over, sir?"

"I hope soon now," I replied, "look, there is Saint Mary's, see all the fishing boats at work, we must set out our own lines and go to work also."

"I never was so tired of a ship before," said Deady.

I was tired myself, and lest I should tire my readers also, with their permission, I'll just drop anchor at Saint Mary's, and try my hand at cod fishing.

CHAPTER 33

Arrival at the Mouth of the St. Lawrence

On the evening of the 4th of September, the fleet which sailed from the Cove of Cork, on the 1st of July, and which during their two months' voyage had encountered such bad weather, were now off Saint Mary's,' Newfoundland; not a breath of wind to fill a sail or cause a ripple on the water, was a novel and pleasing contrast to what we had previously, arid almost without any intermission, experienced; and in eight fathoms of water we resolved to try our hands at a sport, though new to us all, we had often heard of—cod fishing.

To a thorough-going angler, he who would only condescend to throw out a line of the finest texture, with flies appended to it, such as "grouse hackle," "wren's hackle," or the far-famed and much-admired "green drake," such clumsy work as we were now about to dive into, would savour more of "pot-walloping,"—a term, by the way, sometimes applied by critics to unfortunate scribblers, who write not only to amuse others, but themselves also—than genuine sport; nevertheless I do not hesitate to avow, that had those gentlemen been cooped up in a ship for some eight or nine weeks, without much amusement, and, what to many was even worse, without having tasted a morsel of fresh fish, they would not have turned up their noses at the solid and rational enjoyment we were now about to plunge into.

I have before mentioned that, while at Cork, we had purchased a good supply of hooks and lines, and these we now distributed amongst the soldiers and ship's crew; for, though the latter were supplied with some, they were old, and by no means as good as ours. For the officers' use we reserved twenty lines, and I do believe that, making all due allowance for inexperience, no score of lines ever did more execution in the same spot, or in the same space of time. We had no regular bait, and were obliged in the first instance to use pork, but though the fish "took," as the phrase has it, it was but slowly, and it was manifest our neighbours, the regular fishermen, outstripped us greatly.

"Why, sir," said Pat Carey, addressing Owgan, "sure it can't be possible but amongst so many boats some of the 'boys' from Waterford must be there; and now that I remember, sure there was Jack Green's father, and his uncle, and two of his brothers, went out to Saint John's two years ago. Aint that the thruth, Jack?" said Carey, addressing one of Owgan's sharp-shooters.

"Sure it is," replied Jack, "and I'm neither afraid nor ashamed to deny it"

"Why should you?" was the reply.

"What does he mean, Carey?" demanded Owgan.

"Why, sir," replied Pat, "the Greens of Dungarvan were always a dhroll set iv boys, and they were often accused of taking what they had no call to take; and the neighbours used to say they had a taking way with them; and so you see they thought it best to come over here for a while, far as it is from their own home; for, 'pon my soul, it was the general belief in Waterford, if they staid there much longer, they'd thravel farther from home than where they are at present"

It was not possible to mistake this more than innuendo touching the relatives of Jack Green, and Owgan judging he could not have a better guide, though perhaps a better man, resolved that Green should accompany him in quest of bait

The jolly-boat was soon lowered, soon manned, and Owgan, who understood something of boating took the helm, and also a couple of bottles of whiskey; and the party were soon amongst the fishermen. In less than half an hour they returned bringing a plentiful supply of a bait called squid, as likewise half a dozen fine cod fish. These were given them by some Irish fishermen, who refused to take payment for either fish or bait; and though the "Green family" were not amongst the party, it was ascertained they were on the banks, (which, by the way, happened to be the green banks of Newfoundland,) and prospering very much in their new calling.

Before taking leave of these kind-hearted fellows, Owgan was resolved not to be outdone in generosity, and as they would not accept of money, he presented them with his two bottles of Irish whiskey, remarking that, though we were all on the "banks," it was no reason we should be on a "dry-bank."

"By gor," said Jack Green, "that was spoken like a rale gentleman, as you are, Mr. Owgan," and seizing one of the bottles, he knocked off the neck, and presenting the bottle to Owgan, requested him "to dhrink success to the boys."

This request was, of course, complied with, the whiskey was tasted by Owgan, the bottle passed round, and in a few moments it bore, as Green observed, "Moll Thompson's mark."

"What mark was that, Jack?" said Owgan.

"Why, thin, did you never hear it, Mr. Owgan? sure Moll's mark for she couldn't write well, was M. T." (empty). A regular shout of approbation, greeted Jack's wit, and if it were permitted, the fish-owners would have given us all the fish in their boat.

Up to the time of the return of our boat, we had not killed more than a dozen of cod, but the moment our lines were properly baited, the work began in earnest; and without entering into any minute detail, it will be sufficient to say that in about four hours, with fifty, lines, the deck was strewed with upwards of four hundred fish. They were divided into different lots; some for the officers, and the rest to the different messes, sailors as well as soldiers. We had some expert hands amongst us, and the process of cutting open the fish. and salting them, was performed rapidly and well, and afforded us not only rational but agreeable amusement. We lived on fish for the first three days, and old Taylor, who was a great economist, taught our men, how to make the most of them. For this purpose, he caused the heads of some twenty or thirty fish to be cut off, and then be boiled up with biscuit dust, and made a horrid-looking mess of them, which he called "chouder." He and his crew eat voraciously of this. dish, and it might, for aught I know to the contrary, have been delicious, but I never tasted it

Owgan, with his single line, to which only two hooks were attached, killed five and twenty fish; and so keen was he at the sport, that one of his fingers was cut to the bone by the friction of the line. It would be; impossible to give a just description of the voracity of the fish in these latitudes, neither could any computation be made of their numbers; but, from appearances, it might be supposed that the sea was literally alive with cod.

No doubt there must be something marvellously attractive in the shape of food on these banks, and there must be an abundance of it, too, or how could: millions of fine well-fed cod exist? Then, on the other hand, if food was so plentiful, why seek after the bait we fished with? When those fish were opened, their maws were found to contain all kinds of fish: crabs, lobsters, and a variety of others; and yet they would follow our lines up to the surface of the water, and struggle with the captured fish for the bait in his mouth, when, if the truth could be told, the latter would not only resign the bait to his follower, but the hook into the bargain. I asked Jack Green if he could account for this.

"By Gor, sir!" replied he, "it puts me in mind of the young Irish gentlemen, when they do be running after the country girls, and leaving the quality,—skins iv potatoes for the change iv diet." It was a phrase I never had before heard, and was so truly Irish, that I took a note of it at the time.

The wind, which for several hours might be said to have ceased altogether, now got up, and an end was made to our butchery, for so in truth it was. The *Antelope* made signal for sailings and she and the fleet were soon steering their course, with a fair though light wind. How to arrange and stow away our enormous quantity of cod was a task of more difficulty than the hooking of them. However, "by hook or by crook," we packed them into beef and pork tubs, got up from the hold; but the smell was disagreeable, and after we had feasted a couple of days on fish, we began to wish the remainder were once more in their native element, the sea: but this was strongly opposed by old Taylor, who offered to take them all himself, and promised to stow them so securely, and so far away, that we would suffer no inconvenience whatever.

This was a promise easier made than fulfilled; for had his ship, the *George*, been the size of the *Royal George*, it would not have been possible to cushion the stench that arose from below, unless, indeed, our present vessel was as deep under water as her ill-fated namesake; in which case, it would not be of much consequence to her occupants whether the fish smelt well or ill. However, we gave him three or four barrels full, and our own consumption being still considerable, by degrees the nuisance became abated. Taylor was so delighted with the success of his application, that he resolved, while the weather was so fine, and the fleet so well together, to ask his friend the captain of the Peggy Cleary to dine with him. I forget the name of this man, but I recollect he was an Irishman, and as drunken a one, too, as was ever imported into any ship, or exported from his own dear country, and in saying so much, it must be evident he was a drinker of the first class, indeed

To judge from the number of dishes that left the cook's caboose, Taylor must have given his friend a plentiful dinner; and, from the mirthful sounds that issued from the *sal à manger,* it was plain that something stronger than water was made use of to wash down the good cheer. In short, Peggy Cleary (for so I must now call him) showed symptoms of intoxication that were not to be misunderstood. He commenced several songs, but failed—from loss of memory rather than from want of voice, for he sang very well,—to finish any; and as he could not get through a song to his satisfaction, he came on deck just as the soldiers and their wives had commenced their evening dance.

Having obtained permission from the officer on duty to select a partner, he was not either scrupulous or long in making his choice; but the effect of his last tumbler which so closely followed on the footsteps of the dancing, caused him to be in fact the last tumbler himself, and in making a *faux pas,* he pitched head-foremost against the binnacle, and falling flat on his face, broke not only his nose but his leg also.

"I knew," said old Taylor, as he raised his bleeding friend, "how this would end. What good ever befell a man who, having first got drunk, began kicking up his heels like a jackass?"

This unfortunate event put an end to all further amusement, as the staff-surgeon, Doctor Macdonald, who accompanied us, was soon occupied in endeavouring to set poor Peggy's leg right, (it was the left leg by the way,) and his nose upright. The former task was not difficult, for the fracture was not a compound one, and the cause was simple enough^ but the nose was the grand point to get over, being the most prominent as well as the most difficult feature in the business; and, as Hickson observed, the difficulty of getting over the nose was increased ten-fold in consequence of the bridge being destroyed.

"Pon my soul, Mr. Hickson," remarked Taylor, "your observation is an arch one."

All this time poor Peggy was enduring a torture that seemed to be agonizing; but before Macdonald could commence operations in earnest, it was necessary that the blood should be staunched, as it flowed in such copious streams apprehensions were entertained that a portion of the fractured cartilage would be carried away by the flood. However, by frequent styptical applications, the threatened evil was avoided; and by a gentle pressure of the finger and thumb, a very respectable nose was substituted. in lieu of the hideous snout which a short time before, had garnished his face, and which we had at first looked on with horror and dismay.

"All that may look very well, Doctor," said Owgan, "but how will you keep the arch up without some support? The entire foundation is so sapped with blood, that it has lost its consistency." The doctor looked puzzled, for it was utterly impossible to gainsay Owgan's observation.

"If the fellow could be kept quiet," replied he, "we might manage to keep up the nose; but in his present excited state, I really do not well know what to do."

"Oh! I'll be quiet," moaned the sufferer, "never fear me; let me have another glass of grog, that's all. I say, Doctor, I was always an ugly fellow, but now, I suppose, I am the very devil!"

"You are ugly enough in all conscience, now," replied Macdonald; "but not only your looks, but perhaps your life depends on your keeping quiet for a short time. If you do so, matters may go on very well."

"Now Doctor," hiccuped Peggy, "what do you call a short time?"

"Why, a few hours," was the reply.

"Well, then, go to work as soon as you please," was now the prompt answer; and from it there was no difficulty in perceiving that the hint of his life being in danger, had wrought a marvellous change in Peggy's demeanour, and he allowed the doctor to operate,' without stirring hand or foot.

Macdonald cut two small pieces of card, and putting a morsel of fine lint on each end, insinuated one into' each nostril, and thus formed a kind of trestle bridge, and no doubt was entertained by him that all would be right if "Peggy" would only remain tranquil. This: the poor man promised to do, and at his earnest request a looking-glass was brought to him, in order that he might see the ravages inflicted on his physiognomy. He bore the examination with the composure of a stoic, until he saw the frightful hole on the bridge of his nose. He could not, with his eye, fathom its depth, and he made demonstrations of getting his little finger into it This was strenuously opposed by the doctor, and "Peggy" remarked, that anyone who pleased might play "three hole span" on his face.

At length the doctor got him not only out of his hands, but, to our infinite relief, out of the ship also. His exit was amusing enough, for he was scrupulously particular that all respect should be paid him. "Let me," he pompously exclaimed, "go first, and the practitioner (meaning the doctor) can follow."

It was no easy task to slew him down the side of the ship, and get him safely into his boat, but all was accomplished without accident, and we lost sight of him forever.

"Well," said old Taylor, "I'm rid of that 'ere chap, and I'm blowed if I'll soon again be hooked into anything of that sort." He apologized for all the trouble he had caused, and was heartily forgiven; for, to say the truth, we were more amused than annoyed with the gambols of "Peggy."

On this day we spoke our companion the *Atlas*. Bagwell and all his officers and men were well, and, like ourselves, had none on the sick list. We continued our voyage with mild weather, but as usual with contrary wind, and the fleet was considerably reduced in number. Some had sailed for Halifax; others had either separated from us, or had been taken by privateers; and we did not count more than twenty sail out of the vast fleet that had left Cove.

We had scarcely got rid of "Peggy," and he could not have much more than reached his ship, when the weather, which was before so beautifully fine, showed symptoms of a change, and though the wind had never been in our favour, we continued to get on tolerably well, though always on the "tacking" system. However, appearances were now once more against even this, and in a few hours we had a touch of a real gale on the banks of Newfoundland. All that we had witnessed before was mere child's play to the storm we now encountered; not only the decks, but the masts, half-mast high at least, were washed over; our ducks, the remnant of our poultry, were carried away; and two, out of our three remaining pigs, shared the same fate. Two of our best steersmen were lashed to the helm, and no person could show his face on the deck without the certainty of being washed over.

Nevertheless, old Taylor was as steady as a rock; he showed no symptoms of fear, and remained during the entire night at his post, and superintended the relief of the men at the wheel. Morning at length came, and though the storm continued to rage with unabated fury, it was cheering to behold the rays of the sun; but there was not one solitary ship to be seen, all were either dispersed, or had resolved to make the best of their course without the protection of the ships of war. The wind at length became more moderate, the soldiers were enabled to stand on deck, and Taylor resolved to run chance and make the best of his way to the Saint Lawrence. This was a proposal that met the wishes of all, and was indeed our only chance of not passing the remainder of the season on board ship, or at all events not reaching our destination.

"Now, Mr. Owgan," said Taylor, "you may have an opportunity of trying your hand with a Yankee, for I think it more than ten to one we shall have to deal with some of them 'ere chaps. As for the ship and her crew, I wouldn't place either second to any in the fleet, even if they were all together; and the privateer that tries to board us will have a tough job of it. Eh, Mr. Owgan?"

Owgan had not forgotten the former row he and our worthy skipper had on the same subject, and he only remarked that if Taylor would put his ship alongside the Yankee, and give the latter an opportunity of trying her hand, he might be tolerably certain of a favourable result; but no such event occurred, and after three days' sail we found ourselves in the Gulf of Saint Lawrence. Here we were joined by the *Antelope* and four other ships of the convoy; the rest had either gone to Halifax or to Quebec; and the wind being now favourable, we arrived at the mouth of the Saint Lawrence without further adventure or mishap.

Chapter 34

A Love Adventure

We were here hailed by several pilot-boats, each carrying one or more "branch pilots," that is to say, men who were duly authorized and licensed to pilot vessels up and down the river Saint Lawrence; but whether it was that old Taylor preferred our Canadian sailor, "Jerry," or that he wished to save the expense (which is great) of a "branch pilot," I know not, but he declined all offers from the boats, and we all joined in requesting that "Jerry" might be allowed to guide our ship to Quebec, for he seemed thoroughly acquainted with all parts of the banks, and he had produced his father's certificate as a "branch pilot," as likewise his own testimonials as having acted with him for four years.

All matters being thus settled, and "Jerry" regularly installed, he, before entering on his duties, determined to give the crew some grog, and, as a matter of course, he was not himself an idle looker-on. While he and the crew were thus employed, our dance, amongst the soldiers and the soldiers' wives, was going on; the water was as smooth as a looking-glass, and though the tide was strong against us we were making more than five knots an hour.

As we passed the shoals of Manniguagin, the water near the shore, and the entire air on its borders, were actually darkened with wild fowl. To say that there were thousands would be saying nothing, or next to nothing, for there must have been millions. We requested Taylor to let us have a boat to go on shore, as "Jerry" said he would anchor for the night a mile or so farther up, but at the moment the boat was about to be lowered, the ship struck with a tremendous crash on a rock, and threw us into great confusion. Old Taylor ran about like a man out of his senses, while "Jerry" tore his hair, and appeared to be quite distracted.

There was no actual danger of loss of life, but Taylor feared the keel of the ship was injured, and be now began to repent having refused to take in a regular pilot; for he dreaded the displeasure of the owners of the vessel. We advised him to keep his own counsel, and say nothing of the matter, and as "Jerry" assured him the tide was low, we should soon be able' to see the extent of the damage done. "Jerry" was right, for in less than an hour the ship was high and dry, and upon inspection it was found that her bottom was uninjured, with, the exception of the loss of a few feet of copper, which was torn away. This was soon remedied, and at the return of the tide the vessel righted, and we were once more steering for Quebec. Towards evening we anchored, and some of us went on shore; we shot a great number of ducks, and some beautiful widgeon, but, though the seals were swimming about us in hundreds, we did not kill one, though we wounded many.

The banks of the river, though flat, are very interesting, and are nearly covered with cottages as white as snow, and these are so close together that they present to the eye the appearance. of one continued village; and the neat little churches, with their tin-covered steeples, give to the scene a beautiful and, dazzling *coup d'œil*. Behind the cottages, :and the narrow strip of cultivated land in their front and rear, nothing is to be seen but a vast mass of forest, which seems to have no termination. The foliage of many of these trees was beautiful, and appeared to our eye, after so long a voyage, to be the most lovely sight we had ever beheld.

As we neared Quebec, the river became much more narrow, and, warned by our recent mishap, the lead was constantly in requisition; but we met with no adventure in the shape of striking on rocks or grounding; and "Jerry," by his intimate knowledge of the different localities, completely re-established himself in the good graces of all. Even old Taylor looked upon him with a more favourable eye, but I have reason to believe he made an awful deduction in poor "Jerry's" pilotage money in consequence of the damage done to the ship.

At length we came in sight of the beautiful island of Orleans, and had a distinct view of the Falls of Montmorenci, and the spot occupied by Montcalme's army, between the falls and the river St.

Lawrence, where Wolfe and his army were defeated in their attempt to effect a landing. All this was very interesting to us, and we were fortunate in passing near the Falls of Montmorenci at a time when the river of that name is: greatly flooded, as at other times the stream is but scantily supplied with water, and the appearance of the fall which was now splendid, by no means remarkable; for the breadth of the river at top, from each bank, is not sixty feet; but coming down, as it now did, with a rushing foam over a bed of broken rocks at the brink of the precipice, and descending in one uninterrupted and perpendicular fall of nearly three hundred feet, it presented a grand and beautiful spectacle, and it was a matter of much regret to us all that we could not obtain a nearer view of it We had now approached to within about seven miles of Quebec. The river here is about six miles wide, and we anchored for the night

At the first dawn of day on the 4th of October, after being on board ship for three months and four days, we weighed anchor, and soon came in sight of Quebec. To say that we were delighted, would be only saying what everyone can well believe, and we were not much disposed to find fault with the appearance of a place, which those who had before visited it, under less annoying trials than we had experienced, pronounced to be a good town.

To us it appeared beautiful, and the numbers of tin spires that out-topped the different churches, had the appearance, as the sun shone on them, of so many steeples formed of silver. The Canadians have a method of using tin for this purpose so that it never becomes rusty, and I wonder it is not adopted at home.

Our interest was excited as we passed each spot which the gallant Wolfe had rendered memorable in the pages of history. We had a near view of Point Levi, from whence Wolfe bombarded the town, as a mask to his daring and successful enterprise against the Heights of Abraham; we viewed that part of the river, immediately under the lower town, where our army, in the dead of the night, passed with muffled oars, and we surveyed the walls of the town under which the army performed this perilous exploit. Those walls bristled with cannon, at half range from the boats that carried the troops, were enough to deter any but the most audacious general, and the most courageous troops, from hazarding the attempt.

Higher up, but too distant for minute examination, we saw the wild and stupendous Heights of Abraham, where our soldiers clambered up, and where, with immense toil and labour, they dragged up the guns by means of ropes and pulleys fixed round the trees, with which the banks are covered from top to bottom; but we had not time to examine more, as our ship was now about to anchor in the bason, which is so capacious as to be capable of floating one hundred sail of the line.

Here we found several of the ships of our fleet which had been separated from us in the late gales, and amongst others, our companion, the *Atlas*. This transport, as I have said, carried half of our detachment, and as our ship, the *George*, was the one in which the stores of clothing for the entire were packed, it was necessary to see Major Bagwell, and hand over to him that portion which belonged to his detachment.

I, in my capacity of paymaster and quarter-master, went on board the *Atlas*, and here I learned that orders had been received by the major to supply his men from the stores in Quebec; and I thus found myself in possession of a large supply of trousers, shirts, and shoes, for which we had no occasion. This, however, did not cause me much uneasiness, as those articles were fifty per cent, dearer in Canada, than at home, and by giving them to the quarter-master of the first battalion, at a much less price than he could purchase them in the country, I found myself richer by several dollars, than I had calculated upon before I landed.

After the detachment had been duly reported to the officer in command at Quebec, and after having received two months' pay from the paymaster-general, we were ordered to be in readiness to be conveyed to the town of Three Rivers, distant about fifty miles from the capital. The regiment was at this time stationed at the town of Sorelle, fifty miles higher up than Three Rivers, but the barracks at the former were not sufficiently large to accommodate the entire regiment, and were undergoing alterations for this purpose. Meanwhile, our detachment was to occupy Three Rivers.

The period for our stay at Quebec was limited to four days, which gave us ample time to see the town, and the soldiers were allowed to land in small portions, and at intervals, so that each man could have an opportunity of walking on land, which, as may be supposed, was very desirable after so long a voyage. Nevertheless, long as the voyage was, we had but three men on the sick list upon our arrival, and not one man, woman, or child, died during the passage.

The city of Quebec, standing, as it does, on the left bank of the river St Lawrence, is so well known, that it is not necessary I should enter into any minute description of it, and besides this, it has been so often visited by calamitous fires since the period I write of, that it must be considerably changed in appearance. There are, however, some points which I shall briefly touch upon, which I hope will not be devoid of interest to the reader, and which, perhaps, he may not have before read or heard of.

The town is divided into two parts; the lower and the upper town: the latter stands high above the former, which is out-topped by Cape Diamond, which stands one thousand feet above the level of the river. This point, though by nature so formidable, is strongly fortified, and is called the citadel of Quebec. Between the Cape and the walls of the upper town, is the plain of Abraham, and as it was on this spot Wolfe conquered and died, we visited it in the first instance, it is a plain of small extent, covered with stunted grass; in the centre, and about one thousand yards from the walls of the city, are two rocks, on one of these the gallant Wolfe breathed his last.

I had determined to take away a piece of this rock, and having a blacksmith with me, provided with a sledge-hammer and a large chisel, we soon succeeded in knocking off two large pieces, one of which I gave to Mr. Rutherford, of my regiment, and the other I kept myself. I regret to say that, by some accident, I lost it, for it was a relic I prized highly.

I have said there are two rocks in the centre of this plain, but the one upon which Wolfe died is not to be mistaken, as independent of its being pointed out as the same, the great diminution in its size, from the numerous pieces that have been chiselled off it, marks it out as the rock. Having paid our companion and guide, the blacksmith, for his trouble, we dismissed him, and returning through the upper town to the lower, visited those places we thought most worthy of notice.

The house of the governor is a plain stone building, situated in an open square, not remarkable for either regularity or neatness.

We were told that it contained several good apartments, but as it was occupied by Sir George Prevost and his family, we did not ask to see the interior. It is by no means a place having pretensions to strength. In one of the adjoining gardens there is a parapet wall along the edge of the rock, with embrasures, in which about half a dozen guns are planted, but they are of small calibre, and seem as if they were more intended to garnish the wall than for any offensive or defensive purpose. In fine weather, one of the regimental bands of the garrison play every evening in the square, which is the fashionable public walk.

The market of Quebec is very well supplied with meat at a moderate price, but fish and vegetables were in the greatest abundance and variety, and remarkably cheap. All the fish we saw were unlike any in Europe, with the exception of sturgeon and mullet. The fish most prized, and deservedly so, are the masquinonje, the black and white bass, the *poison d'or*, and the white fish. They are all very fine, and of a most delicate flavour. Fruit is to be had in great abundance, as also butter and eggs, and I should suppose that when occupied with less troops than it was at the period of the war with America, Lower Canada must be a very cheap country.

There are several churches, and three or four nunneries in Quebec; the latter are well supported, and well filled with nuns, as they are not subject to much restriction; amongst them are to be found many Irish young ladies. I made acquaintance, while visiting the convent of St. Ursula, with a good old French priest; he was a protestant, and had contrived to get out of France during the reign of terror. He conducted us through the town, and showed us everything worth seeing. With him we visited the engineers' house, and there saw several models of fortifications, amongst them that of Quebec. The priest spoke English so imperfectly, that it was next to impossible to understand what he said in that language, but Owgan was a capital Frenchman, and acted as interpreter.

We also visited the armoury, which is kept in admirable order, and contains several thousand stand of arms. There is also a good barrack for artillery, said to be able to contain one thousand men. It would require a garrison of from six to seven thousand men to defend Quebec, if laid siege to; and it is generally occupied by four or five battalions. The supply of stores and ammunition is great, and the number of guns in battery are very considerable; so that, all things considered, Quebec may be called a fortress of high pretension.

Two, out of the four days we were to remain at Quebec had now passed over, and Owgan and I were ordered to precede the detachment, and proceed to Three Rivers, in order to take up the barracks, and have them in readiness when the troops arrived.

We were offered a free passage in Malcolm's steamboat, the first we had ever seen, but, curious as we were to sail in the boat, we had had so much of navigation already, that we preferred going post at our own expense, and our commandant, Captain O'Hara, allowed us to make our own choice.

Early next morning our *calash* was in attendance; it was an excellent one, with a good horse, and a smart, intelligent-looking driver. He deposited our portmanteau under the seat, and, in high spirits, we took our places, and bid *adieu* to Quebec; but a circumstance took place before we were through the town, that delayed us for half an hour. We were well repaid for the delay, and what occurred gave us ample amusement for the first stage of our journey.

In a former chapter I mentioned the difficulty we experienced, on leaving Cork harbour, in arranging the soldiers' wives that were to accompany us, as also those left behind. There was, however, one young woman who had fallen desperately in love with a fine handsome young sergeant of the name of Anthony, and so sudden was her passion, and so short their acquaintance with each other, that there was not time sufficient left to get them married before we sailed.

We left the girl, as we thought behind, and it was not until we were half way across the Atlantic that Anthony ventured to tell me what he had done. I kept his secret, and was thus hooked into a sort of confidential alliance from which I would willingly have been excused.

On landing at Quebec, the young woman was most anxious that the marriage ceremony should be performed, but not thinking that Anthony seemed quite as warm in the affair as he ought to be, she left him.

This counter-stroke, which was executed as soon as resolved, threw her intended into despair; for he was ignorant of the address of his runaway mistress. He was, however, soon relieved by receiving a letter from her, and with this letter in his hand,—for it was he who arrested our progress—Anthony stood before us. He begged of me to read the letter, and to advise him as to how he should act. The letter was as follows:—

> Dear Pat,—I write these few lines hopping it will find you in good health, as I am at present.
> Och! Pat, God may forgive you as I do, but if you brake all the promises you made me, don't you think God Almighty will shoot [1] you out of heaven.
> Yours, till death,
Sally Grimes.

The latter part of this epistle caused Owgan and myself so much amusement that we nearly fell out of the calash in a fit of laughter that strongly approximated a convulsion. But on Anthony it had a far different effect; for being but a young soldier, and never having seen service, he was anxious, like most young aspirants, to "smell powder," and though he would, I have no doubt, have faced a battery of cannon in this world, the idea of such a warfare being in *petto* for him in the next was too much for his nerves, and he asked me in a tremulous voice for advice.

I told him to marry the woman, without delay, and that I, as commanding the company to which he belonged, would authorise the marriage, and I promised to have the ceremony performed on the arrival of the detachment at Three Rivers; but at this instant the old *emigré* curate joined us, and upon my stating the case to him, he offered to marry the couple on the moment All that was now wanted was the presence of Miss Grimes, and as Anthony promised to bring her to us in a few minutes, we thought it better to delay our journey and have the affair ended.

In an incredibly short space of time Anthony and his Cleopatra made their appearance, and we proceeded to the church, which was quite close; and the priest immediately began to repeat the service from memory, in English, but anything like his attempt

---

1. "Sally," no doubt, meant to say that Anthony would be shut, and not shot out of heaven.

I never before witnessed. I refrained from laughing as long as I was able, but when he came to the words "those whom God hath joined together," and in place of them snuffled out, "those whom Cot hath shined together," it was impossible to avoid committing a breach of order, so I got out of the church as fast as possible, and left Owgan and the rest of the party to get through the ceremony the best way they could. The business was soon concluded. I gave the priest four dollars for his trouble; a better fee, I believe, than he was in the habit of receiving. I, as a matter of course, kissed the bride, received Anthony's salute and grateful acknowledgments; and Owgan and I once more stepped into our *calash*, not forgetting to give the driver a trifle for the delay we had occasioned him.

Chapter 35

Ragged Heroes

The line of travelling between Quebec and Three Rivers, and on to Montreal, is admirable, and quite surprised us; a regular number of post-houses are established at nearly equal distances upon it, where *calashes* or *carioles*, as the season requires it, are always to be found in readiness. Each post-master is expected to have four *calashes* and a like number of *carioles*, and I believe he is subject, by law, to a severe penalty, should he fail in having this number; but, in case of those being all engaged, the traveller can never be at a loss, as there are many more kept by other persons, and, in case of emergency, the post-master has the power to employ them, and they cannot be refused.

This is an excellent regulation, but its excellence is further to be felt by the traveller, because the delay in changing horses in the day is limited to one quarter of an hour, and, in the night, to double that time; and in default of this regulation being complied with, the post-master is liable also to a severe penalty, and he is bound to have you driven at a rate of not less than two leagues an hour. I do not recollect what the charge is, but it is something very small, and you are not obliged to give the driver any gratuity.

The distances between the post-houses vary, but they seldom exceed nine miles, and with a good horse, such as ours, the distance is generally performed within an hour and a quarter. The *calashes* are clumsily built, but are easy and comfortable, and very agreeable to travel in. The horses, though small, are powerfully strong, and have very good action; they are always in good condition, and, like those of Normandy, are easily fed.

We reached the first post-house, nine miles from Quebec, in

about an hour. Our handsome conduct to the driver in no small degree caused him to give us a proof of the goodness of his horse and his own excellence as a driver; this, at first, we supposed to be the only reason, but we afterwards learnt, by experience, the real cause. Both Owgan and myself praised the horse, which, to say the truth, was not more than he deserved, but the Canadians are so vain of themselves and their horses, that if you praise both or either you will be well repaid for your flattery,—no matter how gross. On our arrival at the post-house we were greeted by the post-master and his wife: who were summoned to the door by the sounds of the driver's whip, which he managed to crack in a very superior manner. The driver dismounted, advanced towards the hostess, uncovered, and kissed her cheek, which she presented to him. This ceremony over, we stepped into our new *calash*, and proceeded on our route; the same routine of politeness was observed by the drivers at each post-house, until we reached Three Rivers.

The road, generally speaking, runs near the banks of the St Laurence, and, as we proceeded, we passed through innumerable beautiful little towns and villages, in all of which the inhabitants were occupied in some way or other. I never saw a greater appearance of comfort and neatness, and the scenery along this noble river is, in some places, very imposing and grand.

The peasantry are a fine race of people, and the women, in both dress and appearance, bear a strong resemblance to those of old Castile. The pastures were abundantly stocked with black cattle and sheep, and the farm yards literally crammed with pigs' and poultry of the best description. Almost every cottage was provided with a large fishing net, and each family seemed to have a *calash* and *cariole*,—the former for summer, the latter for winter; and I do not think there can be found on the face of the globe a more comfortable race of peasantry than those of this part of Lower Canada. Their style of farming did not seem to be first rate, but there appeared to be the greatest abundance of every article of food, and they have a ready sale for any surplus, and an easy carriage by water, as flat boats, or *bateaux*, as they are called, are always at their command, and in these vessels they transport their cattle and corn to either the town or port they are intended for.

Towards evening, after a most delightful journey of about six hours, we arrived at the town of Three Rivers. The country near it is level and barren, and we were not prepossessed in favour of either country or town on our first view of both; but we never passed a more agreeable autumn than the one we spent amongst the kind and hospitable inhabitants of that town and neighbourhood.

The streets are narrow, and the houses, with a few exceptions, small and indifferent, and are chiefly built of wood. There are two very respectable hotels, one kept by Monsieur Beaupret, and which, being recommended to us by my old friend, the *curé*, at Quebec, we fixed upon in preference to the other. It proved to be a most excellent house, and, having ordered our dinner, Owgan and I called on the barrack-master, Mr. Wills. He received us with great politeness and good nature, and pressed us to dine with him at his hotel, which was not the one occupied by us. We declined his offer, and, finding that he was stationed at Sorelle, the head quarters of our regiment, and had come down to Three Rivers expressly for the purpose of arranging our barracks and giving them up to me, we requested that he would give us the pleasure of his company at dinner, which he did, and we passed a most agreeable evening.

Early next morning, Owgan and I took up the barracks from Mr. Wills; they were in remarkably good order, and fully ample for the accommodation of both men and officers. This did not occupy us long, and we were advised to visit the convent of St. Ursula, so remarkable for the curious bark-work, for the making of which the sisters of this convent are particularly distinguished.

The bark of the birch tree is what they use, and with it they make several beautiful fancy articles, such as pocket-books, work-baskets, counter trays for cards, dressing boxes, &c., which they embroider with elk hair died of the most brilliant colours. They also make models of Indian canoes, and various warlike implements used by the Indians. A variety of these articles were shewn to us, and we made some purchases, but the prices fixed on what we fancied, were exorbitantly high; however, we could not bargain with these ladies, who, no matter how religious they might be, and no doubt were, most certainly were resolved not to lose anything for either their polite civility or the articles they disposed of to us; and I had but a small portion to shew,—but they were very handsome,—for forty dollars, which I paid for about a dozen articles.

Having taken leave of our religious acquaintances, and had yet two clear days before the detachment were to leave Quebec, Owgan proposed that we should drive on to Montreal. A *calash* was soon ready, and in about four hours, we found ourselves in that city. The villages between the two places were of the same description as those we passed through on our route from Quebec, but we saw nothing that deserved particular notice.

The town of Montreal stands on an island about thirty miles in length, and ten or twelve in breadth; the soil of this island is luxuriant, and the country is very populous. The walls round the town are in a rapid state of decay, but the gates are still perfect. The walls have the appearance of being more intended as a defence against archery than cannon, and it cannot be considered as a place of any strength. The number of houses within the walls bear no comparison with those in the suburbs; but the streets in both are narrow. In the centre of a small square there is a neat pillar erected in honour of Nelson's victory at Trafalgar.

We met a number of officers we were acquainted with, some of them of our own corps; amongst them was Colonel Macgregor, who, with Dr. Young, of the 8th, Mr. Goldsmid, of the dragoons, and others, were busily engaged in rehearsing the play of the "Poor Gentleman." They had hired the theatre, and were determined to have a series of plays during the winter. We dined with our friends, and, after passing a most agreeable evening, set off the next morning on our return to Three Rivers.

On the opposite ride of the St. Laurence, and not far from La Chine, is a village entirely inhabited by a tribe of Indians called Cachenomaga, but, much as we wished to pay this village a visit, we had not time to do so; and we regretted this, as it is one of the largest Indian villages in Lower Canada: the number of inhabitants is, however, small, and does not exceed one hundred of both sexes.

We met many of these creatures in the streets of Montreal, and in the larger villages, on our return, and some of the females, or squaws, were not only well looking, but were really beautiful. The men, generally speaking, were squalid and filthy in the extreme, and their only occupation seemed to be begging spirits and food. We were, however, informed that those savages whom we now saw were but a poor specimen of the North American Indians, and that, when we proceeded farther up the country, we should see them nearer to what they were in their original state, in consequence of their having less intercourse with the Europeans, and not being corrupted by their vices.

We reached Three Rivers without any other adventure, and next day our detachment arrived in two transports. The quay is a good one, and the troops were disembarked with ease. The officers and men looked well, and their clothing, which was new, and had been laid aside during the voyage, presented so great a contrast to the tattered uniforms of those regiments of the Peninsular army that had sailed direct from the scene of their victories, that we were much complimented upon our appearance, and many of the inhabitants told us that when the regiments that came direct from the army of Lord Wellington, made their landing at Quebec, they were at first taken for so many convicts.

It was not difficult to give credit to this account, for it was only natural that a race of people who had never seen soldiers that had composed an army such as that which had fought in the Peninsula for such a number of years, were astonished to see men who had performed those wonderful prodigies of valour, which all the civilized world had read of, arrive on their shores in a state of apparent want of all those requisites which, to the eye of the general and ignorant observer, are essential to a soldier.

In those days, breeches and leggings, and a highly varnished cap and pouch, were the necessary essentials to form a soldier,—and with such materials were the soldiers of our colonies copiously garnished. It may, therefore, be easily conceived what a contrast the appearance of the heroes of the Peninsula presented to those "pipe clay" soldiers, and it cannot be wondered at that the inhabitants of Canada looked upon these men with an intensity of interest mingled with curiosity.

Their tattered uniforms, without anything having the slightest pretension to uniformity; their bronzed faces, huge whiskers, and their general bearing, were of that character that inspired feelings of awe more than admiration. Their old trowsers, some black, some green, and their caps, some perforated with three or four bullet holes, while others, with a portion of them shot away altogether, most unquestionably did not mark them out to the eye of the general and ignorant spectator as a body of men that had trampled under their tread the greatest warriors in the world. But, to the experienced eye, those men possessed all the qualities necessary to form a soldier; their iron frames, without an extra pound of flesh,—their muscular limbs, firm as the hough of a race horse, their arms and appointments all in order, ready for battle at a moment's notice; their knapsacks packed with a neatness that it was impossible to surpass and difficult to imitate, carried on their shoulders with as much ease as if it were a thing of no weight, pointed them out to be, in the fullest meaning of the word—soldiers!

It is a positive fact that on the disgraceful retreat from Platsburgh, when a forced march was made in the night, many of the Peninsular soldiers carried the packs and firelocks of the Canadian regiments, and it was even said that a soldier of the 88th, named Jack Richardson, carried on his shoulders, not only the appointments of a soldier of the 41st Regiment, but also the man himself!

We were not more than a day or so settled in our barracks, when we were visited by all the respectable inhabitants of the town and neighbourhood, and there were many of these; amongst the number were the families of Colonel Gugy, Mr. Coffin, Dr. Short, and Mr. Hart, Dr. Carter, and several others.

A number of dinners were given to us, all of the best description, for, generally speaking, the inhabitants were of independent means, and many, the Harts and Gugys for instance, were extremely rich. We, in our turn, had all the gentlemen to dine with us, and gave two very handsome balls to all our acquaintances. In this manner we passed a most delightful time at Three Rivers, and we left it with great regret.

About this time Fairfield came down from Sorelle, and had for his travelling companion Captain Pring, who commanded our ill-fated fleet on Lake Champlain, after the fall of Commodore Downey, We heard with indignation the shameful manner in which our fleet had been forced into action by Sir George Prevost, before it was in a fit state for fighting. Scarcely half a dozen of the crew knew their stations, much less their officers, and, so unfit were the ships for action, that several of them were without the requisite number of belaying pegs to fasten the halliards to; several of the guns had no blocks behind their carriages, and the first shot fired from Downey's ship was fatal to him.

He was standing behind the gun at the moment it was discharged; the gun recoiled, and its breach struck Downey in the chest and killed him on the spot. Thus fell the commodore, and the confusion became great, not only in his ship, but throughout the rest of the fleet. It would be impossible to describe the motley appearance of the different crews; some were able-bodied sailors, others merchantmen, more Canadians, and many were negroes. With such materials, it is manifest that the equipment of every ship should have been on the best possible scale, but the direct contrary was the case, and, as a matter of course, in about twenty minutes after the action commenced, every British ship had struck her colours.

The Americans, it is true, were roughly handled, so much so that their Commodore, Macdonough, remarked while taking the swords of our captured officers, "that he did so, for form's sake; but," he added, "in a few minutes, we shall have to return you the compliment, as our ships are too much disabled to get away, and your soldiers will carry the fore of Platsburgh, and leave to us the choice of surrendering or being sent to the bottom of the lake."

This was the truth, for Brisbane's brigade of "Peninsulars" were lookers-on at the combat on the water, and a burning thirst for revenge was not only felt, but an opportunity of satisfying it was loudly called for by the soldiers. Before the contest on the lake, the gallant Sir Thomas Brisbane thus addressed Sir George Prevost:—

"Sir George Prevost,—If you will allow me, I will attack and carry the fort of Platsburgh with my brigade, and I will engage to do so in less than twenty minutes from this time!"

But Sir George was deaf to the proposal; the troops were ordered to retire, the stores were burnt, and our fleet as also the fleet of the enemy were left, the latter unmolested and the former captives.

Meanwhile the gallant Captain Robert Nickle, of the 88th, accompanied by his three lieutenants, Hacket, Hill, and Delme, and the light companies of the brigade, forced the passage of the Saranac, although opposed by upwards of two thousand Americans; the river was rapid, the water high, and the soldiers, with their cartridge-boxes under their arms, crossed under a heavy but ill-directed fire. A panic seized the Americans, and they fled in disorder before one hundred and fifty undaunted British soldiers. The troops in the fort caught the contagion, and, either exchanging their uniforms for other clothes, or running away in their shirts, many made their escape. This was the moment to strike; but not a blow was struck, and the advance troops were ordered to recross the river, and join in the retreat of the main body!

Chapter 36

Sentimental Reflections

At length we left our kind friends at Three Rivers, and it would be difficult to say whether they or we regretted it most. We were there for two months, and during that period a constant interchange of hospitality took place. The Gugys, the Harts, the Carters, the Shorts,—in short, all were on the most friendly terms. Malcolm's splendid steamboat took us up the St. Laurence to Sorelle, where I once more saw my old friends the officers, and many of the gallant old soldiers, beside whom I had fought on many a hard contested field.

To those who have never been in the army, or at least served a few campaigns, it would but be a waste of time, pens, ink, and paper, to describe feelings such as those I experienced when meeting, once more, my old companions: but it was a heart-stirring time, nevertheless. To meet again the humble soldier who had shared his last biscuit with you, when both he and you were nearly famished; to meet the men beside whom you had fought, and who covered you on the cold earth where you lay unsheltered, without even a blanket; he who gave his watch-coat to you, placed his knapsack under your head as your pillow,—a hard one, no doubt, but the best he could give you. I say, to meet these men once more was a pleasure.

But many old faces were no longer to be seen. The front rank of my company was occupied by new faces; and I asked my sergeant "Where is Darcy, where is Brophy, where is Cooney?"

"Oh, sir, they're all dead! Darcy had his head shot off at Vitoria; Brophy was killed at Orthes; and Cooney—poor Cooney!—had both his legs shot from under him at Thoulouse." Then I turned to the mess-table, and missed Nickle, ill from wounds; Macdurmott killed at Orthes; and Moriarty, who was buried in the same grave with him. When, I say, one personally experiences all this, it is not surprising if the emotions which these scenes call forth are never forgotten. Promotion, they say, is the life of the army, but it is to be gained chiefly by the death of your old friends. However, I think, and so, no doubt, does the reader, that we have had enough of the sentimental; we must now turn to something gay.

Our detachment brought up from Three Rivers fifteen officers, most of them young hands, and upwards of three hundred men. Colonel Macpherson, one of the best of men, was in command during the absence of Colonel Alexander Wallace, who was idolized by the soldiers, and regarded and esteemed, and justly so, by the officers. Macpherson and Wallace were both Scotchmen, but they differed from many of their countrymen in one essential point. Neither cared a farthing about money, but they both had plenty; and Macpherson, who was fond of gaiety, said we ought to give a ball to the inhabitants of Sorelle, who had been as attentive to the regiment as our friends at Three Rivers were to the detachment that just now joined the head-quarters of the corps.

A ball was therefore decided upon, and we of the detachment resolved not only to ask our friends at Three Rivers, but to go down the St. Laurence in our sleighs, for by this time the winter had set in, and take them back with us.

Sorelle was distant forty-five miles from Three Rivers, so that it is tolerably manifest that to go there and return, and go back again and get back to Sorelle, would embrace a distance of one hundred and eighty miles! but so it was. O'Hara, Morgan, Owgan, Hickson, and myself, set off in our sleighs, and rattled over the forty-five miles of ice at an "ice" (nice) pace in less than four hours! We were expected at Gugy's, and we all dined there. Colonel Gugy, a man of large property, was from home, being in command of a regiment of militia on the frontier, but his good wife made amends for his absence. Never did woman better discharge the duties of her table, which was kept in the best style; and her two daughters, and her two sons, who were with her at the time, were as good as the mother; and should they ever read these pages, they will, I have no doubt, say I am not paying them a mere compliment

In the evening, almost all our old friends came in, and we danced before supper and after supper, and it was six o'clock in the morning before we separated. The next day we promised to dine with Doctor Carter, and the following day was fixed for our return to Sorelle, as our ball was to take place on that night. Carter's party was like all the rest; the greatest hospitality and the best cheer, and we broke up as usual at an early hour in the morning.

We breakfasted with Mrs. Gugy, and I, who acted as the man of business, paid our bill at Ashard's hotel, saw the sleighs all right, the horses fed, the buffalo and bear skins regularly deposited in their respective places, and having done so, joined our breakfast party, announcing that "all was right," and that we might take the road, or rather the river, in ten minutes.

"Yes, but you must take some breakfast first," said Mrs. Gugy. It did not require any great power of oratory to induce me to acquiesce in the proposal, and having masticated tolerably fairly, we all began to bestir ourselves.

Our sleighs, four in number, were arranged as follows:—In the one belonging to Hickson was to be placed Miss Maria Gugy; Morgan took the two Miss Shorts; I had the charge of Miss Gugy, and O'Hara took Mrs. Gugy. Her two sons travelled in their own sleigh, and brought up the rear.

Mrs. Gugy was a good woman, and a good housekeeper also. I observed her placing two large bottles in the side pocket of the sleigh she was about to occupy, and I asked her what she was doing!

"Doing! is it?"—(she was an Irishwoman!)—"I'm doing what you'll say is only right and proper; I'm putting in a bottle of Martinique *noyeau*, and a bottle of cherry brandy." Her precaution was not a bad one, as will be seen hereafter.

Now, though Mrs. Gugy was extremely provident as regarded her *noyeau* and cherry bounce, she completely overlooked the disparity of O'Hara's weight as compared with hers. He was a slight young man, not weighing more than eleven stone, while she, on the contrary, was over twenty-two stone. Besides this, the road we had to travel before we reached the St Laurence, was very uneven, and being a great thoroughfare, there were several nobs or ruts,— the Canadians call them *cahoos*—which caused a great delay, and rendered precaution necessary; but what precaution could balance eleven stone against two and twenty?

Before we had advanced a mile, O'Hara's sleigh was upset seven times, but no mischief was done, for the snow was very high and Mrs. Gugy was very fat. We had not more than a mile or so to go on the high road, and the river once gained we had fine smooth ice to go upon, but before reaching the river an awkward and narrow bridge was to be passed; and long before we reached it I warned O'Hara of the danger he would have to contend with; but he, become callous, perhaps from his numerous upsets, laughed at the idea; and Mrs. Gugy, holding up her *noyeau* bottle in one hand, and a large wine-glass in the other, motioned me to come to her. I required little persuasion from her, for the day was bitter—the mercury thirty-two degrees below the freezing point—and not only I, but all the rest of the party, ladies and all, took such a pull at the *noyeau*, that it was palpable her precaution in having the reserve brandy bottle was one of prudence.

We all resumed our respective stations, and it was evident the *noyeau* had effected what was intended, namely, putting us all in excellent spirits! In a short time we neared the bridge; but though O'Hara looked confident I had my misgiving. He and Mrs. Gugy occupied the sleigh in my rear, and as I, with much difficulty, passed across a huge hole, nearly as large as a gravel-pit, I turned round and advised O'Hara to prevail on his companion to walk across the bridge, but neither would heed me. Mrs. Gugy laughed, O'Hara gave his horse a lash of the whip, and he essayed to pass the bridge at a gallop.

This was perfect insanity, but it seemed as if both courted the fate that befell them; for upon reaching the hole, beforementioned, the horse, a high-mettled one, took fright, and attempted to shy it O'Hara had recourse to the whip, but the horse was by this time quite unmanageable, and making a furious plunge upset the sledge on the top of the battlements of the bridge, and Mrs. Gugy was precipitated into the bed of the river, a distance of about fifteen feet By a miracle neither the horse nor the sleigh nor O' Hara followed her, or she would have been crushed to death.

O' Hara, for what reason he himself could never tell, held fast hold of the reins, but the shock was so great that the horse was thrown on his haunches, and had not the reins fortunately broken, the animal would have fallen upon O'Hara, and killed him on the spot. All this took place in the view of every individual that composed the party, and one and all jumped out of their sleighs and ran to that part of the bridge over which Mrs. Gugy had been capsized. We all called out in a breath, "Are you hurt, Mrs. Gugy?"

"Not in the least," was the reply, "this place is like a feather-bed, it's so soft."

And it was fortunate it was so, for there were eight or ten feet of snow in the bed of the river. We all congratulated her on her escape, and she had reason to be very thankful; for had there not been a sufficiency of snow to break the fall of so enormous a woman, she must have been killed instantly; and had she fallen on her face instead of her back, to a moral certainty she would have been suffocated before aid could be given her. But there she lay uninjured, her face beaming with good-nature, and, as contrasted with the snow, looking like the rising sun.

So far all was well, but to get her out of the river was a task not so easily done as to get her into it. We had no snowshoes, and it was impossible to approach where she lay without them. It occurred to Hickson, who was an intelligent lad, that a couple of our military sashes, if thrown to her, might be tied round her waist, and then by adding the traces of our sleighs to each other, she could easily hook on one end of them to the sashes, and we could thus pull her out. The thing succeeded beyond our most sanguine expectations, and at the end of an hour we had her, uninjured, on the high road.

The first question she asked, after thanking us, was, "If the cherry-brandy was safe?" O'Hara said it was; and it is needless to say we all contributed to make it something less than it was.

On reaching Sorelle, which we did at four o'clock in the evening, we lodged our fair companions in their respective houses, which our friends in the town had prepared for their reception; when, after having rested themselves, and dressed for the evening, we conducted them to our mess-room, where a very handsome dinner was ready.

It is astonishing what great fatigue the ladies of Canada can support without seeming to feel it In the present instance, our friends did not show the slightest symptoms of having travelled over a mile of ice, much less the distance of forty-five miles, which we had performed.

After dinner the ladies were ushered into a temporary drawing-room, and the mess-room was made ready for the reception of our friends, who shortly afterwards began to arrive. Dancing soon commenced; about twelve o'clock at night supper was announced, and after it the dance was kept up to a late hour in the morning.

Next day we took charge of our friends from Three Rivers, arrived there without any mishap, and dined at Doctor Carter's, where a large party were assembled to meet us. As we passed the bridge, which was well nigh fatal to O'Hara and Mrs. Gugy, she requested us to halt, which we did, and the entire party quitted their *carrioles* and took a survey of the spot into which our fat friend had fallen; and in order to commemorate the event, a bottle of *noyeau* was uncorked, and soon shared the fate of the former one, on the same spot, the preceding day.

We passed two days at Three Rivers, and on the third returned to Sorelle, where we learnt that we were to march to St. John's the day but one following. This was a sad change for us, as we had very good society at Sorelle, while at St. John's there was not one solitary family we could visit It was also a severe blow to some old mothers, who had counted sure upon getting their daughters off their hands. Two of our officers were unfortunately hooked into marrying; several others were partly engaged; but an old lady, who thought she had two regularly "booked" for her two daughters, in the chagrin of the moment said to a friend—"Well, the 88th are about to leave us, and I must say the officers are a very fine, and a very promising set of young men!"

Chapter 37

The Connaught Rangers Set Sail for Europe

Having taken an affectionate leave of our friends at Sorelle, we commenced our march to St. John's. The weather, though piercingly cold, was fine, and we reached our new quarters without any particular adventure, save the loss of a portion of the noses of two of the soldiers, which were frost-bitten. I, myself, bad a narrow escape, but by the timely application of snow well rubbed into the skin, I preserved this essential feature, not, however, without sustaining some injury in the shape of a small bump, which remains to this day. The country about St. John's is uninteresting, and bare of trees; the town itself is poor, and the remnant of its fortifications nearly crumbling into decay.

Our old general of brigade. Sir Thomas Brisbane, had established his head-quarters here, and he gave the officers of our corps a handsome dinner. We broke up about ten o'clock, and as there was no barracks for the officers, we took different routes to our quarters, which were widely apart from each other. O'Hara, and three or four more, were proceeding quietly towards their billets, when they observed the house of Beaupret, an hotel-keeper, to be more than usually lighted: besides this, the sound of two or three fiddles were heard, and the passing figures of several ladies and gentlemen told plainly that a ball was going on.

"What glorious fun," said young Morgan to O'Hara, "we'll make one of the party, and keep it up till morning."

Though O'Hara did not exactly relish the proposal, he was unwilling to interpose his authority, and he reluctantly acquiesced.

Hickson and Hilliard also avowed their determination to join in the sport, and the die being thus cast, the doors of the hotel, which were open, were soon entered, the stairs mounted, and in a much less space of time than I could tell the story, much less write it, the entire batch were in the centre of the ball-room.

It may be necessary to state that this same ball was one given by some Yankees who had come down to St. John's on a speculation of furnishing our soldiers with provisions. The thing was regularly got up, and two stewards were appointed to make the necessary arrangements, and to invite those persons whom they desired to have present. Their astonishment was, therefore, great when they saw half a dozen British officers enter the room uninvited. "A capital room this," said Morgan, turning to Fairfield, "I'll dance with that dark-eyed girl sitting in the corner; she looks like a Jewess."

"I hope," replied Tim, "she may take a fancy to you, and prove to be as rich as one."

The observation was scarcely made, when a tall, raw-boned Yankee, about six feet five inches in height, stalked up to the group of officers, and asked, in language not the most polite, even for a Yankee, what in h——l's d————n brought them there?

Fairfield replied, that they had only arrived at St John's that day; that they had dined with Sir Thomas Brisbane, and that on returning to their quarters, seeing lights in the hotel, and hearing music, they thought there was a public ball, and said they wished to join it.

"Well, now, you see, Mr. Britainer, that you're d————y mistaken. This is no public ball, and there are but a few of us come here to 'tea it,' as we Yankees say, so the sooner you make yourselves scarce the better, or we'll take the liberty of kicking you down the stairs." The last syllable was scarcely uttered when Morgan knocked the Yankee down.

A general row now took place, and every man was engaged; but the contest was an unequal one, for the Yankees were in the ratio of five to one. The men shouted, the ladies screamed, and the ball-room was a scene of great confusion. Morgan, a powerful young fellow, in the excitement of the moment, ran to the stove, and pulling down the tube, flung it at the heads of half a dozen Yankees by whom he was assailed; but this evolution was not executed without very disagreeable results. The force of Morgan's tug was so great, that the stove lost its centre of gravity, and it tumbled about the room, discharging its contents, and, in fine, setting fire to the apartment, and burning Morgan's hands most frightfully.

If the confusion at first was great, the reader may well conceive to what a pitch it had arrived at this period. The room was one mass of flame; all the ladies, and several of the men, attempted to hurry out towards the street, but the passages were blocked up and all egress was denied them; for Morgan, Hickson, Hilliard, and Fairfield, were combating fiercely on the lobby. Several of the townspeople came rushing up the stairs, some from curiosity, others to assist in extinguishing the flames, but the moment they made their appearance they were knocked down.

The affair now assumed a very serious appearance, and even the most turbulent and refractory became cool. The ladies, one-half of them fainting, while the others were screaming, and endeavouring to get down stairs, in which attempt they lost the greater part of their dresses. At this moment a sergeant's guard arrived, and forcing their way up the stairs, rushed into the room, extinguished the flames, and righted the stove; but, unfortunately, one lady had her arm broken, and old Madame Zacherry, the widow of a Jew banker, had one of her eyes put out by unluckily falling on one of the soldier's bayonets. Fairfield, who never could, or ever did, let an opportunity pass for his joke, said, "she was worth a Jew's eye yet."

The surgeon of the regiment, Mr. Johnson, was immediately sent for, and he endeavoured to replace the old lady's eye, which was hanging down on her cheek, but the attempt was futile, for Johnson, though a very clever man, and a pupil of Sir Astley Cooper, was inadequate to the task, and the pupil of old Madame Zacherry's eye underwent the operation of the pupil of Sir A. Cooper, and be cut it clean out of the socket!

It may be supposed that so serious an affair was not unattended with a proportionate loss. A formal complaint, drawn up in a voluminous shape by a Canadian lawyer, was sent to Sir Thomas Brisbane. A court of enquiry was ordered to sit and investigate the matter. The court did sit, and the pros and cons as to who was right or who was wrong, were sturdily argued on both sides. It was manifest that the first insult was offered by the Americans, and little attention was paid to their complaint, but Madame Zacherry's eye was a stumbling block, not as easily got over as it was got out, and this was the greatest "eye-sore" in the business.

Upon enquiry it was found that she was poor, for though her late husband had been once a banker, he died a bankrupt, and it was whispered that a little money would hush the matter up, and prevent a court martial, which, end how it might, would be an unpleasant business. About two hundred pounds were made up by the officers, and here the matter ended;

Fairfield remarking that she would give her other eye for half the money—and the business was supposed to be concluded, but such was far from being the case; a new claimant, in the person of a Monsieur Duplos, an apothecary, made his appearance, and stated that his shop, which was immediately under the ballroom, had been nearly destroyed, and if his account was to be credited, he lost as many bottles of physic as would have drenched the stomachs of all the inhabitants of Lower Canada put together. The demand of this man amounted to about forty pounds; but the most curious and exorbitant item was one of fifty dollars for damage done to "Galen's head," which was placed over the door, and had been, as the doctor at least said, new gilt the week before, and looked—as he professionally remarked—"as fresh as a pill." However, the man was paid, and thus finally ended the affair.

The 76th Regiment, which had been for several years in Canada, arrived at St. John's at this time, on their route to England. An universal peace now reigned, not only all over Europe, but over the world also, and we had made up our minds for a long repose in America. We reflected with pride that the invincible army of the Peninsula had been mainly instrumental in effecting this.

We had written to our friends by the officers who were now about to return to their own country, and I had intended writing some pages descriptive of a winter in Canada, but the arrival of the packet from England, announcing the return of the Emperor Napoleon from Elba, and his triumphant and bloodless entry into his own capital, astounded m, and altered all our plans; for the same packet which contained this intelligence, brought the order for us to be transported to the scene where the destinies of the world were to be once more combated for.

All Europe was now in arms, and we rejoiced that we were to be again partakers in the great struggle. God knows why those feelings animated us; for nineteen-twentieths of us had not gained anything, except honour, and of that we had had enough to satisfy those most craving of it.

We had fought and gained nineteen great battles, and we had combated in countless lesser actions. We had received ample testimony that to the Peninsular army our own country was chiefly indebted, not only for the position she held amongst the other nations of Europe, but, perhaps, for her very existence. We knew all this,—for the world knew it, and had proclaimed it; our own statesmen proclaimed it, yet what recompense did we receiver. Absolutely nothing,—except the thanks of parliament fifteen different times. Some of the senior officers, or the favoured few who held staff appointments, or had interest through their connexions, got promotion, or, what to many was more prized, medals; but to the great bulk of that wonderful army all reward was denied!

With all these facts we were perfectly well versed, and it may be asked how it was that we rejoiced at being once more called upon to peril our lives for our country, and fight under the General who had so shamefully neglected our services, and left our breasts undecorated,—save by scars? Nevertheless, we did rejoice; and why? Because "War is the condition of this world. From man to the smallest insect, all are at strife, and the glory of arms, which cannot be obtained without the exercise of honour, fortitude, courage, obedience, modesty, and temperance, excites the brave man's patriotism." [1]

Independently of all this, our feelings of mortified pride and anger were stifled when we were, as I have said, once more called on to fight our country's battles; and on the 4th of June, 1815, we embarked at Three Rivers, and with a fair wind set sail for Europe.

---

1. Napier.

Conclusion

And now reader, I am about to take leave of you for the present at least. In these *Adventures*, I have told you many circumstances you never before heard of, and I hope I have not fatigued you, or trespassed too long on your patience. I have, without being, I trust, too tedious, told you of the wrongs my old corps has suffered. I have, without presuming to write a *History of the Peninsular War*, told you something of the services performed by the Peninsular army; and I am now about to draw your attention to the scandalous manner in which the never-to-be-forgotten services of that wonderful army have been treated by the government and by the Duke of Wellington; leaving the continuation of the *Adventures of the Connaught Rangers* dependent on the favour of which you may think the pages I have now presented to you deserving.

When the war in the Peninsula, and indeed in Europe, was finished in the spring of 1814; when not a hostile shot was heard; and when the Emperor Napoleon was made a captive and placed in the hands of the allies, it was expected there would be an end to any troubled or war-like movement in Europe for a considerable lapse of time; and so there would, had it not been for the bungling manner in which the captive Emperor had been disposed of. His escape from Elba, his return to Paris, and the battle of Waterloo, are events too notorious, and too often mentioned in the pages of history, to need remark or comment from me.

But it is necessary that I should contrast the rewards that were heaped on the Waterloo army, (and, since then, on other armies,) for a few days' campaign, and one battle, with the base neglect that has been shown to the army of the Peninsula, that combated for six years in Portugal, Spain, and the South of France,—an army that gained nineteen pitched battles, and never lost one!—an army that killed, wounded, or took prisoners about two hundred thousand of the most warlike troops in the world! and an army that left behind it, amongst the mountains and plains of the Peninsula, the bones of forty thousand of their once brave companions. This army delivered Portugal and Spain from French dominion, and was the main and principal cause of the success of the great European contest in the spring of 1814; which success not only saved Europe from degradation, but England from invasion,—perhaps conquest!

This (comparatively speaking) wonderful handful of men, amounting, according to the Duke of Wellington's own words, to but thirty thousand, kept, for five years, two hundred thousand of Napoleon's best soldiers at bay, and prevented them from joining in the great struggle then taking place in Germany and in France. One half of this number would have broken to fragments this coalition of emperors and kings, for they were, as the Duke of Wellington, with caustic humour, told Lord Bathurst, "such troops as the allied sovereigns had not yet dealt with!"

Well, the war terminated gloriously; but Wellington, with sixty thousand Anglo-Portuguese, effected more in the south, than did the allied sovereigns, with half a million of men, on the northeastern frontier; and against what description of soldiers did this band of heroes combat for those six years, during which period they gained nineteen battles, and never lost one, and for which victories they received the thanks of Parliament on fifteen different occasions? Four lines from the pen of the Duke of Wellington will best answer the question. "They," (this French army) says the Duke, "captured more than one strong place in Spain without any provision of bullets, save those fired at them by their enemies, having trusted to that chance when they formed the siege!"

"Before the British troops they fell, but how terrible was the struggle! How many defeats they recovered from—how many brave men they slew. What changes and interpositions of fortune occurred before they could be rolled back upon their own frontiers. And this is the glory of England, that her soldiers, and hers only, were capable of overthrowing them in equal battle."[1]

---

1. Napier.

Let us now take a glance at what the probable consequences to England might have been had not this handful of soldiers performed such services as I have stated, and I will give the Duke of Wellington's own words in a letter written to the Earl of Liverpool.

> From what I have seen of the objects of the French government, and the sacrifices they make to accomplish them, I have no doubt that if the British army were for any reason to withdraw from the Peninsula, and the French government were relieved from the pressure of military operations on the continent, they would incur all risks to land an army in his majesty's dominions.
>
> Then indeed would commence an expensive contest; then would his majesty's subjects discover what are the miseries of war, of which, by the blessing of God, they have hitherto had no knowledge; and the cultivation, the beauty, and prosperity of the country, and the virtue and happiness of its inhabitants would be destroyed, whatever might be the result of the military operations. God forbid that I should be a witness, much less an actor in the scene.

"By the blessing of God," and the indomitable courage and perseverance of the Peninsular army, which fought the battles of England in the Peninsula, this calamity was averted; and " the cultivation, the beauty, and prosperity of the country, and the virtue and happiness of its inhabitants," were all preserved and kept sacred by those very men who are now refused a medal by their country, for which they fought, bled, and saved from invasion,—perhaps, I repeat, from conquest! Had that wonderful and invincible army suffered even one single defeat, the Peninsular cause, and the European cause, would have been irrecoverably lost, and England would have been invaded. I will here quote the opinion of the Duke of Wellington in a letter addressed to Lord Bathurst, dated 21st December, 1813.

> With thirty thousand men (British) in the Peninsula, he had for five years held two hundred thousand of Napoleon's best soldiers in check, since it was ridiculous to suppose that the Spaniards and Portuguese could have resisted for a moment

if the British troops had been withdrawn. The French armies actually employed against him could not be less than one hundred thousand men; more, if he included garrisons. Was there any man weak enough to suppose one Third of the number first mentioned would be employed against the Spaniards and Portuguese if the British were withdrawn?
They would, if it were an object with Buonaparte to conquer the Peninsula, and he would in that case succeed; out he was more likely to give peace to the Peninsula, and turn against the allied sovereigns his two hundred thousand men,—of which 'one hundred thousand were such troops as their armies had not yet dealt with.' The war every day offered a crisis, the result of which might affect the world for ages. Napoleon, rising even above himself, hurtled against the armed myriads opposed to him with such a terrible energy, that, though ten times his number, they were rolled back on every side in confusion and dismay. But Wellington advanced without a check—victorious in every battle—although one half of the veterans opposed to him would have decided the campaign on the eastern frontier. [2]

Had matters turned out differently in the Peninsula, Napoleon must have been successful against the allies, and what then? Why the invasion of England, perhaps her conquest, not by the arms of France alone, but by a coalition of all the subdued potentates of Europe, who would have been allowed by Napoleon to hold their crowns on those terms of alliance,—and on those only!

Suppose, then, England so placed,—conquered!—Reader! start not; the thing was possible! Ay, more than possible! Austria, the most formidable military European power, who had fought as many campaigns against France, as any other European power had fought battles, was conquered; Russia, another powerful nation, was dictated to; and Prussia, at one time the greatest military power in Europe, was. all but sponged off the map. We have heard of the confederation of the Rhine, in the heart of Europe, and why not the confederation of the Thames, the Humber, and the Severn; the Shannon and the Tweed? I repeat that this was more than possible, and I maintain that it was rendered impossible by the

---
2. Napier

wonderful and almost incredible valour of the Peninsular army; yet that army and its imperishable deeds are left unrewarded, and the Duke of Wellington, far from advocating its just claims,—as he is in duty hound to do,—gives it the most inveterate and unnatural opposition.

Events in 1815, and events in 1844 and 1845, proved beyond a doubt that the Duke of Wellington thought no more of the services of his tried old companions,—his faithful followers in a hundred fights!—who had, by their valour and constancy, made him a duke, and gained for him all, or almost all, the fortune and rank he now possesses; for, in place of supporting the claim they then made, and now make, for a medal, he has opposed them—in a manner as weak as unnatural; and, in his attempt to quash the claim of his old veterans, he is not very felicitous on the score of memory.

When the Duke of Richmond brought forward the claims of the Peninsular army for a medal, in the House of Lords, on the 21st July, 1845, what was the reply of the Duke of Wellington? In the *Naval and Military Gazette*, of 26th of that month, we read the following:—

> "These" (the granting rewards, such as medals, &c.) "were the acts of the sovereign, and of his advisers; and upon those points I never had presumed to interfere in any manner,—except when called upon to give my opinion," &c., &c.

Now this is a very positive assertion, and would—if correct—be a sort of back-door escape for his Grace of Wellington, yet it would be but a back-door escape after all; but how are we to reconcile this positive and solemn assertion of the Duke with the following letter, as published in the Duke of Wellington's dispatches, compiled by the late Colonel Gurwood?

On the 28th of June, 1816—ten days only after the battle of Waterloo—the Duke of Wellington wrote to the late Duke of York to the following effect, and in the following words:—

> I would likewise beg leave to suggest to your royal highness the expediency of giving to the non-commissioned officers and soldiers engaged in the battle of Waterloo, a medal. I am convinced it would have the best effect in the army.

And again, on the 17th of September, he writes to Earl Bathurst, the Secretary of State for the War department:—

> I have long intended to write to you about the medal for Waterloo. I recommend that we should all have the same medal, hung to the same riband as that now used with the medals.[3]

Now, is there any disinterested man to be found who cannot, at a glance, discover the cause, the main-spring, of this wonderful solicitude—this maiden effort of the Duke of Wellington, to obtain a badge of honour for his army, nine-tenths of which he had never seen before that day, and who, as a matter of course, had never laid eyes on him?

Is it to be supposed that he who could, and did, quietly accept the immense riches, honours, and titles that were showered on him, and gained for him by the best blood of his Peninsular army, without once raising his voice in favour of a medal for his old and tried veterans,—his companions during six years' terrible war, and victorious in every battle!

The men who had carried him, it may be truly said, on their very shoulders, and placed him in the exalted position he now occupies; is it, I say, to be supposed he felt, or could feel, any interest in an army that he had but just seen, and an army that had fought under his command for little more than as many hours as his Peninsular soldiers had fought for years, except for the gratification of his own personal vanity?

If not this,—but who can doubt it?—Why did he write to the Duke of York on the subject? Why! Because he had beaten the great man in person, and he was determined that "Wellington" and "Waterloo" should be banded about on the breasts of his hundred thousand soldiers, more than the half of whom had never seen a shot fired before that day; and many of whom were not only not in the battle, but knew nothing about it for a day afterwards; yet all these men—absentees included—got a medal!

I therefore ask what interest—except to gratify his own ambition—could he take in this Waterloo army, or any other army the world could produce, when he forgot the services, and trampled under his feet the application of an army that made him what he

---

3. Garwood's *Dispatches of the Duke of Wellington*, vol. 12, pp. 519, 636.

now is? [4]

But having written to the Duke of York, as his dispatches avow he did, why did he not say so in his reply to the Duke of Richmond? Does he not, in point of fact, deny in his speech that which we have, printed by his own authority, in his book of dispatches? and his assertion that since the battle of Waterloo "not a shot has been fired in Europe," is perfectly contemptible when adduced as a reason for granting a medal for that battle, and refusing one for the Peninsula. Why has there not been a shot (an hostile one we presume the Duke meant) fired in Europe since then? Because Napoleon was properly secured after Waterloo, and had he been so secured after Toulouse, Waterloo would never have been fought.

But how did the Duke of Wellington know (for I put the good and amiable Duke of York out of the question, as also the ministers,) that there would be no more fighting in Europe? He knew not, nor could he know, any such thing; but in a few months after his beating Napoleon (this was the hobby!) we find his Waterloo army with their medals dangling at their breasts.

We have now in this speech, and in this letter, taken from the Duke of Wellington's dispatches, sufficient to warrant the idea that he was resolved to raise a blush upon the cheek of his supporters; we have now under his own hand,—or at least in the book of dispatches published by his authority,—a complete disproval, a flat contradiction, of what he said in reply to the Duke of Richmond. What then am I to say, or what can any man say, of this speech of the Duke of Wellington? He cannot be right in both cases.

I mean the Duke of Wellington no disrespect by what I have just written; I only take him as I would any other individual man placed in the same circumstances. But the Duke of Wellington on this occasion was a volunteer; he consequently must be more rigorously dealt with than an ordinary witness, and I am not going to

---

4. "I have got an Infamous army, very weak and ill-equipped, and a very inexperienced staff."—"I really believe that, with the exception of my old Spanish infantry, I have got not only the worst troops, but the worst equipped army, with the worst staff, that ever were brought together."—"I am obliged to you for the reinforcements which you announce to us. The greatest object is to have old infantry. The others are better than foreign troops, but they are nothing in comparison with the Spanish infantry."—Gurwood's *Dispatches of the Duke of Wellington*, dated 8th May, and 25th and 28th June, 1815. Vol. 12., pp. 358, 509, 518.

overlook his services in that capacity, as he did the services of his volunteers in the Peninsula. He thrust himself forward when he was not required, or asked to do so, and it would have been much more decent had the Duke of Wellington remained silent, or, when he volunteered an answer to the Duke of Richmond, he should have spoken of his Peninsular army far, far, differently.

I before said, I mean the Duke of Wellington no disrespect, but I say again, if his speech in reply to the Duke of Richmond be correctly reported by the news papers, and if his letters of the 28th June and 17th September, as given in the twelfth volume of his dispatches, be also correctly given, and if the Duke of Wellington cannot give an unqualified contradiction to these two letters, then I say the Duke of Wellington has placed himself in rather an awkward predicament.

I have read with much attention the twelfth volume of those "Wellington Dispatches," particularly that portion of it subsequent to the battle of Waterloo; but cannot find any trace in the Duke of Wellington's letters of any letter from his Royal Highness the late Duke of York, written by his royal highness himself, or by his direction, to the Duke of Wellington on the subject of this Waterloo medal.

We must therefore conclude that no such letter was ever written, for if it was it would, we presume, be alluded to in the volume of dispatches which contains the letters of the Duke of Wellington quoted by me; and we must also come to the conclusion that this suggestion of the Duke of Wellington for the medal, emanated from himself, and that he made the suggestion to gratify his own personal vanity for having vanquished Napoleon in person.

However, all this may not have been so. The Duke of Wellington may have (though the odds are a million to one he has not) some private letter, written to him by His Royal Highness the late Duke of York, in which letter his royal highness, and not the Duke of Wellington, may have made the suggestion touching this medal for Waterloo. We will go so far as even to suppose that the Duke of York actually said in his letter, that is, if he ever wrote it, "My Lord Duke of Wellington, I think your army that fought at Waterloo deserve a medal for that battle, but I would not recommend its being granted by his majesty without first consulting you, and asking your opinion;—what do you think of it?" Mark, this is what I say the Duke of York might have written to his Grace of Wellington, and, supposing that he had done so, the Duke of Wellington could have given an answer that would have been the means of immortalising his name as much as any victory he ever gained,—for he might have said:—

> I feel highly flattered by your royal highness's condescension in asking my opinion on this matter; and, although I think the army of Waterloo well deserving of a medal for that battle, I take the liberty of giving my opinion against the grant of such a decoration.

This answer would, as a matter of course, have brought another letter from the Duke of York, or from his secretary, demanding the meaning of the Duke of Wellington's letter. This could have been easily replied to. The Duke of Wellington might have said:—

> My reason for not agreeing to this grant of a medal to my Waterloo army, is, that no medal has been given to my Peninsular army, which has seen one hundred times the service of the Waterloo army. That Peninsular army has made me what I am, and, on parting with it in 1814, I told it that although circumstances might alter the relations in which I stood towards it for some years, so much to my satisfaction, I assured it I would 'never cease to feel the warmest interest in its welfare and honour,' and that I would be 'at all times happy to be of any service to those to whose conduct, discipline, and gallantry, their country is so much indebted.'
> This promise I will keep to the utmost of my ability, and I cannot be a party to what your Royal Highness will forgive me for terming an insult to my. Peninsular army. I am happy your Royal Highness has given me this opportunity of expressing my opinion on the subject of granting medals, which I could not have done until I had received your Royal Highness's letter, as 'upon those points I never had presumed to interfere, in any manner,—except when called upon to give my opinion.'
> I hope and believe your Royal Highness will think as I do on this subject, and in order to illustrate more clearly the view I

take, I will suppose that, either from illness caused by wounds, or by the failure of health from hard and long service, or from absence on duty in another quarter of the world,—it had so happened that after all my toils and triumphs in the Peninsula, I had been unavoidably prevented from commanding the army at the battle of Waterloo; how should I have felt if I had seen the army that gained that one victory, commanded by a general who had not seen the tithe of the service I had, and that I had seen that general and that army honoured with all the homage and distinction that could be shewn them, while I, myself, and my faithful and well-tried soldiers were passed over unnoticed and undecorated,—as the bulk of the Peninsular army has been,—how, I ask your Royal Highness, should I, or could I, feel? Precisely—I take the liberty of answering—as the survivors of that army now feel; disgusted and stung to the heart's core.

Now, if the Duke of Wellington could shew that he wrote thus, or in substance thus, he would stand in a far different light, and in far different estimation, with his Peninsular army than he does at present; but if on the other hand no such correspondence ever took place, (of which, reader, you will observe I have spoken but hypothetically) will any man have the effrontery to stand forward and say that the Duke of Wellington has not, to make use of a common-place expression, "thrown his Peninsular army over?"

Are they not, as a body, regularly "used up?" And has not their leader in a hundred fights coldly kicked aside, as it were, the ladder which has been the means of raising him to the proud position he has so long occupied?

But when, instead of writing thus, we find him, before he beat Napoleon at Waterloo, telling the Duke of Kent, in a letter dated 13th April, 1815, that it was in the contemplation of his Royal Highness the Duke of York that the whole army which served in the Peninsula, and in the south of France, should wear a medal, and saying that "he had not heard what had prevented his Royal Highness from carrying that intention," the granting a medal to the Peninsular army, "into execution;" but that he would "enquire," (the survivors of that army have not, to this day, heard a valid reason for its being withheld,) and also saying that he had promised the Duke of Kent that he would "recommend that the Royals,"[5] the Duke of Kent's regiment, "shall have one," even, "if it was not intended that one should be given to the whole army."[6]

When, I say, we find him writing thus in April 1815, and then suggesting in June, 1815, after Waterloo, that the army that gained that battle should have a medal, while he then totally passed over the claims of his Peninsular array for a decoration, and since then has uniformly opposed such grant,—I ask can we come to any other conclusion than that the victory of Waterloo, and the beating Napoleon in person, absorbed all his thoughts, and left him neither leisure nor inclination to think of the services of his faithful and unconquered Peninsular army.

Having said so much, I assert, that there can remain but one other apology—still assuming the correspondence, which, for argument's sake, I have sketched, never to have existed—for this discrepancy of the Duke of Wellington as regards his letters, which I have quoted, and his speech in reply to the Duke of Richmond, and that is,— that it has been caused by a lamentable decay of memory.

The Duke, in his speech in opposition to his Peninsular army, goes on to say, "It is perfectly true that the late sovereign was pleased to confer upon the army that fought at the battle of Waterloo, and upon every individual soldier who was present on that occasion, an honour which had never before been conferred upon any body of troops."

It was quite unnecessary for the Duke of Wellington to have told the House of Lords this, for it was known to that body, and it was known to the army, a quarter of a century before; and it was likewise known that regiments not present in the action got a medal! But had the Duke told the House of Lords, and told the army, that he had suggested to the Duke of York the expediency of granting this medal to his Waterloo army, he would have told

---

5. The Royals, though a good regiment, and one greatly distinguished in the Peninsula, was not better or more distinguished than many others that composed that army, yet the Duke of Wellington promises his Royal Highness the Duke of Kent, that in default of this general medal being awarded to the Peninsular army, he—the Duke of Wellington—will recommend that the Royals shall have one; not, it is to be supposed, because the services of that regiment were greater than many others, but because the Duke of Kent asked this favour for his own regiment, with which request the Duke of Wellington promised to comply.
6. Gurwood's *Dispatches of the Duke of Wellington*, vol. 12., p. 307.

that which a great number of people had never heard before; and he might have added, with the most perfect safety, that if he had asked the same favour for his Peninsular army, it would have been as freely granted as his Waterloo suggestion,—and, his Peninsular army will add for him, that it would be granted even now but for the heartless opposition he gives it.

But the whole secret has been already told: Napoleon, the greatest general of this, or perhaps of any other age, was beaten in person; and it would seem that this all-absorbing thought haunted the Duke of Wellington so early as the night of the battle, for Captain Sherer tells us, in his history, that on the night of the battle, when at supper, "Wellington repeatedly leaned back in his chair, and rubbing his hands convulsively, exclaimed aloud—'thank God I have met him! thank God I have met him!'"

How different were Nelson's meek but fervid words after his great victory at Trafalgar! The dying hero's last words were—

"I thank God that I have done my duty!"

But the Duke of Wellington, according to Captain Sherer, was thinking much more of himself and his beaten adversary than of his country! However, he did not forget his army, for, as has been seen, in ten days after the battle he begged leave to "suggest" (in plain English, he asked the Duke of York to give the medal, and it was given) the expediency of giving this medal to his army.

To those who can smile—a Peninsular man cannot—at that part of the Duke of Wellington's speech when he talks of the Peninsular campaigns and draws a parallel between them and those of India and China, much amusement must be afforded them; but I look upon it as a melancholy proof of the facility with which a man can, by the help of mere sophistry, endeavour to overpower the strongest understanding. Such principles and arguments—if arguments they can be called—as those brought forward by His Grace of Wellington, though laughable in theory, are highly reprehensible in practice; and the extraordinary manner in which he attempts to draw a parallel between the services of the Peninsular army and those of India and China, will be best given in his own words. Speaking of the former, he says:—"It is perfectly true that this service in the Peninsula was not an expedition,—it was a war carried on for several years, for six consecutive campaigns, and some winter campaigns," &c.

"Not an expedition!" What presumption for any man to tell the British House of Lords this I no, we should say that the war in the Peninsula was not an "expedition," for we never heard of an "expedition "that cost the country one hundred millions sterling, or of an "expedition "that lost forty thousand British soldiers by the sword, and upwards of two hundred and forty thousand more by wounds and disease; or of an "expedition "that slew or took prisoners about two hundred thousand of the best troops the world could boast of, or of an "expedition" whose commander received a dukedom, and half a million of money for his services. It did not require the Duke of Wellington to tell the world that this terrible war in the peninsula was not an "expedition."

His own brother, the late Marquis Wellesley, in his place in the house of lords, immediately after the battle of Talavera, and nearly five years before the termination of the Peninsular war, said:—"The struggle in which Spain is now engaged is not merely a Spanish struggle; in that struggle are committed the best—the very vitals of England. With the fate of Spain the fate of England is now inseparably blended." And what a mighty struggle was carried on there!

> England expended more than one hundred millions sterling on her own operations; and with her supplies of clothing, arms, and ammunition, maintained the armies of Spain and Portugal, even to the guerrillas. From thirty up to seventy thousand British troops were employed by her constantly, and while her naval squadrons continually harassed the French with descents on her coasts, her land forces fought and won nineteen pitched battles and innumerable combats; they made or sustained ten sieges, took four great fortresses, twice expelled the French from Portugal, preserved Alicant, Carthagena, Cadiz, Lisbon; they killed, wounded, and took prisoners about two hundred thousand enemies; and the bones of forty thousand British soldiers lie scattered on the plains and mountains of the Peninsula. [7]

Now if the Duke of Wellington can make such an *exposé* as this

---

7. Napier.

in behalf of the armies of India and China, (both of which armies have got a medal,) he will do more than any man in the universe can do. But even supposing he did make this *exposé* on the part of those armies, he would be only putting them on a par with the Peninsular army, that he denies a medal to! and all which that army asks for, is to be put on a par with those armies who have received medals. If, on the other hand, the services of the armies of India and China are considered to be of so much more importance than those of the Peninsular army, and that those two armies are awarded a medal while the Peninsula army is denied one, how is it that Napier, Gough, and Hardinge do not receive from their country—as the Duke of Wellington did—half a million of money each, and a ducal coronet?

Because the British nation, and the entire universe, know that the services of the Duke of Wellington and his Peninsular army were immeasurably greater than those of the armies of India and China put together, and also of all the armies that ever left the British shores for the last half century prior to the commencement of the war in the Peninsula. Had it not been for this army of heroes who fought the battles not only of their country, which they preserved from invasion, but were the means of preserving this same India from attack, would we have it now? Many people say not; and those who have read the history of the French revolution, and the history of Europe since that period, may remember that India was a portion of the globe and of our possessions that was, and is, much coveted by France and Russia; but it would be only a waste of words and time to argue a point that cannot be contradicted.

The Peninsular army saved England, and preserved for her all that she now possesses. Their services are now unrewarded, and apparently forgotten, because they are no longer wanted. The Duke of Wellington has got all, or almost all, he now possesses by the valour of that army whose services he now presumes to make light of. His great genius, no doubt, did much,—who doubts it?—but he owes his Peninsular army too much, and he owes his country too much, to allow him to disregard the just claims of the former; and by his advice, and his hostility to their claim for a medal, he is in a great measure the cause of the latter disgracing itself; for I do maintain that any nation who can slight the claims of the men who fought for it as the Peninsular army did for Great Britain, disgraces itself. And if after what I have said,—all of it true,—I would ask. any man, I would ask any number of men—the entire universe, if that were possible—is not the remnant of this Peninsular army worthy of the medal they ask for?

The Duke of Wellington has been described as being a man whose character for greatness has been objected to, inasmuch as that "he was constitutionally cold and impassable, stern in the execution of his duty, careless in rewarding merit, the end his mighty object, the means a matter of indifference." [8] But cold as he is, or is described to be, there was a time when he held different opinions, or at least different language; but when he did so, the services of this Peninsula army were indispensable to him. At that time the Peninsula was not liberated, France was not invaded, and Lord Wellington was not a Duke!

Let us suppose that that portion of his Peninsular army which formed a part of the army of occupation in France had murmured when the Waterloo medal was granted, and when soldiers who had never seen a shot fired before that battle had their medals dangling at their breasts, while the heroes of a hundred fights had no mark—save their wounds—to distinguish them as the men who had tramped under their feet the best troops in the known world. Suppose, I say, that those men of the Peninsula had then put forward their claim, when their services could not be dispensed with, and when, as has been seen, the Duke of Wellington declared that the greatest object was to have with him his old Spanish infantry, what, reader, do you think would have been the result? The instant application of the Duke of Wellington to the Duke of York for a medal for his discontented Peninsular army; and why would the Duke of Wellington then have advocated their claims? Because he then required their services!

It may be asked why I presume to write so positively on a matter like this? To which I give the following letter, written by the Duke of Wellington to Mr. Villiers, on the 30th of May, 1809, on the subject of temporary rank in the Portuguese service. He makes

---

8. Maxwell's *Life of the Duke of Wellington*. It is but just and fair towards Mr. Maxwell to say that he contradicts this picture of the Duke of Wellington, though he gives it a place in his history.

use of the following most powerful argument, which is too convincing and too applicable to the subject on which I write, not to be quoted; and a departure from those views would require a very strong case for its justification. He says, in speaking of the dissatisfaction of his officers on this point:—

> It may be asked, why are they to require satisfaction? To which I only answer that men's minds are so constituted, that when they conceive they are injured, they are not satisfied until the injury is removed. Dissatisfaction on one subject begets it in others; and I should have (indeed I may say I have, for the first time,) the pain of commanding a dissatisfied army.

You see, reader, how keenly alive the Duke of Wellington was to the complaints of his army, when he required their services; and you see now how he tramples on their claims, when he no longer wants them!

This is, I at least think, too plain to require more from me. Others may differ from my view of the matter; but I cannot help that. I have said what the Duke of Wellington has done on the score of his opposition to the appeal made by the Duke of Richmond for this grant of a medal to the Peninsular army; and I will now take the liberty of saying what I think he might, and aught to have done.

When the motion was made for the grant of this medal, he might have said, and ought to have said:—

> My lords, that army fought and gained nineteen pitched battles, and countless combats; the loss of any one battle would have laid Europe and England prostrate! That army created my glory and my prosperity; and if its request for a medal is not granted, I will solicit permission from Her Majesty to present the survivors of it with one myself. To that army you are indebted for escaping the horrors of an invasion—for the prosperity and happiness of your country—perhaps for the very seats you now occupy!

Had the Duke of Wellington said this, it would have been more creditable to him, but he acted far differently; yet, if the officers who now survive of that wonderful and ill-treated Peninsular army, will even now stand forward and fight their own battle, with the twentieth part of the tithe of the zeal they fought the battles of their country, they must succeed. It would be much better to do this than content themselves, as they do, with silent contempt, which, they may take my word for it, has little effect upon the Duke of Wellington.

I have now done with the Waterloo medal, and the claim of the Peninsular army to one. India and China shall occupy but a short space; and when I have given my opinion on the medals granted to those armies, I shall conclude my observations.

Speaking of the India medal, the Duke of Wellington is reported to have thus addressed the House of Lords:—

> It is an historical fact, that a great disaster had occurred in that part of the world, and that for sixty years such a disaster had not occurred as happened a few years ago in the northeast of India. Such a disaster had never before occurred in the past, and for above sixty years it had not occurred at all.

And this is the reason given by his Grace of Wellington for granting this medal to the army of India, and for not granting one to the army of the Peninsula, that fought and gained more than one hundred battles and combats—without ever losing one! In reply to this speech of the Duke of Wellington, the Duke of Richmond observes—"He did not think it was very expedient to tell the army—only suffer a disaster, then rally and distinguish yourselves again, and you will receive decorations to revive your spirits!"—(Hear, hear.)

The Duke of Wellington may be a good reasoner, and as in so grave and learned an assembly as the house of lords this speech of his was listened to, we must suppose the majority of those lords actually thought as his Grace of Wellington spoke; and if so, that is to say, if they thought an army, a portion of which had been routed, worthy to receive a medal caused by such overthrow and defeat, most unquestionably, most undeniably, and most unequivocally, the Peninsular army had no possible claim whatever at the hands of those noble and learned lords, who listened to this speech of his Grace of Wellington.

Now, reader, what do you think of this proceeding? Did you ever, since the day you were born, hear the like before? Of course you never did. You may have heard of a regiment losing its facings for misconduct; you may have heard of a regiment being sent abroad, out of its turn, for bad conduct; or you may have heard of the officers of a corps being scattered about and sent to other regiments for ill-conduct; but, I believe, this is the first time you ever heard of an army receiving a medal—because a portion of it sustained a "disaster!"

Is it not astounding to bear a man, having the experience of the Duke of Wellington, a man of his years and standing, deliberately telling any number of men what he told the House of Lords about this medal? He who could do so, must not only possess more than an ordinary stock of assurance, but must have the most contemptible opinion (and justly so) of an auditory that did not only listen to him, but—the best of the joke—actually believed him, or were afraid to tell him they did not! One of them, the Marquis of Londonderry, had the hardihood to stand up and applaud the speech of the Duke of Wellington; to speak slightingly of the Peninsular officers; and to read the Duke of Richmond a lecture. This line of conduct from any officer who had served in the Peninsula was bad; but from the Marquis of Londonderry, it was—"too bad."

There was a time when the Duke of Wellington held a different opinion on matters of this sort; for, if my memory be not very defective, immediately after the shameful conduct of D'Urban's two Portuguese cavalry regiments at Majadahonda, in sight of Madrid, when Macdonald's guns were captured, and half of the German heavy dragoons massacred, some of them in their shirts, in consequence of the dastardly conduct of these two Portuguese regiments; then, in place of giving them a medal, "to revive their spirits!" these troopers were dismounted, and obliged to march on foot at the tails of their horses; thereby entailing on themselves the reward they merited. Had the Peninsular army earned rewards by being "dispirited," or by being beaten in detail, I opine that Sir Arthur Wellesley would not now be Duke of Wellington, or be living at Apsley House. But I by no means wish it to be understood that I presume to censure our unfortunate comrades in India; the best troops in the world may sustain a reverse from unavoidable circumstances; but I lay the stress I do upon it, to prove the inconsistency of the Duke of Wellington, and to show the weakness of his arguments against his Peninsular army, in his attempt to bolster up this India medal. After getting through a few crotchets and quavers, or, as the late Lord Byron would term it, "with a good deal of rigmarole," his Grace concludes this India affair by saying—"and that is the history of this medal." And a mighty pretty history it is! Before touching on the Chinese affair, let us hear what the *Naval and Military Gazette* says in its leading article of the 17th May, 1845. Speaking of a pamphlet, written and published by me that month, the editor remarks:—

> We are sorry Mr. Grattan has taken the trouble of bringing up the arguments used by the Secretary at War, in order to confute them; everyone knew the unfortunate position in which Sir H. Hardinge was placed at that time, and had forbearance on his own account; we had at that period alluded to," (the motion of Sir A. L. Hay in favour of a medal being granted to the Peninsular army), "written many pages in confutation of the sophistries he was obliged to put forth, but withheld them from a feeling of commiseration. Never was any honourable man placed in a more difficult or painful situation; and we consider the Governor-Generalship of India a poor and paltry recompense to that gallant soldier for what he went through on this very discreditable occasion. We now gladly seize the occasion of the publication of a pamphlet by Mr. Grattan,[9] to renew our remarks on this subject; and we most heartily recommend the perusal of this brochure, not only to every man in the profession, but to every honest and enlightened man in England.

After this extract it would be, I conceive, presumptuous in me to say one word in observation of the speech of Sir H. Hardinge, and I shall now turn to the Duke of Wellington's *exposé* as regards the Chinese medal.

"There was afterwards," says the Duke, "another instance with regard to such medals, with respect to which, I think, from what I shall state, it will be exceedingly clear that they were given on such distinct and exclusive grounds that they will form an exception to the general rule, and I think that I

---

9. *The Duke of Wellington and the Peninsular Medal.* By William Grattan, Esq. Churton.

shall, in a few words, show your lordships a full justification for the distinction that was made—I mean the medals given in the case of China."

His Grace of Wellington then goes on to enumerate, in the gross, the evolutions of our Chinese army and their redoubtable enemies. He talks of "extensive operations performed in that war." He talks of fortified towns, and of rivers, and of an "army! (God bless the mark, an "army" of Chinese!) manoeuvring as if they were troops with cannon in the field."

But his Grace tells us nothing of the renown of those Chinese generals, or those Chinese troops that our officers and soldiers were pitted against He tells us nothing of the losses inflicted upon our troops in this terrible and bloody war; but though his Grace is silent on these material points, this hiatus in his speech is made up for by several accounts we have read of those "extensive operations."

Major-General Burrel, writes in the following terms, giving an account of the capture by our troops of some island, with an awful long name—I think it was, for I have not the major-general's despatch by me, the island of Ning-poo-tchoo-foo-nim-pang. The general says in substance, for I cannot give it *verbatim*, that for six or eight hours his troops were assailed by a fire from some six score of cannon, directed by Chinese officers, and served by Chinese gunners; and that the only impression this fire made on the British troops he commanded, was the impression—that the Chinese knew nothing whatever of the use of gunpowder!

Had the merits of these Chinese troops and those of her Majesty Queen Victoria been tested by the knowledge of the use of gunpowder-tea, how immeasurably greater would the former rank, and what a scurvy figure would our soldiers have cut! But the part taken by the Duke of Wellington in this affair is so truly ridiculous, that I shall only quote a few lines from the *Naval and Military Gazette* on the subject. The editor of that journal says—

> The Duke has since given the Companionship of the Bath to certain captains of Sir Hugh Gough's army, after whitewashing them first with the brevet rank of major, for having shot down a parcel of old women clothed in quilted bedgowns in China. By what obliquity of judgment has a thing

so incongruous been brought about?[10]

I think, having thus disposed of the Duke of Wellington, his Waterloo medal, the India medal, and the Chinese medal, we may conclude with a parting glance at the speech of Lord John Russell, in reply to Sir De Lacy Evans. We will, by way of a parting thrust, take a look at what is going on about this bronze equestrian statue, now placed in front of Apsley House. On the 19th of last August, Sir De Lacy Evans brought the services of the Peninsular army before the notice of the House of Commons. This motion was negatived by Lord John Russell, the prime minister.

The bulk of his argument was that the lapse of time—this was the basis of the refusal—was an excuse for denying a medal to the Peninsular army—and, in short, it was the same as a man pleading the statute of limitation for the non-payment of a just debt Now, reader, what do you think of this answer from a liberal minister? of course you think very ill of it; but what will you say when you hear from me, that within the very same week that Lord John Russell pleaded the "lapse of time" as a reason for refusing a testimonial to the survivors of the Peninsular army, within the walls of the very same house of parliament, and in presence of the very same auditory, a lengthened discussion is carried on between Lord Morpeth and some other members of the house, as to the proper site for the bronze equestrian statue of the Duke of Wellington, lately cast, and now placed over the triumphal arch in London, I will ask Lord John Russell what this statue has been erected for?

Is it not in honour of the services of the Duke of Wellington, and the victories gained by his unconquerable army, thirty-two years ago? Most certainly it is. If, then, it is not too late to erect this testimonial in honour of the duke's services—rendered thirty-two years ago—as commander of the troops that gained those great victories, why is it too late to grant his army the small testimonial it asks for? This statue should either be not erected on the score of the "lapse of time," or we should hear no more of the cant with which we have been surfeited. It is high time that public opinion should put a stop to this farce, and to such proceedings; for while we are told one evening that "the time is gone by" when the claim of the Peninsular army could be listened to, we are edified on an-

---
10. *Naval and Military Gazette*, May 17; 1845.

other evening with a long dissertation between Lord Morpeth and someone else, as to the proper site whereon to place the equestrian statue of the Duke of Wellington, for the very same services, performed at the very same time, by him at the head of this very same Peninsular army, whose claim for a medal is now scoffed at.

I again say, that it is high time to put a stop to all this sham, all this cant, and all this ingratitude. As to complaint or reproach, they are the offspring of weakness; disdain should stifle them; but nothing can or ought to stifle the expression of disgust every honest mind must feel at such want of integrity; and it behoves every man who served in the Peninsula to stand forward, and join in one bold and noble effort to get what may be truly termed—his birthright.

The very rocks amongst which we fought would, had they the power of speech, speak for us; the plains upon which we fought, and upon which we slew and overthrew our terrible enemies, and upon which thousands of our comrades were slain, would, had they the power, advocate our claim; the very graves that contain the ashes of forty thousand once gallant souls—our companions left behind us—would in like manner, could they do so, raise their voices, and cry shame on the man who would not advocate our cause!

But as neither the rocks, nor the plains, nor the graves can speak, and therefore do not, it by no means follows that I, who am not only endowed with the power of speech, but the will to give it utterance, am to be silent; and it is to be hoped an historian will be found, possessing sufficient moral courage and honesty, to state the wrongs that have been inflicted upon an army which rendered services to its country that merited far different treatment.

Appendix

No. 1
THE BATTLE OF BUSACO AND THE THIRD DIVISION.[1]

Having compared the following statements by Sir Henry King and Major Mackie, respecting the two British brigades of the third division engaged in the battle of Busaco, with our own notes and recollections of that conflict, we are enabled, as far as our knowledge extends, to add our individual testimony to that of those competent witnesses.

The extreme difficulty of the historian's task has been frequently admitted and dwelt upon in our pages. The toils and perplexities of that invidious office are so evident, that the marvel is rather how any man can be found to undertake it and succeed, when the subjects are contemporaneous, than that failure or inaccuracy should be the result In the description of battles, the general picture must be compounded of detached sketches taken from the limited views of individuals at particular points; and these fractional parts being necessarily imbued with the tone and bias, and dependent on the opportunities, of the spectator, increase the concision of the artist by whom such ill-assorted elements must be combined into a harmonious whole. That he should often succeed, is, we repeat, more surprising than that he should occasionally fail or offend.

The subject discussed by our correspondents is the part taken by Picton's division in the battle of Busaco, as it is related by the historian of the Peninsular war, upon the faith of documents prefixed to his fifth volume. However it may be shown, by the narratives of our gallant friends above named, that these documents were erroneous

---
1. From the *United Service Journal*.

as far as regarded the Third Division, we are bound to do justice, from personal knowledge, to the anxiety of the historian to obtain accurate and impartial, information concerning the striking event he was then about to describe.

The impression of Colonel Waller, a most estimable and zealous officer, must have been unaccountably distorted when he flew to the rescue of the "Fighting Division" from their grim assailants on the ridge of Busaco! Alas, for his misplaced solicitude! The bear-skin caps and mailed chins of the Frenchmen had no terrors for Lightburne's brigade, or their neighbours, the Connaught Rangers and old 45th,—*nec aspera terrent*;—the former, as their immediate commander, Sir Henry King states, panted for closer quarters—the latter, feeling the collision, struck their foes like a thunderbolt, and while Colonel Waller was galloping for aid, the bear-skins were fleeing like worried sheep to the shelter of their own position and reserves. Since the day of Vimiera such a rout had not been seen—and never was confidence more high or better warranted in any band or body of the British army than amongst the very troops the worthy assistant- quartermaster- general thought doomed to destruction.

The intervention of our gallant associates of the Fifth Division unquestionably applied to a difierent body of the enemy, and to some minor attack or diversion at a later period of the day. The main assault, to which we have just alluded, commenced with the misty dawn, and no sooner was the enemy perceived on the ridge than he was attacked and broken to pieces. But the details of this section of a battle, from which the Third Division derives one of its most glorious and inalienable trophies, are discussed in the following narratives so clearly and concurrently with our own views, that additional comment on our part is unnecessary. Could further doubt exist on the point which forms the subject of this discussion, the despatch of our great leader alone decides the question:—

Mr. Editor,—My attention having been called to a memorandum of the late Colonel Waller, respecting the battle of Busaco, prefixed to the fifth volume of *Napier's History of the War in the Peninsula*, which contains some material errors, I feel myself compelled to give a statement of what took place under my own immediate view, as commanding the second battalion 5th Infantry, in the Third Division on that memorable day. Omitting any preliminary detail, I shall proceed at once to narrate occurrences as they were.

Lightburne's brigade, constituting the left; of the third division, was formed in line on the brow of Busaco before dawn; when daylight allowed, a very heavy column of the enemy was perceived commencing the ascent, and, apparently, directing its march on our front: a cloud of *tirailleurs* were thrown out on its flanks to cover its advance, and the light companies were ordered out to oppose them. At this moment Lord Wellington, attended by his staff and other officers, rode up, and asked where there was a good position for a gun. I pointed out a small rocky eminence in advance, and on the right of my battalion.

A gun was promptly brought up, and opened on the enemy, the Fifth Light Company was now, warmly engaged on the slope of the hill, and the battalion being much exposed, and sustaining some loss from a galling fire, I was directed by Lord Wellington, repeated by Sir Brent Spencer, to retire a few paces. This was done by stepping back, so as to clear the rising of the slope. Lord Wellington then proceeded to another part of the position, Lieutenant-Colonels Colin Campbell, A.D.C., and Charles Napier, being previously wounded in rear of the gun. The enemy's column suffering much from the fire, directed with great precision and effect by Captain Lane, R.A., and from our light infantry, changed its direction by an oblique movement to its left, advancing steadily to the large rocky ridge or projecting point on the summit of the heights, which it attained under a heavy flanking fire.

The *tirailleurs* were soon after repulsed and driven back, leaving many killed and wounded in our front, belonging to the 2nd Chasseurs Légers, a very distinguished corps in the French army. A desultory fire of musketry was kept up for some time, from which we suffered some loss. The change in the direction of the enemy's column brought it m contact with the left of the light brigade of the Third Division, upon and beyond the rocky ridge, above described, which interrupted my view of its further movements.

The enemy did not long retain his advantage. I could not observe whether he had extended his front by deployment on our right; but, apparently, he had no time to form his line so as to "sweep the ridge of the hill" in our front, if such was the intention; for in a very brief space of time he was hurled down the steep, by a most gallant attack from the regiments on our right, namely, the 88th and 45th, and retired with the utmost precipitation and confusion, leaving the glacis of the hill covered with dead and wounded, nor did he attempt to rally or slacken his pace till at the very base, which, from the formation of the ground, (a rather steep though gradual declivity,) was at a considerable distance from the summit

He then continued to retire in more order, but in manifest dismay, nor was any attempt made to renew the attack. The charge, which decided the defeat of the enemy at this part of the position, I always understood to have been made by the 45th and 88th Regiments, and this was, generally received and believed in the Third Division.

From the above plain narration, it will appear that Colonel Waller has erred in the first instance, by, stating that the action commenced by a fire of artillery upon the left of Picton's position; nor did the column of attack, which directed its march on our front, deploy into line previous to ascending the hill, but advanced to the summit in a solid mass. I saw but one of the three attacking columns; that alone demanded my attention. I have always supposed. that a third column of the enemy, (the second having attacked and been repulsed by the right of Picton's division on the Cantaro Pass, while endeavouring to. turn our flank and gain the great Coimbra road,) was, encountered by Leith's division of Hill's corps, and, totally defeated.

Colonel Waller has also erred in stating that "Lightburne's brigade was repeatedly charged, and fairly driven from the rocky part of the position." This never took place. The Second Battalion 5th Infantry was never charged by the enemy, and, consequently, never driven from its position; it remained on its original ground, in readiness, and, I may add, in earnest hope, that the enemy would afford an opportunity to charge, when we anticipated a very different result I have accounted for that opportunity not having been given, by the deviation of the enemy from his direct line of march. The utmost steadiness prevailed in our ranks, nor was there the slightest hesitation or wavering. The enemy was decidedly repulsed, the infantry most gallantly driving back the Chasseurs Légers in our front

I never saw Colonel Waller during the action; nor was any order communicated to me till its close, after the decisive charge had taken place, when the Fifth was ordered to the right, and was thrown back into column for that purpose; but its advance was rendered unnecessary by the total rout of the enemy and his precipitate retreat. Sir Thomas Picton was chiefly in the centre, and on the right of his division, where the brunt of the conflict took place.

I must here remark, that no one is more competent than yourself to appreciate the accuracy of the events I detail, having commanded the light company of the 5th in the engagement

I have written the above without reference to any document, public or private, having indeed none at hand. The lapse of twenty-six years might wear away the recollection of trivial events, but the stirring scenes of active warfare are engraven in more durable characters on the memory, and I relate what I saw, and what I believe to be incontrovertible fact

It is not within my province, nor is it my intention, to enter into a defence of Picton's faults as a man; his merits as a soldier I may venture to assert: his gallantry, skill, and conduct as a general of division were proved on every occasion in the field; and the gallant men led to victory by him, although grieved by his intemperate language and apparent prejudices, will, I doubt not, bear a just testimony to the former, while they deprecate the latter. He fell in his country's service; such a death consecrates his memory; let it obliterate his errors.

In conclusion, I must observe that the confidence placed in the combinations and arrangements of Lord Wellington, preparatory to battle, infused into his soldiers of all grades an enthusiastic devotion and anticipation of victory. No apprehensions of defeat or exposure to attack, in rear or on a flank, were ever felt or expressed: every exigency was known to be foreseen and provided for, and that in the event of repulse, succour was near. This feeling actuated the whole British army in the Peninsula, and was attended by those brilliant successes which distinguished the war, and have inspirited the pages of its historian. I remain, &c. &c.

Henry King, Maj-Gen. Elmdon Hall, Birm, Dec. 17th, 1836.

Mr. Editor,—In a work so extensive as that of Colonel Napier's

History of the Peninsular War, embracing so many and such complicated details, information as to which must be collected from so many different sources, perfect accuracy, as to every point, it would certainly be most unreasonable to expect. It is equally evident that any errors as to minuter points can in no way detract from the value of a work like his, so far as regards his statements relative to the operations of the war on a more extended scale, and the correctness of the conclusions he has drawn from these, the soundness of which must rest on different grounds.

To the public, therefore, at large, or to posterity, it is a matter of but trivial moment, whether in the work in question there are, or are not, errors as to the minutiae of the various actions; not so, however, as regards the corps engaged in the several operations referred to in the work, and more especially as they may affect the feelings of the surviving officers, and of the friends of those who are no more.

It is also evident that when errors as to any part of the details in works of this description are pointed out in the author's lifetime, and either corrected by him or the accuracy of his statements fully vindicated, it must go far in accrediting the work at large, and vouching for its correctness where it is not called in question.

For these reasons I am confident that I shall not have merely the forgiveness but the thanks of this gallant and able writer for pointing out to him some mistakes into which I think he has evidently been misled in detailing the operations in the battle of Busaco.

To the existence of these errors I had occasion to allude in my strictures upon Robinson's *Memoir of General Picton*, inserted in a former number of your *Journal*, and my attention has again been more particularly directed to the subject by the publication of the fifth volume of the work, containing some documentary evidence in the shape of letters from Major-General Sir John Cameron and Colonel Waller, corroborative, as Colonel Napier thinks, of the accuracy of his previous statements. How far they answer their intended purpose I shall leave yourself and readers to determine, on perusing the following comments on them, as they affect the leading features of the battle.

This division in the general arrangements were allotted for the defence of that portion of the ridge extending from the St Antonio road, about a mile to its left.

Having passed to the right of the Mondego at Pena Cova on the 21st September, they encamped neat the village of Conteças, on the Coimbra side of the mountain, till the 25th, when they took up a position on its summit, the right brigade of the division upon and close to the road of St Antonio de Cantaro. The advance being thrown forward to the neighbourhood of this village, were in the evening of that day driven back, when the ravine at the bottom of the ascent became the line of demarcation between the contending armies. During this interval, that is, between the 21st and 25th, a road of communication had been formed along the ridge, on the reverse or Coimbra side, near the summit, but so far below the very top of the ridge, or hog's back, that troops passing along this road could not possibly see what was going forward on the other side.

The evening of the 25th and following day were spent in some skirmishing, and a cannonnade of our guns upon the reconnoitring parties of the enemy, a portion of whose force, the second corps under Regnier, were concentrated upon the road leading from Mortagoa to the village of St Antonio de Cantaro, evidently evincing a disposition to force this point of our position; that portion of the ridge from the pass to the Mondego being of a more rugged and inaccessible character.

Perceiving this obvious intention of the enemy, Sir Thomas Picton had, on the evening of the 26th, so disposed his force (the British portion not exceeding fifteen hundred bayonets,) as to meet the attack anxiously expected the following morning. Nor were we disappointed: as the dawn of day discovered the enemy in motion, a column having, during the obscurity of the night, moved along the bottom to attack, considerably to our left, and nearly opposite to the point where the ridge rises abruptly, or as I have in my previous remarks designated it, the convent-hill, the enemy at the same time making an attack upon the road, and with considerable bodies at intermediate points, with an evident intention of distracting our attention.

To meet the first, the 88th Regiment, which stood upon the left of Picton's force, was instantly moved by Colonel Wallace, and to their support four companies of the 45th, under Major Gwynne, with a portion of the 8th Portuguese following in their track.

Having premised thus much, I shall now proceed to state the several mistakes into which Colonel Napier and his authorities have fallen, and whereby, however unintentionally on their part, very great injustice has been done to the third division as a whole, and more especially to that portion of it which, at the time, I had myself the honour to belong.

These errors I conceive Colonel Napier has himself summed up in his answer to the observations of Picton's biographer, when he says:

> It is now affirmed distinctly and positively that the French did break the 8th Portuguese Regiment, did gain the rocks on the summit of the Sierra, and on the right of the Third Division, did ensconce themselves in these rocks, and were going to sweep the summit of the Sierra, when the Fifth Division under General Leith, attacked them, and the 9th Regiment, led by Colonel Cameron, did form under fire, as described, did charge, and did beat the enemy out of these rocks, and if they had not done so, the third division, then engaged with other troops, would have been in a very critical situation. Not only is all this reaffirmed, but it shall be proved by the most irrefragable evidence.

Now, Mr. Editor, in answer to these several statements of Colonel Napier, thus distinctly and positively affirmed, I beg leave as distinctly and as positively to affirm, that the right of Picton's division never was forced back; that the enemy never did reach the summit of the ridge to the right of his division, and there ensconce themselves in rocks; and further, that the right of Picton's division never was in the slightest danger of being turned. In proof of these assertions, it need only be stated that the brigade of Portuguese artillery, and 74th British regiment, in position on the extreme right, not only never did retreat a single step, but the former never had occasion to move during the day, nor the latter till they advanced at the close of the action, as I shall afterwards have occasion to explain.

Having thus shown that it could not possibly be at this point of the position occupied by the third division that General Leith rendered to the former the essential service they are represented to have done, I shall now proceed to show that neither was it rendered at that point where the most formidable attack was made upon it. This is the more required, because Colonel Napier's description would leave his readers to imagine that it was where, and when, Picton's division was most seriously engaged, that the latter received that timely aid, which, saving them from defeat, left them forever after so beggared of gratitude to the fifth division.

This point, where Regnier's most serious attack was actually made, was not, as Colonel Napier asserts, between the third and fifth divisions, thus endangering, as he thinks, the turning of Picton's right, but on the extreme left, near the convent-hill, nearly a mile from his right. Instead of six guns playing upon them in their ascent, or of there being anything else to justify the account he gives of the astonishing power and resolution with which they scaled the mountain, overthrowing everything that opposed their progress, the truth is, that, having advanced at first under cover of a dense fog, they were totally unperceived until they had made considerable progress up the steep. A fire of some rounds was then opened on them from two guns, by direction of Lord Wellington. This, however, could not greatly retard their progress; so that continuing their course, still under cover of the fog, the first intimation that the troops on the height obtained of their approach was the head of the column just appearing within view.

Neither, as I again assert, did this column ever penetrate the line occupied by the Third Division, or establish themselves on the height. A portion of them, undoubtedly, were ensconced in rocks, but not upon the summit, while the whole of them had much to accomplish before they could have thought of sweeping the Sierra.

The head of the column having just reached the top when seen by Colonel Wallace, he immediately detached three companies who drove the body from the rocks, while he himself, with the remainder of the 88th, and the four companies of the 45th, under Major Gwynne, attacked and drove the main column down the steep, strewing the ground, as Colonel Napier has graphically described, with dead and dying, to the very bottom of the valley, not, however, as he would lead his readers to imagine, after a general *mêlée*, in which these regiments had only joined with others.

With the exception of a portion of the 8th Portuguese which joined in the pursuit, the repulsing this column, which made undoubtedly the principal attack on the third division, and was, in truth, the main feature of the day, was accomplished by the above, not only without any assistance from the fifth division, but even without the aid of any other portion of the third.

I feel the more desirous to note the aid thus afforded by the 8th Portuguese, from the unqualified manner in which that corps is, once again, represented by Colonel Napier to have been broken in pieces. Whatever may have been the case with the remainder of the regiment, I can positively assert that this was not the case with that portion of it stationed on the right of the 88th and 45th. These, so far from being broken to pieces, driven as chaff before the wind, did, on the contrary, maintain their ground, and join in the pursuit, as I have said above. I may mention that a regiment of Portuguese militia, stationed somewhere in the rear, at no great distance from these corps, were panic-struck, and fled almost to a man. They all, in fact, betook themselves to their heels, with the exception of their commanding-officer and another, who, after the action, applied to Colonel Wallace, and obtained from him a certificate to the effect that they had kept their post.

While the 88th and 45th were thus engaged in repulsing this attack, the enemy made a simultaneous attempt on the pass of St Antonio, where, however, they made little or no impression, being at first exposed to a destructive fire of the Portuguese artillery, under Major Arentchild, an officer of the King's German Legion, and afterwards kept in check by the light troop of the division under Colonel Williams, and a portion of the Portuguese. Having, from this cause, advanced but little from the bottom of the hill, this evidently was not the spot where the supposed effective aid of the fifth division was required and given.

This brings me now to state, what, once pointed out to Colonel Napier, I feel assured that every inquiry he may hereafter make will more and more convince him is the truth, which is, that these several operations of the Third Division have been by him confounded and mixed up with that attack in which Leith's division actually had a part. Upon inquiry, he will find that General Leith's affair did not take place till a considerable lapse of time after the contest of the 88th and 45th was over; he will also find that it did not take place on Picton's right, but in reality at an intermediate point between his right and left.

Of this latter contest I have no desire to speak disparagingly, nor any wish to detract from the merit of the Fifth Division. I do maintain, however, that, when compared with the attack repelled by the 88th and 45th, the contest in which Leith's division was engaged was but of minor import. Can a stronger proof of this be asked for than the simple fact that the whole loss of the troops therein engaged amounted only to two officers, two serjeants, and forty-three rank and file killed and wounded. Does this tally with the paramount importance Colonel Napier attaches to Leith's affair? Does this make it appear that the latter had any great share in those operations which put no less than three thousand of the enemy *hors de combat*, as was acknowledged in the intercepted dispatches of their general, be it remarked, equal to that which Napoleon confessed to even at Austerlitz?

I ask Colonel Napier if he can seriously hazard the opinion that the heroes of Austerlitz, established on the heights, ensconced in rocks, and going to sweep the summit of the Sierra, could have been baffled in their purpose, could have been driven from a position such as is here described, and totally defeated, leaving, their adversaries to boast of a victory acquired at so very insignificant a cost as was this loss sustained by Leith's division.

Truly, Mr. Editor, I should have argued differently of these heroes from what was seen and felt of their prowess at another point, and at an earlier period of the day. While, however, I have, documents to prove that Picton was right in calling the affair in which Leith was engaged the last, so: would the smallness of the loss the Fifth Division sustained at least afford presumption that he was also justified in styling it, by comparison, a feeble effort of the enemy.

Rocks the latter may have met with; upon this occasion, and in these rocks they may have been ensconced, and from these rocks may have been: driven by Leith; but what I pointedly and decidedly affirm is, that these rocks, wherever situated, were not on Picton's right, and that the French whom Leith encountered and defeated never were established there. That any portion of the enemy ever established themselves so completely on the heights as to, rest their right upon a precipice overhanging the reverse or Coimbra side of the Sierra, or that considerable bodies of the enemy had descended and were killed there, are, I apprehend, facts that even Wellington himself was not aware of till he saw them in Colonel Napier's book.

How the enemy, having ever gained this immense' advantage, should have suffered themselves to be so easily dispossessed of it as the loss of Leith implies, would, I think, puzzle the gallant colonel and his authorities to account for.

Before I drop this portion of the subject, allow me further to express the surprise with which I learn that Leith was indebted for the good fortune that he had in meeting with the enemy to the accidental circumstance of having fallen in with an officer galloping along, and shouting—"To the rescue, ho!" like an ancient warrior in a border fray, imploring aid, for God's sake, for the third to protect them from danger which existed only in his own imagination.

The more probable reason, and what I have always heard assigned is, that when he came in contact with the enemy, Leith, in obedience to the instructions of the great master-mind that planned and overlooked the operations of the day, was watching the progress of events, that he might give his aid if it should be required, indeed, that this was the case, is proved by what Colonel Cameron has stated in General Leith's own words—

> That the ground where the British brigade was now moving was behind a chain of rocky eminences, where it had appeared clearly the enemy was successfully pushing to establish himself, and precluded Major-General Leith from seeing at that moment the progress the enemy was making; but by the information of staff-officers, stationed on purpose, who communicated his direction and progress, Major-General Leith moved the British brigade so as to endeavour to meet and check the enemy when they gained the ascendancy.

Here we have Colonel Cameron's admission, that the column which General Leith attacked could have been but in very temporary possession of the height, since he states that when first seen they were yet in the act of pushing forward to establish themselves.

Indeed, every concurring circumstance affords strong presumptive proof that Leith, who was on the ridge, two miles to the right of the pass, at the commencement of the action, was moving along the road of communication, entered the position of the third, and passed on the left till he embraced the point of ascent of the enemy's column, which he repulsed. This is evident from the manner in which he formed line by wheeling up into that formation, when he fired and charged. Colonel Cameron also supports this assumption when he says:

> He, Leith, therefore ordered the 9th British Regiment, which had hitherto been moving rapidly by its left in column, in order to gain the most advantageous ground for checking the enemy, to form line, which they did with the greatest promptitude, accuracy, and coolness, under the fire of the enemy, who had. just appeared formed on that part of the rocky eminence which overlooks the back of the ridge, and who had then, for the first time, perceived the British brigade under him.

That the disposition of Leith's force must have been known to Picton, and that this column of the enemy was discovered in its advance, and immediately attacked and defeated by the Fifth division, satisfactorily accounts for its being left entirely to them, without the supposition. Colonel Napier makes, that this was caused by the Third having their hands at the time full elsewhere; a gratuitous assumption, not only unsupported by, but utterly opposed to, facts.

While the importance of his co-operation, in itself, has been magnified out of all conceivable proportion, its importance, so far as it regarded the safety of the third division, is of a purely imaginary nature. The critical situation in which they stood—the imminent danger from which they are supposed to have been rescued by the timely interposition of the Fifth, are rested by Colonel Napier on the belief that, at the time Leith came forward, the position of the Third had been gained by the enemy, who were overhanging the reverse side of the Sierra; while the greater part of the Third

Division, British and Portuguese, were fully engaged at the time. Critical enough, heaven knows, had it been placed in this dilemma. But what is the truth? and I would particularly beg Colonel Napier's attention to the facts, as showing how very erroneous has been the information on which he has proceeded in drawing his conclusions.

So far from the greater part of the Third Division, British and Portuguese, being fully engaged in active contest with the enemy at the time that Leith advanced to meet their last attack—not a Frenchman stood then upon the height but as a prisoner of war—those of the Third who had been engaged in the earlier operations of the day were then resting on their arms, and had been so for hours, ready, if required, to do again what they had done so well before; while the brigade of Portuguese guns, under Major Arentchild, never moved from their station on the right throughout the day.

Colonel Napier must, further, feel that his whole ground goes from under him, as to the supposed danger of the Third Division, from their being so entirely occupied as to render them unable to defend themselves from this attack, when he learns that a considerable portion of it, consisting of Lightburne's brigade, under the command of Sir Brent Spencer, but stationed immediately on Picton's left—with the exception, Mr. Editor, of the light company of the 5th Regiment, commanded by yourself—never found an opportunity throughout the whole of the operations to fire a single shot.

This, certainly, could not have been the case had their comrades of the Third been in the jeopardy Colonel Napier has supposed, burning with eagerness, as we know they were, to emulate their more fortunate companions, and share with them the glory of the day. Seeing, therefore, that the Third were so entirely disengaged—and yet, that none of them took part in this affair, except the 74th British Regiment, and some of the Portuguese, who, while the column was met and repulsed by Leith, advanced against a body, which at the same time threatened our position by the St Antonio Pass—these, with the other reasons assigned, justify the conclusion that the affair itself was not of the importance he imagines, and was determined without the necessity of a more general interposition on the part of the Third Division.

So much, then, for the critical situation of the third—so much for the forcing and the breaking of their centre—so much for the turning of their right—so much for the incalculable service supposed to have been rendered to them by the Fifth Division—and so much for the chance of Picton having had a different story to relate, as to the glory of his troops, than he was left to tell by the favour of fortune and the assistance of the Fifth!

To the whole I answer, that if there ever was a time when there was a risk of anything being told to the disadvantage of the third, truly it was not at Busaco; that their laurels were in danger.

If their credit was not there in any way endangered by any want of courage or by inefficiency in themselves, equally remote from fact is the impression that it was placed in danger upon this occasion by any incapacity or blunder of their leader. To blame Sir Thomas Picton, as Colonel Cameron does, for leaving his right exposed—that is, for it can mean nothing else, for not resting it on a position naturally strong—is, under the circumstances, absurd. It was, in fact, protected, as far as the case would admit; and there was no natural *point d'appui* nearer than the banks of the Mondego, nearly four miles distant.

That Picton occupied the ground he was commanded by Lord Wellington to take—that his right neither was turned by the enemy, nor ever was in the slightest danger of being turned—and that the troops which he commanded afforded the most essential service that was rendered during the operations of the day, upon this portion of the ridge—form the only vindication which he can require.

Thus, Mr. Editor, I have, as I conceive, brought forward sufficient evidence to convince your readers, that the account given by Colonel Napier in his work, and in the several letters of Sir John Cameron and Colonel Waller, presumed to be corroborative of that account, are chargeable with inaccuracies more or less injurious to several of the parties that were there engaged.

As having been so long a member of a corps, subject, I may say, to a systematic course of injustice at the hands of Sir Thomas Picton, it cannot be supposed that I am in any way in danger of being unduly partial to the memory of that commander.

I am sure, however, that, in expressing my own, I express the feeling of every officer of the 88th, when I declare, that no resentment for injuries received from him could lead me to acquiesce in any obloquy that may be thrown upon him where it was not deserved.

Such, however, would be the case did I not come forward to assert that the several documents in question are fraught with injustice to his memory: charging him with faults in the disposition and employment of his troops, which, even supposing they were proved to have been errors, and which has not been proved, could be chargeable only to his superiors in command. In the second place, I have shown that injustice has been done to a portion of the 8th Regiment of Portuguese, in stating in so unqualified a manner that they were broken to pieces—one portion of them, at least, having maintained their ground.

In the next places I have shown, that to the third: division, as a whole, the gallant author is exceedingly unjust. Misinformed as to the real characteristics of the battle connected with the position occupied by them, he has painted as one grand fight and general engagement, on the summit of the Sierra, what should have been represented as a series of bold and strenuous, but unavailing, efforts of the enemy to gain possession of the summit.

By employing the expression—

Meanwhile the French who first established themselves on the heights,

and immediately proceeding to expel them by the agency of Leith, he has rendered it impossible for the reader's mind to separate the earlier, main, and leading features of the day, from, what everything concurs to prove was but a subordinate affair—the last expiring effort of the foe.

It is by these mistakes as to the real nature of the contest, or rather contests, with the enemy, and by thus confounding operations in themselves distinct, as to actors, place, and time, that he is enabled to give the Fifth Division the credit of saving the Third from overthrow, when it was never in the slightest danger. It is by similar means that he has given the Fifth a share in repelling the earlier and principal attacks made by the enemy on this portion of the line, and repulsed by the Third alone, without the slightest assistance being required from, and far less rendered by, the Fifth, which entered upon the ground where alone they met the enemy after the fortune of the day, in every essential point, had been determined,

I say it, Sir, from no invidious feeling, for I believe sincerely that they, and every other portion of the British troops, not only did, but did well all that was required of them upon that day. I leave it, however, for you and for your readers to determine, if it is not a case of hardship, that a division whose total loss, in the whole share of the operations they were called upon to take, amounted only to nine rank and file killed, and two officers, two serjeants; thirty-four rank and file, wounded—the loss of the 9th British Regiment, which by all concurring testimony had the greatest share in this affair, amounting only to five rank and file killed, and one officer, one serjeant, and seventeen rank and file wounded, should have equal credit with, I might say greater honour done them than, the 3rd, who bore the heat and burden of the day—witness the superiority of the loss which they sustained, twenty-two officers, five sergeants, and three hundred and fourteen rank and file, independent of the loss sustained by Portuguese attached to the division, *viz*. fifteen officers and two hundred and fifty rank and file.

Comparisons, Mr. Editor, are proverbially odious; and it is peculiarly painful to be compelled to draw them to the disadvantage of those who have undoubted claims on our respect; but, Sir, when we are told that "the Third Division would have been in so critical a situation but for the assistance of the Fifth;" and again—"if assistance, and British assistance, too, had not come to their aid, their general might have cut a different figure in the despatch to what he did;" when it is further boldly stated—"that others wear the laurels which belong in justice to the Fifth," is it possible for the former to submit in silence? Can the Third be blamed if they are roused by these assertions?—can they be accused of egotism, if, "fighting their battles o'er again, they show how fields were won," proving, as they can, that the laurels which they wear are all their own, gained by their own good swords, which left them no occasion to beg, to borrow, or to filch from others.

It must be acknowledged to be galling to their feelings that an attempt should now be made to strip them of a wreath which they have so long and so deservedly enjoyed. It is the more annoying, that in this particular instance, they are to be denuded of the honours to which they are entitled, that they may be bestowed on those who, although deserving of a better fortune, only came in to glean the field, more plentifully reaped by their more fortunate precursors.

In the fourth and last place, Mr. Editor, after what I have stated in the preceding observations, need I specify to yourself or readers the nature of the feelings with which I read the following passage from Colonel Napier's work? Following up his account of the enemy's first attack, he proceeds to say—

> The leading battalions immediately established themselves amongst the crowning rocks, and a confused mass wheeled to the right, intending to sweep the summit of the Sierra; but at that moment Lord Wellington caused two guns to open with grape upon their flank, a heavy musketry was still poured into their front, and in a little time the 45th and 88th Regiments charged so furiously that even fresh men could not have withstood them. The French, quite spent with their previous efforts, only opened a straggling fire, and both parties went down the mountain side, &c.

What meaning, Mr. Editor, do I ask, can be attached to this, more especially, when taken in connexion with the previous, but most erroneous account of the nature of the opposition to which this column had been subjected in ascending the acclivity, but, that Colonel Napier himself believes, and means to impress his readers with the conviction, that the service rendered upon this occasion by the 88th, and the four companies of the 45th, was limited entirely to the beating back a portion of the enemy that was not composed of fresh men?

In other words, it is his belief that they only beat back men spent, as he says, with their previous efforts—jaded, worn out, and on the point of yielding to the opposition they had previously met. Thus would it appear that these two corps only came in to reap a victory already rendered easy by the prowess of others. Had there been anything to justify Colonel Napier's description—had the French, in scaling the mountain, experienced opposition requiring astonishing power and resolution to overcome—had they then forced the right of the third division back, broken the 8th Portuguese to pieces, gained the highest part of the crest with their hostile masses—had they established their leading battalions among the crowning rocks—had a heavy musketry been continued to be poured into their front—had they gone through all this, before they were met and charged by these two regiments.

Colonel Napier might have had some excuse for characterising it as a charge which even fresh men could not have withstood. There might, in this case, have been some colour for the comparatively negative credit which he has left them of defeating the French quite spent with their previous efforts, and only opening a straggling fire: all, certainly, calculated, to convey to the reader's mind anything but an impression of any vigorous effort being required to overcome them.

Let me only then recapitulate the simple facts, that the column of the enemy to which his observations are intended to apply, was in reality composed of fresh men, who, for the reasons stated above, had met with little or no opposition in their ascent—who previously had no continued fire of musketry poured into their front— no part of which could be characterised as a confused mass.

On the contrary, they were a column composed of the very elite of the French troops, the leading battalions being their 2nd Light Infantry, 36th Grenadiers, and 70th of the Line; and with the exception of that portion of them that occupied the rocks before alluded to, and which only made their assault more formidable, advancing in one firm, compact, and unbroken force, when they were charged so gallantly, at the moment that their heads appeared, and defeated by the 88th Regiment under Colonel Wallace, and the four companies of the 45th under Major Gwynne; and with the exception of the aid rendered by the 8th Portuguese in the pursuit, without the assistance of a single man of any other corps.

Misconceived so far in its details, and mixed up with less important operations, I assert, Mr. Editor, that the account of Colonel Napier is decidedly unjust to the officers and men of these distinguished corps. Consider the nature of the service which they rendered; consider that this attack was the first that the enemy had made upon this portion of the line. While the manner in which it was met and repelled by them, went so far, by its result, to determine the ultimate success and issue of the battle.

Take into account that the rendering of this service was by them effected at a loss of no less than sixteen officers, seven serjeants, and two hundred and sixty-one men, killed and wounded. Compare what Colonel Napier says of them with what he says of others, who neither did so much, or at so great a cost, and I leave any impartial person to determine if, in Colonel Napier's work, the gallant bearing of these two corps stands forward in the bold, and prominent, and commanding manner which in bare justice it has .a right to do.

What was in itself pre-eminently the fight on this portion of the line, is mentioned by him in such a manner as to give it the appearance of a subordinate incident in the fight. Involving it, as he has done, in the tumult and confusion of a general engagement, he has rendered it impossible to recognize that spot—

where Greek met Greek, there came the tug of war,

I ask if his description does what it ought to signalize a conflict, brief, it is true, in its duration, but, while it lasted, contested so fiercely on the part of their opponents; and notwithstanding the infinite superiority of numbers of the enemy, with a courage and determination so great, so irresistible on theirs, as to draw from Wellington himself, who was spectator of the combat, that memorable burst of admiration—

"There, Beresford, look at them now!"

This certainly was an open expression of his approbation, which, whatever he might feel, was as rare from him, as, when coming as it did from the first of generals, and first of judges of all military merit, it was honourable to those on whom it was bestowed.

Having had the honour to belong to one of these, I am sure that Colonel Napier will excuse the very pardonable jealousy with which I now come forward to vindicate their claims, and to guard against anything that could possibly endanger their special right to words, which, as they equally shared the gallantry that called them forth, ought, in my own humble opinion, to be interwoven in the colours, and in letters of gold, emblazoned in the records of these two corps, as the proudest distinction they could possibly attain.

More, Mr, Editor, I need not add, confident, as I am, that the facts which I have stated must be sufficient to open Colonel Napier's eyes, and to let a new light in upon him. I rest in the assurance that the gallant author, in preparing for his next edition, will revise the details of this important battle, and willingly repair what he must now perceive to be his great, though I believe sincerely, his unintentional injustice.

William Mackie, Major Unat,
formerly of 88th Regt.

No. 2

REPLY TO "OBSERVATIONS ON SOME PASSAGES IN THE *LIFE OF SIR THOMAS PICTON*." [2]

Mr. Editor,—I had hoped that the very reason which you have assigned for not reviewing the life of Sir Thomas Picton, would have spared me the necessity of again entering the field of contention respecting its merits; but as the author of that work, I cannot allow the comments of your correspondent M. (in your last number) to pass unnoticed. You say, "It is now too late to review a work which has been so long before the public."

If, Sir, it is too late to review it, is it not too late to cavil at its contents? and may I venture to inquire, by what fortuitous circumstance your correspondent arrived at the conclusion, that the two points upon which he dwells in his communication call for so elaborate a criticism? Has he only just read the work? or has he had no earlier opportunity of expressing his opinion?

He says, that he has "lately read the *Memoirs of Lieutenant-General Sir T. Picton*, recently published;" now the work was published in September, and the second edition in December; consequently, your correspondent has taken an unreasonably long period to concoct his ideas, and I begin to suspect that I shall have to keep up a running fire with all ranks of the Peninsular army, from serjeant-majors to lieutenant-generals, unto my dying day. I feel flattered. Sir, by your remark, which, with true author-like vanity, I will take leave to repeat; that, bating some errors of detail and erroneous conclusions, to be referred to my want of experience and to misinformation, I have "compiled these *Memoirs* with zeal, industry, and intelligence."

---

2. From the *United Service Journal*.

Now, Sir, I beg to inform you, and the public, through your valuable *Periodical*, that since my commencement of the *Life of Sir Thomas Picton*, I have gained a considerable portion of military experience; I have discovered that no two individuals, who have served in the same affair, ever give the same accounts of its details—that sometimes their statements only differ in a trifling degree—at others widely—while in some they are totally opposite. I assert this, Sir, from doleful experience.

My opportunities were extensive, but my disappointments numerous; frequently, after listening to a continuous narrative of events which, by the readiness of their birth, had every appearance of being "the only true and particular account," upon attempting to put them to the corroborative test of contemporaneous statements, they have either been totally put *hors de combat*, or so shaken as to be rendered unfit for historical purposes; and so frequently was I thus led to be dissatisfied and to reject the evidences of the actors in the different fields where the Lion was triumphant, that I began to wonder from what sources an authentic history of the Peninsular war could be compiled.

And this conviction is indelibly fixed in my mind—that no history of the war can be produced, which will not call forth comment and contradiction from some of the numerous actors who witnessed those events with different eyes and feelings; and all that can be said respecting these varied and frequently opposite statements is—what I have already remarked in my "Introduction to the Life of Sir Thomas Picton"—that:

> they contribute to that mass of materials from which, hereafter, when all inducement to partial praise or censure shall have ceased, an adequate history may be drawn of that eventful period.

But let it not, for one moment, be imagined that I have made these observations with the slightest disrespect to that service, of which the noble subject of my labours was so bright an example; my respect for the army, and those who fought by Picton's side, is as sincere as my devotion to the name and character of my hero. Again, it might appear that I am ungrateful to those distinguished individuals, to whom am so much indebted for the interest they took in my exertions, and the valuable assistance which they afforded me in completing the work, I beg that they will acquit me of forgetfulness or ingratitude, and admit the following reasons for what I have asserted:—

Any thinking man, without ever having heard a shot pass within whizzing distance of his head, will freely admit that the report of an officer respecting a battle will depend, in a great measure, upon his rank in the army—for upon his rank depends his situation, and upon his situation the power of making observations.

For example, the officers of a company will be enabled to report when the company or battalion opened fire, when they ceased, when the enemy ran after them, or they ran after the enemy; but this constitutes no portion of the description of a general engagement, and in addressing myself to you, Sir, I have no doubt you will readily admit, from practical knowledge, that a regimental officer, when surrounded by the smoke and roar of the musketry while firing and under fire, has, if he does his duty, very little time or opportunity to make any observations upon the general movements of the army, or even the division to which his regiment is attached: yet, at a distant day, when the battle is over, and he is once more snug in his club or amongst his old cronies, he will give you—because he was there—every movement that took place during the day, from personal observation. Now, this individual, in nine instances out of ten, states only what he has heard, read, or understood, yet from a constant habit of repeating the same story and sticking to the same points, he becomes a downright champion for the truth of his statements.

Let us now get a step higher—to the staff. Here we may obtain a great deal of correct information, for they are moving about in the rear, watching the different dispositions—reporting the impressions made upon, or by the enemy: still but few staff officers are enabled to give an accurate detail of the movements; as *aides-de-camp*, they are hurrying in all directions without time to pause or inquire, frequently obliged to hasten forward to a distant part of the field at the most vital moment upon which the fate of the day depends; upon their return the feature of the battle is changed, they know not why or when, and, before they can obtain any information, are again dispatched to the opposite extremity of the position;

until, at the end of the fray, they know which has gained the day, but not the various manoeuvres which led to that result.

But the general-in-chief or general of division, must know every movement and disposition of his part of the field; and, Sir, I maintain that, if he be ignorant where anyone regiment is (and this is a moderately broad basis) at any one time during the battle, he will inevitably betray this omission, to the serious detriment of his position, and the fate of the day.[3]

Your correspondent roundly asserts that Picton did not know where the 88th Regiment was, the night previous to the battle of Busaco. Now, Mr. Editor, I can forgive any of your correspondents who like to abuse me, or call me anything that a gentleman may hear, but I cannot allow Picton's fame to be tarnished by a breath of reproach. I have brought his memory and reputation again before the world; I dare to hope that I have placed his name in the next niche to that of his mighty leader. For that of Wellington must stand alone; and I cannot calmly witness the efforts of subaltern spleen, or overwrought *esprit de corps*, to wrest from his memory one iota of that reputation which he so dearly bought.

Perhaps a more serious accusation could notice brought against a general of division, than to assert that he was ignorant of the precise situation of one of his regiments; it is as bad as to accuse the Duke of Wellington of not knowing in what part of the field "the fighting division" was disposed; and may I, Sir, beg to know who this officer is who ventures to bring this accusation against Sir Thomas Picton? To which of the three classes did he belong at that period? Was he in the line, on the staff, or in command of a brigade, that he presumes to contradict General Picton in his reiterated assertion—that he detached the 88th Regiment to the left the night previous to the battle?

Indeed, Sir, if we are to admit your correspondent's contradic-

---

3. This is a strong assertion, but it is not borne out by facts. Had Colonel Wallace remained with the 88th Regiment in the position he had been placed by General Picton, the battle, at this point at least, would have been lost; but Wallace did no such thing. He moved his corps from the place General Picton had placed it, advanced against the French column, completely overthrew it, and decided the battle. Of all this, Picton was as ignorant, at the time, as his biographer. While Wallace was occupied as has been described, Picton's hands were full at the "St. Antonio pass," and he could not be (as an Irishman once said,) "like a bird, in two places at the same time."—Author.

tion, we must accuse Sir Thomas Picton of having possessed a most fertile and fallacious memory; for, more than a fortnight after the occurrence, we find him writing to the commander-in-chief his reasons for so doing, in the following words:—

> There being an unoccupied space, of considerably above a mile, between my left and Sir Brent Spencer's division, immediately after sunset (when it could not be observed by the enemy), I detached Lieutenant-Colonel Wallace with the 88th Regiment to take up an intermediate position, and communicate with the hill of Busaco and the main body of my division at the pass of St. Antonio.

In confirmation of this remark, if any be considered necessary, a little further on in the same report he observes—

> A few minutes after, when the day began to clear up, a smart firing of musketry was heard on the left, apparently proceeding from the point where the 88th Regiment had been stationed.

These observations are again repeated in his letter to Colonel Pleydel, consequently Picton must either have been deceived into the belief that the 88th Regiment had moved to the left according to his orders, or else the regiment was there; for, after these remarks, no person who has any belief at all, can doubt but that Picton imagined the regiment was where he states. I have said more than I originally intended upon this subject, but as it appears to me the only part of your correspondent's letter which at all touches the character of Sir Thomas Picton, I have given it my particular attention. Your correspondent's remarks respecting the battle are made with judgment, and I readily bow to his presumed "military experience," although I have little difficulty in reconciling the statements to which he objects as confused and contradictory.

The "rocky point," which is so often mentioned by me in the work, is the rocky point alluded to by General Picton in his report to the Duke of Wellington, which, the General says, was situated "about half-way between the pass of St. Antonio and the hill of Busaco." My reason for so frequently reverting to this point is to disprove Colonel Napier's assertion, that it was on the right of Picton's position, and not to imply that it was the only "rocky point" in the line; for there may be, and I believe are, a great many, although it may be presumed that this point was particularly marked from the others, by Picton using the term "high" in its designation.

Your correspondent then charges General Picton with what the general, in his letter to the Duke of Wellington, most positively denies. I allude to repulsing the enemy's first attack upon the position occupied by the 88th and 45th Regiments; and if your correspondent will again peruse the general's letter to the duke, I feel confident that his good sense will enable him to discover that Picton, when he speaks of the gallant chaise made by those two regiments, and disavows the merit of leading them, adding that he was actively engaged at the pass—I say, that when your correspondent re-peruses these passages in conjunction with the subsequent remark, that "a smart firing was heard on the left, where the 88th Regiment was stationed," that he will be satisfied that Picton did not lead the first charge made on the left;, but that he was personally concerned in repulsing the second attack made by the enemy upon this point of his position.

With respect to the light companies of the 74th and 88th Regiments retiring in disorder, perhaps the less this point is discussed the better. Your correspondent says, they were "retiring in extended order," but doubtless Picton thought the movement more resembled extended disorder; and we know the licence of light infantry movements to be so great, that an actual helter-skelter may afterwards be expressed by some military term implying order.

Your champion for—and I suspect of—the 88th Regiment, has ably conducted their defence; I am not prepared, neither am I inclined, to bring forward any fresh arguments in support of the remarks contained in *The Life of Sir Thomas Picton* respecting this brave regiment; indeed, sir, I would rather not have lent my aid in stigmatizing that or any other corps, but what I have stated, I received from a number of distinguished officers, as well able to judge, and more impartial than your correspondent, who, with proper candour, admits that his remarks are not made "without some feeling of *esprit de corps*" [4]

---

4. Will Mr. Robinson favour me with the name of one officer (out of this host of "distinguished officers,") who will bear him out in his assertion about the "coloured wood."—Author.

Colonel Wallace might have done much whilst the work was in progress, to vindicate his old corps from their so often repeated reproach; for I requested him most earnestly to favour me with his assistance, but unfortunately I received no reply to my communication, which I freely attributed to his advanced years.

Your correspondent says, that General Picton gave the regiment a bad name; but the inference to be drawn from this assertion is rather unfortunate, for Picton was a strict disciplinarian, at the same time that he had a strong sense of justice: consequently, if he gave it a bad name, we are bound to think that it was deserved; and the statement of your correspondent, that Picton convened a dinner to express his regret to Colonel Wallace for the injustice that he had done his regiment, is by far too *ex parte* and improbable to be received upon any other authority than as a report. [5]

Your correspondent, in concluding his remarks, has fallen into a very common error, and one which I fortunately saw in time to avoid, before I commenced the *Memoir*. I allude to the failing so prevalent in compiling similar works. The author falls in love with the character of his hero—in consequence, tries throughout to portray him without faults, and as much like the immaculate hero of a romance as the humanity of the man will admit But this is not doing either the subject of the *Memoir*, or the public, justice; for it is misrepresenting the one, and misleading the other. In conclusion, sir, I have to return thanks to your correspondent for having invited into the field all who ever served with Sir Thomas Picton, that I may have an opportunity of keeping my pen in exercise, and the events of the Peninsular war continued in my recollection. [6]

I remain, sir, your obedient servant,
H. B. Robinson.

London, April, 1836.

---

6. This may be very true, but Mr. Robinson cannot make the same charge against me, because, in an early page of this volume, he will find a correct statement of the fact; and, so far from any friend of the late Sir Thomas Picton seeking to contradict it, he should either admit it or be silent,—for the entire affair was most .creditable to the general.—Author.

6. This is extremely facetious on the part of Mr. Robinson, but not quite grave or dignified enough for the historian of Sir Thomas Picton. However, chacun a son gout. But, has Mr. Robinson fulfilled his promise and kept his "pen in exercise?" In the month of October, 1836, I addressed a letter to the editor of the U. S. Journal. In that letter, which was published the same month, (Continued next page.)

No. 3

To the Editor of the *United Service Journal*.

"But injustice to the living as well as the dead."

"Neither at Rodrigo nor Badajoz did General Picton head his division."

"Badajoz one of the most astonishing exploits mentioned in history."

"The brave Lieutenant Mackie, 88th Regiment, who at Rodrigo so gallantly volunteered and bravely led the forlorn-hope of the third division, notwithstanding the promises of General Mackinnon, which ought to have been held sacred, was altogether passed over by General Picton."

"No officer of the 88th Regiment was ever promoted through the recommendation of General Picton."

Mr. Editor,—The above extracts and the sentiments therein contained being continued to the present time, call forth "justice to the dead as well as the living," and therefore I beg leave to express my reliance on General Picton's honour, and that he actually did earnestly recommend to the commander of the forces every officer of the Third Division who merited it; and if they were not in consequence promoted or otherwise rewarded, that should be ascribed to the cause of the total disregard and wholly unanswered repeated recommendations of General Picton in favour of his own *aide-de-camp*, though most justly due to the general as well as the sufferer, a fine young man, who was so dreadfully wounded as not to be again fit for service. He lives; which proves an inattention to the claims of General Picton, for himself, his personal staff, and his division (so proverbially true,) as living individuals of the division can attest.

General Picton did bravely head his division; and at Badajoz, and far in the fire, fell wounded in the foot on the left side of General Kempt, in the approach to the mill-dam on the memorable 6th of

---

I gave a flat contradiction to some of Mr. Robinson's statements; I affixed my name to that letter, and I challenged Mr. Robinson to produce proof of what he stated in his history. From that hour to the present I have never read one line from Mr. Robinson in reply, and, so far from keeping his "pen in exercise," I begin to suspect he has laid it aside—as Picton's champion at least—altogether.—Author.

April, 1812. When be it proclaimed! Badajoz was taken by the third division, having escaladed and established itself in the castle previously, according to General Picton's own proposition, and "which was one of the most astonishing exploits mentioned in history."

It will be recollected that General Mackinnon was blown up by the mine at Rodrigo; he could not, therefore, subsequently communicate to General Picton the promise he is said to have made to Lieutenant Mackie.

AGAIN, UNITED SERVICE JOURNAL MAY 1833, PAGE 53:

—"The brave Captain Gates, so far from being recommended, was not even noticed by General Picton for his gallant conduct at Fort Picurina."

Fort Picurina was undoubtedly the key of Badajoz, which was the door opened by the escalade of General Picton's division for Lord Wellington's subsequent success!

A Soldier of the Third Division.

14th of June, 1833.

No. 4

Mr. Editor,—I have, in my narrative of the storming of Rodrigo, said what General Picton did not do; namely, that he did not notice Lieutenant William Mackie, of the 88th. I shall now say what, in my opinion, he ought to have done.

On the morning of the 20th of January, 1812, the day after the capture of Rodrigo, he should have sent for Lieutenant Mackie, and taken him by the hand and brought him to Gallegos, the head-quarters of Lord Wellington, and said,—"My Lord, this is the young man who so gallantly led the forlorn-hope of my division last night. He is an officer of first-rate merit,—is the senior lieutenant of his regiment,—and I beg your Lordship will notice him."

Had he done so, would he have done too much? because Mackie was a hero in the very essence of the word, and not only General Picton, but every soldier in the Third Division, knew him to be such; for it was not his leading the forlorn-hope at Rodrigo, gallantly as he volunteered his services on that memorable night, that Mackie had to depend upon to ground his claims to the notice of his general. His conduct at Busaco, at the head of the battalion-men of the 88th, who supported the riflemen of the third division, should have gained him a company! at Rodrigo he ought to have been a major!! at Badajoz, a lieutenant-colonel!!! But what is he now, after a lapse of twenty-three years? A captain, without so much as a medal to mark his gallant—his chivalrous services!

Had the general of his division done as I have said, is it likely that Lord Wellington would have turned a deaf ear to such an appeal? But if he did, surely the general might have issued a division order, expressive of his sense of the services of Lieutenant Mackie; or he might, in presence of his division, have declared his approbation of his conduct; and General Picton never wanted words, when it suited him to give his opinions on a division parade. No, no: the defence attempted to be set up is not maintainable. General Picton had but one course to pursue; namely, to recommend Lieutenant Mackie to the notice of Lord Wellington; and if that failed—or whether it did or not—to notice him himself. In a word, Mackie was one of the bravest and one of the most ill-treated men in the world.

As to the death of General Mackinnon, and the consequent failure of his promise, it is equally untenable. Is it to be supposed that a general who commanded and arranged the attack of his division did not know the name of the officer who led the forlorn-hope of it? And let it not for a moment be supposed that in anything I have written I seek for more than justice—even-handed justice— to the officers and men of the 88th Regiment

If Lieutenant Gurwood, of the 52nd, was entitled to promotion for his gallant conduct—and who will say that he was not?—surely Lieutenant Mackie, of the 88th, is equally entitled to the same favour. Major Manners, of the 74th—belonging, like Mackie, to Mackinnon's brigade—led the storming party, which Mackie preceded with his forlorn-hope! and gained promotion in consequence!

How will "A Soldier in the Third Division "account for this? Mackinnon's death ought to have barred both or neither!

He says, that "the sentiments therein contained," (alluding, of course, to what I have written,) being continued to the present time, call forth "justice to the dead as well as the living;"—no doubt they do, and why not? But how will he account for the pre- motion of Manners and the neglect of Mackie, both belonging—if we are to cavil about the thing, which, by the way, is only childish—to the brigade of Mackinnon!

Does he know that the 88th, independent of what I have before said, have been denied the badge of the battle of the Pyrenees on their colours, and that the 45th and 74th, belonging to the same brigade! are allowed to bear it? Can he give any reason for this slight? Can any of General Picton's staff—I will take Colonel Stovin for an example—give a reason why it is so? He cannot, I believe, no more than anyone else.[1] If he will inquire at the Horse Guards, he will be told by Lord Fitzroy Somerset, that the 88th cannot be allowed the badge of a battle—in which their conduct was marked as being gallant—because the general commanding the third division did not recommend the officer commanding the 88th for a medal! Is this "justice to the living?" Is this justice to the brave 88th? I think not.

The object I have in writing as I have done, is not meant in any way to throw a slur on any particular general; they are, to me, all alike. What I wish for is to uphold the character of my regiment, the 88th; all that I seek for is the same favours for them as have been granted to others—and to have them placed in the same position. I seek for no additional mark—I claim no precedence for that corps; all I ask for is justice! This is all that is sought for, this is all that is expected;—with that the 88th ought to be satisfied—but with nothing less!

I never imputed any blame to General Picton for not leading on his division at the assaults of Rodrigo or Badajoz; on the contrary, I praised him for not doing so. He arranged and directed both attacks with his usual talent; conducted them with his usual skill; but he was not rash enough to head them, well knowing that his directions were of more consequence, and that in the hands of brigadiers or colonels, his men were as likely to do their duty, without the chance of their chief being cut off in a station that would have been better filled by a common soldier. And the circumstance of General Picton being wounded at the "Mill-dam," is conclusive, and bears me out in what I have said.

If General Picton fell wounded at the mill-dam on the River

---

1. See letter following pages.

Rivellas, some hundred yards from the castle wall, it is manifest that he could not, as I before said—he did not—head his men at the assault But in saying what I did say, and which I still assert as a fact, that neither at Rodrigo nor Badajoz did the general head his men, I meant nothing derogatory to General Picton, but wished merely to prove how well soldiers could act under their own commanding officers. If the object of a "Soldier of the Third Division" was to prove that General Picton headed his division at the assault of the castle of Badajoz, his own letter is a disproval of the fact; for he says that "General Picton did bravely head his division, and far in the fire fell wounded in the foot on the left side of General Kempt, in the approach to the mill-dam on the memorable 6th of April, 1812."

Now, General Kempt, who is still alive, and who, according to this authority, fell wounded at the same time General Picton did, namely, at the mill-dam, will scarcely lay claim to the glory of having headed his brigade at the assault of the castle. Taking it for granted that Picton and Kempt both fell wounded at this point, who was the general that led on the Third Division to the assault of the castle? There was no general excepting these two in the division; they both were disabled, long before the division reached the point of attack. It was owing to the bravery of such men as the gallant Colonel Ridge, and Captain Canch, of the 5th, Lieutenant Bowles of the 83rd. and Mackie—the gallant Mackie—of the 88th, the place was taken at all; and so far I am, I think, borne out in the opinion I gave of the folly of generals placing themselves at the head of their men at an assault, when the duty could be as well performed by subordinate officers.

In conclusion, he quotes a passage from my adventures, and I must confess that I can in no way understand the meaning of it;—it is this: "The brave Captain Oates, so far from being recommended, was not even noticed by General Picton for his gallant conduct at Fort Picurina;" and by way, I suppose, of putting a stop to any further "extracts, and the sentiments therein contained," he adds, "Fort Picurina was undoubtedly the key to Badajoz, which was the door opened by the escalade of General Picton's division for Lord Wellington's subsequent success!!!"

Every person at all acquainted with the siege of Badajoz will admit this fact;—but what has it to do with the shameful neglect of Captain Oates?—Nothing, Oates deserved notice and promotion. General Picton could not promote him, but he could have recommended him!—he could have noticed him!! Did he do either the one or the other? This is the point at issue.

As for Badajoz having been taken by the third division, I am not so sure that the Fifth Division would not lay claim to a portion of the glory. In anything I have written, I have, I believe, given the third division their meed of praise. He may do better than I have done for them, and I hope the survivors of the "fighting division" will believe me sincere when I say that I shall feel happy when such a man as "A Soldier of the Third Division" will place their imperishable deeds in a more distinguished point of view than I have been able to accomplish by my feeble efforts.

Dublin, Nov. 20, 1833.

The foregoing letter was written by the author to the editor of the U. S. Journal,

Royal Hospital, 20th July, 1830.

My dear O'Malley,—I wish it were in my power to give you any satisfactory reason why the officer in command of the 88th Regiment did not obtain the medal for the "Pyrenees," but I have no document in my possession which can lead to any elucidation of the cause which withheld that distinction.

That the regiment performed its duty in the usual gallant style which always reflected so much honour on their services, I am most ready to attest as far as my observation could command, and I should consider it equally entitled to the distinction you solicit, with the 45th and 74th Regiments; indeed, on the 28th. when Soult made his great effort against the left of our position, the 88th were the only part of the third division engaged, and it was in the pursuit of the enemy after that day that the whole division co-operated, when, by rapidity of march, and some skilful flank movements through the mountains, they succeeded in securing a number of prisoners.

I am quite ignorant of Lieutenant-Colonel MacPherson's present residence, who might furnish such information as would forward the object of your desire, in which I sincerely wish you success, and wish I could in any way contribute to it.

Ever, my dear O'Malley,

Yours, &c. &c.,

(Signed) Fredk. Stovin.

To Lieutenant-Colonel O'Malley, 88th Regiment,

To His Exoellency General Earl Wellington, K.B , Commander of the Forces, &c. &c.

The Memorial of Lieutenant W. Mackie, 88th Regiment.

Sheweth,—That memorialist, as a volunteer, led the advance of the storming party of the Third Division at the capture of Ciudad Rodrigo, on the 19th of January. That memorialist with his party arrived at the citadel before the advance of the light division under Lieutenant Gurwood; that your memorialist is now senior lieutenant of the 88th Regiment, and has served in this country since March 1809, and that memorialist has never been absent from his regiment.

Memorialist therefore begs from the foregoing circumstances that Your Excellency will take his case into consideration for promotion.

(Signed) W. M.

The above forwarded through Sir James Kempt, at Elvas.—1812.

London, 11th May, 1816.

Dear Sir,—I have the most perfect recollection of your having forwarded through me, shortly after my taking the command of a brigade in the Tthird Division, a memorial stating your services, and particularly mentioning your having led the advance of the storming party of the Third Division, at the attack of Ciudad Rodrigo, and I am quite convinced from the estimation that the late Sir Thomas Picton, then commanding the division, had of your conduct and services on that occasion, and the manner in which he brought your merits to the notice of the Duke of Wellington, that some special mark of favour would have been conferred upon you, if you had not, almost immediately afterwards, been promoted to a company as the senior lieutenant of the 88th regiment.

Your conduct also at the siege of Badajoz, in which you were engaged in operations under my immediate command, impressed me with a very favourable opinion of your merits.

(Signed)　　J. Kempt, M.G.

To Capt. Mackie.

London, 11th Dec., 1830.

Sir,—Major Mackie, late of the 88th Regiment, informs me he has never received any mark of distinction for having volunteered, and conducted the forlorn hope to the main breach in the assault of Ciudad Rodrigo, in consequence of his not having been recommended at the moment, which, I believe, proceeded from General Mackinnon being killed at the time. Major Mackie's conduct on all occasions was so truly meritorious, and I have no doubt that he calculated on receiving, as a matter of course, promotion, if he succeeded, as you immediately succeeded, and took the command of the brigade which he served with. I beg leave to say that you will forward the interest, and do justice to one of the most gallant officers in the service, if you will point out to the commander-in-chief the service Major Mackie performed on that occasion, as I have no doubt he will then receive that mark of approbation which has always been granted to officers and non-commissioned officers who have successfully performed a similar service.

I have the honour to be.
Yours very faithfully,
J. A. Wallace, M.G.

Right Hon. Sir James Kempt, &c.

I certify that Captain William Mackie (then lieutenant), of the 88th Regiment, volunteered, and led the advance of the storming party, at the capture of Ciudad Rodrigo, in Spain, under my command.

(Signed)　　Russell Manners,
Lieut.-Col. and Major 74th Regt.

Whetstone, Middlesex,
Feb. 11, 1816.

The original of the above certificate was transmitted to the Horse Guards in June, 1816.

I certify that Captain Mackie, of the 88th Regiment, served in the brigade under my command in the campaign of 1812, and particularly distinguished himself by the great zeal, activity, and intelligence, which he displayed in the performance of his various duties.

I also certify that upon my joining the Third Division, immediately after the capture of Ciudad Rodrigo, Lieutenant-General Sir Thomas Picton, then commanding the division, pointed out Captain Mackie to me as the officer who led the forlorn hope in the assault of the main breach, which the Third Division carried, and that he particularly distinguished himself on that occasion.

(Signed)   James Kempt, M.G

London, 26th March, 1820.

Edinburgh, 17th Jan., 1820.

Dear Sir,—Captain Mackie, of the 88th Regiment, has expressed to me his intention of forwarding a memorial to His Royal Highness, the commander-in-chief, for some special mark of favour in consideration of his services during the late war, and his hopes, as you commanded (for some time,) the brigade which he served in, and the kind interest you took in forwarding a former memorial for him, that you may be inclined to give your countenance to the application he is now about to make; he has, therefore, requested me to state to you my opinion of his conduct, as having commanded the regiment, which, I hope, will plead my excuse for now troubling you.

I beg leave to assure you that Captain Mackie's conduct has, on all occasions, most fully merited any recommendation I can give. At the battle of Busaco, I selected Captain Mackie (then lieutenant) to command a party from the troops under my command, to descend the hill and harass a column of the enemy ascending to the attack; this service was conducted by him with a spirit and energy conspicuous to every person present.

The readiness with which he came forward, when an officer was called to lead the advance of the storming party at Ciudad Rodrigo, I believe you are acquainted with.

I had so very high an opinion of Captain Mackie's intelligence, that he attended me, in the capacity of *aide-de-camp*, during the period I commanded a brigade in the Third Division, on the Peninsula, and particularly at the battle of Salamanca, where I had every reason to be much satisfied with his conduct; and in every situation of danger, he was always ready and anxious to make himself conspicuous; his activity and intelligence, on all occasions, was repeatedly noticed to me by the late Sir Thomas Picton in terms of the highest satisfaction, and I am sure Sir Thomas Picton was anxious that he should have received some special mark of favour, with the other officers, after the storming of Ciudad Rodrigo, but he, at that time, succeeded to a company as the senior lieutenant in his own regiment, which may have prevented him from receiving any particular mark of favour at that time, and, I presume, Captain Mackie is in hopes of a favourable result to his memorial in consequence of these circumstances.

I beg again to apologise for the trouble I give you, and am, dear Sir,

Your faithful and humble Servant,
(Signed) J. A Wallace, M.G.
To Lieut.-General Sir James Kempt, G.C.B., &c.

Vindication of the Connaught Rangers From the Charge Preferred Against them in the *Life of Sir T. Picton*. [1]

Mr. Editor,—In the May number of the *United Service Journal*, I read a reply from the compiler of the *Life of the late Sir Thomas Picton*, to a correspondent of your journal, who signs the initial "M." to some remarks he had thought proper to make on certain portions of the work written by Mr. Robinson. I was curious, never having read the *Memoir*, to see what your correspondent "M." had written, and I accordingly obtained the April number of your periodical, and there I found the remarks of your correspondent.

Since then I have read an extract from the *Memoir*, which was sent to me, and I am at a loss to guess at the exact drift of the attack made on my old corps the 88th, or the different regiments, in general, that composed the Third Division. Whether it be meant to show that General Sir Thomas Picton was a man of such superior abilities that he did as much, or more, with the worst description of troops in the army, than any other general; or that, by some fortuitous circumstance, he was placed in command over such a set of men, I cannot pretend to say; but it is most true that the regiments which composed the Third Division were as well organised, and in as high a state of discipline as any other division in the army.

But the remarks on the 88th Regiment are so void of foundation, that I think it only right to inform Mr. Robinson, through the medium of your journal, that he has been greatly led astray by his "informant." All this is, however, unimportant, and I think your correspondent "M.," who I take for granted read Mr. Robinson's work before he wrote his letter, has devoted more time and paper, to say nothing of pens and ink, in his reply, than the subject merits.

Whether General Picton called the 88th Regiment "ragged rascals, or Connaught robbers," is of little import to the regiment, or the army in general. Neither is it of much consequence whether General Picton commanded the right, left, or centre, of his division, on the day of Busaco. We are to give the general credit for doing the best he could, and if he happened to be away from the principal point of contest, it was no fault of his; or, did he claim any merit to himself, for the charge made by the five companies of the 45th and the 88th Regiments, it only goes to prove what I have already said, that "regiments can perform this work as well when led on by their own commanding officers, as if generals placed themselves at their head."

I never heard that General Picton called the 88th Regiment his "ragged rascals," but as Mr. Robinson so denominates them, so shall they remain for the present. But, Mr. Editor, if I have said that the points, to which your correspondent "M." has alluded, were of little import to the 88th Regiment, or the army in general, it does not follow that what I am now going to speak about is not of importance to both. It is a point that strikes hard at the honour—the very vitals—of a corps. It is the charge made by Mr. Robinson, in his work, against the 88th Regiment, on the score of their ammunition.

The 88th Regiment, according to Mr. Robinson's "informant," was found frequently, upon going into action, deficient, by the half, of their cartridges, and the men, it would seem, substituted in place of them pieces of wood "cut and coloured," to resemble ball. Now, in what action did this occur? Was it at Busaco, where they with a few companies of their brave companions, the 45th, overthrew the 2nd, 4th, 36th. and the Irish brigade belonging to Regnier's corps? Those four French regiments were at least six times the number of the 45th and the "ragged rascals."

Was it at Fuentes d'Onore, where the 9th French Light Infantry, and some hundreds of the Imperial Guard, were driven from the chapel heights, through the town into the river, and across the river, by five companies of the 88th, and a few men of the 71st and 79th Regiments? Those French troops were about five times the number of the 71st, 79th, and the "ragged rascals!" Was it at the breach of Rodrigo, where General Picton told the Rangers of Connaught (not the "ragged rascals"), "that it was not his intention to expend any powder that evening, that the business should be done with the could iron?"

At this same breach the senior lieutenant of the 88th volunteered, and led the forlorn hope of Picton's division, a major of the 74th followed, with the storming party. Both officers escaped without even a wound. The major of the 74th was promoted, but the senior lieutenant of the 88th was not promoted—not even noticed!

Was this "unqualified praise,"—was it justice? Perhaps Mr. Robinson's "informant" was at Rodrigo, and can tell him something about this! I entertain no doubt that he was there, and that hearing Picton make his splendid, though short appeal to the 88th, perhaps he caught hold only of that part of it which said, that no powder was to be expended, and took it for granted that there was none to expend! Fie!

What a shame for any man, much less an officer, to mislead an author to such an extent, and now, after so long a lapse of time, to lend his aid in endeavouring to crush a regiment that has already suffered such degradation and injustice at the hands of General Picton, as the ill-fated 88th has endured! Did the 88th want ammunition at Badajoz, where Lieutenant Whitelaw, of that regiment, led the advance with the ladders, against the castle, and died unnoticed? Did the men who carried the fort of La Picurina want ammunition?

At the storming of this fort, one of the most desperate affairs, for the numbers "engaged, that occurred during the Peninsular war, a force of five hundred men from Picton's division was taken out of the trenches, this force was divided into three parts, and each attacked the point marked out for it The three officers who commanded were wounded before the fort was carried. The command then devolved upon Captain Oates of the 88th.

This officer was a captain of some nine or ten years standing—a splendid soldier in the fullest acceptation of the word. He found himself in a dangerous situation, as to success; for his ladders were too short to reach the embrasures. He called out to the men, who, by the way, were all 88th, to run the ladders up the counter-scarp, and throw them across the fosse. The men did so, and thus a sort of bridge was formed. Oates put himself at their head, carried the fort, and fell wounded, so desperately that it took one year to enable him to recover and join his regiment At the time he was thus wounded, he was in command of the entire—he, in fact, was commanding officer.

It may be asked, what was his recompense for this service? Just the same as the leader of the forlorn hope at Rodrigo; he was neither promoted nor noticed by his general! Did the 88th want ammunition at Salamanca, where the 45th, 74th, and 88th Regiments, not counting, altogether, more than one thousand five hundred men, and led on by the gallant and chivalrous Colonel Alexander Wallace, of the 88th, overthrew, and knocked the heart's-blood out of the French Seventh Division? This French division was four times the number of the 45th, 74th, and the "ragged rascals." They struck the first blow, and struck it well, on the memorable 22nd of July, 1812; and having said so much so far, may I ask, where, and on what occasion was it, that the "ragged rascals" were found deficient?

It was utterly impossible that such a practice, as that of substituting "coloured wood" for cartridges could have taken place in the 88th without detection; and I never knew an instance of the regiment wanting ammunition in battle. The ammunition of the corps, in common, I believe, with the others that composed the army, was inspected daily, and a certificate of such inspection signed by the company's officer, who made the inspection, on the back of the morning report of the state and strength of his company.

The 88th was too well commanded to allow any relaxation on this essential point. Colonel Wallace, as well as his officers, knew, that not only the honour of the regiment, but the honour of the British army, and the honour of the British nation, was at stake in the contest we were engaged in. But, independent of this, supposing the officers to be so degraded a set of scoundrels, as to be totally dead to any such feeling, as I think did exist, on so vital a point, amongst us all, the lives of the men, as well as the officers themselves, might be forfeited by our thus disarming ourselves, and any colonel, or any set of officers, who could allow so high a crime to pass unpunished, would deserve to be, not only cashiered, but sent to the galleys for life.

If such atrocious conduct, on the part of the officers of the 88th Regiment be true, why did not General Picton immediately report it, and demand a court martial upon them? That would have been but his duty. This would have been doing real justice to the 88th; for by so acting he could have got a colonel and a set of officers over the men that were trustworthy; and a set of officers amongst whom, during the four years of his command, he might have found one, at least, worthy of promotion or notice.

Now, General Picton never having done as I say he should, he must have either connived at the infamous conduct of the regiment, officers as well as soldiers, or the entire story is a mere fabrication.

If the officers connived at, or could be duped by such conduct on the part of their men, they should have been dismissed the service for infamy or incapacity. And if the general of the division connived at such infamy or incapacity on the part of the officers of any regiment under his command, he was equally culpable as they, and should be likewise dismissed the service. It then comes to this, that Colonel Wallace, and the officers of the 88th, as likewise General Picton, should have been turned out of the service; or, that all have been most foully calumniated. There can be no distinction between them. An officer who does not know the merits or demerits of his men is unfit to command them. A general who is similarly circumstanced is equally unfit. The story of the "coloured wood," in point of argument, whether true or false, is the same. If true, the general, the colonel, and all the officers, so implicated, should have been, not only turned out of the service, but degraded, and their names held up to public scorn. If false, both general and officers, as likewise the soldiers, have been foully libelled.

No knot, no matter how closely tied, can be more binding than the charge made by Mr. Robinson against the 88th Regiment and

General Picton. And both the general and the officers of the 88th Regiment must stand or fall together! They are both placed in the same predicament. The fate of the Third Division; the fate of a battle; the fate of a campaign; the fate of the Peninsula! might be decided by the inefficiency of a regiment only half-armed when called upon at the moment of necessity. Thus then, the general who could allow such a practice to be carried on under his own eye, was not fit to hold a command. Both the general and the officers of the regiment, for both must be linked together, so incapacitated, were unfit to remain in the Peninsula.

But where is the man who will say, that Picton was not a fit person to command his invincible old Third Division; that was never defeated; or, that the ill-fated 88th Regiment did not stand by him, and add a stone, I do not say the coin-stone, that has raised the monument of his fame to the pinnacle on which it now stands? Oh I shame! The biographer of General Picton, instead of adding to the fame of his friend, in his endeavour to brand the 88th Regiment with infamy, has committed an historical suicide, and murdered the man whose life he has attempted!

Now, Mr. Editor, to you, who know so well the habits of the British soldier, it would be but taking up your time unnecessarily, to say that the men of the 88th Regiment would, and did, in common with all the regiments in the army, exchange their ammunition for wine, where opportunity favoured such a practice; but the point at issue is, whether the story of the "coloured wood" be true or false; whether, in fact, the 88th Regiment, upon going into action, were but half-armed; in a word—were they an inefficient body of officers and soldiers, not to be depended upon on the day of trial? This, sir, is the real substance of the charge. If true, as I before have said, the general was not a competent person to fill the command with which he was entrusted.

On this point it will not, I think at least, be easy to argue; for no argument, no matter how strong, can, in my opinion, combat the position upon which I have taken my stand. I have not made use of any metaphorical aid to support me. I have but taken the words of Mr. Robinson as true, and upon his assertion alone, whether I am able, on the part of the 88th, to rebut it or not, the character of General Picton is to be judged by those persons who read Mr.

Robinson's work. Those persons are not to look to my defence of the general; for in the defence I am about to make for my old corps, I am defending General Picton also! If I succeed in clearing the 88th from a charge so gravely brought forward against them by Mr. Robinson's "informant," I also clear the general; and Mr. Robinson must not look upon me in the light of a poacher trespassing on his "property," for I can assure him, with truth, that I would not have touched on it at all, was it not that in defence of what I consider as my "property," I have been obliged to cross his hounds.

It is difficult to say, indeed it would be presumptuous for me to say, never having read Mr. Robinson's work, or even if I had, what is his real object of attack against the Third Division in general, but more particularly against the 88th Regiment. If it be meant to show that General Picton had the misfortune to be placed over a set of ill-organized regiments, which did as much as other divisions in the Peninsular army, I thinks with all due deference to Mr. Robinson's better judgment, not good taste, it is not complimentary to those colonels who commanded and led on those regiments to victory in every action.

If it is meant as an excuse for the uniform, the chilling neglect, which the officers of the 88th experienced from General Picton, Mr. Robinson might as well lay down his pen. All the water in the salt sea, much less the ink with which Mr. Robinson writes, could not wash away, or in the slightest manner efface, the facts I have published as to the manner in which the officers of the 88th have been passed over, neglected—unnoticed.

If Mr. Robinson wishes for the particulars of those slights, I will give them to him, and if he finds me wrong in one single observation I may have made; or that I have introduced one solitary name without due authority, I will not only expunge such name, and such observations, but frankly confess I was wrong in what I stated. No man can do more, no man ought to do less. I write to uphold the character of ray old corps, the 88th. Mr. Robinson writes the life of his hero (and, I suppose, friend) General Picton. Both of us may err in our estimate; but truth cannot err! I hope soon to compile these reminiscences, and before I publish them I will send Mr. Robinson the proof-sheets, and if in those pages he shall find just grounds of complaint for what I may say of General Picton, as connected with the 88th Regiment,—beyond that I have nothing to do,—I will expunge it altogether.

This is only just and fair, because any book bordering on historical facts must, more or less, be subject to the scrutiny of the public; and by the judgment of that public it must abide. Posterity ought not to be defrauded of its rights, neither should the living any more than the dead; and if a work such as Mr. Robinson's should remain unnoticed, or allowed uncorrected to pass current now, no one, in after times, could, or would, have any right to deny its being sterling; and our children might see the soldiers of the degraded 88th, and those of the more favoured regiments in Picton's division, cutting each other's throats about a passage in Mr. Robinson's book; or on the score of a badge of merit being denied to the 88th, when we, Mr. Editor, who are now living, know that that regiment merited such badge.

Now, Mr. Editor, what I have asserted in defence of the 88th is true; yet assertion, no matter how strong, is but assertion nevertheless. I have no doubt on my mind that Mr. Robinson himself will give me credit for sincerity, and that by the time he has read this letter through, he will believe that I am in earnest, downright earnest, in all I have said; and I have but. little hesitation in believing that he would take my word for the truth of what I have asserted; and here the matter might rest, as far as regarded Mr. Robinson and myself; but as the "informant" of Mr. Robinson might be a little sceptical on the subject, I shall append a few documents to this letter, by way of index, which will, I think, be conclusive on the subject of the "coloured wood," and even shake Mr. Robinson's opinion as to the soundness of his "informant's" knowledge, or the wisdom of his advice; and as I freely give up my authorities as to the utter falsehood of the charge attempted to be fastened upon the 88th Regiment, I have done my part in the vindication of my old corps, on this point, and of General Picton's also.

EXTRACT FROM THE *MEMOIR OF THE LIFE OF THE LATE LIEUT. GENERAL SIR THOS. PICTON*, IN 1836. BY B. ROBINSON.

'But this was not all,' added our informant; 'for frequently, just before going into battle, it would be found, upon inspection, that one half of the 88th Regiment were without ammunition, having acquired a pernicious habit of exchanging the cartridges for *aqua ardiente*, and substituting in their place pieces of wood cut and coloured to resemble them.'

So soon as this extract reached me, I lost no time in forwarding it to any officer, non-commissioned officer, or private, who had served with the regiment in the Peninsula, and whose address I remembered; but I had a difficult task to accomplish, for so many years have elapsed since we had been together, that it was not easy to find out some of those whose testimony I annex. I was only enabled in part to fulfil what I consider my bounden duty, not only in defence of my own character as an individual, but in defence of the character of my old regiment as a body. But from all to whom I wrote I found a ready reply, negativing the foul charge attempted to be saddled on the 88th. I shall insert these documents in the order they reached me, not paying attention to rank; for where all are equally concerned, I shall pay no more deference, in the list of names, to a colonel than I would to the lowest soldier who served with the regiment. First on the list is a serjeant-major, whose testimony is as follows:—

(No. 1.)

Naas, 3rd July, 1836.

I, Michael Spellicy, late serjeant-major 88th Regiment, can make oath, if necessary, that the gross and false libel put forth from Mr. Robinson's *Life of Sir Thomas Picton*, against the 88th Regiment, is false and without foundation; and I further state, that I was present with the 88th Regiment in all the general actions in which that corps was engaged, and nothing of that kind could occur without my knowledge.

Michael Spellicy,
late Serj.-Major 88th Regiment.

(No. 2.)

Naas, July 3rd, 1836.

I can certify the above statement of Serjeant-major Spellicy to be correct in every part, being myself in the whole of the Peninsular campaign.

William Byrne,
late Private 88th Regiment.

(No. 3.)

Dublin, June 25th, 1836.

I served in the 88th Regiment as private, corporal, and serjeant, from the spring of 1809 until the summer of 1814; that is to say, from the time the regiment first landed in the Peninsula, and subsequently left it for Canada. I was present in every battle in which the regiment was engaged, from the battle of Talavera in 1809, to the battle of Toulouse in 1814; and in all the actions that took place during that time, I never knew one instance in which the soldiers of the 88th Regiment were deficient of ammunition.

They could not be deficient of it, as the ammunition was inspected at the morning parade every day; and as it has been said that the men cut pieces of wood to resemble hall cartridge, I most positively deny, and am ready to make oath, if necessary, that any such practice could have been carried on without my knowledge, and I most solemnly declare that no such practice ever took place.

Thomas Kelly,
late Serjeant 88th Regiment.

(No. 4.)

Naas Barracks, July 2nd, 1836.

I, Henry George Buller, late Captain 88th Regiment, during my service in the first and second battalions of that regiment, from the 24th May, 1804, to 1824, on full pay in those corps, can state positively that what has been stated in the *Memoirs of the Life of the late Sir Thomas Picton*, namely, that the soldiers of the 88th Regiment, on going into action, were found to be deficient of one-half of their ammunition, and that in lieu thereof they substituted bits of coloured wood to resemble ball cartridge,—I know, and can report with truth, that no such practice did, or could have taken place without my knowledge; further, the ammunition of the soldiers was inspected daily; and in short, the story is without the least foundation or truth; and I am surprised any one could have dared to have made such a false statement against a corps that always did their duty in defence of their king and their country.

W. H. G. Buller,
late Captain 88th Regiment.

(No. 5.)

Tymore, 5th July, 1836.

I had the honour to serve with the 88th Regiment in five campaigns, and part of the sixth. I commanded almost every company in the regiment at different times (from casualties). I declare the assertion of ammunition substitution is infamously false. We were always remarkable for having our ammunition and arms in fighting order. The character of the 88th Regiment scorns such remarks.

Thomas J. Stewart,
late Lieutenant 88th Regiment.

(No. 6.)

Kilkenny, July 12th, 1836.

My dear Grattan,—I have the pleasure of receiving your letter of the 7th instant, containing an extract from the Life of Sir Thomas Picton, accusing the 88th of making away with their ammunition, and substituting painted sticks for cartridges, and really, my dear fellow, the charge is so monstrously absurd that no rational man would believe it; and surely if such a practice ever had existed (except in the mind of the calumniator), the officers of companies must have discovered it at their inspections, and, as a matter of course, brought the offenders to punishment.

For my own part, I never heard of any such thing, and, of course, have no hesitation in saying so. I have not yet seen the *Memoirs*, but I am surprised you have not met with it, and perhaps it would be well, before you communicate anything for publication, that you should see and read the part extracted yourself; at all events, here comes my contradiction:—

> Having been informed that, in the *Memoirs of Sir Thomas Picton*, it is stated that "frequently before going into battle it would be found, upon inspection, that one-half of the men of the 88th Regiment were without ammunition, having acquired a pernicious habit of exchanging the cartridges for *aqua ardiente*, and substituting in their place pieces of wood cut and coloured to resemble them,"

I feel myself called upon, as an officer of the regiment, to give the most unqualified contradiction to the above charge, and to state that I served in the 88th Regiment from the year 1808 to

1817, during which period I was present with that gallant corps at the sieges of Rodrigo and Badajoz; at the battles of Salamanca, Vittoria, Orthes, Vic Bigorre, Pyrenees, Nivelle, Tarbes, and Toulouse; besides the affairs of E1 Bodon, La Barba, Hasparien, and others I never went into action without inspecting the ammunition of the company I commanded, and I never knew, never heard, nor do I believe any such practice could have existed without my knowledge. The survivors of the French corps, serving at the time, under Marshals Soult and Marmont, in the Peninsula, could bear ample testimony that it was not by painted sticks, resembling cartridges, their bones were broken or their bodies riddled, whenever they had the *malheur* to come in contact with the Connaught Rangers, whose gallantry upon several occasions excited not only the admiration, but unfortunately the envy also, of particular corps; and I have no doubt that some individual, actuated by the latter feeling, imposed upon the writer of the *Memoirs*.

Parr Kingsmill,
late Lieutenant 88th Regiment.

(No. 7.)

69, London Road, Brighton, July 16, 1836.

I certify that I was on service as lieutenant in the 88th (Connaught Rangers) during the Peninsular war. I was present with that corps in the following engagements (besides minor affairs); namely, Talavera, Busaco, Badajoz, Salamanca, Vittoria, and Orthes. I was frequently in command of a company, and can affirm that the statement contained in the *Memoirs of the late Lieutenant-General Sir Thomas Picton*, to the effect that the 88th Regiment were frequently without ammunition on going into action, having disposed of the same, and substituting pieces of coloured wood, is incorrect.

John Fitspatrick,
late Captain 88th Regiment.

(No. 8.)

Kilkenny, July 20, 1836.

We the undersigned pensioners of the 88th Regiment, having read the extract from the *Life of Sir T. Picton*, stating that the soldiers of that regiment, upon going into action, were frequently found deficient by one-half of their ammunition, and that pieces of wood, cut and coloured to resemble ball cartridges, were substituted in their place, declare that during the long period we served in the 88th Regiment, no such practice did exist; and we are ready to transmit affidavits to that effect if required.

Peter Connor,[2] Corporal.
Joseph Swift,[3] Private.
William White,[4] Private.

(No. 9.)

London, July 29, 1836.

I have been upon active service with the 88th Regiment for more than twenty years; was almost in every action in which it was engaged, particularly in the Peninsula; never absent, except for the recovery of wounds (five in number), and surely must have known, or heard, if such had ever taken place. Now I do most solemnly declare that I never knew or heard of such an occurrence happening in the 88th Regiment, and I never heard the smallest allusion to the same till now; being upwards of twenty-two years since leaving the Peninsula.

J. P. Oates,
Lieutenant-Colonel H. P. 89th Regiment.

(No. 10.)

Royal Hospital Chelsea, July 98, 1836.

Having served in almost all the actions in the Peninsula with the 88th Regiment, I most solemnly declare that I never knew or heard of such a practice in the regiment, and that the above assertion is false, groundless, and entirely destitute of truth.

John Davern,
late Captain 88th Regiment.

(No. 11.)

Ramelton, July 17, 1836.

I, W. C. Seton, late Major of the 88th Regiment, do hereby certify that I served in the above corps from its landing in the Peninsula in 1809, to its entry into Madrid in 1812. I was never absent

---

2. I served in the regiment thirteen years and two months; was in ten engagements, and twice wounded.

3. Served twenty-one years in the regiment; was in every engagement, and once wounded.

4. Served seven years and a half in the regiment; was in seven engagements, and once wounded.

from the regiment during the above two periods. I was present at the battles of Talavera, Busaco, Fuentes d'Onore, the storming of Ciudad Rodrigo and Badajoz, and at the battle of Salamanca, (the two latter in command of the regiment,) and in every other minor combat.

I never heard, or ever knew, or do I believe that such a vile practice could be carried on without my knowledge; and I do, in the most positive manner, assert that the foul aspersion made against the 88th Regiment, by the author of the *Life of the late Sir T. Picton*, to be false and without the slightest foundation.

W. C. Seton,
Major H. P. 88th Regiment, and Lieut.-Col.

(No. 12.)

London, July 30, 1836.

I most positively deny that so shameful a practice and unsoldierlike act was ever practised by the men of the 88th Regiment I served with both battalions of the regiment from 1809 until the termination of the war in the Peninsula in 1814. I never heard a whisper, either since or before, until now, that the men of the 88th had on any occasion expended their ammunition, save in the most efficient and effective manner, as our more honourable enemy, the French, can fully testify.

W. H. Rutherford,
Captain 88th Regiment.

(No. 13.)

Dublin, July 21, 1836.

My dear Grattan,—I have not read Robinson's *Life of Sir T. Picton*; but if the extract you annex be contained therein, I pronounce it, to the best of my knowledge and belief, an atrocious fabrication; and I have a right to do so, having served such a number of years in the 88th Regiment, and having been present with it in the Peninsular War. Our powder and steel we have the credit of making good use of, and this could hardly be effected without special care of both.

Your friend and comrade,
Robert O'Hara,
Major 88th Regiment.

(No. 14.) London, July 26, 1836^

Dear Grattan,—Having served in the 88th Regiment for upwards of twenty-one years, and having shared with it in nearly all the actions in which it was engaged in the Peninsula, it could be easy for me to refute this very improbable statement, did not its preposterous absurdity render it unnecessary. The idea of the 88th Regiment employing itself in front of an enemy, and going into battle, in painting and carving little bits of sticks to represent ball cartridges, and risking their lives by exchanging powder for liquor, and leaden balls for glasses, is so excellent, that it only wants the finishing assertion—that they bartered their bayonets for cork-screws, to complete the picture!

The whole statement is so truly ludicrous, as to provoke a smile of pity at the credulity of the author.

I am very sincerely yours,
Robert Nickle,
late Major 88th Regiment, and Lieut.-Col.

(No. 15.) Stokestown, July 26, 1836.

My dear Grattan,—I have received your letter, and the extract from the *Memoirs of the Life of the late Sir T. Picton*. I served with the 88th Regiment during the entire of the Peninsular campaign, and as I generally had the command of a company, and was almost always present with the regiment, I can have no hesitation in saying that the charge made by Mr. Robinson as to the "coloured wood "and the want of ammunition, is totally false and without the least foundation.

B. Mahon,
late Lieutenant 88th Regiment.

No. 16.—Extract of a Letter from Captain Duncan Robertson, dated Kindrocket, August 1, 1836.

My dear Nickle,—The extract you sent me from a passage in the *Life of Sir Thomas Picton,* lately published, astonishes me more than I can express. How or why such a gratuitous falsehood found its way into this publication I am quite at a loss to conjecture. There have been numberless anecdotes told of the feats and witticisms of individual soldiers of the 88th during the Peninsular war, which had no foundation in fact; but those anecdotes were generally quite harmless, and seemed to have been invented merely to be laughed at. It became, indeed, a sort of fashion among some idle wits in the army, to coin little stories which they imagined to be characteristic of heedless young Irishmen; and the feats related in those invented tales were very generally attributed to men of the Connaught Rangers, who were considered (I suppose more from the title than any other cause) to be the most genuine Irishmen in the army.

However, those idle stories were more amusing than mischievous, and therefore the members of the corps did not heed them nor take any steps, so far as I am aware, formally to contradict them, but the statement in the life of Sir Thomas Picton, of which you sent me an extract, is of a very different description; it affects the character and discipline of the regiment in a most material degree, and it therefore behoves every officer and man who served in the 88th in the Peninsula, to confute this bold calumny as directly and promptly as possible.

The libellous assertion that frequently before going into battle it would be found upon inspection that one-half of the 88th Regiment were without ammunition, having acquired a pernicious habit of exchanging their cartridges for *aqua ardiente*, and substituting in their place pieces of wood cut and coloured to resemble them. What vile varlet could have propagated such malicious falsehoods? Pains ought to be taken to discover and expose the original inventor of this base calumny.

I have served in the 88th Regiment for the space of twenty years, all to a few months, from 1804 to the latter end of 1823, and shared in all its services during that period, and I most positively aver that I never knew or heard of the scandalous practices asserted in this libellous extract from the *Life of Sir Thomas Picton*. I never knew or heard of pieces of wood cut and coloured to resemble cartridges, in a single instance, being found in the pouch or cartouch of any soldier in the regiment during all our campaigns.

After the first campaign I always commanded a company during the Peninsular war, and made it my practice to look at my men's ammunition once every day, which I have reason to think was the practice with every other commander of a company in the regiment. I, like others, found damaged cartridges after long and fatiguing marches, and this would occur occasionally in spite of every care and precaution that could be taken in packing the cartridges in the men's pouches; but I never found coloured pieces of wood, or any other substitute, in any man's pouch, nor did I hear of any such substitute being found in the pouches of the men of any other company in the regiment. Therefore, feeling quite satisfied that no such scandalous practices could possibly have occurred in the 88th Regiment, I can have no hesitation in declaring that the assertion regarding the misuse of their ammunition by the men of that corps, and that too when in presence of the enemy, and on the eve of battle, is a scandalous and malicious libel on the character and discipline of the regiment.

Duncan Robertson,
Late Captain 88th Regiment.

No. 17.—Extract of a Letter from Major-General Sir John Taylor, K.C. B., dated Aix-la-Chapelle, Aug. 5, 1836, to Colonel O'Malley, C. B.

The false and scandalous assertion made in Mr. Robinson's publication it would be quite unnecessary to contradict to any officer who had served in the army of the Peninsula, and above all to any who had belonged to the Third Division; but as the *Life of Sir Thomas Picton* will probably have a large and general circulation, I beg that you will add to the certificates of officers which you have already, my most positive and solemn assurance of the total falsehood of the statement of Mr, Robinson, that the soldiers of the 88th Regiment had, during the period that I commanded the regiment, the practice to which Mr. Robinson alludes, nor do I believe that any such practice, or even a solitary instance ever occurred in the corps.

I am, my dear Colonel, very truly yours,
(Signed)   J, Taylor,
Major-General.

(No. 18.)

Quarley, August 14, 1836.

Being called upon, I testify that the statement in the memoir of General Picton, by Mr. H. B. Robinson, of the soldiers of the 88th Regiment, when in the Peninsula, being in the practice of bartering their cartridges for *aqua ardiente*, and substituting pieces of wood to resemble them, is as false and ridiculous as are other portions of the work relating to that regiment.

(Signed) Wm. Mackie,
Major unatt., formerly of the 88th Regt.

(No. 19.)

Avranches, July 30, 1836.

Having read the above paragraph extracted from the *memoirs of the life of Sir T. Picton*, I declare that I landed with the 88th Regiment in 1809, and with the exception of a little more than a year, at various periods, I continued with it until it embarked at Bordeaux in 1814. That being in the general habit of inspecting the men's ammunition in their pouches, I positively state that, as far as ever came under my observation, the above passage is entirely false. The author must be perfectly ignorant of the manner of packing and preserving ammunition on service, to make such a ridiculous assertion.

I never heard of the soldiers exchanging their ammunition for *aqua ardiente*, when in expectation of coming in contact with the enemy: on the contrary, the soldiers always evinced the most earnest desire to exchange any damaged cartridges for good, whenever an opportunity presented itself.

G. H. Dansey,
Major unattached.

(No. 20.)

Belmont, Innishannon, Aug. 12, 1836.

My dear Friend,—Being called upon by you, as a Peninsular man, to state whether I remember any instances having occurred in the 88th Regiment of men going into action deficient of ammunition, and of their having sold their ball cartridges for *aqua ardiente*, substituting in lieu thereof pieces of coloured wood, I do hereby declare that, although I served with that corps as a subaltern during the greater part of the Peninsular campaigns, I never heard of such a practice in the regiment, nor can I believe that such a deception could have been practised without the knowledge of the officers.

Frederick Meade,
Major unattached.

(No. 21.)

Lochryan, August 22, 1836.

My dear Grattan,—I have just received your communication, and I really do think the assertion that the soldiers of the 88th Regiment went into action with painted pieces of wood in their pouches instead of cartridges, as stated in the work you allude to, is too ridiculous and absurd to require contradiction; and you may rest satisfied that the reputation of the regiment in the field has been too well established to suffer from so absurd and unfounded a calumny; and I am satisfied that every officer, non-commissioned officer, and private, who served in the regiment, do know it to be such; and had the author applied to the French troops against whom they served, they would most probably have fully confirmed this statement.

I am, my dear Grattan, very sincerely yours,

J. A. Wallace,
Colonel 88th, and Major-General.

(No. 22.)

Kingussie, August 28, 1836.

The following paragraph having appeared in a late publication, entitled, T*he Life of the late Lieut. General Sir Thomas Picton*, namely:—

> Frequently before going into battle, it would be found, upon inspection, that one-half of the men of the 88th Regiment were without ammunition, having acquired a pernicious habit of exchanging the cartridges for *aqua ardente*, and substituting in their place wood cut and coloured to resemble them,—

I do hereby declare upon my honour as an officer and gentleman, that this is a false, groundless, and malicious accusation. I consider myself entitled to make this strong assertion, having served as a major of the 88th Regiment nearly the whole of its services in the Peninsula, and was present with the corps in five general actions, in four of which I had the honour to command.

R. B. Macpherson,
Lieut.-Col. H. P. 88th Regiment.

Now, having done so much, will Mr. Robinson think it too great a liberty in my asking him to give the name of his informant? I do not wish to press him too closely—but justice is justice!

Mr. Robinson has written a book, and it must be a well-written one to have gone through two editions in so short a time. I have never seen it, or heard more of its contents than the passage I have been obliged to quote.

He must be a clever man to be able to write a work, the subject of which is the memoirs of any general in the service—the Duke of Wellington excepted—that could have had such a ready sale. I say he must be a clever writer, and a man possessed of great talent indeed; but if he possessed ten times the talent he does—if that was possible—and that those talents with which he is endowed were backed by the talent of all the known world put together, it could not prove that General Picton "gave them (the 88th) most unqualified praise whenever it was deserved: and this was often."

Those are Mr. Robinson's own words.

Now, what praise did General Picton ever give the 88th? When, where, or upon what occasion? What officer of that regiment did he ever recommend for promotion during his command from 1810 to 1814? I will even ask, what officer of the 88th did he ever notice for his good conduct in the field during the above period?

If Mr. Robinson's "informant" will mention upon what occasion "unqualified praise" was bestowed,—if he will mention one solitary instance where promotion was obtained,—or if he can call to his recollection any one occasion where notice of the good conduct of any officer took place, I shall hear more than I ever heard before.

Any writer who builds his argument upon such authorities as I have given in the body of this letter, is not easily to be confuted. He is not to be answered by the general assertions of an "informant." He may want the eloquence of Mr. Robinson to amuse, but, speaking truth, he must always convince

I am, Mr. Editor, your obedient servant,
Wm. Grattan,[5]
Late Lieutenant 88th Regt.

New Abbey, Kilcullen, Ireland,
July, 1836.

To this letter the Author never received a reply from the biographer of the late Sir Thomas Picton; and it is a source of great pride to him to be enabled to add that his friends, whose testimonials against Mr. Robinson's assertion are annexed to the foregoing "Vindication of the Connaught Rangers," subscribed and presented him with a present of plate, of the value of two hundred guineas, "as a mark," to quote the words of the inscription, "of their personal esteem and regard, and also in token of their warm admiration of his triumphant vindication of his gallant regiment from the attacks of the biographer of the late Sir Thomas Picton."

ALSO FROM LEONAUR
AVAILABLE IN SOFTCOVER OR HARDCOVER WITH DUST JACKET

CAPTAIN OF THE 95th (Rifles) by *Jonathan Leach*—An officer of Wellington's Sharpshooters during the Peninsular, South of France and Waterloo Campaigns of the Napoleonic Wars.

BUGLER AND OFFICER OF THE RIFLES by *William Green & Harry Smith* With the 95th (Rifles) during the Peninsular & Waterloo Campaigns of the Napoleonic Wars

BAYONETS, BUGLES AND BONNETS by *James 'Thomas' Todd*—Experiences of hard soldiering with the 71st Foot - the Highland Light Infantry - through many battles of the Napoleonic wars including the Peninsular & Waterloo Campaigns

THE ADVENTURES OF A LIGHT DRAGOON by *George Farmer & G.R. Gleig*—A cavalryman during the Peninsular & Waterloo Campaigns, in captivity & at the siege of Bhurtpore, India

THE COMPLEAT RIFLEMAN HARRIS by *Benjamin Harris as told to & transcribed by Captain Henry Curling*—The adventures of a soldier of the 95th (Rifles) during the Peninsular Campaign of the Napoleonic Wars

WITH WELLINGTON'S LIGHT CAVALRY by *William Tomkinson*—The Experiences of an officer of the 16th Light Dragoons in the Peninsular and Waterloo campaigns of the Napoleonic Wars.

SURTEES OF THE RIFLES by *William Surtees*—A Soldier of the 95th (Rifles) in the Peninsular campaign of the Napoleonic Wars.

ENSIGN BELL IN THE PENINSULAR WAR by *George Bell*—The Experiences of a young British Soldier of the 34th Regiment 'The Cumberland Gentlemen' in the Napoleonic wars.

WITH THE LIGHT DIVISION by *John H. Cooke*—The Experiences of an Officer of the 43rd Light Infantry in the Peninsula and South of France During the Napoleonic Wars

NAPOLEON'S IMPERIAL GUARD: FROM MARENGO TO WATERLOO by *J. T. Headley*—This is the story of Napoleon's Imperial Guard from the bearskin caps of the grenadiers to the flamboyance of their mounted chasseurs, their principal characters and the men who commanded them.

BATTLES & SIEGES OF THE PENINSULAR WAR by *W. H. Fitchett*—Corunna, Busaco, Albuera, Ciudad Rodrigo, Badajos, Salamanca, San Sebastian & Others

AVAILABLE ONLINE AT **www.leonaur.com**
AND OTHER GOOD BOOK STORES

ALSO FROM LEONAUR
AVAILABLE IN SOFTCOVER OR HARDCOVER WITH DUST JACKET

WELLINGTON AND THE PYRENEES CAMPAIGN VOLUME I: FROM VITORIA TO THE BIDASSOA by *F. C. Beatson*—The final phase of the campaign in the Iberian Peninsula.

WELLINGTON AND THE INVASION OF FRANCE VOLUME II: THE BIDASSOA TO THE BATTLE OF THE NIVELLE by *F. C. Beatson*—The second of Beatson's series on the fall of Revolutionary France published by Leonaur, the reader is once again taken into the centre of Wellington's strategic and tactical genius.

WELLINGTON AND THE FALL OF FRANCE VOLUME III: THE GAVES AND THE BATTLE OF ORTHEZ by *F. C. Beatson*—This final chapter of F. C. Beatson's brilliant trilogy shows the 'captain of the age' at his most inspired and makes all three books essential additions to any Peninsular War library.

NAVAL BATTLES OF THE NAPOLEONIC WARS by *W. H. Fitchett*—Cape St. Vincent, the Nile, Cadiz, Copenhagen, Trafalgar & Others

SERGEANT GUILLEMARD: THE MAN WHO SHOT NELSON? by *Robert Guillemard*—A Soldier of the Infantry of the French Army of Napoleon on Campaign Throughout Europe

WITH THE GUARDS ACROSS THE PYRENEES by *Robert Batty*—The Experiences of a British Officer of Wellington's Army During the Battles for the Fall of Napoleonic France, 1813.

A STAFF OFFICER IN THE PENINSULA by *E. W. Buckham*—An Officer of the British Staff Corps Cavalry During the Peninsula Campaign of the Napoleonic Wars

THE LEIPZIG CAMPAIGN: 1813—NAPOLEON AND THE "BATTLE OF THE NATIONS" by *F. N. Maude*—Colonel Maude's analysis of Napoleon's campaign of 1813.

BUGEAUD: A PACK WITH A BATON by *Thomas Robert Bugeaud*—The Early Campaigns of a Soldier of Napoleon's Army Who Would Become a Marshal of France.

TWO LEONAUR ORIGINALS

SERGEANT NICOL by *Daniel Nicol*—The Experiences of a Gordon Highlander During the Napoleonic Wars in Egypt, the Peninsula and France.

WATERLOO RECOLLECTIONS by *Frederick Llewellyn*—Rare First Hand Accounts, Letters, Reports and Retellings from the Campaign of 1815.

AVAILABLE ONLINE AT **www.leonaur.com**
AND OTHER GOOD BOOK STORES

www.ingramcontent.com/pod-product-compliance
Lightning Source LLC
Chambersburg PA
CBHW021823220426
43663CB00005B/115